Obed's Story

Testimony To God's Infinite Grace, Mercy & Faithfulness

Obed I. Onwuegbu, Ph.D

Obed's Story

Testimony To God's Infinite Grace, Mercy & Faithfulness

Copyright © 2025 by Obed I. Onwuegbu, Ph.D

All Rights Reserved. No part of this publication may be reproduced, stored in a retrieval system, or transmitted, in any form or by any means, electronic, mechanical, photocopying, recording, or otherwise, without the written permission of the author.

Published by: Stellar Book Publishing
www.stellarbookpublishing.com

Preface

"... But as for me and my household, we will serve the Lord."
(Joshua 24:15b)

"So now I give him to the Lord. For his whole life, he will be given over to the Lord."
(1 Samuel 1:28)

"The women living there said, 'Naomi has a son!' And they named him Obed. He was the father of Jesse, the father of David." (Ruth 4:17)

Obed writes this book as a witness to show how God has directed, controlled and protected his life to fulfill the promise Obed's parents (Jeremiah Isigwuzo and Rachel Iheomadinihu) made to God for a boy before his conception. Much of his life has been how God has guided him towards fulfilling the promise his parents made to God about him in spite of his sin. A few pages of this story describe what his mother told him. The rest is how and what he lived and wrote to tell. Telling the full story of his life will take volumes to complete. So here is the gist of his story.

First, he thanks God for his Christian parents who gave him birth and the name Obed. Also, he thanked God they were Christians. As the answer to their prayer, Obed hopes he fulfilled the promise they made to give him back to God as a teacher or a Reverend Minister in the Methodist Church. That God answered their prayer with Obed may be the reason his father blessed him instead of his first son. Unfortunately, he died before Obed could recognize him. Obed's mother became a single parent at a young age.

Reading some of the ways his mother treated him at an early age in this book may present her as strict, just the way Obed's children perceive him today. However, his mother was one of the most loving mothers God ever created. She had a difficult childhood because of her father's early death. Her life became more complicated and difficult when her young, rich husband died, and her brother-in-law confiscated the husband's wealth and caused her and Obed to leave his father's decaying mud house and become homeless. With the exception of the time Obed lived away from home during his childhood and early boyhood, he went through her experiences with her.

Amos Nwaoyoyo, his age mate, said in 1977, "As a boy, Obed suffered. But as a grown-up man, he is better than almost everyone else." Obed said he did not have a childhood. Still, he thanked God for the training and experience and would not change any of the "sufferings" for something else, not even the discipline from his strict, loving mother.

He is grateful to all his elementary school teachers who believed and inculcated in him that he was the best and could be anything he wished in life. As a result, they entrusted him with responsibilities. The most outstanding of them were Mr. R. W. Iteke and Miss D. Nkechi Okezie.

Obed thinks he is the apple of God's eye. He supports the statement with a few events in his life. First is his birth and survival. Two uncles cracked his head, and each time, God healed him without medical treatment. He was always first or second in his class throughout elementary school, first in standard five in the circuit (district), and the only successful candidate in all grade six classes from Umuahia Circuit (District) to attend a one-year teachers training college. Also, first at the college at the end with 105 points above two students who jointly came second. During his first year of teaching, he was the only successful candidate from Umuahia Circuit to attend Uzuakoli Elementary Teachers Training College. Jesus came to his house, hugged him, and gave him a scholarship to study in the U.S. and more.

God gave him his wife in his dream more than a decade before he met her in real life. In spite of Obed's effort against God's plan, He carried it out at His schedule. It turned out that He gave him an angel for a wife. He blessed them with four lovely children; people jokingly refuse to believe he and his Sweetie produced because of their height. God is faithful.

Obed is really grateful to all the people he met on this journey so far. To Mr. and Mrs. Nwamkwo Okpokiri, who provided his mother and him with a room to stay when they became homeless. Thanks to dee Okwum, who allowed his mother and him to use his late brother's house when Ebisike vacated it. Thanks to dee Ikeji, who gave them a room when the house became uninhabitable. He is grateful to Mr. Ezekiel Ogunka, who allowed him to use the vacant bed in his bedroom to sleep and thereby afforded him the first opportunity to sleep on a bed alone, though he was in standard (grade) three. Thanks to dee Kanu Nbelekwe a man with a deformed leg from whom, as a boy, Obed incidentally learned how to stake yams. The same is true of dee Ibewunjo from whom he learned how one person could repair a leaking roof with mats. Thanks to Wilson Ezeunara who taught him how to climb palm trees with ropes. Obed cannot thank those people in his village who loved him so much enough. Almost to a person, all the adults had different pet names for him, as though they were sharing in his suffering. God bless you all.

He is gratefully indebted to his maternal grandmother, who named him Anosike (live long). Your love was beyond description. The same is true of his favorite aunt Ukachi. She was the only one whose consoling talk soothed him in the worst days of his childhood.

He thanks his great aunt Nwanyiocha, whom he and his brother affectionately call Nneocha (grandmother with fair skin). She carried him on her shoulders for as long as he can remember. Unfortunately, she left this earth before he could say thank you to her. Thanks to his brother, who, for a period of time, seemed to understand that Obed did not steal his birthright, lived like a brother, and rendered some help in his early education.

Wow, how can he thank the two most important people in his life enough! Rachel, in spite of all your sufferings from childhood, you are the best mother God put on this earth. God gave you everything you needed to overcome every adversity and be the mother He made you be. You were so beautiful in body and character. You led Obed to God. Obed believes you are enjoying the face of the Lord in Paradise. Then came Sweetie, the wife he married in his dream when he did not shake hands with women, and a fellow teacher said she was an angel, not a human. She happened to be both. Our marriage is made in heaven, manifested on earth, and sustained by God. Thank you, God, and thank you, Sweetie. At one time, it seemed he was losing all four children. Satan seemed to have the upper hand. Thank God. Today, God had taken hold of them. No one can take what is in His hand.

Obed's parents were members of and led Amafor Isingwu Methodist, the village church. The villagers loved and respected both of them. His father was one of the rich people in the village and was generous.

Of three siblings, his father was the youngest, and his sister was the oldest. They became orphans early in life, and the sister became his father's surrogate mother. He remained ever grateful to her for as long as he lived. Unfortunately, after the premature death of their father, she behaved as though her brother's family had died with him. Their father bought goods wholesale from United African Company Limited (U.A.C. Ltd), a British company, at the time of his death. He also had a number of people from the village and beyond who carried and sold his goods in distant markets such as Bende and Uzuakoli. These markets are about twelve miles away from home. However, much of the goods were at the U.A.C. stores when he died prematurely. Father's wealth became the family's misfortune and nightmare.

Obed's mother was beautiful with a beautiful voice and sang in the women's choir of the church. If she lived in a later era, she could have made a living with her voice. She was very industrious, the characteristic God used to guarantee Obed's and his brother's survival, where most widows of her age and time would have failed. She was as loving as she was a disciplinarian. Her father died when she was a child. Her mother had three daughters, and she was the middle daughter. After the death of Obed's mother's father, Obed's grandmother took her three daughters to Ogbodi, her birthplace. Obed thought his mother was born in Ogbodi until later in his childhood.

Obed's parents had several children before he was born. Unfortunately, except Enoch, the first-born, the rest died as toddlers or later. Worse still, his mother became stricken with bleeding. It appeared she would never become pregnant again. When medication failed to cure the sickness, his Christian parents resorted to prayer. Most probably influenced by Hannah and the birth of Samuel (1 Samuel 1), they promised God that if He gave them a son, they would give him back as a Reverend Minister or a teacher in the Methodist school. God answered their prayer with a son, and they named him Obed.

As simple as the name is, many people in the village called him a variety of names derived from Obed. The most common is Obida. Even now, Obed does not know what Obida means. Some called him Obinnaya. This means the father's heart desires. There were so many that he was not sure what his real name was in his early childhood. Of course, his grandmother, great-aunt, aunts, and uncles all called him different names. For example, his grandmother named him Anosike, which means live long; his great aunt called him Iheanacho (what we desired); and his favorite aunt named him Okwudiwa, in reference to what people said during his mother's ill health. Okwudiwa means the birth is the suitable answer to whatever anyone said regarding her sister's ability or inability to have more babies remaining with the person.

Before Obed could know and enjoy his father, death snatched him. With his death, the family's future seemed doomed. The merchandise he bought had not been cleared from the U.A.C. stores at his death. His oldest son Enoch, who started school earlier than all his age mates, was in standard (grade) one. There was no oral or written will. They were not literate either. In that part of the world where a woman had no voice at the time, the responsibility to claim the goods fell to Uncle Ehiogu.

Aware that the goods were at the U.A.C. Store, Uncle Ehiogu went to claim them. The Englishman in charge of the company branch at Umuahia refused to release the goods because he heard his brother had children. He demanded to have cosigners to guarantee the children would be taken care of. Uncle Ehiogu took Mr. Udeagha Agbara and Chief Inegbu Agbara, the village chief with him. They went and signed a letter stating that Uncle Ehiogu would take care of the children. The widow did not know anything about these transactions. The signatures sealed the mother and children to a life of misery, refugees, physical abuse, and false accusations of Obed's mother and misuse of her husband's wealth.

It seemed as though his father had a premonition of his death that year and paid his brother's whole year of school tuition at the beginning of the year. There was Obed's mother without a father or a brother, and the one man who was father, brother, and husband for a short time was gone forever and never to be seen or replaced. She was one month pregnant when her husband died. That compounded the problem. Because of the prominent position he occupied in the larger family and his role as a civil leader in both the church and village, they named the baby girl Ahia. Ahia means market, which is the abbreviation for a long name that means no matter how important a person may be, the person's absence from a market does not prevent the market from holding. She might not have lived to see her fourth birthday because of malnutrition and malaria. Because of financial difficulties, Obed's mother leased land and her clothes to pay his brother's tuition. Sometimes, the school sent him home until he paid the tuition. As a result, he repeated standard (grade) four. He failed standard five and dropped out of school. Indeed, things got worse.

Table Of Contents

Chapter 1

    Introduction 1

Chapter 2

    Neglects And Dreams 7

Chapter 3

    Learning Through Life Difficulties 19

Chapter 4

    Enugu Through Class Two 23

Chapter 5

    My School Life Begins 30

Chapter 6

    Standards 1 and 2 at Eziama 35

Chapter 7

    Standards Three and Four

    Mission Hill 46

Chapter 8

  Home Again

  Home Again And Standard Four 55

Chapter 9

  Standard Five And Mission Hill 63

Chapter 10

  Standard Six

  Mission Hill 70

Chapter 11   82

  Nto-Ndang PTC 82

Chapter 12

  Teaching Fulfilling Parents' Promise 94

Chapter 13

  Uzuakoli Elementary Teachers' College 108

Chapter 14

  Final Year At ETC 125

Chapter 15

  Teaching As A Trained Teacher 130

Chapter 16

    Headmaster Umuoriehi Group School 138

Chapter 17

    High Elementary College (HEC) 144

Chapter 18

    Final Year At Uzuakoli 152

Chapter 19

    Josiah's Engagement And After Effects 164

Chapter 20

    Akanu Item Teaching After HEC 169

Chapter 21

    From Akanu Item to Alayi. 184

Chapter 22

    Transfer to Umukabia 190

Chapter 23

    Going to America. 200

Chapter 24

    In America 209

Chapter 25

    Vermont, My Second Home 222

Chapter 26

    Honorary Citizen of Nebraska Twice 238

Chapter 27

    Salt Lake Bound 257

Chapter 28

    On The Road Again 279

Chapter 29

    Central Connecticut State 1970-72 282

Chapter 30

    Central Connecticut State 1973-1975 298

Chapter 31

    Last Semester In Connecticut 318

Chapter 32

    Transit to Nigeria 324

Chapter 33

    Living In The War Zone 333

Chapter 34
- Ibadan Federal College Of Education 353

Chapter 35
- Founding Federal College of Education, Oyo 356

Chapter 36
- Authorized Chaos 372

Chapter 37
- Acting Principal Destined for Removal 391

Chapter 38
- Lost Wars 405

Chapter 39
- In a Lion's Den with God 413

Chapter 40
- Entrance Examinations And After Effects 425

Chapter 41
- Glaucoma Treatment 432

Chapter 42
- In The USA. 438

Chapter 43

    Court Cases. 442

Chapter 44

    They Were God's Angels 447

Chapter 45

    "Dr., You are clean." 464

Chapter 46

    Last Days in the Ministry of Education 495

Chapter 47

    Back to the USA 513

Chapter 48

    Living with Blindness 528

Chapter 49

    In the Will of God 542

Chapter 50

    New Pastor And Results 556

Chapter 51

    Living With Enlarged Prostate 566

Chapter 52

   Visit To Nigeria 569

Chapter 53

   Experiences 582

Chapter 54

   What's Your Name 611

Chapter 55

   July 31. 617

Chapter 56

   Celebrations. 625

Indices 630

Chapter 1

Introduction

"And it shall come to pass afterward that I will pour out My Spirit on all flesh; Your sons and your daughters shall prophesy, Your old men shall dream dreams, Your young men shall see visions;"

Joel 2:28.

This phase of my journey began with two of the most significant dreams of my life, one during my time at Akanu Item Methodist Central School and the other at Umukabia Methodist Central School in Nigeria. After completing my High Elementary Teachers' Training course, the Methodist Mission assigned me to teach at Akanu Item Methodist Central School. It was there, before the end of the first term, that the headmaster, who also taught the standard six class, became gravely ill and had to be hospitalized. In his absence, I found myself juggling not only his standard six class but also my own standard five class, alongside the additional responsibilities of acting as the headmaster.

In the midst of this demanding period, and in a place regarded as remote even by Nigerian standards at the time, I had a dream—one that would forever change my life. In the dream, I was in the United States of America. Upon waking, I felt a pang of regret. *What am I doing in this rural place, dreaming about being in the United States?* I wondered to myself. I quickly dismissed the dream, recording it in my mental archive of "unattainable dreams" and drifted back to sleep. This dream, however, lingered in my thoughts, even though it occurred three years before I wrote the letters discussed later.

In May 1963, I sat down to write five applications for admission and financial aid, addressing them to five different colleges and universities in the United States of America. With a mixture of hope and anxiety, I posted them, one by one. As the weeks passed, the replies began to trickle in. The first four responses echoed the same disheartening message: "You are late, especially since you are asking for financial aid. Apply before the end of December." Each rejection felt like another weight added to my shoulders, and I began to wonder if my dream of studying in America was slipping away.

Then, at last, a letter arrived from Lyndon State College in Vermont. It was different. The College didn't reject my application outright. Instead, they asked for a biographical sketch and three letters of recommendation. It was a glimmer of hope, and I eagerly complied, gathering the requested materials and sending them off as quickly as I could.

In June, my letter of admission finally arrived, signed by Mrs. Susan C. Gallagher, the admissions officer at Lyndon State College. While the letter confirmed my acceptance, it also brought disappointing news: I had not been considered for financial aid because I was neither a Vermont resident nor a U.S. citizen. Despite this setback, I held onto the hope I found in the words of that letter. I thanked God for the admission and immediately responded, determined not to accept "No" for an answer when it came to financial assistance.

In my reply, I expressed my gratitude for the admission but shared the story of the Syrophoenician woman and Jesus Christ from the Bible. The Greek woman, though not a Jew, asked Jesus to heal her sick daughter. Jesus initially responded by saying that the children's food should not be given to dogs. However, the woman humbly replied,

"Yes, Lord, but even the dogs eat the crumbs that fall from the children's table." Moved by her faith, Jesus healed her daughter (Matthew 15:21-28). I used this story to illustrate my persistence and faith, hoping that Lyndon State College might reconsider my request for financial aid. I posted the letter and waited.

On the quiet evening of July 31, I felt unusually drowsy. After locking the doors and windows, I lay down and drifted off to sleep. In my dream, a man walked into the room and asked, "Did you say you want to see Jesus Christ?" Without hesitation, I replied, "Yes." The man left and soon returned—with Jesus by his side. In the dream, I stood up, and Jesus embraced me. When I awoke, I felt a wave of disappointment wash over me, realizing it had only been a dream. Still, I went back to bed, pondering the significance of what I had just experienced.

The next morning, August 1, I eagerly shared my dream with fellow teachers. Excitement bubbled within me as I told them, "I saw Jesus Christ in my dream." Their reactions were a mix of curiosity and humor. "What did He look like?" some asked. Others teased, "You and your Bible." But before the day was over, by 1:30 p.m., the mail arrived. Among the letters was one addressed to me from Lyndon State College. I opened it with trembling hands. The letter, signed by Mrs. Gallagher, brought incredible news: the Vermont State Board of Education had awarded me a free tuition scholarship and permission to work ten hours a week.

Overjoyed and feeling as if I were floating on air, I went around the school, letter in hand, announcing the good news to everyone. Mr. Okeke, the headmaster and one of my recommenders, smiled and said, "O. I., Paul is no longer the last apostle to see Jesus Christ—you are." I thanked him, overwhelmed by the profound connection between my dream and this life-changing news.

Although I was eager to leave, I couldn't depart immediately because of my "bond"—a contract I had with the church. The dream, and Christ's visit, had changed me and my world for good, but practical matters still remained. With two weeks left before the end of the second term, I used the time wisely. I sought and obtained permission from the Methodist Church for a study leave and sold my motorcycle to help fund my journey. I also wrote to my best friend, Emedom, who was studying at Dartmouth College in New Hampshire, U.S., and shared with him the dream that had profoundly affected me. In his reply, Emedom wrote, "If you hadn't said you saw Jesus Christ, I would have thought you saw Chineke—God, the Father."

Though it was just two weeks, they felt like two long months as I prepared for my departure. Part of my preparations included sending three hundred pounds to my brother in Lagos to help cover my boarding and travel expenses. The final day of school arrived, and I remember waiting anxiously for the transport that would take me and my belongings home. Each minute seemed to stretch endlessly, but eventually, the vehicle arrived. We loaded up my belongings, and I said my farewells to the school.

Sunday was my sendoff. On Monday, I embarked on the journey to Lagos, traveling by lorry from Umuahia—a journey that spanned two long days. I was on my way to secure a passport and visa, the final steps before my dream of studying in America could become a reality.

The consulate didn't inquire about my sponsor, and within 53 hours, I was back at my brother's home in Lagos, arriving at around 2:00 a.m. and waking everyone up with my unexpected return. Later that month, we purchased my plane ticket, and then all that was left to do was wait. On October 2, the people from my village gathered to hold a sendoff party for me.

Leaving home was bittersweet. My mother had already shed a few tears when I left, and now it was my sister-in-law's turn. She cried quietly before we left the apartment for Lagos Airport. A few hours later, we said our final goodbyes, and I boarded the PAN AM flight. On October 3, 1963, after two brief stops in Accra and Dakar, I was airborne, headed to New York City. We landed in the early hours of October 4, greeted by a ferocious cold wind that hit like a wall. It was a struggle to maintain my balance as I walked from the plane to the waiting room, the cold a sharp contrast to the warmth I had left behind.

Soon after, I was on a Northeast Airlines flight to Boston. The name stirred memories of my British Empire history lessons, reminding me of the Boston Tea Party. Finally, I arrived at Montpelier Airport, the capital of Vermont. Exhausted but filled with anticipation, I took a cab to the bus station, only to watch in dismay as the bus to Lyndonville drove off, unaware of my arrival.

After a short walk, I stepped into a warm store, grateful for the shelter from the cold. I introduced myself to the man working there and explained my situation, requesting his help. Kindly, he dialled the College and handed me the receiver. On the other end of the line, Mrs. Gallagher answered. "I am Obed, the Nigerian student, and I'm at Montpelier," I said. "Where in Montpelier?" she asked. The store owner quickly informed her of my location. Later that day, Mrs. Gallagher, accompanied by Mr. Bob Mishaud, arrived to pick me up.

By the time we reached the Vail campus, students were finishing their dinner. I was ushered into the dining room, where I had my first meal at Lyndon. Around 9 p.m., a bus took the male students, including myself, to our dormitory. A bed awaited me, and I discovered I had two roommates. That night, I experienced something new—sleeping in a room with the heat on and heavy blankets to ward off the cold.

The following day, Saturday, the College bus took us back to the Vail campus for breakfast. It was there that I met Ali, an Arab student, who kindly offered to take me to a store to buy a winter jacket and a Russian-style winter hat. Later, he suggested we go to a movie, and assuming he would pay, I agreed. To my surprise, I ended up paying for myself, and it was also the last movie I watched during my three years at Lyndon.

October 6 marked my first Sunday in Lyndon, and I attended the People's Methodist Church. There, I met Janet McKnight, who introduced me to the fourth-grade Sunday school class and asked if I would teach them. It was an unexpected but welcome opportunity, and I gladly accepted.

Part One

Chapter 2

Neglects And Dreams

> Then Midianite traders passed by. And they drew Joseph up and lifted him out of the pit and sold him to the Ishmaelites for twenty shekels of silver. They took Joseph to Egypt.
>
> (Genesis 37:28)

My father, Isigwuzo, had two older siblings: Nwaekenna, his sister and the oldest, and Ehiogu, his older brother. They became orphans at a young age, which profoundly shaped their lives. Onwuegbu, a half-brother and the oldest son of their father adopted my father as his own son. Additionally, my aunt became a surrogate mother to my father during this difficult time. When he became a Christian, my father adopted the name Jeremiah. Similarly, my mother, Iheomadinihu, adopted Rachel as her Christian name. They were both Christians when they got married.

Due to my lack of knowledge about this adoption, I went by Obed Isigwuzo throughout my elementary education. Even my sixth-grade graduation certificate bears the name Obed Isigwuzo. Later on, I changed my last name to Onwuegbu, following in the footsteps of my older brother Enoch, who also goes by Onwuegbu.

My father, Jeremiah Isigwuzo, was a wealthy and generous man. He was well-loved and respected in the village, alongside my mother, Rachel Iheomadinihu. However, my father died prematurely, and I was so young that I barely knew him. At the time of his death, the goods he purchased were still at the United African Company (UAC Ltd, a British company). My uncle Ehiogu, his older brother, went to claim these goods. The Englishman in charge of the store required him to bring co-signers to ensure that the proceeds would be used to care for my father's family. Uncle Ehiogu brought along Chief Inegbu Agbara and Udeagha Agbara, who both promised they would oversee this responsibility.

Once Uncle Ehiogu obtained our father's goods, he acted as though my father's family had perished along with him. He, along with his two wives and children, lived in luxury while we struggled. The wealth they enjoyed was destined not to last forever. As time passed, living became a struggle and even a nightmare for my mother and her children.

My mother resorted to pot making, a trade she learned from my grandmother. Although clay was inexpensive to buy, it was heavy to carry. The process of making pots involved several stages, from raw clay to finished product. Each load of clay was carried on her head, and the clay itself was purchased from a village about six to seven miles away from our home. When dug from the ground, the clay was wet and heavy, and carrying it exacerbated my mother's chest problems.

At home, she would break the clay into small pieces and pile it together, keeping it hidden from the sun. Two or three times a day, she would heavily water the heap for a total of three days to ensure it softened properly. For the pots, fine grains of sand were essential, and my mother would collect sand from a section of the village main street. As I grew older, I helped her gather the sand for preparing the pots.

Eventually, I became strong enough to carry the clay myself and participated fully in the process. Once the clay was sufficiently soft, my mother swept a designated area of the yard where she prepared it for pot making. She used a special kind of basket, pouring sand into it and shaking it vigorously. The fine grains of sand fell through the basket, while larger grains, pebbles, and dirt were retained. These larger particles were discarded, marking the beginning of the heavy-duty work.

With the sand spread out, my mother moved the wet clay on top of it. Methodically and rhythmically, she would dance on one leg—usually the right foot—continuing this movement until the clay flattened and covered the sand completely. After the first dance, she gathered the flattened clay and piled it back at the center of her workspace.

Next, she took the basket and spread the sand a second time. This was followed by another round of dancing and flattening the clay. At this point, it was crucial to test the quantity of sand in the mixture, as the amount of sand determined how much she would sprinkle on the third round.

After the final dance, she divided the clay into smaller heaps, with the size of each heap dictating the size of the pot to be made. These pots would typically hold between four to eight gallons of water, and their utility directly influenced their sizes and prices.

Preparation is complete, and pot making begins. There were no machines involved; everything was made by hand. Living in the equatorial zone has its advantages and disadvantages. The heat from the sun allows the pots to dry quickly, but if they dry too fast, cracks can form during firing.

The pot-making process requires two forms of firing. The first occurs in the house, aiming to transform the brown-looking pot into a black, hardened version. This stage also tests the pot's durability; if it contains too much or too little sand, it will not pass this crucial test.

The fire used during this stage is moderate, significantly less intense than the large final fire in the second stage.

The second stage takes place outdoors on the street, resembling a pyramid structure. Baked mud blocks are placed on the ground, creating a stable base. Wood is arranged between the blocks to create a foundation for the pots. The first layer of pots is placed directly on the blocks, followed by a second layer, which contains fewer pots than the first. Dried shrubs are placed on top of the pots, and firewood is stacked around them, forming a large base that narrows upward like a pyramid.

Once everything is in place, the fire is ignited from the ground up, baking and hardening the pots as my mother watches the flames. If any pots appear undercooked—meaning they do not exhibit a red hue—she quickly tosses additional combustible materials into the fire from a safe distance, ensuring the flames intensify.

As the fire begins to die down, my mother uses a pole, about four to five feet long, to carefully remove the pots from the top layer. The next step involves painting the pots while they are still hot. She uses a thick, yellowish, cooked substance to apply the paint. While some pots are sold locally, most are transported to Uzuakoli market, which is twelve miles from home.

I took the time to describe this process to illustrate the labor and time that this trade requires. My mother was also a dedicated farmer, growing our staple foods. In her early years, she managed everything on her own, with only occasional help from my grandmother and maternal aunts.

Our father and his brother jointly owned land in the village and in Isieke Ibeku, located about seven miles from our home. My uncle grudgingly allowed my mother to farm part of the land that belonged to my father. She planted yams, cocoa yams, maize, beans, and two kinds of vegetables, ensuring our family's sustenance.

When she wasn't busy making pots or farming, my mother traveled to distant markets, such as Orienteghe and Afoumuda, to sell or buy items like egusi (melon), pepper, and groundnuts. Despite her busy schedule, she stayed home on only a few occasions: while making pots, on Sundays, when she was sick, and during general holidays like Christmas and Harvest Thanksgiving celebrations.

My mother struggled with chest problems, and carrying heavy loads without sufficient rest exacerbated her condition. With her as the sole provider, our world came to a screeching halt when she fell ill. It took several days for the news of her sickness to reach our grandmother and aunts, but once they heard, help arrived swiftly.

Even before her illness, life was challenging. My mother primarily planted and harvested carbohydrate-rich crops, supplemented by seasonal vegetable proteins, which were often short-lived. Animal protein was a luxury we could rarely afford, with small, dried fish and crayfish being the only exceptions. Unfortunately, circumstances worsened instead of improving.

During this difficult period, Udeagha Agbara, who was of the same age as my father and one of the signatories for the release of our father's goods, had a vivid dream. In it, he saw my father, visibly angry, warning my uncle: "I notice your wicked acts against my family. You may get away with murder, but if you fail to take care of Obed, I will kill you." My uncle interpreted this warning as a directive to prioritize my care, believing that it meant, "Take care of Obed and let others fend for themselves."

From that point onward, he began inviting me to dinner with him and his sons, three of whom were older than I. He even allowed me to sleep on his bed. Before I turned five, he would take me on his bicycle to his stall at the market, where he sold mgbasa (women's wrapper cloth) daily. As we ate, he would instruct his children, emphasizing my presence by saying, "I know I am talking to Obed. He is the one who will benefit from this instruction."

While my world seemed bright with my maternal uncle, my brother took out his frustrations on me. Being much older and stronger, I was unable to defend myself against his beatings. He struck me as if I were the cause of our father's death and, therefore, the source of all his problems. It felt as though he wished I would simply die and leave home. Was he envious of the way our uncle treated me? As I grew older, I learned that our father had blessed me, which only fueled my brother's resentment. I often wondered if I had become his Jacob or Joseph.

There was one occasion when he beat me so mercilessly that, when I finally managed to get up, I grabbed a nearby knife and threw it at him as he ran away. It struck his leg, and I braced myself, expecting him to retaliate and kill me. However, he did not.

On another occasion, Mrs. Nwaburuche Ekeledo witnessed my brother beating me and intervened, separating us and admonishing him. She didn't stop there; she returned later to warn my mother, saying, "If you don't separate these two, you will come home one day to bury the younger one." I learned of her warning from my mother when I was older.

This tension at home often led me to spend weeks with my grandmother and youngest aunt in Ogbodi. I cherished my time there, and my aunt quickly became my favorite. It was during these stays that I met my great-aunt, who would carry me on her shoulder to various places.

From time to time, I would spend weeks with my grandmother and youngest aunt. It was during one of these stays that I made one of my childhood "famous" statements about cassava. This root tuber grows underground and can be eaten in various forms. One popular way is as sliced cassava, which is harvested, cooked, and then sliced thinly, resembling potato chips. The sliced pieces are placed in a basket and taken to a running stream in the evening, where they are left overnight. The following morning, the owners retrieved the cassava, thoroughly washed it, and took the cassava home.

While I was staying with my aunt and grandmother, she brought home freshly sliced cassava from the stream and spread it out in the sun to dry. I watched her, hoping she would give me some to eat fresh. Instead of asking her directly, I said, "Amafo people do eat sliced cassava fresh," referring to my village. She laughed and offered me some, fulfilling my wish.

However, my brother's hostile reaction to me during my visit to Nigeria in 2009 reminded me of his past beatings. While I was there, two cousins in our compound got into a fight—one was much older and bigger than the other. The smaller one cried for help. My sister-in-law was the first to get up, and despite my brother yelling at me as if I were a small boy, "Sit down! Where do you think you are going?" I ignored him and rushed to separate the boys.

Uncle Uwakwe, a paternal uncle, had a son who was much younger than I. My youngest aunt, Gunu, the daughter of our grandfather's youngest wife, was babysitting him. A few of us children sat on the ground outside playing when, somehow, I got sand in Gunu's eye. She cried out, and Uncle Uwakwe soon learned that I had caused his babysitter to cry. In anger, he cracked my head with the knuckle of his middle finger, and blood trickled down. I ran home in tears. My mother could only quarrel and shed tears for me; I didn't even receive any treatment, but God healed me.

This incident was just the first time an uncle would crack my head. For more than eight years, my mother did not speak to him. He eventually broke the silence by apologizing to her with a gift of yams on a new yam thanksgiving ceremony day. By that time, I was in standard (grade) four.

As children, we were enchanted by the bushes and the thick forest we called Okata. Our older female cousin, Elizabeth, guided us through the nearby woods in search of mushrooms. We would harvest three kinds, with the best being called Onyekamete, which translates to "who prepares better soup than I?" After gathering mushrooms, we would venture out on our own to collect firewood. We affectionately referred to her as Nne, meaning grandmother. The children in our compound became more familiar with the bushes and the surrounding forest than any other children in the village.

Our yard, surrounded by walls, provided more space than other families in the compound. As a result, it became a gathering place for children at night, where we would share moonlight stories and play games. At that time, there was no electricity in our villages, making moonlit nights precious, even if they were short. Under the glow of the moon, we would tell fables about the animal kingdom and their interactions with humans. Two of our favorite activities were hide and seek and a game called Gwam, gwam gwam, which means "tell me, tell me," often played before a question was even asked.

Nnete, a girl from Obowo, about eight miles from our village, was smaller than my brother but bigger than I. When I visited home from the U.S. in 2009, a man in the village, who was the same age as my brother, still teased him by calling him Nnete's husband. One special celebration occurred whenever my mother returned from the market; it was the joy of sharing the treat she brought home. One evening, she returned with a delightful surprise: three crayfish—a large one, a medium one, and a small one.

She gave me the crayfish to share, and I decided to give the big one to my brother, the medium one to Nnete, and kept the little one for myself. Unbeknownst to me, she was testing my generosity. With a smile, she then presented me with a second crayfish, even larger than the one I had taken.

As children, two of our main chores in the village were fetching firewood and water. One day, Nnete and Asabituka took Iroanya and me into the bush to gather firewood. Iroanya was about my age, though slightly taller. During our outing, we got into a quarrel. When he ran from me, I chased after him. Asabituka, ever the instigator, teased him, saying, "Stop and fight! He's your age. If it were me, you'd be running your mouth. Face him!" But Iroanya refused to stand his ground, and eventually, I stopped chasing him. Soon after, Nnete quietly slipped away, retreating to her home as our situation became more difficult.

Our parents owned two houses. The smaller one had just two rooms, its walls made of mud and roofs thatched with mats woven from palm wine leaves. Due to the heavy equatorial rains, these roofs required constant repairs and replacements. In our culture, it was customary for the man of the house to undertake such maintenance, or for the woman to hire someone to do it. My mother, however, was unable to perform the repairs herself or afford the necessary services. As a result, the smaller house became the first casualty. Its roof eventually collapsed, and the walls crumbled.

Desperation began to take hold of my mother, leading her to question and doubt God. Ultimately, she ceased attending church services and participating in church activities. During this troubling time, she had a dream where a voice called out to her, saying, "Rachel, Rachel, pray to your God. Whether it is well or not, pray to your God. Do not forget or ignore your God. Pray and pray to your God." Heeding this message, she resumed her Christian life. Yet, even with her renewed faith, life continued to grow increasingly difficult.

My brother was still in school, but as he progressed to higher grades, the costs increased significantly. The expenses for school uniforms, books, and tuition, known as school fees, became a heavy burden for our mother. The academic year was divided into three terms, beginning in January and concluding around the second or third week of November, with three-week breaks in April and August, and about seven weeks off between November and the end of January. Each January, students would return to school clad in new uniforms, armed with new books, and ready to pay the term's fees. The fees for the second and third terms were due at the start of each term, and failure to pay within two weeks of resuming classes resulted in suspension until the fees were settled.

There were times when my mother couldn't pay these fees at the beginning of the second or third terms, leading the school to send my brother home from standard four until he could settle the debt. In some cases, she even used her wrapper and clothing as collateral to borrow money for the fees. Unfortunately, these financial struggles sealed my brother's fate in standard four, forcing him to repeat the standard (grade). Despite this setback, he managed to succeed after his repeat. However, when he faced the same challenges in standard five, he refused to repeat again and ultimately dropped out of school. As a result, I became the first in our family to graduate from elementary school, a bittersweet milestone overshadowed by the loss of our two remaining sisters.

During specific festival days, we would receive visits from men from neighboring villages. One of them was Mr. Onwubiko from Umuosu, whom we affectionately called Nnanna, meaning "grandpa." I later discovered that he was either a brother or a relative of our father's mother. Another frequent visitor was Dedem Osuagwu, who I initially believed was my mother's father. He visited us often and showed more concern for our well-being than anyone else, although I didn't fully grasp our connection at the time. Dedem Osuagwu turned out to be the nearest kinsman who, in the absence of my grandfather and any uncles, received my mother's bride price. He was the one to receive the seven hundred pounds that my mother was falsely accused of giving to her relatives. Yet, no one dared to confront him about it or speak of such accusations in his presence. Dedem Osuagwu hailed from

Amachara, my mother's birthplace, while other relatives visited less frequently.

The deteriorating condition of our big house, coupled with my mother's declining health, ultimately forced us out of our father's home. Fortunately, my mother had an older cousin, Ikodiya Nwankwo, who was married in our village. Her brother, Gbogbo Agwu, had taken my brother to live with him in Port Harcourt. As the remaining house became increasingly unsafe, my mother and I moved into a small room provided by Ikodiya and her husband, Nwankwo Okpokiri.

This single room became our living space—our living room, bedroom, and kitchen all in one. One by one, we moved what valuables we could salvage, taking only what was necessary and could fit within our new home. The rest was left behind to perish with the old house. Our new place was just a few hundred yards from where we had lived, but I was still quite young during this transition and cannot recall every detail. However, I was about to grow up quickly, and I wish I could say that our circumstances improved, but they did not; in fact, they worsened.

By the time we became homeless, we had learned at least two lessons that have stayed with me. The first was a bitter truth: while our mother was away at the farm or market, Uncle Uwagbokwu committed some unpleasant acts in her absence. When she returned and we informed her, she confronted him in anger. He stormed into our yard and physically assaulted her, and we were powerless to intervene. From that moment on, regardless of what anyone said or did in her absence, we resolved never to tell her.

The second lesson I learned resonates with the sentiment Paul expressed when he wrote, "I have learned to be content in all conditions..." (Philippians 4:11-13). This understanding of resilience became a guiding principle as we faced our challenges.

Unbeknownst to us at the time, God was weaving His grace and goodness into our lives during our homelessness. My mother and I escaped not only physical but also mental and emotional abuse, as well as false accusations from our uncles. In His divine timing, God brought us back when it was safe, and He provided us with better and larger homes in place of the old ones we lost.

Among the special celebrations in our community were the Sunday Market days, which occurred every eighth Sunday, the New Yams Festival, and Christmas. The latter two were annual events, and our uncles' families prepared lavish dishes that filled the air with the aroma of rice, stew, and fufu soup as they entertained guests. Although our mother could not afford such delicacies, we never went hungry. She prepared fufu and cow bones, from which we scraped any remaining flesh, cracked the bones to extract and savor the marrow, and chewed on the cartilage. The scent of our mother's kitchen was almost as inviting as that of our uncles' wives.

We quickly learned to avoid visiting our cousins on these festive days. In an effort to console us, our mother often shared the story of a poor woman from Uzuakoli. During a festival known as Ilaoso—meaning "stampeding"—the Uzuakoli people enjoyed their celebrations after filling their stomachs with food. While others feasted on rich dishes, the poor woman had to satisfy herself with simple fare. As they danced, she sang, "Stomach, tell what you ate! Stomach, tell what you ate!" This tale taught us to be content with whatever food our mother prepared, imparting one of the most valuable lessons of my life.

I grew up believing that people ate for two reasons: first, to quell hunger, and second, to fuel their activities. As long as the texture and taste of our food were agreeable, nothing else mattered. Yet, as life unfolded, I realized things would get worse before they improved.

Chapter 3

Learning Through Life Difficulties

"She said, 'Please let me glean and gather among the sheaves after the reapers.' So she came, and she has continued from early morning until now, except for a short rest."

(Ruth 2:7)

"I have been young, and *now* am old; Yet I have not seen the righteous forsaken, Nor his descendants begging bread."

(Psalm 37:25)

Bombs on the road of life are challenges. Take them as they come. Do not avoid them. Each time you succeed, you become smarter, and wiser, and life is more enjoyable and easier.

After my brother flunked out of school, a distant uncle from Ogbodi invited him to live in Port Harcourt. My mother, eager to see him settled, gathered what seemed to me as a child to be a mountain of food and supplies and made the journey to visit him. But when she returned, she looked devastated. She hadn't been told why she was needed there and was blindsided by what she learned: my brother was being questioned by the police.

My mother's relative, worried about the situation, had called her to assure my brother that honesty was his only safeguard—that as long as he told the truth, he'd have nothing to fear. With that done, she returned home carrying the heavy uncertainty of my brother's future. Only when news came that he was free did that anxiety finally ease.

Later, my brother remained in Port Harcourt when my mother and I moved in with Dee Nwankwo and his family, where, as always, there were children to play with. Finally, my Uncle Onwumere Ikeji offered him a new beginning in Lagos, where my brother went to live under his care.

I still visited our old compound and played with my cousins. That particular year, however, I was saddened to discover that they had gone to school while I was left behind. It wasn't too bad, though, because despite my affluent cousins being in school, the children I played with daily were not. I had hoped that since my mother knew my cousins were attending school, she would send me the following year. But that didn't happen. Instead, I drifted from one home to another.

My first "displacement" was to my oldest maternal aunt, Onwuamaghihe, at Umuawa. As was customary, young children were expected to babysit the infants of better-off relatives. I was tasked with caring for her infant daughter. After two or three months, I returned home.

In the village, there was Jonah Ogbonna, who owned a hotel at the Umuahia township market. At that time, the hotel was a makeshift stall in the market where food was prepared and sold. The structure was made of mats, and while it served its purpose, it was a disaster waiting to happen. Without electricity, a water system, or a fire department in the township, it was a perilous place, especially with the flammable mats that made up the walls and roof. The seating and tables posed their own fire hazards.

Jonah negotiated with my mother, and I went to live with him. He and I slept on a mat on the floor each night. That marked my first experience with child labor. He paid my mother a meager nine pence—about 10.5 cents a month. After several months, I ran back home. Unfortunately, my time at home was short-lived, and I soon found myself moving again.

Wilson was about the same height as me, and for a time, we thought we were the same age. But as we grew older, we discovered that he was actually older. Like me, Wilson wasn't attending school. Instead, he worked as a houseboy for an Aro couple. He convinced my mother to hire me out to another Aro man for seven pence, about eight cents a month. One might assume that, given my experience washing dishes at the hotel, my wages would have improved with my next job. Instead, they dropped. The man paid my mother only seven pence a month. Again, this employment didn't last. I ran home before the end of the third month, despite Wilson's repeated pleas and cajoling.

As much as I enjoyed my new friends, I still missed my cousins. So, I visited our old home from time to time. On one of those visits, I noticed that Uncle Ehiogu had planted yams in our yard. At first, it didn't mean anything to me. But when I told my mother, I watched as tears filled her eyes. I still didn't understand why she wept, and she never told me. It's hard to say what motivated my uncle to plant yams in our yard, but they didn't grow—no foliage, no seeds. After a few years, he replaced them with palm wine trees, but they fared no better. If he thought that planting things in the yard could somehow erase the memory of his dead brother and family, he was mistaken. It failed.

As long as I was home with my mother, eating and growing, I helped her with many of her activities. Soon, we children joined some older kids in a money-making venture. The township market, which served as the center of commerce for many villages, attracted people from a twelve-mile radius and beyond. With no nearby source of water, children from surrounding villages carried pots of water to sell in cups at the market. The younger ones like me were lucky if we made half a penny a day. So, going to the farm, helping carry clay, selling water, and assisting with the other commodities my mother sold at the market became part of my daily routine.

I was experiencing life at a faster pace than children older than me. One day, Isaac Ikeji came to our house with a request from his older brother, Akwarandu, who lived in Enugu. He wanted me to come and live with him. My mother refused the request, as she had plans to send me to school the following year. Isaac returned later, promising that I would start school in Enugu the next year. My mother agreed, and I traveled by train with an adult companion to Enugu. Dee Akwarandu was at the railway station to meet us and take me to the one-room apartment where he lived with four other people. Of the four, three were adults, and one was in his late teens, all from Mgbaja, a village just under three miles from my own. That became my home for the next seven or eight months.

Chapter 4

Enugu Through Class Two

"Behold, the hour is coming, indeed it has come, when you will be scattered, each to his own home, and will leave me alone. Yet I am not alone, for the Father is with me. [33] I have said these things to you, that in me you may have peace. In the world, you will have tribulation. But take heart; I have overcome the world."

(John 16:32-33)

My people say a young traveler is wiser than an old man. If you look hard and long enough at disappointments, you will see hidden blessings. I believe that is what Paul meant when he said to give thanks for everything. ("giving thanks always for all things to God the Father in the name of our Lord Jesus Christ," Ephesians 5:20)

Uncle Akwarandu was waiting for me at the Enugu railway station when the train arrived. Together, we crossed a football field and walked through a narrow street until we reached his one-room apartment, which he shared with four others. By then, it was late afternoon, and as we stepped inside, I noticed a high school student already in the room. Soon, the rest of the tenants trickled in, each settling into their own space. I wondered who they were, but they stayed quiet and went about their routines.

The room held two twin beds—a sight that surprised me, as this would be my first time living with electricity. Another difference was the separate kitchen, where each tenant prepared their food independently. Evening came, and one by one, they each made and ate their dinners separately. Only two beds and five people—I found myself wondering where everyone slept.

The answer became clear soon enough. My uncle took one bed, and Dee Anyalewechi, one of the other tenants, took the other. The rest of us spread mats on the floor, ready to rest in whatever space we could find.

Unlike his brothers, Uncle Akwarandu had never stepped into a classroom as a student. Instead, he worked as a coal miner, a job that fascinated me as much as it filled me with questions. He wore a black hat with a peculiar hook at the front—something I initially thought looked funny, until I understood its purpose. The hook held a lamp, which guided him through the pitch-dark tunnels where he spent his days, or sometimes, his nights.

Within a week of my arrival, Uncle Akwarandu introduced me to three older boys. These boys, with a mix of friendliness and authority, became my guides in Enugu. They quickly showed me what my responsibilities were and explained how I was to accomplish them.

Enugu was divided into various zones, each with its own name. We lived in the Ogui zone, directly across from the railway station. No buildings stood between our house and the station, which meant that from our front step, we could see every train engine and coach that passed through, every person moving around the station, and the large piles of coal the railway corporation had stacked for its operations.

Jacob, one of the three boys Uncle Akwarandu introduced me to, taught me an important task: how to collect coal for cooking. There were two types of coal available. Sometimes, the trains would burn coal and deposit it along the rail line. As long as we stayed out of the workers' way and didn't endanger ourselves around the trains, we were free to gather as much as we could find. But this kind wasn't always available.

When the rail line deposits ran low, boys would often get into trouble, tempted to steal from the railway's reserved coal piles intended for the engines. Those who got caught would face punishment—either a harsh flogging or detention until someone came to claim them. My cautious nature kept me out of trouble in this regard.

The other two boys, Onyeukwu and Isaac, taught me about navigating the sprawling Ogbaete market, where one could find everything imaginable and learn the ways of trade in Enugu.

Gari, a staple food for the Igbo people across Nigerian cities and towns, would occasionally become scarce in Enugu. Besides the owner, our house had three other tenants. One was a railway worker with his family, who rented a room in the back. Another was a man from the Enugu region who occupied a back room and rented a front room as a small bicycle repair shop. He had a knack for finding gari at a good price whenever it became hard to find in the area.

One day, he decided to send a relative living with him to Ahia Eke to buy gari, and Uncle Akwarandu sent me along. What I thought would be a simple trip quickly turned into a small adventure. Along the way, we came upon what appeared to be a group of armed bandits. They stopped every passerby, asking where they were coming from. Some travelers were detained while others were allowed to pass. Fortunately, we made it through unbothered.

About a mile later, we passed a large, white mansion that looked out of place among the modest huts surrounding it. My guide pointed it out as belonging to Lawyer Onyeama, likely the first Igbo lawyer. Our trip turned out to be worthwhile—gari was much cheaper there than at Ogbaete market. But the journey took the entire day.

Behind our building, there was a school, which also owned the football field that separated between our house and the railway station.

Despite my training in finding items at the market and bargaining for good prices, I rarely went there. It wasn't because we had storage or a refrigerator—those were uncommon luxuries. Rather, it was because many goods could be bought right from home. All one needed was a good ear, patience, and a knack for bargaining. Hawkers would carry items on their heads, calling out to announce what they were selling. The moment they set their load down, bargaining would begin. Goods from hawkers were often cheaper than in the market since they didn't have to pay stall fees. For fresh meat and gari, though, it was still best to visit the market.

Another stark difference between Enugu and the village was the water system. In the village, women and children fetched water from streams for all household needs. Enugu had running tap water, but it wasn't connected directly to homes. Instead, taps were scattered at central locations across the township. People would line up with buckets and pots from early morning until noon and again from early evening until late at night to collect water. Many households had large pots and barrels for storing it.

Like the Samaritan woman in John 4, I learned to fetch my water between noon and late afternoon, a quieter time when most people were away from the taps.

Uncle Akwarandu was in charge of making soup, and once prepared, a pot of soup would last about four days. I learned to make the just the way he liked it, and I took care to have his food and hot ready before he went to or returned from work. He enjoyed a hot and I made sure everything was in place for him.

The youngest child of our landlord attended the school behind ing, and I often watched him and the other students play. I m, eagerly waiting for the day I'd be in a school uniform alongside them. Christmas arrived, and Uncle celebrated by cooking rice and gifting me a frock shirt. Given my age and size, I didn't need a pair of shorts or pants unless I was attending school, so I didn't receive any. Pants were a privilege for schoolchildren, so I patiently waited for the year to end, hoping to start school soon.

On Christmas day, I watched the ceremonial ethnic dancers parade through our street. Every occupant of our room was home, and the day seemed to hurry by. A few weeks later, the school year began, but I was still watching from the outside. I couldn't bring myself to ask my uncle why I wasn't in school. I wasn't in Umuahia Township, so I couldn't run home, nor did I have a way to contact my mother. To my surprise, word of my absence from school somehow reached her.

One day, I saw a young woman approaching our building, and the closer she came, the more familiar she looked. Being so far from home, I hadn't expected to see anyone I knew in Enugu, but then she called my name. That confirmed my suspicion—it was Nmiya Nwankwere, a relative who had recently joined her new husband in Enugu. She had a message for Uncle Akwarandu, who was still at work: "Tell him daa Hemere wants you to come home to start school." She left before my uncle returned.

This happened to be one of the weeks he worked during the day, and I was relieved that I would finally be going home to start school. Despite my excitement, I still prepared his food and boiled water for his bath. When he returned, I mixed the hot and cold water for him. After serving his meal, he ate, and just before I put the plates away, he stepped out with the cup of water in his hand.

As he drank, I told him that Nmiya had come and mentioned that my mother wanted me to come home and start school since I was not attending school in Enugu. Without warning, he struck me on the head with the mug. Blood trickled down my face, and I cried uncontrollably. There was no one there to console me.

To justify his cruelty, he falsely accused my mother. "Your mother took seven hundred pounds your father buried in his room before his death and gave it to her relatives. Whose money does she want to use to send you to school?" he spat.

Monday Nwaobiala, one of the men who lived in the room, was standing nearby. Hearing the accusation, he became enraged. "If she took the money, isn't it her husband's? Are you going to kill him because of his father's money? Why don't you just send him back to his mother?"

The uncle, avoiding the confrontation, retreated into the room. The next morning, I don't even remember if I had eaten or bathed. He handed me two shillings and told me to walk to the train station across the street and buy a half-ticket to Umuahia.

With no treatment for my wound—no bandage, no care—I made my way to the train station. God, in His mercy, healed me. But when I reflect on why he didn't send me to school that day, the answer is clear: finance. He couldn't afford the school uniform, books, shoes, and fees, let alone the loss of the constant help I provided him.

Of the two shillings he gave me, one shilling and ten pence went toward my ticket. I stepped into the coach and began the long journey home, burdened by my wound, but with a sense of relief in knowing that I was finally going home.

By early afternoon, the train pulled into Umuahia. It stopped, and I stepped down onto Umuahia soil once again. The two-mile walk back to my village felt long, but when I finally reached home, I handed my mother the two-pence change. The moment I shared my story, tears welled up in her eyes.

Her face spoke volumes, torn between joy and sorrow. She was happy to see me, but my wounds and the pain of what had happened to me deeply troubled her. Unfortunately, I didn't start school the following day or week, as the first term had already ended by the time I arrived. I had to wait for the beginning of the second term to begin my studies.

Looking back now, I'm grateful I didn't attend school in Enugu. For one, I never attended a single church service during my time there, which might have hindered my spiritual growth. It's possible I wouldn't be the Christian I am today if I had stayed. Furthermore, less than three years after I came home, Dee Akwarandu returned. Unfortunately, he didn't live long after his return and never saw me become a teacher, let alone a doctor.

In 1976, Jacob, one of the men who had lived in the same one-room apartment, saw me and refused to believe I had earned a Ph.D. "It can't be," he said, "It's too early for you to have a Ph.D." This was six years after I received the degree. I didn't argue with him; I simply smiled.

Waiting wasn't a matter of resting or wasting time, as the first-term holidays coincided with the fall farming season, particularly the planting period. During this time, students helped their parents plant yams, maize, and beans. By the time I arrived home, there were still about two weeks of holiday left. Mother and I made the most of this time, working in the fields and attending local markets, buying and selling goods.

Part Two Grade School

Chapter 5

My School Life Begins

"Boy, I was mighty happy when the first day of school came, and the bell rang. I walked toward the school grounds as one of the pupils, eager for the day ahead. I arrived before most of the students. Soon, the schoolyard filled, and we all swept the grounds and tidied the classroom before the second bell rang. Villagers, who didn't own clocks, provided schoolteachers with timepieces to keep the children and their parents on schedule. Once everyone was ready, the teacher lined the students up, and we marched into the classroom for devotions."

"At that time, in that part of Nigeria, the school system began with what was called Infants One, equivalent to pre-kindergarten. It was also referred to as Class One. In our one-room school, there were two grades—Infants One and Two, or Classes One and Two—taught by a single teacher. After a brief 'interview,' the teacher placed me in Class Two. What a joy! Finally, Obed was registered as a student and was going to listen to a teacher in the classroom. Even better, my cousins, who had started school two years before I did, were now only one grade ahead of me instead of two."

"A week or two after school started, it happened again. It seemed as though I wouldn't stay home to enjoy my mother. My teacher and my mother agreed that I should live with him and his wife. Both of them were either in their late teens or very early twenties. So,

I moved in with Mr. and Mrs. Iweha. The best part of this move was that I still lived in the same village as my mother, and you know what that meant—I could run home any time I felt dissatisfied. I had certain advantages and responsibilities that other students didn't. Students fetched firewood and water for the teacher, but I didn't. They swept the school grounds daily, but I didn't participate. In a village where clocks were nearly nonexistent, the teacher rang the bell to signal when to come to school and when to attend church. Ringing the bell and carrying the books to and from school became my responsibilities. Ringing the bell was an advantage because I learned how to tell time. Since I lived with the teacher, I was never late and avoided punishment for tardiness. What I couldn't figure out was why he chose me when there were other students, older or the same age as I was. Like the rest of them, this arrangement wouldn't last through the year. This was the first time I'd lived and slept in the same room as a husband and wife. I thought she would cook the food, and I would do the dishes. Instead, she prepared the soup halfway, cooking it until she added meat, fish, melon, and leaves. I finished the cooking. I did most of the other tasks while they played in the room. As a boy, I thought I should be playing, not two grown-up people. But I endured through the second term."

"Final year examinations were always comprehensive, covering everything the teacher taught throughout the year. However, there was also a midterm examination during the second term, which covered all the material taught from January to the week of the examination in June. This was also the case in Class One, the first year of school. From Class Two through Grade Six, the final year examinations were both comprehensive and external. The classroom teacher didn't know who set the questions or graded them, and only received the results a day before school closed for the year-end holiday. About seven or eight weeks into the second term, we took the midterm exam. The result surprised almost everybody. Njikonye came first, and I came second. From *that point on, it seemed like he and I competed for academic leadership, even beyond Class Two."*

"When the third term began, the wife seemed sickly often. They never called each other by their names, only using 'nwanne,' which means sibling. I didn't know that their play was affecting her, but it increased my load of work. I decided it was time to quit and ran home. I thought she was getting fat and lazy, but she was pregnant. All efforts by my teacher to bring me back failed. He determined to make a 'federal case' out of it.

He decided to make my life uncomfortable. His first attack was verbal. He came to class and said an Igbo idiom: "A man who gets his mother's slave woman for a wife does not know that marriage costs." The implication was obvious. But did he forget my services to them? I cooked while they played in bed. One of my survival skills was that my mother had taught me how to cook. I did the dishes, swept the rooms, pounded everything that needed pounding for the soup, and rang the bells. These tasks were much more than I would ever do for my mother. His threat didn't matter to me.

The school premises, which were the same as the mission grounds, were divided according to the number of boys at the school. He put together three boys' portions and told me to sweep them. There was no one to appeal to, so I accepted it, especially since it was only for a fraction of the third term. Others swept the grounds for two years and lived."

"In a Christian school, Scripture was the first lesson of the day. Arithmetic followed, and on Mondays, Wednesdays, and Fridays, physical training (P.T.) was next. One of the activities was wrestling. My teacher decided to subdue me. He chose Chineme Ogbonna, who was older and bigger than I was, to wrestle with me. Within a short time, his back was on the ground, and I was on top of him. My teacher could not believe what he saw. With his eyes wide open, he looked at

me, shook his head, and pointed at me, saying, 'Isi adighi gin ma,' meaning 'Your head is not right.'

Even after decades, when I returned from the U.S., and he saw me, he still smiled, pointed his finger at me, and made the same statement. A woman passing by when I wrestled Chineme down was so impressed that she stopped and gave me one-half penny. That was the only wrestling prize I ever received, even though I was the champion in the 135 lbs. class at Lyndon State College. Roy, the P.E. Master, did not give me a dime or a pin. At last, I was home, and my stay with my mother was permanent. For one reason or another, my teacher retained me as the class monitor. I carried books from his house to the class before and after school."

"Students did almost everything for their teachers. For example, he took some of the boys to Isieke, the home of his parents-in-law, on a Saturday. We worked on their farm, about seven miles from our home. They fed us lunch. He could be funny, maybe because of his youth. Teachers were paid poorly, but he must have saved enough money toward the end of the year. He bought a new pair of white shorts and socks that reached his knees. He wore them to church. When he came to school the following Monday, he was beaming with smiles. Before he sat down, he asked us, 'Did you notice how glamorous I looked in church yesterday?'

The term was winding down, and the examination day was fast approaching. As stated earlier, the class teacher did not set the questions, nor did he correct them. As a rule, we would not even take the tests at our school. We trekked to Mission Hill, the nerve center of activities in the Umuahia Methodist Circuit (District). The examination lasted two days. We returned to school and waited about two more weeks before the results were ready. A day before the school closed, our teacher went to Mission Hill and brought the results. The students were still at school when he walked back from the one-and-a-half-mile distance. He saw me, smiled big, flashed the five fingers of his right hand twice, and raised his index finger. If he thought I understood what he signed, he was mistaken. I did not. The mystery that went over my head the previous day became clear the following day when he announced the results. Eleven out of the fifteen in our class (grade) were promoted to Standard One, while four would repeat the class. Njikonye and I exchanged positions. I was first, and he was second. That also marked the end of my schooling in the village. We would transfer to Eziama group school the following year."

"*The first term holiday is for planting. The third or Christmas holiday is for harvesting what was planted. It is also the dry season, hot and humid. Yam is the main crop harvested during this holiday, usually before Christmas. I will discuss my involvement in farming as I grew older in later chapters. As the only child in the home, I was compelled to learn to be both the son and daughter. The openings on the roof forced us to move again.*"

Chapter 6

Standards 1 and 2 at Eziama

"Go to the ant, O sluggard; consider her ways, and be wise."
(Proverbs 6:6)

"It is better to go to the house of mourning than to go to the house of feasting, for this is the end of all mankind, and the living will lay it to heart." (Ecclesiastes 7:2)

My mother was very loving. She starved herself to feed her children. To provide for us, she went to the farm and market even when she was sick. But when she disciplined us, she spared no rod. As I said at her funeral, "She loved like Jesus and disciplined like the Spartans." It seems to me today that her discipline style was a way of asking for appreciation. As she used to say, "I was young and beautiful when your father died. I could have remarried, but for you. I did not want you to live with some other woman who would give you food by measure."

Three levels of education systems existed in Nigeria at this time, namely, elementary schools, secondary schools, and teachers' training colleges. There were no universities. The Christian denominations owned all elementary schools. They also owned most of the secondary and teachers' training institutions. Therefore, schools were named after the denominations that established them. So, all Methodist institutions were prefixed Methodist. For example, the three levels of Methodist elementary schools were named Methodist Infant School, Methodist Group School, and Methodist Central School. So were all the other protestant and Roman Catholic institutions named after them.

Elementary schools consisted of three levels. The first level was the infant level, the equivalent of pre-kindergarten and kindergarten in the U.S. This is the one I graduated from. The Infant School was usually owned by one village. The next level was the typical Group School. A group school belonged to several villages that could not afford to finance the buildings required for the schoolteachers and classrooms individually, nor could it afford enough children to populate it. Several villages joined their efforts together and built and administered the school. A typical Group School remained a Group School, and it had three to four teachers. This was the case with Methodist Group School Eziama, where we went the following year. Another class of Group School was in transition to becoming a Central School. Many villages came together and built big schools in central locations. These schools started from the infant classes through grade six. Central Schools grew gradually. Before any group school was granted standard (grade) six, the Government sent inspectors to ensure it met all requirements. This included teachers' quarters, classrooms, and football and netball fields. Mission Hill was in a class of its own. This is where we took our final year examination and where we wished to be. But we had to go to Eziama first.

Having survived the Christmas holiday, the bell was quick to ring the day school started. I was equally eager to trek to Eziama Methodist Group School to begin the new year in a new class. I was going to meet my cousins Chikara and Mwoko, who started school two years before I did. But they would be only one grade ahead of me. They were in standard two, and I was in standard one.

The bright morning January sun was shining when we arrived. Soon, Mr. Isaac Chimaraoke rode in on his bicycle. He was from my village and the headmaster of the school. Besides, he was the standard one teacher. At the school were students from about seven villages and two or three from the personnel at Mission Hill. By the end of the school day, he made me his class monitor. But thank God I was not going to live with him. Again, I enjoyed the privilege of not fetching water and firewood. However, it was my responsibility to make sure that others did and to report those who failed. Also, I carried his basket, which contained books and other materials, to school in the morning and returned it to his house after school. In spite of the many students from other schools and villages, Njikeonye and I led the academics class.

Meanwhile, I learned a few things about Christianity from my mother. One of them, in particular, made the dream she told a big surprise to me. That she stopped her Christian activities, especially prayer, baffled me. Her condition must have been terribly difficult. As far as I knew, she had an attitude towards prayer. She prayed when we ate. The first thing she did on entering the church building was kneel and pray before she sat down. Her first action when she got home was to pray. Below are the instructions that illustrate her attitude toward church attendance. I am a prayer warrior today because of my mother's prayer attitude.

In those days, boys performed two duties on Sunday mornings. They swept the street, and the bigger boys and girls fetched water while mothers prepared breakfast. The children took their baths, ate, and went to church. Many churches had teachers, and the teacher rang the bell three times on Sundays. The teacher rang the first bell at seven, the second at eight, and the last at nine. To get me to church in time, my mother told me that God's angels came to church at 9 am, counted people in the church, numbered the people, and left. Anyone who was not present at nine when the angels counted was considered absent from church that Sunday. I taught prayer at EV Free in Salt Lake City, and the pastor, who was busy with some members in the office, walked in late to the class I was teaching. I told him my mother's instruction, and the class roared. In 2011, my niece in London told me that my mother had also given her the same instructions.

Going from Amafo village Infant School to Eziama Group School added some responsibilities. There is a road about one mile long, which connects the village to the Umuahia to Owerri highway. Male students in standards one through six swept the road every Saturday between 6 a.m. and 7 a.m. Anyone who failed to attend or even came late was fined. There was another one, which was voluntary. It was the church choir, and I joined it. The choir practice was always held in the evening.

Knowing that other children stayed home and played, life seemed to pass without me. I was in school, which I enjoyed, or on the farm or at the market. Fortunately, I liked most of the activities, especially going to the distant markets. I boasted about them and now I believe that buying and selling helped my problem-solving in arithmetic. But as the days and months and, yes, years passed, and the loads increased in weight and scope, I became overwhelmed. On some occasions, my mother would decide to pull me out of school because there was a need for me to go with her to the farm. Here are a few instances that drove me to the breaking point.

My mother and I left the house early one morning and trekked to our farm at Isieke Ibeku and worked till the evening time. We were tired and carried heavy loads on our way home. By the time we traced the seven-mile distance to our village, it was dark. Still, my mother would not wait but went to report a case to Dee Ojoemelam, the oldest man in our old compound, who also was the oldest man in the village. The old man gave her a cup of palm wine. She was not a drinker. Drinking on an empty stomach did not help. She was dizzy when she came out. She was still dizzy when we arrived home. She told me to start a fire for cooking. To start a fire requires one to take firewood and go to someone else's kitchen, stick the wood into a stove with a burning fire, wait until the wood catches fire, and then bring the burning wood to start the fire at your stove. Hungry, tired, and weak, I thought, "Which other child of my age would work as hard as I did, carry heavy loads, and come home to have the responsibility of cooking?" I refused to do it.

She recovered and made the fire. After she had cooked the meal, she ate it and denied me the meal. Early the following morning, she ate, locked the door, and gave the key to Nne (grandma) Nwangbede, our host's mother. I did not know who she gave the key to or what instructions she gave the person. I got so hungry that I thought I was going to die and yet could not enter the locked room. I lay flat on my back on the ground outside the house, crying, "I am going to the land of the dead with an empty stomach. I am going to the land of the dead with an empty stomach." Then, the old woman threw the key to me. I got up, unlocked the padlock, found food, and ate.

As far as health was concerned, my mother did not know nor did she practice "a stitch in time saves nine," or "prevention is better than cure." As a result, when she got sick, she continued to labor until she was completely exhausted and unable to move. Then, she became bedridden. She wanted and compelled me to practice what she lived, and I hated every bit of it. What compounded the problem was the mentality that fever was a sickness of its own instead of a symptom of malaria. So, when I had a fever, she made me go to the farm or market with her. Her philosophy was that when a sick person walks about in the heat of the sun without treatment, he or she gets healed. She behaved as though the sun had a healing magic. But it did not always work for her or me. I could not understand why other children stayed home even when they were well, especially during holidays, and I could not, even when I was sick. However, I endured it through standard one.

In spite of all the students from all the other villages and schools, Njikonye and I still dominated the class academically. I took the first position in the midterm examination. As usual, we trekked to Mission Hill for our final-year examination. The result favored Njikonye. He was first, and I was second. It was the long eight-week Christmas holiday. We were still at our one-room "exiled" home. Besides going to the farm and the township market called Beach and helping in carrying clay home, I ventured to Afoibeji, the shortest of the long-distance markets I eventually attended.

Standard two students were the successful standard one students, and those who failed the standard. Reverend Badi had been transferred and took his sons Albert and his brother with him. Again, the teacher made me his class monitor. Mr. Isibuaku, our teacher, lived opposite Mission Hill School. Only the main road separated his street from the fence that surrounded the school. We used to weed his long street of weeds.

The first term ended, and the planting season holiday started. That someone suffered from malaria and got immunity does not prevent one from getting malaria again. All it does is reduce the severity. Once the mosquito that carries the germ bites an individual and injects the bacteria, it starts to attack the victim. I was sick and had gone to the farm the previous day. Walking fourteen miles to and from the farm and the sun did not heal me. Instead, I got worse. There was no medicine in the house. My body was still hot, which was the only way the body temperature was measured. Yet my mother insisted on my going to the farm. She told me that she saw me in her dream before she got pregnant with me and told me she did not want me. I felt unwanted and like I had had it. Life was not worth living. I told her so and more. I will die and get out of your life so that you live your life the way you want. I took off running into the bush to die. She ran after me, carrying a broken-fired pot with a brownish-yellow color that was never used for cooking. People in the culture believed this kind of pot had mythical powers. When she caught up with me in the bush, she took it and waved it around my neck and said, "This pot will prevent you from reincarnating as a human being if you ever fail to pay me back my breast milk you drank before you died." She left me in the bush and walked home. Fearful that what she said would happen to me if I died, I cried more and went home. I believed that shook her and softened her attitude.

Within a short time, Ebisike, a blacksmith from Obowu who had lived in this part of our village for many years, decided to return to his village. As a blacksmith, he made hoes, knives of different sizes, and three-legged stoves. He was a native doctor, i.e., spiritus. He occupied a home that belonged to Okorie, Okwum's dead brother. When he left, the houses became vacant. Dee Okwum allowed us to occupy them. My mother and I moved into them. Two or three years before, dee Onwumere, whom my father helped to educate, took my brother to Lagos. We learned that dee Onwumere, who worked for the railways, had been transferred to Zaria, a town in northern Nigeria. My brother was learning a trade. It was necessary for him to complete his trade. Therefore, Uncle Onwumere left him with Mr. Amadi Udu in Lagos.

When the second term began, the teachers decided to make one change to how our school was governed. The school would have a prefect. He would be in charge of the school. In the absence of the teachers, supervise the activities of the students and report to the appropriate authority. We thought they had decided who the student they wanted was. To our surprise, they said that they would not appoint the prefect, nor would there be any election. They wanted an individual to volunteer. All eyes were on the older and bigger students, especially Obediah and Chionye. It seemed as though they did not hear the announcement. The headmaster repeated it. After a long wait and no response from either of them or someone else, I raised my hand and was declared the Prefect. I also retained my position as the class monitor.

"Go to the ant, O sluggard; consider her ways, and be wise." (Proverbs 6:6)

Wilson, mentioned in an earlier chapter, had also started school. As an older boy, his oldest brother had taught him how to climb the palm tree with the ropes, a trade the poor class learns. I got interested in this art. He took me to a dwarfed palm tree for several days and taught me how to climb the palm tree with the ropes. It came in handy many years later.

With our spacious new home, Mother had room for the clay. The ample ground space between the two houses provided more than adequate room to spread and dance on the clay in preparation for making pots. The extra room provided shelter for the pots from the excessive heat of the sun and rainfall. Things were improving when suddenly my grandmother, who lived alone, became sick and came to live with us. My youngest aunt had married and was nursing a baby. My older aunt lived farther away. Besides, my mother was the favorite. I came home from school one day, and my grandmother was at home. She had come to live with us and was seriously ill. Her health was fast deteriorating. Should she die at our house, there was no land to bury her or people to carry her corpse to her home. There was only one thing to do. After a short stay, my mother walked her to and took care of her at Ogbodi, her birthplace, where she died after a short time. I was on my own at this time. My mother, aunts, and male relatives buried her there. We sank to our lowest financial level with her burial and other expenses.

Taking care of Grandma became my mother's primary duty during her sickness. My mother's money-making ventures such as pot making and marketing were suspended. We lived on what she harvested from the farm, such as cassava and vegetables. She started with pot making after the burial. But the process took weeks. Consequently, we ate the most unnourishing soup I ever ate in my life. Normally, a typical Igbo soup contains crayfish, fish, meat, stockfish, and maybe snails. Of course, palm oil, salt, and pepper are taken for granted. That soup contained only the basic ingredients, namely salt, pepper, oil, and a lot of vegetables. It tasted like medicine. My mother was almost in tears as we ate. I ate it without complaint. The result was a reward after the pots were sold. She bought pork, a rare thing in our meal. I was getting older, growing, and attending more distant markets. As the year progressed, it became obvious that I would survive the worst year of my life. Finally, the third term arrived.

Surprisingly, all the older and bigger boys cooperated, even Nkemakolam, whom we called Kema. He was older but small and was never afraid of the whip. Whenever it was his turn to be flogged, he stood before the teacher, folded his arms in front of him, and turned his back to the teacher. In the end, he blinked his eyes, walked back, and took his seat, making the teacher feel as though he had wasted his time and energy. Our teacher hated that and called him names. The annual pilgrimage to Mission Hill, called the final year examination, came, and we eagerly made it. I was first in the midterm examination, and Njikonye was second. The final year examination result produced a shocking surprise. Ekwebelem, who sat between Njikonye and me on the long bench during the examination, was the first. He was not even one of the bright students in the class. We did not mourn for long because we would be students at Mission Hill the following year. Most of the successful students rushed to Mission Hill to hear the school's headmaster announce the results of standards three and four, while those who failed cried and went home. It was bad news for my two cousins, Chikara and Nwoko. They failed and had to repeat standard three. That meant I would be in the same standard as them the following year.

Though my mother made many pots, she did not carry many of the pots to the market by herself. A few were sold at home. Many people from the village carried empty baskets to Uzuakoli market, twelve miles away, where she sold the pots and carried the bulk to the market. She also bought commodities from the market like everyone else. Since I was not old enough to trek to Uzuakoli, I met her on the way with an empty basket and carried some of her load. That pleased her very much. She rewarded me with a special treat. She sold the items she bought at other distant markets.

One of those markets was Orieteghe, a distance of about twelve miles from home. She sold ukazi leaves, groundnuts, and pepper there. We planned to go to this market. She left early to trek to the market. But because of me, she planned to leave earlier than she normally did. The baskets we carried were prepared the previous night. Unfortunately, the same problem that drove us out of our original home, namely, torn mats on the roof, plagued us in the new home. However, this was dry, not rainy season. The moon shone very brightly. My mother woke up and saw the bright moonlight shining into the room and woke me up. Though she knew it was not daybreak, but because of the cock crew, she thought it was close. We took off.

We trekked through six villages without hearing or meeting any human or animal. On reaching a big stream, we heard two creatures she called mermaids jump into the stream. That scared my mother. Finally, we reached Umunwanwa, and it dawned on her that we had left home too early. By God's grace, we were near a church building. It was Umunwanwa Methodist church building. The doors were unlocked. We went in, put benches together, and had a long sleep before we heard voices outside. Like the Priests of the Old Testament, we had shelter in the house of the Lord. We were only about five miles to the market. For my mother, the incident overshadowed whatever she sold or gained. Because we heard the splash of what she believed to be two mermaids into a big stream we passed, she said, "What is wrong with me? One of these days, I am going to lead another man's son to death. God forbid! Things must change." It never happened again.

That was not the first time. Once, we were at our farm at Isieke Ibeku. Anyone who has been in the equatorial zone knows that the sun shines until it suddenly disappears. My mother and daa Martha another aunt worked separately at their farms. They worked until the sun "cooled" down. By the time we walked two miles, we could not recognize "the color of the palm of our hand," as they say. A man jumped in front of us suddenly and shouted, "It is Ohuhu people O!" He ran away from us toward our home. We were terrified. Four miles and about one hour later, we saw him at Obohu, our stream, with a short gun on his shoulder. We concluded that he went to borrow or rent a gun from our village to hunt with.

One day I went to our old compound to visit my cousins. My maternal senior uncle had planted palm wine tree seedlings on our father's compound. These trees are usually grown in swamps where water runs or ponds surround them throughout the year. It did not mean anything to me. I saw Chikara and looked at his map books. There was his map book and the map of Nigeria he drew. I stepped out and drew the map on the ground, and inserted Rivers Niger and Benue. I thought they represented a tree and its branches. In my mind, the distributaries were roots, and I inserted them. At that point, Mba, another cousin and the smartest of all of my uncle's children, came out. He had completed standard six and was waiting for the results. Impressed by my drawing, he called Chikara and Nwoko. "Come and see the map Obida drew. He is only in Standard Two. You failed Standard Three and cannot draw the map." They did not pay attention. Mba and Chikara are the same age and older, while Nwoko and I are the same age. Having spent enough time with them, I returned to Uhu Ezeunara, my current home.

Chapter 7

Standards Three and Four

Mission Hill

*God promised to build David a sure house
(1 Samuel 2:35, 2 Samuel 7:27).*

Mission Hill was the school every schoolboy and schoolgirl in Umuahia Methodist Circuit (District) desired to attend. It must have been the oldest central school in the circuit. The Methodist Mission might have built it. Therefore, unlike other central schools, it was not the property of any village or group of villages. Also, the school was located next to the manse, the headquarters of Umuahia Methodist Circuit. The students came from about an eight-mile radius. It was the only Senior Central School i.e., the only central school that started from standard three instead of Infant One. It chose the brightest students from its feeder schools and sent away the rest to search for admission somewhere else. Each standard had A, B, and C classes. For the first time, Njikonye and I were separated. He was in standard three A and I was in standard three B.

Standard three was different from previous grades in one major way. From class one through standard two Igbo was the language of instruction. English was taught as a subject in standards one and two. However, the English language became the medium of instruction for all subjects in standard three except the Igbo language. Also, for the first time, we had more than one teacher teaching the class. Though Mr. S. Jaja was our main teacher, Mr. I. I. Ogbonna taught us History. There were three classes of standard three.

Because of the large size of the school, the students were organized into four groups called houses. These houses were named after four former British Reverend Ministers who administered the Umuahia Circuit. They were Williams, Smith, Dodd, and Brewer. These houses had different colors and each boy wore the house color on his boxers. The houses competed for points in sports, games, and keeping the premises clean. The boys wore their colors during sports and games. Once I got my boxers, I wore them permanently and never went out naked.

Our first history lesson was about one Dr. Mungo Park who explored the River Niger. If you remember this is what I thought was a tree with a branch and roots several weeks earlier. This teacher said they were the Rivers Niger and Benue. Then followed the confusion. This is a part of the note he wrote on the blackboard, which we copied. "Dr. Mungo Park a young Scottish Doctor of Medicine… He discovered the course of the River Niger and died at the rapids of Sansanding in 1805 in West Africa." Mr. 110, as his colleagues called him, because of his initials I. I. O., entered the classroom the second time and started his lesson with a review of his previous lesson. No one else except me answered any of his questions. He marched the rest of the students to the front of the headmaster's office and reported them to the headmaster for not studying the note he gave them and could not answer his questions. The headmaster allowed him to detain and punish them after school. They cut grass. Though I answered the questions, I only recited what I heard as he lectured and remembered as I copied the note. The confusion was "young Doctor of Medicine." Ph. D., D.D., etc. were unknown to us. The only doctor we knew was the one at the hospital. The *Doctor of Medicine* was confusing. He didn't explain *Scottish and explorers*. What is Scottish and who is an explorer? But he blamed the students.

The roof of the house we lived in gave every sign of not surviving the coming rainy season. My mother could not afford to maintain the two houses and we had to move again. This time from Ezeunara's compound to one of the oldest compounds in the village from where our great-grandfather moved to where my father built his house. There was a vacant room in Ikeji's yard. His daughter, who lived there, got married. We moved into the room. For the first time I slept alone on a bed in Ezekiel's room. If I thought I had missed my childhood, this time I was going to be an adult. We had been far from the center of activities when we lived at Ezeunara's compound. Now, at Ikeji's home, we are separated from all the village's important activities by only a thin fence. The village square and the mission grounds were right by us. Going to choir practice and church and hearing the first bell at 7 a.m. on school days were advantageous. On the other hand, to hear other children play and be unable to participate was both tempting and even sometimes agonizing. Some of my days looked something like this:

My mother and I got up early and started pounding corn (maize) before other people woke up. This was in preparation for agidi. Usually, the pounding started the previous night. After the first round of pounding, the corn was put in a big pot of water and washed; the husks were removed first by hand, and then the water was filtered to remove the small husks that could not be removed by hand. This husk that was removed at night received a second pounding in the morning to separate, reduce, and catch as much of the husk as possible from the real food. It was put into a pot of water again and washed. The same process of washing and removing the husks by hand and filter was repeated. We got rid of the husks in two ways. 1. Add oil, pepper, and onion and mix them together, and wrap small parcels of it, boil, and sell them. 2. Throw the husk out as food for goats and chickens. The water that contained the starch was allowed to stand while the starch settled and condensed. Then I got ready to go to school. My mother trekked to Uzuakoli market a distance of twelve miles.

Once school was over at 1.30 pm and as the class monitor, I carried the teacher's books and any students' books the teacher had to correct to his house. I hurried home to complete the agidi business. I kindled the fire, boiled water in a pot that held about five gallons, and then poured the wet starchy corn into the boiling water and stirred it. Within one hour, it was cooked. I made small parcels, each about four ounces of the whole pot. That took about another hour. As the parcels cooled, they hardened. By the time I finished parceling most of them were hard. I moved every one of them into the room and locked the door. These were to be sold at the market the following day. My next task was to take an empty basket and meet my mother somewhere, even if it was less than four miles from home. I relieved her of some of her heavy load. She always bought some treat for me knowing that I was busy.

Amos, my age mate, surprised me in 1976 after I returned from the U.S. with my family. I did not know that they recognized my struggles. He remarked, "Obed suffered as a boy, but since then, he has been ahead of almost everybody."

The school year almost ended as a failure. As usual, the first term ended without any major examination. The second term was different. June arrived and there was the midterm examination. I was first in my class, and Njikeonye was first in his. I also participated in games and sports. The school population was divided into three groups for the purposes of games and sports, namely, senior, intermediate, and junior. Each House participated in each of these groups, and I was in the junior group. One of the games I enjoyed was football (soccer).

On our return for the third term, my House was scheduled to play two junior football games in the first week. Soccer shoes were a luxury parents could not afford, nor did we know that soccer players wear shoes. As a result, we played football and walked every distance barefoot. I sustained a cut on my right foot during the first game. It was not treated. A few days later I pleaded with the House captain to excuse me from the second game, but he refused and forced me to play. A few days later after the game, germs were festering in my foot. By the weekend my right foot was swollen. I managed to be in school the following Monday and was one of the students who went to the hospital from the school. At the end of the day, that was the last treatment I received for many weeks that followed. My leg was swollen from the foot to the knee. I could not walk. My body temperature was burning, and I lay on the floor next to the fire twenty-four hours a day and seven days a week.

It was during this illness that I seemed to learn how and what killed my siblings. My mother cried constantly. As she cried, she repeatedly said, "He is going to die like the others. It always starts with high fever and then they are gone." Malaria starts with a high fever. I concluded that they died of malaria and malaria complications. I could not walk the three miles to the hospital. She came home one day with some pink-looking grains. Umunnakwe, a man who was a soldier during World War II, gave them to her. They called it German potash. First, she added it to warm water and washed the ulcer with it. Then she spread some inside it and bandaged it. The swelling went down in a few days. It started to heal. In less than two weeks the fever was gone, and I walked about with the aid of a stick. The final exam was on the horizon. I still could not trek the one- and one-half miles to Mission Hill. I could not stay home without taking the final year examination, which was comprehensive and external and still hope to be promoted on my performance in the midterm results. My mother made the decision.

The final year examination lasted three days. She carried me on her back to the classroom. My classmates rushed to greet me. My class teacher, Mr. Jaja, came and said, "I am sure you will do well." His comment annoyed me. I thought I was his best student and was there to do only well. My mother left me and went home. She came back later in the afternoon and carried me home. She repeated the same act the second day. On the third day, she carried me to school, but Chikara, my cousin, carried me home. With the examination over, I stayed home until the day the result was announced. Mr. Umunnakwe Amaefule, through whom God healed my ulcer and saved my mother from burying another son, visited me when I returned from the U.S. I gave him some money and he wondered what it was for. I reminded him what he did. He had no recollection of it. He said, "You boys, Ezeka, another man in the village, had thanked him for the same reason." I stopped sending him money after I heard of his death.

While I recuperated, I envied other boys who played at the mission grounds on Saturday and Sunday evenings. In our compound lived daa George with her two children, a girl and a boy. The girl was the older of the two. Without failure, the boy sounded an alarm every night before they ate dinner. The girl knew how to trigger the alarm and it rarely failed. Everyone knew when they were about to eat when the boy started shouting, "Hey! Hey! Hey! Ejionu! Ejionu!! Ejionu!!! (Ejionu is the sister's name). Daa George, their mother, responded with shouts of, "Chileke! (God) Chileke!! Chileke!!! …" One of the evenings, I said to their mother, "Daa George, if you call down God here, what will you tell Him?" She looked at me with a straight face and said, "Obida, if I call down God here now, your mother will take Him over. She will not allow me to say one word."

A few weeks before the results of the tests were released, I had recovered enough to walk about with the aid of a walking stick. The last day of the school year was always an important day. The schools announced the results from class one through standard four. I got ready for school and slowly trekked to Mission Hill. Soon the students filled the premises and swept the grounds. The bell summoned the students to the hall. The teachers assembled, and the headmaster walked to the platform. There was dead silence.

Because of the large population of the students at Mission Hill, the headmaster did not call the role of all the successful and unsuccessful students. Instead, he announced the first three successful students from every class of standards three and four and those who failed. He also announced the names of students who were not allowed to return to the school the following year either because of bad behavior or because their failure was below tolerance. I knew I did well, but I could not tell how well. The headmaster took standard 3A class and Njikeonye was first. Next was Standard 3B. When he said first Obed Isi…, before he could finish saying Isigwuzo the students erupted with cheering shouts and clapping of hands. He looked askance and confused. A teacher went to the platform to tell him what the tumult was about. The student who was absent from school the whole third term and was carried to the exam room took the first position. On my way home I wore an expressionless face. Reaching the village some women were sympathetic. "Oh, my son if it was not for your sickness, you would have passed." Other students with me replied, "Who Obed? He took first." The woman said, What! Wow. My mother, who was home expecting an ordinary pass, had to be convinced. After she became convinced, she sang the rest of the day. I wrote to my brother and informed him about my result. He poured ice water on it with, "Standard four is not standard three."

I wondered what was special about standard four and why it is not standard three? Whenever Abel Okroafo, who taught standard four, came to our standard three class and requested our teacher to give him a student to answer a question his students could not answer, my teacher always sent me. I wondered if standard four would change when the school year started.

I am a Christian, attended a Christian school, and sang in the children's choir. Dee Elezue, another man from the village, called me.

I met him and he invited me to follow him to the home of dee Ojoemelam. Dee Ojoemelam was from our compound and the oldest man in the village. Dee Elezue was a soldier during the second World War and fought in India. He returned with a black box he claimed saw the underworld and foretold the future. Dee Ojoemelam was sick, and instead of going to the hospital, he invited dee Elezue to tell him which of the gods caused his sickness and how to appease the god. Dee Elezue took me along. When we got to the house, he brought out his black box. Once he opened it, he chanted something and told me to look at the dark, shining surface. Whatever he had compares favorably with the iPad of today. "Do you see anything?" he asked. "No," I said. "Do you see a man coming out through a door?" I said, "Yes." Even though I still saw nothing. Ask him why dee Ojoemelam is sick and what he should do to get well.

I needed to think quickly. I remember that my standard one teacher once said that the native doctors are frauds. "They don't see anything. They merely go by seasons. If it is a farming season, they claim that it is Njoku, the farm god. If it is the rainy season, they blame Egbe Eluigwe, the god of thunder, etc." I said it was "Ala" (the village god). Since he was the oldest man in the village, I said the god wanted a cock that was at least a year old and a jar of palm wine. He wanted to know what else the man said. My answer was, "Nothing." He chanted again and told me to raise my head up. He said that I missed one thing, the kola nut. With that he dismissed me. I walked out and did not look back. Convinced that the native doctors were frauds, I did not even tell my mother or anybody else about my experience, mainly because I was afraid of the man.

Just a few days before Christmas there seemed to be a slight chance of a change in our fortune for the better. A man from the village who lived in Lagos came home on Christmas vacation. He sent for my mother. She returned with a parcel. When she opened it, there was a small bag of rice, corned beef; there was a small bag of rice, corned beef;

there was a small bag of rice, corned beef, and a picture of my brother. He dressed in a pair of trousers, shoes, and a long-sleeved white linen shirt without a tie. My mother was so proud and thankful to God that no place could contain her. She sang and danced, and every woman in the compound joined the chorus. By nightfall, she was in a different world in thought.

She looked at the borrowed room we lived in and asked, "What happens if I am in this room when my son comes home on vacation? Is he going to sleep here with me?" Her answer was, "God forbid it." Her final answer was to plan to build a two-room house in my father's yard. I was old enough to play a part in the project.

Chapter 8

Home Again

Home Again And Standard Four

Before the school year started, my mother contracted dee Nwokeohuo Ebule to build a two-room house in my father's yard. We supplied much of the labor and materials e.g., carried the sticks, fetched water for making mud, and bought mats for the roof. Also, I helped him with tying the sticks and placing the mats on the roof. By the middle of the first term, we moved to our own home. For the first time, I had my own room and bed. My mother had the other room which also served as the kitchen. Cooking was done in her room during the rainy season and, at times, outside the room during the dry season. Once more, we were united with my cousins, and all three of us were in standard four.

As far as I could tell, there was only one significant change in my school life in standard four. For the first time, I had a lady as my teacher. Miss Nkechi Diamond Okezie completed her Elementary Teachers' Training Course at Oron and we were her first students. Again, she made me her class monitor. She was a small lady. There were three older and bigger boys in the class who made her life miserable. Two of them were repeating the class, and the third lived with Mr. Fombo, the most feared teacher at the school. These three provoked her to flog them. Because she flogged them with the whole of her upper body and still did not make them feel the pain, they made fun of her. More often than not, that disrupted the class.

On the home front, there was a change in my activities. For a reason I do not recall, I stopped singing in the choir and switched to teaching Sunday School. I know Scripture was one of my best subjects in school. The whole Circuit had one Sunday School syllabus. Miss Thomas, an English lady, was in charge. All the Sunday School teachers in the Circuit met at Mission Hill every Friday from 3 p.m. for about one hour. These teachers ranged from a few students in standard four to untrained schoolteachers. Miss Thomas taught us the lesson on Friday, and we taught the Sunday school students on Sunday. By the end of the year, she liked me and gave me a leather-bound New Testament. Her handwriting was the best I have seen. Shame on me, I do not know what happened to that Bible. From then on, I have taught Scripture.

My people say that titikpo i.e., the young lizard, told its mother not to pray for its growth but for life because whatever lives and eats grows. I was living and eating and growing. That brought more responsibilities at home and school. Having a house meant I had become the man of the house. I had to take care of the roof. There are two ways to provide mats for the roof. One can buy already-made mats. We could not afford to buy them. The second is to go to the swamp and cut palm wine fronts and come home and weave the mat. I relied on this second method. Uncle Ehiogu made this possible. He used to take me along with his sons to a swamp at Amafo Ihungwu, a distance of about four miles, to cut palm wine leaves with which we made the mats. Repairing the roof is also a man's job. But normally it takes two people. One man stays inside the house to lift up the mat on top of the leaking mat. Another man stands outside the house with another mat to insert in between the leaking mat and the one that is lifted up. But I had to do the two-man job alone. Providentially, there was dee

Ibewunjo a bachelor and middle-aged man who lived next to us. He devised a means of repairing his house alone. He cut two rods of about four inches each. He went inside and raised the leaking mat. He suspended the mat with a flat stick about four feet in length. He used two short sticks, each about four inches long and one inch in diameter as a wedge between the leaking mat and the one above it. He walked out and used a long bamboo stick to insert the mat. In the process, he pushed down the two four-inch sticks then went inside and tied the mats to the railing inside. He became my incidental teacher. With this knowledge, I could take care of the roof without involving my mother most of the time.

Besides sweeping from the mission grounds to the Umuahia Owerri main road (highway) every Saturday morning, schoolboys in the village added one more project. Instead of open-air latrines, they decided to replace them with pit latrines. The knowledge that people could avoid many common diseases by replacing open-air latrines with pit latrines inspired them to action. As usual, it was by competition. My village comprises four compounds, namely, UmuEnwere, UmuEgbe, UmuOgbometeghe, and UmuOpete (umu means children). One of the important projects the village did on a set date was weeding roads. Of the four compounds, two are large and two are small. Entering the village from Eziama, one passes through Umuogbometegh, a large compound, and Umuegbe, a small compound. These two always form a unit. Beyond the mission are Umuenwere, a large compound, and Umuopete, a small compound, and these two form another unit. The first two always weeded the right side of the road. Once the bell rang in the morning, the race to see who won began. By 9 a.m. everyone was home. This was the same mode the students used in building the pit latrines. They contributed the materials and provided the labor. They and the village were proud when they finished.

My foot healed completely. Instead of participating only in the junior group at Mission Hill, I participated in both junior and intermediate groups in football, volleyball, and rugby touch.

At this time, some student teachers came from the Women's Teachers' College, Old Umuahia (WTC), to practice at Mission Hill. One of them taught our class. As the class monitor, I went and brought her a stool. A few minutes later I completed my assignment and was fidgeting. I continued to pull the leg of the boy on my left. All his response was to move his foot as though some ants were biting him. I knew something was not normal. When I looked up to see why he reacted as he did, the student teacher was touching the class teacher, and her finger was pointing straight at me. All six eyes met. They were still smiling when I buried my face on my desk. I think the student teacher learned from then that I was the teacher's spoiled student. I had not seen anything threatening about standard four. Almost every textbook we used was written in Britain, e.g., Longman's Arithmetic, Oxford English, Book Four, Evans Hygiene, and the King James Bible. One day I read a topic in my Oxford English book that I did not understand. I requested the student teacher to teach the class the topic. Unfortunately, she did not teach the topic before her three-week teaching practice period ended. A short time after she left, we had our midterm examination. The midterm examination was internal. However, because each standard had three to four classes, different teachers set different examination papers. Different teachers taught different subjects and they followed the syllabus. The teacher who set the test on English included the topic the student teacher failed to teach us.

Less than two weeks after the examination, the results were out. I was first but scored only 71 percent in English. I wrote to the student teacher and complained that my low score in English resulted from her failure to teach the topic I requested. I told her that I was still the first. I surprised her by writing her first and last names in full.

WTC is less than four miles from Mission Hill. She replied within a week.

First, she wanted to know who told me her first name. My answer was simple. Your colleagues called you Chiadi. I have a cousin whose name is Chiadikobi. So, I concluded that Chiadi is the abbreviation for Chiadikobi. She congratulated me on being first and was not surprised. However, she wondered why I did not tell her how I performed on the topics she taught. Before I received her reply, I wrote to my brother and informed him that I had taken the first position in the midterm examination. I did not hear "standard four is not standard three" from him again.

Of the three classes of standard four, standard 4C, our class had the worst result in the midterm examination results. In those days Nigerian high school seniors took what was called Cambridge Certificate Examination. I believe the University of Cambridge in England set and corrected the papers. The results did not reach Nigeria until sometime the following year. While they waited for the results some of them became interim teachers. Because our teacher was not good in Arithmetic one of them who was hired as a teacher at Mission Hill was assigned to teach us Arithmetic. I carried my teacher's books to her house one afternoon. She assigned me something to do for her. Soon after Mr. Nmereole walked in and ordered me to leave. My teacher objected and I stayed. When Mr. Nmereole came to teach Arithmetic the following day, I, as the class monitor, gave him a piece of chalk. He allowed it to fall to the floor. That was the excuse he needed to flog me for not leaving the house. He left the school after he received a successful result. Whom do you think I saw at Umuahia Market in 1972 when I visited Nigeria from the U.S.? Someone introduced his wife to me. "Tell your husband that you met Dr. Onwuegbu, Obed. It was in Miss Okezie's house at Mission Hill when he ordered me to leave. Miss Okezie told me to stay put. He flogged me when I came to class because he did not get what he wanted. Tell him that in a few years, I will return to Nigeria. I will make sure I find the school his children attend. Even if they are in a university, I shall go there and leave only after I flog them."

Before the end of the third term my teacher bought me my first tea set: a teacup, a teaspoon, and a saucer. I gratefully accepted my gift though I could not afford tea or coffee. A big surprise awaited us when we returned from our term holiday. Because our class performed poorly in the midterm examination, Miss Okezie was sent to teach one of the standard three classes and Mr. Fombo, the most feared teacher at the school, became our class teacher. He was also the "Singing Master" (music teacher). By the time a student spent four years at Mission Hill, he or she mastered the Methodist Hymn Book. He was mercilessly harsh. He was so brutal that students took out their anger and retaliated against Billy his son. But that did not deter him. For example, Moses Nwaogwugwu was the best football player among all the juniors at the school. Moses was sick with malaria and did not come to school for about three days. He still looked sick when he returned to class. Mr. Fombo flogged and kicked him with his hands and feet until Moses escaped his hands and ran away from him and never came back to school again. I did not escape his whip. I attended church classes one day in the week in preparation for my baptism before school started. I went to school late on one of those mornings. He flogged me. As he flogged me, I tried to explain why I was late. "I went to class for baptism," I said. He ridiculed me as he flogged me and said, "I went to church. I went to church!" As I wrote the last sentence, I wondered what he might have said or done if I told him, "Mr. Fombo, you are persecuting me because I am a Christian." For the whole term, he smiled only once. The one dry smile came out of his mouth when Maggie asked him the meaning of mature. He looked at her and said, "You are mature." The class laughed and poor Maggie sat down." He laughed.

My mother and Uncle Uwakwe were still not speaking to each other because he cracked my head with his middle finger many years earlier. He repented of his cruelty to me and made peace with my mother. So, during one new yams harvest Thanksgiving ceremony he gave my mother yams to ask her pardon. They started to talk to each other again, after more than eight years.

As I grew, my responsibilities expanded. In our kind of agricultural economy, men provided the big sticks to stake the yams. That meant that I had to go to Ebite, the village common land, and cut sticks for our yams. Usually, one dragged such sticks out to the side of the road. Unfortunately, another boy had cut and dragged his sticks and placed them by mine. I described my heap to my mother. On seeing the two heaps, she decided that an adult cut my heap and carried the inferior heap. Fortunately, I was with her the next time. Before this time my mother exchanged labor with men to stake our yams. They staked our yams, and she weeded their farm. I was becoming the Jack of all trades.

Back at school, I was about to learn some facts about the examinations we took. Headmasters in Umuahia Circuit (District) met at Mission Hill and appointed the teachers who set questions for different subjects and standards. They also decided who corrected the papers and who collated and calculated the marks for classes two through four. Then the scores were returned to Mission Hill. Mr. Fombo was one of those who collated and calculated the final grades. As the best Arithmetic student in his class, he assigned the job to me. While other students worked on the school farm, cut grass, or did some other things after the examinations, I was in his house calculating and adding marks. He had faith that I would not make mistakes, though I had no calculator, and that I would not tell anybody the secret. Thank God, I did not disappoint him.

Soon the school year was over. The headmaster performed the rituals of the last day. As usual, he started with standard three A. Four

C was the last class, but I lost my first position to Dick Nwankwo. My mother bought gifts and thanked Mr. Fombo. It did not make sense to me until I realized that both my mother and brother were worried about standard four because my brother failed and repeated the class. Our long Christmas holiday followed, and all students and most teachers went home.

The holiday brought a new adventure to my life. Until then my contribution to pot making ended with helping to carry the clay, fetching sand, and running domestic errands connected with the process. This holiday I was big enough to carry some pots to Uzuakoli market twelve miles from home. Two factors were responsible for my venture. The first was to boast to other boys and girls that I had been to the market. The second was the sweet yam my mother always bought at the market. Also, there was the Esomonu family which was a friend of my parents. The wife used to send sweet yams to me through my mother. Of course, there were a few other older boys and girls who trekked to the market from the village. Later on, I trekked to the Afoumuda market. My mother bought palm oil for sale from the market. I am not aware of any other boy or girl from the village who went to Afoumuda.

I had outgrown selling water by the cups at the market. When I was not at the farm or market, I joined my cousins Chikara and Mwoko at the United African Company compounds. The UAC bought palm produce, kernels, and oil and shipped them to Britain. Before they were inspected by produce inspectors, the kernels were spread in the sun to dry. Once the inspectors pass them, they undergo another process of filtering and bagging. The boys were paid by the number of bags they filled. I did this on Saturdays or during holidays. I always gave my mother the little money I made.

Chapter 9

Standard Five And Mission Hill

"Before I formed you in the womb, I knew you;

Before you were born, I sanctified you;

I ordained you a prophet to the nations." Jeremiah 1:5

Mission Hill had undergone transformation when we resumed classes in January. More than half of the teachers had gone on transfer. The Mission had transferred my lady teacher and the headmaster to Umuda Methodist Central School. My standard three teacher was studying at Uzuakoli Methodist Elementary Teachers' College for two years. Even Mr. Fombo was gone. Many high elementary (Grade Two Teachers) who taught standards five and six were gone, including my favorite, Mr. Onyecherelem. I liked him so much that I imitated how he walked and looked forward to being in his class.

Before school started, we heard rumors about the new headmaster. Some of his colleagues called him Lord Iteke. His real name was R. Wilson Iteke. They said he taught at the secondary section of Methodist College Uzuakoli. He was a short, proud man and used to say to his students, "What puffs you up? Is it tallness? Iteke can jump up and slap you." Then he slapped the student. When he disagreed with the Principal, he asked for a transfer and left the College. He was a good artist and drew many of the subjects, including human beings and trees, from the Igbo readers we used in school. He was coming to Mission Hill from Port Harcourt. He also knew Uncle Onwumere Ikeji at Uzuakoli College. Yet the biggest surprise awaited us on the opening day.

That sunny January morning, the students, boys in white shirts and brown khaki shorts and girls in green dresses, march to the school. Students, old and new faces, filled the school grounds by 8 a.m. The bell rang at 8 a.m. All the old students lined up according to their new classes, believing that things remained the same. The headmaster walked to the front of the students and announced the changes. First, he selected the best from each class based on the examination results of the previous year to form a class or two for each standard. For example, out of three classes of standard four at Mission Hill and two from two feeder schools, he formed one class of standard five of 35 students. Then he announced that two or three former feeder schools, including Umuawa and Umuokpara had become Central schools and told those who were not admitted to seek admission there. He decided to teach Standard Five, our class. Again, I became his class monitor. By appointing me his monitor, I also became the school's general monitor. Mr. Iteke became the most important teacher and headmaster of my school career.

A large reduction in the school population also led to a change in the number of Houses. The four Houses and the English names they bore became history. Dodd and Smith became A House, while Brewer and Williams became B House. Boys in standards five and six from villages continued to live in the school dormitory. Living at Mission Hill as a boarder meant more responsibilities for me. As the General Monitor, I was also the timekeeper. I rang the bell at 6 a.m. to wake up all the boarders to perform their morning duty. I rang the bell at 7:00 to get them to prepare and eat breakfast and rang the bell again at 8:00 for the school assembly. After the morning devotion, I kept the time for the change of lessons, recess, break, and end of every activity, including announcements. I rang the bell to tell the boarders when to eat every meal, when to take their siesta, when to study at night, and when to blow their lights out. There was no electricity. Teachers submitted their class registrars, schemes of work, and notes of lesson books to the headmaster on Fridays. I carried them to his office at his home. I distributed them on Mondays and gave each class chalk.

Mr. Iteke introduced new organizations at Mission Hill. The first was Sunray Club, and I became a member. Unfortunately, only very few students were interested, and it fizzled out. Then he followed it up with a Boy Scout Club. I became a member also. We were able to form two companies. He was a well-known scout master in Eastern Nigeria; recognition came easy. One of the visitors was the Commissioner of Scouts for Eastern Nigeria. He came at a time when Mrs. Adanma Okpara, the wife of the Minister of Health who taught standard six at Mission Hill, was on maternity leave. They and two of us patrol leaders were in our scout uniforms when we visited her and her baby at Umuahia Township. On our way to see her, a chicken a bicyclist hit lay dying by the road. We took care of it.

We had watched other schools, especially the Anglican and Roman Catholic schools, march to the tune of their school bands on Empire Day with admiration. Mr. Iteke made us proud when he bought one of the best band sets in the District. We at once embarked on learning how to play the instruments. At first, I chose the flute but changed to the drum. For some reason, our pride was short-lived. It seemed the school could not afford it.

Mr. Iteke was an excellent teacher and an effective disciplinarian. Yet he rarely used a whip. His handwriting was superb. The blackboard was at least eight feet long, and he wrote straight from one end to the other. He amused himself with some of the student's writing. He smiled and said, "If I trained my chicken, it would write better than some of you." However, having chosen the best of the students, he did not spend much energy getting them to understand what he taught.

Much of the time, he disciplined students with his mouth instead of the whip. Here is a story that illustrates his method.

Iheanacho was the Vice Captain (VC) of *A* House, and Isaac was a member of his House. Isaac proved stubborn, and Iheanacho reported him to Mr. Iteke. Expecting a quick decision from the headmaster, a few of us followed them. After the VC reported the case to the headmaster, the headmaster acted as though he did not hear what he said and turned against him. "Iheanacho," he said, "I am waiting for the day someone will bring you here. That day, you will know that you are not above the rules of this school." While he spoke to Iheanacho, Isaac smiled and made faces at the Vice Captain, unaware that the headmaster saw him. Then Mr. Iteke turned to him and said, "Isaac, what puffs you up? You are not smart in school. You are too short. Iteke is short, and his shortness is a good one. You are short, and your shortness is a bad one. Your father is poorer than Iteke. …" Before he said one more word, Isaac stretched his hands and pleaded to be flogged. "Please, Sir, flog me and don't say any more." We all, including Mr. Iteke, laughed as Isaac pleaded. He warned Isaac against doing anything that would bring him to his office again.

Njikeonye and I were in the same class again after two years of separation. But the competition was no longer between just two of us. There were at least three more in the class. However, when the midterm examination came, I was still the first. Except for a few boys from the township, all the boys in our class lived in the dormitory. Because of the empty classrooms and vacant teachers' quarters, three of us, Ubadire, the Compound Chief, Amos, and I, were allowed to occupy one of the vacant teachers' quarters. The Compound Chief was the most senior student officer; the two Captains were under him. My duty as the timekeeper took on additional significance when all the adjacent schools came to Mission Hill to take their final year examination.

Living in the dormitory meant my mother had two kitchens to support. She gave me one shilling of three pence per week. My cousin Nwoko got two shillings a week, nine pence more than I. Unfortunately, his was not enough for him. One term he used his school fees as well and had to beg Gbo Gordon to pay his school fees. Like me, his father was dead. My advice to him to spend less on meat met with a comparison with one Chibuzo whose father sold meat at the market. However, I was able to save enough money for my scouting activities. As long as I did not ask my mother for extra money, she was fine with my activities. Besides, I was contributing in different ways. At times, we went to the farm and market together. At other times separately. Some other times, I went to the U.A.C. yard with my cousins. My brother was employed and could send some gifts or even money. We also farmed on our father's land. I planted some banana trees and one orange tree on our street. Our kola nut tree, which did not yield fruit for many years, suddenly started to flower and yielded nuts. That was also a source of income. Besides our uha trees that shed leaves once a year and their fresh leaves used for soup, it was also a source of income. It seemed that God Himself was welcoming us back to our home.

The final year examination was around the corner, and Mission Hill was still the center of activities. Though all the headmasters and or their representatives met at Mission Hill for planning, every central school administered the tests at their school. But it was exactly the same test for every standard in the denomination. Feeder schools still came to Mission Hill to take their tests. Mission Hill was the coordinating center for all the examination activities for classes two through standard four for all the schools in Umuahia Circuit. Even as a teacher of standards five and six, I never knew who set and corrected the examination papers for those two standards. The students were the first to take the examination papers, but the results were not out until about the third week of January the following year.

With a new set of teachers, one might think that Obed would not get involved in collating and calculating the results. That turned out to be wishful thinking. Mr. Uko, a new teacher at Mission Hill who was in charge that year, assigned the task to me. Unlike the previous years, I had to wait till the new year to hear my result, especially since my name would not be heard from the platform.

There was still one market called Orieukwuamoji, which I had not been to. It is about 16 miles from home. Nobody from home attended it. But some people from Ogbodi, my grandmother's home, did. A cousin of my mother Ada Orioha, who lived at Ogbodi did. She and my mother arranged for me to go with Daa Ada Orioha. I went and slept at Ogbodi overnight. We trekked the remaining fourteen miles on the market day.

I carried groundnuts still in their shell. My mother instructed me to sell them by the cigarette cup she gave me, one cup for one ejenma, i.e., one Manila. Ngwa women bought and planted groundnuts on their farms. The market was already in session when we arrived. Once we arrived and the women saw my groundnuts, they surrounded me, eager to buy everything. I covered my bag and bargained. Instead of selling a cup for one ejenma, I got them to pay three manila for two cups. Within thirty minutes after I arrived, my groundnuts were sold. I was delighted and wished I could fly home at that moment to show my mother my achievement. But I had to wait for daa Ada. Looking at me in amazement, she exclaimed, "You can do this, and your mother struggles alone." I thought, what does she mean by struggles alone? I waited for her, and by the time we reached her home, it was dark. I slept there.

Early in the morning, when I woke up to go home, my legs were swollen. But I had to trek home. I started, but it was difficult. By the time I reached Ogwumabiri ukwuacu i.e., halfway home, I could not move anymore. I stopped. I was aching and, at the same time, eager to show my mother my achievement. My money was also heavy. It must have been after eleven in the morning when I reached home. My presence alone delighted my mother. But my swollen leg dampened her spirit. My achievement and joy, I believed, lessened her concern. With rest and without any treatment, my legs healed.

Before the holiday was over, standards five and six results were out. My village is the second nearest village to the school. The news of the results attracted students and parents to Mission Hill. I knew I did well on the test. So, I did not think I should worry. Was I surprised at how well I did? I was first not only at Mission Hill but for all standard five classes in the district. I visited Nigeria from the U.S. in 1972 and visited the University of Nigeria, Nsukka, for the first time. I spent the night with Obioma Imo from my village. We strolled around when he saw Ihuoma Philip, the Acting Bursar, and asked him, "Do you know Dr. Onwuegbu?" Ihuoma smiled and replied, "How can I forget Obed? If not for him, I would have been first in all standard five in Umuahia Circuit." He attended Umuokpara Central, not Mission Hill.

Mr. Iteke taught the total person. Any student who failed to succeed under him might not succeed under any other teacher. As reluctant as I was to become a teacher, he influenced me in choosing to be one and the kind of teacher I became.

Chapter 10

Standard Six Mission Hill

My final year at Mission Hill started with more responsibilities. Mr. Iteke appointed three students to lead the student body. Dick Nwankwo was the Compound Chief, Amobi Nzenwata was the Captain of *A* House, and I was *B* House Captain. This was in addition to everything I did the previous year. All the students, including the captains, were subjects to the Compound Chief. Dick was a member of my House. Suddenly, a test of the will developed between us.

As I stated earlier, the Houses competed for points in different areas, including neatness. The school divided dormitories and the kitchen between *A* and *B* Houses, and the teacher on duty inspected them every morning after the students left for classes. Dick unfailingly left untidy space, and my House was penalized for his mess. After several warnings, I gave him grass to cut. Insisting that I was under him, he refused to do the punishment. But he made a foolish mistake and reported me to Mr. Iteke. He regretted his move when the headmaster told him that when he was in my house, he was under me and must obey my orders. "But when Obed comes out to school, he is under you. If you don't like that, you move to *A* House." He moved out of my house.

Mr. Iteke made us compete for articles he planned to give away. At one time, he brought his old fountain pen to class and set a test on Arithmetic. He promised to give it to the first student to finish with the correct answers. I took it. The same thing happened when he gave away a ruler.

Every school day started with morning devotion. The headmaster followed it with his pep talk. He often said, "I know all the things you do. Look here, the smartness in you is the foolishness in your teachers." I thought he could not know until I became a teacher. He was also fond of saying, "If you are a tiger, come to me as a tiger. Don't come as a sheep. Don't pretend." Before he dismissed the assembly, he said, "You did not pay me for this." I cannot leave out his most famous and frequent saying. "A cow does not know the use of its tail until it is cut off."

For example, Sunday Chikezie was the school's best goalkeeper. We had a football match against another school. Sunday was late, and the game was delayed for a few minutes. When finally, he came, Mr. Iteke made him take off the goalkeeper jersey and gave it to Ekwebelem who had never been a goalkeeper to keep the goal. We still won the game.

I was in the dormitory one day when the headmaster sent for me. I walked into his living room and saw a familiar face standing by him. We recognized ourselves. It was Jonah Onyegbule, who was in standard five and assistant captain the year I was in standard three at Mission Hill. He came for admission to read standard six with us and had been admitted. Mr. Iteke reintroduced him and asked me to take him to my house. Jonah became a friend and a better replacement for Dick. From the first time we saw him, his nickname was Nwadicheiche, which means the boy with different manners. He came to the newspaper table one day during our first year at Mission Hill and saw those of us in standard three, and declared, "Our infants are at the table." He had not changed and was still liked and likable.

As the term progressed, Mr. Iteke told me and made me feel that there was nothing I could not do well. If he saw any student playing with me instead of studying, he said, "Are you fooling with Obed? Tomorrow, he will pass, and you will fail. Go ahead and fool with him." To my surprise, some of my classmates speculated that I passed examinations with medicine, i.e., magic. One Ibeku boy looked at me with such hatred that if looks could kill, he would have me dead on the spot. But he could not say a word to me. The fact that two High Elementary student teachers from Methodist College Uzuakoli on teaching practice acknowledged that I was smart did not help matters. The second term and midterm examination came, and I was first again. This midterm result was different from all other elementary midterm results.

The Methodist Mission used to employ standard six graduates as teachers and train them at elementary and high elementary colleges. At a certain stage, the Mission changed its policy. It established Preliminary Teachers Training College. This training lasted for one year. The standard six midterm examination results in all Methodist schools determined the candidates who took the entrance examination to the College. The first, second, and third highest performers in every standard six class qualified to take the test. Therefore, as the first, I qualified with Njikeonye Ugenyi and Njikeonye Iheukwumere. But we had to wait till the third term to take the entrance examination.

Meanwhile, my extracurricular activities, especially farming, had advanced. I could cut big sticks to stake the yams. But they were too bulky for me or my mother to pin them deep into the ground to prevent the wind from uprooting them. Walking to the Mission one day, I saw dee Kanu Nbelekwe staking his yams. He was deformed in one leg and could not lift the bulky sticks to pin them deep into the ground. He had a short stick almost as short as he was, which he used to open the ground first and then lift the bulky stick and push it into the hole. That was the solution I needed. I adopted his method.

After my mother and I returned to my father's yard, it seemed that my uncle decided that God had assured our survival and started accommodating us. Since he and his brother, our father, owned common farmland at Isieke Ibeku, he invited my mother to participate and also share the responsibility of feeding workers. Harvesting yams took several weekends. Preference was given to weekends because schoolchildren participated. A typical weekend yams harvest started on Friday. The adults went to the farm on Friday. The men dug out the yams from the ground, and the women brushed off the soil and laid them in heaps, and covered them with leaves. All the adults and every child who was able to carry yams went to the farm on Saturday morning. Every individual ate breakfast at home. The farm was seven miles away from home, and the children made three trips that Saturday.

Once we trekked the first seven miles to the farm, all the children loaded their baskets and carried the first load to the stream at home, offloaded, and walked back to the farm. While the children were gone, the men harvested, and the women brushed the soil off the yams. One woman, my mother or one of my uncle's two wives, was designated to feed the crew. When we returned to the farm, we were sure food was waiting for us. We ate lunch ,loaded yams again and went off. This was always the most difficult trip. The sun was hot, the ground was hotter, and we trekked barefooted. We ran with loads on our heads when we walked on hot roads without sheds and slowed down on tracks with trees and sheds. Again, we deposited the yams at the stream and hurried back to the farm for the last trip of the day. Usually, the load was light. Mothers also carried yams at this time. Some of the children usually carried firewood. The sun was no longer as hot as earlier, and the ground stopped burning the feet. We congregated at the stream, washed the yams, and carried them to the open common barn more than one hundred yards away. My uncle gave each family yams through the mothers. The day's work was done, and we went home.

Soon, boxing was introduced at Mission Hill. I joined the club. Later I received my brother's picture in his boxing suit with the name Enoch Wild. He informed me that Uncle Jacob was also a boxer in Lagos. Though I enjoyed boxing and did well in it, I had no more opportunities to advance once I left Mission Hill.

The third term arrived, and we took the two most important entrance examinations I knew, namely, Methodist Secondary College Uzuakoli and Nto-Ndang Methodist Teachers' Preliminary Training College.

Mr. Iteke also taught singing to standards five and six. During one singing lesson, he was teaching a song in the Methodist Hymn Book. I did not understand the beautiful lyrics, nor did I like the tune. The hymn was, "Captain of Israel's host and guide ..." Now I understand the lyrics and enjoy the tune. But then the thirty minutes seemed like hours. I rang the bell once as a warning to inform teachers that they had five more minutes before either a lesson change or the end of the school day. If it was the end of the day, I rang the bell for as long as I liked. Singing was the last lesson of the day. A minute or two before the end of the lesson, I took the bell and rang it for as long and hard as I could. I still giggle as I type this story, as though it happened yesterday. Mr. Iteke looked at me, clapping his hands and calling me as he waved me out with his hand and warned me, "Get out from here. The day I hear you sing or even hum this hymn at this school, I dismiss you." I took the bell, the clock, and my hymn book and hurried out. Trying to avoid him the rest of the day, I ran as fast as I could to the classroom and carried his books to his house. On my way out of his house, we met. I was still wondering what he would say or do when he looked at me and smiled. "You want me to kill you at this school?" That was the end of the matter. I wondered why I would bother singing a song I did not care to learn. I used this as an example of wrong punishment that turned out to be reinforcement with my graduate students.

Several weeks after we took the entrance examination to Uzuakoli the result was out. All six or seven of us who took the first test were selected to travel to the College for the second round. Unlike trekking the twelve miles when we went to the market, we traveled by train this time. We paid our way. One of the duties of the captain was to supervise members of his House during morning duty. Some of my house members swept the road from the school to the Manse. As I supervised the students one morning, the Reverend Minister's clerk saw me and said, "Obed, you took the entrance to Nto-Ndang PTC." Ignorant that the result came through the Reverend's office and that his clerk had seen it, I replied, "Yes." I proudly added, "It was easy, and all three of us will pass it." He said, "You are sure of that?" I said, "Yes." Two days later, the headmaster announced the result during the assembly. Obed was the only candidate selected from the whole Umuahia Circuit. The rumor that I passed examinations with the help of medicine developed wings. But no one accused me to my face. To Mr. Iteke it was all in my head. What we did not know is that was the way to fulfill the promise my parents made to God before I was conceived. When I hesitated to accept admission to attend the College, God used Mr. Iteke to convince me. He said, "If, for no other reason, you can say that you are the only successful candidate from the Circuit." As the Provost (President) of Oyo Federal College of Education for Special Education, I visited my home in 1986 and visited David Ukaegbu, one of my classmates at Mission Hill. I knew he did not recognize me, and I could not have recognized him if I had met him elsewhere. I called him David. He wanted to know who I was. To confuse him the more I replied, "Dr. Onwuegbu," because I went by Obed Isigwuzo in elementary school. Having thoroughly confused him, I said, "I am Obed." He got excited, "Obed Isigwuzo!!" "Yes", I said. "We thought you passed exams with magic." I asked him, "What changed your mind?" He said, "We know better now." He had become an accountant by profession.

As a scout boy with the knowledge of Morse code, I developed an interest in the post office. I no longer went to the post office simply to buy stamps and post letters, or claim my registered letter, or cash my money orders. I went and watched and listened as the staff sent telegrams. I thought and daydreamed of the day I would work in the post office as a messenger.

It must have been during the second term holiday when we noticed an additional unit at the U.A.C. compound. A new noisy factory was operating. It was an orange squash (orange drink) factory. Oranges that rot in the villages were being picked, bagged and sold by the scale. At first, we walked in, and out of curiosity, we helped. Later we were employed. We stood steady. The machine cut the oranges into two halves, and the conveyor belts carried them to us. We took each half and pressed it against a spinning iron piece, which squeezed the juice out. We threw the peel to another belt that carried them away. We were not paid much, but we ate as many oranges as we wanted. Our earning ability, as well as opportunities, was expanding.

About two weeks after we returned from Uzuakoli, the headmaster received a letter from Mr. Ashby the headmaster of the secondary school. He was coming to Mission Hill to interview the candidates. We were all very happy except that Njikeonye Ugenyi's name was missing. It seemed impossible that he failed when less capable students succeeded. Uzuakoli was the college every boy in the Methodist schools desired to attend. The school was still in session, and every student, including Njikeonye, got dressed for school. By 9 am, the college Principal was at Mission Hill. After some formality with Mr. Iteke, we went to see the Principal in what used to be a standard six classroom. When he finished and was about to dismiss us, I told him that there was another Njikeonye who took the test at Uzuakoli but was not called to the interview. He was surprised and sent for him. I went and called Njikeonye. He interviewed him before he left. A short time later, we learned that Njikeonye Iheukwumere passed to go to

Umuahia Government College. This was the only College in the region that could minutely be said was better in some way than Uzuakoli. Soon Ogbonna Inegbu received admission from Uzuakoli. Njikeonye and I decided that if he passed, we were sure of admission. He came from the same village and was of the same standard. He had never been as smart, let alone smarter. However, he looked younger than his age.

Jonah had one influence on me. He had several clothes he wore after school. I did not. There was only one way I could afford new clothes, and that was by myself. I dared not ask my mother. I started saving more from my weekly feeding money. By the beginning of the third term, I had saved enough to buy some yards to give to Jonah's tailor to sew a shirt and a pair of shorts for me. I planned to take them home on a Saturday. Knowing that my mother would be upset to hear that I saved money and did not give it to her and instead spent it on me, I lied to her. I told her my brother sent me a parcel and I needed to go to the post office the following Saturday to get it. Thinking about it now, several things could have aroused her suspicion. How did he get my measurements? Why did he not write or ask about her in my letter? But I used my clothes. I know my children will not read this paragraph. If by mistake they do, they may not understand it.

Suddenly, a tragedy struck. I walked out one morning to inspect the work of members of my House on duty. Someone from the village saw me and told me my cousin Mba was dead. Mba was the brightest of all my uncle's sons and the only son of his mother. I ran to the headmaster's house weeping and obtained permission to go home. I wept as I ran home. On arrival, everyone in the compound was crying. Mba lived and died in Lagos and was buried there. Dee Amadi Udu sent the telegram about his death the previous day to dee Agonmo. It was late in the evening when he received it. Therefore, he waited till before daybreak the following day and woke up my uncle before the cock crew. With some difficulty, he managed to control my uncle, and they planned how to tell his wife. On my arrival, I saw Mba's mother crawling on all fours like a baby, mute with tears streaming from her eyes, having exhausted herself crying. Dazed and confused, she crawled a distance of more than the length of a football field to the main street, weeping as though in search of the son with other women walking by her. I spent the day at home with the rest of the family members.

Several weeks later, Njikeonye Ugenyi received a letter of admission from Uzuakoli. While I waited for my result, I wrote to my brother, who directed me to ask dee Brown Ekeledo to telephone the Principal of Uzuakoli. I walked to the GBO Company office where he worked. He was in the front office at his small desk. I told him why I was there. He picked up the phone and pretended to ask for the Principal of the College. His next statement was, "Thank you." He looked at me and said, "The Principal traveled." It was a little more than two years later, when I became a student at Uzuakoli, that I realized that he simply played a prank on me because there was no telephone service at the College then.

Soon, it was the annual pilgrimage of teachers and students who congregated at Mission Hill because of the final year examinations. The headmasters and or their representatives decided who set and who marked the final year examination papers for class two and standards one through four. Even though standards five and six students took their examination a week or two before other students, they still attended school till the last day. Again, all the examination papers the teachers corrected were brought to Mission Hill. Mr. Uko, the standard four teacher at Mission Hill, had several schools and subjects to collate and calculate. Once again and for the last time, I became his calculator. Fortunately, I finished in time to go camping with the Boy Scouts. It was overnight camping. When we returned to Mission Hill on a Saturday midday, the headmasters were making the final decision about the results. I heard a familiar voice calling "Obed." When I turned, it was my standard four-lady teacher. We were happy to see each other again. She was in charge of the ladies preparing food for the headmasters and was ready to feed me.

My experience at Mission Hill cannot be complete without this paragraph. Euginea was a girl in my class. Immanuel, her brother, was also in the same class. For one reason or the other, she liked me and told everyone else but me. Unknown to her and me was the fact that Jersey, another girl in my class, liked me also. Knowing that I had not shown any interest in any girl, Jersey tried to find out if Euginea and I were really friends. She concocted a story about Euginea and me and asked her about it. Surprised at the false story, Euginea came and asked me about it. To prove that Jersey lied, I hid in a corner of an empty classroom and asked Euginea to trick Jersey into the empty classroom. Immediately she walked in and saw me, she shouted and ran away. Unfortunately for them, I had no interest in girls at this time.

My disappointment with Uzuakoli had hardened my mind against Nto-Ndang. If they don't want me at Uzuakoli, I will not go to Nto-Ndang, which was my stand. Mr. Iteke started his labor of advice and pleas. "If for no other reason, you can say that you are the only successful candidate from Umuahia Circuit. Besides, I know that you will pass the entrance examination to Elementary Teachers' College at your first trial. Then you will be a student at Uzuakoli." I agreed to attend Nto-Ndang.

Why did I hesitate to go to Nto-Ndang? Recall that only the best three students from each standard six class took the examination, and only sixty students from all Methodist schools were admitted to the college each year. Many who took the examination and others who did not qualify had been admitted to Uzuakoli secondary school. One might say that it was only a one-year college or that teachers were not paid much. None of those concerned us. Our problem was an employee of the Methodist Bookstore, the biggest bookstore in Umuahia, and the headquarters of all the Methodist bookstores east of the River

Niger. The employee did not play good football, i.e., soccer, and was not handsome. We, the students, called him Nto-Ndang. Associating him with Nto-Ndang also gave the College a negative connotation at our school.

The last day of the school year was always special. My last day at Mission Hill was extra special. My House won the year-end prize over A House when the school calculated all the points from sports, games, and cleanliness. Removing Dick from my House paid off. The reward was that the school paid seven shillings and sixpence for the first six copies of the House group photograph. For the first time, the school bought gifts for the Compound Chief and captains. The Chief and the captains received the same book, and in addition, I received a biology book. The headmaster justified the gift of the additional biology book by saying that Obed was the only candidate from the Circuit who passed to go to Nto-Ndang and was waiting for the result of the interview from Uzuakoli. He concluded, "It is certain he will be in college next year. Then, he announced the result and dismissed the students. Standards five and six students went home and waited for their results.

As the school population decreased, so did the need for space. On the other hand, the bookstore staff was growing, and they wanted more space. My cousin Chikara and I heard that they planned to build more houses for the staff and were employing students to make cement blocks for them. Besides, they paid better than what we made at UAC. Company. Chikara and I applied and were employed. Besides better pay, we worked only five days a week. By the end of the holiday, we had made enough money to contribute toward our needs. Meanwhile, I waited for my brother to send me the ten pounds Nto-Ndang would cost. Instead of sending the money, he wrote to me and asked why the College would cost only ten pounds a year. "Why do you not tell me if you have a scholarship?" Therefore, I traveled to the college without paying tuition.

I used my holiday earnings and the money my mother gave me to buy the list of things the college requires of students. The list included school uniforms, shoes, white pairs of shorts, eating utensils, and knives for cutting grass. I was buying some of the things at Umuahia township market one day when another boy came to me and introduced himself. Emedom Ogbonna had seen me at Uzuakoli during the second test, and I had the same list as he did from Nto-Ndang. We talked and parted. Before I traveled to Nto-Ndang, Gbogbo Odikemere, one of my uncles, told me about one Mr. Ibegbulem from the village who was the headmaster of the College. He also gave me three shillings to buy bread. I used Chikara's school box as my suitcase the morning I left.

Failure to gain admission to Uzakoli was painful for other reasons. Two years earlier, when I first went to Uzuakoli market, two relatives, dee Way, and dee Sunday, came to greet my mother at the market. Both of them were students at Uzuakoli Methodist Secondary College. They were handsome and always dressed smartly in their uniform. I admired them. It did not occur to me that I could be a student at Uzuakoli at the time. When two years later, it seemed that my brother could afford the money, and I had the ability to pass the entrance examination; to be denied the opportunity seemed unbearable. Also, as mentioned earlier, there was the Esonu family at Uzuakoli. Both husband and wife were good friends of my family. They were fond of me before I even went to the market. They sent me gifts through my mother. They gave me more when I attended the market. I thought I would have a second home at Uzuakoli. But I took comfort in that the two boys who succeeded were not smarter than I. I did not know God was working out His plans to fulfill the promise my parents made in my "failure."

Part Three
Teachers' Colleges, Training, And Teaching

Chapter 11

Nto-Ndang PTC

"' For the mountains shall depart
And the hills be removed,
But My kindness shall not depart from you,
Nor shall My covenant of peace be removed,'
Says the Lord, who has mercy on you. (Isaiah 54:10)

'No weapon formed against you shall prosper,
And every tongue *which* rises against you in judgment
You shall condemn.
This *is* the heritage of the servants of the Lord,
And their righteousness *is* from Me,'
Says the Lord." (Isaiah 54: 17).

Nto-Ndang means the children of Ndang. Nto-Ndang is twenty-one miles from Umuahia, my hometown. The people are

Anangs, a different ethnic group from the Igbo ethnicity to which I belong. Nto-Ndang village has a notorious history. As Anangs, they do not understand our Igbo language, nor do we understand theirs.

Igbo people from many villages that make up the area called Umuahia went to Efiayong by bicycle on a three-day journey to buy bags of crayfish. Nto-Ndang is the first non-Igbo village they passed when they went and the last on their way home. The Igbo traders knew that some of the Anang people were dangerous so they armed themselves with sharp machetes and rode in groups of three and four or more. Among the traders were some members of the Christian Science sect who did not believe in violence. Therefore, they did not arm themselves. There were two of these Christians in a group of three on their way from the market when they reached Nto-Ndang.

A group of armed villagers waiting for them ambushed and attacked them. The one-armed trader defended himself gallantly before he was overpowered. Before they killed him, he had done enough damage that caused blood to flow freely along a large space, and the crayfish was thrown along the road. The next group of Umuahia traders who arrived at the scene stopped, and so did all the groups. They all decided to carry their bags of crayfish to the Umuahia market and return for revenge. They refused to report it to the police. On their return, they traced the blood, and when the blood stopped, they entered the village and killed and burned houses. The nearest police station was at Ikot Ekpene, ten miles away. By the time the police arrived, the Avengers had paid the murderers in kind and left. After the dust settled, the government built a police station in the village by the road. The Methodist Mission built the College on the other side of the road, almost opposite the police station.

It was about the third week of January; elementary school had started, and the standard six results were still not out. That did not prevent the students from traveling to Nto-Ndang College. The lorry deposited me at the entrance of the College. With my bucket and pillow in one hand and Chikara's school box in the other, I walked to the compound. First, on my right was a large block that turned out to be the two classrooms. Passing the classrooms on the right, one saw the whole College of about eight buildings. At the center of the compound was the football field. There were three students dormitories labeled A, B, and C, each meant for twenty students. The College assigned all the students to hostels before we arrived, and mine was C House. On the left side of the field was the headmaster's residence. A big house further inside on the right behind A and B dormitories was the Principal's house. Between the headmaster's house and C House was the big house partitioned into two: a small side was the kitchen, and the big side was the dining hall. We soon learned why the tuition was so low.

There was no electricity or running tap water at the College. The College provided the students with raw food items, and the students fetched firewood and water and prepared their food. Of course, there were organizations to govern campus life. Each dormitory had a captain and a vice-captain. I was neither a captain nor vice. For cooking, there were six groups of ten each, and I was a group leader. That meant I ensured that my group received its fair share of the food items, supervised the cooking, and shared the food after it was cooked. This second part of my duty led to a clash between my vice-captain and me later in the year. I was also the Sanitary Inspector and the Games master. The last office did not mean much since we had only the game of football (soccer). All I did was organize and referee the game.

Before nightfall, almost the entire student body was present. Since I was the only student from Umuahia Circuit, Emedom, whom I met at the Umuahia market, was the only familiar face at the College. He came from Uzuakoli Circuit. Later in the term, the College admitted Chijioke from Umuahia. This was a favor to Mr. Ibegbulem because of Mr. Ibegbulem's relationship with Chijioke's cousin. By this time, the standard six results were out. One of the new central schools had learned that its students would not receive the standard six certificate because it did not meet Government requirements. The College expelled two students from the school. I discovered that of all the students who took the entrance examination, I was fourth among the successful candidates.

I introduced myself to Mr. Ibegbulem before the end of the first week. He acknowledged knowing my father and spoke well of him. Why did I not know anything about this man from the same village? He lived in a village separate from mine. At one time, these two villages were one. Our village grew larger in population and space. Where we live is Amafo Isingwu, and Isi means head. His village is Amafo Ihungwu, and Ihu means face. The names indicate that while the two villages are separated, they are still one; one is the head, and the other is the face.

This knowledge cleared one mystery for me. After my mother and I returned to my dad's yard, my uncle used to take us boys to the swamp only a few yards from Ibegbulem's house to cut palm wine leaves for weaving mats for the roof of the house. I wondered how we could own a swamp that far from our village. It was many years later that Mrs. Ibegbulem told me that her husband told her that my family is the nearest blood relation in my village. Though I was ignorant of that fact, he became my surrogate father.

Mr. Udo, a very short and stout Efik man, was the Principal. He taught arithmetic, my favorite subject, and some others. Mr. Ekanem was the clerk but was at the college temporarily till he passed his Cambridge Certificate examination. Besides methods of teaching various subjects, Mr. Ibegbulem also taught Rural Science. This was a new subject to us with new terminology. Several weeks into the first term, a man from my village dee Onwugbarauko who was on his way to the crayfish market, brought me the tuition fee my brother sent.

By the end of the first term, we knew some of our surroundings. We all knew the stream from where we fetched our all-purpose water and even very often had our bath. One of the first Efik sentences I learned was dikaa idim kenyere nmong, which means Come let us go to the stream to have our bath. I even said it to the Principal. He simply laughed and said, "No." Emedom became my good friend. Also, Akpan, who is not Igbo became my good friend. On the other hand, another Akpan in my C house and Enyina, who lived in the same dormitory with my friends, proved difficult to get along with. Apart from classroom activities, the first term ended almost without any major event.

Both Uzuakoli and Nto-Ndang closed on the same Friday, and that meant Ogbonna, Njikeonye, and I were home the same day. We planned to visit Mr. Iteke at Mission Hill the following Monday while the school was in session. When we reached the door of his classroom and hesitated to walk in, he enthusiastically invited us in as though we were his trophy to show to his class. A few minutes later, we were on our way to the market. We were a few steps away from his class when he called me back. In a subdued, low voice and as though he was sorry, he said, "Njikeonye took first with only three points above you." I thanked him. With that, I became the first to graduate from grade school from Isigwuzo or even Onwuegbu family.

While I was on holiday, we received a letter from my brother. He would be coming home on leave during my second week of holiday. We were overjoyed, especially my mother. She prepared her delightful food on the day he was expected. My cousin Nwoko and I went to the railway station, but that was not the day the through train from Lagos was scheduled to pass through Umuahia. They called it "through train" because it passed through small railway stations without stopping. My mother was in a mourning mood when she heard that it was the wrong date. Every hour of the remainder of the day might as well have been a day of its own. The day passed, and Nwoko and I were at the railway station again. As I saw the engine passing the station platform, I wondered if I could recognize him. The engine and several coaches passed the spot where we stood, and Nwoko saw him waving his hand at us. He shouted, "There he is! There he is!" We ran to meet him, and he climbed out through the window. He went and claimed his bicycle and luggage. We carried his suitcase and other things, and he rode home. I wished I was home when he arrived to see my mother's reaction. A few days later, he gave me a ride on his bicycle to the market and back. It seemed as though we never had one disagreement as children. I watched as many relatives from the village and other villages came to see him. About nine days after he arrived, I left him with the one bed we shared and returned to the College.

It may sound funny to say that one of the gifts God gave me is my brain. As a result, whatever the teacher said in the classroom was enough for me to do well in the examination. Unfortunately, I thought everyone should understand the teacher as he taught them to pass examinations. So, when Nwaogu Nmeribe, the Vice Captain and a member of my group consistently stayed in the classroom to study while others cooked, I got angry at him. He stayed in the classroom until the bell rang for people to come to the dining hall to eat. Then he ran like he had a wedge between his legs. One day, I decided that we had enough of this university student. I took out his share of raw food before the group cooked the rest. I told the rest of the students in my group to eat their food after the grace and leave him with me.

Soon, the bell rang, and he was in the dining hall. When he uncovered his plates after the grace, he saw raw food staring him in the face. He fumed. I explained my actions. "Other Captains and Vice Captains come here to see and even encourage their groups. No one has ever seen you except when it is time to eat. Are you in a university, and are we your slaves? Take your food and cook it yourself."

He was angry and stormed out. The next thing was that the headmaster called me to his house. When I walked in Nwaogu was there. I explained myself again. I don't expect him to fetch water or firewood or to cook. But like other Captains and Vice Captains, I expect him to show his face during the cooking and encourage those who cook. Like Mr. Iteke before him, I was right, and Nwaogu was wrong. I went and ate my food. Unlike Dick, he did not request a transfer to another group.

Less than two months after I left my brother in the village, I received a letter from him. He was back in Lagos. The unexpected, pleasant news was that he was betrothed to a girl in standard (grade) four. By this time, I had become familiar with the Ibegbulem family. He sent Onwe, his adult male servant, to the village to help build his house. I helped with some of the domestic chores the house boy performed, such as fetching water, grinding casava, and frying it to make gari. I also used his old bicycle to run errands to Umudike, a village in Igbo, land sixteen miles from Nto-Ndang and five from Umuahia.

Umudike was an important educational village with two important educational institutions. One was an agriculture research institution in animals and seeds. Rural Science teachers such as Mr. Ibegbulem trained there. I rode to the School of Agriculture to get him certain materials from Mr. Egbe. The other institution is the Government Secondary School, the only one that could claim to be minutely superior to Uzuakoli Secondary School in some respect. I used to run errands for Mr. Ibegbulem from Nto-Ndang to Mr. Egbe who was stationed at Umudike.

Mrs. Ibegbulem had a brother, Iroawuchi, who graduated from Nto-Ndang the previous year. He was teaching at Ogbuebule, another Igbo village nine miles away from Nto-Ndang. I returned from Umudike one Saturday, and his sister pleaded with me to take food for him. It seemed that he would starve to death if I did not. I agreed. But as I rode to his house, I wondered about my future. Who would supplement my salary if I found myself in his situation? When I arrived, it was late to return to the College, besides I was tired. I slept there and rode back on Sunday.

If we thought that by going to college, we had outgrown the famous mighty Methodist midterm examination, it stood and smiled at us in the face. By the middle of June, the Principal told us to get ready for the midterm examination. The one subject I enjoyed most was Arithmetic. It included stocks and shares, simple and compound interests among other topics. I finished the test, which meant for two hours, in about thirty minutes. At the end of the examination, I felt the tests were relatively easy and no one else complained. Well, we came to learn how to be teachers. So, our next project was teaching practice. The College drilled us into its expectations. We filled out forms and chose the schools in the areas we wished to practice. The second term holiday was three weeks, and our teaching practice began on Monday afterwards and lasted for three weeks. I chose Eziama where I was schooled. The College gave each of us the equivalent of three weeks of feeding money.

At last, another term ended. The students went home on holiday. The midterm examination results were not out yet. We wondered if the results would be sent to us while we were on holiday.

The Holiday was uneventful and passed as we waited for the beginning of the teaching practice. However, I did go to see my future sister-in-law. She was and is still beautiful. I loved her from the moment I saw her. The parents named her Nwanbu, i.e., her first child. At the end of the holiday, I trekked to Eziama Methodist Group School just as I did five years earlier, except this time, I was a teacher instead of a student. I still fetched water at home from the stream and performed chores.

When I reported for duty, Mr. Mba Iheukwumere was the headmaster and standard one teacher. He assigned me to teach his class. I spent the three weeks with his class and enjoyed the students, many of whom came from my village. One other thing that changed at Eziama was how students addressed me, Sir, instead of Obed. As they say in America, "It seemed as though I was moving up in the world." Soon I was on my way back to the College.

My mind was on the midterm examination results when I arrived at the College. Once I reached the dormitory and deposited my things on my bed, I hurried to Mr. Ibegbulem's residence with the hope that someone would tell me something about the results. After about one hour, which seemed like a day, and nothing was forthcoming, I left. I thought that I failed or performed so poorly that they were disappointed. I spent the rest of the day on my bed, lost in thought. A long Sunday came and passed. When Monday came, Mr. Ekanem, the clerk, was in the office. Of course, he opened the door, and the signboard was also out. Students walked to see the results. I thought that I did well but not as well as the board showed. I was first with 105 points above Akaiso and Ironsi, who jointly came second. I marched to Ibegbulem's house. "I came here last Saturday hoping you would tell me the results. Instead, you spoiled the weekend for me and made me miserable. You could not even congratulate me." "But you did not ask," was the reply. I knew Mr. Iteke would appreciate that and wrote to him. He did.

Enyina was Anang. But his name is an adulteration of the Igbo name spelled Enyinna. As my people say, the beetle flew and landed a few feet from the chicken who pursued and pecked at it. The beetle asked the chicken, "When did our enmity start, while I was in the air or now that I landed?" In the same way, I did not know when or how my enmity with Enyina started. But he was out to prove his hatred for me.

Sunday Nwagbara, an Igbo student from Uzuakoli, was my friend. He had an older brother who drove cows with other herdsmen to Ikot Ekpene. His brother advised him to wait for him at the police station near the College to receive some pocket money. They planned to arrive at Nto-Ndang between 8 and 9 pm. Sunday invited Morris and me on this day to accompany him. Unfortunately, Sunday's brother and his companions did not arrive until past 9 pm. We were sitting at the police station at 9 pm when the bell for "lights out" rang. Usually, the Captain on duty went around the three dormitories and checked to make sure that every student was on his bed. Enyina was the Captain on duty. When he came to my dormitory and found me absent, he rejoiced and wrote my name down. He did not write the names of Sunday and Morris who lived in the same dormitory with him.

He was so elated that he boasted about what he was going to do with me. He would submit my name to the Principal, not the headmaster. He hoped that might lead to my expulsion. My friend Akpan lived in the same dormitory and relayed every word to me the following morning. Enyina reported the case to the Principal that morning. Later in the day, the Principal, in his jovial manner, called me, "Ete Obed, I have a little matter to discuss with you."

I was ready when I walked into his office. He told me what I already knew. "Please Sir, may I ask you a question," I asked. "Yes," he said. I asked to know how many names Enyina submitted to him, and he said one. I admitted that I was not in the dormitory at 9 pm when the bell rang. I told him where I was and why I was there. I also gave him the names of the other two students who were there with me. I asked him to enquire from the policemen on duty that night. Then I added, "Enyina is setting his trap to catch me. I am praying that he catches me. The day he does, he will be sorry." He told me to go. Later, he called Enyina and warned him. I was not punished, and that was the end of his animosity.

Mrs. Ibegbulem was expecting their fourth child. In anticipation of the baby's birth, they brought her mother to the College. There was no hospital at Nto-Ndang. However, there was a maternity ward at Obot Akata on the way to Ikot Ekpene. Less than two weeks after the mother arrived, she had the baby. They expected a boy but had a girl. She was the third girl, and they named her Nwadiutao, which means child is sweet. I became more involved in their domestic work including taking food to her for the few days she was at the maternity ward. A week or two later, the mother went home. One of the fun memories of the time was their son's understanding of the hymn, "Trust and Obey". Johnny thought the hymn said, Trust on Obed. Nma, his mother, would laugh and say, "My son, you better not trust Obed."

Our days at Nto-Ndang were winding down. Akpan, Enyina's friend, lived in the same hall I lived. I did not know whether they attended the same elementary school or not. From what happened the previous night of our departure, it seemed that Akpan knew that Enyina had a dislocated left shoulder that had not healed properly. Enyina came over to our hall. He talked with Akpan in their language, which I did not understand. Soon, they raised their voices. Most of us, especially those who did not understand them, paid no attention as we continued to pack our belongings. The next thing I noticed was Akpan beating Enyina mercilessly. Enyina could not defend himself with one hand. The next moment, their tribe's students were shouting, "Akpan Ben akpaa o! Akpan Ben akpaa o!" This means Akpan Ben is dead! When I looked up Enyina was chasing Akpan Ben, who was jumping from one bed to the other, using his hands to shield off the knife Enyina used to cut him. I ran after Enyina and held his one healthy hand, and took the knife from him. Thank God it was not a machete, but a flimsy grass-cutting knife students used only to cut grass. Yet, it did some damage. Soon the police who heard the shouts were at the College and took both of them. The students who understood their language were invited to the police station as witnesses. Both of them slept there. I saved the lives of my self-proclaimed enemies. They were still at the police station the following morning when we left the College for the last time.

The best thing about attending a teacher training college in those days was that one did not have to look for employment. The fact is that we were not only employed but the one-year training was also counted as one year on the job. We were also paid five shillings monthly more than anyone employed the same year without the training. Besides, the Mission would inform us of our posting before school started. So, we went home and waited.

Chapter 12

Teaching Fulfilling Parents' Promise

Once we completed the training, we automatically became employees of the Methodist Mission. Also, though we were not assigned to any school, our salaries started on the first day of January. However, by the end of the second week of January, we knew where we'd be teaching. The Methodist Mission sent me to teach at Umunwanwa Methodist Central School. Note: Before October 1, 1960, the world knew the Methodist Church Nigeria as the Methodist Mission. End of note. When Mr. Ibegbulem saw me, he cautioned me about Mr. Ekpo, the Rural Science Master at the school. He said that the man was a difficult man to work with and then added, "I am not worried. You can work with the devil and still succeed. I would be worried if it were Chijioke."

Teachers were mainly classified into two groups, namely, trained and untrained. The Mission was responsible for transporting trained teachers to their schools. Though we had a one-year training course as teachers, we belonged to the class of the untrained. That meant I had to transport myself and whatever belongings I possessed to my station. I could not afford to carry my bamboo bed, small dining table, two chairs, suitcase, cooking utensils, and bucket to my school. My cousins from the compound and maternal aunts at Ogbodi and

Umuawa carried them to the school. My house was about fifty yards from the church; my mother and I slept in the night, and the moon deceived us to leave home too early for Orienteghe market. I lived in the smallest building in the teachers' quarters.

It was a mud house with four small rooms. A wall partitioned the building into two. I occupied the left side with one living room and one bedroom. Like Samuel and Hannah in 1 Samuel 1:27-28, my teaching at Umunwanwa was the beginning of fulfilling the promise my parents made to God before my conception. One day later, Ezekwem Okorie, who had occupied the other half of the house with his two young brothers, returned. I discovered that they came from Eziama Osa, a village separated from mine only by a narrow bush path. To my delight, I later discovered he was a Christian. He was not trained, and his church activities kept him in teaching, if not he would have been dismissed. Many untrained teachers were dismissed after they failed to pass the entrance examination to Uzuakoli Elementary Teachers' Training College after the third trial. But those who were active in the church were retained. Besides, his father was a leader at his village church.

Knowing that the food I came with was the last help I expected from my mother or anyone else, I planned how to spend my meager salary. My monthly pay was two pounds sterling, and the government took five shillings as tax. That left me with one pound and fifteen shillings. Three factors determined my planning. The first was Mr. Iteke's assurance that I would pass the entrance examination to Uzuakoli Elementary Teachers Training College the first time I took it. I did not wish to disappoint him, and if I succeeded, I wanted to contribute to the financing. Second, I had to eat. Believing that people ate to stop hunger and be able to work, I decided to eat twice a day. Finally, from this time, I was obligated to help my mother. With respect to saving for college, there was no bank at Umuahia. Therefore, I could not open a bank account. However, teachers devised a way of saving what they called a lottery. Each person contributed as much as the person could afford every month based on their salary. Those with the most urgent needs received the contribution first. The amount ranged from one to three pounds a month. I decided to subscribe one pound a month and to receive my share last.

As for food, I was determined not to exceed ten shillings a month. I lived alone, and deciding to eat two meals a day, I prepared my first meal in the morning, dished it out, covered it, and left it on my table, and went to school. I came home during a break between 11 am and noon and ate my first meal of the day. My next meal was between 6 and 7 pm. Feeding actually cost me less than eight shillings ($1.12) a month.

Usually, I bought what I needed at the small Umunwanwa market in our backyard. The most important item I bought from this market was honey. The people harvested wild honey and sold big bottles of undiluted honey for one shilling. Once every month I went to Umuahia big market and bought the items I could not find at Umunwanwa. Daa Iroanuka, my aunt, helped me with my purchases at the market. In addition to selling dried crayfish to me, I gave her my money and told her what I needed. She bought them for me. Consistently and surprisingly, I spent less than ten shillings a month on food. That made it easy for me to give my mother a few shillings every month.

This was the period of spiritual growth for me, and Ezekwem, my neighbor, had something to do with it. His praying habit reinforced what I already learned from my mother. He told me that he prayed at specific times of the day. Also, as a boy, I witnessed my mother's prayerful attitude both at home and church. I had also witnessed God's answer to a prayer. Daa Mabel Onwuneme, a barren woman in my village, became pregnant after some preachers prayed for her. Ezekwem lit his candle and incense when he prayed. Using candles was not a novel idea since there was no electricity. So, I copied him. Since I had no convenient place to pray, I went to the carpenter section in the Umuahia market and described a prayer stand for a carpenter who made it for me. It had a box twelve inches square and three inches deep for my Bible, candle, incense, and a place for the candle to burn. The box was on one carved leg of one-and-one-half feet that stood on a base. After I read that Daniel prayed three times a day, I decided to pray six times a day at three-hour intervals beginning at 6 am. Many things happened in my life during this period and after. Here are a few of the things that happened while I was at Umunwanwa.

As I said earlier, Ezekwem's activities with the Mission saved his employment.

Reverend Nwana baptized me when I was in standard four. The church preacher in the village taught the class. In the same way, people who wished to take communion went to classes before they took communion. Ezekwem represented Reverend Nwanna at the school. Reverend Nwanna had scheduled to come to Umunwanwa to give communion to members of four churches and the teachers. Ezekwem invited me to participate. I disqualified myself, and here is why. "For as often as you eat this bread and drink this cup, you proclaim the Lord's death till He comes. Therefore, whoever eats this bread or drinks *this* cup of the Lord in an unworthy manner will be guilty of the body and blood of the Lord. But let a man examine himself, and so let him eat of the bread and drink of the cup." (1 Corinthians 11:26-28.)

It is the way my mother's generation understood the verses i.e., I must be perfect before I could receive holy communion. This is what compelled me to disqualify myself. If you are a Christian, you know that the verses do not command you to be perfect but to believe. My mother told me that some members walked out when Reverend Dodd preached those three verses. Even Paul, who wrote this, said he was not perfect but was pressing on. Thank God someone in my dream that week took me to a high elevation, sat me on a high stool, washed me, and told me to receive communion. I did. In addition to other reasons people have given for the birth of Jesus in the manger, I suggest the following as the main reason. The manager was where animals for slaughter were fed. Jesus Christ came to be sacrificed for the sins of mankind. "I will put enmity between you and the woman and between your offspring and her offspring; he shall bruise your head, and you shall bruise his heel" (Genesis 3:15 ESV). That was fulfilled on the cross. However, unlike animals who were killed against their will, Jesus Christ gave His life to redeem sinful, dead humans. Therefore, Jesus said, "No one takes it from me, but I lay it down of my own accord. I have authority to lay it down, and I have authority to take it up again. This charge I have received from my Father" (John 10:18). Also, "... Jesus said to them, 'Truly, truly, I say to you, unless you eat the flesh of the Son of Man and drink his blood, you have no life in you.'" (John 6:53 ESV). By this, it is certain one has to eat the flesh and drink the blood of Jesus Christ first to become righteous. One cannot live or become clean from sin without the blood of Jesus. Therefore, thinking and acting that one has to be perfect in order to receive communion is the reverse of Jesus' teaching. He also instructed them to eat the bread and drink the wine in remembrance of Him.

As I read my Bible, I came to Exodus 19:15, which put me in trouble twice. The Lord instructed the men of Israel to refrain from touching women for three days before they met with Him. I decided to see God every day. As a result, I refused to touch or shake hands with any woman. I reasoned that if God demanded the men of Israel to refrain from touching women for three days to meet Him for one day and I desired to meet Him every day, I should keep away from them at all times. Below are two examples of the troubles I landed in. The first was at school. There were four lady teachers at the school. Three of them lived on the school premises. They went to school together and passed by the front of our house. I was an insignificant, most junior and the youngest of the male teachers. These unmarried women shared the same big house. The youngest of the three was in standard five at Mission Hill when I was in standard three. We were even in the same Brewer House. Miss A. came from Osa. Miss N., the leader, came from Ogbodioke, a village next to Umunwanwa. They accused me of rudeness and making fun of them whenever they passed by our building to Mr. George, the headmaster. The leader said that I closeed my door and shouted, "Akaa, they have come-o," as they walked by.

Mr. George sent for me in their absence and told me the accusation. He made fun of the matter before sending for them. When they came, it appeared as though only the leader was offended. When she finished, the headmaster looked at me half serious and half jovial, and said, "Mr. Onwuegbu, be nice to the ladies. Do not close your door whenever the ladies approach. We have beautiful ladies at this school. You should be friendly." I said, "Yes Sir." The second incident happened at home in my compound. One of my older cousins Ebere and his wife had their first baby, a boy. The birth of the first child is a big cultural event, especially if the baby is a boy. Culture demanded that women from the wife's home bring food items sufficient to feed the nursing mother for the first few weeks after birth. On arrival, every member of the compound was invited to thank and shake their hands as a sign of welcome, acceptance, and gratitude. Like everyone else I greeted them, thanked and praised them until it was time to go round and shake their hands. I refused to comply. There was uproar. I simply said I didn't do it and walked out. It did not sit well with people. Some even began to speculate that there might be some truth in the rumor that I passed examinations with charms.

On the other hand, I learned to help those who were in need. Here are three of them. Ubakala village is between Umunwanwa and Old Umuahia. At Ubakala was a woman who lost her two legs from the knees down. Her house was by the road. She sat close to the road with a bowl for people to donate whatever amount of money they were willing to give her. I decided to put a certain amount aside each month for her. I gave it to her on the days I went to the Umuahia market.

Nwaoha Nwosu was an orphan from a prominent family in Umunwanwa and was in my class. I did not even know the family at the time. He was also smart. A whole week passed in the third term, and Nwaoha was not in class. At first, I thought he was sick. Then, I asked why he was not in class. I learned about his problem. He was an orphan and lived with his paternal uncle and aunt. He had a fight with his cousin. He overpowered his cousin. The cousin's parents kicked Nwaoha out of their home. He went to live with his maternal grandmother at Ogbodi Oke the next village to Umunwanwa. She could not afford to pay his school tuition. I sent a message to them asking him to come to school. When he came, I paid his school tuition. To show her gratitude, the grandmother sent me a bottle of palm oil. I told Nwaoha to return it to her. Tell her to sell it and use the money to feed you and ask her to pray for me.

This third incident happened in my village with an old widow and in my compound. Dee Ojoemelam lived to be the oldest man in my village. He and his wife were the sweetest couple. It was rare that one saw one without the other. They were so much in love and believed in reincarnation that she had the confidence that when they died and reincarnated, the husband would find her, and they would be husband and wife again. We never knew her name and only called her by the name she called every boy in our compound i.e., dum. Dum is pronounced doom and means my husband. When dee Ojoemelam died, she looked lost. Though he had an adult son, the son must have been from his first wife. She had no child of her own. She saw me on the street and asked if I had any money for her. I gave her the three shillings in my pocket. She was grateful. That amount may mean nothing today, but when one realizes that I lived on less than eight shillings a month without farm products, which she had, one knows it could help. But she did not last long after her husband's death.

One day, Ezekwem, my neighbor, and I were out in front of our house talking. Mr. Ukwu, one of the older and high elementary teachers at the school, walked towards us. He called my name and said, "As I walked towards you, you grew very tall and big. If you watch the friends you make, you will be a great man." When he left, I asked Ezekwem what he was talking about. Ezekwem replied with his own question. "Do you know he is an occultist?"

Even with my one-year training, I was classified as untrained. The three youngest and most junior members of the teaching staff belonged to this class. That meant that we had to take tests for two reasons. The first reason was to retain our jobs. For me, that meant moving from C/D to C. For the life of me I never knew what these letters stood for. Those who failed this examination lost their jobs. A second examination was the entrance to Elementary Teachers College Uzuakoli for men and Oron for women. To prepare for these examinations, the Mission arranged for the most senior members of the trained teachers to lecture those preparing to take the tests. The lectures were free and compulsory. Our lectures covered Arithmetic, English, and methods of teaching. Miss Igbo, Miss Nwosu, and I were the students.

All three of us took the job retention test. But, Miss Igbo did not qualify to take the entrance examination. Of course, where else would the test be held if not Mission Hill? Mr. Iteke had gone on transfer to Ndoro. Since the examinations were on Saturdays, I trekked home on Friday and went to Mission Hill from home. The retention result came out first, and I was successful. That would raise my salary by more than sixty percent if I taught the following year. But who wanted to teach? It was not me.

Meantime, my family was poised to grow by one. My brother had earned enough money to pay the bride price to take his wife home. He sent the money, and my mother, Uncle Uwakwe and a few others in the compound went and fulfilled almost all the most essential cultural requirements. A date was set for us to take her home. Custom dictates that this ceremony occurs in the evening and lasts till the early hours of the following day. People argued over every little remaining gift, such as what to give to her mother, grandmother, age group, father, and others. I wondered if the demands and arguments would end or not. But they did.

Seeing my sister-in-law in our home filled me with joy. Considering what we suffered during childhood, my brother was not expected to marry. Even if he was, not that early, I called her my Happiness. Even today, I still call her my H. Because of how we react to each other, I call her my *sister-in-law* before Sweetie i.e., my wife. She said, "O no, she is your sister, not sister-in-law." She lived with my mother for almost one year before she went to Lagos to live with her husband. She spent the year attending domestic school to learn sewing, cooking, and other things.

Joel 2:28, among other things, speaks of older and the young dreaming dreams and seeing visions. My dreams were like visions. Some of the dreams happened within the hour I woke up. Some took weeks, some months, and years, and one took over a decade before it was fulfilled. Here are a few of them, starting with one that happened immediately after I woke up.

The school's second term holiday was over, and I returned on Friday instead of Saturday or Sunday. My neighbor, Okorie, and his brothers had not returned. Night came, and I went to bed. I was warned in my dream that Miss A. would come to my house that morning for sex. I was not aware that she was on the compound. Immediately, I got up and opened my window; she was less than ten yards away, walking toward my door. I quickly opened my door and met her halfway in the open. She was still in her long nightgown. We stood there and conversed for many minutes before she returned to her building.

This next dream lasted many weeks. Several weeks before we received the results of the entrance examinations, I dreamed that the headmaster would call me and give me two envelopes. He asked me to take mine and give Miss Nwosu one. They turned out to be the results of the entrance examinations we took. We were successful. The headmaster returned from a visit to the Supervisor's office at Mission Hill in November and sent for me. Smiling broadly on my arrival, he congratulated me and gave me two envelopes, one for me and the other for Miss Nwosu; we were both successful, she to Oron and I to Uzuakoli. I rejoiced, especially because I did not disappoint Mr. Iteke. Once again, I was the only successful candidate from Umuahia Circuit. In four successive years, God had placed me in the number one spot as though He wanted me to know that I was obligated to fulfill my parents' promise.

What made my success special was the process of choosing the candidates. There were two stages of the process. First, the candidate passed the written examination. Then, the Mission through the College, investigated the character of every successful candidate at his home village and at the school he taught. Detective work was done on his church activities and character in general. I was certain that I had no problem at school. However, there seemed to be a problem in my village because there was a division at the church.

Dee Odikemere and dee Nwabuisi led a faction while Gbo Jonah led the other. I visited home from Umunwanwa, and a wise aunt, daa Ngbafo, said to me, "Both sides will come to complain to you. When they finish, simply say, "Is that what happened?" That was the attitude I adopted. While still on holiday, the Reverend James Jackson, a Scottish man who was the Chairman of the Eastern part of the Methodist Mission, came to preach at the church. None of the parties wanted anyone from either faction to interpret for him. Both factions accepted me as the interpreter. Because I knew there were better-educated people in the church that day who could do a better job than I, I, like Gideon (Judges 6:15), was nervous and shaken all over at the beginning. Soon, I recovered confidence and composed myself. With that, my Sunday school teaching and participation in the choir, God gave me success in the selection.

This next dream took more than two years to become a reality. I walked home one day, and my mother told me that Jonah had been arrested. Jonah was the older student in standard five when I was in standard three, but he returned to Mission Hill to complete standard six with me. Because of his activities in the church, he was employed as a church teacher. What is the difference between a church teacher and a schoolteacher?

School teachers are the employees of the Mission and the Government. They teach school students, preach, and can become Reverend Ministers. A Reverend Minister was in charge of a Circuit. There were dozens or even scores of churches in a Circuit. The Minister could not attend or manage these churches alone. Therefore, churches that could afford teachers employed them. These teachers always earned less than schoolteachers. They did become Catechists and even Reverend Ministers if they were good. Jonah was employed at Umuire as a church teacher.

I asked why Jonah was arrested. Her answer stunned me. He was doing the job he was employed to perform, ringing the church bell when it cracked. Those who were already unhappy with him called the police and had him arrested. I went into my room, closed the door, and prayed for his freedom. I dreamed that he was not penalized. The case dragged on for years. In the end, he was set free of all charges.

This final example seemed strange in content and the period I dreamed of it. After I became a psychologist, I wondered what Freud would have said about it. One can see why it was easy for me to accept Ezekwem's interpretation. It took more than a decade to materialize. At a time when I did not associate or shake hands with any woman, I got married to a white woman. There was no white person at Umunwanwa or the many villages surrounding it. I was not aware of any Nigerian who married a white person. It was a dream that appeared it could never happen, I thought. Ezekwem gave me a "perfect interpretation." He said, "She is not a human being. You are married to an angel." I believed him.

Did I meet Mr. Ekpo at Umunwawa? He was as Mr. Ibegbulem described him. I had his son in my class. His favorite expression was *akataka*, which has no real meaning. Ezekwem and I abbreviated it *akaa* and called each other Akaa. Akaa is the same word the woman teachers accused me of saying when they walked by our building. Many years after my family and I returned from the U.S., someone introduced the son of "Akatata" to me. He shouted, "That's my teacher." We shook hands, and I learned he had his Ph. D. When I met his parents, they did not recognize me. Mr. Ekpo was one of the senior teachers who lectured us, and I did not have any problems with him.

During one of the end-of-term holidays, I went to see my uncle Ehiogu. He seemed tired or sick. He looked concerned and worried and said, "Tell your brother what I say to you. When your father died, he had his goods at the U.A.C. Stores. I went to claim them. The white man in charge of the stores refused to release them to me without witnesses to ensure that the proceeds would be used to take care of my brother's family. I came home and took Chief Inegbu Agbara and Udeagha, his brother, with me. They cosigned with me. But I did not do what I promised. Today, I regret my actions. I listened to bad advisors. If I had educated even one of you, things would have been better. Tell your brother that I am sorry. Forgive me."

I sat astonished at his confession, unable to speak and simply nodding my head. As I sat there, I remembered my late uncle Akwarandu who cracked my skull and falsely accused my mother of giving seven hundred pounds to my father buried in his room to her relatives. I wished he was there to hear the confession. But he died prematurely. Also, I wished that Monday Nwaobiara, who tried to rescue me, was there. But he too was dead in a lorry accident. I wondered why he confessed. Was he afraid that my brother and I, who seemed to be doing better than his sons, might one day take revenge? Already, there was finger-pointing at my brother at the death of Mba in Lagos. At last, I said, "It's okay. I will tell my brother." I did not think it civil for a small boy like me to say to my uncle who was my father's elder, "I forgive you." I sat for a little while and left. Today, I love him for his confession and pray that God forgave him as I did.

Finally, the school year was winding down. November came, and for the first time in my school career, I was not concerned with taking examinations but instead supervising them. As usual, those who made the decisions about who set or marked the final year examination in Umuahia Circuit papers met at Mission Hill. However, since Umunwanwa had become a central school, students took their examinations at the school. Also, central schools in Umuahia Circuit sent students' sheets and marks to Mission Hill for distribution to the markers.

The end-of-year holiday included at least the last week of November, all of December, and about three weeks of January; the Mission paid the teachers their November and December salaries in November. I was selected to receive my lottery in November. This worked out well for all the teachers because the rest contributed the least amount, one pound out of their salary. As for me, I was going home with all my savings. My two months' salary was three pounds ten shillings after tax.

It costs twenty-four pounds to study a two-year Elementary Teachers' course at Uzuakoli. When I received my ten pounds lottery and salary, I had thirteen pounds ten shillings. My total savings at the time were more than sixteen pounds. Unaware of my brother's financial condition, I requested assistance in the sum of ten pounds. He offered it. I paid Uzuakoli in full.

The pupils took the tests, and the last day of school arrived. Early in the morning of the closing day, some of my pupils carried my few belongings to my village. Later in the day, the headmaster announced the results. Among the successful students in my class were Mr. Ekpo's son and Nwaoha. Unfortunately, that was the last time I saw Nwaoha. I do not know if he ever went back to school. We all said our goodbyes, and I trekked back to Amafo, my village.

While the holiday lingered, Christmas came and went. Dee Amadi, who lived in Lagos, came home on vacation that December. At the end of his leave, he took my H., and presented her to my brother. A second ceremony was performed in Lagos.

I walked out to the village's main street one day, and there was dee Nwoko Ihekweaba walking with Mr. Solomon Jaja, my standard three teachers. Elementary school was in session then. Dee Nwoko said, "Obed, I thought you started teaching." "Yes, Sir, but I am going to ETC Uzuakoli." So soon? My former teacher said, "If anybody can do it, it is him." It turned out they had passed to go to High Elementary of Uzuakoli, but that was why they were not in school. I had to discover that for myself at Uzuakoli.

Chapter 13

Uzuakoli Elementary Teachers' College

When a new student crossed the Methodist Uzuakoli Elementary Teachers' Training College gate and entered the compound, he was in a different world. If he was proud that he was one of a handful of the smartest sixty candidates selected out of many hundreds, he was forced to forget it. From the moment he entered the college grounds, he ceased to exist as a human being with a name. He became a "fox" with a long tail and walked on all fours. Also, he learned a new language and social order.

Here are a few examples. A fox did not enjoy any senior joke. A senior joke was any statement a senior student made that made people laugh. If a fox laughed with "humans," he was punished. It was an offense for a fox to look at a senior through the wrong corner of "its" eyes, though he was never told what corner that was. It was important for the fox to bear in mind that the rule was "obey before complain." That translates to do your punishment before you complain. The fox ran whenever the bell rang. One of the worst offenses was for a fox to make any noise in the morning when the bell woke up the foxes to fetch water from the stream. It was interpreted as rudeness and an attempt to negate the sleep earned not in 1956 but since one thousand nine hundred and fifty-six years ago. "You are down" meant you committed a punishable offense and would be punished. There was no end to the offenses nor the language. These were laid down the first evening after dinner in the dining hall. Besides the military aspect was the rigorous academic life.

There were more than twenty subjects to study. It was not sufficient to know a subject. For instance, we learned to solve arithmetic problems at all levels: simple and compound interest, fractions, stocks and shares, speeds and times trains overtake or cross from opposite sides, and more. Then, we studied the method of teaching arithmetic. This was true of every subject we studied, be it history, English, geography, or any other. The emphasis on the method of teaching almost got me into hot water.

One of our tutors, whom the students nicknamed Method of Teaching Seriousness, taught physical education. Unknown to me was that he was preparing to take his advanced physiology paper for the University of London General Certificate. He came to class with his textbook Wyeth Physiology and lectured by reading through it. I thought they teach us methods of teaching, and this man is doing everything they say we should not do. I chuckled. He looked up and saw me smiling. He looked like death and said, "Obed, how many years did you teach before coming here?" I said, "One, Sir." He shouted, "One year! One year!" I thought I had committed the unpardonable crime and remained standing and silent. He added, "You think you are still in elementary school." "No, Sir," I replied. The storm was over, and he succeeded in or almost succeeded in teaching me why he was called M. T. Seriousness and not to cross him. My first pleasant surprise was about finance. Soon after our arrival, the office informed the students that of the twenty-four pounds we paid, twelve was for the first year. The college told us to go to the bookstore and get books worth four pounds. We also had two pounds available for each of the three terms to spend at our discretion. That was good news indeed. That was enough money for me to meet all my financial needs.

One of the phrases we learned the night of arrival at Uzuakoli was "standard bundle." The phrase described the bundle of firewood the senior students expected from the foxes each Saturday. The firewood was rejected if it failed to measure up to the standard. Uzuakoli boys fetched and sold the standard bundles to most of the students, especially those who taught for several years and saved money before they were admitted to the College. I determined not to spend one penny on firewood.

One Saturday, Egonu and I decided to spend much of the day cutting enough firewood to last several weeks. Egonu attended school at Mission Hill and was in standard six when I was in five. He also attended Nto-Ndang a year before me and taught in Ndoro Circuit. We entered Uzuakoli at the same time. We were cutting down the dried trees when that tropical rain drenched us. We decided there was no need to return to the College and continued cutting. Soon the rain stopped as though the sky simply poured some buckets of water down, and the sun was shining again. Surprise! Surprise! The owners of the farm came. Egonu and I decided that we were Efiks who did not understand our Igbo language. They accused us of stealing their wood. We replied, "Mkomke Igbo," I don't understand Igbo. They told us that they would report us to the Principal. I laughed as we continued to harvest the wood they did not really use at home. Egonu asked, "Obed, why are you laughing?" I whispered back, "How are they going to report us when they don't have our pictures or our names." He cautioned me; you will make them know that we understand Igbo. We finished cutting, carried the woods out in a few trips, and bade them goodbye in Efik. We never heard anything about them.

My first academic term was almost a disaster. As M. T. Seriousness suggested, I acted as though I was either at Mission Hill or Nto-Ndang. I was 21 out of thirty in the class. What made it dangerous was that Uzuakoli ETC had what it called the weeding system i.e., if a student failed during the first year, that was the end of him at the

College. I played football, participated in sports, especially long distances, and taught Sunday school. One of my new subjects of interest was Arts and Crafts. I became fascinated with making cane chairs and made two by the end of the course. I also made a table with compartments but without a single nail. When the first term ended, I could not believe my position. I was twenty-first out of thirty. I thrived in elementary school and even at Nto-Ndang without knowing how to study. I quickly learned to at least attempt to study or be thrown out. It was a wake-up call. Though I was never first or second, or even third for the remaining five terms, I never went below ninth.

Emedom, one of the good friends I made at Nto-Ndang, was one of the few from our set who made it to Uzuakoli in the first trial. The first-year students had gone out to the field for physical education exercise. It rained earlier, but the rain had stopped. The grass on the field was still wet. Emedom, a first-year student, asked M. T. Seriousness for permission to use the staff tennis court instead of the wet field. He denied the request. A few minutes later, a final-year student made the same request, and he granted it. "Sir, we made the same request earlier, and you refused to grant it," Emedom said. Poor Emedom did not know that he had committed the unpardonable sin. Mr. MTS burning with anger, asked, "Whom did you ask that question?" Then, he commanded him to follow him. He took Emedom to the end of a football field under construction, waved his two arms backward and forward, told Emedom to cut the grass in the area and uproot the palm trees, and walked away. From where he stood and how his hands moved from his back to above his head, one wondered if there was any end or measurement that would satisfy MTS. I helped Emedom to uproot one palm tree and cut as much grass as we could. I took Emedom to MTS' house during a break to see his wife.

On our arrival, we entered the house, and I clapped my hands to announce our presence. His wife walked out of the dining room. Immediately, she saw me. She said, "Obed, are you the person who said the thing to darling?" He had already reported the crime to her. Without hesitation, I replied, "Who said it doesn't matter. If you and your darling keep us alive, we will live to have and call our own darling." While she was still smiling, Emedom added, "If he (MTS) kills me here, no one will help him carry my corpse home. He will carry it all by himself on his head to my parents." I told her the endless area he gave with a wave of his hands and what we had done so far. "Well, watch your mouths. I'll see what I can do." We thanked her and left. That was the end of the matter.

    Remember that about two years earlier, while I was in standard six, I was expected to be admitted to the secondary section of Uzuakoli College. Also, recall that I went to Mr. B. Ekeledo at GBO, and he took the receiver of his phone and "talked to the Principal." It proved to be a fake. The College did not have any telephone or running water. Uzuakoli consisted of three colleges, namely, the High Elementary College (HEC), Elementary Teachers College (ETC), and the Secondary school, which included Higher School, the equivalent of junior college in the U.S.. Each of these had its own principles. The most senior of the three was the Principal of the whole College. Reverend McGarr was the Principal of ETC and succeeded Rev. Wood as the Principal of the entire College. We were at Uzuakoli when the Principal installed telephones and running tap water at the College. We had another luxury at Uzuakoli. For the first time, I studied at night under electric lights instead of a kerosene lamp or oil light without glass, and with all the smoke in my eyes.

    It was not because Uzuakoli town or the surrounding villages had electricity. They did not have any. But the College had its own plant which it turned on at 6 pm every evening and off at 10 pm. We were all required to own kerosene lamps for emergencies when the plant failed to operate and it malfunctioned often. The food was much better than we had at Nto-Ndang. Two male cooks prepared the meals, except for boiling the beans. First-year students (foxes) lined up their standard bundles of firewood for inspection at 4 pm every Saturday. The same foxes were scheduled two at a time to boil the beans, and about one hundred twenty students ate for lunch. However, the beans were boiled during the evening when every other student was studying. There were two large iron pots boiling at the same time. A student took care of a pot. The student stood by the raging fire and turned the beans to prevent them from burning. If the beans burned, the students continued to boil beans for days until they learned to cook beans. Boiling the beans was also used as a form of punishment.

On arrival at Uzuakoli, we noticed that Mr. Ibegbulem, who taught Rural Science at Nto-Ndang, was teaching Rural Science at Uzuakoli etc., among other subjects. Mr. Achiugo, the tutor students nicknamed MTS who taught physical education, was also in charge of games and sports. Emedom participated in sports, and I participated in games and sports. I had an accident during football practice and cracked a bone in my left arm. When I reported to MTS, he simply told me to wait at the edge of the field. At the end of the game, the man who taught all kinds of first aid and how to give them walked away unconcerned. I walked back to my room. By the late evening, the pain had become unbearable. I could not sleep. I was restless and paced the floor. Finally, I did what I thought I could never do. I marched to Reverend McGarr, the Principal's house. When he saw me, he called his wife because I worked with her on Sunday school matters. "Not her, Sir, I came to see you," I said. I told them my problem. It was too late to take me to the hospital. They gave me some aspirin tablets and asked me to be ready early the following morning to go to the Lepper Colony Hospital, where there were medical doctors and nurses. I scarcely slept that night.

Early the following morning, the Principal and I were at the Uzuakoli Lepper Colony Hospital. Two people, a white male medical doctor and a female white nurse, took me to a room. I was pleasantly surprised to know that the man was a Jew. They determined that I had a fracture. The Principal left me with them and promised to come and get me in the evening. A few minutes later, I was on a table. The doctor gave me an injection in my arm. The next time I seemed to have a glimpse of my surroundings, I saw the doctor holding me on my left arm and the nurse on my right arm as they led me to a bed in a different room. As we walked, I uttered the only sentence I remember uttering, "Into Your Hand, I commit my spirit, Lord." I slept most of the day. When I finally regained consciousness, I discovered that my left arm was in a cast. The Principal came and took me back to the College. I carried my cast home for the first term holiday. It was removed at the Umuahia General Hospital.

    The method of teaching was so important at Uzuakoli Elementary Teachers College that it was practiced from three different angles. The first was the theory taught in the classroom. Secondly, the students went to observe teachers once a week at an elementary school called Demonstration School, built just for that purpose, only a few hundred yards away from the College. The tutor and his students watched the teacher and returned to the College and critiqued the teaching. The third practice is where the students went out as student teachers for a period of three weeks. Before we left for the first term holiday, we were prepared for our teaching practice. I chose to practice at Umuawa Methodist Central School, a distance of about three miles from my village. My "anti" hand shaking and touching of women was intact. When we got there, some women student teachers from Oron Elementary Teachers Training College were also sent to practice at Umuawa. Enyinne from Umuda the next village to mine, was one of the female student teachers from Oron. She showed interest in me. I ignored her. Several years later, while at High Elementary Uzuakoli, after my virginity went overboard, I went to see her. She literally ran out of her room. She ran to a woman, probably her mother, and shouted at me, "You now have interest in me?" I waited in vain to explain things and finally left.

If we thought my fracture was a major accident, Emedom's illness said we had not seen anything. He ran the 100 and 220 yards while I competed in the 440 and 880 yards and the seven- and one-half miles marathon. Emedom came back from practice one evening and complained of pains in his thighs. The following day, he could not attend classes. For some days, I carried his food to his room. He refused to allow me to report to the Principal. It reached a point where I had to carry him to have his shower and go to the toilet. As his friend, I cared for him though there were at least two students from his elementary school who also were his classmates. I went to the Principal against his wish. Once again, the Principal drove two of us to Uzuakoli Lepper Colony Hospital. The diagnosis was gloomy. They kept him at the hospital. On our way to the College, the Principal told me that we and Emedom's room head would be at the hospital by 8 a.m. the following day to take Emedom to Itu Nbang Hospital, more than eighty miles away. He was annoyed that the room head did not inform him in time. He told me to inform Emeruwa, Emedom's room head, to get ready to travel with us to answer any questions the doctors might ask. I informed Emeruwa that night.

Early the following morning Emeruwa and I walked to the Principal's office and waited. Soon he was out and drove us to the Lepper Colony Hospital. They released and wheeled Emedom to the waiting vehicle. The Principal and Emeruwa sat in front of the pickup while Emedom and I sat at the back. We drove from Uzuakoli to Ituk Nbang on dirty and dusty roads. By the time we reached the hospital, Emedom, and I looked as brown and dusty as the roads we drove on. After a short talk with the officials, someone wheeled Emedom into the hospital and he was admitted.

Just before our departure, Emeruwa and I were arguing about who should sit with the Principal in front of the vehicle. The Principal walked out and asked what the argument was about. Emeruwa complained that I was dirty and wanted to sit in front with the Principal.

He told him to go to the back of the truck. I sat in front. Emedom stayed at the hospital for almost two months. According to him, it was about five weeks before he walked around his bed. The nurses and staff cheered and clapped their hands when he did. It seemed his disease was a new one, and the doctors experimented with various drugs and ordered others from Britain. Many staff and student nurses at Ituk Mbang Hospital transferred to the Queen Elizabeth II Hospital at Umuahia after it was built.

By the end of my first year, I had learned to use different carpenter planes and saws. Woodwork was taking up a good percentage of my six-pound allowance at the college. I also learned how to make photo albums and fishing nets. Though Mr. Orumagbo, the Arts and Crafts tutor, was not the favorite of many students, we liked each other, and I learned a lot from him. Despite spending much of my money on materials I used for Arts and Crafts, I still managed to buy the books I desired, e.g., Sherlock Homes short stories, Beyond Pardon, and the English Oxford Dictionary. These and all other belongings were stolen during the Biafra-Nigeria War.

Life could be unbearable for the first-year student if he fell out of favor with one or more finalist students. The relationship between Egonu and Amanambu nicknamed Mbu is a good illustration. There was an avocado pear tree close to the dining hall. The only way one could avoid seeing it was to walk with one's head dropped down or with closed eyes. Mbu often waited for Egonu on this spot. Egonu's appearance was a sufficient reason for Mbu to accuse him with, "Egonu, you are down for looking at the avocado pear." Looking at Mbu to explain or demand to know how he could be looking at the ground and at the tree at the same time, earned him, "For looking at me through the wrong corner of your eyes." At such times Egonu looked at me and said, "He is going to kill me here."

Because of the scarcity of preachers in the Methodist Mission, the College offered a course to train "local preachers." These are volunteer preachers for Reverend Ministers in charge of the Circuits sent to different churches each Sunday. I registered for the extra-curricular course and was trained as a local preacher.

Unexpectedly, I received a letter from Kano, a city in the northern part of Nigeria. It was from Miss Okezie, my standard four teacher. She had been teaching in the North and was returning to the East. On learning that I was at Uzuakoli ETC, she wrote me and wanted to know if I wanted anything from Kano. I lay on a mattress for the first time at Nto-Ndang. Knowing that they grew cotton in the North and that the cotton mattress was cheap in the North, I requested a cotton mattress. Aware that her train would pass through Uzuakoli to Umuahia, she gave me the time the train would arrive at Uzuakoli and asked me to wait for her.

Students feared being called to Reverend McGarr's office. To be called to the office meant one thing i.e., expulsion. No student wanted to go to that office. I did not know what possessed me, and I went to that office that morning not once but twice. My first request to be allowed to go to the railway station was greeted with a gentle "No." His face turned red at my second appearance before I finished my request; being the stammer he was, he breathed deep and said, "Look here, my boy. The answer is no." I left his office and returned to the classroom. To make sure that I did not go to the railway station and determined to dismiss me from the College if I dared, he drove the college vehicle to the railway station and back. I had hoped to receive a gift from my former teacher. That had to wait until holiday time.

Internal competition in sports and games reigned among the three sections, HEC, ETC, and Secondary, that made up Uzuakoli College. Sports were divided into two, namely general and marathon. To my knowledge, ETC never won the general sports championship. But it was a different matter with the marathon. The motto was "Not at my time." That meant that the championship shield for the marathon would not leave ETC at my time. As a result, we practiced every

Saturday morning between 5 and 6 a.m. The best fifteen runners represented the College. A total of 45, 15 from each section, ran on the sports day. Any runner who completed the marathon first received 45 points, and the last received one point. The last point was always difficult to determine because some runners fainted along the way. Anyway, that did not matter because, by the time the 30th runner crossed the finish line on the field where the marathon ended, all ETC runners were there. We retained the shield at my time. My best position was 5 out of 45 (41 points). Unfortunately, the marathon was eliminated when I was at HEC because a student at ETC fell during practice and died.

Surprisingly, when the final year students began their final year examination, the foxes began to look and act like human beings. Some of them began to perform certain human functions the final year students performed. That was the case when I inherited the two duties Onyechere performed. He was the Sunday School Superintendent and also in charge of water supply. The latter meant that when the first-year students fetched water, he ensured that the order was obeyed. I was reinforced with these positions because I washed his dishes after meals. From when I supervised fellow foxes to about the same time the following year, those were my official duties. My duty as the Sunday School Superintendent necessitated my meeting with the Principal's wife weekly. I walked in one day to see Mrs. McGarr, and she said, "Why do these students pester me with, you mean Mr. Onwuegbu, whenever I ask for Obed?" I said, That's my last name." Once she had the answer to the question, they stopped asking her. Unfortunately, the Principal's health compelled him to leave the country prematurely. The Principal's wife used to tell me that Britain was too cold for her. I did not understand what she meant by cold weather until I lived in Vermont, U.S.A.

Achinivu became the Principal. As a result, he became the first Nigerian to hold the post. He lived to become the Principal of the whole College. Unfortunately, he died of a heart attack a few years after he became the Principal of the College.

One of the points of pride of Uzuakoli graduates is the ability to do what they perform well and to endure. But before graduation, the badge is the pride. Secondary school students wear it on their caps during the first term of the first year. The badge is also worn on the blazer. However, a student merits the purchase and wear of the blazer in his senior year at the College. When a student at ETC was sure his academic standing was secured enough to permit his return for the final year and had the money to buy the blazer, he ordered one. A tailor came and took the measurements during the last week of the third term. It would be an unpardonable sin for me to attend Uzuakoli College and not own the blazer. So, I ordered one.

There is a superstitious belief about the day a person dies in my section of the Igbo culture. There are eight days in the Igbo week called izu. Two of the eight days are called Eke. One is a big Eke and the other is called a small Eke. It is believed that only wicked people die on Eke days. My uncle Ehiogu died on one of them. Before anyone who died on one of these days was buried, old people went to native doctors (spiritualists) to find out which of the angry gods killed the person to appease the god. Dee Ogunka saw me on the street on the day my uncle died, waiting and asked, "What is the need for looking behind? Is it a crime for somebody to usurp his brother's wealth?" I concluded that he must have been one of the "bad advisors" who advised my uncle to usurp his brother's wealth to the neglect of the family. Note: To look behind means to go to spiritualists. He was the oldest man in the compound, even older than my dead uncle. After he spoke, my uncle was buried the same day without "looking behind." I was still a student in the U.S. when dee Ogunka died. My brother said that he also died on Eke Day.

On the eve of the last day of college for the year, the ceremonial cutting of foxes' tails was observed. Various activities dominated the morning of departure, two of which were the inspection and loading of the lorries students prearranged to convey them home. There was only one thing Nto-Ndang students enjoyed better than Uzuakoli students. It was that Uzuakoli students slept on three planks of wood each, ten inches wide and six feet long, placed side by side without mattresses, while Nto-Ndang students slept on beds with mattresses. The planks are piled up the last morning before the inspection. Individuals ate their breakfast when they were ready. The last organized activity of the morning was the inspection of the rooms. By the time it was done, almost every student who traveled by lorry had his belongings in it, and those who traveled by train were ready to go to the railway station. The College had a hairdresser. He gave different names for the same hairstyle and haircut for each holiday. For seniors, it was Goodbye McGarr, and for others, it was Excuse me, McGarr. Whichever haircut an individual received did not make any difference; the journey began at the end of the inspection.

On arrival at Umuahia Motor Park, my two cousins Nwatiti from Ogbodi and Nnenna from Umuawa were waiting to carry my suitcase and bucket home. A pleasant surprise awaited me on arrival. My H. was home very pregnant and a grown-up woman instead of the young girl who left home a year ago. However, she was in the company of those other girls she played with before she went to Lagos, towering over all of them. They ran out from Uwagbokwu's yard to meet me. By the time I was home on holiday, she had been at home for a few weeks and registered with Amachara Methodist Hospital, which trained midwives. Her pregnancy was in its last few weeks. So, I walked with her to the hospital in the next two weeks.

December 25 is the universal and the beginning of the Christmas celebration in my area. After December 25, each Klu Klux Klan celebrates its Christmas day. For example, the big Nkwo belongs to us, and the small Nkwo belongs to my H's village. Her mother came to our celebration and insisted that she come to their celebration four days later. But that was not to be.

For a non-Igbo to understand what follows, he or she must know the mentality of the time i.e., the second half of the twentieth century. To the Igbo mind, especially the women, childbearing is such a natural phenomenon that the pregnant woman did not require assistance beyond what her experienced women neighbors could offer her. It is not a sickness that requires a doctor or hospitalization. So we went to bed that night, and her labor started. I know my wife will find this difficult to believe, knowing how light I sleep now.

There were two old women experts in baby delivery in my compound. My mother went and invited them over to our yard. Other women came over. I did not know how long they were there before I woke up and opened my door. When I asked what was going on, one of the women said, "Obida, is this the first time you heard this commotion?" I said, "Let us go to the hospital right now. No more waste of time." Reluctantly, they organized, and with two lamps, we set off. The women took one lamp and walked in front of the men, which was a few yards from the two parties. They were sure that we would not walk three miles before the baby was born. Less than one half-mile distance into the journey, they ordered us to stop advancing. Soon we heard push, push, followed by a baby's cry. Many more minutes later, the women were singing and calling the names of the adult males in the compound, telling them that they had a male child. Again, we allowed them to take the lead and took the rear. It was still too early, but people still woke up. The celebration started, and everyone in the compound woke up and came over. The women planned and selected a few of them to go to inform the parents of the new mother and her relatives of the birth. That was another big event of its own. Customs demanded that the bearer of the good news identify the gender of the newborn. For a male baby, one of the women carried a matchet painted with white spots. Another woman played the drum while a third carried a medium pan with muddy white chalk water as they sang as they went. Almost every woman they met on their way dipped her right fingers into this chalk and brushed it on both cheeks as a sign of good luck. They were on their way before sunrise.

In my culture, taking care of the new mother for the first three months after she gives birth was so important that failure to do so led people to refuse to give their daughters in marriage to men from that compound. I soon learned that the responsibility fell squarely on my shoulders. That morning, while my mother cooked, I walked to the carpenter section of Umuahia market and bought a crib. That was new to the women because the baby was expected to sleep with the mother on the same bed. Soon, the joy and smooth running of the family received a jolt and a crack. Less than two weeks after the birth of the baby, my mother was infected with chicken pox. I had a big decision to make, especially when the three of them slept in that small room.

To those who were not educated about infectious diseases especially chicken pox and smallpox, these diseases are dangerous only to those who fear and try to avoid them. So, I committed an almost unpardonable sin when I tried to isolate my mother from her only grandchild. Believing that she would enjoy him better and for a longer time if he lived, I did the only thing I had to do.

Having failed to convince her to move to late Uncle Ehiogu's empty house, I went to the office of Sanitary Inspectors at the township and reported to them. They sent one officer with some equipment and sanitizer with me. He sanitized both my uncle's house and the room she shared with both mother and grandson. He explained the situation to her and moved her. By God's grace, no one else contracted it. They came back about two weeks later, and she was healed. She returned to enjoy both her daughter-in-law and grandson. The crisis was over. During those first few weeks, all the domestic lessons my mother taught me when I was a boy came in handy. I became the man and woman of the house. I prepared and served meals to my mother and my H. I fetched water from the stream and firewood from the farm. Our mother-in-law came to help. She and I went to our farm at Isieke to harvest cassava. She stood up and watched me as I uprooted the cassava. I looked at her in annoyance but did not say anything to her. My mother did this work with me when I came with her. You are young and should do it, I thought to myself. Later I learned she was in her early pregnancy after suffering an earlier miscarriage. One of the days I carried my basket of cassava, I saw Mr. Iweala, one of the tutors at Uzuakoli College, and he teased me. "A big teacher in training is carrying a basket of cassava on his head. Wait until you return to the College." We laughed. By the time the long holiday was over, my mother had fully recovered, and my H could perform certain chores. To show gratitude for how I took care of his wife and new baby boy, my brother asked what he should do for me. I requested money to pay for my blazar.

There are certain things some people or customs designate as below certain "dignity." Carrying something like cassava on their heads at that stage of my life was one of them. But I ignored the norm and displayed such behavior again and again. For example, when Uncle Uwagbokwu refused to allow Chukwuma, his son, to carry a jar of palm wine to my H's home, that I was a teacher did not prevent me from carrying it on my head. The last time I did it was in Lagos on my way to the U.S.A. A sendoff party was planned, and people from my village in Lagos were invited. My brother asked me to buy a carton of beer and pay someone to carry it. People in his yard could not believe their eyes when they saw the high elementary teacher who would be flying out to America in two days carrying a carton of beer on his head.

I was ready to return to Uzuakoli, knowing, as the saying goes, that everything was under control. Before I left home that morning, I carried the crib and the baby over to my room to save my mother or my H the trouble of carrying it.

Because I fetched my firewood and never spent a penny buying other items students waste their money on, I used the six pounds and the money I saved from teaching practice to buy things I needed. I mentioned items for my Arts and Crafts and some books earlier. Dee Dick A. Emelike was a student in Britain when he died. His brother dee Monday gave me Wyeth the book MTS read to us as a way of his teaching human physiology. It was a mystery that dee Monday gave me the book at that time. I am not from his compound. Yet, there were at least three boys, two of whom were my age and in secondary school, who could have used the book. But he gave it to me. That is a demonstration of my people's love in the whole village for me. I saw another book on the subject and asked MTS if I should buy it. His answer was, "No book is a waste." I bought it. It was simpler and well-illustrated with sketches. I studied and crammed most of the sketches.

Chapter 14

Final Year At ETC

I was completely in charge of the Sunday School at the College and water management at ETC; The latter endeared me to the cooks. They marked my bowl and almost always gave me extra meat. That made it easy for me to leave some meat for the fox who washed my plates.

Mr. Achinivu succeeded Reverend McGarr as the Principal of ETC. I cannot say what or how it happened, but for whatever reason, the Principal's family took me as one of theirs. They loved me so much that a few years later, when I went through what I thought was my worst disappointment by merely observing me, the wife investigated and called me. I know they lived at Mission Hill when I was a pupil there. But they had nothing to do with the school. I am not even sure they knew I existed.

My relationship with the Ibegbulem family that started at Nto-Ndang grew stronger. His wife had given birth to their fifth child, a son Obike who is a medical doctor at this writing. Every student had his plot to farm and account for the crops and the tools the College assigned them to farm. I assigned the tools to them. It was also my duty to ensure they returned the tools they received at the end of the year. The birth of the second son and the fact that the first three children were in school in Igbo land brightened the future. He frequented his home in the village to supervise his building. They were also friends with the Achinivu family.

Amazingly, after the Christmas holiday, we returned to Uzuakoli ETC as human beings to train foxes the College assigned to us. One of the novels I bought while at ETC is *The Basket of Flowers*. It is about a little girl who experienced a very difficult life. There was an opening in her roof. The moonlight shone through the opening at night. She felt that God was watching over her through the opening. I read the book three times, and each time I wept. I think it reminded me of the night my mother and I left our home too early because of the moonlight. The book was also lost during the Biafra-Nigeria War.

A few weeks after college life resumed, the tailor who took our measurements for the blazer brought them. We claimed them and that further distinguished us from the foxes. Later on in the year, the Principal of Trinity College at Old Umuahia came and preached at Uzuakoli Methodist College. The Trinity College is sponsored by three denominations, namely, Anglican, Methodist, and Presbyterian, and it trained Reverend Ministers. At the end of his sermon, he invited students for individual counseling. I went because I was interested in becoming a Reverend Minister. Besides, I asked for advice about my "anti" behavior towards women, pointing out that I was a virgin. He did not see anything wrong in shaking hands or even befriending them. When I left him without arguing my case, I wondered about Exodus 19:15 and even Paul who said the same thing.

One Christian students' organization, the Students Christian Movement (SCM), flourished at the Uzuakoli campus at this time. Also, at Old Umuahia next door to Trinity College was the Women's Teachers Training College established by the same three denominations, which owned Trinity College. WTC also organized SCM on its campus. Both Colleges organized annual exchange visits. It was the turn of Uzuakoli to visit Old Umuahia and we did.

Those women prepared more teaching aids than they needed. The opposite was true of the males. I did not have any drawings. Our practical teaching examination was fast approaching, and the women had finished. During this examination, the examiners inspect all the apparatus the student teacher prepared in the two years, and in the case of the women in the four years, most of them were at the college. We helped ourselves by borrowing from the women. During the SCM visit to WTC, I borrowed some drawings entitled Nature Says Wash from Nwaoroni Nwagwu. All kinds of animals were busy cleaning themselves. All the arts and crafts were exhibited in the dining hall for the examiners to inspect. That was only one aspect of the external teaching examination, and students were not present during the inspection.

There were other novelties at Uzuakoli. Each student submitted three articles of clothing every Saturday at no extra cost. The washer men the College paid washed them. Optional was the purchase of cod liver oil at a low price. Students lined up empty bottles on Saturday mornings. Full bottles awaited them when they returned to claim them. I used to come home with enough for my little nephew. One of the first things I did after I reached home was to instruct my sister-in-law on how to give it to him. Finally, the practical examinations came.

Teaching, physical education, and the exhibition of arts and crafts count for one. However, no one who failed the classroom teaching passed the examination no matter how well he performed in the other two. Another practical was Rural Science. This was the first of the practical examinations. The white man came from the Umudike School of Agriculture at Umuahia. What I did not know is that he almost failed me, but Mr. Ibegbulem prevailed.

Americans say that we Africans talk loudly. As student teachers, we were not only taught to talk loudly but also encouraged to shout loudest in the P.E. field. Watching about twenty student teachers practice and command invisible pupils on the top of their voices during preparation, looked like nothing short of madness. Within two days, it was all over, including classroom teaching. Once the practicals were over, students concentrated on preparing for the written examination.

By the time the final examination came around, Method of Teaching Seriousness' physiology had become one of my favorite subjects. We took his final test. He saw me as he walked passed and first surprised me with a smile. Then he said, "Obed." I answered, "Sir." Still smiling, he said, "Do you know that some students answered my questions (all essay questions) without sketches?" I smiled and thought, I must have impressed MTS beyond expectation for him to tell me my result in advance. About two decades later when I was the Provost (President) of Oyo Federal College of Education for Special Education, we held a national workshop at Alvan Ikoku College of Education. MTS was the Dean of the School of Physical Education. He walked into the hall during break. I introduced him as my former tutor at Uzuakoli. Many of the participants were graduates of my College. They greeted him warmly and asked, "You taught this great man?" He replied, "It was in those days when they allowed us to teach them. Today you don't allow us to teach you." They answered, "He is our father, and you are our grandfather."

As usual, the start of the final examinations also meant the transfer of power and responsibilities from final-year students to first-year students who were transitioning from foxes to humans. So, Onyekwere, who washed my plates, inherited the Sunday School and water management. The end of the examinations also meant the end of the Elementary Teachers' Course. When I got home, my brother was already home from Lagos on leave. When my family and I returned to Nigeria from the U.S. in 1976, the Government abolished Elementary Teachers' Training Colleges from the Nigerian education system. Today Preliminary Teachers' Training College, Elementary

Teachers' College, and High Elementary Teachers College have all become history.

Chapter 15

Teaching As A Trained Teacher

Completing the Elementary Teachers Course placed me on a higher level than my first four teachers, who were not trained. It also came with certain privileges not available to them. The immediate benefit was the availability of transportation. I did not have to negotiate for transportation because the Mission arranged it. All that was required of me was to know my school, the date and time the vehicle would arrive, and be ready. Another benefit was the raise in salary. While we waited for the results of the final year examination, the first year's salary was raised by more than one hundred fifty percent. A third privilege was a better living quarter.

There were certain decisions to take as the day schools reopened approached. I lived alone in my first year of teaching. At this level, I was expected to have a houseboy. Anozie, Uncle Uwakwe's son, was the likely candidate. It was because of him that his father cracked my skull open with his middle finger. For one reason or another, he was not doing well in school and, at that time, was too big for his class. Though reluctant to take him with me at first, my brother prevailed, and I took him with me. By the end of the second week of January, I learned that I was posted to Methodist Central School Ozuitem. The news also came with the date of the move. Teachers were expected at their stations by the end of the third week in January. My mother packed enough food to last the two of us for at least a week and a half. This was because teachers were paid in the last week of the month.

It was early afternoon when the pickup truck arrived. I had added the beautiful cotton mattress my former teacher bought for me to my belongings. I also took one iron cooking pan and two plates that belonged to my brother. My old bucket and plank box, which I used as a suitcase, completed the load. Also, I added a wooden bed, two tables, and cane chairs. Anozie sat at the back with the belongings while I sat in front with the driver. We arrived at the school less than two hours after we said goodbye. Some friendly faces showed up, directed us to a clean house, and helped us to move in. We thanked them.

Within two hours of our arrival, while we were still unpacking and arranging things and asking questions, another pickup arrived. Those friendly faces went out again to help. I joined them, and it was a grade three lady teacher, another name for those successfully trained Elementary Teachers. That meant she was my senior. I left with the others immediately after we were through. Later that evening, she came to "thank" me. "Don't mention it," that's what they did for me when I arrived. I did not know that I had become a marked target.

Monday arrived and the headmaster began to admit students. When he saw Anozie, my cousin, he refused to admit him because of his size. I sent him home and requested my mother to get me Ukachi Ugbaja. Ukachi's older brother is the same age as Anozie but Ukachi and Anozie were in the same standard. It took a little more than a week before Ukachi came and was admitted to school.

I shared a duplex with Rufus Ogbonna. He went to Nto-Ndang a year before me. However, he was not able to pass the entrance examination for Uzuakoli ETC for training. Many of us who went to Uzuakoli were influenced by our tutors who studied for higher education. As a result, once I received my January pay, I registered with Woolsey Hall in England for private tuition to prepare for the

Preliminary English test for the University of London General Certificate in Education. Unknown to me at the time was that Rufus had done the same thing the previous year but had failed. Finally, we took the English preliminary examination. Unfortunately, he failed again. He pleaded with me not to make my success public because he was not on good terms with the headmaster. He believed the headmaster would make his life miserable if he knew that I succeeded, and he failed again. So, I kept the news of my success between the two of us at Uzuitem but told other people outside the area.

Before I knew it, this lady teacher I would call Hain was seriously interested in me. Remember the life I had lived up to that time, especially in relation to women. I did not know that telling her I was a virgin and not interested in women made me more attractive to her. For some time, I refused to welcome her to my house. I pointed her to three other bachelors on the staff. There was the grade two teacher who was the vice headmaster, Mr. Ogbonna, who had more hairs on his chest than I have on my legs, and Harcourt, who owned a gramophone (record player) where she could dance. Remember the prayer stand I bought in my first year of teaching? I knelt there some nights and prayed and wept and wondered why this woman would not leave me alone.

She had seen my prayer stand with the Bible, the candle, and incense on it. I was reading one late evening when her sister walked in and handed me a letter from her. Part of which said, "I do not intend to mislead you. If I do, God will punish me." It went on, I am going to be sick this week. Don't ask. My naivety and fear of the woman from a clan my people claim to be full of poison made me give her a part of my Udara fruit. I learned later her motive had been sexual from the beginning.

I was mean to her when it finally happened. I lost my virginity to a woman I had no intention of marrying. I did not finish it. Rather I slapped her to the floor. She got up and left. I walked to my prayer stand and wept and prayed. For the next few weeks, we did not talk to each other. Finally, she came back and apologized for her actions. She said, "I thought you were going to die because you violated the rule of your medicine. After two weeks, and you are still alive, I changed my mind." She taught me how to kiss and have sex. My resistance to her went overboard.

Mr. Nwankwo, the headmaster, was one of those early graduates of Uzuakoli College. He and Mr. Igwe, the School Supervisor, were on a first-name basis. He married daa Nwamuru from my village. Mr. Nwankwo scheduled teachers on duty. I brought that ETC discipline to the school. Devotions started at 8 am. When other teachers were on duty, students were not late if they were on school premises before devotion started. As a result, morning devotions were sometimes suspended to clean school premises. For me, that was unacceptable. My rule was that if a student did not participate in cleaning and sweeping the premises, the student was late for school. Such students were detained after school and punished. The school was on a small hill overlooking low land between it and another hill on the opposite side from which most pupils came. When I stood out of the building at school, the students saw me and ran to sweep the grounds. As a result, students rarely came late to school the week I was on duty. It did not seem that the headmaster noticed nor was impressed. That did not deter me. Suddenly the school was informed that a government traveling teacher was coming to inspect the school. The high elementary teacher was on duty, and that Friday was the day headmasters went to get teachers' monthly pay. The traveling teacher was expected early the next week, and the school was a mess. The headmaster handed over the school to me to ensure it was cleaned. That was a vote of confidence. The students did a better job than I expected.

As the teachers met to receive their pay, the headmaster revealed the secret in the cleanup. A traveling teacher would be visiting. Our training at Uzuakoli ensured us that as long as we were doing our duty, we should not fear any government visitor. I had taught my lesson, given my students the assignment, and was going around the class to inspect their work when the headmaster and the visitor walked into my class. They did not say anything. I ignored them. They spent only a few minutes and left. As they walked out, I heard him ask the headmaster, "Is he trained?" The reply was "Yes." The traveling teacher replied, "No wonder."

The grade three lady teacher went away one weekend to see her longtime boyfriend. On her way home, she came in and said congratulations!

"On what?" I asked.

"You have not heard?"

"Heard what?"

"Your grade three result is out, and you are successful."

I thought I did not even dream about it. About two weeks later, Njikonye and Ogbonna, my classmates in elementary school who were at the secondary section of Uzuakoli, came and confirmed the news. We had a mini celebration before they left.

Passing the examination also meant an increase in my salary. I had gone from twenty-four pounds per annum to one hundred pounds. By the end of August, I received a huge arrears payment that covered January to the month of payment. I took the money I had saved up to that time and the arrears, the largest sum of money in my life, and traveled to Umuahia. My plan was to buy a Raleigh bicycle and save what remained in the post office. My plan suddenly changed when I reached Umuahia.

Some rich traders bought boxes filled with parts of imported bicycles wholesale and sold them as single bicycles at the market to individual buyers. Isaiah from my village repaired bicycles at the market, and I used him as a middleman to buy my first bicycle. I decorated it with a bag with the inscription Uchechi, which means God's will. Also, I changed the seat and replaced it with a long, soft, and popular seat they called KKK. It shocked me to read about the Klu Klux Clan in the U.S. I wondered if they made the seat.

As I proudly rode my bicycle on the way to the post office to open an account, I saw a sign that read, The British Bank of West Africa. They were in a makeshift. Some bank employees had recently come from Lagos to open a branch at Umuahia. One of the men was dee Nwokoma, who came from my village. They were about to close. He took my money, gave me a receipt and a temporary number, and advised me to come the following day for my passbook. When I arrived, it was ready, and my number was 25. My mother could not believe that I owned a bicycle, a thing she thought impossible even two years before. I also gave her money. Mr. Ibegbulem owned a bicycle that had lasted decades, which he still rode. The seat felt like a stone when one sat on it. I gave him the new seat my bicycle came with and a bottle of Whisky.

Miss Hain shared the same two-room apartment with another lady teacher. She turned out to be a spy on her for daa Nwamuru, the headmaster's wife. One evening, when Hain came over to my house, her housemate went to daa Nwamuru, who in my custom was an aunt, and reported to her. Soon she was in my house and caught us in bed red-handed. The following day after school, she called me to one of the empty classrooms and queried me. She started by saying how my fellow students at Uzuakoli said I did not show interest in women. I told her my story and why I gave in. "You know better than I know. My parents had seven children, and only two of us were alive. You know where she comes from. If she kills me with poison, you will be one of the first to ask why I didn't yield." She did not have much to say. That was the end. Miss Hain got married within a few months and left the school. Daa Nwamuru was the only child of dee Asiegbu and daa

Chinyere, and I did not know her father. Her mother treated me like a grandson. She was dead by the time I returned from the U.S.

Soon after we returned from the United States, I went to the township market. There was daa Nwamuru standing and looking towards our village. She had traveled about twenty miles from where she was married to stand there. I walked up to her and greeted her. I knew she did not recognize me then. I tried to reintroduce myself. I became a distraction to her, and I left her alone. Today, I seem to know her mind. She was retracing the road she had traveled all the years, even visualizing the room she slept in as a girl and thinking that was the last time she would be there. Today, I would offer to take her to the village in a car, even if she did not want to get out of the car. But that was the last time I saw her.

God had done the impossible. I did not think that at that time in my life, I would be able to own a bicycle and have money in the bank. I made a little feast for the teachers to celebrate the success of the teachers' results. Then, I aimed higher and registered with Wolsey Hall for the ordinary level of the University of London General Certificate of Education. One of the courses I registered for was Mathematics. It consisted of Algebra, Arithmetic, and Geometry. Unless one went to secondary school in Nigeria in those days, one did not learn anything about Algebra and Geometry. I included the course because Arithmetic was my best subject in school. Having no one nearby to explain why the minus sign was more powerful than the plus in algebra and why it changed the answers created my first problem. My impatience and inability to study compounded my problem. The fact that I had less than five months to prepare for the examination did not deter me from registering. December came, and I followed in the annual pilgrimage of GCE examination takers. When the result came out, I discovered I was not immune to failure. I knew I did not deserve to pass.

Ozuitem is made up of about four villages. About three of my classmates at Uzuakoli were from Ozuitem. They came from different villages of the clan. Emedom used to tease them. There was a short bush track that passed by the college fence Ozuitem people traveled by to go to Uzuakoli market. In the afternoon, when they trekked home, Emedom said to the students, "Your people are running away from civilization." Then one of them Ojoemelam teased Uwanuakwa, another Ozuitem student, "Your village people saw a VW Beetle car running on the road and exclaimed surprise 'Wow! If this little car can run this fast now, it will be unbeatable when it grows to be an adult car." Uwanuakwa usually looked at both of them with disdain.

By the time the holiday was over, I learned that I was on transfer to be the headmaster of Eziama Methodist Group School. This was only about one mile away from my mother's kitchen. Not only that, but I was also a student there a few years ago. Even the teacher who taught me in standard two was still there and would be under me because he was untrained. I was still thinking how awkward and embarrassing the situation would be to correct his notes and scheme of work (unit of lesson) when I learned that the Mission changed my transfer to Umuoriehi Group School. This is even older than Eziama. I was relieved that I did not have to correct my teacher's notes of lessons. Again, all I had to do was to be at my station when the vehicle came to carry me and my load. Umuoriehi is only about two miles from my home, but the vehicle would travel from Ozuitem a distance of about twenty miles.

Chapter 16

Headmaster Umuoriehi Group School

Once again, the Mission arranged and moved me along with my belongings to Umuoriehi. Only two of the four teachers lived on the school premises namely, the headmaster and one other teacher. On arrival, I noticed that one of the teachers was older and senior to my standard two teacher. Though he had not taught me, he had been a teacher in my village. I could not avoid having someone I addressed as Sir on my staff. The second one was also known to me; he was older, untrained, and had taught for many years, but I got away with calling him Mr. The fourth was a lady from Uzuakoli. Umuoriehi village had a church but without a teacher. As a trained local preacher, I volunteered my services and became an unpaid church teacher as well. I also preached at other churches according to my schedule as a local preacher. For certain reasons, I enjoyed Umuoriehi for the short time I was there. But the two most important reasons for the enjoyment had nothing to do with the school. One of the reasons I enjoyed the place was the opportunity to preach every Sunday. Another reason was the presence of five women from my village married there who loved me, and one of them was my aunt. There was also daa Ada Ndimele, my mother's cousin from Ogbodi.

Living close to my mother, I had the advantage of visiting her often. In most cases, I stayed till evening. Once, I stayed till late evening and ate my dinner with her. At the time, Nigerians drove on the left side of the road like Britain. Those who rode bicycles also kept to the left side of the road. Near my school and my home were two small hills with a shallow but long valley between them. The light of a car on the first hill points directly to the valley and is not visible until it is at the brow of the second hill. I was descending the second hill with the light of my bicycle on and stretched my right arm, signifying that I was turning to the right to my school, when I saw the bright light of a car at about fifty miles per hour and a blast of the horn and screeching brakes. I thought that was my end. Miraculously I found myself thrown back with my bicycle to the shrubs on the left side of the road. All I heard as I lay there was the voice of the maniac English woman driver, the natives called Ogodoro, who was in charge of Amachara Methodist Hospital, say, "You bloody fool!" I shuddered, and for a moment, I could not move. Slowly, I got up. People rushed out to see who was killed in the crash. I dragged my bicycle and myself to my house. I wondered what my mother would have done. Even now, I still shudder and thank God whenever I remember the incident. When I became a student at HEC Uzakoli, the English teacher assigned us the topic A Narrow Escape. As an essay, I wrote about this experience and received 9 out of 10.

If there was one reason for which God brought me to Umuoriehi it was this. I wrote earlier that my mother had two sisters. By this time, her oldest sister was dead. The last statement my mother's sister made to me before she took her last breath was, "Obida (the name she called me), you, Enoch, and Godwin are the only people Nnenna (her daughter) has in this world. Take care of her." That was a week after the fourteen-year-old girl got married. About one year later, I was at Umuoriehi, and she was pregnant, very pregnant. It was time for me to shoulder my responsibility, and God provided the opportunity.

She and her husband lived in Umuahia Township. The Queen Elizabeth II Hospital, one of the best in the country, was only less than one mile from their home. But they chose to bring her to Amachara Methodist Hospital, less than one mile from Umuoriehi but more than two miles from where they live, for delivery. Once she was admitted, her husband informed me. From that time until the birth and discharge, I took care of her needs, including food. There was no medical doctor at Amachara, but it trained midwives. It was not that the husband could not take care of her. It was more convenient for Ukachi, who lived with me, to carry food from Umuoriehi than for Ukairo, her husband, to bring food from the township. I also enjoyed the satisfaction that I served her. There was Ada Ekwe, a midwife in training, who she said took very good care of her. She started calling her nwunye dee. My cousin called me dee, and nwunye means wife. So, she called Ada dee's wife. Ada and I became friends. However, I promised myself not to fall into another sex relationship before our intentions to get married came, and we never had a sexual relationship. My cousin's husband paid the financial expenses for his wife and son.

It seemed that I was back to my former days of seeing the future in my dreams. It happened one afternoon as I took my siesta. I dreamed and saw these three devil-looking creatures in ekpo masks. They said to me, "We have done it to Reverend Inenoma." This is the Reverend Minister in charge of Umuahia Circuit. Wondering about what these devils did to Inenoma when I woke up, I walked out. A man walked to me and asked me, "Did you hear what happened to Inenoma?" When I asked, "What?" He replied, "His wife just died at Amachara Hospital." I knew what the devils did to him. The three devils had counterfeited the visit of the incarnate Lord and the two angels in Exodus 18, with the opposite result. A few days later, I saw Ada Ekwe and told her about my dream and how I knew about the death of the Minister's wife. She said that the whole hospital staff was stunned and shocked by her death. It was unexpected. No one could tell what killed her.

It was time to take the entrance examination to High Elementary College, Uzuakoli. Emedom, my friend, came and spent the night with me at Umuoriehi. We rode our bicycles to Mission Hill the following day for the examination. As smart as he is, before we went to sleep, I said my silent prayer. "Dear loving Father, I pray that the two of us will pass the entrance examination this time. But if You choose to send only one of us, let it be Emedom, in Christ's name. Amen." I told him about Ada Ekwe. My local preacher's schedule showed that I was to preach at a church close to his home in a few weeks. We planned to see Mr. Ekwe, Ada's father, that Sunday to ask for his approval. I accomplished the two tasks that Sunday.

A car stopped on the main road one day and asked for me. It was the new Supervisor of Schools. I was surprised that he would not even visit the school. With his window rolled down and an outstretched hand, he gave me an envelope with my name on it. He had transferred me to Ibere Central School, a school that was recently granted standard five, and they wished to grant it standard six the following year. I was to help make that happen. Later the following week, the pickup came, and I was on the move again. The only thing worth writing home about Ibere at that time is that it was the cocoa plantation headquarters of the Eastern Region of Nigeria. Ibere seemed like a locked-up prison during the rainy season. There was a steep, slippery hill immediately after Ndoro. Two factors made it most dangerous. The first was the soil that was more slippery than wet clay. At one time, I had to use my bicycle as a wedge in front of me, using the pedal and wheels as support while I walked behind. The more dangerous of the two is the gulf at the bottom of the hill. The gulf was not a part of the road but only a few yards away. It was the burial ground for any vehicle that fell in it. I am almost sure that any driver that fell in with the vehicle did not live. My isolation was made easy because I had bought my first radio, a PYE.

As far as we were from Umuahia, the Umuahia township market was still where one met familiar and friendly faces. I met Emedom at the market on Saturday. He told me that the HEC result was in the Supervisor's office, but he was not releasing it. He heard through the headmaster of Ndoro Methodist Central School that the supervisor was demanding a three-pound bribe from each of the successful candidates before he would release the results. He claimed that HEC is not ETC we entered free. He encouraged me to make the payment but not to tell anyone about it. I paid the money. But their luck ran out when they approached Ufere Ozoemelem, one of our ETC classmates. He went straight to Uzuakoli and reported to Mr. Achinivu, our former Principal. Their little secret became public knowledge. Mr. George, my first headmaster the year I started teaching, was the first to ask me about it. But I did not ask and never received a refund.

Though the school was situated on a nice flat piece of land, that seemed to be the only worthy thing, there were seven teachers on the staff when I arrived. Three of them may have been in their late fifties or early sixties. I already knew two of these by the mention of their names. Mr. Eleke was the father of my classmate at ETC Uzuakoli, and the other had a son who was a teacher but was denied entrance to Uzuakoli because of bad behavior. The headmaster was a total stranger to me. I shared one side of the only duplex with Mr. Esobe, while the headmaster occupied the other end with his family. There was one young woman and another young man. By the year's end, there was no sign of government inspectors. The good news was that I was Uzuakoli-bound. Providence brought one of the pickups that periodically visited once in a while. It was towards the end of the term. We arranged for the driver to pick me up when he came the next time. He came the Saturday after school closed, but because he had something else in the vehicle and feared his engine might not climb the steep hill, he left Ukachi's bed behind with the promise to retrieve it on his next visit. He never fulfilled his promise.

If by now the reader feels that Umuahia market was a place students and people on holidays went to spend away time, the person would not be totally wrong. However, I rode home from the market one afternoon. Ukachi told me that a Cameroonian was at Uncle Ehiogu's house. I went over to see him. He sat alone in the living room. He did not speak my language, and Josiah and Chikara, brothers of the lady he was in love with who spoke English, were not living in the village. Our conversation revealed that he had fallen in love with my second oldest cousin Elizabeth. She was married to a man from Ogbodi who took her to Cameroun. Irrespective of who he was and how he became the new suitor, my duty was to welcome and make him comfortable. I had Ukachi prepare food for him. Daa Amiriola, my aunt and Elizabeth's mother, showed him one of my late uncle's bedrooms where he slept. He left the following day. I did not hear from him or her for some time.

I did not have many days when I had nothing to do and went to the market. I spent some days studying for the GCE examination and some with Emedom or on the farm. But the holiday had an end, and it was over.

Chapter 17

High Elementary College (HEC)

Students knew that High Elementary students belonged to a class of their own at the College. One realized from the railway station that differences existed between high elementary students and the rest of Uzuakoli College students. While the rest of the students carried their loads on their heads, HEC students hired people and paid them to carry their loads. They could afford to pay. There were two categories of High Elementary students. There was a group that graduated from ETC and taught before they became HEC students. They continued to receive their full salaries as though they were in the teaching field. But they paid a little more than three pounds each month to the College. The second group was made up of secondary school graduates. This group did not receive a salary but a meager allowance. However, at the successful completion of the course, the group received better pay than their ETC counterparts.

Unlike the ETC and the Secondary Sections where foxes were admitted, the HEC men were all gentlemen. Though they wore the usual khaki shorts and white shirts to classes, there were no regulations about what they wore after school hours or about the shoes they wore. The first-year students still supplied the firewood. It was unthinkable for any of them to fetch his firewood. Uzuakoli boys made their money selling firewood to them.

Going to HEC Uzuakoli meant that my PYE radio would lie idly unused. My mother could not use it. Mrs. Ibegbulem requested to have it for her kitchen. I gave it to her. They had another baby boy appropriately named Chimarobi, which means God knows the heart's desire. Through examination and performance, Mr. Ibegbulem distinguished himself and earned the teacher's grade one certificate. The Methodist Mission decided to establish another preliminary teachers' training college at Agbani. With his status as a grade one teacher and experience at Nto-Ndang, he became the founding Principal.

Mr. Halse, an English man, was our Principal during our first year at HEC. I was a member of the cricket team he coached. For one reason or the other, I became his favorite student. He took me to interpret for him when he preached. He preached in English, and I interpreted in Igbo at the Uzuakoli Lepper Colony service. One Sunday after the service, the Rev. Dr. Davis organized a buffet dinner for the white people at the service and invited me. I was between Mr. Halse in front of me and Dr. Davis behind me. Mr. Halse looked at me and pointed at the food items, and asked me to compare them with gari, the stable food of Nigerians. I looked at him and said, "This is to you as gari is to me." He pretended as though he did not hear me and asked, "What? Before I could say a word, Dr. Davis replied, "He said that this is to you as gari is to him." That was the end of the conversation. I also taught his steward and cook Scripture every Tuesday.

Mr. Halse was full of surprises. He at least surprised me three times. True, I never saw his wife in trousers. But one evening we were playing a game of cricket when an English couple who taught at the secondary school came to HEC. Both of them wore trousers. Mr. Halse walked over to me and, in a whispering voice, said, "Look at her. You can't tell whether she is a man or woman." I looked at him and smiled. At another time, he embarrassed me in the classroom. The class ordered a geography book. It came from Britain. He told me to go to the bookstore and claim my copy. I knew another student,

Nnawuhe, who also ordered the book and told him. He went with me, and we each claimed one. Mr. Halse never told me that the price was higher than we paid, nor did he tell me not to take any other student. He came to class looking angry. He ripped into me and called me a nuisance for going to claim the book before the proper price was assessed. After expressing his anger, he told the class the new price. When he saw me next, he apologized and told me he had to say that to prevent anyone else from going to claim it at the same price.

The Gold Coast had obtained independence from Britain under Dr. Kwame Nkruma and changed the name to Ghana. Britain was doing everything it could to retain Nigeria as her colony, or at least the northern part. It appeared to find an excuse in the founding of the African Continental Bank. Dr. Azikiwe was the Premier of the Eastern Region and founder of the Bank. Eyo, who worked for the Bank and even earned more than the Premier, lost his job. He invited the British Government to investigate the Bank. The British Government rejoiced and set up an inquiry to investigate.

Once again, we were playing cricket, and Mr. Halse walked close to me and said, "They found that rogue guilty." To me, the rogue was out of context. I asked, who is the thief? He said, "Azikiwe." He continued, "He stole the money." I said, "But the money is in Nigeria. It did not leave the country." Like our other conversations, it ended abruptly. The only thing the inquiry achieved was expanding the vocabulary of the ordinary Nigerian by QC i.e., Queen's Council.

During my first year at HEC, I declared my candidacy for the Ministry, which meant taking written and practical examinations to study at Trinity (seminary) College. At the same time, I prepared to repeat the University of London General Certificate ordinary level. Then the college chaplain, Rev. Collingwood, and seven HEC student members of the Students Christian Movement (SCM), including me, arranged to travel to Otukpo, a town in the northern part of Nigeria, on an evangelical campaign. Rev. Collingwood helped in the preparation, which took a few weeks. Less than twenty-four hours before our departure, he claimed to be sick and turned over the leadership to me.

Two pleasant surprises awaited me on arrival. First, there was the Reverend Egemba Igwe from Umuda, the village next to mine. He welcomed the team. He was one of the rare Nigerian Ministers in the Methodist Church with a degree. As we strolled in the late afternoon, I saw my second surprise. There was a white man coming toward us. I looked, and it was Rev. Johnson, who used to live at Mission Hill. He was the Minister in charge of Umuahia Circuit when we were pupils at Mission Hill. I called him and greeted him and reminded him of the trick (magic) he performed for us with his finger. He pulled his finger and made it seem as though it disappeared. He smiled, did it, and fooled me again. His finger looked as though it disappeared.

The people were mostly animists. Our first meeting was at a square, and on two sides of the place were two small shrines. When I saw them, the one scripture that came to my mind was Paul on the streets of Athens and their numerous gods. I used Acts 17. That became the theme of our campaign. We went to many villages and were welcomed wherever we went. The success was acknowledged on campus. All three sections of the College came to the College hall to hear about our experience. That might have led to another adventure for Easter of the following year.

By this time, my interest in completing the HEC course was waning in proportion to the rate my interest in the Ministry was growing. I rode my bicycle to Trinity College to take the written tests. After the morning papers, I rode to the market. My cousin's husband handed me an envelope, and the sender was the West African Examination Council. Immediately, I knew what it was, so I tore it open. The first words that caught my eye were "Cert. Awarded." I praised God, consoled my cousin by marriage, and sympathized with him about his failure. I was back at Trinity College to complete the afternoon papers.

Delighted and excited with the GCE positive result, I rode back to Uzuakoli immediately after the afternoon papers were over. Unfortunately, the result had two opposite effects.

On my part, I thought that it was a confirmation that I should not continue with the HEC course. But to others whose opinion I valued, the result said that I should complete the course and go on to get a degree before entering the Ministry. Yet they would not say anything as long as I was taking the tests. The results of the written examination were released, and I was successful. Later, the Mission assigned me to preach at Umuahia Township Methodist Church. The objection mushroomed. Mr. Achinivu started by contrasting Rev. Igwe, M.A. with another minister who had not even graduated from ETC. It seemed that others were waiting in the wing to see what happened with the sermon. I passed the first two tests (written and sermon). I preached well. Then there was only one more test i.e., to present myself to the Synod, the governing body of the Methodist Church. The pressure mounted. Mr. Ibegbulem and others joined. However, I was determined to go through the whole process. I attended the Synod at Oron and was accepted.

What I call a miracle happened before the end of the day. Oron is an Efik town. I did not know anyone there and could neither speak nor understand the language. By the time I arrived at the motor park after the interview, there was only one lorry left going to my Igbo land, and it was traveling to Aba, not Umuahia. Aba is about forty miles from Umuahia. I paid to go to Aba. I knew a few men from my village who lived at Aba, but I did not know their addresses. I had hoped to travel from Aba to Umuahia that day. That hope was dashed on our arrival at Aba because the last transport to Umuahia had left. The thought of sleeping in a hotel was foreign to me. Even if it was customary, I did not have the money. I did the one thing I could.

I walked into the town. There was one glimmer of hope in me as I roamed the streets of Aba, looking at every face I passed. I expected to recognize a familiar face, whether from my village or not. Suddenly, there was the face of a man sitting in his corridor that appeared familiar. I could not believe my own eyes. I blinked and stared again. It still looked like the face of Jacob, my youngest uncle, who was supposed to live in Lagos. I closed and opened my eyes again and looked again. The face was his. The soap factory he worked for in Lagos had transferred him to Aba that week. God provided me with a place to lodge that night. I shared my experience with him. He was as surprised as I was. My journey home the following day was smooth.

By this time, my relationship with Mr. and Mrs. Ibegbulem had matured into what I perceived as a son-parent relationship. I went to the market with the family. Usually, I took Mrs. Ibegbulem to the market on my bicycle during holidays. One day, we bought something from a trader, and he gave me more money than the change called for. I gave him back the extra money. Mrs. Ibegbulem looked at me with a smile and teased me with "Okpara Chileke" (the first son of God). During that Christmas holiday, we agreed to take a family picture. I arranged for the photographer to come. Their six children were dressed for the occasion, but husband and wife looked as though they had just woken up from sleep. We went ahead and had the picture taken. The two faces looked as if they were in mourning. A few days later, I rode into town and brought copies of the picture. I learned what the problem was.

Mr. Ibegbulem and his family lived at Agbani at this time but spent the Christmas holidays at home. As usual, I carried his wife on my bicycle to the market and back whether he was home or went with us or was away. One day, while he was at Agbani, I took his wife to the market. Mark from Ohia made what I regarded as disrespectful remarks. I later rebuked him, and he apologized. We all believed that the matter was settled there and then. But Ukairo Igbokwe, my cousin's husband, thought he had something to gossip about. One morning Ukairo and Mr. Ibegbulem traveled on the same train.

Ukairo twisted the story and told Mr. Ibegbulem that Mark and Obed were fighting over his wife.

As if that was not bad enough, Mr. Ibegbulem's reaction made matters worse. He suspected his wife of having an affair with me and planned to catch us. He felt sure that we would not do anything during the day with his six children, an aunt, three half-brothers, and others around. Nighttime would be it. He returned two days earlier than he told his wife to expect him. At another time, he stayed at Mission Hill till late at night and knocked at her window. He did not see me or any other person. At another time, he pretended to travel to Agbani, only to wait at Mission Hill and return late at night or a little after midnight. After three or four attempts that ended in failure, he confessed to her and told her the story.

As she told me the story, I felt betrayed and utterly disappointed. I felt I had lost my trust in thinking he could replace my late father. I thought of the services I had rendered to him from Nto-Ndang, and before I knew it, I was in shock. I started shaking in that heat from the sun, and for a short time, my body temperature was as though I had a fever. Without a word, I took my bicycle and rode home. Determined to sever all relationships with him, I lay on my bed and wept. I told Emedom and his comment or advice was stupid when he said, "Go ahead and do it." My holiday was ruined.

Mr. Spray, the Principal of the College, surprised me one day. We crossed paths, and I greeted him. He said, "Hello, Obed." I thought, "Thank God I am not doing anything wrong. How did he get to know me?" Mr. Halse was in his mischievous behavior again. He knew he was returning to Britain for good at the end of the year. He also knew that Mr. Omeoga, a Nigerian, would succeed him. These facts were not known to us students. In his attempt to create problems for Mr. Omeoga, he promised lofty excursions to the Port Harcourt glass factory and Enugu coal mine the following year. When the College resumed, both the College Principal, Mr. Spray, and the HEC

Principal, Mr. Halse, had left the College for good. All three sections of the College were under Nigerians. Mr. Achinivu, the Principal of ETC, also became the Principal of the whole College. Mr. Omeoga became the Principal of HEC, and Mr. Odokara became the Principal of the Secondary School. There were still about six Britons at the College.

Chapter 18

Final Year At Uzuakoli

Every student was required to attend church service on Sundays at Uzuakoli. We were in church one Sunday when the thought of what Mr. Ibegbulem did overwhelmed me. The tears came again. When the preacher asked us to close our eyes for prayer, I walked out and returned to my room. I wrote what I believed was my last letter to him. Among other things, I told him that he hated me and accused me of incest. That I misplaced my trust in him and that Sir Arthur's round table was dissolved. He read the letter and, according to his wife, blamed her for telling me about it. Then, he wrote an apology to me and pleaded for forgiveness.

Something else was going on at the College. It was a Saturday afternoon. The HEC Boarding Master lived close to the students' dormitories. I was walking to my room when I came face to face with about five wives of some Nigerian teachers coming from the boarding master's house. Mrs. Achinivu led "the procession." She had a piece of kola nut in her hand. Once she saw me, smiled, and stretched her hand, she said, "Obed, my son, come take and chew. It is a gift from your God." Her statement stopped me cold. I looked at her, turned forty-five degrees, and walked away without saying one word. She must have been surprised. Whatever happened, and by whatever means, there was some communication between her and the Ibegbulems, and she was aware of my situation. In my mind, I thought, "If Ibegbulem would do this, who would blame Achinivu if he shot me with a gun for receiving a piece of kola nut from his wife."

A few days later, I received an urgent message. Mrs. Achinivu, the College Principal's wife, wanted to see me. I thought she was going to scold me about my rudeness to her. I thought of taking Emedom with me but decided against it. She had all the facts, but she had to be herself first. She offered me a seat and sat down. She said, "I wondered what devil got into you to treat me the way you did." All I offered was a wry smile. She said I misplaced my anger. "You should have blamed the gossiper." I disagreed. She joined the pleading band. Before I left, we resolved that I should forgive and let go.

Before long, the wind of discontent was blowing between the ETC graduates in HEC Training and the Eastern Region Government over the payment of salaries. The government gave two reasons for its unwillingness to continue to pay salaries to our class of HEC students. The first was the condition of the students. Compared with former students who were paid salaries, our group was young and almost one hundred percent single, while the opposite was true of our predecessors. As a result, the government thought we did not need the money. Secondly, the Government announced Free Universal Primary Education (UPE) that was free. It needed money to run the program. Many ETC students in HEC used the money we were paid to order shoes and other expensive items from overseas. Others made better use of the salaries. If there was a third factor, it was the fact that the secondary school graduates HEC students also received allowance, not salary. How be it, that the Government decided to stop the payment of salaries to ETC graduate students.

The ETC students reacted with organized resistance groups in the region. This was the problem only in the Eastern Region. The other two regions were not involved. Okwong, an Efik, was our secretary. He represented Uzuakoli at the regional meeting. He could not attend meetings in a different town and classes at Uzuakoli at the same time. On his return, the Principal suspended him. We hid him on the campus and fed him while we continued our negotiation with the authorities. When the negotiation reached an impasse, we declared a strike and left the College. Out of the many Colleges in the Region, only Uzuakoli went on strike. It seemed that the strike achieved only one thing, namely, reconciliation between Mr. Ibegbulem and me.

The strike provided an opportunity for me to visit, and with pressure from the Achinivus, I did. I was there for a few days when a tragedy struck. Chimarobi, the youngest son, had a high fever. One of the older sisters carried him on her back when another one noticed that his eyes had turned, and he no longer had black color and started shouting. We all ran out. The little boy was convulsing. His parents snatched him from his sister and took him inside the house. There was no hospital at Agbani. They had to wait till early the following day to drive to Enugu. That meant a sleepless night for all the adults. Before daybreak, Onwe, the house servant, had prepared a rice meal. As soon as he finished cooking, we packed the food into a waiting car. The parents, the driver, and I were on our way to Enugu with the boy. His body was as hot as an oven by this time.

On arrival at Enugu, one could conclude that Mr. Ibegbulem had made up his mind not to go to the General Hospital because it would take too long before a doctor saw the boy. He instructed the driver to take us to a private hospital. The doctor was at his desk when we arrived. He took the boy, treated him, and laid him down. He went and sat down, and Mr. Ibegbulem walked a short distance to see Mr. Achara, the Methodist School Supervisor. Several minutes later, I looked at the baby, and there did not seem to be any breath left in him. I walked close, and he was dead. I walked over to the mother, and she did not know what the condition was. "You have not eaten since last evening. It is high time you ate," I said. I dished out food for her. Once she started to eat, I told her that I was going to get Mr. Ibegbulem to come and eat, too. I walked to the doctor and told him that the baby was dead, "But do not let the mother know until we come. I am going to get her husband."

Mr. Ibegbulem was with Mr. Achara in his office when I got there. I gave him the sad news and told him what I did. He shed tears, and they stood up. Mr. Achara cautioned him. "Mr. Ibegbulem, pull yourself together. You are not going to further break that woman's heart with your tears." We walked out.

She was still oblivious to the condition of the baby when we returned. We walked into the room with the doctor. He examined the baby and said, "I am sorry. The child is dead." The tears streamed. We took the corpse and returned to Agbani. Mr. Ibegbulem made plans to carry the corpse to the village in Umuahia for burial, a distance of about eighty miles.

He also arranged for someone to take care of the children at Agbani. More tears flowed once we reached Agbani. However, once the parents were sure that the children were provided for, they took some clothes to wear at home. By then, it was late afternoon. The three of us, the driver and the corpse, were on our way to Umuahia. By the time we were half the distance to Umuahia, it was dark, and by the time we reached the compound in the village, everyone was sound asleep. We did not need to knock at any door to wake up anyone to tell them about our arrival. Before the vehicle entered the compound, Mrs. Ibegbulem cried so loud that every man and woman in the compound rushed out with whatever they wore to bed. In the Igbo tradition of mourning, every woman joined the chorus. There was no more sleep for the night. We buried the child the next day. One or two days after the burial, we returned to Agbani. Tragedy overshadowed and even healed the wounds of suspicion.

In the second week of the strike, the Principal wrote a letter to individual students demanding that they return to the College immediately or assume they were dismissed. When the letter arrived, I was at Enugu Football Stadium. An English football team was touring Nigeria. It defeated the national team, trounced the Western team, and came to the East. The stadium was packed full. There were still hundreds of spectators outside the stadium wanting to be allowed in. Suddenly, the referee walked to the field and blew the whistle. The police officers and football officials at the gate swung the gates open. Hundreds of the spectators at the gate, including those of us without tickets, rushed into the stadium. The Eastern team played better than the British team. A few minutes before the end of the game, the referee, a white man, awarded a penalty kick to the British team. Ibiam, the Eastern goalkeeper, caught the ball. Father Fisher, the referee, rewarded the kick. The British team scored. The following day, the headlines read: Father Fisher defeats East 1 to 0. In reality, more important than Father Fisher was the British goalkeeper who stood between the poles and caught the ball like a magnet attracts iron. I learned a few things that day that helped my game. At the end of the game, I went to the railway station to buy a ticket to Agbani. The ticket master would not sell one because the train was a "through train" and did not stop at small stations like Agbani. But it slowed down to exchange staff. I knew that as long as I ran in the same direction as a moving vehicle, I would be all right. I entered the train without a ticket and got off at Agbani when it slowed down. It was already dark at the time. I walked to the College and to the house and received the letter from the Principal. The following day, I was on the train again on my way to Uzuakoli.

The reader should by now have concluded that the forces against my attending Trinity College had prevailed. Every serious student would concentrate on studies to cover past grounds. But as Mr. Halse described me as "a happy-go-lucky student." In addition, I added photography to my extra-curricular activities. This was a time-consuming activity. I learned to develop and print pictures. I received the prize for the best work in photography at the annual student awards.

Again, the College Chaplain and the Students Christian Movement planned an Easter outing. We arranged to go to Umuagu Methodist Church, a village about eight miles from the College. Reverend Collingwood was to preach on Easter Sunday. Once again, at the eleventh hour, he claimed to be sick and asked me to substitute for him. I began to wonder if he was really sick or if that was a way to get me to preach under different conditions. It worked out so well that students teased him on our return. "Go and learn how to preach from Obed." He also taught our English Literature class. He was fond of asking me to read so often that students asked why I should read all the time. Even as recent as October 2009, Emedom still told his family that he scored higher than I on a test my friend Collingwood gave.

It seemed all the students returned that weekend. Okwong was on campus. Immediately, the principal called a meeting of all the students who had gone on strike. The first announcement was that the decision of the Government to stop the payment of salaries was final. It would stop that match at the end of the fiscal year. He reminded us that we were under bond. In those days, a student at ETC paid only twenty-four pounds for the two years they spent in training, of which twelve pounds was given back to the student as spending money. They received books worth eight pounds. They were fed and given kerosene every Saturday. Washermen washed three articles of clothing each week for every student. When the expenses for students were calculated, training each student cost the Mission and the Government a lot of money. The one way the government made sure it recovered the money it spent on the students was to make each student sign a contract that bonded each of them to teach for two years for each year he was in training. If we resumed classes, there would be no repercussions. To be sure the students behaved themselves, he would give us a blank sheet to sign, and he would write in what we signed later. I objected. "Sir, I will not sign anything without first reading the contents." He was surprised that I said that and asked, "Obed, don't you trust me?" "I do, Sir, but I will not sign the blank paper." A few more minutes passed, and he dismissed us. That was the end of the matter. That was also the end of the payment of salaries to HEC students in the Eastern Region of Nigeria. Our class felt lucky that we were paid a salary for fifteen of the twenty-four months in training. However, our allowance was about twice the allowance the secondary school graduates received.

College Sports Day was a big event at Uzuakoli. The all-college marathon was one of the events I participated in. The ETC students were in their "not at my time" mode practice when one of them fell and died. Since he came from Umuda, the village next to mine, I had to go to the burial. The College canceled the event because of his death. I still enjoy other sports and football. Our HEC team went to Awka and played their team, but they lost 3 to 1. Many of them wore shoes, except for Ikerionwu on our team, who wore canvas; the rest of us played barefooted. We knew we were scheduled to play our secondary school team the following Monday. However, we were not ready to play another game that soon and asked for a postponement. They insisted on playing the game as scheduled or forfeiting the points. We decided to play.

As I walked toward the field, I saw Mr. Odokara, the principal of the secondary school. He said to me, "Obed, You go and try, but you have lost the game before you start." I told him, "We'd rather fight than yield the points." He said, "Go and try." After a few minutes, the two teams lined up on the field. Within the first five minutes of the game, there was no doubt as to who would win the game. Our team looked like the best and youngest team of HEC the Secondary School had ever played. By halftime, we led by two goals to one. When the last whistle blew, the final score was HEC three and Secondary School one. I believe that was the first time HEC defeated a Secondary School football team. Unfortunately, I did not see their Principal after the game to tell him why we refused to forfeit the points.

Though the village loved me, I grew up in a small circle of friends. Njikonye and Ogbonna were my classmates throughout elementary school. They attended the secondary school section of Uzuakoli, while I attended the teachers' section. They were my constant companions. I did not visit even prominent homes, as was the custom, especially during festivals. Mr. and Mrs. Ibegbulem invited me to accompany them to Chief Fredrick Anosike's home one festival Sunday. When the three wives of the Chief saw us, they started to dance. All three of us were surprised. Mr. Ibegbulem asked why the dance. They, in unison, answered, "Obed came to our house." Mr. and Mrs. Ibegbulem looked at me as if to say, "Are you a celebrity?" They entertained us, and we left.

Njikonye is a distant cousin. I came home one late afternoon during one of the holidays. There was not much to do. I strolled to his home. People were crying. His youngest brother was dead. He was healthy that morning when his mother left him. He was running about in the afternoon when he fell, knocked his head on the hard ground, and died. The mother was still not home. Our immediate problem became how to inform her that the healthy boy she said goodbye to in the morning was dead. We told all the neighbors to leave her house. We lay the body on the bed, and Njikonye and I walked to the main road, a distance of about one mile, to wait for her, pretending that we were strolling.

We did not wait too long on the main road before we saw her walking toward us. Our presence cheered her up. Smiling at us, she said, "Obida, are you and your cousin just enjoying the evening breeze or what?" I said, "Yes." Walking home with her, she told us about her activities and why she was late coming home. As we approached the church building, she lamented the anguish she felt on that spot that morning. Daa Akwaoma Umunnakwe, a woman of her age, was crying when she reached the spot because she lost another child. She planned to go and comfort her once she put down the load on her head. Daa

Akwaoma bore many children. As I write this sentence, I do not know if any of them lived beyond their teenage years. Daa Ojure's comment about daa Akwaoma opened a little window of opportunity for us to talk about death in general and how bereaved people endure it. By the time this discussion was over, we were at her doorstep. The faces of her other sons told the story. Unsure of what she might do with the load on her head, we took it off her head. She threw herself on the dead son and started crying. All the people who dispersed returned. Others and I spent the night there trying to comfort her. It was Sunday at dawn. I walked home to see my bicycle still outside, wet with the dew. My mother was angry at my absence without her knowledge, though I had never done such a thing before. However, she was sorry when she learned the fact. In Nigeria today, that bicycle would have been stolen.

I was on holiday from Uzuakoli, and the Cameroun man who visited the compound alone at one time was in the compound again, this time with the cousin he intended to marry. We greeted. The following day, I went to the market, and when I returned, there was a used tie and a worn-out, un-ironed shirt on my bed. Ukachi told me that the cousin and her husband gave them to me. I felt grossly insulted. I took them, rushed to my uncle's house, and sadly for them, they were both sitting in the living room. I threw their gift on the bed where they sat. Offended and thinking about how her father usurped my father's wealth and drove us out, the ingratitude of my hospitality to my cousin's fiancé on his last visit, and the denial that God had reversed what they thought would be our place in that compound. I said to her, "What is this insult? Do you know who I am? Do you know my status? I am a paid high elementary student. When you go out, ask what that means. This is what you people intended it to be. I would be begging you, wearing and eating your leftovers. You even refuse to recognize that God changed your plan." She was dumbfounded. I walked out. Her gift reminded me of her older sister's insult and the reason my mother gave for refusing to get married to another man after the death of our father.

Recall that my mother said she was young and beautiful when our father died and could have remarried if she wanted. But she did not want another woman to give us food by measure. As an older boy, I visited Uncle Ehiogu's oldest daughter and her family on one of the festival days. She gave me the leftover foofoo and soup of some guests. It seemed as though she were saying, "You are supposed to be dead, and you want me to feed you." That was the last time I visited her home. I understood what my mother meant and appreciated her more.

After my cousin and her boyfriend visited, Nwaekenna, my father's oldest sibling and only sister visited the compound with her daughter. They were about to enter Uncle Ehiogu's yard when she saw me. She turned and walked into our yard. Before I greeted her, she called me Obidayi. Without any hesitation, she plunged into their usual false accusation and attack against my mother. "Your mother has told you not to recognize me as your Adanne." Adanne affectionately means my grandmother's first daughter. However, I will substitute the first aunt for it in this chapter. I was flooded with anger at that point, remembering that Uncle Akwarandu had cracked my skull earlier when I was a boy and accused my mother falsely of passing on my father's wealth to her relatives. I said to her, "Stop! You are not my grandmother's first daughter. You might be that to my father, but certainly not to me. You do not even know who I am. You drove my mother and me out of this yard with the hope that we would be dead by now. You brought gifts to Josiah, Chikara, and Mba (my uncle's living sons). Have you given me any? If you did not see me standing here, would you have come here? That was about ten years since my mother and I returned to our yard. Listen, before you set your foot in this yard again you must obtain permission from my mother. If she permits you to come, then come in. Without her permission, do not step into this yard." At the end of my reply, she knew she had no moral ground or even pretense to stand. She walked away. I never saw her in our yard again for as long as she lived. Daa Amiriola, my Uncle's first wife said, "Obida is like his father. He will say it as it is." When my mother came home, I asked her what my dad looked like. She said, "Look at yourself in the mirror. You will see him." But I visited her (my father's sister) in the company of my brother after I returned from the U.S.A. I told her that my brother compelled me to drive him to see his father, not my mother's first daughter. At that time, she was not able to walk.

Amafo Isingwu, my village, completed a church building. It was started building a long time ago. The fact that I did not know my father and he was the chairman of the building committee gives an idea of how long it took to complete. It was huge and elegant. It was and still is the most beautiful, biggest, and costly church building in the Circuit. Equally surprising is the size of the village that built it. Mr. Uku from Rivers State, who taught at Mission Hill one time, gave an example of a synagogue to his class. In describing the church building to his class, he said, "I passed through Amafo and saw a big synagogue building at Amafo. I could not tell whether the synagogue built Amafo or whether Amafo built it." There, it was finished and ready for dedication. Though I was either unborn or too young when my father started it, I was going to participate in the dedication ceremony.

In our absence, the dedication committee had planned that Njikonye and I would stand at the main door to welcome the dignitaries that including Dr. M. I. Okpara who became the Premier of the Eastern Region of Nigeria. The Reverends Egemba Igwe and Inenoma officiated at the dedication. It was a grand occasion. The dedication committee announced the building cost five hundred thousand pounds. The doubters argued that a village of less than a thousand people could afford to build such a house. The Premier confirmed that it could cost even more. How did the village build it?

The village was divided into eight groups according to the traditional days of the Igbo week. There were stones around the village.

The men went into the bushes with big axes and broke the stones into the sizes the women could carry. The women carried the stones to the mission grounds and broke them down into smaller pieces. There was fine sand in the stream that seemed to increase as soon as any part of it was removed. The men dug the sand out, and as soon as it dried, the women carried it to the mission. Block-making belonged to the men. Almost all the labor and materials except those that were manufactured were supplied by the people. The building was as high as a four-story building. Miraculously, a single person did not get hurt during the building. The dedication day proved to be a very proud day in the village.

Chapter 19

Josiah's Engagement And After Effects

Josiah, my cousin, is the oldest son of Uncle Ehiogu. He was a teacher at Bornu, a town in northern Nigeria. He fell in love with an Igbo woman teacher whose home was only a few miles from our village. She was a member of the Seventh-Day Adventist denomination. All the major Christian denominations in Nigeria trained their own teachers and administered their own schools at this time. The Seventh-Day Adventist (SDA) owns a college that is about sixteen miles away from my home, less than a mile from the market I attended as a boy. This woman gained admission to the HEC section of the college. While I was at Uzuakoli HEC, she attended Ihie SDA HEC. At the College was her classmate Nwachi, and two of them became good friends. I did not know anything about Nwachi until the day they visited me during the second term holiday. After I entertained them, I walked them to the mission and said, "Should you make it impossible for me to see you again, goodbye." My cousin's fiancé insisted that I walk farther with them, which I did. By the time I left them, we were at Umuda, halfway to her village. With the visit over, I thought that was the end of it. Surprisingly, it was the beginning of something else.

The holiday was over, and I returned to Uzuakoli. A few weeks later I received a letter from Nwachi. Among other things, she asked why I did not write "those who are living?" I tore up the letter and threw it away. Within the space of two weeks, I received a second letter from her. This time, she declared her love and asked for a reply. Reluctantly, I replied with a discouraging theme. My cousin's fiancé told me that Nwachi's fiancé was a student in the U.S. I did not believe that a Nigerian woman would leave a graduate to marry a grade two teacher. Not mincing words about my feelings, I contrasted myself to the man in the U.S. "I understand that your fiancé is in the U.S. Please accept one pound that has been willingly offered to you and leave one shilling alone. Twenty shillings make one pound. I thought that was the death nail. The reply came before the end of the week. She would not marry him and gave many reasons. Then, I made my usual mistake of seeking advice. Emedom assured me that it was ok since I was not the one initiating and asking her to leave him. I accepted her friendship. We exchanged letters almost every other week. I almost succeeded in getting the soccer team to play her college. But that was our last year in both colleges.

"Obed, Obed, do you have any money left?" That was the call that woke me up from my siesta. That was Emedom, and he continued, "Everyone is dying. Do you have any money left? If you do, give it to me; let me buy bread for us to eat before we die." I told him to take the three-pence in my pocket. He did, bought the bread, and ate it alone. There was a bad flu in the country, which might have been the first time. There was no effective treatment, and people were dying everywhere. However, the college was not affected. The fact is that a man riding his bicycle fell off and died. Emedom had to make fun of it in order to get my three pence to buy bread. Emedom made fun of anything he chose. For example, we walked out of the evening service one Sunday and two Efik students were conversing in the Efik language. Emedom marched to them and intruded, "What language is this? Who told you that God understands your language?"

Then it was the practical teaching examination when Government Examiners came to the College. Besides classroom teaching, they also evaluated students' physical education performance with their pupils on the field. The field was divided to accommodate about twelve students and their pupils at the same time. Before the Examiners came, the students practiced without the pupils yelling commands no one listened to or obeyed. Emedom called me and said, "Come and see mad people!" Despite his joke, it was real. With the practical and written examinations over, we left HEC the last set of HEC students who received one full year's plus salary while in training.

This chapter will not be complete if I fail to mention the fact that Njikonye and I did our three-week teaching practice at Mission Hill. It was most satisfying that we taught in the same classroom where we sat as standard five and six pupils. Unfortunately, Mr. Iteke, my beloved teacher and headmaster, had gone on transfer. I had one more pleasant experience with him while I was at Uzuakoli HE College. I rode my bicycle to visit him and his family one day at Ndioro. He was so pleasantly pleased and surprised he could not believe it. He mentioned some of his former students who were nearby and had not visited him. He insisted that I stay and eat lunch. I obeyed. His wife prepared a fresh meal for me because they had already eaten when I arrived. When I got up to go, he gave me five shillings. I protested. "Sir, I am a salaried high elementary student." His reply was, "After all, are you not Obed?" I accepted my five shillings with gratitude. Wednesday evenings were Bible study evening time at all three centers at Uzuakoli College. As a result, students ate dinner at seven instead of six pm. On one particular Wednesday, we at HEC came to the dining hall. It was past 7 pm when the students ate dinner. Most of the students were present. We took our food from the racks, sat down, and sang the grace. The compound chief, who was also a student, came late. Instead of saying private grace, he ordered everyone to stop eating and sing what I regarded as his grace. I felt that to be the arrogance of power and continued to eat my food. He determined to punish me. He told me to come and cut grass. I refused. Usually, when a student failed to do his punishment during the week, he was not allowed to break bounds on Saturday. So, the following Saturday, after a general inspection, the Boarding Master, Mr. Ekwe, announced that I could not break the bounds that day. By this time, I had fallen out with Mr. Ekwe. To tell them that I was ready to be expelled, they were still on the lawn when I took my bicycle and rode out to leave the College boundary and rode back. They did nothing.

Shortly before the end of the holiday, I was resting on my bed in my one-room portion of the two-room house when I heard, "Gbogbo, gbogbo there is a woman who wants to know if you are at home." Before I got up Nwachi was in the room. This was the woman who fell in love with me before I wrote the first letter and we decided to marry. She had traveled many miles to come. We kissed passionately with intimacy. Her plan was to see me first, then go to spend the weekend with her friend. By midafternoon my brother's wife, who was home from Lagos with my two nephews, was home from the market. I decided to walk Nwachi to Umuawa village, the home of her friend's grandmother. When we got there, the friend who lived with the grandmother was not at home. She had traveled to the College. She told me that her friend had fallen in love with two brothers at the College. In an attempt to leave a note for the friend, she brought out a picture from her bag. It was a picture of her and a man she called Ed. When I asked who he was, she said he was her cousin. I challenged the blood relationship based on their posture. She maintained her claim.

As a member of the SDA, she could not travel the following day, Saturday. She could not even travel at a certain time on that Friday. That meant she had to stay with me until Sunday. My explanation about why she came back with me and could not travel until Sunday was acceptable. She provided me with a flimsy excuse when she asked me to become a member of the SDA. I laughed. She asked, "Obii, why are you laughing?" Still thinking about the picture, I said, "Suppose I became a member today, and tomorrow you marry someone else." "Is that why you are laughing?" Through my brother's wife, I told my mother that we were debating membership in SDA. I got Emedom to come and meet her.

Sunday came, and we attended the big Methodist church in my village. My cousin Ogonnaya and I walked her to the railway station, and I bought her a second-class ticket to her home. Unknown to her was that her father had gone to the College and seen her friend there. When the dad asked about the friend, and she indicated that she saw her, he confronted her with the fact. She admitted her absence but not the whole truth. She was impressed by and contrasted the friendly atmosphere in my family to the one she was said to be betrothed. My reply to her letter was the last communication until after the holiday.

Chapter 20

Akanu Item Teaching After HEC

As usual, before the end of the holiday, I learned that I had been posted to Methodist Central School Akanu Item. Prior to the publication of the postings, Mr. Amadi Udu, a man from our village, had requested that I take Sunday, one of his sons, to live with me. His second son Chibuzo had completed standard six and was waiting for the result but failed to gain entrance to any secondary school. For two reasons, he needed to repeat the class. First, there was no provision for private candidates to take the entrance examinations. Second, the boy needed private tutoring, and I would provide that free. But he would pay the school fees and his feeding money, which he determined to be an amount. My older brother had also decided that I would take Chikezie, Uncle Uwakwe's second son, with me. He was my responsibility.

God had moved me through the rungs of the teaching status ladder of the time at the fastest pace. As a high elementary teacher, I had progressed from carrying my belongings to my station to being conveyed by a pickup truck to a big lorry. The Mission made all the arrangements, paid for it, and informed me of the schedule. On the day of departure, Mr. Udu sent his second and third sons to live with me instead of one son. Later on, I learned his reason. I heard that he said he carried my load first, and it was my turn to carry his. Since he was a much older man, I wondered if he was one of those who carried my father's goods to distant markets and asked Uncle Uwakwe about that. His answer ridiculed the idea. "Amadi could not carry himself. How could he carry loads?" I discovered what my load was later.

Remember I stated earlier that Uncle Onwumere, who took my brother to Lagos, was transferred from Lagos to Zaria in northern Nigeria. For the fact that my brother was learning a trade, he left him in Lagos, where he lived with Mr. Udu. It was now my turn to live not with one but two of his children.

It was during this holiday that I committed one of my sins of omission. Daa Mgbafo and her one surviving child, a son, lived next door to my mother and me. We are in the same age group. He started school two years before I did. But because I skipped a grade and spent less than eight months in one, and he failed in standard three, we read three, four, five, and six in the same years. We were in different classes until standard five, when we studied in the same classroom under Mr. Iteke. She allowed this only surviving child to do almost whatever he wanted. His soup was lavish when compared with mine. As students, we lived in the dormitory from standard five through six. His mother gave him two shillings a week while my mother gave me nine pence less than he received. While I saved from my one shilling three pence, his two shillings were not enough for him.

By this time, the son was living alone and could not maintain his high taste. As the only child, he was also expected to help his aging mother, who was struggling. Unfortunately, he had run into trouble with the law twice and served terms. Like us, his mother had reached a point where she could not take care of her roof anymore. But unlike us, she left the village and returned to her brother in her village of origin. I was sleeping one afternoon when she came to the house. Ukachi was there. She wanted to see me and told Ukachi to wake me up. He refused. Their argument woke me up. I pretended to be asleep still and did not get up until after she left. I knew she was about to ask me for some financial help, but I did not give it. God provided another opportunity one day at the market. It was raining. She walked into a store where I sought shelter from the rain. She complained about the treatment Ukachi gave her and what a disgrace her son had become when compared with me. I comforted her and paid for a taxi to take her home.

    The departure date to travel to Akanu arrived, and all three boys waited for the lorry to come. However, Ukachi was not one of them. Rightly or wrongly, he still owes me a grudge today. But I could not take care of four teens alone. By midmorning, the lorry was at my doorstep. Once it was loaded, the boys hopped in, and we were on our way to Akanu Item. Within three hours we were at Akanu Item Methodist Central School. The headmaster who came out to greet me Mr. Aruogu was a man I met at Uzuakoli when he was an HEC student, and I was at ETC. He showed me my quarters and the load was discharged. I was his vice headmaster. He taught standard six and I taught standard five.

    There were twelve teachers on the staff. All was well until one morning when I walked to school, and there was a message from the headmaster. He had fallen very sick with asthma and was taken to the hospital. I became the acting headmaster in charge of the school. Besides, since there was no other teacher to teach his class, and that was not a system where substitute teachers were available, I had to teach both standards five and six. I thought it was a sickness that would last for a few days or longest, a week. It lasted for weeks, then months, and a term and more. The university undergraduate students were on vacation. Mr. Ndukwe, a former teacher at the secondary school at Uzuakoli and a student at the University of Ibadan, was hired to teach standard six for part of the term before the holiday. It was not till towards the end of the third term before the headmaster returned to the school and, by the doctor's orders, was not allowed to resume duties that year. Fortunately, almost all the teachers were cooperative.

Before the headmaster fell ill, he admitted Chibuzo as a standard six student. Shortly after school started, the standard six result was out, and Chibuzo was successful. The headmaster told him to withdraw his name. But since the major objective in registering him was to enable him to gain entrance to a secondary school, the headmaster allowed him sit in class for the duration he needed to register and sit for the examinations.

Meanwhile, Nwachi had indicated in one of her letters that her father was against her marrying a non-SDA man. In reply, I suggested that we meet him and discuss the matter face-to-face. She declined the offer and asked for time. I believed that Ed, not her father, was the problem. In reply, I rehearsed the history of the relationship, especially by reference to one shilling and one pound. I was harsh because she was the only woman to visit me and slept with me at home. When she failed to reply, I traveled to her school. They were on break when I got there. She invited her friend, who taught at the school, to be present. In less than fifteen minutes, the discussion and relationship ended. She still denied that Ed was the problem. Notwithstanding, she married Ed.

Before the trip to Nwachi, I had two of the five dreams I had at Akanu Item. On the way from Akanu to Alayi are two steep and slippery hills separated by a narrow valley. These unpaved hills were dangerous when wet. I saw in my dream that after we descended, our lorry could not ascend the other hill. I also noticed that no one was hurt in the attempt to offload both men and loads. Since it had been three or four days before I traveled, I forgot the dream. It did not rain on the day we traveled either. But when we reached the exact spot the lorry stopped in my dream, the lorry stopped and started sliding backward. The driver stopped it before any damage was done. We got off and walked to the top of the hill. The driver then drove the lorry and its cargo to the hilltop, where we joined him again.

My second dream was at home. Of the three boys who lived with me, Chibuzo was the oldest; Sunday, his brother, and Chikezie were the same age. I spent the rest of Friday at home without telling my mother where I had been. That night, I dreamed that the boys fought. There were no broken bones or scars on their bodies, nor did anybody complain when I returned. So, with the result of my disappointing trip, I let the sleeping dog lie. I even doubted if it actually happened. A few months later, after Chibuzo had gained entrance to a secondary school, he left Akanu and returned to his father in Lagos. Chikezie and Sunday quarreled. Sunday reminded him how Chibuzo beat him up. Chikezie acknowledged the beating but added that Chibuzo is older than him, but he beat Sunday up, though they were the same age. I put two and two together and knew what happened. Chikezie was beating Sunday up when Chibuzo came to the aid of his brother. More importantly, my dream was real. Nwachi married Ed and gave me her reason more than a decade later. She said the women from my clan at her College promised never to allow me to marry her.

Item people are famous as traders. There are at least four villages that make up the Item clan. It seemed that Akanu was the least educated. Many Item people live in Aba, the largest city in Abia State. People believe that any item one cannot find at Aba market cannot be found in any other market in Nigeria. Many Item people start life at Aba. Several of the children live at Aba till their teenage years then return to Item to start school. Consequently, Akanu Item Methodist Central School had adults in standards five and six. The people were also notorious for killing one another by poison. Two of the adult pupils were in standard six. One of them was the senior prefect of the school to the envy of the other. Disobeying his orders did not satisfy him. He fought him. That violated not only the prefect but also the authority of the school. I gave him six strokes on his buttocks before the whole student body and staff. In less than two weeks, the prefect was dead. Every person in the village believed that this other man killed him by poison. I wept at his funeral as I spoke. At home, I wondered if I had caused his death and if I should have done something differently. As I pondered over it, I had another dream.

There was an assembly of all the male adults of the village. I did not know who called the meeting. But I was invited, and it was on the school grounds. Present was the pupil and a man they said was his elder brother who came from Aba. The assembly was to decide the guilt or innocence of both the pupil and me. The older brother did not even allow me to speak. He stood up and walked to the center of the assembly, owned up, and condemned his brother for killing the student. The assembly dismissed, and I woke up. I was helpless to do anything. No one came forward to accuse him publicly, and even if they did, that was a case beyond the school. I had no grounds to dismiss him from school. He stayed till the end of the year.

Two incidents endeared me to the school board members. I did not and still do not know how long the board tried to get the school ledger, which showed the records of how much money the village deposited with the office of the supervisor of schools and the balance sheet and failed. Without any special effort on my part, I, the acting headmaster, brought it to the board. The second was a test of character and will.

The village was building a block of four classrooms before I came. Mr. Achara, the School Supervisor, lived far away in Enugu and would not come to Akanu to inspect one block. He delegated me to inspect the block. The contractor visited the school and requested that I approve the unfinished job. When I objected, he went and bought drinks and put money in an envelope, and brought one of the members of the school board to my house. I welcomed them and offered them seats in my living room. Immediately, the member of the board asked for glasses. Knowing their motive, I asked, "What for?" He reminded me of one Igbo saying. "Headmaster, you don't reject the drink, but what comes after the drink." I said, "While that may be so, I don't drink. So, there is no need for a drink." "If you don't drink, two of us can drink," he said. I was irritated and said to him, "Not in my house." Then, he presented the case he knew had failed. He presented the envelope and requested that I approve the building. I rejected the envelope, refused to approve the building and told him, "As a native and member of the board, you can approve the building." He did not, and I earned his respect. I wrote my report to the School Supervisor.

As long as I thought there was a glimmer of hope for reconciliation between Nwachi and me, I maintained my strict, cold relationship with any other female. The two women teachers at the school did not hesitate to brand me "wicked." They visited my neighbor Anozie. During one visit, when things were quiet and I thought they had left, I said to Anozie, "These women come here with their noise and disturb people. The men they will marry may never meet our wives." But they were still there and kept quieter while he concurred. Suddenly, one of them got sick.

She was a member of the sect that does not understand the Bible and mistook James' admonition in chapter five: "Is anyone among you sick? Let him call for the elders of the church, and let them pray over him, anointing him with oil in the name of the Lord," to mean that Christians should not use medication. As a result, she refused to treat a small wound. It became a mighty sore. She lived alone and could not take care of herself. I was the Acting Headmaster in charge of the school. I had to do something.

There was no tap water. She could not even get out of her room let alone go to the stream to fetch water on weekends. I sent one of the boys to fetch water for her and help her with some of her needs. The women decided there was some humanity in me after all. She also applied medication and was healed. Still the distance was not bridged.

Having succeeded in the ordinary level of GCE, I ordered four advanced subjects: Economics, Ancient History, Geography, and

Christian Religion. I also ordered the books from Woolsey Hall, England, before I left Uzuakoli. The year was ending, and I still did not have my textbook. Yet I had registered to take the examination. As poor as I was, I wrote and threatened them. "There are banks in Nigeria. If I wanted to save my money in the bank, I would deposit it here. If I don't receive those books soon, I will hand over the matter to my family solicitor." The books arrived within three weeks. But it was already too late. I was teaching two standards, the Acting Headmaster, tutoring the boys, and had four Advanced University of London GCE subjects to prepare for in a few months. It was an impossible task. I was also referred to in my HEC results. The reference did not pain me as much as my failure to get credit in Arithmetic, my best subject. I was referred in practical rural science, though one of my credits was in written rural science.

One late night, I stumbled upon the Voice of America on my shortwave radio. The male voice was announcing names and addresses of Americans who were interested in pen pals and the countries they wished to have friends. I got the name of a thirty-two-year-old lady teacher in California and wrote to her. We were teachers and had a common interest in photography. At one stage, I requested that she send me the addresses of some universities and colleges. She did, but I kept the addresses and did nothing with them. However, I dreamed one night that I was in the United States. When I woke up, I regretted that it was only a dream. Like my dream of marrying a white woman several years earlier, I dismissed it from my mind.

As a local Methodist preacher, I had to present my credentials to the Reverend Minister in charge of the Circuit when I arrived. My first problem was the distance between Akanu Item and Ovim the residence of the Minister. My second problem was that I was not familiar with the "poisonous" area, especially because the church fed the preacher lunch. But Akanu Item Methodist Church was next door to the school and had no church teacher. I attended church services there and preached on many Sundays. One Saturday, I dreamed, and, like Paul and the man calling him to come over to Macedonia and help us (Acts 16:9), a man came to my house and invited me to preach at the church. The following morning was Sunday, and Mr. Anozie and I were conversing over the wall that separated our bungalow. "I should be getting ready for church. Someone came here last night in my dream and asked me to preach because they had no one to preach for them." He asked, "And you think it will happen?" Before I completed the sentence, "You never can tell," there was a knock at my door. When I opened the door, the man at the door was pleading with me to come and preach. I accepted. Of course, Mr. Anozie heard the request. From that day on, he called me Joseph the dreamer.

I had registered to retake my English test at Umuahia. There was Nwachi on my arrival for the same thing and she could not believe that I was referred in English. That was the first paper of the day, and I thought I did well. She was not married, but still engaged to Ed. We were cordial. But that was the last time we saw until I returned from the United States. Rural Science became optional, and I did not have to retake it.

Three guests visited me at Akanu Item, and Emedom was one of them. He is a talented artist. While at Uzuakoli he entered and won second prize in a national art competition. When he went to claim his certificate and the panel saw the shoes, he drew by looking at them with dots; they regretted it and confessed that if they knew that he drew by looking at the shoes, they would have awarded him the first prize. Consequently, when he left Uzuakoli he applied to the Art Department of Ahmadu University for admission. At the time, Arts was a three-year certificate course. He was admitted. At the same time, the Eastern Government appointed Mr. Omeoga, our principal at HEC, as chairman of the Eastern Scholarship Board. Emedom and others from Uzuakoli applied for scholarships and received them.

Some American art lecturers came to the department to teach. They refused to leave well enough alone. They fought hard and prevailed, changing the three-year certificate course to a four-year degree course. Emedom benefited from the change and became the first of our classmates to be admitted to a university for a degree course. Before the change, he had visited me at Akanu. As Mr. Iteke said of me, "After all, are you not Obed?" I knew that after all Emedom is Emedom and gave him five pounds. He made what I regarded as a foolish remark. Instead of "thank you," he said, "You are putting me in debt." He spent about a week. I thought he did not say that at Uzuakoli when I bailed him out. He was the treasurer of Ohuhu Students Union and could not balance the cash account at the end of his term. I gave him the balance.

My second visitor was Mba Esomonu of Uzuakoli. We called dee Esomonu dee Esonu. My mother told me that dee Esomonu's mother came from one of the big compounds in my village, and he was a good friend of my dad. My dad stored the goods carried to Uzuakoli market but not sold in dee Esonu's home. I knew dee Esonu, although he was dead at that time. The friendship had passed from parents to children, and more importantly, daa Orihe Mba's mother continued to send me gifts. When Mba showed up at my door, there should not be any suspicion. Indeed, it was a pleasant surprise. We enjoyed ourselves for about a week, and he left. Several months later, I learned that there was trouble in his village, which he was trying to avoid. The period he spent with me was sufficient for the storm to blow over. He left when he felt safe to go home without saying a word about it. My third visitor was Chy, Emedom's fiancée. Her visit was ordinary. She knew where Akanu Item was, and though she was an HEC student, I did not give her any money.

Once again, I put myself in a predicament. There were knocks at my door at about 8 pm. I could not remember when anybody had knocked that late before. I decided to get the door myself. When I opened it, it was one of the lady teachers, not the one who was sick. Knowing that there had been trouble at her quarters before and she had never come to my house, let alone that late, I asked, "What's the problem?" She smiled, greeted me, and said, "None." "Are you sure?" She replied, "Yes." With me still blocking the door, I asked, "And you want to come in?" She said, "Yes." I allowed her in. I offered her a seat and a cup of coffee. She declined the coffee. I waited in vain for her to tell me why she came. I thought I knew what she wanted and moved close to her. We walked from the living room to the bedroom. When it was over, I was regretting it. Ojike, who shared the other side of the house with Mr. Anozie before Anozie went on transfer, eavesdropped as the lady answered my questions. He opened his window and, with his light shining, watched to see her go.

The following day found me more miserable than the night. Maxwell and Rachel were at Amaokwe Methodist Central School. Amakwe Item is only a few miles from Akanu Item. I decided to go and share my burden of sin with them. I rode my bicycle to their house after school. As I told them what happened, tears flowed. Baffled by my behavior, his wife said, "Obed, pull yourself together. Everybody does it all the time. It happens at this school." I said, "I am in charge of the people there." I am glad she did not say, "You should have thought about that before you did it." I don't know if my "confession" helped me, but it did not happen again. If the lady teachers thought that I was a eunuch, she found out the truth.

The Headmasters at Item schools travel to Ovim, a distance of about fifteen miles on accounts days, to collect teachers' salaries. In return, the headmaster invited the teachers to his home and paid them. I did this for the time I acted as the headmaster, and my instruction was the same: "Please count your money here before you leave my house to make sure you received the correct amount." One day, I went to Ovim for account and, on my return, invited the teachers to receive their pay.

Before I paid them, I repeated my instructions. Ojike was one of the early teachers to be paid. He went to his room without verifying the amount he received. While I was still paying others, he returned and complained that he was short by five pounds. I asked him to sit down until I was through with everyone else. If I had five pounds left, then I would give it to him. He was angry and accused me. I ignored him until I was through with the others, and there was the five pounds. I gave it to him. He accused me of dishonesty in cheating his people. He claimed that I educated Chibuzo at the school without paying his school fees. Though it was getting dark, I took my lamp and went round the village. I invited members of the school board through the few members whose houses I knew. Within a short time, they came.

I told them why I invited them. One of them called him. He accused me of three offenses. I distrusted him and kept him until everybody was paid. I educated my cousin at their school without paying his school fees. The third was my song, which annoyed him. They asked him if he heard the instruction. He said he did. They asked him to justify his demand for special treatment. He had none. At this time, the headmaster who handled Chibuzo's case was convalescing at the school premises. I told them what happened. I paid the fees before the standard six results were out. Because Chibuzo was successful, the headmaster refunded the fee. He was not admitted, and he is not a student here. I requested them to send someone to his house. They refused and said they believed me. Chibuzo was not even at the school. He left the school once his successful result of admission to Christ the King College (CKC) was out and returned to his father in Lagos. What about my song?

Ojike did not own a radio, but I did. There was a lyric played by the Nigerian Radio very often. I liked the song but substituted my own words for theirs. My words said, "Uto (Uto is Emedom's middle name), our mates are wearing hoods; it remains us." That was offensive to him. But he gave no reason. The people warned him. "Yes, you are our son. This man has done more for us than anyone before him. The member who most vigorously defended me was the one who came with the contractor. "We have tried him, and he shines like gold." But I knew what his real problem was. It was the lady teacher who came to my house at night. He wanted her. He knew that both in looks and education he lost. So, he would not say what his real problem was.

I went home one weekend, and my mother was moody. When I inquired as to the cause, she started to weep. Then she said my favorite aunt was in prison. Young, my aunt's nephew by marriage, was beating Nwatiti, my aunt's daughter, and my aunt went to rescue her daughter. Young got hot in the process. He called the police, who arrested my aunt. The magistrate sentenced her to three months, and she was serving the term at Okigwe. I asked what my aunt's husband did about the whole matter. Her answer was nothing. All I could do was to comfort her. I returned to Akanu Item and was unable to do anything. My only option was to wait and do what I could do for her in three months. At the end of three months, I traveled home. Knowing that prisoners wear government uniforms, I bought her clothes and wrappers for a change of clothing. God's judgment surprised me when I reached home. The very day my aunt was released from prison, Young, the man who sent my aunt to prison, was himself sentenced to the same prison at Okigwe to start a three-month sentence for a crime he committed. Even unbelievers acknowledged God's hand in the events. My aunt was grateful to receive her clothes. I was happy to see her and grateful that God is God.

The Gold Coast had won independence from Britain, and Nigeria was on the threshold of winning her independence. Britain set two conditions that had to be fulfilled before independence was granted, namely, a plebiscite and an election. The result of the plebiscite was a mixed bag. Germany lost its territories in Africa after the First World War, and Cameroun was one of the territories. Britain received Western Cameroun, which was amalgamated into Northern

Nigeria i.e., Bornu State today and Southern Cameroun. The North voted to remain as part of Nigeria, while the South voted to rejoin the Eastern part administered by France. As a result, the strongest national political party in pre-independent Nigeria, the National Council of Nigeria and the Cameroun's was renamed the National Council of Nigerian Citizens to maintain the initials NCNC. There were three main political parties in Nigeria at the time: the NCNC, the Northern People's Congress (NPC) based in the North, and the Action Group (AG) with a strong base in the West. The result of the elections would determine which party controlled the central government at independence. Except for the NCNC, the other two parties, the NPC and the Action Group, contested the federal seats mainly in their respective area.

Since I was the Acting Headmaster of my school, I also became the returning officer at the polling station at my school. I supervised the polling station on the voting day. It was late afternoon when Chuks of Aba, the NCNC contestant for the constituency, walked in and introduced himself. There was no doubt in anyone's mind that he was winning the race. He smiled and made a request. The only opponent was an unknown member of the Action Group party who was losing badly. Mr. Chuks asked me to empty the man's box into his to make sure that the man lost his deposit. "That is against the law," I said. He said to me, "We make the laws." I replied, "And we obey them." He had nothing else to say and left. He and the NCNC won the elections in the East.

Dr. Azikiwe, the national President of the NCNC party, and Chief Awolowo, the national leader of the Action Group, won the elections in their respective constituencies and went to the Federal Parliament. Dr. M. I. Okpara became the Premier of the Eastern Region Government and the national leader of the NCNC, both positions formerly held by Dr. Azikiwe before the elections. Chief Awolowo held on to his position as the national leader of the AG but made Chief

Akintola the Premier of the Western Region. The national leader of the NPC was content to stay in the North and allow his lieutenant to run the Center. That was Nigeria after the elections when Britain granted her independence on October 1, 1960. The end of my holiday brought changes.

By this time, there were two High Elementary teachers in my compound, Josiah and me. Josiah taught in the North, where our uncle Onwumere also lived. Udobi, our uncle's first son, knew and feared Josiah. Our uncle had been a teacher before becoming a railway employee. Udobi was getting to the age when he would start taking entrance examinations to secondary schools. My uncle asked him to choose who to live with, my cousin Josiah or me. He chose to live with me. Though Chibuzo left, I still had three cousins to live with. At school, a new Headmaster was sent, and a woman teacher who completed her HEC course and waiting for her result was also sent to the school. The lady teacher came from Amachara my mother's birth village. According to custom, that made her my distant cousin. Customarily, that seemed to rule her out as a wife or even a girlfriend.

I rode my bicycle to Amaokwe again to see Max and his wife. I knew they had more friends and knew more people than I did. I asked them to recommend a potential fiancé and even mentioned a name. Rachel, Max's wife, looked at me and asked, "Obed, what is the matter with you? There is one there at your school looking and waiting for you to open your mouth and ask her. You want her to come and beg you?" "She is from my mother's village," I said. "I can't marry her." She demanded to know if she came from the same compound as my mother. I did not think so. When she knew that the answer was no, she encouraged me to ask her, "She is waiting for you to ask." I hesitated, and abruptly, circumstances changed and compelled me to ask. I received a letter of transfer.

Chapter 21

From Akanu Item to Alayi

By any standard, Alayi Methodist Central School is situated in a better location than Akanu Item. Akanu seemed to be the end of the road or even civilization at the time. The transport we saw at Akanu was the lorry, which brought some of the Akanu people who lived at Aba home every Saturday evening and left early Monday morning. On the other hand, Alayi is separated from a major road by the school fence. It is also about fifteen miles closer to my home than Akanu. My letter of transfer specified the date and time of day the lorry would arrive.

The headmaster and I had established a good relationship within the short time we were together. He expressed his appreciation and wished me well. Before I even asked Miss Mwagwu to be my "intended," I had told the Headmaster that she was my cousin. "Please take good care of her." Then I went to say goodbye to her. By then, she knew that my mother was from her village. I said, "I would like you to be my intended." She looked at me and said, "I am not ready to get married." I told her that I was not ready either. It is for the future. She agreed. She reluctantly kissed me goodbye. The lorry was ready, and we drove off. I learned later that I was the first man she kissed.

On arrival at Alayi, I discovered that I almost had no place to lay my head. One end of a duplex with two bedrooms and a living room that should have been my living quarters was occupied by two junior teachers. To make room for me, the Headmaster moved the two to one bedroom and left one bedroom and the living room for me and my three cousins. The two junior teachers and the Headmaster were from the Item clan. My three cousins slept in the living room. I did not see any need to make any fuss since I was not married.

My grade five pupils had been without a teacher for three weeks and were delighted they had a teacher. Unfortunately, they had to wait until my cousins were admitted. The two in standard four had no problem. But the headmaster refused to admit Sunday in standard five. He told me that standard five was full and that I should take my case to the school supervisor at Enugu. If he thought that I would not take him up on his challenge, he was mistaken. I traveled to Ovim and from there to Enugu by the early train that reached Enugu by noon.

I went straight from the railway station to the Supervisor's office. He was still in his office. He recognized my face from my previous visit when Mr. Ibegbulem's son died in Enugu. I told him why I was in his office. He was angry. "That's why he sent you here from Alayi?" He did not have time to dictate the letter to his clerk. He wrote it himself. Among other things, he asked him, "You could not promote one pupil to standard six? If you were him, would you teach?" He gave me the letter in an open envelope. I thanked him and hurried to the railway station and bought my return ticket. But instead of stopping at Ovim, I went to Umuahia. For one good reason: this late train reached Ovim at night, and I was neither familiar with nor comfortable going from Ovim to Alayi in the dark. Though the train reached Umuahia later at night, Umuahia was my home. I bought a ticket to Umuahia and slept there. I returned to Alayi the following day. To save the Headmaster embarrassment, I closed the envelope. But his face revealed the content of the letter. All he muttered was all right. He admitted my cousin Sunday, and I taught my class.

It was the season and almost late when teachers' results were released, and I heard they were out. Miss Nwagwu was referred in

English. She had not heard about the results. Besides, Friday of that week was the last day for referred candidates to register for the next examination. It was a Wednesday, and the only way I could get any meaningful message to her was to go to Akanu myself. The school was over at 1:30 pm. I rode my bicycle to Akanu, first to the Headmaster, and told him my mission and obtained permission to take her with me. Then, I went and informed her. There were tears in her eyes. I conveyed her on my bicycle to Alayi.

On arrival at Alayi, my cousins prepared food and served us. She continued to weep and refused to eat. I could not eat with her sobbing in front of me. I could not tell why she felt so bad. There could be one or two things. When I told Nwanyi Sunday Onwubiko my classmate at Mission Hill who came from the same village as Okom, that I intended to marry Okom, her response was, "Two brains." She was known for being the smart one. The second was that her brother-in-law contributed much to financing her education. She felt that she let people down. We did not eat or sleep throughout the night. I spent the night trying to comfort her.

Dawn was late coming. When it arrived, she got ready to travel to Umuahia for registration. I got ready for school. I gave her three pounds, one pound ten shillings for registration and the other half for a taxi if she had to use one. We walked to the road. Within a short time, a VW Kombi bus arrived, I paid for her trip, and she was on her way to Umuahia. I returned to the house and ate my breakfast. It was time for school. I walked into my class, and it seemed that my pupils were in mourning. Throughout the day, my class was as lifeless as the grave. Even the answers to my questions were dull. There was not a smile or noise. I wondered what was wrong with them but said nothing. Immediately after the 1:30 pm dismissal bell rang, I left the classroom and returned to my house. Soon, she was home, this time hungry and with a smile on her face. We ate.

It was a Thursday, and I was not prepared to ride the distance to Akanu and back. She spent the night at Alayi. I walked into my classroom on Friday morning and smiled. The whole class erupted into laughter and clapping of hands. When I asked what the matter was, they, in unison, said, "You are happy again." It occurred to me that I was the reason my class seemed dead the previous day. I walked back to the house. "Did you hear that noise?" When she said yes, I explained the reason. "You and your students," she said. I returned to my class. I rejoiced at the end of the school year because though the final year examination was comprehensive and external, all my students were successful. No other class achieved that at the school.

School closed on Friday morning, and the junior teachers who shared the two-bedroom bungalow left immediately. I had my belongings in the house. Therefore, I locked it. When I returned from the holidays with my cousins, the junior teachers had forced the door open. We went in without saying a word about the door. I told my cousins not to unpack. While we were on holiday, two other high elementary teachers who were my seniors had been transferred. I had become the vice Principal, and two women who completed the HEC recently were sent to the school. The two houses those two high elementary teachers left were vacant and locked. I decided to go and greet the headmaster and also make my presence known. After I greeted him and he did not say anything about those two houses, I made two decisions. I would not share one more night in those two rooms with those two teachers. Since it was lawful to force doors open at Alayi, I was going to do the same thing to one of the houses under the assumption that if he had the keys, he would have given them to me when I visited him. That was exactly what I did.

He was incensed and reminded me that he was a Headmaster at Umuokpara when I was a pupil at Mission Hill. Then he ordered me to move back to the quarter I left. Recognizing that his words were without effect, he reported to the headquarters. Two other

Headmasters came and investigated. They agreed that the two junior teachers should not have shared the quarter with me. I did the right thing when I returned and visited the Headmaster. I was wrong in breaking into the house. I should move out of it. I told them that I would go on transfer before I did that. They told me that if I went on transfer, I would pay for my transportation. I accepted. They also told me to find a school for myself. I went to two schools in Ovim Circuit, but none of them needed a high elementary teacher. I met Reverend Mba, and he was delighted to have a local preacher. He sent me to Umukabia Methodist Central School. I returned to Alayi and packed my belongings.

So far in my teaching career, I was made to spend only one year or less at a school. I walked to the road and waited for any empty lorry traveling to Umuahia. I did not wait long before an empty lorry drove up. We bargained and reached a price. The driver drove to the school premises, loaded our belongings, and off we went. A few hours later, the lorry was at Umukabia Methodist Central School. I knew most of the teachers, and even some of those I did not know knew my name. There was a shortage of quarters, but I did not have to share what I had with two other teachers. In addition, I was only about seven miles away from my mother. We settled in, and I rode my bicycle home to inform my mother about my new station. She was delighted. I returned and asked Reverend Uzu to include me in his preachers' schedule. He hesitated, and I went to his boss, the Reverend Mba. He was irritated. "Uzu doesn't know you?" He gave him a mild rebuke, and I was scheduled.

Okomonu (Miss Nwagwu) and I agreed that we would be husband and wife when the time came. Getting the consent of relatives became an impossible task. My intuition that I could not marry from my mother's village was an obstacle for my mother. Concerned that she would raise that objection, I first inquired from daa Ojure, a relative who came from the same village as my mother and married in my village. She encouraged me to go ahead. My mother held a different view but was not dogmatic. My mother later explained that she was not really concerned about me. However, it was believed that both my brother and I reincarnated from her village. My brother, who was believed to be her father, was the one who had problems with his relatives, not me. In other words, her mute opposition was because of my brother. The economy of Okom's education generated fierce opposition from her sisters and brother-in-law.

Her oldest sister, George, was married to the man who helped finance her education. Their oldest son, Lucky, was already living with Okomonu. She had a younger sister who lived in Lagos with her husband and son. This sister said that Okom's education prevented her from being educated. They decided that the burden of educating everybody else in that family, from siblings and half-siblings to grandchildren, rested on her. To mention marriage was a death nail to their hopes. So, the sister in Lagos, out of envy determined to sabotage the idea of Okom's marriage and nip it in the bud.

I spent a few days of my holiday in Lagos. Chikara, one of my cousins, lived with my brother in Lagos at the time. He took me to see this woman. She was not at home, and we left a message. A part of the message was that a potential future brother-in-law came to see her. On hearing the message, she raged and vowed to prevent it. "Who does she think will educate the children in that family? She prevented me from getting my education, and now she wants to rush into marriage." Within a short time, she was at Umuahia.

Chapter 22

Transfer to Umukabia

Today, Salvation Came To This House

(Luke 19:9)

(To understand and appreciate the rest of this book, first read Exodus 33.)

As usual, I enjoyed my students. My sorrowful day at Alayi and its effect on my students taught me an important lesson. "Keep your problem to yourself. Do not take it to the classroom." I started a little poultry farm at Umukabia. The pure English or imported chicken was susceptible to native diseases. But when they are mated with small, native chickens, the breed becomes big and resistant to diseases. I had the new breed. They were big and beautiful. Suddenly, they started to disappear whenever they went to the backyard. I learned of a neighbor who was the culprit. I also learned that his young son attended my school. I identified his son and sent a warning through the son to the father. "Tell your father to leave my chickens alone. If my chickens go out and fail to return, when you come to school, you will not return." Less than fifteen minutes later, the father was on the school premises complaining about my threat to his son. Other teachers tried to calm his fears. "You know Mr. Onwuegbu is from Amafo, and that is how they talk." I said, "This is not what you people call Amafo talk. If my chickens fail to return, your son will not come home from this school." I did not lose any more chickens from that day.

Like his brother Chibuzo, Sunday did not gain entrance to any secondary school while he was in standard six. He was good in arithmetic, but his English was not good enough to take him over the bar. His father misplaced his anger on me. I don't know what gave him the idea that I was proud. He did not even ask me what caused his son's failure. He told people, "He is only a grade two teacher and boasting. What about those who will attend university?" In other words, his children are university-bound, but Obed is to die a grade two teacher. It seemed he was right because I took the four advanced papers again and received the ordinary-level certificate. However, all my students passed again.

There was a knock at the door one Saturday morning. When I opened it, there stood Okomonu with a cold face. Surprised that she walked the distance from her school to mine that early and with a serious look on her face, I asked what the matter was. She answered, "When we get to my house." She refused to eat breakfast. I got ready and gave her a ride on my bicycle. Shortly after we arrived at her house, she told me her story. Her sister came home from Lagos and told her what she claimed I said in Lagos. Among other things, her sister told her that I was preparing to go overseas and study. After which, I would return and marry an illiterate because she is over-educated for me. That a person I thought was smart would believe such a tale surprised me. "You believe her!" "Well, she is my sister, though some of the things she said do not make sense to me," I asked if she told her friend who shared the living room with her. She said that you would not say such a thing. "Someone who has seen me for only a few months does not believe that I could say such a thing. But you believe I said it?" "She is my sister. Why would she make up such a story?" She demanded that the whole thing be called off. There was a Bible on her table. Knowing that the Bible said that we should not swear, I asked God to forgive me for placing my hand on it and said, "If I said what she said that I said, my world would go backward. If I did not, and she lied against me, God would punish her." I left. I wrote to Chikara in Lagos to investigate. Her husband revealed the facts of the matter. By the time I received the reply, the sister's healthy son was dead. I gave Okomonu the letter to read. A few weeks later, she came to see me. She informed me of the compliment Miss Ada O., the lady teacher who visited me at night at Akanu Item, paid me. She had told her, even without the knowledge of our relationship, that I was the only one among the male teachers who respected the lady teachers. The rest of them behaved as though the ladies were there to be used at their pleasure. When I asked if she told her what she did with me, she said, "No, what?" I deferred the answer.

Meanwhile, I was getting restless about entering a university. Some days, Psalm 6:6 was my companion. My neighbor and a classmate who was not as smart as I seemed to have qualified. I overheard him discussing me with another classmate, the Vice Captain, to whom I served raw food to at Nto-Ndang. Nwaogu said, "We know he is smart." My neighbor replied, "He doesn't study." But I did not have the heart to practice his method. He wrote what he would teach in the year within the first few weeks on the blackboard for the students to copy. The pupils studied the notes while he studied his lessons from Woolsey Hall. I lay on my bed and shed tears.

Emedom was at Dartmouth, New Hampshire, USA, attending a students' conference. He wrote me a heartbreaking letter. Chy, his girlfriend, had not written to him, and he was failing his courses. "Have you ever known me to score forty percent on a test? In the name of friendship, please go and find out what is happening." After I read the letter, I hopped on my motorcycle and rode to her school. I assumed that she had not written and demanded to know what her problem was. She swore that she had written to him and promised to write again. My reply included a request for the addresses of some colleges and universities. I chose five from his list and the list my pen pal sent to me. This was May.

My two cousins were no longer living with me. Udobi had gained admission at Government College Umuahia, and Chikezie left shorthand, and typing, I sent him to learn and went to live with my brother in Lagos. He found him a job. I was living alone, a reminder of my first year as a teacher. The difference now was that I had a kerosene stove, an iron, and student helpers.

One afternoon, while some of my students were still preparing food for me, Max and his wife came to see me. That changed the plan about what to cook. Less than 15 minutes after they arrived, my brother, who was supposed to be in Lagos, walked in unexpectedly and unannounced. Soon, the food was on the table. I said to Max, "You say the grace. My prayer does not pass the roof these days." He prayed, and we ate. We simply enjoyed ourselves. I did not even talk about my brother's unannounced vacation. They all left about the same time.

By the middle of June, I had received replies to four of my applications. They were all negative with one piece of advice, "since you are asking for financial help, apply before the end of December." Lyndon State College was the last to reply. It asked for three letters of recommendation and a biographical sketch. When I went to Uzuakoli, HEC, the Englishman, Mr. Clutterbock, who had become the Principal, said to me, "Why are you going to the U.S.? You received all you need from here." I looked at him and wondered why I was not sitting in his seat as the Principal of the College. "Really," I said. He said yes and wrote the letter. I read it tore it, and threw the pieces away. This was the teacher who gave me nine out of ten for my essay. Mr. Iteke, Mr. Ibegbulem, and Mr. Okeke, my Headmaster, wrote the letters. I wrote my biographical sketch and posted it. What I called a miracle happened when I went to get my letter typed. The sky was dark when I started my journey to the township. As I rode my motorcycle, the rain was following behind me, but it could not catch up with me. Once I reached my destination, it poured hard. By then, I was in the typist's office, and my motorcycle was under the shed. The rain stopped when I was ready to go. I went home dry.

I visited Okomonu one time. She told me that she was Ogbanje. The only way I can describe it is that it is a disease of unbelievers. Curing it entails sacrificing to Satan. I told her that I did not believe in it and would not participate. Irrational behaviors are attributed to this sickness. She was not pleased. She invited me one day to meet her sister and brother-in-law, who were home from Aba. I accepted.

The oldest sister and her husband were in their living room when we arrived. She introduced me. The brother-in-law was offended and complained that I was about to take a picture with his sister-in-law before I obtained permission to marry her. "What! An ordinary picture makes you angry? I wrote your wife and asked for her permission to intend her sister." The wife said, "You want to drive me out of my marriage." I realized that talking about marriage with this woman threatened the whole clan. I gave them my piece. "Here is your sister-in-law. You educated her so that you would marry her and her sister. Go ahead and marry her and her sister. Any day I come to you and complain to you that since you did not allow me to marry your sister-in-law, I could not find a wife, do whatever you want to me. Marriage is not my immediate need. It is education. I have been with her for about three years now. Ask her if I have known her as a man knows a woman?" I got up and was on my way out and heard what sounded like a compromise. "If you two want to get married, you behave yourselves." By that time, I was outside the house without saying goodbye to anyone.

Outside was Nwaola, the daughter of daa Ugoji, my mother's relative. A cousin I did not know was married there. It was her parents who provided us with the first shelter when we escaped from my father's falling house. She called my name. Obida, idikwa nma, (how are you). She was married to a Jehovah's Witness man in that family. My reply, "manma," was a reply to an older person, and it surprised them. I later learned my greeting made them think I was a boy. Whatever she told them might have contributed to their change of mind. A few days later, Okom was in my house again.

Sometime in early July, I received a letter from Lyndon State College. The College offered me admission but would not consider me for either a free tuition scholarship or permission to work because I was not from Vermont nor a U.S. citizen. I received the news with mixed feelings. Therefore, refusing to accept the reason for rejecting my request for financial aid, I thanked them for my admission. Also, I told them the story of the Greek woman and Jesus. A Greek woman had a sick daughter. She went to Jesus and pleaded with Him to heal her daughter. Though Jesus ignored her, she continued to beg. Jesus turned to her and told her that food meant for children should not be used to feed dogs. She acknowledged her gentile citizenship and added that while the children eat, the dogs pick up the crumbs that fall from the table. Jesus told her to go home because her faith had healed her daughter. When she reached home, her daughter was healed (Matthew 15:21-28). I posted the letter. Not knowing what the reply would be, I wrote to my brother to lend me two hundred pounds and Uncle Onwumere to lend me one hundred pounds.

As I waited for the replies to my letters to Lyndon, my uncle, and my brother, I decided to go and see Okomonu. It was evening and a threat of rainfall. Thinking that the rainfall would delay, I rode off on my motorcycle. I was on no man's land between Uzuakoli and Ovim when the sky let loose. It felt like someone was pouring water down with a bucket from heaven. My engine got soaked and stopped running, and it was dark. There was no village or house to take shelter. I prayed. "God, if You don't want me to marry this woman, save me, and I will not. Please save me in Christ's name. Amen." The rain stopped, and a VW Kombi bus going towards Item appeared. They took both me and my motorcycle to Alayi. On the bus was also the headmaster of Okoko Item Methodist Central School. The bus drove towards Abiriba, and the Headmaster became my companion on my motorcycle. My first attempt to start the motorcycle met with failure. As Providence designed it, Alayi is on a hill. There is a long descent toward Item. I put the gear on neutral and allowed the cycle to roll down. Halfway, I turned the engine on, and it started.

When I stopped at the headmaster's house to drop him off, a voice said, "Obed, what are you doing with my sister?" "Achighaku have you asked your sister what she is doing with me?" I asked. She was one of those four lady teachers at Umunwanwa the year I started teaching. She was married to the headmaster I gave a ride to. About twenty minutes later, I was at Okomonu's house. A little after noon the following day, I decided to leave. She gave me the bag of gifts I brought to her. "Are you rejecting my gifts to you?" She said, "Yes." I bade her goodbye. It seemed God approved and accepted the promise I made before He stopped the rain. The following day, I gathered all her pictures and sent them to her by registered mail. By the weekend, she was at my house to learn the meaning. "The relationship is over. I have had enough. When you rejected my gifts, you rejected me also. Goodbye." She said that if she knew my reason, she would not have come. "Now you know." When she left, I thought that was the end. But it wasn't.

Though she did not tell me why she rejected my gifts, I knew her reason. In the past, when I lived at Akanu and Alayi, two places that were far from Umuahia's big market, I bought peak milk by the carton. I gave her 24 of the 96 tins. At this time, I lived alone and near the market and had no need to buy milk by the carton. I only gave her six tins and two loaves of bread. She did not only expect the 24 tins and the other goodies that accompanied them in the past, but she was also blind to the fact that I was in the process of trying to save for my education. About two weeks later, there was a knock on my door. When I opened it, it was her. I told her that I had a visitor from home, and she could not stay. She turned and left. She never gave me anything all the years we went together, not even a handkerchief.

I went home one Sunday. Morning service was over. I had my little camera. Everybody was leaving the church building when I saw my mother on the steps and decided to take a picture of her. She did not powder her face, and I told her to hold on. She waited on the steps. I ran to Mr. Ironmuanya's house, the church teacher, and filled my palm with powder. I ran out, and as I rubbed the powder on her face, some women shouted, "Obed, leave another man's wife alone and go and marry your own." My mother laughed and said, "You are all jealous. Leave him alone." If she were Jesus, she would have added, "he is doing it for my burial." I used this picture to announce her funeral decades later.

I sat in my living room on the evening of July 31, tired. For a reason I cannot tell, I got up, locked my doors and windows, and walked to the bedroom my cousins slept in when they lived with me. I sat on their bed, felt drowsy, and lay down. Soon, I was dreaming. A man walked into the room and asked me, "Did you say you want to see Jesus Christ?" I said, "Yes." That turned out to be the most important *yes* of my life. I realized today that when I said *yes* to the question, I said yes to every plan God has for my life. He went out of the room. The next moment, Jesus Christ walked in, and I got up. Jesus Christ walked to me and hugged me. Like Jesus Christ in the home of Zacchaeus to tell him that salvation came to his home (Luke 19:6), I woke up, and it was only a dream. I sighed and walked over to my bedroom, regretting that it was only a dream. This dream changed me and my world. I slept till morning on August 1st. Although it was a mere dream, I announced my dream with enthusiasm. Fellow teachers were quick to ridicule me. "What did He look like?" "You and your Bible" were two of the many indelible comments. By 1.30 pm that first day of August, the mail came. I received one letter, and it was from Lyndon State College. When I opened it, the College had reversed its decision.

It gave me free tuition, a scholarship, and permission to work ten hours a week. I read it over again and shouted out the content of my letter to every ear around. Those who teased me in the morning were amazed in the afternoon. Mr. Okeke, the headmaster, said, "O. I., Paul is no longer the last apostle to see Jesus Christ. You are."

Before my dream and the good news from Lyndon, dee Onwumere had replied to my request. He said he did not have the money because senior service was not what people thought it to be and urged me to let him know my plan. Since I had no other plan than what I told him, I did not write again. It was the second term, and it did not end till the second Friday in August. I had to complete the term, and I did. I had written to Emedom about my admission at Lyndon and the refusal to consider me for financial aid. Then, after my dream and the reversal and I informed him, he wrote, "If you did not see Jesus Christ, I would have said that you saw Chileke," i.e., God the Father Himself.

Nigeria was getting ready for its first general elections since independence. A number of us in the area had been chosen to be trained as officers at the poles. My cousin Josiah wrote a letter to me. He sounded desperate and helpless. Above all, he pleaded for me to forgive and forget whatever wrong had been done to me in the past and come to Jos as a witness in a case against the woman he was betrothed to. The wrong he referred to was his father's misuse of my father's wealth, which, at that time, meant nothing to me. This was the woman who introduced Nwachi to me and told me that Nwachi was to me what she was to my cousin. In her case, my cousin had done all the customary deeds required to consummate a marriage. She completed her HEC education and went back to the north, but not to the same school my cousin was. She wrote to him and accused him of "allowing the love that existed once to dwindle to nothingness." Though I was in the middle of the training, I abandoned all and traveled to Jos.

New revelations awaited my arrival at Jos. The woman had a baby out of marriage. Besides, she was also expecting another baby, still unmarried and by another man without any prospect of marriage. She still insisted that it was my cousin's fault. When we got to court, I recognized her lawyer as one based in Umuahia and one who traveled by the same train as me. She could not hide or deny her pregnancy. My cousin's lawyer took advantage of that. Her lawyer tried to take advantage of the English magistrate who judged the case.

Igbo custom requires certain gifts for the bride. Many of those are by cash. For instance, rice and clothes. So, when I said in court that she asked for and received five pounds of rice, her lawyer countered, "You mean, for all intents and purposes, she received and ate five pounds worth of rice alone?" I asked him what he meant by all intents and purposes. He said, "You are a teacher, right?" I asked him, "Does my being a teacher mean that I know the meaning of every English phrase and idiom?" The English magistrate stopped writing and looked at me with admiration before he continued. They finished with me that day. The following day I left Jos and stopped at Bukuru, where I spent a day with Dick Agbara. When I got back, I had lost my job at the polling booth. My cousin won the case, and the woman refunded what she received.

Shortly after I left HEC, I went to Uzuakoli College. I saw Mr. Achinivu, who was the Principal of the entire College. Speaking of his position as the Principal and the salary, he said, "I shall soon be making a thousand," i.e., a thousand pounds a year. Unfortunately, he died within a few months of a heart problem. Within a short time, Reverend Mba also died suddenly. Between the deaths of Mr. Achinivu and Reverend Mba was the death of Mr. Nwagwu, Okomonu's dad. I had not been welcomed by the family and had no ground to be present at the burial. I gave Okomonu money to help. About a month after the burial of Reverend Mba, I was on my way to the United States.

Part Four
America And Dreams Fulfilled

Chapter 23

Going to America

I was the first person from my village to go to the United States, though six others, including Uncle Onwumere, had been to Britain. I knew I needed a passport and a visa. But I did not know what the process was. There was no passport office at Umuahia. I wrote to my brother in Lagos and requested him to work on it. A few English women (white)married to Nigerians had given Nigerians the anti-British relationship and monopoly of husband to the exclusion of other relations attitude. In the Igbo culture, what belongs to one belongs to all. The unsolicited advice to me was, "Do not marry any of those white women."

I had forgotten my dream in which I married a white woman. I did not know that God had ordained my marriage. I rode my motorcycle to Aba to see Ngozi Nwogu. There was a man in her house when I got there. I took her aside and asked her hand without telling her anything about my impending departure to the U.S. I knew that if I told her, she would want to pay her own bride price. She hesitated and said, "No." Not knowing what the man was there for, I asked her, "Is this your final answer, or do you want me to come back tomorrow?"

She said, "You can come." On my way back to Umuahia, about three miles to a gas station, my motorcycle ran dry. God seemed to say, "Do you not understand that I have a wife for you?"

Still, I was on my way to Aba the following day. Can you believe who I saw? It was the woman to whom I lost my virginity. She was a teacher at the same school; she teased me. I told her why I was there and about my impending journey to the U.S. Her husband was also planning to study in the U.S.. But he never made it. Then I saw Ngozi. My presence the previous evening was an incentive for the man to commit himself. At that time in Nigeria, anybody but a teacher was referred to as a husband. When she saw me, she was bold and firm in her no. When I told her that I had lost my hat and my dry gas tank, she said, "You deserved that." I almost said I'll see you when I return from the U.S. Instead, I said, "You do not deserve me," and drove off.

I went to the Queen Elizabeth II Hospital for a medical examination for my passport and visa. The hospital was built by three protestant denominations to the envy of the Roman Catholic Church in Nigeria, and it was a first-class hospital. It also trained nurses. I had given the hospital a little money the previous year. The man who received it asked if I wanted it to be announced. I said no. All the medical doctors at the hospital were white. The woman doctor who examined me was surprised that I was not previously registered with the hospital. She requested the laboratory to take my blood and x-ray of my chest. Soon, the x-ray results came back, and she was not quite pleased with the result, so she sold a few tablets to me. A few minutes later, the bloodwork was in. She observed malaria infection sold me more tablets, and ordered me to take the tablets and report back in a week. I have a problem swallowing pills even now. I took the pills for the chest. Since I was not running any fever, which is a sign of malaria, I took only a few of the malaria pills. On my return, she was pleased with the x-ray but not with my malaria. She sent me to a male doctor for my physical and rescheduled me. I did not have the time to go back.

I had to sell my motorcycle, which I had not used for one year. My cousin, the son of my father's sister, brought his friend to my house, paid me fifty-five pounds, and took it with them. When I deposited it into my bank account, I had over three hundred pounds in my account. I planned to retain my account number with the Bank of West Africa at the Umuahia branch. Therefore, I left more than three pounds in the account and sent three hundred pounds to my brother in Lagos through Mr. Ezekwem Nwachukwu from our village, who worked for the bank in Lagos and lived in the same apartment building as my brother. I arranged with Emeruwa, my cousin, to come and carry my belongings and me home on the evening of the last Friday of school. I also planned my sendoff for the following Sunday.

Friday arrived, and students came and went. That was my last day at Umukabia Methodist Central School. I packed and waited and waited. A few hours seemed like a few weeks. It was getting dark when, finally, the lorry drove in, and my mother accompanied my cousin and his driver. As we loaded the lorry, I looked, and there was Okomonu again at the door. She must have been surprised that I was leaving and pleased that we had not left before she arrived. We were all traveling through Umuahia township. I asked her to get on the lorry. I also asked my cousin to stop the lorry at the township in order to find a taxi for her. The mission was accomplished at the township. She went to Amachara, her home, and we drove home.

The following day was Saturday. I went to the market to buy the food items for my sendoff. At the market was Isaiah from my village, who owned a shed where he repaired bicycles. I had introduced Okomonu to him. I also left my bicycle in his shed whenever I rode it to the market. There was a message from Okomonu waiting for me at Isaiah's shed when I got there. She had traveled to Aba and asked me to meet her at her sister's home. She must have mistaken my unwillingness to treat her harshly because of my love for my mother and because she had no brother, and I intended to be that brother as weakness. I ignored the message. Ngozi's sister saw me at the market and complained, "Obed, you are going to America, but did you not tell anybody?" To which I replied, "I went to Aba two times to tell Ngozi. She did not want to hear it." Sunday was my sendoff party. It was a modest party.

Mr. Ibegbulem chaired the party. Mr. Oji Igbokwe, who was of the same age as my father, expressed the sentiment of those who did not come. "Obed is our number one son. But he did not invite anyone to his sendoff." Immediately after the party, Mr. and Mrs. Ibegbulem, Johnny, their son, their driver, and I drove to the township and took a group photograph. When I got home, Nnenna, my cousin, was still waiting for me. I changed clothes. My mother, with a few tears in her eyes, and two other persons, saw me off with Nnenna carrying my suitcase. We were close to Mission Hill when they returned to the village. I collected the pictures and spent the night with Nnenna's family in the town. Having given my mother some money, I instructed her to ask Isaiah to sell my bicycle and give her the money. Christopher was to sell my Philips radio and give her the money. I left Umuahia the following morning by lorry vide Onitsha, a journey that took two days then. I was on my first step towards America.

Tuesday morning, we were at Idoh Motor Park in Lagos mainland, as it was called in those days. I went to see Ben, who works for Mainland Hotel. He called my brother and told him that I was with him. Since I knew where my brother lived, I carried my suitcase and surprised his wife, who was not expecting me. We were in the one-room apartment where they lived with their four children. I gave my brother 46 more pounds from my sendoff party. I began to learn new lessons about traveling abroad.

To my surprise, only one thing was sure. My brother had received the three hundred pounds (money) I sent through dee Ezekwem. Dee Ezekwem complained that his own bank did not trust him and made him get someone to co-sign with him before they gave him the money, though he had more money with the bank than what I sent. What mattered was that my brother had the money. He had also arranged for me to sleep in a distant relative's house. I walked over each night after dinner.

For the remainder of the month of August, I frequented the passport office on the Island from Ebute Metta daily. I had no success. I visited the American embassy and learned that the officials there would not even deal with me until I had my passport. It was the same lesson I learned at the PAN AM Airline office. On the night of September 4th, I had a dream. The passport officer gave me my passport. I was up very early on the fifth, walked over and knocked at my brother's door. Before they asked why I was up so early, I told them my dream. Soon, I was ready and on my way.

During my first week of dealing with the passport office, I decided not to waste my money on bus fare anymore. By the time I walked to the office, the officers were busy. I saw an Efik man who lived on the street where I was staying. We had seen each other often but had not met. That day, we met, and I introduced myself and told him why I was there. He remembered my file and told me that it was ready. He said the only reason it was being withheld was the officer's reluctance to sign it. He described the office and the man and told me to meet him. Before I turned to go, he added, "He is Igbo." That informed me that the man was from my tribe.

When I walked into the office, the man was at his desk. I greeted him and introduced myself and my mission. He doubted the letter from Lyndon. He asked, "How can they give you free tuition and permission to work? This is unusual." I looked at him with dismay. I wondered if he thought that I had written it or that I had bribed someone at the college to write it. I stammered when I tried to speak. He said, "Are you going to cry because of a passport?" He signed it with his green ink and gave it to me. I thanked him and walked out with the passport, thinking that my problem was solved. I guarded it with my life as I walked home. My first eloquent statement, when I got back to the apartment, was to slam the passport on the table. With broad smiles on everybody's face, I told my story.

On the following visit to the American Embassy, I enthusiastically carried my ignorance intact, thinking that I would get my visa that day. The man looked at my passport and with one question, "Where is your Form I-20?" He chipped away a small part of my ignorance. "What is that?" I asked. He told me to write the College. Before I left, I asked if there was a possibility that the College did not have the form. He assured me that as a state college, it did. I walked out deflected.

It took letters written at Lyndon State two weeks to reach me at Umukabia, and I was going to write and wait for the reply. I estimated four to five weeks. Meanwhile, the College had opened its doors to students even before I wrote my letter. Yet I had no other option. I wrote my letter with my Lagos address. Once at the hospital, they took my blood again. They still noticed the lingering malaria infection and sold me more pills. This time, I completed the course. By this time, the College had written and sent the form to both addresses, namely Umukabia Methodist Central School and Lagos. When it seemed the hospital was about to give me a letter of recommendation, they said they found something else in my blood. Though the College had written to tell me that I was late starting the fall semester, I wondered what to do with the hospital. Even one of the staff wondered if they wanted a bribe. Again, I dreamed. Lagos Road was blocked by an immovable enemy. Take another road. I woke up and decided to travel to Enugu, my region.

To my pleasant surprise, the American consulate was located at Oguiyi, right opposite the house I lived in as a boy. It was too late to do anything that day. The American man I met was friendly and told me the hospital he would send me for a blood test the following day. I tried and located the hospital. While on the premises, I saw a man from

Osa, i.e., the next village to mine. I told him why I was there. He took me to the lab technician. To get him to do it quickly, he demanded a fee. I paid it. After we left him, I went and spent the night with Godwin, the only son of my favorite aunt and his family.

The consulate was not open for long when I showed up the following day. In my short conversation with the American, I said that I was already late. He said he knew. I left my passport at the desk in the office. When I reached the hospital that morning, the doctor was alone. I gave him the paper from the consulate. He looked at me, invited me to a room, and drew the blood himself. I left the room. Soon, he rushed to me and demanded to know what happened to the blood. Looking at him with equal, if not more, surprise, I said, "The blood! Are you going to draw it again?" By the time I completed my sentence, he had disappeared. Then I heard, "Obed." I turned, and there was Emedom. He went to the consulate, saw my passport, and asked if I returned my passport from the U.S. They told him that I had not left and where to find me. He had just come back from the U.S. At that point, the doctor came and told me that my result would be sent to the consulate. Emedom and I left, found a taxi and went to see Mr. and Mrs. Ibegbulem at Agbani. It was about 4:00 pm when I returned to the consulate. My passport was where I left it and a woman was at the desk. I greeted her and introduced myself. "Congratulations." She told me that I was going to cold Vermont. I had no idea of what cold she talked about. I did not see any other paper sitting by my passport. When I opened the passport, I saw a stamp with a capital F inside it. Is this the visa? She confirmed, and I thanked her and left. It seemed that I came to Enugu to see Emedom before going to the U.S. I took a taxi to Godwin's apartment. I asked for and received one pound to complete my fare to Lagos., I went straight to Ogbaete Motor Park, and was on my way to Onitsha.

My hope of traveling to Lagos that day was dashed when we arrived at Onitsha. The bridge across the River Niger from Onitsha to

Asaba was not built then. There was only one way to cross the Niger, and that was by ferry. All lorries, cars, cargoes, and people who crossed the Niger from Onitsha to Asaba at that time went by a steamboat that ferried them through. By the time we reached Onitsha, the last ferry had gone. Our vehicle was not Lagos or even Asaba-bound. I was left to fend for myself. God provided again. One of the employees at the port was a native of Ubakala, a village close to mine. He offered to take me home. I spent the night with him and took his address.

    My host knew the schedules of the boats. I was there early in the morning and bought my ticket to cross over to Asaba. As the boat moved, I walked close to two men who stood by the car they traveled. Dressed like the schoolteacher I was, I requested a ride. One of them demanded to see my passport as proof of my story. I gave it to the one I thought owned the car. He said to me, pointing to the other man, "Give it to him. He asked for it." They gave me a ride to Benin City and dropped me. I walked to the post office and sent a telegram to my brother to pay for my flight to the U.S. I planned to travel to Ibadan and from there to Lagos by train. Again, I had to change my plan because the Nigerian Railways called a strike that day. I traveled by lorry. There was a heavy rainfall that night. It was about 2 am when the lorry dropped me near Oyibo Market. I walked to the yard where my brother and his family lived. For the first time, the gate was unlocked. The rain had stopped when the lorry dropped me. I arrived after 2 am and surprised everybody with my knock at the door. The telegram had not arrived. It arrived later that day, and it was a waste of my money.

    My money had paid for every expense so far, including fifty dollars I traveled with. I still had to buy my plane ticket, which cost one hundred and seventy-five pounds. My money with my brother remained only a little over one hundred and two pounds. He added about 72 pounds of his own to buy the ticket, and I was set to go. I had the last few days of September to waste in Lagos. I wanted to see the parliament in session. I went to the Senate, and there were debates about the creation of the Bendel Region (State) with Chief Asadobe presiding in place of Dr. Azikiwe. Also, I went and saw Mr. Uzodinma Nwaobiala from my village, a member of the Action Group Party who was implicated in the party's treasonable felony, charged with Chief Awolowo, the party leader, and sentenced to imprisonment. I saw the Chief in person for the first time that day. I returned to my brother's apartment to wait. He announced a sendoff party for October 2

He gave me money to buy a carton of beer and hire someone to carry it home. I bought it and carried it on my head. When I reached the yard, people in the yard could not believe their eyes that this high elementary teacher on his way to America carried the carton on his head. The party was held that night for people from my village. That was also my last night in Lagos.

Chapter 24

In America

I felt like I could not wait till October 3, but I did. As a matter of fact, I slept better. I ate my last lunch of that decade in Nigeria that afternoon. By late afternoon, I was in my suit with my PAN AM bag hanging over my shoulder, ready to go. My brother, his wife, and I walked to a bus stop and from there to the Lagos Airport. After a while, the passengers were called to board. We said our goodbyes, and I walked to the plane and stepped on it for the first time in my life. Soon, we were airborne. We made two stops in West Africa: Ghana and Guinea. We flew all night, and by the early hours of October 4, we were at New York City Airport. Four Nigerian students were on the plane, three males and a female who was flying to Canada. That was the last I saw them. I was in America.

The cold New York fall wind greeted me as I stepped off the plane. I experienced the cold weather I'd read about in geography. I struggled to hang onto my bag as the wind tried to snatch it from me. I walked towards the airport terminal building. As I got close to the door, to my surprise, it opened by itself, and I walked through. Realizing that I was to fly to Boston made the Boston Tea Party, which I had read in the British Empire, history real to me. It was afternoon, and we were in the air again. We flew from Boston to Montpelier, the capital of Vermont. It was about 4 p.m. when the plane landed. The sun was shining, yet the cold penetrated the body. I wondered if that was the same sun that made people sweat in Nigeria.

Having claimed my suitcase, I took a waiting taxi to the bus station. We were close to the station when the bus driver, oblivious to my arrival, took off. The taxi driver dropped me there anyway. I took my suitcase and walked into a store and told the man inside my story and requested to use his phone. He obliged. When the phone rang and someone answered, I requested to speak to the Admissions Officer. She was prompt. I said, "This is Obed, the Nigerian student." "Oh yes, where are you?" I told her I was in Montpelier. She wanted to know where in Montpelier. I told her I didn't know and handed the receiver to the gentleman in the store. She advised me to wait there. I thanked the man in the store and waited. About one hour later, a car drove up and stopped. In the car was Mrs. Susan C. Gallagher, the Admissions Officer, and Mr. Robert Michaud, the Business Manager. They drove me to the Vail Campus. Students were already eating dinner. I joined them. After dinner, the college bus drove most of the male students to Burke Campus, where I met Eugene from New Jersey, and Jerry from New York, my two roommates. Friday, October 4, was my first full day in the United States of America.

More surprises were in store for me. I was running from the heat of the sun when I left Nigeria. On the other hand, the heat was running in the room I was going to sleep. In addition, there were blankets on the bed. The College bus was ready the following morning to take students to Vail for breakfast. I went and also stayed for lunch. We also went there for dinner. I also learned where things like the library, the bookstore, and a few other things were. Ali was an Arab student at Lyndon when I arrived. He also owned a car. He took me to Saint Johnsbury (St. J) to buy a winter coat and hat. After, he offered to take me to the movie. Naively thinking that he was going to pay for it, I accepted only to discover I was on my own. That was my last movie until my last summer in Vermont. Sunday came, and I went to church at Peoples Methodist Church on Church Street. Mrs. Janet McKnight was waiting for me to teach the grade four Sunday school class. I taught it for one year. I also gave the Australian, who was the Minister, my card that introduced me as a local preacher in the Methodist Church. I was ready for Monday.

Here was Obed on Monday in his suit again and on the bus and everyone in a sweater or jacket, "What are you dressed up for?" I had no answer. It was October 7, exactly one month since classes began. I went to Mrs. Gallagher, who introduced me to the Dean, Dr. Long, the President, and handed me over to Mr. Stockwell, the chair of the Science Department, to give me the placement tests. Unknown to me was that the College scheduled the freshmen class photograph that day. I joined them. I was the only one in suit. After the placement test results and the certificates I presented, I was almost a sophomore. I registered for the 200-level courses except mathematics, where I registered for a 100-level course.

I wrote my first letter to my brother from the U.S. In reply, one of his statements said, "Remember I am here (Nigeria) alone." In other words, I am his only living sibling. That statement remained indelible in my mind and influenced my behavior toward him for as long as he lived. I even returned to Nigeria with that letter after 12 years and 3 months.

One of the first classes I attended was the English literature class. Mrs. Bisson taught it. She sounded funny. I wondered what kind of English she, in particular, and Americans in general, spoke. I thought, "Is this the type of English I will hear in all the classes?" I told her that I did not understand her and requested her to slow down. She made sense in her reply. I wondered why she would not talk like that when she lectured. Mary, another student who sat next to me, volunteered to explain the lesson to me after class. She then explained to me that the lecturer was talking Chaucer's English. At one time, the professor read my paper and told the class that I wrote English the way it should be written but could not speak it. The class turned out to be my favorite class that semester. She also became my favorite Professor. I called her Mrs. Chaucer till her death. Then I discovered that my math class was boring and a waste of my time. By the time I realized that I could switch to College Algebra, another three weeks had gone by. I still did it and that earned me an F at the end of the semester.

By the end of my first week at the College I had been assigned to work in the library as an assistant librarian. I put in 10 hours a week. One day as I walked towards the library, my path crossed a female student's path. She said to me, "you are mean. All I want is for you to be my friend." I was not sure I had seen her before. I shrugged my shoulders and continued walking without saying one word. If I saw her again, I might not recognize her. Among other days, the librarian scheduled me to work on Friday nights. Friday evenings turned out to be dating evenings for the students. At first, I was alone in the library. Then, a lonely female student walked in.

She smiled and we greeted. It was the girl who accused me of being mean. She did not come to read. We were still talking when a male student, Rich, walked in and started talking and weeping. He could not understand why this white girl would choose me, a black student, over a white male. Lois would have none of it and walked out. I tried to comfort and assure Rich that I did not come to Lyndon to get married. I thought I calmed him down. But Lois still did not want to have anything to do with him. About a week later, the full-time library assistant, who was my supervisor, and I were working and talking when a man walked in. She called him Charlie and introduced me to him. He was her husband. A few weeks later, she told me that Charlie was mad that the two of us were alone and conversing when he walked in. Then he came home one day and apologized to her because Bruce Hudson, a student at Lyndon who attended Peoples Methodist Church with me and his co-worker, told him he could not meet a nicer man. Bruce and Nancy, his wife, entertained me at their home. I wondered if American men felt insecure with their women and if the library was a good place for me to work. I thought about what Nigerian newspapers would write if they became aware of the stories and what effect that might have on my family. For a time, things seemed normal.

This was the era when the hippie movement was in its infancy. The student government election campaign was at its peak. Two hippies who were running as President and Vice President advocated no rules at the College. I was not running for any office but wrote against their manifesto. The gist of my paper was, "I would love to live in any place without rules, provided everyone knew how to behave. But such a place and people do not exist. Therefore, there must be rules and punishment to keep people in line." The administration, faculty, and most students appreciated the paper. The hippies lost.

The elections were over, and there was a dance to celebrate the victory. Also, there was a king and queen to be crowned. Many of the students came with dates and some without. I went to see what Americans did. Lois came without a date and so did Rich. I did not notice either of them. I was sitting down among other students when Lois came and asked me to dance with her. I accepted and danced with her. Rich saw us dance a few times. He waited until I left the hall and followed me. He rained abuse on me for dancing with his girlfriend. I got angry and wondered if he mistook my sympathy for him as fear of him. I told him that I was not afraid of him and that he was not smart. She does not like and does not want you. If you threaten and abuse me again, you will be sorry. I left the Vail Campus by the 9:00 p.m. bus for the Burke Campus. Less than ten minutes after I reached my room, the phone rang. When I picked up the receiver it was Lois on the other end. She expressed her anger when she thought that I left because of Rich. I assured her that I left at my time. I believe Rich got the message and that was the end of the irritation for both Lois and me.

There were certain student organizations on campus. Only one, The Protestant Christian Organization, appealed to me and I became a member. Margery Streeter was the chair. There were two other women in the group who took an interest in me but who I did not recognize at the time. November was at hand and Thanksgiving was fast approaching. I was trying to make sense of the near disaster with Rich and Charlie over their women when Mary in the Christian group saw me and said, "Obed, I will take you home for Thanksgiving." Without any hesitation, I said, "No, thank you. I will not go." One would think that was the end of the matter. But it was not.

It was the end of the hour and students were walking from one classroom to another. I was on the steps of one classroom when I saw Gary, my roommate from New York and every student seemed to be unusually in a hurry. He said to me, "You came, and our President is murdered." The next person to speak to me about the death was Mrs. Gallagher the Admissions Officer. She said, "Our President is assassinated." That was November 22, 1963. Strangely enough, my reply was, "By a foreigner?" She said, No." The College was closed until after the funeral. The bookstore manager invited me to spend the funeral day with the family. I learned a few lessons that day. One was about law and the mind. Her husband was a lawyer. He cautioned that the police should not close their mind to the possibility that the real killer was there watching them instead of the man they had in custody. The second was about food or coffee, to be specific. Coming from Nigeria, where I always drank coffee with milk and sugar, the lady asked me if I wanted to drink my coffee black. My answer was yes. Well, I asked for it. I drank black coffee for the first time, and it tasted medicinal. I thought but could not ask, "Why don't these Americans know that the color of coffee is coffee, not black? I did not drink half of the cup. Nevertheless, I learned my lesson.

Mother Mac was the College nurse. I became one of her favorites and the students knew it. Mary reported her offer and my rejection to her. I went to see Mother Mac one day, and she said, "Obed, do you know that the College is closed for Thanksgiving? Do you have a place to spend the holiday? Mary said she offered to take you home and you refused." All these students were white and race relationships in the U.S. in the early sixties were anything but what to write home about. What would this white woman tell her parents when they saw me, bothered me? But I had no other choice. I agreed to go with her. Mother Mac relayed my answer.

 Lyndon State College is only 50 miles south of North Troy, Mary's home. North Troy is on the border between the U.S. and Canada. Mary's dad was also a pastor. Not knowing where I was going or what to expect, I took a few clothes and by mid-afternoon I was ready. Soon, the pastor arrived, and we were on our way. I got excited when they showed me the dividing line between the U.S. and Canada and made a request. Because it was only about two hundred yards from their home, I asked if Mary and I could walk into Canada so that I could claim to have been there. My request was promptly granted. On arrival at the border, the guards demanded to know our citizenship. They would not allow the Nigerian to walk over. My civil and historical lesson that as a Nigerian and a member of the Commonwealth, I am also a citizen of Canada, did not help. They, in turn, lectured me. "Once you step into Canada, you will need a visa to come back here." That threw ice on my ambition. But all they did was to force us to take the back door. Mary's dad drove us through an unguarded road into Canada. I picked a little pebble, which I posted to Peter Ezeocha as a gift from Canada. We attended the dad's church on Thanksgiving and Sunday. They were very hospitable. He drove us back to Lyndon on Sunday evening. Mary saved me a search for where to spend my first Thanksgiving in the U.S. I also learned the difference between our Harvest Thanksgiving in Nigeria and Thanksgiving in the United States of America. Forty-eight years later, I wrote to Mary and thanked her for the hospitality and invited her and her family over. Sweetie and I are still keeping our door open.

With the cold increasing that October instead of abating, I wondered what winter would be like. One of the students asked if I had seen snow before. I said, "No." A few days later he came to the library and invited me to see snow. I put on my coat and Russian hat and walked out. I stretched my hand, opened my warm palm, and let it drop. To my surprise, it melted before I examined it. I went back to the library. After it accumulated and solidified, I discovered that the snow I could not hold in my hand for a second did become as hard as a stone. It snowed from October to May. I also learned that Fall is another name for Autumn.

The big Christmas break was near. Before I thought about it, God had completed every arrangement. Reverend Peel, who was in charge of the Students' Christian Protestant Organization, informed me that I would represent Vermont Colleges at Athens during the holiday. I was thrilled and exhibited my ignorance once again. Not knowing there is Athens in the U.S. and having studied Greek history, I enthusiastically wrote home and told them about my impending journey to Athens in Greece. The College arranged for me to stay in a hotel till December 24, when Dr. Long, the President, picked me up. I spent Christmas day with his family. I was to travel from there on December 27.

As the Christmas holiday drew near Marj Streeter, the President of the Christian club, announced that the National headquarters had chartered buses to take participants to Athens. All the participants from New England would meet in Boston. I had my bus ticket from Lyndonville to Boston and back. Suddenly, I realized I was Ohio State bound, not Greece. The male hostel and Burke Motel that housed male students had become too small for them. The College entered into an arrangement with the Burke Motel and one hotel downtown to house the excess students. The College moved me to one of the rooms in the hotel during the first few days of the holiday. I did not know how the students used the place. But when the President came to get me, the manager said he wished the other students were as caring as I was. That was another plus for me.

When we reached his home, Mrs. Long and their two daughters Jane, a medical student, and Judith, a Ph. D. Psychology student, were present. He introduced me to them and them to me. A short time after he and I went to a nearby hill covered with snow to snowboard. When we returned to the house, Jane was cooking, and Judith was decorating the Christmas tree. She invited me to help with the decoration. I obliged. Soon, dinner was ready, and we ate. Christmas was fun. I understood the song "I am dreaming of a white Christmas," which has no meaning in Nigeria. Dr. Long drove me to the Lyndonville bus station the following day, and I was on my way to Athens, not in Greece but in Ohio.

Once we were in Boston our bus was full. We drove all night. Marj Blake from New Hampshire sat by me on the bus. We were still on the road at breakfast time the following morning. The driver stopped and we went to eat. She helped me order my food. We became friendly and parted at the university campus. When I compared the campus with my little Lyndon, it seemed like a city. Before the end of the first week of the conference, Marge and I met again and talked again. She knew I came to the U.S. from Nigeria less than three months ago. I learned that she was a senior. She did not have a boyfriend and her father wanted her to look for a millionaire to marry. I was aware of at least three men from my Ohuhu clan who came to the States the same year. I hoped to see at least one of them. I did not. However, there were pleasant surprises for me. There was Jane Ubi the daughter of a well-known Catechist in the Methodist Church who came from only a few miles from my village. She said her children called spaghetti worms. Going round, I saw John Ogbu and Eko, two of my classmates at HEC Uzuakoli. It seemed like we planned a reunion.

There were some political discussions and other matters. It was only a month since the death of President Kennedy. It was a topic of interest. I learned more from the songs than from scripture and the Scripture lectures. It was time to part and all these Americans were kissing here and there. Marj came to kiss me goodbye. I refused to kiss her and explained that "we don't do such a thing on the streets." It was not long before she wrote to me. My refusal to kiss her was a major topic. She researched and read about a Nigerian in Britain who refused to kiss a woman on the street. It seemed she had found a poor man for a husband instead of the millionaire her father asked for as a son-in-law. Meanwhile, the semester was over. I lamented my poor performance, no A, one B, and one F. Other students and even lecturers made my excuse for me. "You came late, and you are in a foreign land." Once again Reverend Peel got involved in my holiday. He arranged to take three Vermont students from three Vermont Colleges, including me, on a short holiday trip. His VW Beatle conveyed us. I did not know what he had in mind when we started. The other two students were American white. First, he took us to the Nigerian consulate in New York City. I overheard the Nigerian saying, "Let him suffer it. When you tell them that it is not easy, they think you are trying to prevent them from getting their education." I realized he was asking for a scholarship for me. The man at the window denied his request. We drove off disappointed. We had fun driving to New Jersey. We ran a "race" against a family in a station wagon. Besides a family of about five or six and their load inside it carried a boat on top. We overtook them each time we descended a hill. They overtook us whenever we ascended. At every ascension, we pretended to push our VW to prevent them from overtaking us. They waved and encouraged us to push harder.

Finally, we were at Fairlawn, New Jersey. Reverend Peel drove to a house. He stopped and went in alone, leaving the three of us in the car. The man he introduced as a psychiatrist was also his cousin. I believe he went in to warn the family about the presence of a black man in the company. We spent the night with the family. He was a Christian. We enjoyed our stay, and before we left, he brought a number of suits, shirts, and ties and asked me to take all or choose what I wanted. I chose a black suit, a polo shirt with fish at the pocket and a plain tie. He looked at me and my choice and said, "You are a conservative eh." I smiled and thanked him. Though he was about my height, he was bulky and wearing his pants without covering them with a coat or sweater. The pants would have made me look like what we call "Papa Dash me" in Nigeria because of the waist size of the pants. We enjoyed our adventure and returned to Vermont.

My first summer in the U.S. was close at hand and students were talking about summer jobs. I started my own hunt. But I could not go beyond the student admissions office. When the college closed for the summer, I still did not have any job. Mr. Stockwell, the Chairman of the Science Department, decided to repair the roof of his house and invited me to work for him. My woodwork at Uzuakoli came in handy. He was so impressed that in the middle of it all, he gave it over to me. At about the same time, the College asked me to apply to a Christian camp in Cape Cod as a counselor. I did and Mr. Stockwell was one of those who recommended me. I got the job. Thus, I was to spend my first summer in Cape Cod, Massachusetts.

On arrival, we had a little orientation in preparation for the arrival of the campers. I was assigned to take care of the twelve-year-old boys. I was shown my cabin. Reverend Johnson was the owner. He was seventy years old, and his wife was seventy-five. This camp was located at a place they called Snake Pond. By the time the children arrived, we were ready for them. I had white, black, Puerto Rican, and Chinese boys and enjoyed every minute with them. Since I did not have a car or know where to go, I spent my days off at the camp. At times I put on a life jacket and used a boat on the pond. They called the area Snake Pond because it was snake-infested. However, the people claimed the snakes were not poisonous. Although they claimed that the snakes were not poisonous, I refused to enter the bush. To me the only nonpoisonous snake is a dead one. We went fishing in the ocean one day. I almost didn't catch any fish until the last second before we left.

The senior staff surprised me at the end of the camp with the Counselor of the Camp Award. That meant that I received the pay of a sophomore instead of a freshman counselor. The parents of my boys also gave me gifts, including the bust of Martin Luther King, Jr. The military jets flew overhead many times day and night maneuvering in readiness for the Vietnam War. In a discussion at the camp, I reminded them what I learned in history. The author of the book I used for the British Empire said, "Neither Britain nor the colonies knew when the American War of Independence began." Stated differently, the war started before either party realized it was at war. History might repeat itself in Vietnam.

One of the camp leaders came from New Hampshire. He offered to give me a ride at the end of the camping season to the farm where he stayed. He drove through Plymouth and took me to see the replica of the Mayflower. That really brought my British Empire history alive to me, especially looking at the stone with 1620 carved on it. Unfortunately, his friends on the farm did not appreciate the presence of a black man on their property. He denounced them and took me to the bus station the following morning. Within a short time, I was at the Lyndonville bus stop. There were still about two weeks left before classes began.

As much as I enjoyed the camp and my boys, I discovered that the pay was good if I wanted spending money only. Even though I received higher pay than I should have made if I had not been the counselor of the camp, I needed to make more money. God provided work at the College. Mr. Michaud, the business manager, employed me to work with the College crew. For the remaining two weeks, I worked for the College at $1.25 an hour, the minimum wage at the time. That was by far better than the eighty cents an hour I was paid during the school session. I spent two more years at Lyndon State, and each year, the camp invited me to work for it. But I could not because of the pay. As a private student, I had to earn enough to pay for boarding, buy books and clothing, and meet other needs.

On one of those early days, Lyndon's soccer team played a visiting team. Dr. Long took me to the edge of the field and introduced me to Coach Bell. He invited me to practice with the team. He had not seen anyone in his team play as well as I did. He ordered the number 1 jersey for me. That was my number at Lyndon. The Protestant Christian Club also elected me the President, a position I held for the remaining two years I was at Lyndon. In the middle of the winter, the college bus left the Vail campus for Burke Mansion. Less than 200 yards from the hostel, heavy snow, and slippery roads prevented the bus from moving. All the students got off and left the bus on the road and started walking. Walking on the snow-covered hill was almost impossible for me. The students took a shortcut and entered the bush. As we climbed the hill holding onto the leafless sticks, I discovered that I did not have the right kind of shoes, and every step I took, it seemed I slipped two backward. Soon I was alone in that dark night. At one point, it crossed my mind that I might not even make it, and I started praying. Finally, I was on the grounds of the mansion we lived in. I thanked God and walked in. I walked to the shower and thoroughly warmed myself up. I bought a good pair of snow boots instead of the rubber that covered my shoes. On the whole, my first year was a success.

Chapter 25

Vermont, My Second Home

President Kennedy had sent Americans as part of the Peace Corps to many countries, including Nigeria. One day, Mr. Stockwell told me about one of them, Sally Holden, the daughter of Dr. Holden, the Vermont Commissioner for Education, who was in Nigeria. But he did not know what part of Nigeria. A few weeks later he gave me her address. She was in Western Nigeria, and I wrote her. I promised to be her pen pal in America if she would be mine in Nigeria. She accepted my offer. We communicated several times before she returned to Vermont.

Shortly after she returned, she invited me to her parents' home. Her younger sister drove me from the College to her home. I was not the only visitor. The brother came with a girlfriend and there was another Nigerian, a Yoruba man. Sally enjoyed her stay in Nigeria. The ascension of the White Mountain was our major activity the following day. 1964 was a general election year. The Governor's inauguration ball was scheduled. Sally invited me to take her to it.

This time Sally came and got me. However, the invitees were expected to go and congratulate the Governor-elect. We dressed up and I wore my NCNC Party attire with Dr. Okpara's bust and looking colorful. By the time we got there, the line was long. I expected the Commissioner to take his family and me through without delay. Instead, we joined the line at the tail end. We were there for a few minutes when a policeman saw me. He walked straight to me, thinking that I was an important somebody, and asked me to follow him. Without giving a second thought to whether my date and her parents were behind me or not I took off. After I took a few steps, I heard Dr. Holden ask, "Obed may we follow you?" Almost embarrassed I said, "Of course, I thought you were behind me." Soon we were back to the house and waited for the evening and the dance to begin. I enjoyed the dance but that was the last time I saw Sally.

Either the College smelled danger for me in the library, or they realized I needed to work more hours, or both; I was moved to janitorial duty. I had all the keys to all the offices and instead of ten hours, I worked up to twenty-three hours some weeks. I even worked while classes were in session. It was not uncommon to hear fellow students ask me, "Obed, when do you study?" At one time, the Genetics lecturer, Dr. Dubazeck, wanted someone to take care of the guinea pig laboratory. I applied for the job. He looked at me and asked, "Do you want to buy New York City?" I need money to pay for my boarding, buy my books, and other expenses, and I make only 80 cents an hour. In reply, he said, "Oh, I am sorry. I thought you had a full scholarship." He gave me the job. I learned to use my time when I worked so many hours and carried more than the normal class load of fifteen hours. Except for the first year, when I carried only fifteen hours a semester, I did not carry anything less than nineteen hours a semester. Interestingly, the few semesters I made the Dean's List were the times I carried the heaviest loads, worked most hours, played soccer, and knew I had no time to fool about.

I was also engaged in lecturing high schools and church organizations. There was one female student who attended Peoples Methodist and was invited by the female church organizations with me. Her name was Jane. She sang and I talked. I took a liking for her. Soon she was engaged. The engagement did not last. In all my lectures, one thing stood out that is with all their education, Americans were the most ignorant of other countries, especially the countries of Africa, as the reader would see later on in this chapter. Though they describe the Indian tribes in America, to them, a tribe could number only in the hundreds or, at most, a few thousand. When I told them some tribes in Nigeria numbered more than 10 million, they thought it impossible. I also found some encouragement from one Reverend Dr., who came from St. J., to take me to lecture his congregation. He knew I was a private student. He told me that he educated himself. He added, "Those of us who educate ourselves enjoy education better." It was both encouraging and comforting to hear that this doctor had my experience. The maple products I returned with were too sweet for me. My friends enjoyed them.

I enjoyed most of my classes. However, there were about three of them where I knew the instructor cheated me. One was the Appreciation of Art. First, I did not know that the lecturer was not a Christian. He made derogatory remarks about church window glasses and the candles. He hated the decorations in churches. Then he punctuated every criticism with, "Beauty is in the eye of the beholder." I countered with my own argument. Vail Campus is on a hill that overlooks hills and valleys. "Look at the beautiful site here. Suppose someone who does not know and does not appreciate beauty says there is no beauty in it and says it is ugly. Should we conclude there is no beauty there?" I did not get any grade below a C in any of his assignments. However, he gave me a D- as my final grade. Fellow students told me to report him to the Dean. I asked if D- meant I had to take the course again. When the answer was no, I told them to forget it. Then there was Mr. F who acted as though no black student should get better than a C grade. After I received my Ph. D. and was employed as an Assistant Professor, I visited Lyndon. I shook his hand and introduced myself as Dr. and Assistant Professor. He was still an instructor.

If the first two were endured irritants, the third was a wound I could not bear in silence. Esther, the head of the Department of

Education, hired a retired superintendent of schools from New York to teach a five-hour course. The doctor was a very good instructor, and I enjoyed him. He gave one main test. Only two of us got an A on the test. I got a B+ on my paper and a B on a quiz. More than two-thirds of the way through the semester, he fell sick and left. With only a few weeks left in the semester, the college hired Bev, a seventh-grade schoolteacher, to complete the course. She asked the class to write a term paper on a unit. She gave me a C for a grade. I could not believe her and reported to the head of the department. While that was going on, the College planned to send final-year students on teaching practice. I requested an exemption because I taught before I came to the College. The head of the department decided to send me to teach in this woman's class for some weeks for evaluation. I had no choice.

    I was majoring in teaching Mathematics and Science in junior high. My evaluation was to be based on teaching a unit in one of the two areas. She pleaded with me to teach a unit on Africa since I came from Africa. That is what I taught. I enjoyed the class and received an autographed album from the class. What the students wrote revealed their perception of the teacher. Many of them wished I was the class teacher. "Obed was friendly to all. Obed did not discriminate against anybody. He got everyone involved." Again, I found their knowledge of Africa very limited. It seemed that all they knew about Africa came from the Tarzan movie, not even filmed in Africa. Tribes and jungles make up Africa. When asked how Africa could contain the largest hot desert in the world and still be all jungle, they had no answer. When told that the population of some countries in the west, like Denmark and Norway, is less than one-third of the major tribes in Nigeria, they could not believe it. Finally, they asked the questions coming from adults.

    One such question, "Obed, why don't African countries support the United States against communist countries at the United Nations?" I told them that was an interesting question and asked them to research the answer. The answer they gave was better than anything I could have given them. In the end, the teacher gave me an A, and they granted me an exemption from teaching practice. However, she did not change the C grade. I remained unhappy with her and the chair of the education department, especially after I learned that the GPA is important for admission to graduate school, and this was a five-hour course.

I had been in the United States for one year and two months in December 1964 when I received a letter from my brother in Lagos, Nigeria. He complained that the Yoruba people he worked with were trying to poison him. In an attempt to defend himself, he had spent all his money and had no money to celebrate Christmas for his family. There, I was a private student working at 80 cents an hour, and I owed the college my boarding fees. I sent him ten dollars. In reply, he said the bank gave him three pounds, eleven shillings, and five pence. That amount was enough for anybody to enjoy Christmas in Nigeria in those days. I thanked God I was able to help him. Once again, Reverend Peel selected me to represent Vermont State Colleges at another Christian Conference, this time in Lincoln, Nebraska. It was a Methodist National Youth Conference. I spent my Thanksgiving holiday with the Gallagher family and Christmas with the Long family. We traveled by bus to Chicago and by train from there to Lincoln. We were there for about two weeks, and I enjoyed every day I spent there. I also met Chibuiko Ujo, who was a year my senior at Mission Hill and attended the secondary section of Uzuakoli College. As Marj Blake feared, another female student asked and received my address when we reached Chicago on our way back. However, unlike her, that ended with only the Christmas card exchange.

The Dean of the College and his wife came to see Mother Mac one evening and saw me eating my dinner, and it was Cheerios. He commented, "Obed, you are eating another breakfast." I smiled. Mother Mac said, "Obed made your list (Dean's List)." He said he had not looked at the list. Several weeks later, he called me to his office and gave me a form to fill. When I looked at it, it was a scholarship form from the Nigerian Embassy. I thanked him but refused to fill it. At first, he was surprised. I told him that if I filled out the form and got the scholarship, they would recall me after my first degree, and I did not intend to return to Nigeria with only a first degree. Then he said, "Whatever you want." I thanked him and left the office without filling out the form. Thinking about it now, I realize it was the same All-Sufficient Christ Who gave me the scholarship that directed me to refuse to fill out the form.

I always enjoyed sports and games. As stated earlier, I ran long distances, boxed, and played soccer, volleyball, rugby touch, cricket, and even civilized wrestling in Nigeria. I wore the number 1 jersey in soccer at Lyndon. Twice, I was hurt on the field. The first was at Keene, New Hampshire. The player kicked the ball to my right eye, and I was at close range. I could not see for some minutes. Even when I returned to the game, I could not gauge the distance well. The second was at Lyndon. As usual, I was at close range when the player banged the ball on my private part. I fell to the ground with pain. Within a few seconds, the referee was on his knees by my side and asked what went wrong. Gathering every breath, I could, I said, "My baa naa naa." The referee left me and fell down laughing. Soon, two of my teammates were on the spot asking the same question. I gave them the same answer. They fell down laughing. Then Coach Bell was on my side, asking the same question. I said, "My baa naa naa." He left me and fell to the ground laughing. I thought, what is the matter with these Americans? They told you what they call the thing, and when you mention it, do they allow you to suffer and hug the ground laughing? Finally, the Coach asked, "Do you want to come out?" I thought, "Who, me?" The female students, not males, would surround and ask me, especially if they already know the answer." I said no." Even after they knew the answer, the female students wanted to hear it from me. They were good to me, though.

The people I met in Vermont were so good to me that if I had gone home after my stay in the State, I would have concluded that all Americans were angels. I spent a Thanksgiving with the McKnight family, the lady who gave me the grade four Sunday school class to teach. When she knew that my mother brought me up alone because of my dad's early death, she wrote my mother and congratulated her on the wonderful job she did bringing me up as a single mother. They were prouder than my relatives in Nigeria would have been at those times when I made the Dean's List. The local newspaper never missed any goal I scored or lecture I gave. This led some students to play some mischief. I thought another student did it. But a student from New York, who is now a Mormon, many years later visited me in Salt Lake City and claimed to have done it instead of D. So, forget the name.

There was a bust of a pig at Lyndon Center that someone painted red. Whoever did it claimed that my name was always on the paper. Nobody knew that he was at the College. He decided that his name would be read for good or bad. He decided to paint the pig red and did so. He did not hesitate to confess and give his reason for doing it. The paper printed the story, and he achieved his objective.

I made two terrible mistakes with "my women friends." I asked the one who first loved me and had a dispute with a former boyfriend, and another girl over me to give me her mother's address. She did. This is a mother she brought to my room during Homecoming weekend. I wrote such a stupid letter of rejection, which I thought was a piece of advice to her daughter through her. I mention this here to offer my apology to both of them. I am sorry. Please forgive me. Then there was Fay, who I liked, and she said to me, "Obed, you are handsome." I said, "I know that." Her big friend said, "Obed go and marry yourself." Mary was always nice to me, especially during summer when I walked to the stores. She usually gave me a ride to the College. Nevertheless,

I never asked her to come in or took her out because I did not think she wanted me to. She saw me on the morning I left Lyndon and said, "Wherever you are going, don't behave the way you behaved here." I said, "Thank you."

Holly was a typical American student. She had watched Miss Blake in the lobby of the main building and said, "She is beautiful." I neither confirmed nor denied. She must have read about the slave trade somewhere. She wanted to know when I first wore clothes. I said it was the day my plane landed at the New York Airport. She wanted to hear the whole story. I told her, and she believed it all. She wanted to know where we lived. "Top of trees," I told her. "What about the American Ambassador and the staff?" "We honor them with the largest trees." How do you get your mail?" "That's easy. Throw down a rope, and the mailman ties it to the end of the rope. You draw it up." At the end of the Q&A, I took her to the library and gave her one of the magazines I brought. She saw a picture of Lagos from the air. She said, "I have been watching you and wondering where you learned how to behave. Now you are my brother." Before the semester ended, I received another surprise. Instead of Ed, a fellow white student, who was interested in her, she told me that if I agreed to be her boyfriend, she would stay in college. When I denied her request, she left. Some of them typed my papers for me, while some ironed my clothes. I know I did not knowingly set out to be a snob to any of them. It was my culture, ignorance, and determination to put any other things second to my education. For instance, I thought I was paying a compliment to one who graduated and came to see me when I wrote, "You looked so beautiful I almost kissed you." She was so angry and wrote, "And you discovered I was not good enough for you." To you all, I apologize and ask for your forgiveness. However, I did develop an interest in the President's younger daughter. She was not interested in me.

There were two male students besides Rich with whom I had a problem. Vermont was too cold for most blacks. As a result, there were only about three black Americans at the college when I arrived, two males and a female. If not for the American classification, one could not look at her and call her black. Danny was not quite liked. At that time, American whites discriminated against black Americans, but they were in love with blacks from Africa. For example, I wore my NCNC Agbada clothes one Sunday morning to church. I walked past a house, and soon, a car stopped by me. The two women offered to give me a ride. I declined. They pleaded, "Please do us the favor. We are from Texas. See, we are not dressed. We are still in our nightgowns and saw you and came to give you a ride." I allowed them to drop me at church. Danny hated such "royal" treatment to a man like himself and what he received. He misplaced his anger on me. He tried to intimidate me. Twice, he tried and failed. The third time I walked into the library, where everyone was reading, he left his seat and met me at the center. He started to abuse me in a quiet voice. I butted his face with my head and challenged him to touch me. He went back to his seat. I took a sheet of paper and wrote a report of his attacks to the Dean, promising to fight him to the finish if he attacked me again.

A white student who seemed to be popular was elected the President of the student body. He often got drunk. One evening, he got really drunk and walked into the lobby. With his friends around him, he abused me and pushed me. I decided to box him; the only thing they would do was deport me. At that moment, Coach Bell appeared and told me not to do anything. He saw everything and must have reported it. I understand his GPA at the end of the semester was .02. That was his last semester at the College.

The State completed building the President's residence at the Vail campus. Dr. Long and his wife moved in. It was winter with snow everywhere, and the Longs planned to take a few days off for a vacation. They asked me to stay at their house and take care of their two big German Shepherds. I agreed. While they were on vacation, a former Lyndon student who was studying for his master's degree at

Springfield, Massachusetts, visited Lyndon. He said he saw a Nigerian student who said that he knew me. He told me his name and gave me his telephone number. I called him from Long's number. Nwabuisi was not home. I left the number. I was still in the house when he called long distance through the operator. As we talked, I warned him to stop because of the cost, but he insisted on talking. When we stopped, the operator told him he owed ten dollars. He did not have ten dollars. The phone rang, and there was Nwabuisi asking for help. I reminded him of my warning and offered to pay five dollars. Pleased with the condition of things when they came back, Mrs. Long gave me ten dollars. I refused the gift. "It is an honor that you chose me of all the students and entrusted your house to me. And you want to pay me for it?" However, I told her about the five-dollar bill on her phone. Nwabuisi was my senior at HEC Uzuakoli and only a few miles from my village in Nigeria. The girl he married would not marry him until she knew he was going to the United States. As a result, he did not pay the bride price before he left Nigeria.

After a while, I wrote to Ngozi, a girl I wanted as a wife, shortly before I left Nigeria without letting her know that I was going to the U.S. I let her know that God was "giving me what I deserved" in America. She replied without delay and enclosed a sweater. I thanked her and told her the sweater was not warm enough for Vermont Winter. Before I knew it, she was trying to get her passport. As Nwabuisi said, she was willing to pay all her expenses. She sewed a uniform of Agbada for two of us and sent mine. Then there was the coup, and she wanted me to help. I reminded her of what she told me at Aba when I lost my hat and had an empty tank, and had to drag my motorcycle. After we returned to Nigeria, I learned that one of my nephews briefly stayed with her.

The Lyndon State soccer team played Keene in November. I met a Yoruba student who recently came from Nigeria. He painted a gloomy picture of the political situation in the country. He said people were being thrown into prison for trumped-up charges while political opponents were even murdered. I wrote to Godwin Anozie in December and told him the news I heard and wished the Army would do something about it. It was the end of the fall semester, and I turned on the radio and heard there was a coup in Nigeria. We were on vacation when I heard it on January 15. I called the Yoruba student and informed him. He had not heard it.

During vacation, I used to live in the big Vail men's hostel with the two house mothers, Mac and Scram. This was the building with all the offices, the library, the bookstore, the gym, the dining, the laboratories, the two lobbies, and most of the classrooms. Sometimes, Mother Mac traveled to Cleveland to see her daughter and grandchildren during the Christmas holiday. Since I spent much of my free time watching television in her living room, the place became lonely when she traveled. I wrote my cousin Godwin in Enugu, Nigeria, and asked him to tape highlife music and Harcourt's songs and send them to me. He did, and the highlife song became a companion. Mr. Harcourt's songs could not play, so I threw the tape away. I was in this big building alone one night when I heard the door that led to the outside open. I rushed down to see who it was. It was Mr. Michaud, the Business Manager. He looked at me in amazement and shook his head. "You are rushing down here unarmed? You must be living right."

Then, I performed one of my mischievous actions one day. The Yoruba man I met at Dr. Holden's home gave me the name and telephone number of Veronica, an Igbo student at a university in New York. I wanted to talk to someone. I took her number, went to the kitchen, and used the phone, which belonged to the catering service. She was not there. I did not tell the service supervisor. The College was on vacation. Though the amount was minimal, when the manager looked at the bill, he knew someone used his phone. He looked at me as though he was saying, "I know what you did." I looked at him like, sorry, but I am not going to say anything. Soon, he had a padlock on his phone.

Mathematics and science subjects were taught only in secondary schools in Nigeria. As a teacher, I did not go to secondary school. Lyndon was almost exclusively offering a Bachelor of Science and Mathematics in education. I decided to take as many science subjects as I could fill in my schedule. Chemistry was my favorite, followed by genetics. I could have enjoyed astronomy, but the lecturer spent most of the time calculating distances between planets. For the first time, I was able to use the laboratory and dissect and grow things. Our visit to the astrology lab at St. J opened the universe to me. Physical Education introduced me to the world of "uncivilized" wrestling. However, I won the championship for the class of 135 pounds. I experienced a negative transfer of learning in baseball. I played cricket at Uzuakoli. The objective is to defend your wicket. In baseball, there is no wicket involved. Yet when the ball came straight at me, I deflected it instead of batting it. Having overcome my earlier mistakes, Coach Roy wanted to recruit me to the team, but I already had too many irons in the fire. I declined. I found psychology very interesting and took as many hours as I could.

In a small college like Lyndon State, every senior knew what every other senior was planning to do. While others looked for jobs, I talked about graduate school. At one time, Willie asked what degree I aimed at. I said Ph. D. He smiled and said, "How can a crazy man like you be a doctor?" When I went to receive my distinguished alumni award, I invited him to see that I was not as crazy as he thought I was. He and his wife Mary could not make it. Finally, I had to decide what to study in graduate school. To the disappointment of Dr. Dubichek, my Chemistry professor, I chose Educational Psychology. My first choice was the University of Vermont (UVM), but UVM did not offer Educational Psychology. Mrs. Bisson suggested her Alma mater Columbia. I could not see myself in New York City. Reluctantly, I applied to the University of New Hampshire. *Reluctantly* because that is the home of Miss Blake, who thought I came to the United States to marry her even before I graduated with my first degree. She reasoned that her mother was the one who had the degree when her parents got married. "I am not your father," did not make sense to her. Finally a few weeks before graduation, I applied to the University of Nebraska in Lincoln and two others.

In less than three years, I graduated from Lyndon State with B.S., Ed. While I waited for the results of my applications to graduate schools, my brother wrote to me. Amadi, his first son had passed his entrance examination to Government College Umuahia. Umuahia was one of the best secondary schools in Nigeria. My cousin Udobi was already there. I was very pleased with the news. Then the University of New Hampshire admitted me but without financial assistance. Someone in the LSC admissions office called my attention to the Institute of International Education Fellowship (IIE). I applied and filled New Hampshire as my institution. Dr. Long wrote a magnificent letter of recommendation that went with it. The tone of the letter from the President of the College convinced me that IIE would award me the fellowship.

Before our graduation day, Lyndon State received the good news it had waited for some time. It was nationally accredited. We became the first class to graduate from nationally accredited Lyndon. I used to join the College labor crew immediately after my finals were over. This time I waited till the graduation was over. That was my happiest day in the U.S. so far, and I wished my blood relatives were there. However, I had many well-wishers and received many gifts, including a bracelet for my wrist from the Longs, a briefcase from Mother Mac, and a book from Mother Scram. I had my second date at Lyndon, Michelle, for the graduation ball.

Shortly after graduation, the University of Nebraska offered me admission. The program was broad and more tailored to my needs and cost less than New Hampshire. I wrote to IIE as though they had awarded me the fellowship and asked for their permission to transfer to the University of Nebraska. They replied in the spirit I wrote i.e., as though they had awarded me the fellowship and granted me the permission to transfer. In the meantime, I learned one more expression. John and I went downtown for breakfast. When we finished eating, he asked the waitress, "How much damage did we do?" I never considered my eating as damaged before. All the same, she gave us the bill and we paid before we left.   Later, the University of Nebraska admitted me, and the foreign student's office sent me a form to fill out and requested my picture to be enclosed. One of the questions asked if I was married. I answered, "No". The one immediately following it asked, "How many children do you have?" I felt that it should have prefaced the question with, "If you are married." Therefore, I answered with, "How do you do that?" I know that question is irrelevant today. I told Bud, my boss, about the form. After he told me that someone answered the question with sex, he took out a booklet from his pocket and gave it to me. The title read, What Every Man Should Know About Every Woman. The cover was red. I opened it and it was blank.

It was almost three years since I arrived in Vermont and went to my first movie by mistake. In about a month I would leave to go to Lincoln, Nebraska. Mr. Stockwell's nephew asked me if I wanted to go to a drive-in movie. I agreed to experience it. Though I enjoyed it, it was my second and last movie in Vermont. It was Jack Lemon falling off a roof because of a woman, but he survived.

During vacation when I worked with the college crew, my hourly pay was $1.25 instead of 80 cents. This enabled me to feed and save for the next semester's expenses. The summer of 1966 saw two more responsibilities in my schedule. I was going to graduate school, which cost a lot more than undergraduate and without the certainty of financial aid. Secondly, I bore the burden of helping my brother to educate his children. I planned to leave Vermont in the last days of

August. I had worked for as long as I could and saved as much as possible. Two weeks before I traveled, I knew I would have over $800 in my account by the last payday. I sent $300 to my brother. I was happy when he wrote to say that the bank in Nigeria gave him 107 pounds, 5 shillings, and 8 pence. That was a lot of money in those days. That was my annual salary as a second-year grade three teacher before tax.

My graduation brought more pressure from Blake from New Hampshire. I refused to write to her. One Sunday, she arrived after I had gone to Church. Mother Scram saw her and, knowing that I was fed up with her, warned me. She only stopped after there was a knock at my door and when I opened the door, it was her. I was rude to her. She stopped coming but continued to write. One year after I went to the University of Nebraska, she sent me a sweater through the Graduate College Office. A woman in the office teased me for not giving her my address.

In July, the radio announced a counter-coup in Nigeria. This time the Igbo people were massacred, soldiers and civilians alike. Pregnant women were ripped open, and the babies in the wombs were taken out and cut to pieces. Gowon, who led the counter-coup, announced there was "No basis for Nigeria to continue as a country." Britain and the West got what they wanted i.e., to subjugate the Igbo people and continue their colonization of Nigeria. Oil had been discovered in commercial quantity in the South and they wanted it at all costs to the Igbo people who drove them away in the first place. They persuaded Gowon to remain in the country and started the re-colonization with him as their stooge.

Emedom wrote to me and reported that Okomonu told him to write. She had asked him to ask me to forget the wrongs inflicted on me. He told her that he would write but warned her that though we are best friends, we do not tell each other what to do. When she wrote, the closest she came to an apology was that no one else could have borne the treatment I bore. I demanded the truth and an apology from the sister. Also, I asked if she was still a virgin. That was the end of our communication.

The University of Nebraska had a foreign student organization that welcomed international students. The Foreign Students Office gave me the name and telephone number of Mrs. Jo Ritzman to call once I arrived in Lincoln, and she would pick me up. Having bought my bus ticket, I packed my suitcase and a carton of books. Most of the freshmen came on my last day at the College, and with them were some of the seniors. In front of me was Lois. I stood there frozen, debating whether to say goodbye or not and wondering how she would react to me. Before long she and her friend were out of the gym. The following morning with tears in her eyes, Mother Mac and I bade goodbyes. While I waited for a ride to the bus station, Mary, who gave me rides to the College, said to me, "Wherever you are going, don't behave the way you behaved here." I thanked her. With that piece of advice, I left Lyndon. That was the end of the communication between the two women in Nigeria and me.

Chapter 26

Honorary Citizen of Nebraska Twice

Between the last week of December 1964 and the end of the first week of January 1965, I was in Lincoln, representing Vermont Methodist College youth. We were awarded honorary Nebraska citizenship at the end of the conference. In addition, we were invited to join Nebraskans in the celebration of their centennial in 1967. Neither of the two events was in my mind when I left Lyndonville by Greyhound Bus that morning. After a few hours, I said goodbye to Vermont.

After two days and one night on the road, I was in Lincoln. With my suitcase and box of books secured, I dialed Mrs. Ritzman's number. Less than thirty minutes later, she picked me up. She took me to the foreign student's office the following day. I was wearing the same clothes I wore in the picture I attached to the form I filled. Unaware that the form I filled was passed around and made news, I expected no reaction. I did not know whether Mrs. Ritzman told them that we were coming either. But once I stepped into the office, the women there roared and said, "There he is, he looks like his picture." I realized what happened to the picture I enclosed. We began to discuss an apartment and job for me. I stayed with Mr. and Mrs. Ritzman for about a week before I moved to the first apartment. I discovered it was not really an apartment and went back to the Foreign Student's Office. There was no room in what they called "African House," because African students lived there. Finally, Mrs. Boykin, one of the foreign students' advisers, asked me to go to see a basement apartment in her parent's house. It was on 1919 E Street. It cost $40 a month. I rented it and moved in.

At about the same time, the foreign student's office found me a job in the Orthopedic Department of the University as a lab assistant that paid $1.65 an hour. Dr. Mihedah had written a proposal to study human teeth and their effects on the shape of the face. She proposed to study the rhesus monkey, which they say has features closest to humans. She received the grant, and I was to assist her with the study. I fed the monkeys, caught and held them for her to give them injections to put them to sleep, helped her extract their teeth, and took x-rays and pictures of the faces. I washed and sanitized the cages they stayed in. I worked 20 hours a week. I registered for the full graduate load of twelve hours a semester.

As I walked out of the Foreign Students Office one day, I saw a man going in. We passed, I turned and looked at him and he did the same thing. We smiled and approached each other. We discovered that we were not only Igbos from Nigeria, but from the same Umuahia clan. He graduated from Wesleyan University in Lincoln and was coming to do his graduate work at the University of Nebraska. I learned that Sydney Ugwunna went to Awka Teachers' HEC. We became good friends.

It was not a surprise that the University made me pay out-of-state tuition fees. Yet, I felt I should be treated differently for two reasons and called the Governor's office. A female voice answered the phone, and I launched my protest. "I was made an honorary citizen of Nebraska and invited to come and celebrate your centennial with you. I am here now to answer the invitation as a graduate student, and I am being charged out-of-state tuition. What happened to the citizenship?

Can the Governor's Office do something about this?" She asked me to wait. A few minutes later, she told me that I was connected with the Secretary of State's Office. The result of my inquiry did not change my status or the amount I paid. But it led to my friendship with Hon. Frank Marsh, the Secretary of State of Nebraska at the time, and his wife Shirley, who attended Trinity Methodist, the same church I went to.

Getting my identification card (ID) almost proved impossible. I walked to the window of the student's affairs office and requested a student ID card. I gave the officer the information he needed and spelled my last name for him. He gave me a date to come for the card. He had the card ready when I returned. Unfortunately, he misspelled my last name. I pointed out the error, corrected it, and left the card with him. When I returned the third time, he had made another mistake. Again, on the fourth time, he still was not without error. I realized his problem. The poor man was trying to substitute his English alphabet for mine. Where I have 'nw' and 'gb,' he substituted 'wn' and 'bg.' He turned to me and said, "Why don't you change this to John or Smith? We would have been done long ago?" I laughed and wondered if he was MR? I printed my last name again. When I returned for the fifth time, I got my ID.

Soon the Host Family Organization assigned me to my host family. Mr. and Mrs. Robert Frey and their three children became my family in Lincoln. The oldest boy was about twelve and the little girl was about four. It was fun being with them. Mr. Frey worked for Sears, and I think Mrs. Frey was a teacher. We were all disappointed when Sears transferred him to Baltimore, Maryland. Another family volunteered to be my host family, but I declined. However, I agreed to visit and ride their horse. I spent the rest of my time in Lincoln without an assigned host family. It was experientially better as I was able to choose where and when I went out without feeling I offended someone who prepared for me.

I was surprised to see Mr. Marsh at Trinity Methodist. Even more surprising was to see him as a member of the church choir. Nancy McCune and her family also attended the same church. She was the chair of the University host family organization in Lincoln. I became a friend of the family. She was one of the Americans who wrote to my mother, praising her for the great work she did in bringing me up as a single mother. In reply, my mother wrote her that I was her little boy. Nancy teased me for as long as she could with "my little boy." Soon God blessed me with the Institute of International Education (IIE) Fellowship. Then the senior minister of my church, Reverend Dr. Berg, invited me for an interview on his radio talk show about an American "know-it-all" who visited Lagos, the capital of Nigeria at the time, for a few days and assumed he knew everything in and about Nigeria. I accepted. The man had been in Lagos for about three days. On his return to the U.S., he claimed that education was not important to Nigerians. "The important thing to them is the Arrow shirt. The streets of Lagos were filled with them, etc." That was the worst white lie anyone could have told when I knew firsthand that parents in my village and family pledged land and even clothes to borrow money to send their children to school. Reverend Dr. Berg was so impressed that after the radio talk show, he drove me to his house and gave me a signed copy of his autobiography, *A Piece of The Blue Sky*, with the phrase, "with respect." Later on, he asked if I wished to be ordained as a minister because I gave the church my card from Nigeria, which indicated I was a local preacher in the Methodist Church. I said, "Not yet."

After Gowon declared a "Three-day surgical operation on Biafra," I called Festus Obioha, an Igbo who earned his Ph. D. that summer, to ask what we should do. He surprised me when he said, "I have suffered enough already and don't want to be bothered anymore." What could he have suffered this early, I wondered? Later I learned that he had sent his pregnant wife home with the hope of going home immediately after graduation. I felt that to be an excuse. Writing about him reminds me of the story Sydney once told me. He said that he and Festus went to the zoo one day. While they were at the monkey section, a white man came. The white man looked at the monkeys for some minutes and turned and looked at Festus, who almost looked like a monkey, for some minutes. After the man repeated his observation a few times, Festus called Sydney and asked him to observe what the man was doing, after which he told him it was time, and they left the monkey section. He could not control himself laughing as he told the story. We organized the Biafra Association in Nebraska and Festus never participated in its activities.

Rita was an English woman married to an American soldier during World War II. I believe she was in charge of social events for one of the television stations in Lincoln. Thanksgiving was knocking at the door again. Rita and the foreign student's office arranged to have some foreign students eat breakfast at the studio on Thanksgiving morning. I was one of the few students selected for the event. It was prerecorded a day before Thanksgiving. It went so well, and she thought I was the star of the show; she invited and used me in other social events, including a visit to the penitentiary and the discussion of the 1968 Nebraska Democratic presidential primary, which Senator Robert Kennedy won.

Before Christmas, the IIE awarded me a scholarship to attend leadership training at Este's Colorado. I had very high hopes when I accepted it. I was the only lab assistant in the office. Sydney was the only person I could trust to substitute for me during the two weeks. So, I arranged with him to take care of the monkeys while I was away. We also agreed that he would receive the pay for the period. A day before I traveled, I took him to the lab, and he watched me feed the monkeys. I locked the door and gave him the key.

When we arrived at Estes Colorado, there were fewer people than I expected. There was a Chinese student at the conference whose statements did not end without the word "kicks." Unfortunately, a good portion of the time was wasted by the leaders on "the characteristics of American women who date foreign students." I felt insulted and asked them if they called us there to tell us how or which American woman to date. "If I want to date American women so badly, I will go and stand by the Nebraska Hall door and ask every female who passes through for a date. By the time I asked a hundred, I will get a date. I thought you researched what made the Washington, Lincoln, and Kennedys and came here to share the information with us. My problem is not how to find American women. My problem is how to keep them out of my life." We left the dating game and discussed what we, as children, thought we would be when we grew up. My real benefit was outside the conference room.

In my study of geography, I read about hot springs and geysers. But I could not understand or imagine how steam could come from underground. There I was, looking at the steam rising from the ground in many places, like smoke, as though the dead were boiling something from their graves. The first few minutes were worth more than the years I spent reading what I did not understand. At the end of the conference, the organizers assigned the conference attendees two to a family. My family was a young couple who lived in Loveland. They had a young friend couple who came over to visit with us. His wife spoke English the way it should be spoken. When she finished, I said to her, "I am sorry, I did not understand you. Are you an American? I was more interested in and admired how you spoke than what you said." Before she answered, our host said to the husband, "Oh, watch out for that guy." She said she was an American and a speech teacher. I flew back to Lincoln the following day after an enjoyable evening with our host.

A big unpleasant surprise waited for me in the monkey lab. But it was not apparent when I unlocked the main door. Then I opened the door to the room where the monkeys were kept. Two of them were outside the cage, jumping up and down, and the monkey food in the bags was scattered all over the floor. They were chattering away. My presence got them excited. I put on my thick gloves, caught them, and put them back inside their respective cages. I re-bagged the food, swept and mopped the floor, and hoped my boss did not come to the office while I was away. My disappointment in Sydney was spelled out in my refusal to pay him any amount, and he did not protest.

I was particularly interested in two classes during registration, namely, education of the gifted and intelligence tests. Of the courses I registered for, these two were mainly about I. Q. Part of the intelligence course was giving the Benet and Wechsler and Stanford Benet to adults and children. In the course of giving the tests, I discovered what I felt was cultural bias. But what I could not understand was the notion that this I.Q. remained constant and does not change. Then, I encountered an interesting five-year-old boy.

This boy was the last of five children. As the mother said, "He had his two, and I had my two. This son is ours." This boy had lived in the city of Lincoln all his five years. The question is, "Where do you get milk?" His answer from experience was, "from the refrigerator." His answer was not the best answer. The best answer was and may still be the cow. I could not give him fewer points because the book said the cow. We discussed his answer in class and agreed that he should not be penalized. I asked him another question from the same book. "Boys wear shorts. What do girls wear?" He looked me right into my eyes and said, "Obed you are not supposed to talk about such things." Since there is no provision to pursue his objection, I did not ask why not. There were others about eggs and Columbus. The course raised more questions about intelligence tests and I.Q. than it answered for me. I decided to do individual research on intelligence tests and I. Q.

Professor Mary Krider taught the intelligence test course. About the third week of the class, she said the class was too large and asked if any student was willing to switch over to the Saturday class. When no one volunteered, she asked if I would. I told her that I worked on Saturdays. She asked, "Why don't you starve?" "My mother did not teach me how to starve," was my answer. She said she felt terrible later on. She told me that she asked herself why she said such a thing to me, especially since I was the only black person in a class of 14. She and her husband took me out for lunch and adopted me after the course. She almost freaked out one day. I took one twelve-year-old girl to the lab to give her a test. I called her mother. She asked, "Obed, what did you call that girl?" Knowing what she meant, I tried to calm her nerves. I said to her, "Her name is Ruth and Ruth is the mother of Obed in the Bible." She relaxed and allowed the test to proceed.

By the end of my first year at Nebraska, I decided to take a three-hour summer course. I would do a three-hour research study on intelligence tests and I.Q. Before then, I had Dr. Orton as a teacher and liked him. He seemed to know so much about I. Q. that I requested him to chair my master's committee, and he accepted. One of his favorite statements about I.Q. was that "to be a doctoral candidate, one must have at least an I.Q. of 132." There, I was aspiring to earn a Ph. D., and I had not taken any of these life-and-death tests. Consequently, I did not know my I. Q. Believing that he knew so much about I. Q., I requested him to supervise my research study. He accepted.

Granted that the course was a three hundred level i.e., doctoral course, he raised no objections. When I completed my research, I became convinced that I. Q. is neither the quotient of intelligence nor constant as they claimed. I. Q. changes, which is why the tests are revised as often as they are. One of the studies I read was done in Washington State. Two locations, one on the hills and the other in the valley, were studied for some time. Development started in the valley, where roads and schools were built first. The children in the valley scored far higher I.Q. than the children on the hills. As development extended to the hills, the gap closed. Another study about Australian immigrants in the USA showed a reduction in the differences between dominant and minority groups. These scores about the same I.Q. proved that the claim that I.Q. does not change was based on the misinterpretation of data. Even more interesting to me was that creative people do not score very high I.Q. I walked into the office of my supervisor and said, "Dr. Orton, what you call intelligence test I can now call cultural test." I did not know that I broke the eleventh commandment. After he read my paper, he said, "Though you ran into 'pretty' studies, I Q. is still authentic." He accused me of wanting to throw away what they had without replacing it and gave me a C for a grade. That contributed to my going to the University of Utah to complete my Ph. D. I have proposed replacements for "what they have." They are found in my books entitled, *ABCD of Intelligence And Behaviors Implications for Education* and *Authentic Intelligence And Functions*. I. Q. is called a misnomer and replaced with Q. I. T., standing for Quotient of Items on the Test.

The year of the celebration of Nebraska's centennial, 1967, arrived, and the State was in a festive mood. The men grew beards. I also did. The Foreign Students Office took a picture of me in my thick beard and in what Nigerians called TOS and sent it along with the information sent to its freshmen. There was a competition for prizes. Some urged me to enter the competition, but I refused.

I was the only African at Lyndon State and a member of a handful of blacks that never exceeded five in any given semester. When compared with Nebraska, one could say that I arrived in Africa. There were about twelve Nigerians, seven of them were Igbos and there were three more Igbo students at Union (an SDA) College. There were about four Yoruba men and women and an Efik woman. Oh yes, I almost forgot two couples from Bendel State of Nigeria. There were others from other parts of Africa. Some parliamentarians from West Africa touring the U.S. visited Lincoln. African students at the University had an evening with them. Accompanying them were some Nebraska legislators. The pictures of how Africa is portrayed in the movies one watched on the television were disgusting. I asked them why these moviemakers did not film the cities as they filmed the "jungles?"

One of them took offense and barked, "We were here before you. You don't want us to be friendly?" One of the Nebraska legislators intervened. "He is not asking you not to be friendly. He wants the facts to be balanced." The man had nothing more to say.

With so many Igbo students at hand, we organized the Biafra Students Association, which was later on changed to Biafra Association because there were other Biafrans in Nebraska who were not students. John Aniaza was elected the first President, and I was the Secretary. We received the bad news that Nigerian soldiers entered the university town of Nsukka and used the library books as firewood to cook goat meat. Biafrans referred to them as barbarians. Somehow, there was some good news from some other sectors reported in the London Sunday Times.

I applied for the position of a Graduate Assistant in the department before the end of my first academic year and got it. That reduced the number of hours I worked in a week. It also provided time for me to be effective as the Secretary. I wrote a short history of Nigeria to show the consistency of the British policy of divide and rule, which led to the war. The same policy guided its actions during the war. It was fighting the war to maintain its hold in Nigeria. The Soviet Union was, unfortunately, supplying arms to Nigeria in competition with Britain to have influence in Nigeria. Then, I requested that departments and individual lecturers donate books to the University of Nigeria, Nsukka library. John walked to my office one day and read the paper I had written. He congratulated me on the paper and encouraged me to send it to other departments. Soon, there were books everywhere.

It was not long before I received two letters, one from New York and the other from Michigan. New York proposed a national conference of all Biafra Association branches in the U. S. to be held in New York City. In reply, I supported the idea of the conference but suggested Chicago because of its central location, which is in place of

New York City. The letter from Michigan complained about Mba Uzoukwu. I could not believe there would be two men bearing exactly the same name. I wrote Mba and asked if he was another Mba Uzoukwu or "the Mba" from my village. I knew he laughed his head off when he read the letter. New York replied and changed the venue to Chicago.

My next letter was to President Johnson. When he failed to reply, I complained to my friend Frank Marsh, the Nebraska Secretary of State, a Democrat. All I asked was for the U.S. to intervene and bring a peaceful resolution to the war in Nigeria. Mr. Marsh took the letter and sent it. I received a reply from him. In my naivety, I learned that the U.S. does not interfere in British affairs. Egypt flew Nigerian war planes against Biafra. I wrote Golda Meir, the Prime Minister of Israel, and complained that Egypt was using Biafra to train its pilots. She thanked me in her reply. On one of those rare evenings when I watched the news, I heard Eric S. of CBS tell one more lie about Africa. The first time was his statement that Lumumba was killing every educated person in his country. This time, he claimed that the Igbos killed the most popular politician in Nigeria. So, they merited the killings they got. Mrs. Ritzman said when she heard him, "Obed will write him." I did not disappoint her. I wrote a few Senators, including Fulbright, the chair of the Foreign Affairs Committee. Mrs. Ritzman used to say, "I wish we could use our pens the way you do."

Many in my evening class, including the professor, knew that I came from Biafra. In response to the professor's request, I lectured the class on the war between Biafra and Nigeria. A short time after, someone from the Peace Corps came to recruit. I knew many of the students doubted the facts I presented to the class. The man did not know that I was from Biafra, nor did he know that I had lectured the class on the causes of the war. There, he was trying to justify the need for them to become Peace Corps and citing examples. He claimed that they set the world on fire. South America and Nigeria were good examples. He claimed that the Igbo people in Nigeria were educated, occupied government positions, and owned properties. They set the northern people against them. The students went from giggling to laughing. He stopped and asked what the matter was and was embarrassed to know that I was Igbo. He quickly switched to South America. I wondered what this white American would do if the Indians, blacks, Asians and other minority races in the U.S. join forces and attack the whites because they are the educated and owned the property in the U.S. When I sat on the pew on Sunday, Reverend Berg preached on prejudice. I remembered the suffering of the Igbo people in Nigeria because of British and Western prejudice against them and wiped my tears with my handkerchief. I dashed out immediately the service was over. Someone must have seen me wipe off the tears and reported to the clergy. Later on that day, the associate pastor came to see me. By then I had recovered.

Finally, the day of the conference arrived, and I represented Nebraska at Chicago. The national executive had received a record of General Ojukwu's speech and the Biafra national anthem and brought them to the conference. We had a surprise visitor in the person of Dr. Mbadiwe. Mbadiwe was the Federal Minister of Trade in the Old Republic. He claimed to be the the personal representative of General Ojukwu, the Head of State. What do you know? My eyes were looking at Mba from my village and Comfort Nwagbara of Amachara. It was a successful conference. We raised money for Biafra and made decisions on how to proceed. Towards the end, we danced, and my partner was a woman from Ubakala, a village that is about four miles from mine. I invited her to Lincoln.

The woman came the following weekend. I had completed my master's program and enrolled in courses for the Ph.D. I was ready to get married. She was ready to get married that day. But the story she told me threw a sheet of ice on the idea. She came to the United States from London. She was married to an Igbo man who became mentally sick. She did not even send him back to his parents. She left him there and came to Chicago. I thought she had a mental problem of her own. I wondered if she would leave me and fly to Paris if I got sick instead of sending me home to my people. When I drove her to the railway station that day, it was the end.

I came home one day, and a letter was waiting for me. It was from Nwabuisi in Springfield, Massachusetts. He had also completed his master's program and planned to travel to Canada. However, he wished to see the U.S. first. He planned to be in my apartment on a certain date. When he arrived, he was as "sick as a dog" with the flu. My white neighbor from across the street invited me to dinner. A family of five with three hungry boys. I thought that they might have cooked for six but not for seven. I declined the offer and explained why. They would not take no for an answer. We went and had an enjoyable evening.

Nwabuisi and I slept on the same bed for the short time he was with me. I breathed in all his germs. Within a few days after he left, I was as sick as I had never been since I arrived in the States. I could not move and had no appetite for food. News reached the foreign students' office. Mrs. Boykin, the female student advisor and the daughter of my landlady, heard about it and came to my aid. By then, I was recovering. I was on my bed when she walked in. She wanted to know how I was doing and what I wanted for food. I requested donuts. She smiled and bought me donuts. About two days later, I was up and did one of those Obed things. I went to the standing mirror to look at myself. I said, "Let me see how I would have looked if I were dead." At first, I looked serious. Then, on second thought, I convinced myself that I would have a smile on my face. I smiled a bit and said, "That's better." Meanwhile, knowledge of my request for donuts made news at the foreign student's office. The familiar roaring laughter of the young women in the office greeted me as I walked in. I thought they were cheering my recovery. No, it was my request for donuts. "Of all things you could ask for, you asked for donuts?" they asked in unison. I simply laughed along with them.

Mr. Tieman was the Republican Governor of Nebraska. He invited the foreign students to the Governor's Mansion. That might have been the tradition in Lincoln. We enjoyed the day. The Biafra Nigeria war was heating up. The Biafra Association in America decided to celebrate the first independence anniversary. We ordered a large Biafra flag and invited many people. It was successful. The Nigerian Embassy in Washington, DC, must have heard about it and asked Nigerians in Lincoln to organize a similar gathering. It sent a representative. They also had a sizeable audience.

Mr. and Mrs. Frey, who attended Trinity Methodist, invited me to a dinner one evening. Also, at the dinner were two of their daughters and one boyfriend. It was a lovely evening. After a while, I excused myself. I was driving to the university library when I turned on my car radio and heard that Dr. King Jr. was shot. I turned and drove back to my apartment. His death was confirmed later.

There were four Nigerian couples in Lincoln, including Sydney and his wife. There were also two single women from Nigeria, but they were not Igbos. I was interested and determined to marry an Igbo woman. I asked Sydney and his wife to help find one. His wife was more than happy to do so because she had a friend in the east who had visited them the previous year. She promised to invite her for a visit. The reply was disappointing. She got pregnant and had to marry the man. I invited the Yoruba woman out and could not hold her hand and did not shake her hand. Then, a Biafran couple on study leave invited the Anang woman I knew was interested in me to dinner in their apartment. Though I gave her a ride to and from, I did not think we were made for each other. I wrote Chikara, my cousin in London. I knew a student in London from Umukabia whose father was a friend of Uncle Onwumere and worked with him for the railways. Daa Igbenma an aunt was married at Umukabia. So, I wrote Chikara, my cousin, to locate the student since he also lived in London. When that failed, Sydney volunteered to write to his sister, who also lived in London. It was easier to find Igbo women in Britain than in the U.S. He wrote his sister, but the reply was not forth coming. Having completed my master's degree, I was determined to find a wife. But I could not find one within the boundary I set.

A few days before the 1968 Nebraska Democratic Presidential Primary, Rita asked me to be a member of the panel to discuss election returns. I was surprised that I was the only student on the panel. Another surprise was the presence of a British parliamentarian. In a chat before the discussion, he said that the Biafrans knew what they were doing and expressed doubt that Nigeria could defeat them without outside help. Senator Kennedy won the primary in Nebraska and flew to California after. He also won the primary there but tragically was shot the same night. He died the following day.

I had my run-ins with animals in Lincoln. First, it was my monkey. One of the monkeys scratched me. I went to the University hospital and was treated. When I was returning home on a Saturday morning, a small dog bit me. The woman who owned the dog pleaded, and I went back to the clinic. As the nurse treated me, I said, "I hope I don't come back with a chicken bite next time." She could not contain her laughter. Then came the biggest animal, a policeman. The side of the city I lived in was not only black-free, but it was also poor white-free. It was Spring, and I was walking home. A policeman on a motorcycle saw me and stopped. He walked towards me and ordered me to identify myself.

I knew the only reason he had for stopping me was my color. There I was a Biafran, a country the United States did not recognize and without a passport. I was left with nothing else but to comply. I took out my wallet and gave him my university ID card. He read it and saw that I was a graduate student with a name he could not pronounce and was less than one hundred yards from my address. His demeanor changed. He handed the card back to me and muttered, "Thank you, Sir. We want to make sure that you people in this area are protected." I walked away without a word.

As I walked home, I was angry that a policeman stopped me simply because I am black. If I had a car I would have driven back to the University to report. I did not have a telephone either. That was my first business the following day. Without a delay, the Foreign Students Office complained to the police and received an apology and a promise. Another American white saw me walking home and said to me, "You are not an American black. Where are you from?" Looking at him with misgiving, I asked him what he meant. He claimed that I walked like an African. His curiosity was satisfied when he learned that I was from Biafra.

During my first summer in Lincoln, I registered for a driver's license course. At the middle of the course the two physical education graduate students who were my instructors decided to play a joke on me. They drove me to the licensing office and told me to take the test. I thought they were kidding. But they were serious. I took the written test and passed. A police officer entered the car, they drove to the place, and asked me to drive. When we came back, he said I passed. My instructors were more surprised than I was. "Obed you passed!" I asked if that was not why they took me there?" "No. We brought you to have an experience for the real thing." They allowed me to drive the car to their department. That was the end of my course.

After suffering through two cold snowy winter seasons and police harassment, I decided to buy a car. I could no longer go on helping my brother without thinking of myself. I grew tired of waiting for the bus in the cold snow. I asked Mr. Ritzman to help me buy a car. He gladly accepted and found a used Ford Galaxy 500 for me. I paid $700 for it. I had a minor accident the day I took possession of it. That was the only accident I had during my driving days that I caused. Only some of the young women at the Foreign Students office jokingly muted a complaint about my driving.

By the middle of the Spring Semester, the chairman of the department called me and told me that I was not admitted to the doctoral program and that even if I decided to do another master's program, Dr. Orton would not be my advisor. I told him that I would never ever consider another master's program. Mother Krider asked me to apply to the University of Utah. I did and asked her, the chairman of the department, and my boss in the department, Professor Kirken to write letters of recommendation for me. They did. Soon I received a letter of admission from the University. It was like a repeat of my experience at Lyndon. We used a book by the chairman of the Department of Educational Psychology and Measurements at the University of Nebraska. He left the department the year I arrived. Dr. Orton used a book, Essentials of Educational Studies, written by the Director of the Bureau of Education, which is a part of the Department of Educational Psychology at the University of Utah. But he was not there when I arrived. I had to wait till after graduation before I moved.

John was not re-elected as the President of the Biafra Association in Nebraska. Someone else replaced him. I retained my position as the secretary. All of a sudden it seemed that the war had turned in favor of Biafra. We heard that Biafran forces had liberated Bendel State and declared it the Republic of Benin. But instead of marching to Lagos, they waited. Later we learned that they waited for the Yoruba western state to declare its independence. But that never happened. I packed all the books I collected for the University of Nigeria, Nsukka, and all items that belonged to the Association and gave them over to the President. Also, I discovered that of the three Biafrans at Union College, one of them, George Anyataonwu, attended Uzuakoli HEC right after my class. We became friends. He was graduating from Union College that Spring and had applied to the University of Nebraska for graduate study. Like Uzuakoli he would come after I left.

Graduation day came and I was happy to receive my M.A. in Educational Psychology and Measurements. The state awarded me my second honorary citizenship, this time with the other graduating foreign students. I left the department that day and did not go back until two years later when I returned as Dr. Onwuegbu, with the Ph.D. behind my name. I learned later that I was expected to work for my boss that summer. I looked for a summer job but did not succeed. There was a permanent job in my field that was offered to me. But how could I work for two months and make them start another search for a replacement? I told the office my plan. They thanked me. I spent the summer without a job.

I did it again. Though I was not sure of my financial future I sent money to my brother when I wrote to tell him about my graduation. I was extremely thankful to God to hear that he received the $150 before he left Lagos to return to Umuahia. I had not serviced my car since I bought it. It had no seat belts either. Up to that point, I had not driven on the highway, and I was going to Salt Lake City from Lincoln through Highway I-80 West. I decided to service the car and put a seat belt on the driver's seat and did so.

I wrote to a few people at Lyndon, including Dr. Long, the President, and Mother Mac. My favorite sentence was, "I think Obed I. Onwuegbu, Ph.D., will look nice to read." As I wrote it, I remembered one of my tutors at ETC Uzuakoli. He had no degree. He said there was no comma after his name. It was Mr. Achinefu's period.

Once again, I chose to leave in the last week of August. For the first time, I heard about the Utah Mormons. My landlady, who was white and, in her eighties, expressed concern about the Mormons in Utah. "I shall not rent your apartment. If you get there and those Mormons don't like you, come back. It will be here for you." I thanked her and wondered who the Mormons were. The funny side of the story was that they had horns. But it sounded like a fact. I thought about when they told me in Vermont that I was going to Indian country as I prepared to go to Nebraska.

Right about the time I was ready to leave, Sydney's sister in London asked a woman from their village in London to write to me. She was a nurse and looked like her brother who was two years my senior at Mission Hill. Even if I had time to write her, I had no address since I was moving to Salt Lake City. Therefore, I did not write. But in a way, I had been inadvertently rebellious to the dream God showed me about who He made for me for a wife. One might say God was getting me prepared to meet my wife. Before I left Lincoln, I said to Sydney that I would not marry anyone with less than a master's degree. The night of departure arrived, and I packed much of my belongings in the trunk of my car. When I went to bed that night, I was almost ready to travel.

Chapter 27

Salt Lake Bound

Early on a Thursday morning, I packed whatever belongings remained in the back seat of my car and drove off. Before I drove out of the city of Lincoln, I filled my tank and drove to I-80 W. I was on my way to the University of Utah in Salt Lake City. My journey since I came to the U.S. continued to be westward. I was still on the road at midafternoon without stopping to eat. Somehow in my attempt to find a place to eat, I left I-80. Tired and wobbling on this less traveled road, the driver in the car behind me blew his horn to warn me. I drove to the side and parked.

I discovered I was in Wyoming. After a few minutes' rest, I drove off again. I found a place and ate and looked for a place to spend the night. I spent the night in Wyoming. After a good night's rest and sleep, I was on my way to Salt Lake City. I saw the colorful University of Wyoming buildings and was impressed, almost wishing I was going there. Soon I was back on I-80 W again. It was after midafternoon when I reached the University of Utah. By asking questions I found the housing office. They gave me a listing of apartments for rent. My people say that someone who asks for directions does not get lost. My questions led me to the student cafeteria, where I ordered and ate my dinner.

Looking through the list and not knowing how far or near to the University the apartments were, my only guide was the price. One at $35 attracted my attention. Yet I was mindful of the possibility that "Mormons with horns" could say no to this black student. So, I called, the phone rang, and Mrs. Hooten answered the phone. I said, "This is an African graduate student. The University gave me your number. Is it against your religion to rent your apartment to a black graduate student?" There was a long silence followed by, "You can come to see it." The address said 3300 South and some number on 2700 East. By the time I found the address it was late evening. When I rang the doorbell, Mrs. Hooten came out to meet me. We greeted, and she took me to see the one-room apartment. As she showed me the apartment and I looked it over, she said, "It is getting too late for you to continue looking today. Even if you don't like it, you can sleep here tonight. But if you like it, I will take off $5, and you pay me $30 since you will drive to the University every day." I thanked her and assured her that I liked the place. I unloaded and stretched out the hideaway bed. It looked nice and I settled for the night.

The following day was Saturday, and I determined to see if there was a Methodist church in Mormon land. There was a church building across the street from where I now lived, but it was not a Methodist church. I drove off. A few blocks later, on 3300 South and 2300 East, I saw a lovely building that said, Christ Methodist. I could not be nearer to a church than that, even if I planned it. What do you know? The stores to buy my food and other things were only a few blocks away from the church building on the same 3300 South. I drove back to the apartment, pleased and thankful to God that I was well located. Sunday came, and I wore my TOS Benson clothes to Christ Methodist Church. Reverend Yelken walked down to my seat, introduced himself, and greeted me. Christ Methodist became my church for the next two years. I became an active member. I taught Sunday School and belonged to the College and Career Group of the church. This was a group of young adults who were in college or had graduated and were working but not married. But a married couple, George and Linda Rathbun, led the group.

Monday was orientation for foreign students. To my great surprise I was subjected to a test in the English language. After the result they suggested that I teach English as a second language. I declined the offer. I registered for twelve hours, the normal graduate full load. For the first time since my arrival in the States, I found myself in a term instead of a semester system.

Unlike Nebraska, where there were many Biafrans and Africans, I was the only Biafran at the University of Utah, and about three other African students. Also, there was Oscar, an Anang from Cross River State of Nigeria, who was also a Mormon. That meant I was left to make the case for Biafra alone in Salt Lake City. I debated two American college history professors. One of them claimed that America was not even ready to rule herself when she declared independence from Britain. Therefore, Biafra should not declare itself independent no matter what. I thought the argument made him look foolish. But I could not tell him that with the camera on.

Mr. Warsaw, who owned a store chain, raised funds he said were for both Biafran and Nigerian children, though I was the guest of honor. Some organizations, including my church, invited me to lecture them on the Biafra Nigeria War and I accepted. Nixon campaigned and won the Republican presidential nomination and the presidency by promising to end the genocide in Biafra. But once he won and became the President, he forgot Biafra.

The College and Career Group took an overnight trip to Arches National Monument. I used to fly with my hands as my wings in my dreams while I was in Nigeria. This place looked like where I flew over. When it was time to go to sleep, these Americans spread their sleeping bags on the ground. This Biafran refused to lie on the ground. I spread my sleeping bag on the top of the picnic table and refused to sleep on the ground. The Americans could not believe that I was afraid to sleep on the ground having come from Africa (the jungles). But I refused because of snakes and crawling insects. However, they got over it. In our small College and Career group were at least five women two of whom were teachers. Two of them were also named Sue. One Sue was a teacher and her career appealed to me. However, I was attracted to the other Sue who was still a business student. Also, I liked her contributions during the discussions. The International Students Organization planned an end-of-term get-together, and I invited Sue Williams, the student, to go with me. She accepted. At the end, I took her home with a handshake. I believe she enjoyed herself. Then the group asked me to speak about the conflict between Biafra and Nigeria and invited people from First Methodist also in Salt Lake City. Only two women came from there. One of them was a teacher and graduated with her bachelor's degree the same year I did. She lamented that she came from Wyoming and, for the years she had been in Salt Lake, had not had a date. They left after my lecture. I walked out to get her phone number only to see her car leaving the church premises.

Meanwhile, I developed an interest in Sue Williams and asked her for a date. We went to my little apartment first. She cooked this spaghetti that tasted as though it was out of this world. My people say that the way to a man's heart is through his stomach. I thought God had found me a wife. After eating we went and saw the movie Gone With The Wind. This time we kissed goodnight.

Sue Williams was also the most beautiful among the women in the group. I asked her in my nonceremonial way to marry me. She said, "I love you but not for marriage." I did not know that she had a soldier boyfriend in Vietnam. In the meantime, I wrote the nurse in Britain. She replied and enclosed her picture. I replied without my picture. I warned her that when she got my picture, she should not think I was as handsome as the picture depicted me. Emedom, my best friend, said I look better in the picture. I also wanted to know if she attended Mission Hill. She did not.

Though I was the only Biafran in Salt Lake City, it was not too long before I discovered two families who were like family to me. One was Bud Krider who was Mother Krider's son and his family. The next was Bob Downing and his family. Bob was the grandson of my landlady in Lincoln Nebraska. These two visited me and invited me to their homes. Mother Krider came to Salt Lake that Christmas and visited me. I showed her my grades, and they were all A's. She was so proud she almost took the card to show them at her department meeting in Lincoln. Dr. Della-Piana offered me a position as a research assistant in the Bureau of Educational Research of the department. There were three of us in the office. I had met Muffin and someone I thought was her boyfriend at the international students meeting. She showed up in this general office one day. I learned that she was a Roman Catholic. I know that Roman Catholics want you to join their denomination before any marriage can take place. I invited her to go to Christ Methodist with me. She declined. Once in a while we saw each other and greeted. Sue continued to say that her love for me was not for marriage and even announced to the group that she was going back to Washington, DC where she worked for the FBI after high school before she came back to go to college. We were still good friends.

I attended black students meeting on campus. The presiding president was beautiful. I took her name. At the beginning of the second term, when I called her, she had dropped out of school. I was more annoyed than sympathetic. What is the matter with these people? They would not stay in school, yet when they see you with a white woman they cry. I was sleeping in my room one afternoon when the door opened, and I heard my name. It was Muffin. We talked for a few minutes, and she left.

By this time the war between Biafra and Nigeria was raging on. Only four African countries had recognized Biafra and none outside

Africa. The late Dr. Julius Nyerere, the President of Tanzania, whose government was one of the four, issued his famous factual statement. "The OAU represents more foreign interests than African interests." The OAU was to meet in Algiers, the capital of Algeria, that year, 1969. I wrote the members suggesting that they meet their obligation by finding a peaceful resolution to end the war. I suggested a number of things they could do. An African geology graduate student, who said he was worried that I was going to flunk out because each time he saw me I was playing bridge, came to me at the end of the term. He wanted to know what grades I got. He could not believe that I made all A's. I gave him a copy of my letter to the OAU. He read it and wept. "You are an African and this smart, and you will not be the president of Nigeria one day because you are not corrupt and do not have the money to buy votes." The conference ended without a resolution on the war. People continued to suffer and die while oil companies and the West calculated their profits.

By the middle of the third term of my first year at the University of Utah, organizations were electing officers. As I walked out of the library, MaryAnn, the current President of the International Students Club, and her friend met me. They wanted to know what my GPA was. I asked, "What!" They knew what I meant and pleaded. "Please tell us because we want someone to run for the office of the President of the Club. Muffin's boyfriend may win it and we don't want him to be the President." All the women, including Muffin, were political science majors. Still unwilling to run, I told them I did not have the time to campaign because of my involvement in the course of Biafra. They would not take no for an answer but insisted on knowing my GPA. "It is 4.0". "Wow!" they shouted and asked me to leave the campaign to them. Several weeks later they called me and told me I had been elected the President. I accepted.

I am determined to complete my doctorate program in two years. I had developed a real interest in the psychology of human development and learning. Also, my interests in science and mathematics were yearning for satisfaction. I registered for a course Dr. Woodruff taught on teaching. At first, I asked many questions that sounded like debates. Privately some of the women, who probably were teachers, urged me to continue to ask him those questions. Before the end of the course, I fell in love with both him and the course. I got an A for the course and took my card of all A's to him and requested him to be the chair of my doctoral committee. He accepted. When I told Dan, another doctoral candidate in the department who was there when I came, that Dr. Woodruff agreed to chair my committee, he asked if I was out of my mind. How can you satisfy him? He claimed that Dr. Woodruff knew his subject so well he did not know how to teach it.

The doctoral committee comprised five members, three of whom came from my department and two from outside the department. Dr. James of the department of education taught a course on how to teach science and I took and enjoyed it. I also took a course on how to teach mathematics. I recruited the two to my committee. My boss, Dr. Della Piana, was also a member of my committee, and so was Dr. Sloane. I chose my topic for my dissertation, presented and started to work on it. Some told me to complete my coursework first. I ignored their advice.

Dr. Sloane called me one day. I was surprised when he asked if I was prejudiced against white women. I said yes if they are ugly. He gave me a name, telephone number and an address. Is it called a blind date? When I picked her up, the first few sentences that came out of her mouth spelled trouble. She was a graduate student. She said her parents told her that she was smart, and she knew she was not. They told her she was beautiful, and she knew she was not, and she did not trust them. Then she looked at me and declared, "I don't trust you." I thought, "Am I supposed to work for your trust?" I asked her, "Do you want to go home?" She said, "Yes," so I took her home and left her to report to Dr. Sloane.

The International Students Club was mainly run by the President and an adviser named Mod. It took students to the copper mine for orientation and had a day designated as an International Day. I retained the visit to the mine. When compared with Nebraska there were not many countries represented at the University of Utah. It was not surprising because no matter what race one was, as long as one was not a Mormon, one was a Gentile and did not count. It was so bad that when I assumed the office of the president of the International Students' Club and was invited to speak at a gathering, I said to the audience, "It is better you don't admit international students to this university than admit them and discriminate against them. These are people who are going to be leaders in their own countries. You make more friends for the Soviet Union than you'll ever know." At the end of the gathering, a man came and asked me if I needed any financial assistance. I said, "No." I reorganized the club. My Executive Committee included the President and Secretary of every international club on campus that the University recognized. The International Day was extended to International Week. Different nations were assigned different days of the week. Saturday was the last day, and every nation had a booth and presented different dishes. Students borrowed films from their embassies. One of the outcomes of the international week was a cookbook of international dishes. However, the jewel of my tenure was a radio program I entitled, "They Came To the U." Once a week, a different international student discussed the culture of his or her country to educate Utahans.

I came out of a building one day, started my car and shifted the gear to reverse, and it would not move. I did not know that cars need maintenance. I discovered there was no oil for it to operate. Someone helped me push the car out. I drove to a gas station and learned that cars needed to be maintained. They also changed the oil, but by then, the engine was leaking oil. I borrowed $200 from the church for the repair. The Minister hesitated and asked how I intended to pay it back. When he learned that I worked, he gave it to me. I paid back my first debt in time.

Every person in the College and Career group knew that Sue Williams and I were friends but did not know to what extent. The international students scheduled an important get-together. I asked Sue Williams to go with me. She said she was studying for her tests. I asked Sue Arnot and she agreed. At the eleventh-hour Sue Williams called and said she would go. There would not be enough women at the party, so I took the two. At the end of the party, I dropped off Sue Williams and Sue Arnot and I went to my apartment. She asked me if I drank beer, and my answer was "no." She wanted to know if I held it against someone who drank. Again, my answer was no. Since I did not have a beer, I volunteered to take her home. She wanted to know if I would like to go to the university theater if she bought season tickets. She was a teacher, and I, as a student, could not afford it. I came home from school one day and there was a small box at my door. When I opened it, there was a small animal made of chocolate for Valentine. Muffin brought it and left it at the door.

We learned that life in Biafra was getting worse instead of better. As the secretary of the Biafra Association in Nebraska, such information came through me. As poor as I was, I sent my brother fifty dollars. His reply seemed like God made me send the money. He told me that he used two hundred forty Biafran pounds of the money ($10) to bail his wife from jail. I thanked God that the money solved a real problem.

Not surprising, Biafra could not fight Britain, Nigeria, Egyptian pilots, the Soviet Union, and American tactical support and win the war. Biafra destroyed the Onitsha Bridge with hundreds of Nigerian soldiers and equipment on it. Most of them perished. All of a sudden, Nixon, who campaigned on stopping the war of genocide in

Biafra, was talking about sending help to Nigeria to repair the Onitsha Bridge. I wrote to him and told him what I thought. When he failed to reply, I wrote to Dr. Billy Graham, who I understood was his spiritual adviser. I got a reply that did not address my concern.

The London Sunday Times was my main source of news about the war. At one time it had a picture of a Nigerian soldier, Biafran soldiers captured. He claimed that they were told that Biafra was defeated and that they were going to keep the peace. Then, the son of Churchill, who was a journalist, interviewed General Ojukwu, who told him that things were looking better for Biafra in the Owerri sector. After I returned to Nigeria, a Nigerian Major told me that Biafran forces encircled the Nigerian army at Owerri. If Biafra had captured them, the war would have ended there with a disastrous defeat for Nigeria. But Biafra did not have the weapons.

Sue was still hesitant. One evening she was going home from work and stopped by. The phone rang and I picked it up. It was Muffin at the other end. Once Sue heard who was on the phone, she perked her ears up and stood behind me. I said, "Hi politician." She said, "I am not a politician. I am a woman." She claimed her womanhood several times and hung up. Sue left without any comment. Later she agreed to marry me and told me about the conversation between her and her mother. She went home angry at the woman. Her mother told her that as long as we were not married or even engaged every woman had a right to pursue me. I tried to give Muffin some hope. I asked Sue to marry me, but she did not say yes. She said, "But you have asked the big question." Finally, Sue said yes. Shortly after she said yes, a woman stopped me and introduced herself.

She was a graduate student and had been a Peace Corp in Gabon West Africa. She met a few Biafrans there and they were eager to return to Biafra to fight. She came from California and invited me to visit her to introduce me to her landlady. When I asked where she knew me, she said she was in the class I lectured. I was annoyed with her but did not show it. "Have you not seen me since then? I took the piece of paper with her name and telephone number. Too late, I thought, and never called her.

There was one more episode before Sue said yes. Her boyfriend, who was in Vietnam, returned from the war and wrote her. He addressed her as an angel. I busted her bubble when I said, you are Sue, not an angel. She came over one Friday evening for what she thought was the last time we would see as friends. She heard the soldier boy had called in her absence. We said our goodbye, called a breakup. Saturday morning, I was outside talking with the daughter of my landlord when Sue showed up with her hair in curlers. There was a change of mind. She would marry me after all. God had ordained it. We started all over again less than twenty-four hours after the breakup.

After she agreed to marry me, I called Bob Downing, the grandson of my landlady in Lincoln, to help me choose a diamond ring for her. Bob obliged, though he was home with MS. We chose the one I could afford, but it was beautiful, attractive, and looked delicate. She came in one evening on her way from work. We were standing and talking when I took her left hand towards her back and slipped the ring on her finger. She swung the arm in front and there was the diamond. We kissed and hugged. She drove home and my phone rang. It was her mother with a thank you. A day or so later the other Sue called and congratulated me. She said she knew it would happen. She said she knew she was not returning to DC. She added, "Elliot and I just broke up." Elliot was a member of the College and Career group.

My fiancé was a good student and liked by the college administration. She would graduate at the end of the semester, and they were interested in offering her an appointment. The FBI office in Washington DC she worked for before she returned to Salt Lake to attend college was also interested in getting her back. Though the College offered her a job she seemed more interested in the FBI job. She said to me,

"Let me go to DC. Maybe when I get there, I will feel miserable. Then I will come back." My reply was simple. "There are two things, Washington and me. You can't have both of them. You can have Washington or me. So, make your choice." She accepted the offer at her college. Then we had the last trial on her graduation day. The ceremony was over, and she walked alone in the hall filled with people. I walked to her and spoke to her. She ignored me acting as though she never met me in her life. I thought this woman was wearing my ring and she was ashamed to talk to me before people from her college. She would not walk with me in public. I decided to terminate the relationship. I left and changed her picture with the picture of the Nigerian nurse in Britain. She came to my apartment in my absence and saw the picture. She replaced the picture with her picture and wrote, "I love you!" That was our last hurdle. We set our wedding date a week later than we originally planned. Knowing the many deaths on Labor Day weekend, I refused to die on the road. We chose September 5 for our wedding date.

    My apartment was advertised for nonsmokers and nondrinkers. I did none of those nor did my fiancé. For some reason, I came home early one afternoon, and there was my landlord in front of the pool at my front door smoking. The Mormon was distraught to see me. Throwing away the cigarette was not an option. He muttered at my greeting. I wondered why a man probably in his late fifties would be hiding to smoke. I believed he planned to catch me red-handed doing something as I caught him smoking. Sweetie, my fiancé, the name I called her, and I were quietly eating the food she prepared. Without any knock, the door opened. When we looked, there he was staring at us and, without any greeting, passed and took a jar of fruit and left. I told Sweetie what I thought he was about.

    As we prepared to wed, I asked Bob to be my best man. He agreed. I asked George Rathbun, the leader of the college and career group, and Oscar Udo, a Nigerian of Anang tribe and a student at the

U, to be the groomsmen. Kay, my sister in-law, was the maid of honor. Joy and Kathy, Sweetie's friends, were the bridesmaids. Christ Methodist women provided the meal. A number of things were new at our wedding.

Mother and Father Krider flew in from Nebraska to represent my parents at the wedding. Mother Krider said to me as we took the family picture, "Two years ago, this could not have happened here." That was because only two years before did the U.S. Supreme Court rule that black and white marriages were legal. The tuxedos my best man and I wore, were white jackets and black pants and were a new style. The shape of our cake was experimental also. About a month before the wedding, we thought we would go to California for our honeymoon. My soon-to-be bride looked at my Galaxy 500 oil-leaking car and said, "This car cannot take us to California, let alone bring us back." I started to look for a car in different lots. While searching, God intervened again. Sweetie's neighbor Jayne Riccardi heard about an older woman who owned a Chevy Malibu with about 5,000 miles on it. She said that she paid $3100 for it but discovered the car had more power than she could handle. She wanted $2300 for it. I agreed to buy it and learned a shocking lesson. What is honorable in Nigeria is a discredit in America. One has to be a debtor in America to be creditworthy. Banks would not lend me money because I had not borrowed or owed money before. Then I learned about the University Credit Union. Even more important, I was told that I could join it that day and borrow money the same day. I did both and paid for the car. I had to sell my Ford. I drove to a lot. The owner of the lot looked at the body and refused to have anything to do with it. He watched as I started the car. The sound of the engine attracted his attention. He told me to stop. When I stopped moving, he listened to the engine more and asked how much I wanted. He would only pay $200. I sold it to him. He drove me home and asked why I sold it. I showed him my Malibu when he dropped me off.

Knowing that my fiancé recently graduated, and I was in debt, we changed our honeymoon plan. Instead of going to California, we chose to go to Yellowstone National Park. As expected, the wedding was beautiful. Being in Salt Lake, there were only two black faces: Oscar and me. Dr. Woodruff, some people from her college, including her boss, MaryAnn, and a few people from the International Students Office, most members of the church, and students, were present. Almost all the guests stayed as long as we were there. Finally, we cut the cake and I gentlemanly helped Sweetie to eat her cake. Like the sweet angel she became after we got married, she gently put my cake in my mouth. The guests were still there when we left and went to the place where we had hidden our car. Note: Two weeks before our wedding date, I received a letter from Chikara, my cousin in London. This is the relative I tried to find all these years but failed. Reverend Igwe had traveled from Biafra to London and my brother gave him my address in Salt Lake City. He also enclosed his phone number. I called him and we spoke for three minutes. Marrying an Igbo woman was out of the question. End of note.

We went to Bob Downing's home and got our car. Arriving at a hotel in Salt Lake where we thought we had booked to spend the night, we discovered it was the wrong hotel, and it had just been robbed. We went to the correct hotel where I performed the American ritual of carrying the new bride over the threshold. It was one of the most enjoyable peaceful nights. We ate our breakfast and did a little shopping the following morning and were on our way to Jackson Hole. On our arrival at the motel, I took out the keys from the ignition and gave a pair to Sweetie, saying, "In case I lose mine." I put my pair back in the ignition, stepped out of the car, and locked the door with my pair in the ignition. She saved us from the problem of searching for someone to retrieve our key. Sunday saw us watching the Old Faithful Geyser at Yellowstone. Again, the abstract geography lessons I could not understand in Nigeria came alive. I saw live bears walking with their cubs. On our return, our gifts and other belongings were waiting for us at our new apartment. The College and Career Group also gave us flowers. We were Mr. and Mrs. Onwuegbu in our own apartment. She went to work, and I went to school. Before the term started, I applied to the University for Financial Aid. The office denied my request. The reason it gave was that I bought a car. I continued with my $ 200-a-month research assistant job. In spite of my financial situation, I enclosed $50 in my brother's letter when I informed him of my marriage.

The news about the war between Biafra and Nigeria was getting worse by the day. I dreamed about the defeat of Biafra while I was in Lincoln. I had hoped it would be my one dream that would not come true. But when I read that the Nigerian army was at Aba and Owerri, I knew that my hometown, Umuahia, was next. Though Biafra manufactured some weapons, its own salt, and refined its own oil, it was no match against the forces that defeated Germany and her allies in World War II. Therefore, it was no surprise when, in January 1970, the world heard that Biafra was defeated. Western newsmen and their cameras made fools of themselves as we learned later. To illustrate the starving Biafran children, the newsmen threw candy to the ground. As the children picked up the candies, they took pictures of them. We mourned the loss. The picture prompted us, and I believe other Biafrans outside Nigeria to send money to relatives. Thank God the fear that Nigerians might steal it, was alleviated when my brother wrote to acknowledge receipt of the money. More important his family and my mother were all safe. Our only consolation, if there was any, was that both Dr. Okpara and General Ojukwu were out of the country at the time of surrender. As I said then, I say now, Hannibal saw the head of his brother thrown into his camp and declared, "The doom of Carthage." The defeat of Biafra was the doom of Africa.

Having gone through rote learning in Nigeria and contrasting it with my experience in the U.S., I chose teaching and learning as the topic for my dissertation. The topic agreed with my specialty in the psychology of human development and learning. I had completed my study for my dissertation and was writing it. Sweetie was an expert in typing, and it fell on her to type it. She was cute typing and said the sweetest thing, "I don't know if you married me just to type your dissertation." A little over three months after we got married, she went to her doctor, and he told her she was pregnant. About two months later, one smart-alecky high school student, Paula, at Christ Methodist saw me and said, "Obed see what you did?" I asked her, "What did I do?" She said, "You got Sue pregnant." "No, you did not see well. She ate too much," I replied. But I don't think I convinced her.

As Sweetie typed my dissertation, I prepared my resume. In the midst of it all, we heard from Mr. and Mrs. Ritzman. They were driving from California and would be passing through Salt Lake returning to the Midwest. They wanted to see us but not for lunch. I had my grade sheets spread out when they arrived. He looked at them and, laughing, said, "Obed you had a D- in Art appreciation. I told him why. I left him in the house and took his wife to get my wife from work. Knowing how hard I worked for the cause of Biafra in Lincoln, a good part of our discussion was on that. Sweetie was really pregnant at this time. Food could not be used as an excuse anymore. The three of them got to know a little about themselves before the Ritzman's left.

One of the two institutions I applied to at this early stage was Central Connecticut State College in New Britain. My main reason for applying to the college was its location in the east. I calculated that I was closer to home by a few thousand miles. It did not take long before they called me for an interview and promised to pay the airfare. On arrival at Bradley Airport, Bob Stowe was waiting for me. The interview was conducted on the same day as I requested previously. I flew back to Salt Lake the same day. Within two weeks after, I received an offer as an Assistant Professor. Thus by the end of the first week of March, I had a job, but I would not start until the first day of

September. To graduate I had to complete and defend my dissertation and complete two other courses.

The 1960s and 70s were the era of the Vietnam War and caused unrest in U.S. universities and college campuses. Dr. James Fletcher was the University of Utah President. There were riots on most campuses. He formed the President's Advisory Council made up of all the Presidents of the student organizations the University recognized. I was a member of the Council. That council helped to avert riots at the University of Utah. Once or twice, we met with Governor Rampton. However, I would cease to be a member of both the Council and the International Students Club at graduation.

George Ndo was another doctoral candidate in the department. He shared an office with Keith. I discussed some of my findings with George, and he was helpful. Finally, I discussed my dissertation with Dr. Woodruff, and he was satisfied with it. A date was set for the defense. I saw Dan and told him I was done with writing but did not know what the committee would say. He asked, "Who did you say is your chairman?" "Dr. Woodruff," I replied. "What did he say about it?" "He is all right with it," I replied. He told me to go and relax. "Who can say no to what Woodruff says is ok."

At this time, I had a narrow room as my office. Oscar visited me there while I wrote my dissertation. His wife was pregnant also and he was graduating Ph. D. Sociology the same day with me. His wife gave birth to a baby boy before Sweetie. Unfortunately, the baby died in sleep. I was in my office waiting for Dr. Woodruff on the day of the defense of my dissertation.

By the way, Dr. Woodruff was the Distinguished Professor of the department. Mother Krider called him Dean Woodruff. I assumed he was a Dean at BYU at one time. He called the committee to order and talked for a few minutes and then called me in. I did not spend ten minutes with the committee before he dismissed me. In less than five minutes after, he invited me in with "We are not going to kill you." When I sat down, I was greeted with congratulations. Dr. Woodruff announced my grade, and it was A. I thanked them and walked out Dr. Onwuegbu. I called Sweetie. It is not today that you know who is at the other end before you remove the receiver. When she answered I said, "This is Dr. Onwuegbu." We rejoiced. Her mother was the next person I called. My Sweetie and I went home that day and celebrated with the only thing we could afford, pizza. But we enjoyed it. She thought she was through typing for me. If she meant typing on the typewriter, she was right. Now she types on the computer. A few days later, Dr. James saw me and asked, "Obed, how does it feel to be a doctor?" "I have not experienced any change," was my answer. Before long I received my two remaining grades, and they were A's. I saw Dr. Stone, who gave me the only B I received from the university, and said, "Dr. Stone, do you know that you gave me the only B on my record at this university; the rest are all A's?" With a smile, he said, "That shows you are human." We laughed and parted.

Though I attended Trinity Methodist in Lincoln I did not teach Sunday School. But I preached at Nebraska City on one Student' Sunday. I also preached at Midvale United Methodist Utah and later discovered that was the church the grandparents of my future wife attended.

I encountered the police three times in Salt Lake City. The first time was about two weeks after my arrival. Driving through downtown, I thought I saw a warning for a stop sign and slowed down. When I got to the junction, I did not see the stop sign. There was no vehicle coming from the other roads, so I cautiously drove through the intersection. Once through the intersection a police car was flashing its light behind me. I stopped. Of course, he saw my Nebraska license plate and followed me. He demanded to see my driver's license and I complied. He asked if I saw the stop sign. I said "I looked for it and did not see it. Maybe I should get some glasses." He laughed and drove off. If I thought that all policemen in Salt Lake were gentlemen, I discovered that I fooled myself.

As the President of the University International Students Club, my Executive Committee and I organized a Christmas party that was attended by many students and even parents of American students. I was driving home with Sweetie at the end of the party when a police car saw us and followed us. We were at the center of the intersection when the light turned yellow. He turned on his flashing lights and followed our car. His problem was that he saw a black man with a white woman. In his haste to stop a black man from "kidnapping" a white woman, he failed to see that I wore foreign clothes until he came to my door. "You ran a red light," he said. I asked, "What!" He changed the red light to, "That young girl is almost sitting on your lap." I asked him, "She is sitting on my laps with her seatbelt on? That young girl happens to be my wife." He was dumbfounded and could not say one more word. He went to his car and drove off. The third was a campus police. It was not uncommon that every parking space behind Milton Bennion Hall at the University was taken. In such cases, people waited in their cars, especially if it was toward the end of classes. That was the case the day I waited in my car. The policeman drove to my side and stopped. He ordered me to move my car. I told him why I would not. He gave me the foolish argument that a stopped car is a parked car. Embarrassed by his argument as there were others waiting in their cars, he drove off.

Graduation, wow! God has exceeded every expectation of the night of July 31 when I saw My Savior Jesus Christ in that dream. While on the plane flying to New York, I said to three other Nigerian students with me that it would take me seven years to complete my education. God granted me my request, from October 1963 to June 5, 1970, when I received my Ph. D. The goal had been accomplished. Who is like my Yahweh? The euphoria of being called a doctor was not that fresh because several weeks had passed since I defended the dissertation.

A few days before the big day, I received the gown, the hood and the cap and took pictures. The University requested three names of newspapers that would announce my graduation. It was easy to choose one in Vermont, one in Nebraska, but I reluctantly chose one in Nigeria though I called it Biafra. As we lined up to march in, one question was in my mind. My bachelor's degree said, "rights and privileges." The master's degree added "and honor." I wondered what the doctorate degree will add. As I reached President Fletcher, we recognized each other and smiled broadly. He gave me the diploma cover and we shook hands. When I sat down and opened it the diploma was missing. A minute or two later, a professor from my department walked to me and gave it to me. The addition was "responsibilities." The Ph. D. did not stop me from reading. It started me to read what I want to read and to challenge and correct what I disagree with. When the ceremony was over and my employment ended with the Department of Educational Psychology, Sweetie and I awaited the arrival of our first baby the following month.

Dr. King, who took care of Sweetie during her pregnancy, calculated the delivery date to be July thirteen. So the day came, and I drove Sweetie to the hospital. Gail was his great nurse. It was not until late in the evening when the serious contractions started. But the baby refused to come on the 13th. One of the nurses with us monitored the heartbeat and declared, "This is the heartbeat of a boy, not a girl." The other nurse warned her to watch her mouth. But I had already told Sweetie that my dream predicted a girl. We chose the name Melody Adanma based on the dream. We chose David, should my dream fail to materialize. It was past 11 pm when they asked if I wanted to witness the birth. I hesitated and then said yes. They wheeled her in and gave me a hospital gown to wear. I put it on, and the doctor was by her. They were set and the pushing began. Our Melody came into the world crying at 12:07 am on July 14, 1970. The nurse looked at her and said, "She is hungry and will not wait to be spanked to cry." When they put her on Sweetie's belly and announced, "It's a girl," she looked at me, smiling said, "We'll try again." I knew she meant for a boy, but I thought not now in front of all these people. It surprised me that all the pains vanished at the birth of the baby.

The doctor and nurses performed their duty as I watched. It was time to wheel Sweetie to her room. Passing by the nurses' station, they gave Sweetie a phone to call her parents to tell them they had become grandparents. Once they settled mother and baby I went to my car and drove home oblivious of what I wore. Even after I parked my car and walked into the apartment, I still did not notice what I was wearing. I turned on the light and tried to unbutton my shirt and realized I was still wearing the hospital gown. Puzzled at my blindness all the while, I sat down and had a good laugh. When I took it back later in the day, the nurse said, "You were not nervous, were you." We laughed. When they came home from the hospital we still had until the last week of August before our move to Connecticut.

Relatives and friends came to visit our baby girl. We had not yet informed our landlady of our intention to leave at the end of August because it was still July. Fearing that we might be there for another year she called us the name she gave us, "happy couple" and reminded us that she did not rent the apartment to couples with children. She was happy to learn that we were leaving the last week of August. In the meantime, the many gifts we received at our wedding and baby showers lay waiting to be packed. After taking two weeks of vacation to have the baby, Sweetie returned to work and gave her two weeks' notice of resignation. I took care of the baby. We still attended Christ Methodist through our last Sunday.

On hearing that I was employed to teach in Connecticut, Nancy and Mrs. Ritzman organized a welcoming party in Lincoln. There was a question about where my family and I would stay. I knew we would stay with the Kriders my adopted parents. However, Mrs. Boykin wanted us to stay with her family. I declined the offer though she was the female foreign student adviser and the daughter of my former landlady in Lincoln.

We serviced our Malibu for the journey. The day before we left Salt Lake, we rented a medium U-Haul trailer and packed everything we needed in it that evening, ready to move the following morning. We were ready to follow I-80 again except that this time it was to the east.

Chapter 28

On The Road Again

Early that morning we got up, and packed whatever remained into our car, and by the time we finished eating our breakfast, my parents-in-law, sister, and brother-in-law were there to wish us a safe journey. The last person to enter the car before her parents were our five-week-old Melody. With hugs and kisses, we bade everyone goodbye and were on our way. I was on the road again, except this time, I had a family. Amazingly, our daughter traveled very well.

We left Salt Lake owing two debts, namely the car loan and Sweetie's college loan, but that did not prevent us from sending money home (Nigeria). As my people say, the chicken scratched the ground front and back and asked, "What is greater, the past or the future? The future" is the answer. With the salary Central Connecticut College offered me, we had no fear about paying off the debts. On arrival at Cheyenne, we decided to spend the first night there, though the sun still shone. We entered a restaurant to eat and put our daughter, who was in her baby seat, on the table. The family at the next table fixed their eyes on us. Upon receiving our food, I noticed their faces brightened when we held our daughter's hands and said grace. In the end, we had a peaceful and restful night.

Lincoln, Nebraska, was our next destination. By mid-afternoon, one and a half days later, we were in Lincoln. Our first stop was Sydney Ugwunna's home. Unfortunately, there was no one home. We left the former Air Force Base and drove into the City of Lincoln. Our first stop was 1919 E Street, the home of my former landlady. The old lady pleasantly received us. After several minutes, we excused ourselves and drove to the Kriders' my adopted parents' home, where we spent our two days in Lincoln. From here, we made telephone calls to inform people of our arrival.

Nancy McKune and her children were the first to visit us. As usual, it was a pleasant visit. Sydney came alone. We decided to visit the University. He insisted on my taking the abstract of my dissertation with me. He wanted me to show it to my former adviser. I did. When we arrived he was not in his office because it was summer. Sydney was completing his master's degree in biology. While at the University I met two other Nigerians, John Aniaza and Okugo. Okugo, another Biafran, came to the department as I was leaving. He was angry at Biafra for losing the war and at the department for denying him the opportunity to complete his doctoral program after two years. He was determined to go home. Commenting on the denial, John Aniaza, who was getting his Ph. D. from the Department of Economics, said, "I am not sure they would have allowed me to complete my degree if I were in your department." Then, I was shocked to see Antwart still in the department completing his dissertation. This was a man who received his M.A. from Oxford, England. But because an M.A. from a British university is usually awarded on the basis of one's performance on the bachelor's degree, Nebraska did not recognize his M.A. He had to go through the American system. He had completed his doctoral dissertation while I was there. His chairman, the same one I had, said to him, "You had almost all A's. You should write a better doctoral dissertation than this." He started all over again, and two years later he was still at it. I looked at him, shook my head, and thought to myself. Thank God I do not have that patience.

The following day, some friends in Lincoln, including Deputy Governor Marsh and his wife, Nancy, Jo Ritzman, and her husband,

and the Kriders held a party in our honor. We expressed our gratitude. The following day was Sunday, and we contemplated attending service. Then I learned that Reverend Dr. Berg, who was the senior Minister when I attended Trinity Methodist, was no longer there. We decided to travel that morning. We left Lincoln early that Sunday after breakfast and spent the night somewhere in Pennsylvania. It was from here that we drove to Connecticut the following Monday. By midafternoon, two days later, we were in New Britain. Not long after, we drove to the Central Connecticut State College campus. I went to the office to see if any arrangements were made for us. They gave me a listing and a newspaper clipping. I lived in a $30 apartment as a bachelor. We lived in a $75 apartment as a married couple. I was hoping for a $100 to $125 apartment in New Britain. What I saw ranged from $400 to over $700. It was getting late. We ate dinner and drove to a motel in Newington and slept there.

While at the motel, we read through the advertisements, especially housing. I had decided that Sweetie was going to stay home and take care of our daughter. Though I could afford the $ 500-a-month apartment, it would come at the cost of other things. We chose the top level of a two-story house in downtown New Britain that was furnished for $200 a month. Mrs. Legasi, the owner, met us on arrival and was pleasant. When we climbed up, it was big and clean, with three big bedrooms, a big kitchen, a good-sized living room, and a bath. We rented it. Within two blocks were three churches, one of which was Trinity Methodist. We unpacked and settled at 32 West Pearl Street.

On our way to our new home, I noticed a gas station with U-Hauls parked there. After we unloaded, I looked at the address the U-Haul Company in Salt Lake City gave me, and they matched. I drove to the station and gave it to them. Thus, five days after we left Salt Lake City, we settled in New Britain where we spent the next five- and one-half years.

Chapter 29

Central Connecticut State 1970-72

My contract with the college stipulated that my appointment would start on September 1. On that day, I found myself in the faculty parking lot in front of the campus police office and walked to the Psychology Department office to report. I saw a door on the right with four names. When I glanced at them, mine was one of them. I walked into the secretary's office. She gave me a key to the office and told me to go and register my car with the campus police. I discovered that, among other things, the registration included fingerprinting. When I returned to the building unlocked the door, and entered the office, I noticed that two of the four desks were already occupied. I chose the third. Further examination of the card showed I had twelve hours of classes to teach each week. I was also required to indicate three hours during the week when students could meet with me for consultation. In addition, I had a mailbox in the secretary's office. The department had already ordered the textbooks for my classes, and I received my copies.

Before classes began, I met my three officemates, June, Bill, and Thomas. Bill graduated from the University of Utah with a degree in experimental psychology. Our paths did not cross while in Utah. You recall my first day at Lyndon when I wore a suit by accident. At

Central, I wore it Monday through Friday and on purpose. My four classes were equally divided between the psychology of human development and human learning. I enjoyed my classes more than other lecturers, maybe because of our daughter's age. I confirmed and discredited the text from my previous knowledge and what I observed in her.

While we were in Salt Lake City, I lived and operated as a Biafran. I received a letter from the U.S. government offering me citizenship if I wished to become one. I declined the offer. When I started work at Central Connecticut, the College told me I had to apply for permission to work and for renewal every six months or for permanent residence status. Sweetie teased me. "They offered it to you free, and now you have to pay for it." I applied for permanent residence and got it. We had hoped to receive my first paycheck at the middle of the month. But it did not happen. However, we survived. At the end of the month, we paid our rent and had surplus money left. I opened a bank account with Federal Savings Bank. We still owed the money Sweetie borrowed for college and the bulk that remained out of the money I borrowed to buy my car. It was getting to Christmas. I sent my brother a hundred and fifty dollars. When he replied, he acknowledged the receipt of the money and asked for a sweater. Our first Thanksgiving in Connecticut was uneventful. Sweetie had reconnected with Ann her supervisor at the FBI Office. At this time, Ann and Larry and their daughter, Eileen, lived in Boston Massachusetts. We planned to spend our first Thanksgiving in New Britain with them. We got ready to travel to Boston. When we walked out and put the key in the ignition, the car refused to start. Nothing we did would start the car. Soon, the tears were running out of Sweetie's eyes. That did not move the engine. We gave up trying, and she called and informed them of our situation. We spent the day in New Britain. The following day, the car started as though we bought a new engine. We thanked

God and wondered what would have happened on the road if we had traveled.

We were already attending Trinity Methodist Church nearby. Still thinking of moving to Africa, as many Americans say, we did not hurry to become members. However, we noticed that quite a few members of the church were also from the College, e.g., Don Bennion, Todd Sagraves, Jim Snaden, and the Library Director. Some from this group and others, such as the Thompsons and the Kims, formed an international group that met during holidays such as Thanksgiving and Christmas. Excellent friendships developed out of this group. We also got to know Judith Kahane, who had been in Nigeria as the wife of a diplomat and had supported the cause of Biafra during the war. Judith Kahane taught in the department of philosophy, which we understood was a part of the psychology department before they decided to expand. It must have been through her that I heard of an American who was going to Port Harcourt Nigeria. I gave him $150 and the sweater my brother requested and five dollars to register the parcel to my brother when he reached Port Harcourt. My brother wrote and acknowledged receipt of the money and the sweater.

The first chance I got, I took Sweetie and our daughter to Lyndon State College. On arrival at Lyndonville, we saw this lady walking on the sidewalk, wanting to cross the street. It was Janet McKnight the lady who introduced me to the grade four Sunday school class and asked me to teach it the first Sunday I was at Peoples Methodist. I slowed down and drove zig-zag like I was drunk. She stopped, and I stopped and walked out; she laughed and declared, "I wondered who this nut was." We greeted, and I introduced Sweetie and Melody. Off we went toward the College. From the time we arrived, they treated us like royalty. My Sweetie was so surprisingly pleased that she asked if I was the President.

I walked to Vail's main building, and who did I see? Dr. Holden, the former Commissioner for Education whose daughter was a peace corps in Nigeria, standing in front of me. Having surprised ourselves, I said, "Dr. Holden," and he said Obed. He asked where I had been and where I was coming from. I told him and asked about Sally his daughter. "Sally is at home." I thought she was not married or working. I asked why he was at Lyndon? He was there as the interim President until a successor for Dr. Long was found. Of all the student's faces I saw, I recognized only one. He left college, joined the Navy, served and returned to complete his degree course. I saw some of the instructors and professors. One Ferguson, who behaved like the highest grade a black person can score on a test is a C, called me Obed. I stretched my hand, and as we shook hands, I said, "Dr. Onwuegbu, Assistant Professor, knowing that he was still an instructor. We attended service at Peoples Methodist on Sunday. There were many familiar faces. Many friends were there also and came round to greet us. The pastor surprised me when he asked, "Are you Obed?" Wondering who he was, I answered affirmatively. He reintroduced himself. He was one of the three students who traveled to New Jersey in Reverend Peel's car. He completed college and seminary and was now the pastor at Peoples Methodist. He had grown big. Our reunion was brief and pleasant. My family and I spent the day and returned to New Britain the following day.

Summer was approaching, and the chairman of the department called a meeting to discuss summer teaching. There were not enough courses for everyone who wanted to teach to get six hours i.e., two courses. Those who were there before us argued that they should get their six hours and the newcomers should go without. I argued in favor of assigning a course to everyone who wanted to teach and then a second according to seniority. Bob was one of those against that. His reason was the retirement benefits were based on the total yearly amount a person made before he or she retired. To humor the argument, I put a twist on retirement. "Retirement results from being tired too many times. Why not take a rest this summer and prevent getting tired too many times? That way, you would not need to retire early." It brought the laughter it was intended for. But it did not solve the problem. They had their way. However, before the semester ended, the chairman had a course for me to teach. I taught inner-city mothers how to interact with their young children.

Sweetie sold Fashion Two Twenty Cosmetics, which is a brand of makeup, while she lived in Salt Lake City. She discovered Angie and her husband Norm, who made the sale of the product their occupation. To occupy herself with something, and maybe more importantly, to supply herself with the product she loved, she got connected to Angie and her husband. We took a bottle of Melody's food during one of our earlier visits. Coming home, still a few miles on our way, Melody finished it and was still hungry. She cried so hard and long that it seemed forever. Sweetie tried everything to comfort her. Soon, Sweetie was sobbing, and I had two people to comfort. I was relieved and happy when we unlocked the door, and she fed her. At another time, we went to Angie's, and she gave Melody a stuffed dog and called it "oof oof." After a while our friend Don and his wife Gene came over with their son, who was three months younger than Melody, to see us. He was crawling at the time. David crawled on his fours. Melody looked at him and looked at us and called him "oof oof." We laughed and explained the language.

Melody was turning one that Summer. Her grandparents, aunt and uncle came to celebrate it with her. We all enjoyed the visit. Before we left Vermont, we sought out Mother Mac. She was sixty-five in my last year at Lyndon. In spite of her age, Dr. Long, the President, appreciated the job she performed as the college nurse and kept her. When we came in 1971, she had retired. We learned she was at Monroe, a small town in New Hampshire, and visited her. My parents-in-law, sister, and brother-in-law saw much of New England. However, one incident made the visit a memorable event for my father-in-law. Mind you, this was a man who fought in World War II, and his plane was shot down. While a POW, he built a radio and listened to the progress of the war until American forces liberated them. We visited the Empire State Building, looked at the Statue of Liberty, and visited the United Nations. None of these excited my father-in-law as much as what we saw by accident. I was driving and got lost. All of a sudden, we found ourselves in Manhattan. I drove to a police station to ask for directions. A few minutes later, we were looking at Yankee Stadium. My father-in-law could not believe that his eyes were looking at the Stadium. I could have charged him for my error, and he would probably have gladly paid. That was the topic of our conversation on our way home and after.

Also, we communicated with Mother Krider in Lincoln, Nebraska. She had planned to go to Washington, DC for a psychological conference. She took the opportunity to see us. We enjoyed and appreciated the visit, the first since we saw her last in Lincoln. Unfortunately, that was the last time we saw her. A year or two later she sent us a telegram that announced the death of her husband. We were in Nigeria when she remarried.

Another faculty member at Central I got to know was Mrs. Kinney. She taught African history. Her husband was the President of a junior college. She was a member of the Educators To Africa Association (ETAA). She got me interested in it, and I became a member. She was very interested in Africa and Africans. They had two African students, a Kenyan and a Ghanaian, who lived in their home. At a later date, she informed me of a trip the Organization was planning to West Africa sponsored by the United Nations and asked me to consider making the trip. For me, the main attraction for the trip was the cost of the ticket, only $200 round trip compared with the $490 I paid to fly to the U.S. I could not pass it up. As the date of travel drew near, she was diagnosed with terminal cancer. She withdrew from the trip.

As Summer approached, I found myself in two other projects besides my intended travel to Nigeria. First, there was the Wheeler

Affiliates at Plainville. Its mission was to train students who would work with children, especially in early childhood education intervention. The Executive Director invited me to participate in the selection of the candidates. During the interview, a white woman candidate made a disparaging remark about a black person she encountered somewhere. I was the only black person on the panel of interviewers. The rest looked at me, and one accused the woman of prejudice against blacks. The rest concurred. To their surprise, I defended her. I explained that she narrated her experience and should not be penalized for it. That endeared me to the Executive Director. I became a permanent part-time staff member of the organization. They requested a passport photo size of me. I thought it was for my file and gave it to them. But they had something else in mind. Second was the summer school.

I was typing in my office one afternoon when Dr. Bill Meyer passed. He stepped back and said, "The Summer schedule is out, and I have my courses. Go to the chair, and he will give you yours." I went to the office and asked the chairman. He said it was not out, and he did not have it. I was totally disappointed in him for lying to me. I lost faith in him. At the end, I had a course to teach.

When my parents-in-law, sister, and brother-in-law came in July, they did not know that Sweetie was pregnant again with our first son, and we did not tell them. The picture I took of her with the Christmas flowers I bought for her showed a very pregnant Sweetie. By the time we celebrated Christmas in 1971, we were debt-free. I had paid off both my car loan and Sweetie's college loan. We waited the celebration of a son. I dreamed of a son and chose the name Chinedum, and my brother suggested Isigwuzo. Isigwuzo is our father's name. On January 13 exactly one day before Melody turned one and half years, our son Chinedum was born at New Britain General Hospital. As Sweetie said at the birth of Melody, we tried again and got a boy. We celebrated and the folks in Utah rejoiced at the birth of their second grandchild.

After my brother received the money and sweater I sent him in May 1971, he informed me that he was planning to marry a second wife. I was offended. Here I am, denying my family simple pleasure like going to a movie, to help him and his family. Yet, he was planning extra pleasure in a second wife. I made it clear to him. "If you marry another wife, I will not know her and her children." I did not send him money that Christmas.

I had two problems to solve before I traveled. The first was easy to solve. Melody just turned two. Chinedum was six months old, and Sweetie was pregnant with our third child. There was no way she could take care of all the responsibilities alone. Our solution was to fly them to Salt Lake two days before I traveled. My summer class was the second. There would be about a week left of summer school when I traveled.

Realizing the conflict, I took care of it when I prepared the handout I gave to my students on the first day of class. "I shall lecture you till the last week of class. There will be two tests and a term paper. Your grades will be based on the tests and term papers. You will share the contents of your term paper with members of the class in the last week, and the sharing will not influence your grade." I planned with an Associate Professor, Dr. Don Bennion, who was also the Associate Dean, and Dr. Suad, who was an Assistant Professor in the department before I came, to supervise the presentations. After the tests and grading of the papers, I assigned grades to each student and gave the grade book to Dr. Bennion for final assignment at the end of summer school. Two days before I traveled, I took my family to Bradley Airport in Connecticut from where they flew to Salt Lake City. On the day I traveled, Dr. Bennion drove me to New York JFK, where I met and flew with other members of ETAA. Our first stop was at the University of Ghana at Logan. I spent the night and flew to Lagos the following day with some other Nigerians. American members stayed in Ghana for two weeks before flying to Nigeria.

Before boarding at JFK, I noticed the exchange rate of the pound to the dollar. This was cheaper than any rate I could get in Nigeria. I took advantage of it and changed most of my dollars and bought three hundred pounds. The news of the atrocities people of Rivers State committed against Igbos during and after the war was still fresh in my mind. For that reason, I decided against flying to Port Harcourt. Having misjudged the distance between Benin City and Onitsha, I chose Benin Airport over Enugu. It was almost dark when we reached Owerri. There was no vehicle going to Umuahia. The one vehicle for Aba promised to travel through Umuahia. I paid the fare only to discover it was a prank. They drove to Aba straight, and the scars of a defeated people were everywhere. It seemed that Nigerian soldiers stopped the vehicle every mile or two on that dark night. I checked in at Unicoco Hotel.

I got up early in the morning, had my shower, dressed, checked out, and carried my suitcase to the motor park. The vehicles at the park looked like a dump rather than vehicles worthy of the road. A forty-mile journey took more than two hours because of the ditches on the road, the condition of the bus, and the soldiers who took pleasure in reminding Biafrans they were defeated. At last, I was at Umuahia Motor Park. Once I took out my suitcase from the bus, three small boys surrounded it struggling to see who would carry it. I had only one suitcase and only one of them got it. When I stopped to get a taxi and paid him, he was unhappy because he expected more. At that point, Chinenye Obobo, from my village, drove up with his taxi car. I asked him what I should pay the boy. He told me and I paid the boy. He drove off. Even without the war, nine years of absence would have made a difference. With the war, things really looked absolutely much worse than when I left. A few minutes after he drove away from the township towards the village, he remembered that the women were attending their quarterly women's Christian fellowship and concluded that my mother would not be at home. I asked if he knew where they were meeting. He said it was at Umuoriehi. We drove to Umuoriehi church. It was a big disappointment when we got there and learned Ohia was hosting it. Though I informed my brother of my visit, I warned him not to tell my mother. If she heard about the plan and failed to see me, she would conclude I was dead. So my visit was a complete surprise to her. When we got home, my sister-in-law was home. My mother, who was on her sick bed, thought she was dreaming when she heard her daughter-in-law call ulunnedim, i.e., my mother-in-law's younger son. I answered. I paid Chinenye and settled down. My presence was more than half the medicine my mother needed to get well.

Soon the news of my arrival spread beyond the village and even Umuahia. The first few days of my arrival witnessed the burial of a popular and funny teacher, Mr. Ogbuagu, made even more popular by his son Bob. Many people went to the burial and heard about my visit though I did not attend. Mr. and Mrs. Ibegbulem from Agbani with Mrs. Onyije and Emedom and his friend from Aba, and others visited me. When I attended church the first Sunday, I was home, I saw that the walls of the church building bore the marks of bullets. Then I learned why Umuahia was the last major battleground. It became the capital of Biafra after the fall of Enugu. The war museum, which was General Ojukwu's bunker, and office is at my village land today. It is only a block or two from one of my plots.

All the things I left when I traveled to the U.S., my glass bookshelf, my desk, cane chairs, cushion chairs, big table, and the pride of my craft, the table I made without one nail but only glue, were all stolen. Not one of the books I spent much of my earnings remained. In spite of all, I was grateful to God that my mother and her family were alive. I walked out to see the roads and the township. Of all my years before I went to the U.S., I never saw the roads as bushy and unkept as they were. As I walked, a car stopped in front of me. When I looked it was Rachel, Maxwell's wife. A Nigerian army sergeant rudely interrupted our conversation and demanded a ride. I looked him in the eye and denied him the ride. Rachel lamented, "That's what we suffer here as a defeated people." When I left her, I traveled to Government College Umuahia to see Amadi, my nephew. On my way home and climbing the little hill at Osa before my village, a cyclist stopped behind me. I turned and there was dee Okebugwu, an uncle by marriage. That reminded me of the ritual we displayed as little boys to show our respect and ability. I walked backward and took the bicycle from him. He was coming to bid me welcome. Once we reached the top of the hill, he took his bicycle and rode home before me, delighted that I still respected him and played the part of the boy. Showing his joy and congratulating me in the traditional way, he took out a bottle of White Horse whiskey from his bag and bade me welcome.

Within a few days after my arrival, my brother came from Abakeleke his station. I gave him one hundred and fifty pounds for him and his family. We were little when our dad died. He is the oldest and was only in standard one (grade one) when our father died. I did not even know my father. My brother cannot get over the fact that our dad blessed me instead of him. As little children, we did not know how and where he was buried. I decided to hold a memorial service for him. I gave my brother the money he estimated it wouldcost. Members of the village church came after the morning service and celebrated his life. Those who knew him paid tribute to his leadership and generosity.

It was time to venture outside Umuahia, and no place was more attractive to me than the University of Nigeria Nsukka. I had collected books for the university library while in Nebraska when we heard the Nigerian soldiers used its library books to roast goats. Obioma Imo, my agemate from my village, also worked in the finance department. I traveled to the university. Obioma was still in his office when I arrived. He took me home. He took me around to show me the campus. The next familiar face I saw was Ihuoma Phillip, Acting (interim) Bursar. Obioma asked him, "Do you know Dr. Onwuegbu?" Ihuoma laughed and said, "O yes. How can I forget Obed? If it was not for him, I would have been first in all standard five classes in Umuahia Circuit (District)." Surprised at his comment because I spent so much time in his village as a boy with Ukachi my favorite aunt who lived next door to his parents, all I could say was, "You can't forget that." I walked to see Dr. Nwagbara next and saw some of the tanks Biafrans manufactured during the war. I took my camera and took pictures before someone stopped me. Someone tried, but I had taken two snaps before he completed his statement. Then I traveled to Enugu.

A surprise awaited me at Enugu. I lived in Enugu as a boy, even before I started school and got my visa there. As mentioned earlier, Enugu was the capital of the Eastern Region of Nigeria when I left. At the time of my visit, it was the capital of East Central State, one of the three states carved out of the Eastern Region. Walking along the street, I saw Mr. Achiugo, my former tutor at ETC Uzuakoli; he was studying for his M.A. at Springfield, Massachusetts, U.S.A. when I was at Lyndon. He saw me and gave me a ride on his combi bus to his office. He worked for the Ministry of Education. He complained about the politics at Nsukka as the reason for joining the Ministry. Then he boasted of what he felt was a great achievement in the school system. They had changed the holidays to coincide with the Western summer holidays. That was cosmetic to me. But what could I say? He took me to the motor park after telling me about his losses during the war, including the car he returned home with from the U.S. By late afternoon, I was back to Umuahia. The visit was depressing, but I had firsthand information. I took as many pictures as I could.

While I was home, Uncle Onwumere Ikeji came home on vacation. As was the custom, I went to greet him. I walked into his living room and greeted him. He surprised me with his reply, "Yes, do I have to apologize to you now?" For what I asked. He said, "Oh. Before I left his house, I realized he was referring to my financial request to him and his inability or unwillingness to give me money before I traveled to the U.S. But the fact was, I was never in need because God took me to the U.S. and maintained me there. If anything, I had sent money home. However, I decided to spend two days in Lagos with his family.

First, I had to spend a day at Aba with Emedom and his family. They were not even a full block away from the hotel I spent my first night on arrival to Nigeria. He worked for the textile factory that employed him before the war. However, the Americans sold it for one dollar to the Federal Government after the war. He took me round to see some of his friends. When I asked the whereabouts of Mrs. Achinivu the wife of our late ETC Principal, he drove me to her shed. She expressed her delight at my sight and her disappointment in Emedom. She said Emedom stopped because I brought him. She said that was the first time he ever stopped though he lived at Aba. Unfortunately, I had no gift for her. The robust woman had lost so much weight. Emedom drove me to Aba Motor Park the following morning, and I was on my way to Lagos through Onitsha. Between Owerri and Onitsha, I saw the charred chartered Roman Catholic mercy planes that flew food to Biafra which Nigerian planes destroyed as it unloaded. By early evening, I was in my uncle's apartment at Akpakpa Lagos.

Again, I was interested in seeing another Nigerian university, this time the University of Lagos. It was vacation time, and the doors were locked. I walked around, reading the names on the doors. I recognized Dr. Nwosu from Umunwanwa, an old boy from Uzuakoli who graduated from Harvard. I knocked and no one answered. That gave me hope that other Igbo people might be on the faculty. A short time after I returned to my uncle's apartment, I had three unexpected visitors. As usual, the door was open when they walked in and greeted. When I looked, I saw Njikonye, my relative, and Elijah, both from my village, and a woman with them. We greeted and Njikonye introduced the woman as his fiancé. She was from Bendel State and her sister was also married in my village. Mba, her brother-in-law, her sister, and their children were also in the States. They brought some gifts for me to take to them. I was glad to see them. The last time I saw Njikonye was in Enugu about a week before I traveled to Lagos on my way to the United States, and he was an engineering student at Nsukka.

Coming to Nigeria was emotionally draining. Learning of the number of people from the village who were killed in the pogrom in the north, most of them young, my cousin Joy, a student nurse who was killed when the Queen Elizabeth II Hospital was bombed, and the condition of things was depressing. On the other hand, the resilience of the people to rise again was encouraging. It was time to leave the country again. I bade relatives goodbye and went to the airport by taxi. Our chartered plane was ready. There was no limit to what the passengers could carry. The plane was overloaded. When the Nigerian who checked my passport read my name, he sought a way to extract a bribe from me. He tried to make fun of my Dr. "Everybody in the U.S. is a doctor," he said. What are you sitting here for? Why are you not there? I asked. Then he said my inoculation was not stamped. "You did not turn me back when I arrived. Now that I want to leave with all my diseases, you want me to stay and spread them. You don't make sense." He gave me my passport. Soon we boarded. Because of the load the plane carried, we stopped on an island before we landed at JFK. I waited till early in the morning before I called Sweetie. She and Don came to get me. The sight of my family and Don, for a moment, eased the stories of despair I had experienced for the past three weeks. Off we went. After we left New York City, Don told me about the problem my absence caused at the College. The picture I gave to Wheeler Affiliates was after all not a private matter. The newspaper flashed it on the front page of the day's news with the details of my employment with Wheeler Affiliates. Besides it gave the details of my trip with ETAA and the UN as the sponsor. It did not end there. It printed my congratulatory message from representative Ella Grasso.

Both the chairman of my department and the Assistant Dean of the School got excited and attacked me in their report to the Associate President for Academics. Among other things, they accused me of ruining the reputation of the College. They based their report solely on the report of the chair of the department and my absence. There was no mention of my handout or the arrangements I made. Before I drove Don to his house, he handed a copy of the complaint and reported it to me. The report did not suggest any act of discipline.

My first task was to reply to the report. Prior to this my annual evaluation had been very good. I did not think this would change it. I replied and enclosed my handout to the students and described the arrangements I made to supervise the students' presentation. I submitted my reply to every officer they copied. The only reply I received from the Associate President for Academics was verbal. He saw me and said, "We are proud to have you here." I thanked him.

When I opened the envelope Wheeler Affiliates sent to me and saw the check enclosed, I was disappointed. I decided it was not worth the headache. I wrote my letter of resignation and took it there myself. When I reached the office, unfortunately, the Executive Director was absent. I greeted those present left my letter on his desk and drove home. A few days later, I received his reply. It started, "Dear Obed, you should know we were all stunned and disappointed to read your decision …" He pleaded for me to reconsider my decision. He wanted us to get together and arrange what was best for me. When we did, he offered me a position at the associate professor level. I declined the offer but agreed to be prorated on that. I had become a consultant to the Clinic. One result of the feud was a rule from the main office. Such outside employment shall receive approval to be authentic. I went to the Associate President for Academics and received the approval.

The two previous academic sessions saw me heavily involved in the department. However, I became active in campus activities. I became the Foreign Students Adviser and a member of the Greater New

Britain Campus Ministries; I withdrew from some of the departmental committees. Also, I started a number of projects and had a work-study student who needed to be busy. I was busy at my church also. To test the waters, I asked my students to evaluate me as a teacher. It was very good, especially since I asked them to critique without their names or numbers. Tom, one of those who shared the office with me, thought I was crazy. A year or two later the College started student evaluations of the faculty. One older woman student in my psychology of learning class said, "You said don't use your name and number. I don't know why you frighten students away on the first day of class. This is a most interesting class." I told her my reason. Some came here to look for wives or husbands. In the absence of those, the rest study.

Mrs. Kinney was still suffering from cancer when I returned and had lost one eye through the operation. She had requested me to take many pictures and I did. The cancer lasted for about two years, and she was gone. I discovered at the memorial service that one of the women at Wheeler was engaged to one of the Kinney's sons.

Shortly after Sweetie and the children returned from Salt Lake City and I from Nigeria, she had our first miscarriage. Her doctor could not determine the cause. Several months passed, and she was pregnant again. A few months later she had another miscarriage. Again, the doctor could not explain it. Though we planned for a daughter and two sons before we got married, we decided to stop trying for a third child.

At last Sweetie's dream of spending a Thanksgiving with Ann and her family was fulfilled. Ann was not only Sweetie's supervisor at the FBI office, but she also led her to become a Christian. At this time Larry, Ann's husband, was a seminary student in Boston. We enjoyed the reunion. Our Christmas took an international flavor. Our group comprised Americans, Koreans, Chinese, Mexicans, Italians, and Nigerians, and maybe one Indian. Soon the year and fall semester were over.

Chapter 30

Central Connecticut State 1973-1975

Computers were becoming available to institutions. Bill and Tom, my officemates, went to summer school to learn how to use a computer. A popular opinion mushroomed that computers might replace human lecturers in the classrooms. The rumor heightened my interest in teaching and learning. I designed a study to compare four methods of teaching. Without revealing my reason, I requested the chairman to assign all my four classes in one area of psychology, human learning, or human development. However, I did inform him that I would use four different methods of teaching. Amazingly he agreed without asking for details. But I had to wait till the following semester.

When I took over the job of the Adviser to the International Students, they celebrated International Day. I reorganized and changed it to International Week. Each country received materials such as films and, in some cases, speakers from the embassy on the day assigned to the country. Also, the College allotted enough funds to take the students to Washington DC for sightseeing, usually the last two or three days of the week. We visited the Smithsonian and the monuments and watched the Congress in session. I took them to Cape Cod during my last summer at the college.

Many of the students had some significant problems and reported the same to me. One day, I called Carol, their counselor, at her house. She told me she could not talk at that time and gave me the telephone number of where she was going and asked me to call her there. I did. When she answered, I listed the problems and suggested solutions. She took the list to Dick the Dean of Students. The Dean invited the Associate Dean, Carol, and me to a meeting. At the end of the meeting, the Dean thanked and praised Carol for her foresight. She smiled broadly and swallowed the praise without acknowledging that I was the source of the foresight or even giving me any recognition. I was satisfied that the problems were resolved before they surfaced in the open. So, I said nothing.

Meanwhile, Wheeler Affiliate developed two psychology courses to teach students in the areas of human development and early childhood education. They hired Bill and June two of my officemates. They agreed to teach each of the three-hour courses for $750. When the Office Manager called me to teach Early Childhood Education, I asked what he paid. He told me what he paid my colleagues. I declined the offer and added, "I will not teach for anything less than a thousand dollars." He refused to pay me a penny more than he paid my colleagues. We agreed to disagree. About a week later, the phone in the office rang. The Manager was at the other end of the phone when I picked up the receiver. He recognized my voice and asked, "Is that Biafran Jew there?" "Who wants him?" I asked. He said the Dean of the College refused to allow anyone else to teach the class and told me to teach it. I did. Later in the semester, the Executive Director gave me a note that congratulated me and said, "The students informed him that I was their best lecturer and was there on time every lecture day."

My fall semester classes at the College started with the usual four classes of three hours each. Since my Alayi experience with my standard (grade) five pupils, when I spoiled their day with my personal problem, I have learned to be mindful of the feelings of my students.

As I taught my psychology of human development one day, I watched one of my female students. She reacted to some of my statements as though they were daggers to her heart. She hurried out of the class immediately the last word left my mouth. I stopped her at the door and asked what her problem was. With tears in her eyes, she narrated all. Mod and her husband had three sons. They took them out one day and went close to the bank of a river. She thought one son pushed the other into the river. Her husband jumped in to save the drowning son but instead drowned. When she attended service the previous Sunday, the sermon was on the duty of the father in the home. She came to my class, and the topic was the same, i.e., the duty of the father in the home. There she was with two young boys without a father. I spent several minutes with her. I also told her that I was the International Students Adviser and invited her and the boys to the events that week. I talked to her from time to time. A few years later, after I submitted my letter of resignation, I saw her and asked how the boys and her were getting on; she said fine. She told me that she was dating again. On hearing that I was resigning, she bought a placard for me entitled, The Five Most Important Things in Life, and the last was "I," indicating my concern and care for her family. Then she enclosed a note that said, "Thank you for being here when I needed you." The placard is in Nigeria as I write this book.

Trinity Methodist decided not to wait for me to become a member to get me involved in the leadership. Without any objection on my part, they elected me to the Board. From there I became the chairman of the Education Committee of the church. It became necessary to employ a youth director at the church. A woman was employed. For the fact that I was not a member of the church, I played a limited role in her supervision. The church was disappointed with her performance and let her go. We replaced her with a man. At about the same time, Trinity, my church, and the Congregational Church that was across the street had a joint Education Committee. Dr. Kinney was the chairman of the Congregational Committee, and I was the chairman of the Trinity Committee. We became the co-chairs of the joint Committee. The Congregational had a youth pastor, Gus. Many agitators at Trinity did not like Gus. They wanted to withdraw from the union because of him. I knew that Trinity benefitted from the union more than the Congregational church; for one thing, we did not have the money to hire a youth pastor of our own at the time. So, I invited nonmembers of the committee who were in favor of the union to a scheduled general meeting.

As the youth pastor, Gus attended separate meetings of the two churches. When our Minister tabled the question of the union, Gus spoke. He said there was no need for the meeting to discuss the matter because his church had decided to sever the relationship. Suddenly, Dr. Kinney and Gus attended our meeting unannounced. Dr. Kinney complained that we canceled the arrangement we made jointly with his church without any regard for their feelings. I was offended. I felt that those people who disliked Gus were justified. "Gus, do you have anything to say?" When he said nothing, I said, "Dr. Kinney, Gus stood here when our Minister announced the topic for discussion and told us not to discuss it because his church had decided to sever the relationship. He is supposed to be a pastor and trustworthy, etc." Gus had nothing to say. Dr. Kinney was embarrassed and offered an apology.

When I visited Nigeria, my brother had about nine living children. Their first daughter died before I traveled to the States in 1963. I continued to send him money. By then, I had money in two banks, and one of them was at Corbin's Corner, West Hartford. I drove there one day to send him money. A woman was backing out of her car and hit my car. The damage was more than she expected. She looked at my car and asked, "Did I do all this damage by myself alone?" Surprised by her question I replied, "I did not see anybody else helping you." We called the police. He took the names of our insurers, and her insurance took care of my car. The accident did not prevent me from sending the money.

In at least one of the excursions to Washington DC, many of the foreign students expressed their frustration and inability to understand American slang in the classroom. I promised to take care of it. After we returned, I decided to organize an informal students-to-student interaction group with American and foreign students, without lecturers or grades. The best way I could get volunteers was through the college newspaper. The editor agreed with me and published it. Carol, the Foreign Students Counselor, took offense. She did not tell me, nor did she call me. I was dismayed to see a copy of her letter to the Associate President for Academics, which she also copied the Deans of Students and my school and the chairman of my department. She complained that I was duplicating a problem she was already solving. She claimed that she had set up a course with the English Department to teach foreign students grammar and composition. She totally missed the need I was trying to meet. As insulting as her letter was, I refused to call and tell her what I thought about her and chose to reply to her letter. First, I let her know that she sought publicity through the back door. I told her that I did not believe that she did not know the difference between the use of grammar and slang. Then I told her what her problem was. "You are angry and disappointed because I did not go through you as I did before. You recall when I called and gave you a list of potential problems and answers; you passed the list on to the Dean of Students, who called a meeting. After the meeting he thanked you for your foresight. You smiled broadly and swallowed every praise. You did not even have the decency to say, "Obed has something to do with this, let alone that it is all Obed's doing. You are now crying because I did not go through you and give you a credit for promotion you don't merit or foresight when you do not even have sight. I was a foreign student and I understand their problem. Next time call me or come to my office." I sent copies to everyone who received her letter. The administration did not even reply to her letter. When she realized her failure with the Administration, she called the officers of the International Students Club and showed them my letter to her and sent the officers to me. But she did not tell them that I wrote in reply to her letter. When they saw the letter to which I replied, they apologized to me for bothering me. "Didn't she know you would reply?" they asked. That was the end of the matter. When the Associate Dean who attended our meeting with the Dean read my reply, she invited me to her office and apologized for praising the wrong person. As I wrote the last sentence, I realized God was using both the complaints by the chair of my department and Carol to the Administration against me and my replies to those letters to positively expose my performance to the administration.

As in every city, there were some families at our church who needed rides to church. Sweetie and I volunteered to give two of them rides. One couple was middle-aged. Later on, he accused his wife of adultery and they divorced and did not come to the church again. However, there was SueAnn, a young lady with her young daughter, who Sweetie met at the church nursery. Her daughter Allison is about three months older than our son Chinedum. Cliff, her husband, was in prison in Pennsylvania at the time. She went to see him from time to time. We took care of Allison in her absence. We became good friends. It turned out that SueAnn was one of those naïve, uninformed Americans who believed that Africa started and ended with Tarzan. She asked me the same questions Holly at Lyndon State asked,

"Obed, what will you wear when you get back to Nigeria?"

"What Tarzan wore."

"Where would you live?"

On the top of trees.

Where do the American Ambassadors live?

We give them the biggest trees with large branches.

Where would Sue, i.e., my wife, put her Tupperware and how do you get your mail?

By this time, I had scrambled her brain, and she was feeling sorry for Sweetie. Then I told her the real story.

We decided to move to another location in New Britain. We also decided to buy our own furniture. We achieved both. One of the advantages of our move was that we did not leave our building to do our laundry. We were also closer to the College, and the shopping center was practically in our backyard. There was even a little green space for Chinedum and me to play soccer. Those who wanted to swim had a swimming pool. But we were a few blocks farther away from Trinity church. More importantly, our children had other children of their ages to befriend and play with. However, we had only two bedrooms. To supplement we bought a hideaway bed for a couch.

One day the phone rang, and Sweetie answered it. It was a John she did not know looking for me. When I took the receiver, it was John Ogbu, my classmate at Uzuakoli, who I met at Athens, Ohio, in December 1963. He was teaching at Berkley and had come to Yale in New Haven, Connecticut, to do research. He came with Linda his wife. They invited us to their home. When we arrived, he surprised me with okwe also called asigo (a game the Igbo people play that uses seeds. I was good at it, but it was a long time since I played it last). We played it. I knew he was surprised to see me excited when I saw the carved wood. He was amazed when I easily won the game. I thought he would request a second game, but he did not. While we played the game, Sweetie and Linda visited. Before the end of the Summer, they returned to California.

Then the semester arrived for me to try my four methods of teaching. I had four classes of human development for thirty-two students each. The first class I lectured in my usual method of teaching.

The second class, I divided into small groups, and each group was assigned a number of chapters to read, discuss, write questionnaires, and interview children, parents, and teachers, and present their findings to the class. In the third class, I lectured from the book and allowed the students to ask questions whenever they wanted. For the fourth group, I applied my knowledge of programmed instruction with frames, searching by reading chapters, and discovering the answers. By the end of the semester, almost one quarter of the fourth class had withdrawn. They were hostile. One of them told me that his father worked to earn a living; I should work to be paid. I wondered if he would say that to the computer. The class I lectured from the book did not complain before me but opened their books and read along. Even my explanation about the four methods of teaching did not satisfy these two groups. However, since I graded by curve there was not much noise. The real comparison was between my lecture and the group methods.

The class I taught by my usual lecture method enjoyed the class; nothing extraordinary happened. I was overwhelmed by the joy, extra energy, enthusiasm, and innovation the class I divided into small groups and assigned chapters displayed. The students displayed intensive cooperation and eagerness within the group to discover and learn new things. Some of them invited their friends to the class to observe what went on in the class. Two of the many things they discovered through the interview are 1. Every child is different, and 2. The "average child" is a textbook creation. The results influenced my method of teaching to the extent that some members of the faculty in my department wanted to know how I taught my students. For example, Dr. Vlahakos asked, "Obed, how do you teach your classes? My students want me to teach my class the way you teach." Dr. Stowe said, "Obed, we hear good things about your classes." A female student walked into my office one day and greeted me. I asked what I could do for her. She said other students told her about me. They told her that if she wanted the knowledge, she should come to my class but not hope for a high grade. She added, "I need both the knowledge and the grade. What do you advise me to do?" I did not think I was stingy with grades. However, I told her that if she worked hard, she would earn a good grade. She registered in my class. At the end of the semester, she earned a B. She came and thanked me.

Do you know anything about American football? I did not until I went to the University of Nebraska in Lincoln. When I was at Lyndon State College, I called it mass wrestling and shunned it. At Nebraska, I became a cheerleader. Even after I got married, I watched football, and my wife watched me. By the way, do you know the college football game of the twentieth century and who won it? Do you know where it was played?

I was teaching at Central Connecticut State in New Britain. The Thanksgiving football game was between Nebraska and Oklahoma at Norman, the home of the Oklahoma Sooners. I walked into my class confidently and enthusiastically announced that Nebraska would defeat Oklahoma. We spent a few minutes on that, and I thought it was over. Then Vern, one of my students, came on the next day of class and told me that her husband wanted her to bet me. When I asked what the bet would be, she said, "I will get A if Oklahoma wins and F if Nebraska wins." When I accepted her challenge, she said she was afraid of me and would not bet me. I refused to allow her to withdraw it. We went home for Thanksgiving vacation to watch the game. The game was a thriller. Johnny, the Nebraska running back, caught the kickoff and ran it from post to post to give Nebraska a 7-0 lead. He scored another touchdown during the game, but the referees took it away because someone pushed him out of bounds before he ran to catch the ball for a touchdown. When the game ended, Nebraska won by 4 points. I carved a big "F," which I put in my winter jacket and carried to the classroom. I waited until every student was in the class and called Vern out. The whole class started laughing. I pulled out the big "F," and the class roared. When she saw it, she walked back to her seat laughing. I took it to her as a present for her and her husband. She reminded me that she did not bet me.

Professionally, I belonged to the American Psychological Association (APA). Also, I belonged to two subgroups, namely human development and learning, and was listed in *Who Is Who of American Men And Women of Behavioral Sciences 1973*. One of the committees I cared for in the department was the Curriculum Committee. Central Connecticut State at that time had a student enrollment of more than 13,000 and offered bachelor's and master's degrees and six-year certificates in some fields, especially education. I believe it to be the oldest state higher institution in Connecticut. At the time, a plan was on paper to turn it into a university, which it is today. The Department of Education enrolled the most significant number of students, and almost all of them took the Psychology of Human Development. When I arrived, all the lecturers used the same text. When I asked, "Why?" I received an unsatisfactory answer: "It is easy for the students." I asked about Munson and Munson and was told, "It was too difficult for the students." I argued that was why I was there, to explain it to them. When they refused, I used my choice. That did not go well with the woman who ordered the textbook. I argued that if the department wanted to teach the same thing with the same text, it should have employed its entire faculty from the same university. As long as we came from different institutions with various backgrounds, to insist on using one text violates my freedom of choice. The matter seemed settled.

I completed one of my papers entitled "The Bathroom Theory of Instruction" and submitted it. It was accepted for publication with a demand that I change the title. I did, though I had explained that the name was because the idea came to me while I was in the bathroom. Another paper entitled "Piece Meal the Problem of Practical Psychology" came back with a request to do more work on it. In the meantime, I had two other projects, a book and a proposal, I worked on with Kim as my work student helper. She put in only a few hours a week.

Therefore, I put Piece Meal The Problem of Psychology aside. The chair had completed his term, and it was time to elect a new chair. I wrote a paper that criticized how the department functioned and stated what I would do to enhance the curriculum and students' participation.

Some people, led by the chair, took offense, especially because the Administration saw the paper. The usual procedure was for departments to hold one election and submit the first three names to the Administration, which chose one out of the three, not necessarily the first or second. Once the chair and his group saw my name among the three, they changed the procedure. Frightened that the Administration would make me the chair if my name appeared as one of the three, they decided to hold three elections. Each time, they would choose number one. Knowing they were terrified of me, Dr. John Taylor, the second most senior member of the faculty, advised me to withdraw my name from the ballot, and I did.

About this time, I received a letter from frustrated Johnny Ibegbulem. He complained that he could not gain admission into any university in Nigeria and asked for help. I gave him addresses. Later, he wrote to tell me that Johnson State College in Vermont had admitted him. Sweetie and I took the children and drove to Vermont where we saw him in the library. We spent time with him and invited him to Connecticut. Our hideaway bed served the purpose it was purchased for when he came. He spent a few days with us, and among other gifts, I gave him the thick woolly coat I used at Lyndon. That was the last time I saw him in the States.

Mere, one of the three names passed on to the Administration, who later became the departmental chair, and Dith, both members of the department, became infatuated with themselves. (Mere and Dith are not their real names). Both were married and had children. Mere was a retired military officer with adult children. Dith was a middle-aged woman. The two divorced their spouses and got married. The woman whose husband was in the English Department of the College retained her maiden name. Mere's position as the chair of the department became the opportunity to make this woman the chair of the curriculum committee, even though she was only an instructor. Two events would precede Mere's assumption or even appointment to office. First, Bill proposed the addition of behavior modification to the department curriculum committee, and it adopted it. I proposed the implications of the psychology of learning in the classroom. They did not adopt it because it was educational psychology. I designed it as a summer graduate course for teachers. It was a full class. Mere became the chair that Summer. At the end of the class, I asked the students to critique the class without their names and numbers. They rated the class so highly that I decided to make it public. I took it to the Dean of our school. He read them and asked, "Are there bad ones?" I gave him the worst. It said, "I know Dr. Onwuegbu is one of the better professors at this college, but the praise this class heaped on him is too much." He was impressed and I walked out. Mere was in the chair's office when I returned to the department. I gave him the papers to read. He did not read half of it when he said, "How much did you bribe them to write this," with a wry smile on his face. The class was filled again in the second summer, and the department was ready to make it a regular graduate course at number 499.

    Listening to the news and my experience with Wheeler Affiliates and other sources assumed that inner-city students fail to perform well in schools. But unlike the general or even universal conclusion that they are victims of low mentality and consequently low I. Q., I believed and still believe that low performance is caused by the environment, not low mentality. For example, time wasted in watching TV instead of studying and lack of meaningful family interaction. I have proved that with three of my books: Discover Teaching, Teaching That Guarantees Learning, and ABCD of Intelligence and Behaviors Implications for Education. I wrote a proposal to work with parents, their children, and some city advocates in the City of New Britain to improve the student's performance in school. I chose a few behaviors to be learned and how to reinforce them. The city employees and parents would learn these first, followed by the children. We intended to measure the results by improvement changes in work, attitude change, school performance, and improvement. To submit the proposal required a budget. I gave a sum of what I thought it might cost and took it to the Director of Research for discussion. He sent me to Al his assistant.

Al itemized the costs. I had recorded the inner-city employees as volunteers in my budget because I scheduled them to work during office hours. I submitted the proposal to the Connecticut Board of Education. Bill, the experimental psychologist, read the proposal and said, "I wish I had written this." Shortly after the submission, the Director of Research called me to his office. When I walked in, he showed me a page and said, "These people asked some questions about your proposal, and I am sorry Al is not here to answer them." I thought Al had given him the false impression he was writing my proposal. Before he said anything else, I interrupted him. "What! Who is Al? What does he know about my proposal? Is itemizing the costs of writing my proposal?" He gave me the paper without one more word. Kim was in my office when I came back. I answered the questions, and she typed them. I took the reply to his office and handed it to him. He read it and declared, "I'm impressed. I'm impressed Dr. "Onnn" (however he pronounced my last name). I thanked him and walked out. He must have told the Associate President for Academics about the proposal. The Associate President for Academics saw me, congratulated me, and expressed his delight. He said it was the first time he saw anyone include parents in their children's education. In the end, the Board did not fund it. They requested that I include the city employees in the budget instead of listing them as volunteers and resubmitting it the following year. Dr. Vlahokos suggested that I frame the letter.

Another topic of interest to me was music and its effect on those who use it when they study. Study after study showed no differences in the performances of those who use music and those who do not. Yet people continued to ask the same question year after year as though repeating the question would change the answer. It did not make sense to me. So, I designed a three-by-two paradigm to study the problem. I accepted the answer that there is no difference in their performance. Then I asked three questions: 1. Who uses music when the person studies? 2. What does music do for the student? 3. What kind of music does such a person use? Doug, who was the College TV Director, attended Trinity Methodist with me. I approached him and arranged to have him involved in the study. I hoped to find two kinds of people who use music when they study, namely, 1. Those who are threatened and are nervous at the onset of a task, and 2. Those with competing stimuli (like noise). Though music would do different things for each group, the result should be the same i.e., better concentration and result.

While I was planning my study, John Ogbu called me again and told me that the Nigerian Government sent representatives to the U.S. to recruit Nigerians, and he had applied and planned to go for the interview. He gave me the details, and I applied.

The 1973 Arab-Israeli War and American support for Israel ushered in the Arab oil embargo on America. That had a significant impact on the economy, primarily on the industrialized states of the north. The result affected different classes of people in Connecticut in various ways. As a state employee, I had good and bad news. First, I received a letter from the President's office conferring tenure on me from September 1, 1974, with the congratulatory message that accompanied it. Later, another letter of regret came. It announced the inability of the state to promote any of its employees that year because of the bad economy as a result of the oil embargo. Enclosed in the letter was a list of the names of the department faculty and the order in which they were ranked. It was an unbearable insult to my person. Of about nine Assistant Professors to be considered for promotion to Associate Professor, three of them were Americans and the rest were foreigners or at different stages of becoming citizens. Looking at the list, I saw that all the three Americans who came the same year as me and shared the same office with me were listed before me. Suad, who was there before we arrived and shortly married an American, was number four, and I was five. I did not see how any of them could be rated better than me. I protested.

Accusing the committee of discriminating against foreigners in general and me in particular, I challenged them to justify the basis of the ranking. I warned that they would be in court defending themselves that day if the state had promoted any of them before me. They never told me that promotion would be based on citizenship, etc. I sent the letter to the President and copied the Associate President for Academics, the Dean of the School of Arts, and the Chair of the department. Soon, the order came for the senior members of the department to look into the matter. The chair claimed that I left my summer class and traveled to Africa. I told them what happened and how I took care of it before I left, and instead of what he thought, the Associate President told me I was a credit to the College. I said I did not tell him because I lost faith in him when he lied to me about the summer courses. Dr. LaPine raised his hand and pretended to slap me. I stood up and warned him directly and the committee, "This is the last time you will try such an insult before me. If you dare try it again, I will punch out your teeth." I walked out. Upon reaching my office, I called the Associate President's office and reported what happened in the kangaroo court. He called while they were still there. They had no defense. When I saw the Associate President next, he said again, "We are proud to have you here. To be a full professor, you must do something that should be nationally recognized." In other words, my promotion to Associate Professor was assured; however, I had to prove myself to be promoted to full professor. Whatever he said to them terrified them enough to prevent them from submitting my name as one of the three to be considered for the chairmanship of the department.

Melody was ready for Pre-K. Sweetie took her to Stanley school. This is a grade school owned by the College for the purpose of teaching practice and observation. As a part of the college, the principal and assistant professor were also members of the college faculty. When Melody and Sweetie arrived, he put our daughter's name on a waiting list. Believing that he had no ulterior motive, I accepted his decision. Several weeks later, Don Bennion took his son David to the same school for admission to the same class and registered him. David was about three months younger than Melody. Don told me about the registration. I called the Principal and asked why my daughter was on the waiting list. He lied to me as he did to Sweetie. I asked if any class of people was meant for a waiting list at the school. When he asked what I meant, I asked if he knew Don Bennion. "I am sending my wife and daughter to that school tomorrow. If my daughter is not registered, you and I will be standing before the College Authority to settle your case of discrimination against my daughter. If I am not satisfied, you will find yourself in a court of law. Melody was admitted the following day.

My family spent one Christmas holiday in Salt Lake City. Since I did not buy either my bachelor's or master's class ring, I went to the University of Utah to order my Ph.D. ring. They told me they had never done it before. I urged them to try it. They did. About a month after I ordered it, I received it. While we were in Salt Lake City, we had a snowy Sunday. My parents-in-law lived on a hill, and one could see almost the entire Salt Lake Valley from their balcony. During winter, the hill is treacherous. My father-in-law put chains on his tires. So, it was that snowy Sunday, and other cars got stuck on the hill. The people were trying to dig out their cars, and my father-in-law came with his car lights on, indicating he would drive through. One of the men gesturing for his attempting the impossible said, "Come on, wise guy, let's see how you will make it." We drove by, laughed, and clapped our hands. My quiet father-in-law simply laughed.

We were thinking of changing our car that we bought second hand and used for five years before the oil embargo was in full swing. Many of the car dealers were eager to rid their lots of the big cars. Car buyers were equally desiring to avoid the gas guzzlers, as the big cars were called. One dealer outside New Britain cut the cost of his Pontiac Catalina very low. I drove to the lot with the family. By the time we got there, they were all bought. The salesman we spoke to showed us a Pontiac Grandville. The price tag was over $7,200. It was bigger than the Catalina. He promised to sell it for $5,000 to get it off the lot by the end of the month. He showed us all the features plus the Mercedes engine. He reduced the price to $4,750. I still refused. He asked for our address and telephone number. I gave them to him. Right after dinner, our doorbell rang. When I opened the door, it was the car salesman. We started the bargaining all over again. He wanted the car off the lot by the end of the month. I did not offer him more than $4,700, and he agreed to sell it. However, he was disappointed when he learned that he would not be financing my car. When it was time to go, we shook hands. He said, "It is a pressure to do business with you." I went to my bank the following day, withdrew money, and paid him.

Though the various lecturers who taught the psychology of human development taught their classes as they wished, all the students watched the same films in a big hall under one lecturer. She selected the film and asked questions. At one of the department meetings, I suggested a review of the method used in teaching the course. The department agreed to appoint a committee to look into the matter. The chair appointed a three-man committee. Dr. Lapine, an Associate Professor, the chair's wife, an instructor, and I, an Assistant Professor, formed the committee. The chair and his wife went home and decided what they wanted, and he made her the chair of the committee. Every suggestion put forward was greeted by her with "her husband would not like that." I called for an adjournment. Once I reached my office, I wrote a letter of resignation from the committee stating that the chair knows what he wants to do with the course. He should submit his proposal to the department instead of through the committee. Lapine saw me and said, "I wondered how you were taking that." I passed without a word. Behind me, the chair said I wanted to fire his wife. Before me, he urged me to join them with my expertise in learning to conduct a study, he did not name. Many of these groups are still among our best friends in the States today.

Then I applied to the Nigerian consulate in New York for a job with the Federal Ministry of Education. John Ogbu had applied before me and was interviewed. I was invited. When I got there, they did not know what to ask me when I told them my specialty and the courses I taught. Finally, one of them said, "I am sorry. I am the only person in the group with some knowledge in your area. What is the difference between inductive and deductive teaching?" I thought I was back at HEC Uzuakoli again and started to lecture them on the folly of their mission. A few minutes later they dismissed me. I thanked God it was over, and they had no job for me. But I was mistaken. Several weeks later they offered me a job as a Senior Education Officer with a promise to pay all expenses to transport all my belongings to Nigeria and the plane fare for my family and me. The transportation was more attractive than the position. I put aside the whole package and continued without acknowledging the offer. Soon Mr. Anozie wrote me from Nigeria and informed me that my name was already in the newspapers as one of those recruited by the Federal Government. He encouraged me to accept the offer. I still treated them with silence.

Our International group became our family in New Britain. Most of them came from our church. As a group, we went to Catskill Game Farm in New York with our children. Twice Don and his family and my family traveled to Vermont to see the fall maple leaves and ride the wagon trains. The scenery is always beautiful in October before the leaves fall off the trees.

I kept my letter from the Nigerian consulate a secret from the College. The chair assigned me one developmental psychology course and my graduate learning course for the Summer. We planned to spend two weeks of our summer in eastern Canada. As a member of the American Automobile Association (AAA), I listed the cities we wished to visit and asked the Association to plot the route and make reservations for us. They obliged. Soon the package arrived, and we waited for summer school to come and go. That also became history. We drove from New Britain that morning. Our first stop was Ottawa, the capital of Canada. When we arrived at our hotel, they were waiting for us. It was early evening when we checked in. Melody and Chinedum traveled well, and we all enjoyed our "luxurious" new car that gave us only fourteen miles to the gallon on the highway. We enjoyed the evening. We wanted to watch the changing of the Guard the following morning. We also achieved that. What excited the children and even me was the sight of the double-decker bus. We watched the Changing of the Guard, and I explained the relationship of Canada to Buckingham Palace and the customs. The place was filled with visitors and tourists like us. Our next stop was Montreal.

Two places in particular interested us in Montreal. The first was the World Fairs and the second was the Cathedral. The Cathedral was beautifully decorated with rows of colorful burning candles displaying red, yellow, and white roses. The site took me back to my art appreciation class at Lyndon State, and I wondered how the instructor could not see and appreciate beauty in such an arrangement. Walking around the grounds, we saw the statues that told the story of the crucifixion. Among the visitors were some nuns. They acted pleasantly surprised to hear me describe the scene to our children, especially when I pointed out Simon of Cyrene who helped the Lord carry His cross.

Our next attraction was the World Pavilion. We saw the Dome, a magnificent creation of the globe that I cannot even describe. We then drove to Quebec City. We spent much of our time in the City. One of the scenes we enjoyed was the historical artifacts of the war between France and England. Melody climbed one of the cannons mounted in defense of the City, and I took a picture of her on it. Looking out through the window of our hotel in the evening, we saw carts drawn by some huge horses. I was tempted to take the family for a ride. But we were running low on cash. Besides, we had planned to visit a wax museum, the following morning before we left. I gave up the idea. By sunrise, we were on the road in search of the museum. After a long search without success, we turned homeward. To my surprise, I discovered that the car was not only guzzling gas but also oil. By early evening we were at St. J. in Vermont. We stopped for dinner. We were eating when Dave, my classmate at Lyndon, walked to our table and asked me, "Didn't you graduate from Lyndon?" I called him Dave and added, "I'm Obed." He asked if I did not say I was returning to Nigeria after graduation. "Yes," I said and reminded him that I planned to travel by bus across the ocean. When that proved impossible, I went back to school. We had a good laugh, and I introduced my family and told him where we had been, where we were going, and what I had done. It was dark by the time we finished eating. We retraced our way to New Britain. It was midnight by the time we reached our apartment.

Chapter 31
Last Semester In Connecticut

About two weeks after the semester started, a student walked into my office and introduced himself. He was Igbo. He was admitted to Central and given a visa to attend Central. On arrival in the States, he went to another institution in California. Immigration got hold of him and threatened to repatriate him if he did not return to Central. I gave him a ride to my apartment, and my wife fed him. Unaware of the kind of visa he had, I advised him to register with the dormitory. He seemed to have settled in my apartment. I refused to house and feed him and gave him twenty-four hours to find a place. He met the deadline. In less than a month he came back and begged to use my phone. He had violated the terms of his visa again. He was working against the terms of his type of visa and immigration was after him for the second time. He wanted to call the Nigerian Representative at the UN. I granted his request. Anyone can find my name from any corner of the globe today. He did and called me in 2012. He is still in the U.S.

Finally, I accepted the appointment Nigeria offered. I called John, and to my surprise, Nigeria did not know what to do with his field and did not offer him any job. We invited him and Linda, his wife, to visit us. When they came, they brought bad news. Several minutes after they arrived, John invited me to take a walk. He told me that he and Linda were getting a divorce. He did not think Linda wanted to have babies. He was not even sure she was not a lesbian. Linda was giving Sweetie her version. To her, John was losing a wife. We discussed our impending move to Nigeria. I felt sad but helpless to do anything. When I heard from John again, he had gone home and married Ada. When I announced our intention to move to Nigeria at Church, many told me to stay. One librarian told me that America needed me more than Nigeria. I said, "If God wanted me to be an American, I would have been born American."

When the semester started, the College expected me to continue with my various commitments. I had chaired the Personnel Committee of the Greater New Britain Campus Ministry the previous year. The members expressed satisfaction with how I handled matters and nominated me for the President of the whole ministry. I declined and told them I did not think I would be there the entire school year. But if you want me as the Vice, I will accept. They made me the Vice. Lee, the Director who received his Ph.D. and wanted to be placed on the same salary as a full professor, resigned and took a job somewhere else. We were in the process of hiring a replacement when I left. As though there was a conspiracy to keep me in the U.S., the University of California at Chico wrote me and asked me to apply to head its African Studies. Within a short time, one University in Chicago wrote me to apply for the position of Associate Professor. McCook Hospital asked me to head its children's department. When the Vice President for Academics went through the list of those who applied for promotion and did not see mine, he sent me a memo asking me to submit mine. It was getting to the end of September. I took my three-month letter of resignation notice to the Associate President and gave it to him. He expressed his regret and asked to know why I resigned. I told him. I put the chairman's copy in his box in the secretary's office.

Muhammad Ali and Joe Frazier were preparing to fight for the World Heavy Weight Championship. The prefight showmanship was on the TV. Ali came to entertain the world. Frazier, on the other hand, took the fight to be a matter of life and death. Ali made fun of Frazier, who looked angrier. Ali looked at him and told him that he was too ugly to be the world champion. Ali opened his briefcase took out a stuffed skinny gorilla of about five inches, and showed it to Frazier. He dangled it before his face and declared, "I will get the gorilla in Manila." That forced a smile out of Frazier for the first time during the interview. I enjoyed Ali and wished him well. We did not watch the fight on the TV. However, I dreamed about the fight three times that night. Each time, Ali won the fight. That was the first time I had the same dream three times the same night. I got up early in the morning. When I opened the door, the newspaper had Ali's picture as the world champion on the front page and he did win.

Sweetie was involved in the Children's Ministry at Trinity Methodist. Trinity received a new Minister whose wife ministered to the church through dancing. Sweetie also joined her. They floated gracefully with outstretched arms as the music played before the pastor preached.

December 31 was the effective date of my resignation. We were gradually preparing to leave. My visit to Nigeria more than three years earlier was still fresh in my mind. I was returning to Nigeria with ditches on the roads. Unfortunately, I was returning with my Pontiac Grandville. I had to put it in its best road-worthy condition. First, I took it to the dealer and reminded them they had not taken care of the oil leak. God led the manager to walk over as I discussed the problem and looked at the record. Surprised at how early I reported the problem and the failure of his men to do the repair, he promised to take care of it. I did not tell them my plan to leave the U.S. On my return to claim the car, the manager told me they put a new engine in the car. It was free. However, I had to pay for the labor. Then I took it to a muffler place to put new heavy shock absorbers on it. I changed all four tires. I went to Sears and bought a toolbox. Since I was not sure the kind of cooling liquid used in the car in place of ordinary water was available in Nigeria, I bought three gallons of the yellow liquid.

Meanwhile, the Nigerian Embassy had sent us four tickets and permission to send our belongings through a shipping company. The choice of the date of travel was ours. We woke up one morning and picked up our newspaper to read. On the front page was another story of another north-engineered coup in Nigeria.

This time it was a bloodless coup. Gowon, who had ruled Nigeria since July 1966 when his northern soldiers massacred Igbo men, women, children, and even the unborn, was out of power. He was attending a Commonwealth Heads of Governments Conference when the news was announced. He expected the news. The British Government knew of the plot and warned him. Unable to do anything about it, he sent his family to Britain before he traveled. Mutula took over the reign of Nigeria with Obasanjo as his second in command. That did not affect either my employment or the arrangement to travel.

In disgust of the chair and his new wife, the woman who served as the secretary to the department, asked to be transferred to another department and got her wish. As usual, the International group celebrated Christmas. Before the holiday I had one more student incident. The female student made an appointment to see me. When she came, I was facing my desk and asked her to sit down. She would face me if she sat down. Instead of taking a seat,, she looked at my bookshelf behind me. She pretended to be searching for a book. Suddenly, I heard her sniffing. She was weeping. I invited her to sit down. When she did, she unburdened herself. She was the first to attend college in her family. She said that she knew she was not college material. However, her father had pinned all his hope for getting a college graduate in the family on her. Yet, she did not believe she would make it. All I could do was to encourage her to go on.

Gradually I emptied the bookshelves of all my books and carried them and every personal belonging in the office home. Having arranged with a shipping company to come and take our belongings, I thought that I would start work before our belongings arrived and made a different arrangement to transport my books. I shipped them through the post office. I went to the human resources office to settle my accounts. I withdrew all my contributions including retirement. When it came to Social Security the good lady told me to leave it alone. "You have paid enough to earn your social security pay wherever you may be when the time comes." I let the sleeping dog lie.

Unaware that our friends were planning a surprise send-off for us, we were invited to Dr. Jim Snaden's birthday celebration. We accepted. To make sure we did not opt out at the last minute, Don and Gene Bennion cooked up an excuse about their car and requested a ride to the Snaden's that evening. Carol, our neighbor, came and borrowed one of the food items she used. It was snowing when we left the premises to get the Bennions. It snowed through most of the night. When we reached the Snaden's home, there were many cars around, but the house was quiet because they knew of our arrival time, and one light was on. The Bennions knew what was going on, but Sweetie and I were in the dark. We rang the doorbell, and the lights went on simultaneously with shouts of Surprise! Surprise! Sweetie knew what it was all about immediately. But to this foreigner, it took a few minutes to sink in. It was a beautiful and memorable evening with beautiful people and gifts. The most memorable was a beautiful album filled with pictures and writings. One of the big surprises of the evening was the presence of Marge, the former wife of the chairman. Note: When I visited Central Connecticut in 1982, the chairman had retired and was no longer married to the woman in the department for whom he left his wife. The story is that he called Marge, his former wife, one day and asked for pardon and said, "If you will take me back, I am ready to return." His adult children objected, but she convinced them and received him back. End of Note.

The shipping company came on December 31 and took our car and everything we gave them. Thank God we arranged door to door shipping without which most of our property could have been stolen at Apapa Lagos wharf.

1976 was the second centennial celebration of the United States. My wife and children are American citizens. That is a once-in-a-lifetime event. They would start that year in the United States, and I would take them to where they did not know. I suggested to Sweetie to stay with the children and come after the celebrations. She preferred to travel with me and declined the offer. I accepted her decision. By the evening of December 31, all our belongings except the suitcases we took on the plane and our television set had been taken from our apartment. They were on their way to Nigeria or given away.

We spent the night at the Thompson's home with our suitcases. We had celebrated the new year with them. We also spent January second, our last full day in New Britain with them. The neighbors in our group came to say goodbye. Our friends took us to JFK Airport.

So far God has accomplished every dream He showed or disclosed to me from Umunwanwa through and beyond Nebraska, e.g. marriage to a white woman, going to ETC Uzuakoli, the U.S.A., the visit by Jesus Christ in my dream and results, Ali's victory and the defeat of Biafra, all to demonstrate His faithfulness.

When we got to the Airport, we discovered that the Nigerian Airline did not book us to fly that night in spite of several calls and promises. However, after a short wait they assigned us seats and loaded our suitcases. We hugged and kissed, and the women shed tears and we parted. My family waited for boarding.

Part Five
Back To Nigeria

Chapter 32

Transit to Nigeria

I left Nigeria on October 3, 1963, to come to the U.S., and on January 3, 1976, exactly twelve years and three months, I was leaving the U.S. to return to Nigeria with a family of four. Praise be to God. Still, I was filled with trepidation. For one reason, I was taking the family to a different and worse Nigeria than the one I knew. That was the main reason I wanted them to stay in the U.S. until after July 4. Then it was time to board.

The change was obvious. In 1963 the PAN AM I flew by was almost empty. In 1976 the Nigerian plane was like any market in Nigeria. One could tell immediately on stepping onto the plane that the passengers were traders. The excess baggage they carried filled both the overhead and below-seat spaces. Both the passengers and the agents on the ground ignored the weight limits. Later that night we left the U.S.. Our plane stopped in Guinea and we felt the West African January heat of the sun. After spending some time there, we took off and arrived at the Lagos International Airport. We collected our luggage but no one from the Ministry was there to welcome us. January 4 was a Sunday.

Doing what any person in my situation should do, I went to the desk and said, "I am Dr. Onwuegbu a Federal Ministry of Education officer. Could you please announce our arrival and ask any Ministry representative to meet us?" He did and soon someone showed up. He promised to get someone from the Ministry to pick us up and asked us to wait. After two hours without any sign of a person or a car, I decided to pay for the taxi. He promised to send us to a hotel. I stayed at Ebute Metta, where my brother and some other Igbo people lived, when I left Nigeria more than twelve years ago. I requested a hotel in the area. Unknown to me was the fact that he was representing an employee of the Ministry for the purpose of assigning new Ministry employees to hotels prearranged for the purpose of sharing the hotel pay. He directed the taxi to a hotel at Ebute Metta. I paid the taxi driver, and we were checked in.

Chinedum has always been a picky eater. Even his doctor in New Britain at one time excluded milk from his diet. We were concerned about what he would eat from the onset, and he did not disappoint us. As Providence would have it, he took a liking for rice and fried plantain, both were common. We occupied two adjacent rooms, the children in one and Sweetie and I in the other. We had a good restful night. After our breakfast, we took a taxi to the Federal Ministry of Education Building. When we got out of the taxi car, the premises looked very familiar, but I could not say why. Later I discovered it was the former American Embassy building I visited several times in 1963. When the military took over the government of Nigeria, it accused the U.S. government of spying on the building and took the building over. We walked into the building and registered my arrival date.

When I walked into that reception room, I knew I was not in the United States anymore. No one smiled and no one asked, "May I help you?" Instead of giving me a smile, or asking me to report to a school, they told me to report daily to the same room. I was not alone.

There were many faces from many different countries who were housed in hotels, fed, and paid for doing nothing. Wondering how long the waiting would last, we returned to the hotel now assured that the Ministry would pay the expenses.

Suddenly, I had the flying nun at my back on our bed, with her finger pointing in a certain direction. Sweetie said, "Honey look," in a whispering voice. I looked and looked wondering what in the world caused my wife to fly like lightning behind me and kept her there. Sweetie's flight frightened whatever it was, it hid itself. I could not see anything. What is it? Finally, it came out again and it was a mouse. When I got up to get something to kill it, it disappeared again. My wife was determined not to climb down from the bed until the thing was dead. We played cat and mouse until it was dead. Sweetie climbed down, and I thanked God for its death, threw it out, and prayed that we did not see any other mouse in that hotel. God answered my prayer.

Taking my family to the Ministry every day was not a wise thing to do. So, most of the days I left them at the hotel and went alone. One of the days I told a taxi driver where I intended to go. He and his friend mischievously drove to a different section of Lagos. Suddenly they saw passengers and stopped. When I opened the door, I was at Oyinbo market close to the Mainland Hotel. Looking at them as mischievous fools, I walked away without giving them a penny. They did not have the guts to ask me to pay them either. That was an opportunity for me to walk to the yard where my brother and other Igbo people from Umuahia lived from where I traveled to the United States for the first time more than twelve years ago.

There were no Igbo people around. I walked back to the hotel. Nine days after we arrived in Lagos Chinedum turned four years old. Celebrating the birthday was almost impossible. Sweetie was able to buy a cake at a store and we took it back to the hotel and had a semi celebration.

Two weeks after we arrived in the country, for the first time I saw a familiar face at the Ministry. He came from my village. I called him Mlewedim, the name I knew him. He came, greeted me and politely told me that he changed his name to Elijah. He was a messenger in the Ministry. A few days later, Njikonye and Elijah from my village who visited me in 1972 at my uncle's apartment, visited us at the hotel. At this time Njikonye was married to the girlfriend who accompanied them in 1972. While in Lagos, we got in contact with Emedom and Chy, who had moved from Aba to Lagos. They took us out one evening. At another time, they took us to see Mr. Uta, who married Ogonnaya, one of my cousins from the village. She died the previous year during childbirth. It was through Ogonnaya that I got to know Ngozi. Emedom looked at Sweetie and said to me in Igbo, Your wife is beautiful." I said, "Thank you." Mr. Uta had made an album of the burial ceremony. We left after a sober evening.

About the end of the second week, I was eager to see my mother and for her to see my family. I was also bored and tired of doing nothing and demanded to be posted. They thought I was crazy for not enjoying idleness that cost me nothing. That was the first clash I had with Nigerian employees, and it was the beginning. When they insisted they had no station to post me, I told them to send me to East Central State. They looked at me as though I was out of my mind because that was the state the war affected most. The Yoruba Principal Education Office in charge looked at me as though I had committed suicide and said, "That is your choice and to East Central you go." Having agreed to send us to Enugu, they gave us a date. They would buy the tickets and provide transport to the airport. Later I discovered that the Ministry employees were offended and angry at me because I was leaving, and my leaving put both the hotel owner and them at a financial disadvantage. They made me pay for it.

They took us to the airport as planned but I was left on my own. Though we had not added any weight to our luggage we were charged for excess load. I paid it believing that I would be refunded. That turned out to be a wishful thought. We collected our suitcases on arrival at Enugu. It took some time to connect with the state ministry. However, once we notified them, it did not take long before we were conveyed to the Ministry headquarters. Once Sweetie and the children sat down, I walked to a woman officer who had it out for those officers she perceived to have run away from the state to other parts of the country immediately after the end of the war. She jumped on me. "You are now coming back to this state. You all ran away from here immediately after the war thinking we would all die. We are still here and alife." I looked at her in unbelief. Her attack once more reminded me of the story of the beetle and the chicken mentioned earlier. I wondered when and where this woman's hatred started. I looked at her and replied. "Woman, if you fought this war here the way I fought it from the U.S. you would have won it. You lost it, live with it." A single word did not come out of her mouth about the war again. By then, Godwin Chimaroke, a man from my village, had become aware of our arrival, and he was a senior officer of the Ministry. He came and helped secure for us a chalet in a government hotel. We had a sitting room and two bedrooms. I sent two telegrams, one to my brother at Abakeleke and the other to my mother at Amafor, my village, that reported our arrival at Enugu.

Very soon people from my village started to visit us. One of the first people was Gbo Gordon from my compound. My brother came from Abakeleke within the week. One evening, we went for dinner, and Melody did not want to eat. We cajoled her to eat a little. By midnight she was burning with fever and shaking. Sweetie took her temperature, and it was 104 F. Sweetie put her in the tub and sponged her with cold water while I walked to the front desk. There was no one at the front desk. A sign indicated I should go to Room 5. I knocked and a man answered. I greeted him, introduced myself and requested him to search his registry. "Do you have any medical doctor at this hotel? If you do, may I have his name and room number please?" He searched and gave me a name and the room number. I hurried to the door and knocked. He opened the door. I apologized for disturbing his sleep introduced myself and informed him that my family recently arrived from the U.S.. Then I described Melody's high fever and what my wife was doing. He kindly gave me two tablets of quinine and told me to give her one immediately and the remaining one early the following morning. Then take her to Enugu Teaching Hospital. I thanked him and hurried back to our suite. Sweetie gave her the tablet, and within a short time, the fever subsided. We all went to sleep. Daybreak brought much improvement in her condition. After she took the two tablets the fever was almost gone. We took her to the hospital, where she received a thorough checkup and treatment. Though she lost her appetite for a few days, she recovered completely.

Before the end of our second week at Enugu all the people from my village who lived at Enugu organized a welcome party in our honor. Among those present were Ogbonna Inegbu, my classmate in elementary school, and dee Solomon Chikara, who worked for the government newspaper in Enugu. Mr. Chikara brought a team from the newspaper who wrote an article about the party and took pictures. We cut and sent some copies to my parents-in-law and some friends in the States.

Our stay in the suite was costing the government too much. So after about a week in the suite, they moved us to the regular hotel room. As Godwin said, "We put you there so that your wife and children will know that we have what they have in the U.S." I told him that he spoiled my fun. I told people in the U.S. that you gave Americans the biggest trees. Instead, you gave my wife a chalet. While we were in this large hotel building, I met a man from Umuahia. I heard about him when I was a student at Uzuakoli at a time when he was a university undergraduate student. But we did not meet, and if we had crossed each other's path, we might not speak to each other because we were in different worlds class-wise. He arrived from the States with his two sons. On hearing my name, he told me more about himself. He married my elementary school classmate at Mission Hill. The wife told him all about me. She even saw me at Umuahia two days before I left Umuahia to travel to the U.S. They were in the States together, but he and the sons left her behind to complete her master's degree. He then told me the story of one of his sons and the lizard.

Anyone who grew up in Nigeria, whether in the city or village, grew up with lizards. A lizard is a small reptile about three to four inches from its head to where its tail starts and only one inch wide at its stomach. It is useful because it feeds on bugs. It runs around in the yards and climbs the tree when it feels threatened. Then came this American boy, seeing the lizard as it ran about on the hotel grounds got him excited. He requested the father to get one as a pet for him. It took the father some time to convince the son that no one made a pet out of the lizard.

As a federal officer loaned to East Central State, I was allowed to teach or work only at a teachers' college. This restriction was in place because the Federal Government had planned to implement its Universal Free Primary Education (UPE) grade two teachers colleges to train teachers. Even Enugu did not know where to send me. After another two weeks of idleness, waiting became unbearable. I went to the office and volunteered to go to colleges to find any that might need a teacher. They suggested two and gave me the addresses. I was to pay for my transport and request a refund later. One of the names was Umuavosi Amavo Aba Grade Two Teachers College. Aba is only forty miles from Umuahia my home. I chose to visit the college first. From Enugu to Aba is about 120 miles and I arranged with a taxi driver to pick me up the following morning. When we got to the college the Principal was absent. But someone assured me of their need for a lecturer. I promised to come, and we turned around and left.

We stopped at a gas station in Umuahia, my town, to fill the tank. When I looked out through my window there was dee Nwoko Onwuneme from my village almost at my face. To prevent him from seeing me, I looked the other way. Because my family was not with me and I did not plan to visit the village, I did not want anyone to see me and go home and tell my mother. So secretly and quietly I slipped through Umuahia and even through the short road that leads to my village. My successful trip paved the way to my station. While we waited for the Ministry to make transport arrangements two incidents occurred. First, I learned that Dr. Akanu Ibiam, the first Nigerian Governor of Eastern Region, lived nearby. The Students Christian Movement (SCM) at Uzuakoli College invited him to speak to us when he was the Principal of Hope Wardell College, Calabar. He was a fine Christian and renounced his British knighthood during the Biafra Nigeria war because of the British Government's support for and supply of massive weapons to Nigeria against Biafra. I went and enjoyed a short visit with him. The second was a visit to the University of Nigeria Nsukka. I was introduced to one of the Deans as a psychologist. He arranged to interview me for a post in the Department of Psychology. A short time after we returned to Enugu, the waiting was over.

A Ministry driver driving a combi bus knocked at our door one day, we loaded the bus and were on our way to Aba. I had heard that my mother panicked when she received the telegram, I sent to her. She claimed that telegraph messages are only used to report the death of a person. This day I determined to see her. We went through Umuahia. One- and one-half miles before we reached the center of Umuahia township we branched to my village a few hundred yards away from the main road. When we reached the compound, my mother was not home. But she was in the village. We did not even send anybody or message. Those who saw us informed her of our presence. She hurried home. Assured that we were alive and well, she saw her daughter-in-law and grandchildren, and she was elated. Sweetie kissed her. Before we left, I promised her a visit that following Sunday. Our next stop was at the College. Again, the Principal was not in, and someone had to deputize for her. We were sent to the ENTA Hotel.

On arrival at the hotel, Mr. Onyeado, the proprietor of the hotel, was not sure whether or not to lodge my family because there was no official letter from the Principal. It was a Friday and he had to wait until Monday before he could hear from the College. In the end he did accept us, and we would be there for months. Our son had a terrible time with food. He specialized in toast with peanut butter, rice, and plantain. ENTA Guest House Hotel proprietor introduced us to Indian curry. The official letter came from the College on Monday to the hotel and Mr. Onyeado was pleased to have us for as long as the government was willing to pay him.

Chapter 33

Living In The War Zone

First Year On Return

Like the rest of my family, I had returned to experience a new Nigeria different from the one I left over twelve years before. It was worse in the area they called "the war zone." Policemen carried guns instead of batons as they did before I traveled to the U.S.A. The soldiers carried guns and stopped traffic every few miles. The whole place looked like an army camp. I traveled about ten miles by taxi every morning to the College.

Soon after we arrived at Aba, the rumor we heard at Enugu about a new state within East Central became a reality. The birth of Imo State was announced. Owerri was the capital to the disappointment of those who had hoped that Umuahia would be the capital. The ministries and ministry officials carved out of East Central, made up of mainly the personnel of Imo indigens, were sent to Owerri to start the new state. Many of them had no accommodation at Owerri and were temporarily stationed at Aba. The Ministry of Education was one of the ministries sent to Aba. The personnel filled the hotels at government expense.

Before long Sweetie was trekking to Aba market to buy certain things. On one such trip she met one older English lady, Miss

Backhouse. She had been in this part of Nigeria for over thirty years. She stopped and gave Sweetie a ride. From her the many expatriate women at Aba knew that another white woman was in town. It was through her that Sweetie learned about Auntie Margaret School. Our investigation confirmed it was a good school. We sent our children Melody to kindergarten and Chinedum to PreK.

As I expected, I soon discovered that Senior Education Officer was an insult to my level of education and experience. Some Indians who graduated Ph.D. and were five years my junior, recruited from the States at the same time I was were Principal Education Officers, two levels my senior. Of course, my name as an Igbo (Biafran) gave me a definite disadvantage before the recruiters. Even at the College, a man who graduated with a bachelor's degree after I did without any further education or publication, was my senior. I petitioned the Federal Ministry of Education arguing that at least I should be an Assistant Chief Education Officer. Meantime Imo State Ministry of Education advertised the post of a Chief Education Officer. I also applied for the position. I was invited to the interview at Enugu.

Though the publisher in Boston, U.S., had said that publishing my book Humanizing Education would force him to throw away every book he had published, I was not discouraged. In fact, his comment had the opposite effect. I modified it for Nigeria and entitled it Discover Teaching. It became my teaching text. If it was new to the publisher in Boston, it was a fairy tale to the students at Umuavosi Amavo and their teachers. One grade two teacher without a degree got annoyed that I corrected a student's teaching lesson note after he had done so. At one time, all the students, teachers, and the Principal gathered in the classroom as I prepared the students for external teaching examinations. They could not believe some of the things I said.

The first difference I noticed was the caliber of students. At my time the students were first class students. For example, the students who went to Nto-Ndang for teacher training were first, second, or third in their classes. As a result, eighty percent of them eventually obtained a degree or more from universities. Those admitted from secondary schools to teachers training colleges made grade one or two. But in 1976, most of the students in Grade Two Teachers' Colleges either failed the school certificate examination or had grade three. As a result, the standard was lower because there were universities in the country that admitted the best high school graduates and the government wanted to train anyone who attended secondary school and was willing to become a teacher. Here are two examples of the problems I encountered. Teachers behaved as though if the student failed it was solely the student's fault. When I taught them to write the instructional objective (what they knew as the aim of the lesson), that measured the result of teaching by the level of the learner's success, that was unacceptable. One of the students asked, "Do you mean that if I do everything I can, and the student still fails it is my fault?" This is what brought every teacher and student to my class. Another is the statement, "If at this level you cannot illustrate and demonstrate what you teach in practical terms, you probably don't understand it."

This is not a book on teaching. Therefore, I shall not answer these questions in detail here. I repeated the statement the student made, namely, "If I did everything I could..." That is the problem. You are doing everything! Is the student to sleep, watch, play, or what? The learner does nothing except watch the teacher regurgitate a concept he does not understand. They challenged me to make democracy and friction practical. Anyone who understands these two concepts knows they are the easiest to demonstrate. But the military had ruled Nigeria for too long without elections. The Principal and teachers appointed student prefects without students' elections. I got them to elect leaders from among themselves. Then, by questions and answers, they demonstrated by, of, and for the people. The concepts became self-explanatory. Rolling different objects of various degrees of shapes and smooth and rough surfaces on the grass, floor, and tables took care of friction.

The students demonstrated the concepts and explained them in their own words. There was no more the question of the teacher doing everything herself without student participation.

In the meantime, the Federal Ministry of Education replied to my letter through the Principal. I never knew her qualifications. I knew she did not have a degree. She read the reply, misconstrued the content of my letter, and acted offended. To show me that she was the boss she assigned me to mark the register, a duty that should be assigned to the most junior member of the faculty. I did not say a word, nor did I mark the register. When the Federal Ministry of Education rejected my petition, I wrote the Federal Service Commission. I came home from the College one day and Sweetie told me that the shipping company brought our belongings, but they were not at the hotel. I asked where the car was. They did not bring it and I had to go to Lagos to get it.

I took the particulars of the car and went to Lagos. It was bad news. It was not a question of ownership. The government demanded me to pay 8,750 naira as import duty and that was more than three times what the car cost to buy. I went to the Ministry and everyone I met was a Yoruba. Rather than help, they frustrated me. I went back to Emedom's house and slept there. I left Lagos by bus in the morning for Aba. Before noon we were at Ore. It rained the previous day, and the road was slippery. A trailer fell and blocked the road. That was the only road that connects the east to the west. Vehicles stretched miles on both sides of the trailer at a standstill. There was no telephone service to inform Sweetie or Emedom where I was or what was happening. It was getting dark, and the Yoruba people started hawking food and drinks. I bought one corn on the cob. Fearful of poisoning myself with the water they sold I bought a can of beer. I tasted beer for the first time in my life. The first swallow was more than enough for me. I threw away the rest and went back to my seat. The sun was shining the following day when the state Commissioner of Police rode his

Mercedes Benz flanked by armed policemen in police trucks, made a two-minute photo at the scene and vanished. It was late afternoon before the vehicles started moving again. It was late in the night by the time I reached ENTA Guest House.

I completed preparing the students for the teaching examination and went for the interviews at Nsukka. The Dean of the College was willing to offer me a job as a Senior Lecturer, but Dr. Adiele, the Acting head of the department, who was a Grade One lecturer, objected and put me on the same level he was. I refused the offer. Mr. Uzoma, who was the Supervisor of Schools in the Anglican denomination when I was a pupil at Mission Hill, had become the Chair of the newly created Imo State Civil Service. He presided over the interview for the Chief Education Officer selection. As the Supervisor of Schools, the college where I was teaching was under him. He and the Principal thought they had a savior for the College in me. His comment at the interview was, "You want to sit behind the desk instead of teaching?" I immediately knew that he did not know the duties the Chief should perform. But I respected his age. If he and the Principal thought they won, they had a rude awakening awaiting them.

I took every penny in my bank account and the arrears the government paid me, which covered my salary since we arrived in the country. I still needed a few hundred naira to make up. Then I discovered that the Chief Accountant had taken more than eight percent of my money as rent when I had no place to stay. Besides they tried to force me out of the hotel before they gave me an apartment. First, I met the Chief Accountant about the deduction for rent. When he argued, pointing to the paragraph about rent deduction, I said to him, "If I expect you to read this and understand it am I expecting too much from you?" He yielded and promised to cooperate with me fully from that day on. Imo Government ordered all its employees to vacate the hotels. The employees extended the order to me without providing me with a place to live. My wife had found a house in the Government Reserve

Area (GRA) meant for senior government officials and expatriates for ₦200 a month. They refused to rent it and continued to spend over eighteen hundred naira a month at the hotel. I refused to move and demanded to go to Lagos as a Federal Officer. They accepted my challenge. I also took a petition I wrote to the Head of State that making me pay import duty on my car was a violation of the terms of my contract of employment. In the process of trying to collect enough money to get my car, I asked my brother if he bought the land I sent $2,000 to buy for me. He said, "No;" and added that he used the seven hundred fourteen pounds plus (£714 plus) to educate his children in secondary school. Also, he used part of it to help Nnamdi (his brother-in-law) at Uzuakoli College with the hope that he would help him educate his own children. I wondered aloud before my mother how he could work, use all the $200 I sent to him for his personal use and the $2,000 I sent him to buy land for me in less than seven months.

With my money and petition to the State in my hand, I was ready to travel to Lagos again. A member of the faculty read the petition and declared, "Dr., you missed your calling. You should have been a lawyer." I spent the night with Emedom and his family. I was not surprised that the Secretary to the Head of State was a Yoruba man. I told him my mission and the petition I brought with me. Envy was written all over his face. He accused me of returning to Nigeria with an airconditioned car so that I could roll up my windows and avoid seeing the filth on the streets." Completely ignoring the terms of the contract, he demonstrated his tribal animosity against my name as an Igbo. I asked him who put the filth there and wanted to know why he did not clean it? His attitude already showed me what to expect of him. I knew the letter would not go beyond his desk. Therefore, I gave him the duplicate and kept the letter with me. He did not even notice it was a duplicate.

Determined to see the Head of State before I paid the money, I walked towards Dodan Barracks, the office and residence of the Head of State. On arrival, I noticed the whole place was fenced round, and I did not see any sign to the entrance. I saw a military sergeant and asked for the entrance. He looked at me over,, and I was not wearing a suit or the Nigerian flowing agbada, and asked, "What do you want the entrance for?" He was incensed to hear me say, "I want to see the Head of State." He blurted out, "You want to see the Head of State who sees other Heads of State and Ambassadors!" I asked, "How many heads do those heads of state and ambassadors have?" "Who are you?" he asked. "I am Dr. Onwuegbu," was my answer." "Oh! You are a doctor. There!" He pointed to the entrance. When I walked through the gate there were soldiers and guns ready for any situation. Having learned that doctor carries a certain respect with it, I introduced myself as Dr. Onwuegbu. The officer in command asked what I wanted. When I told him, he informed me that the Head of State was not in the office. He demanded to know if I had an appointment. When I said, "No," he took the letter and promised to deliver it. That ended my first trip to Dodan Barracks. This time Emedom was traveling to Umuahia and gave me a ride home.

Our car had been at Apapa Wharf for about a month, and my letter to the Head of State for more than two weeks without a reply. I went back to Lagos. First, I went back to the Barracks, and they were angry that I expected a reply that early. I went back to the Ministry not knowing what God had prepared for me. I met Okugo, the Igbo I met at Nebraska, who could not complete his doctorate in Lincoln. He told me that he spent a year in Germany. After a short chat about him and my problems he took me to a lady and introduced me as Dr. Onwuegbu. Her eyes opened wide, and looking at me, she asked, "Are you the same Dr. Onwuegbu who wrote that letter to the Commissioner and did not even care to type it?" It happened she was the officer who replied to my petition. She was also Igbo. She must have been educated in the U.S. also. She wanted to know how long I was in the States. "Twelve years and three months," I replied. "That's the problem," she said and offered me a seat. I continued, "I don't know why I came back. I would be an Associate Professor now."

I gave her the letter from the Imo State Ministry. She read it and became angry. She rebuked them and warned them. "If Dr. Onwuegbu, with his qualifications and experience, were a foreigner, you would have kept him in the hotel for years. He is not leaving that hotel until you provide a furnished house for him." I told her how much I was going to pay to repossess my car. She said they were joking, and I would not pay a penny. She wrote a note, walked to another office, and returned with a paper she gave to me and told me to take it to a government clearing office. "They would release your car to you." I could not believe what was happening. I could have hugged and kissed her. But I was "new" to a "new" Nigeria. I thanked her and went to the Wharf. If the Yoruba officer at the clearing office thought I would bribe him to do his work, it did not succeed. After all his complaints about what I did and did not do, he gave me the paper. I went to the Port Authority and received my keys to the car. I did not know that they emptied the tank before loading the car onto the ship. I tried to start it without success. With the strokes of her pen Mrs. Ann Akpofure had solved two of the three biggest problems I faced in Nigeria since we arrived.

By the time I got the car ready for a drive, the offices had closed. I drove to Emedom, and we changed the oil that night in readiness for the long drive to Aba the following day. I drove Emedom to his office that night. Commenting on the smooth ride on the bad roads, he said the road that destroyed his small car could not shake mine. I left early the following morning and was not stopped throughout the Yoruba and Benin regions. A few hundred yards to the Onitsha bridge the police stopped me. They wanted to see my driver's license. I took out my Connecticut license and told them it was an international license. They looked at it and waved me goodbye. I drove to the village and my mother and brother were in the house. I asked my mother to get in the car and drove her around with her sitting in what Nigerians call the owner's seat. Then I drove to Aba to meet my family, thanking God I had accomplished the goal for which I brought the car to Nigeria, namely, to give my mother a ride in the car. No one, including me, thought it a possibility.

On my arrival at Aba the blast of the car horn at ENTA Guest House brought the family to the window with smiles. It was a Friday, and I did not have to go to work the following day. However, I drove my family to my village on Sunday. Coming back, we saw some members of the college faculty on the college premises. I honked but they did not know who was calling their attention. When I drove in on Monday, all the students rushed out in pursuit, cheering, clapping their hands, and chanting, "One in town! One in town!"

While I was in Lagos trying to get my car two events took place at the College. The Federal Commissioner for Education visited the College. There were two other Federal officers at the College, but they were recent graduates. If he said anything or asked about me was not made known to me. When I gave the the letter from Mrs. Akpofure to the Imo State employees, they seemed to be determined to leave us in the hotel indefinitely. The second event, which took place while I was in Lagos, was the external teaching examination. The examiners stayed at a hotel at Aba. One of them slept with a woman at the hotel. During the teaching examination, he discovered that the woman was one of the students. He failed her because of that. I could not believe the Principal allowed the married man to get away with that, but he did. Unlike Jesus who forgave the woman caught in adultery (John 8:1-11).

With my car in hand, I became mobile. That also meant encounters with the police, soldiers, and crazy drivers. The police stopped me one time out of curiosity about the size of the car or the license. They debated about the Connecticut plate before me. One of them asserted, "It is one of those plates they give in Lagos." Lagos was the capital of Nigeria at the time. Then they asked me to go. With the soldiers, it was a different story.

We were on our way to the village one day. We had passed the College and approached a three-man soldier's post. Two of them looked unconcerned and one could not make up his mind about what to do. At the last minute when we were only a few yards from him, he raised his hand. I turned on my blinker and drove a few yards past the post before coming to a stop. He walked to the car, still nervous, and blurted out, "Where are you going?" I was annoyed and wondered if I had to obtain his permission to go anywhere. "Don't be silly. Is where I am going your business?" He turned back muttering, "You are abusing me." Sweetie said as we drove off, "Isn't it too bad that you have to go to that extent to get a sense in them?" At another time and place, the soldiers stopped cars about a mile on each side of the road. It took us about one hour from where we stopped at the tail end of the line to reach the spot where the soldiers stood. Once we reached the spot, the soldier ordered me to get out and open the boot. I sat in my car and pressed the button that opened the boot. He yelled at me to get out! I told him the boot was open. He did not know, nor had he seen a boot opened like that before. He continued to yell and order me to get out. His officer walked to him and ordered him to go and inspect the boot and muttered, "It is people like you we are trying to protect." I drove away wondering why they would allow a drunk with a gun in his hand on the road.

There were many accidents with many fatalities on Nigerian roads. One could blame the fact that there were no speed limits on the roads. In reality that is a minor cause. Besides the condition of the roads and drivers buying their licenses, one of the experiences I had significantly contributed to my resignation. On my way to work one morning, I was close to the college gate and turned on my blinker. Ordinarily, even tankers avoid my "luxurious" car for fear of who might be in such a car. But that was not the case that morning. I slowed down and turned left to enter the college premises. A Peugeot taxi car with eight passengers was screeching its brakes with the passengers shouting at the driver. The car stopped a few yards behind the tail of my car. With all the noise and imminent danger, I held my brakes with force only to be held back by my seatbelt. The taxi reversed and drove past. I heard the passengers say, "He had his blinker light on showing where he was going." I thanked my God. My insurance was still the one I had in Connecticut.

While we were still at ENTA Guest House I said to Sweetie, "Let us try one more time for another baby." She agreed. I prayed for a baby boy. She became pregnant. Some Americans recommended a Christian hospital on the outskirts of Aba with Dr. Whitaker, an English man in charge, and with Nancy, an American nurse who worked with him.

Mr. Ibegbulem had been a teacher for almost fifty years and had retired. However, because both state and federal governments had not paid his retirement benefits, he continued to teach in order to maintain his family. The Imo State Government owed him ₦18,000, and the Federal Government owed him ₦24,000. The Imo State Ministry employee in charge would not pay him unless he gave them a bribe. He was unwilling to bribe them and was distressed over the whole thing. I told him not to worry and promised to travel to Owerri the Ministry headquarters. On arrival, I went to the Chief Accountant, who previously promised to cooperate fully with me in the future, and told him why I was there. Reluctantly he called a junior officer and told him to give me the money. As he went, he muttered, "He has to send a whole doctor to come and get it for him." I said to him, "If you had given it to him without demanding a bribe, he would not have sent even half a doctor." Amazingly the envelope was ready. He took it out and gave it to me. I thanked the Chief and left. Mr. Ibegbulem was all smiles when he saw his check. I thanked God I was able to help him. I could not do that for him from the States.

I thought about the dangerous road I drove daily. The memory of the drunk soldier with a gun in his hand pointing at me was indelible in my mind. I was working and earning a monthly salary that did not meet my monthly needs. I had to supplement with my savings. What would I do when I emptied my savings? If I died on the road what would happen to my family? The Federal Service Commission was taking its sweet time to reply to my letter. I drove to the College one day and remembered the insult of being assigned to mark the register. Though months had passed, I had not marked the register, and she did not have the guts to ask me why. I tore a sheet of paper and resigned. I took it to her office and handed it to her. She promptly became a preacher and my adviser. She said she heard how much I loved my mother and pleaded for me not to return to the U.S. Thank you was my reply and walked out. We moved into the house the Imo State Ministry refused to pay ₦200 a month.

Of course, people from my village who lived at Aba read the newspaper and knew what my people at Enugu did and would not go unnoticed. So, they held a party in our honor. One of the gifts was a carved palm fruit harvester with the fruit on his head and the climbing rope on his shoulder, indicating a successful end. One of those present was Jemima Nwakudu who owned the hotel at Aba where the party was held.. She took a liking for my family and visited us from time to time. Each time she brought a carton of soft drinks to "my wife" (the customary name for a loved woman married in the village) and "my children." I paid a little of her kindness back when her dad died in our village.

I went home one day, and my mother said, "I am the mother of a doctor and I still sleep on a bamboo bed." I drove to the market and bought her an iron twin bed, a cotton mattress, and a pillow. Chidi Ikeji walked into our house one day with the same familiar problem. East Central Government had awarded him a scholarship to study in the United States but would not release it without him giving them a bribe. With Imo as a separate state and Chimaroke from the village as a senior officer in the Ministry, dee Onwumere, his father, sent him with the hope that Chimaroke would help. But he did not help. I took him to the Ministry. When I walked into the Permanent Secretary's office the face was familiar. He was in the secondary section of Uzuakoli when I was at HEC. I smiled, greeted him, and said, "Dr. Onwuegbu and an Old Boy." Old Boy means former student of Uzuakoli (an alumnus). That settled it. I told him why I was there. He called an officer and told him to release the scholarship paper. As we walked to the storeroom he said to me, "Stop here. You cannot follow me to the room." I replied, "Yes lord," but he said, "I should follow you." They all, including the poor officer, laughed. Soon I walked out with the scholarship paper. Chidi was on his way to his father. I went home one weekend and sought a room to sleep in, in my uncle's house. To show his gratitude for getting his son's scholarship released, he and his wife gave me their bed and chose to sleep on a small bed. I could not believe them. Rejecting the offer, I said to him, "What is this? So, if Udobi (his first son) comes to my house, you expect me to give him my bed? I will not do it." I went and slept on the small bed. By the time I resigned, I had seen enough of the delusion Nigeria chose as a way of life. The oil was booming. When I left Nigeria bribery was a taboo and a crime. On my return, it was openly practiced from the highest to the least official. One had to bribe a messenger to see his boss. The ministry officers received percentages from car manufacturers and imported cars that would not be allowed to enter any port in the Western world. Morality and education were on their downward trends. I wrote a paper entitled, "Functional Education in Nigeria" and condemned those practices and suggested remedies. About two weeks after I submitted it to the Academic Star for publication the editor wrote to me. He complained that he could not publish the paper as I submitted it. He might have been afraid of the military that ruled the country. My reply warned that if he deleted any of my essential points, I reserved the right to submit it to another publisher. When he published it, the paper was as I submitted it. Those who knew me congratulated me. A few went as far as to promise to send me some facts if I was willing to use them. Neither the Army nor anyone else complained openly.

To my dismay, I noticed so many problems, educational and otherwise, waiting for solutions. I decided to stay self-employed. I was going to be a consultant to governments and institutions on education. I would continue writing and also counseling individuals on psychological matters. I wrote my first children's book. It was how to teach children to tell time. With the Universal Primary Education (UPE) at its peak and the state governments buying textbooks, I knew schools needed the book. This was important because most homes in the villages did not own clocks. The book was good. They knew they needed it, but they demanded me to give them a ten percent bribe. When I failed to negotiate to pay the bribe, the officers rejected my book.

In one case, I went to Port Harcourt, the capital of Rivers State. I knew people of that state were hostile to the Igbo people during and after the war. I also knew that many of the educated people went to Uzuakoli College. On my arrival at the Ministry of Education, I could not believe the name of the Commissioner for Education. It was Albert Badi my classmate in standard one. Instead of filling out a form to see him, I took my card and wrote Old Boy (he attended Uzuakoli also) and classmate at Osa. It was a reunion and I congratulated him. After telling him why I was there he called an officer and asked him to take care of me. I did not offer any bribe and that was the end of that. As expected, I met two officers of the State, who were my roommates at Uzuakoli. They behaved as though I was an enemy.

We shared a fenced yard with a British couple Mike and Jillian. A Dutch nurse Barbara, who was the matron of a school of nursing at Abiriba, came to visit them. In addition, she needed someone to help her with a curriculum on Human Development. Mike sent her to me, and I solved her problem. Meanwhile, two letters arrived at the College where I taught from the Federal Government addressed to me.

The first letter came from the Federal Ministry of Education in response to my letter of resignation. It threatened that if I resigned, I was liable to refund the Ministry all the expenses the government incurred in bringing me back to the country. I heard about it and ignored it. Shortly after, a second letter came from the Federal Service Commission through the Ministry. It upgraded my status from level ten to level twelve from the day I assumed duties in Nigeria. The Principal was in possession of the two letters, and I did not care to go to get them.

I pursued two other projects with the Imo State Government. Most of the so-called rich people in the State and their wives worked outside the home. They hired maids to care for their children. In all the cases the maids were illiterate and lacked the basic knowledge of human development and early childhood education. I proposed a program to remedy the situation and asked the government for permission to open a training school. At first, they denied me the permit. A second project is what I called Science On Wheels. One of the courses I took at the University of Utah was how to teach science in junior high. Besides, my first degree was in teaching mathematics and science in Junior High. The Government had funded a project on how to teach science in junior highs. My class was one of the participating guinea pigs. It was practical. I noticed the lack of science teachers and equipment in secondary schools in Nigeria. Besides, my nephew, who had graduated from high school, read part of the studies in the book. Commenting on many of the topics said, they did not study the materials meant for junior high schools in the U.S. Science on Wheels would train several science teachers and equip some trucks and ensure that students would receive good science education at less cost. Imo State was not interested. I went to Cross River State thinking that the name I heard was a man who was my senior at Uzuakoli, but he was not. He sent me to two English men who represented their companies in Nigeria. When I saw the Imo State Ministry of Education Permanent Secretary next, he asked me to resubmit my application for the training school. I asked why he rejected it the first time. He claimed to have received bad advice from his officers. He also told me that the Federal Ministry of Education wanted me to return to serve it in a new capacity.

Chinedum suffered from a persistent cough. We took him to Dr. Whitaker the English medical doctor who was in charge of the Mission Hospital at Aba. But he failed to diagnose him correctly. He wrongly put him on a course of tuberculosis treatment. May came and our third child was due. The hospital gave us a date. I drove Sweetie to the hospital about mid-morning. We spent the entire afternoon without anything serious happening about the birth of the baby. We walked the ground till evening. Nurse Nancy was scheduled to return to the States the following day and Mrs. Nwakanma had taken over the management. She lived near the hospital. When evening came, she asked me to drive her home so that in the event she was needed I could come to get her. When the contractions were frequent and close, I drove to her home and informed her. By the time I got back, Sweetie was lying down to give birth. I walked into the room and the nurse was horrified. She ordered me to get out of the room. I told her it was my duty and right to be present when my wife gave birth to our children. "How are you going to explain to this child why I was not present at his birth when I witnessed the birth of his siblings?" The baby was about to show up. She asked Sweetie, "Do you want him here?" She replied, "He can stay." Seconds later, and before Mrs. Nwakanma arrived, Munachimso was born. The midwife survived the shock of a man at the "secret" birthplace. It was late at night when I got home. At dawn, I informed our children that they had a baby brother. The news brought joy and disappointment at the same time. They were happy about the birth and that mom was doing well. Chinedum was especially happy that he had a little brother to play with. On the other hand, Melody, who hoped for a little sister to play with was disappointed the baby was a boy. I consoled her when I told her the boys would be fighting for boys' toys while she would have all the girls' things to herself. Nancy saw the baby that morning before she left for the U.S. Sweetie gave her the telephone number of her parents. She carried the news of the birth and that the baby's middle name was Delbert, the maternal grandfather's name.

After mother and son came home, I drove to the village and gave them the good news. My brother's wife visited us for a few days. When she left, I paid her transport and gave her a few naira. Disappointed with the amount of money I gave her, she sent it back to me without a word. I received it without one word. I did not know what she expected me to give her. There I was without a job, paying ₦200 a month for rent, private school fees for my children and maintaining my family. They did not even ask how I fed my family. All they cared for was how much I gave them. My mother came and we enjoyed her for a few days. She and Sweetie got along well and communicated by pointing and mimicking.

Nigeria had planned to establish a college of education to train special education personnel. The Federal Ministry of Education sent some of its employees to Britain, some for three months and others for six- or nine-months training to learn "the administration of special education." The Ministry decided to open this college at this time. Though I had resigned months earlier the Ministry wrote to me. It transferred me to Ibadan Federal Advanced Teachers College for Special Education. As usual, I ignored the letter and pursued other interests, including the return to the U.S. I also applied to the Ford Foundation in Lagos for employment. But there was no opening. In addition, I wrote a publisher in the States to see if he could open a branch in Nigeria. All he would promise was a machine to copy books.

After many months of no income, caring for my family with one extra mouth in the person of Onyema, my brother's second son to feed, and with my funds almost depleted, I borrowed ₦2,000 naira from Mr. Ibegbulem. When the hope of selling my book to the States and the science project seemed doomed to failure, the idea of returning to the States loomed larger in my scheme of things. I submitted my manuscript entitled, "Discover Teaching" to a publisher. He looked at it and asked if I was writing a dictionary of education and returned it. That he did not understand the manuscript was an encouragement to me. I believed that I had something new the country needed. I expressed my gratitude to Ugonma Nwanaoruo, my former pupil at Umukabia Methodist Central School, who typed it.

Onyema, who was living with us, applied for a job and was invited for an interview. He performed well at the interview and was invited for a medical checkup. The manager and the doctor conspired and failed him because he did not bribe them. I decided to take them to court. First, I had to prove that Onyema was healthy. I drove to the doctor and introduced myself as Dr. Onwuegbu. With my eyes fast on his, I stated my reason for being there. "My nephew Onyema came to you for a medical checkup, and you declared him unfit. I want to have him treated for whatever sickness he has. May I have your report?" He became evasive. I told him I was going to prove his conspiracy to ruin the boy's life where it would cost him and drive off. My next stop was at another medical doctor who was trained in the USSR. We met there at Aba. He and his Russian wife returned about the same time we did. He was not in, and I left a message telling him why I sent my nephew. When he got my message, he declined to examine Onyema. He explained that if I had not told him my intention to go to court with the result, he would have done it. Indirectly the doctor got the message that everyone was not going to bribe him and the manager or allow them to ruin their life and passively accept it. Later, after I left Aba, Onyema worked for the firm.

We had made a few friends, especially those educated and the expatriates. One of the Briton accountants employed by Nigeria was stealing Nigeria's money but was unwilling to allow his Nigerian secretary to type what he was about to steal. He asked Sweetie if she would be willing to work with him. She declined his offer. I felt my last resort was to return to the U.S. Sweetie asked me to go and see what the Federal Advanced College at Ibadan was like before I made my final decision. By this time, I had taken one more project in Amafo Isingwu my village.

While I was in the U.S., Amafo Isingwu built her own central school. Max was the first person to write to me about the school. He said that other villages were trying to imitate the pattern. I thought of how to improve learning in the village. The best way was to make a library and books available. I wrote the churches I attended and served in the U.S. and requested books old and new, especially in mathematics and science. Also, I called on my age group, which at that time had more educated persons than any other age group in the village, and asked for their help in building what we called a cottage library. We decided to remodel the old Sunday School building. By this time the project was near completion. Bags of books were arriving, especially from Christ Methodist Church in Salt Lake City, Utah. Soon it was completed. Imo State was invited for its dedication. A Chief Education Officer represented the Government at the dedication. The village was proud and Odionyenfe K. Ekeledo volunteered to pay the salary of the librarian for the first six months. I also served on some committees in the village at this time. During this first year, Amadi my brother's firstborn and first son, was in a grade two teachers college at Owerri.

A man who sold Volvo cars and imported different brands and sizes invited people from Aba and the suburbs to the unveiling. Sweetie and I were among those invited. It was the dry season, and the temperature was well in the high eighties at a place without any air conditioner. Sweetie and I dressed simply. As we got ready to leave, Onyema, who lived with us, started to laugh. When I asked why he was laughing, he said, "When you get there, everybody else will be in suits and agbada." I responded, "At my level, if I imitate people instead of people copying me, something is wrong." As Onyema said, all the people at the gathering, except us, dressed in their suits and agbada. They also sweated. But we did not. When we came home, I teased Onyema. "You should have been there, everybody sweated and fanned themselves. We did not and enjoyed ourselves." As some women in my village said, "You returned from America and made your mother a young woman again." I had improved her diet. Besides, I supplied her with a carton of Vita malt from time to time and one-a-day vitamins. With her in mind, I decided to investigate the Ibadan Federal Advanced Teachers College as Sweetie suggested.

Chapter 34

Ibadan Federal College Of Education

I traveled to Lagos and spent the night with Emedom. I went to the Federal Ministry the following day to get information about the location of the College in Ibadan, the largest city in West Africa at the time. Not a single soul knew where the College was located. The story was the same at the Ministry of Education Ibadan. Half of the day was gone, and I was frustrated. At last, the Permanent Secretary found one person who said the college was temporarily located at Oyo, but he did not know the location at Oyo. I raced to the motor park and there was a taxi loading to travel to Oyo. I paid my fare and entered the taxi.. As was usually the case, we had to wait until he had the number of passengers he wanted. Once he got the number, he took off like a bullet on the winding narrow road. As we passed one narrow bridge the driver suddenly slowed down. As we ascended a small hill, we saw a VW Beatle car on our left side of the road. It looked parked without a top. The driver was sitting at the driver's seat dead. He had been pressed from the front and back of the car. Beyond him on his right was a valley and in it was the body of a wrecked lorry. There were no police nor any sign of an ongoing investigation. Once he passed the scene of the accident, he resumed his speed as though it could never happen to him. I prayed as we went. Shortly after that, we were at

Oyo Motor Park. The news was the same, no one knew where the college was. I walked about until I saw a man who suspected a building and directed me to it. It was a small apartment complex with no college sign. I walked into what looked like a living room with two desks and a typist. I asked if this was the College. The typist confirmed it was. I asked if the Principal was in the office. The Executive Officer walked out. After we exchanged greetings, I introduced myself. He told me the Principal had traveled to Lagos on official duty. The bursar also came out. They noted that I was there to report for duty. However, I learned that the earliest the students would arrive would be the first week in October. Some members of the faculty were already at the apartments and others at a hotel. They were ready to book me into a hotel. I rejected the offer and asked them to note the date I reported. "Tell the Principal I reported and will be back before the students come." I walked out and took another taxi to Ibadan. It was already late to get transport to the east. I went back to Emedom's house in Lagos. As far as I knew the College existed only on paper. I traveled from Lagos the following day, grateful to reach Aba, and spent the evening with my family. I determined to try it.

Sweetie was cooking and feeding Onyema in our home. Yet he was acting as though she was usurping what belonged to him. Luckily for him, he was not bold enough to be rude to her. We went to the village, and I left Sweetie, the children, and my mother at home and walked to the square. When I returned, there were my mother and Sweetie picking and cleaning palm fruits, which many educated Nigerian women would not do. That was like many people in the village watching me when I climbed the palm tree with ropes to cut the palm fruit. I laughed, and my mother laughed and said, "My white daughter is picking with me." That was big news in the village. Asabituka whose son was a medical doctor in the U.S. said, "Tell my son if he sees one like yours to marry and bring her home." The idea of don't marry a white woman became history even if it was for a short time. As Sweetie says, if there had been any disagreement between us, the whole village would have been on her side. My mother was not happy that we were going to Oyo but could not do anything about it.

Dee Onwumere, who retired from the railways, had completed building his big house at home. I asked for permission to store some of our belongings, including our beds, refrigerator, and other things, in some of the rooms in his house. He granted the permission.

Having arranged for the storage of our belongings and given Sweetie sufficient money in addition to the small amount I deposited in another bank in her name, I prepared to travel to Oyo. I left her with the car and three young children all under eight years. Melody, who was the oldest, was only seven years and two months, and Munachimso, our youngest, was about three months. We hoped that I would secure a house within three weeks and return to pick them up. We packed my suitcase, and I was ready to travel to Oyo.

Chapter 35

Founding Federal College of Education, Oyo

Going to Oyo from Aba was not a straightforward journey because Oyo is not on the eastern main artery road to the north. So, one traveling to Oyo from Aba had to travel through Ibadan in the west. Before dawn Sweetie and I were awake. By the time I was ready to leave the house for Aba Motor Park, Melody and Chinedum were awake. We hugged and kissed goodbye. Like vultures striving for the carcass of dead animals, the ocho passengers (passenger seekers) at the park were about to tear my suitcase as they struggled to get me to travel by their car. When I sat down to travel it did not occur to me that my goodbye kiss to my family was for a long time. The taxi took off, and by midafternoon, we were at Ibadan Motor Park. The struggle for the suitcase was repeated. On arrival at Oyo, I stopped the taxi in front of the building that housed the offices and some of the faculty. Without hesitation, they assigned me to the hotel, and a driver drove me to it. I discovered the rest of the faculty who could not be accommodated in the one building were sent there. Mr. Azodo, an Igbo and the Principal, was not at the College or Oyo town. I soon discovered why. There was no good hotel in Oyo with good facilities. Therefore, he stayed at a hotel in Ibadan from where his driver drove him to Oyo every morning.

The Principal and I met the following day. It was some time before I learned why the Ibadan Advanced Teachers College for Special Education was at Oyo. In the meantime, I learned that Oyo had provided the Federal Government with two sites for the college to use as temporary accommodation, one secondary school, a part of which the College turned into the academic site. The other at Durbar became the residence. The College was doing some refurbishing work on the two. The progress was slow, and the Principal had postponed the opening twice and asked for a third time, which the Ministry denied. The contractors were hurrying to complete the offices, the library, the kitchen, and the student's dining hall. The Principal called a meeting to get the faculty ready. He passed a sheet of paper with the names of the faculty and demanded dates of the last promotion, level, and date of employment. He was the only officer whose administrative duty had been assigned to. He was a Chief Education Officer. There was no Assistant Chief Education Officer. However, there were five Principal Education Officers, and I was the most senior of the five. He needed to appoint officers to help him administer the College. Following the protocol of the Ministry in appointing two acting positions in a college in Yoruba land, he designated me his Vice Principal. Recognizing the animosity that appointing three Igbo officers as the Principal, Vice Principal, and Dean of Students would generate in Lagos among the Yoruba people who controlled the Ministry, he bypassed Allen Uche, another Igbo, and appointed Babalola, a Yoruba Dean. He appointed Allen to chair the Science Department, Makinde, another Yoruba, to chair the English Department, and Dr. Adima to chair the Special Education Department. The Yoruba people at Lagos perceived my acting appointment as Igbo domination of an institution in their backyard. They refused to even reply to the request for confirmation. That notwithstanding, we performed our duties as though we were confirmed.

About this time, Alliance Hotel opened at Oyo. Though substandard by four-star hotels, it was better than any hotel that existed at Oyo. The Principal came to stay at the hotel and took me with him. A week before the students arrived, I called a meeting of the heads of the departments as they were called then. I discovered the vacuum in the Department of Special Education. We were to set up the class schedule for each department. The chair of the Special Education department's first two degrees were not even in education. However, he did his doctoral studies in mental retardation. As a result, he had no introductory courses to offer. We still managed to choose some courses and I set up the class schedule. By the time the students arrived, the hostels, the Principal's office, and the general and Vice Principal's offices were ready. There was a scarcity of houses to rent for the faculty. As in all things, the Principal assigned the newly available apartments to faculty according to seniority. When the staff and the Principal were moved to the offices at the academic site, the first-floor apartment they used as offices became vacant. By my position as the next most senior officer to the Principal, I should occupy it, but there was Mr. S. Mensah, a Ghanaian whose son suffered from cancer, and the building was only a stone's throw from the Oyo General Hospital. He pleaded to occupy the apartment in case of emergency. I surrendered it to him. Unfortunately, the boy died in Ghana before his family joined him at Oyo.

Finally, October arrived and the date the students were given to arrive was upon us. They started to trickle in from all parts of the Federation. I was there to receive them. The first student was an Igbo woman Julie. When another Julie from the north arrived, I called the first one number one. Before the day was over, the majority of the students, about thirty of them, were on the premises. The first test of the will or challenge came from the kitchen during the first week. The Yoruba woman in charge of the food acted as though the kitchen was beyond the authority of the Principal. She defied the orders of the Principal and declared her independence from the College. She did not care about students' complaints regarding food, in a country where almost all student riots are about food. The Principal told his driver to take the two of us to the home of the Assistant Superintendent of police in charge of Oyo Police Station. He gave us a police officer to remove the woman from the kitchen. On our way to the kitchen, we dropped the Principal at the academic site. The woman was smart and did not resist but left and that was the last time she was at the College. Her assistant took over.

Several weeks after the students arrived, the College planned students' government elections. The Principal appointed the Dean of Students to plan and supervise the election. The Dean chose Olanikpeku, another Yoruba man on the faculty, to assist him. They made the bylaws, set the date for the elections, and conducted it. Unfortunately, as they proceeded, the result did not turn out as they expected. They had expected a Yoruba student to be the secretary. However, Fred, an Igbo student, was elected. They tried to nullify the election of the secretary.

Meanwhile I had overstayed my temporary visit to Oyo. Our children, especially our daughter, missed me and began to misbehave. My wife sent Onyema to Oyo with the report. He was born in Lagos as were at least five of his other siblings. Onyema spoke the Yoruba language fluently. He was in my office when the Dean and his Yoruba assistant walked into my office. I introduced Onyema to them as my nephew. They assumed that like me, he did not understand their language. They continued the plot against Fred in the Yoruba language in my office, claiming that the post of a secretary was so important only a Yoruba should hold it.

Then they turned to give me the report of the elections. According to them, all the offices were filled except the office of the secretary. Fred was elected. However, because only one person, instead of two, nominated him, they asked for permission to nullify the result and hold another election for the one post. Unaware of the plot, I granted them the request. A few seconds after they left my office, Onyema exposed the plot to me. I was annoyed with him. Why did you not tell me in Igbo while they were here? They do not understand Igbo (my language). I sent him after them to tell them in Yoruba that I wanted to talk to them. When they entered my office, I told them to come to my class at 1:00 pm and announce the decision they made. By that time, my investigation had revealed other facts. Asah, a Yoruba student, nominated Fred, an Igbo student, for the office of Secretary, and Fred was elected. When the Dean and his helper saw the result, they were displeased. They approached Asah, the Yoruba student who nominated Fred, and offered him the office of the Secretary. Asah rejected the offer. He was not interested and only nominated Fred. If Fred had one person who nominated him, Asah had not a single person who nominated him. Yet they offered him the post. I waited. They came to my class at the appointed time. I introduced the topic and handed over the class to them.

Satisfied that they had achieved their objective and were about to leave the class, I stopped them. I reminded them of the cause of the army coup that led to the Biafra Nigeria war. It started with election fraud. I thought they claimed the war was fought to end election fraud based on ethnicity. That is what these two are practicing right in front of me. As long as I am here, I will not tolerate it and it will not succeed. The students cheered and clapped their hands. The two walked out and I continued teaching.

I was not in Nigeria during the war. Many of the Igbo students seemed to suffer from a defeat mentality and told Fred to stop asking for his right. I admired his persistence. I sent Onyema back to Aba with a promise that I would be at Aba to bring the family to Oyo within a week. Meanwhile the question of the Secretary was settled. No Yoruba student wanted it. Fred withdrew his name. Another Igbo student Emeka was elected to the post.

Yes, Americans say Nigerians talk loudly. It was expected that the Principal should be back from Lagos, but it was distasteful to hear him say to the Dean, "All right dear, I will see you on Monday" after what happened in his absence. It was a weekend.

While we were in the hotel, the Principal traveled to Lagos. Unknown to me was what happened in Lagos. It seemed he planned to keep it a secret for as long as he could. However, he could not control events within the environment. Electricity and water were sporadic; now you see them, and then they disappear. He returned from Lagos and there was no running water. The student President came and reported to him. His only option was to borrow a water tanker from the Federal Government Girls High School in the town. He delegated me to go with the Student President to the Principal of the school. The Principal was from Bangladesh. On seeing me she said, "Doctor, you know your Principal is on transfer. He said you are capable and willing to do the job even without pay." I had not been paid for almost four months because I did not bring my last pay certificate with me. She gave us the tanker and I returned to the hotel and the Student President to the kitchen.

The information became my dilemma. Why did the Principal not tell me? Lagos knew it. Oyo knew it and the student body will become aware of it once the Student President gets there. Keeping it a secret from me looked like an ostrich that hid its head in the sand while exposing the rest of its body. On our way to the hotel, I debated whether to ask the Principal about the news or not. I decided to make him understand I knew. Looking at his face I said, "The Principal said you are on transfer." He could not hide his anger and flared up. "She should mind her own business and shut up her mouth." Yes, he had been transferred to Aba in his state as the Principal of the Federal Secondary school there. He would take December as his vacation time and report in January.

We continued to settle down and prepare for his sendoff. His trips to Lagos were also curtailed. One of his last duties was writing his handing over notes. Before this time his signature was the only one on all financial transactions. Before he left, he made the bursar a co-signer.

I waited until Monday. The Principal walked into my office and handed me a report the Dean had given him. He underlined certain sentences and phrases and asked me to reply to the report. One of the statements the Principal underlined was, "I heard him say he is the best-qualified man to be the Principal of the College." The Dean did not say to whom or where I was talking when he heard me. He claimed that American degrees are inferior to Nigerian degrees. I replied but wondered how that man could write and sign his name on such a report. The Principal's reaction did not impress me either. I wondered why he did not ask the two students to write their accounts of the events. I replied to the report.

He invited me to receive the handing-over note. As we performed the ritual, he surprised me. He revised the report the Dean wrote. "You know," he said "the Dean came and confessed that you are right. But he said it was not his idea but his assistant's." As I looked at him, he added, "But you went along with him." I wondered when the Dean confessed before or after he knew the Principal was on transfer. When the Principal rated my annual performance, he gave me all A's and wrote, "Dr. Onwuegbu is endowed with rustic honesty" and he recommended me for double promotion. By then, it was late because by becoming the principal at level fifteen, I had received a double promotion.

Shortly after that, I traveled to Aba to get my family. There was joy at Aba on my arrival that I was not lost or even dead. Melody ran and held me. Sweetie and I hugged and kissed, and Chinedum tagged along. I went in and saw Munachimso. I had not collected my last pay certificate and my letter of upgrade from Aba Grade Two Teachers College, and without them, I could not be paid. I drove to the College and collected them. After about three days, we were ready to travel to Oyo. We loaded what we needed to take with us in the car and were ready to go at dawn.

We said goodbye to our neighbors and Aba the following morning and were on our way to Oyo. We were at Onitsha when one of the tires at the back burst. I thanked God it happened at the best place. We took out a tire from the trunk and a mechanic inflated and fixed it. I had replaced the four tires in New Britain with tubeless tires. We got lost at Ibadan and had to retrace. It was getting dark when we found ourselves on Ibadan Oyo road. We drove to Jobele about fifteen minutes to the college's residential building and suffered a second flat tire. It was already dark, and the villagers were at their market with their bush lamps. It was a time of decision. I had to get my family to the hotel, but how?

As I stepped away from the car with the promise of coming back to take them to the hotel, our two older children started to cry. I could not help imagining what they thought. "He left us at Aba for so long and now he is leaving us on this dark road." I had to do what was best for them. I did not stand there for more than a few minutes when a trailer truck drove up. I flagged it to a stop and asked for a ride. The two-man crew offered me a ride and dropped me in front of the lecturers' quarters. I thanked them and ran upstairs, knocked, and banged at Allen's door. He pretended to be dead. I pleaded that my family was on the road and needed a ride. The two children who lived with him and his wife laughed as I banged and banged and pleaded. Mr. Veerasingham, a foreigner who lived on the same floor but on the other side of the building, heard me and came out. He said, "Even if Allen was dead the banging would have awakened him," and offered to go and get my family. I was grateful and thought, "If Allen, an Igbo, and an old boy of Uzuakoli were the only people at Oyo, my family, as tired and hungry as they were, would have slept on the road that night. We drove to Jobele. Mr. Veerasingham drove the family to the hotel, and I slept in the car. Chimso was only five months old at the time.

In spite of the breakdown, the accident could not have happened in a better spot. We parked less than three yards from the market. It seemed like the people watched my family in my absence while my family watched them, and if they understood the language heard and participated in the selling and buying. I knew God watched over them. Yet when they drove away in that car towards the hotel, I thanked God and felt the assurance of their safety and wellbeing. It gave me joy and inner peace. I closed the doors of the car, locked them, and went to sleep. I did not even know when the market dispersed. Hunger did not even keep me awake. Awake but still in the car with the morning sun shining the following day, the college car with its FGN license zoomed and almost passed but came to an abrupt stop. It was the Principal making his ritual trip to Lagos. We greeted and he continued his journey.

A short time later, another car stopped at the same side of the road. When the driver emerged, he was the Associate Director of the hotel we lodged in. I locked my car and rode with him to the hotel. They had taken good care of my family the previous night and that morning. I expressed my gratitude. My family and I became permanently reunited. While we were at the hotel, the Associate Director tried to help bring the car to the hotel. No mechanic knew what to do with the tubeless tire. We hired a man to watch the car the following night and paid him five naira. The people of Jobele almost attacked him mistaking him for a thief. We rescued the car the following day when we inflated a tube and inserted it in the tubeless tire and drove it to the hotel.

It seemed the presence of the College, even if it was temporary, galvanized the people and inspired them to start building small apartment units. The College rented some of them and started moving the faculty out of the hotels. The College rented one house for me to share with another family. When I saw it, it was painted in psychedelic colors. It was so different and brightly colorful that even a blind person could differentiate it from all the other buildings in the vicinity. I looked at it from a distance and rejected it. If you want me in that house, remove all those red, green, black, and yellow colors and paint the house green. If not send someone else there. The bursar resisted but the Principal overruled and ordered him to obey. It was painted green and furnished, and we moved in. A few days before we moved in, I went to the Nigerian Electric Power Authority (NEPA) office and requested someone to go and read the meter to make sure I was not charged the electricity bill someone else used. The man urged me to move in with the assurance that it would not happen. No one should charge you for electricity you did not use.

We were not in the house for more than two weeks when NEPA turned off our electricity. I walked into the office and met the same Yoruba man who assured me that I would never be charged for an electricity bill someone else used. I wanted to know why I did not have light. He claimed I owed ₦480 the equivalent of $720 at the time. When I reminded him what he told me, he shocked me with his answer. When I said, "At least you should have been honest with me," he shot back very angrily: "Honest! Are you not a Nigerian? How can you talk about honesty?" I could not believe what I heard. I asked what he said?" He repeated himself. I am an Igbo, not Yoruba. I grew up where honesty was respected and nurtured. But his statement reinforced the Dean's behavior. I promised never to pay for it. I learned from the Principal that an army captain lived in the house and failed to pay both the electric and water bills. The College took care of the debts. The statement about honesty reminded me of the report the Dean wrote. I was beginning to learn the character of the people I came to live and work with.

I got Amadi, my brother's first son admitted to Lyndon State College while I was still at Aba. Lyndon gave him a free tuition scholarship. I had to pay for his boarding. Because I did not have a job at the time, I requested a delay for one year, which they granted. He went the following year after I went to Oyo. Chinyere, his sister, failed the final high school certificate examination and came to live with us at Oyo. I sent her to Olivet High School. She received her certificate there. Her behavior became unbearable, and I sent her home. Later I traveled to see her father to talk about her behavior. He stormed me with his confession. He said he believed that our maternal grandmother reincarnated in her. Therefore, he allowed her to do whatever she wanted without any discipline when she was growing up. "Oh! You allowed a child to grow up doing whatever she liked?" God performed a most gracious miracle for me on the day I drove to see him. I drove on a narrow bush road. On reaching a sharp right-angled curve, I could not even see the part of the road in front of me. I put my foot on the brake. Within a minute of placing my foot on the brake, I saw a little girl on the right side of my car. The next second the little head was in front of my car. I held my brake. If my foot was not on the brake, she would have been crushed. An old man who watched the scene raised his hands and declared, "Your God is with you." It took me some minutes to let the car move as I shook and wondered what would have happened. Then, another daughter of my brother, Ihuoma, also came to live with us. She also failed her school certificate examination. I also sent her to the same high school. She also succeeded. I employed her at the College. She was smart and took the entrance examination to the College. She performed better than most of the candidates. She also had a total of five credits, two more than the three required for admission. However, at this time, the College admitted only teachers, and she was not a teacher. I did not admit her. However, when I reached Lagos I reported her situation to the Coordinating Director. He wrote a letter to my Registrar that authorized him to admit her. She became a student at the College while living with us.

The College prepared and gave the principal a good sendoff party. He requested to use the Principal's official car while he was on vacation. I yielded and he took the driver also. I performed as the

Principal, the Vice Principal, and the chair of the Department of Education and taught at least one course. When the founding Principal left the hotel for his vacation, he was the last to leave the hotel. Every member of the faculty present had an apartment. Before he left, he and I went to the Alaafin's palace, greeted him, and had a photograph with him.

At about this time, and while I was still owing Mr. Ibegbulem, Amadi, my brother's firstborn, and I had future plans to further his education. I asked him to apply to Lyndon State College. He did and I recommended him. He was admitted. But I could not afford to send him that year. I asked for a postponement for one year. They graciously granted it. The bursar processed my salary and arrears and paid me. It was much more than the ₦2,000 I owed Mr. Ibegbulem.

I traveled home to pay Mr. Ibegbulem his money and see my mother. When I saw him, he was unhappy with me. Looking at the expression on his face, I paid him the money with the percent interest the bank paid at the time. He received the money but still had disappointment written all over his face. I thanked him and left. A short time after I arrived home, I saw Nkemakolam one of the few childhood friends in the village. He said my brother complained to him that Chikara and Obed, who he helped, had abandoned him and did not help him to educate his children. My brother was at Abakaliki, and I could not take Kema as we called him and make my brother repeat himself before me. I stopped walking and said, "He did not say that!" Kema said, "He said it." Then I said, "He did not send me a penny in the U.S. I sent him thousands of dollars. The last I sent to him was $2,000 to buy land for me and $200 for his family. He claimed to use all the money to educate his children and also helped Nnamdi, his brother-in-law, at Uzuakoli College with the hope that he would help him educate his children. Therefore, he did not buy a plot for me. Even now I plan to send his son to the U.S. next year. He wondered if my brother knew that. He was angry and told me to demand my $2,000 from him. I was so angry and told my uncle Onwumere about it. He reiterated Kema and told me to demand a refund of the 714 pounds, 5 shillings, and 8 pence he said the bank gave him for the $2,000. On the whole, I had given him more than four thousand dollars before I returned to Nigeria in January 1976. But I did not demand the refund of the $2,000. If I were planning to send him to the U.S. instead of his son, I would have dropped the plan for his ingratitude. But I ignored him.

Walking out of my office one late afternoon, I saw two members of the faculty walking towards the office, and they were with a third man. One of the two introduced the third person. When I asked if I could help him, Adima asked if I had not heard the name of the man before. Then he was introduced as the Acting (interim) Principal. I welcomed him, walked back to my office and took the key to the Principal's office, unlocked it, and ushered him in. He sat in the Principal's chair. In the short conversation that followed he revealed that he had not received any official information. He came on the rumor he heard. He had, however, planned to visit Lagos the following day. It was getting late for him to travel, so we checked him into the Alliance Hotel. He promised to see me the following day by 8.00 am.

As usual I was in my office before the time we set. I had planned to go to Lagos the same day with a list of requests including faculty and staff. Nine o'clock came and went and there was no sign of him. It was almost ten when he walked into my office. He claimed to have overslept and demanded to address the junior staff. I told the EO to call the junior staff to the general office. The theme of his speech was, "I have heard how badly the current administration treats you. Be patient things will change when I come."

I believed he was dangerously drunk with power and without a brain. What kind of man would be here on a rumor and say what he said without any investigation? After he left, I invited some of the members of the junior staff I considered to be leaders and asked why they would not allow the man to arrive before they complained. They all denied knowing him or that he was even in town. Finally, the bursar told me that the Dean drove to the hotel that morning to see the man. By noon, one of the drivers and I were in Lagos, and the man was getting his rumor confirmed. I presented my request, and the Chief sent me to the Assistant Chief. I was not in the office for more than three minutes when the Acting Principal designate walked in, asked to see the paper, took his pen, and signed it under my signature. He sheepishly said to the woman officer, "See how hard I work in both places." The Yoruba woman smiled without a word. If I had any doubts about my first impression of him, they vanished.

Unknown to me at Oyo was the character of the bursar at the College. He prepared vouchers for my signature to fill his pockets. I became suspicious and traveled to the east. It was another two to three weeks before the Acting Principal designate assumed duty at the College. I went to the founding Principal's home and asked his advice. The bursar is flooding my desk with vouchers to sign. Did you not pay for the work done before you left and is it safe to sign them? His answer was unsatisfactory. On my return to Oyo, I told the bursar to stop preparing vouchers until the new man came. He hated the orders but could not force me to sign them.

Before the Acting Principal designate went to the hotel during his first visit, he and I agreed on a date when the college lorry would go to bring his belongings. I counted the days. I had the EO make the arrangement. He also prepared the house the founding Principal rented for himself for the acting principal designate. He also made arrangements for him and his family to stay at Alliance Hotel on arrival. Two drivers took the college lorry on the eve of his arrival and drove to the north to get them.

Two unfortunate events took place while we waited for the arrival of the Acting Principal. First, the College Executive Officer (EO) walked into my office looking concerned. His report explained his concern look. Yusuf, a man employed to work in the college kitchen slapped a pregnant woman who also worked with him. I asked if he did any damage. He did not think so. I ordered him to dismiss him. He did.

Shortly after, Yusuf was in my office. Before I looked at him, he was on his knees, weeping and begging. I warned him. "Yusuf, I can beg better and cry better than you. I am not reinstating you because of your crying and begging. I can cry and beg better. I am reinstating you because I do not want to ask my Lord Jesus Christ to forgive me my sins and He points to you and says that I did not pardon you when you requested me to forgive you." That notwithstanding, I warned him that it must never, never happen again!

Second, on arrival at the College one morning, I could tell there was something wrong in the Administration building. The EO met me before I entered my office. The night watchman had reported a burglary that happened during the night to him. His story was unbelievable. I told him to get the night watchman to tell me the story himself. He called him. I demanded to know what happened. He said that he saw a thief carrying two fans from the general office. He ran after him shouting, "Thief, thief," and he ran away with the fans. We spent the next few minutes in questions and answers.

Q: The thief carried a fan in each hand?

A: Yes Sir.

Q: The thief did not drop any of the fans?

A: No Sir.

Q: He still outran you?

A: Yes Sir.

Q: The doors and windows were locked when you received the keys?

A: Yes Sir.

Q: The thief did not break any of the doors and windows, right?

A: He did not Sir.

Q: The thief did not take the keys from you?

A: He did not Sir.

Q: Have you eaten your breakfast?

A: No Sir.

I told him to go and eat, then come back and tell me what happened. He went and came back and told me the same story. I called the police and handed him over to them. He was tried and imprisoned.

Chapter 36
Authorized Chaos

1978-79

"Honesty! How can you speak about honesty? Are you not a Nigerian?" This statement was lived over and over before me during this period, with pride and impunity.

On the arrival of the Acting Principal at Oyo, the drivers took him and his family to Alliance Hotel. They spent the night there. He had the option to spend up to four weeks at the hotel, but after inspecting the house the founding Principal rented and furnished with the best carpet and furniture, he moved into the house after spending a night at the hotel. He still claimed the four weeks' money as though he had spent the time at the hotel. I patiently waited for his first day in the office.

The Principle's messenger had the key to the Principal's office with instructions to unlock the door upon the Acting Principal's arrival. My messenger was also instructed to inform me when the Acting Principal came. With all the instructions obeyed, I took the handing over note Chris Aazodo, the founding Principal, gave me and the key to my office and went to see him. After greetings and a short chat, I gave him the handing-over note. He glanced over it and signed it. I placed the key to the Vice Principal's office in front of him and said:

"You called the junior officers on your first day of visit to this College and condemned this administration on false information. You did not even wait to come and see things for yourself or investigate. That's the key to the Vice Principal's office. Choose whoever you want to work with as your Vice." Looking askance that I was willing to give up the office they revered so easily, he pleaded with me to stay on. In the course of his plea, he lied again. He claimed to have overslept, and no one told him anything. Believing I would not work with him for long, I took the key and left the office.

True to the Yoruba way, he loved money. The people who sent him to the College must have known so. They were willing to share the booty. My headmaster, Mr. Iteke, used to say to us students, "If you are a tiger, come to me as a tiger, don't come to me as a sheep." In the case of this man, he was a lion that presented itself as a lamb.

The second week after the College opened, I noticed that the non-Yoruba speaking students, i.e., the majority of the Christian students, had no place to worship. The founding Principal was a Roman Catholic. So, I organized a nondenominational Christian church. After the Acting Principal arrived and learned about the church, he volunteered to be one of the preachers. By gaining access to the church he became his own spy and later tried to control who preached and who should not preach at the church. I scheduled him to preach from time to time.

He returned from Lagos one day and complained to me. He was informed a Mr. Oluigbo was coming to the College as his Vice. From what he heard about the man, he did not want him as his Vice. He would prefer I continue as his Vice. Oluigbo, like me, is from the Igbo tribe and an Assistant Chief Education Officer like him. The two of them were Art majors except that Oluigbo had a six- or nine-month training in special education. I rejected his offer. But I stayed as the Acting Vice Principal until the Vice Principal arrived. However, I removed all my personal effects waiting to hand over the key on his arrival.

When he arrived, he behaved as though he had achieved his lifelong objective. I watched as he drowned amid the Yoruba conspirators. My people say that an insect was burning in a fire and claimed to be letting out excess fat oil. He spoke like a chatterbox without a brain and claimed to be loved. The Dean convinced him to rate me C's and D's on my annual performance evaluation. He invited me to his office to sign it. I looked at the paper and asked if he wanted me to sign it. When he replied, "Yes," I said to him, "You are stupid. I am going to paste this paper into the library for the students and faculty to read. They will be your judge." He snatched it from my hand and tore it to pieces.

Shortly after, the Dean wrote a history of the College and paid glowing tributes to the founding Principal, the Acting Principal, and the Vice and lavished praises on himself. Students and faculty wondered how he could write the history of the college and miss my name. As if that was not enough, they produced a new faculty roster where they placed me on level ten instead of twelve. I waited for them to subtract one penny from my salary. They did not. Suddenly, the war shifted from me to between the Dean and the Vice Principal, and the Vice Principal ordered him out of his office; and later, the war shifted to between the Acting Principal and his Vice.

From the behavior of the Acting Principal, one could conclude he did not hear, let alone know, anything about special education before he came to the College. His Vice took full advantage of that. The Acting Principal scheduled a meeting to plan the curriculum for the College and wanted me to chair the meeting. He invited me to his office. I was on my way when I heard his Vice arguing against my chairing the meeting. "Dr. Onwuegbu is a Principal Education Officer. I am the Assistant Chief and the Vice Principal. Therefore, I should chair the meeting." At that point, I was almost in the office. The Acting

Principal saw me. With the back of his Vice towards the door, he did not see me. The Acting Principal got up and closed the door and said, "I'll see you later." The Vice did not know who was at the door. The meeting was called, and the Acting Principal chaired it. It was a disaster and ended without any resolution. If the Vice Principal's proposed curriculum were adopted, all the Yoruba members of the faculty would be transferred because they all taught history, biology, and English. None of them was in Special Education at the time. They all turned against him. He even rejected the psychology courses I submitted. He argued that he took only one psychology course in Britain.

It was not long after the new Acting Principal's arrival that boxes of science equipment for teaching chemistry and physics disappeared because the College did not teach those subjects. But the students were not fooled. I walked into the Vice Principal's office one day and he had a radio on. He was in his glory. He claimed to be the glue that holds the College together. When I asked how he pointed to the radio as his reward for trying to save the Acting Principal. He then showed me a sheet of paper with the names of students he received from the Acting Principal. The Acting Principal wrote the names and gave them to him. They were the names of student leaders who were about to riot because they alleged the Acting Principal embezzled College money. He asked him to intervene on his behalf. I asked if the Acting Principal put the request in writing. He looked at me as though I was out of my mind. I walked out.

A World Bank representative came to Nigeria at the invitation of the Federal Government. The objective was for the World Bank to participate in the financing of the College. By profession, the woman who represented the Bank was an economist. She spent her first day in Lagos before the Yoruba man in charge of research in the Ministry brought her to the University of Ibadan where we met. Finally, we met at Oyo. The bone of contention at the discussion became what to do with the graduates of the College. She insisted on sending the graduates to grade two teacher's colleges to teach student teachers so as to get the maximum effect of the dollar. All the participants but me agreed with her. When I asked what would happen to the special needs children already identified, they told me the children could wait. When I refused to vote with them, I became the object of ridicule. At the end of the meeting, I wrote a minority report stating the reasons for my objection. I ended my report with the fact that I worked where she came from and contributed positively. I went to Lagos with my report and was waiting to see Mr. Inyang the ADE in charge of teacher education. The World Bank lady came to see Mr. Inyang and saw me. She wanted to know what I was doing in Lagos. I told her that I wrote a minority report against the decision of the committee and had come to submit it. She said, "If it is any comfort to you, on our way back to Lagos we reconsidered the matter and agreed that you are right." I assured her that I would submit the report. I did and that was the end of the World Bank involvement at the College. Then the Yoruba man who brought the woman saw the folly of sending the man as the Acting Principal to the College. He said whoever sent him there was his worst enemy. They sent him to sit between a psychologist and a special education teacher where he knew nothing. They still left him there.

Shortly after the World Bank representative and the Ministry officials left, an English man visited the College. The founding Principal had arranged with the English man to visit but was on transfer by the time he came. I had completely removed myself from every aspect of the administration. I designed two research projects and another book for grade two teachers' colleges. I used the library instead of the general staff room. I was on my way to the library on the morning the Acting Principal introduced the English man to the faculty and students when he called me back. He introduced me to the man and asked me to work with him to produce the curriculum.

When we finished, every course I recommended was included, and so were all the subject courses such as mathematics, English, arts, etc., but there were no physical science subjects. As we worked on the project, the Englishman surprised me with a request; "Don't let anyone know that you worked with me on the project." In the end, the Acting Principal invited his Vice, the Briton, and me to his office for final approval. As I explained the courses and the need for them the Vice blurted, "Dr. Onwuegbu did not explain why he included these courses to us." To which I replied, "You did not even give me the chance to speak. This is the only country where someone who spent six months on a subject knows better than another who spent years. You expect students who will spend three years at this College to study the one psychology course you studied in three months."

The Acting Principal called on me to "paint a portrait" of the Englishman on the last day of his visit to the College. I used the opportunity and chided those who hid behind where they received their education. "My people say that a woman outgrows saying, I am the daughter of A or B to I am the wife of C or D. It is high time we started showing what we do with our education and stop hiding and talking about where we received our education. No one asked Mr. T. where he was educated." I thanked him and wished him a safe trip home. I went back to the library. My book, *Discover Teaching*, was floating, looking for a publisher.

Soon, two members of the faculty, Mr. Uche and Dr. Adima, were about to leave the College. Dr. Adima was going to the University of Ibadan Special Education Department and Mr. Uche to Okene Federal College of Education. The College planned a sendoff party for them. The Acting Principal praised Adima but told Uche he was difficult to understand. Since I did not want to commit perjury against myself, I refused to say anything about either of them. The man who succeeded Dr. Adima heaped praises on him. Surprised at his speech, I asked him after the party if he was speaking about the same man he liked to destroy? He said, "It was a sendoff speech, which meant nothing." The Vice called me "proper arch Igbo man," because he was waiting for me to say something to aid him.

Having completed the second one of my study proposals, I thought I deserved a rest. I walked from the library to the staff general office one day. Within a short time after my arrival, I heard the Dean, who had not spoken to me since the student's election, call "Dr. Dr." If there was another Dr. in the room, I would not have looked at him. As my people say, when a snake enters the house, a wife remembers her husband's name. "Me?" I asked. "Yes," he pleaded. He pleaded with me to go to the Principal's office with him. He said we had to go and separate the Acting Principal and his Vice before they exchanged blows. I asked if there was any physical fight. He said no. By the time we got there the Vice Principal was in his office. I asked the Acting Principal what the problem was and if he wanted us to intervene. He said the Vice almost slapped him. We went over and talked with the Vice and with the Acting Principal again. I thought the matter was settled. But that was the beginning. The Acting Principal sent one of the Yoruba members of the faculty to Lagos with his own version of the story. Unknown to non-Yoruba members of the faculty was that an inquiry had been set up to investigate the dispute.

Deceiving the Vice Principal in order to catch him unprepared was not enough for the Acting Principal, he extended his deception to the entire faculty. He called an emergency faculty meeting to inform them about the visit. But instead of telling us the real intention of the visit, he told us to get our notes of lessons and schemes of work ready for inspection. When the investigators arrived, they were not the team of inspectors we expected. They only called the Dean and me to the Principal's office. From there they took the two of us to another room, interviewed us separately and recorded our responses, and dismissed us. They scheduled another visit with the Acting Principal and the Vice. Both the Dean and I sat through the second visit from the beginning to the end. The truth was almost absent. At one time I said,

"If this case must be settled, people must start to tell the truth." The Acting Principal changed "almost slapped" to "actually slapped". They asked me and I told them that I did not witness the quarrel. But both of them and the Dean told me they did not touch each other. When they asked the Dean, he claimed to have witnessed the Vice slap the Acting Principal. The secretary turned to the Dean's previous testimony and read where the Dean stated "almost slapped" to him. The Dean was dumb. Then the Acting Principal told another super lie he thought would destroy the Vice. He accused the Vice Principal of organizing Igbo students to overthrow his administration. Oluigbo was incensed and with "excuse me," he hastened out of the room to his office. When he returned, he had a sheet of paper in his hand. It was the same sheet of paper the Acting Principal gave him and pleaded that there would be a riot if he did not intervene on his behalf. Most of the names were Yorubas from the Acting Principals tribe, and there was only one Igbo student, Fred, on the list. More important was the Acting Principal's handwriting. He did not stop there. He said, "When Dr. Onwuegbu became aware of the request from the Acting Principal for me to intercede, he asked if the Acting Principal made the request in writing. I did not understand him then. Now I know why he asked the question. I prevented the students from rioting when they accused him of embezzling their money. Now he is using it against me." The Acting Principal had nothing to say. The Chief Education Officer who led the team had enough.

He let them know he was disappointed in their lies in spite of Dr. Onwuegbu's plea for the truth that fell on deaf ears. The Acting Principal's plea was he thought it was going to be more severe than it was. They left, and we waited for the result.

I drove to the College the following day and walked into the Vice Principal's office. The Acting Principal was sitting on the Vice Principal's desk. Once he saw me, he said, "The Vice Principal has been transferred." I said, "Really?" He confirmed it and added, "They want him to report to Lagos immediately for posting." For the first time that chatterbox did not say one word. The College was unofficially in the hands of the bursar, the Acting Principal, the Dean, and the chair of the English department, all Yorubas. Their policy was to make money at all costs. For example, the building which housed the admin offices was rented for ₦6,000 for the first year. When they renewed it, the rent went to as high as ₦27,000. So did most of the other houses the College rented. They brought one of the water tanks Mr. Azodo bought to the academic site and used it as a gas tank. That was where they filled their cars until the auditors stopped it. No one did any business with the College without giving them a bribe.

Finally, the report was out. It condemned the Acting Principal and the Dean for attempts to deceive the team through lies. Among other things, it recommended the immediate removal of the Acting Principal. In addition, he should not head any institution for at least the next two years. However, since the Yorubas controlled the Ministry, they ignored the report. He became bolder and even reckless.

Recall that the Acting Principal reported the case between him and his Vice to his brothers in Lagos. When an Efik, instead of a Yoruba, chaired the committee, which investigated the case, found him guilty, he looked for a scapegoat and found that in Fred. Fred was the student they denied the post of the student government secretary because he was not a Yoruba and the only Igbo student whose name was on the list the Acting Principal supplied to his Vice. He was also from my clan though they did not know that. The Acting Principal told the student President, who was a Yoruba, that it was Fred who reported the case to Lagos and urged him to get the student government to censure Fred. The council held its first meeting and Fred was informed.

For one reason or another, God led me to the administration building, where I heard Fred and the Acting Principal shouting at each other not only as equals but like two women quarreling over a man. I opened the office and ordered Fred out. By then I heard enough to know what the fight was about. He was trying to trap Fred and dismiss him from the College. Without saying one word to the Acting Principal, I left the office, drove home took my tape recorder, and drove back to the academic site. Classes were still in session. I set up the tape recorder in the student government office. One after the other, I interviewed all members of the student government starting with the President. Yes, it was the Acting Principal who told the President that Fred reported the case to Lagos.

Scarcely had I finished the interview when the last class before break ended. The Acting Principal stood outside the administration building and invited all members of the student council to his office. Thinking he had achieved his objective, he reported his encounter with Fred and solicited their cooperation. They shocked him with the news of my interviewing them and taping their answers. Furthermore, they warned him that they told me the truth and would not cooperate unless he got me to erase the tape. He dismissed them and sent his messenger to call me. When I arrived, he shamelessly told me what the students said and then asked me to erase it. I looked him in the eyes and denied his request. "The tape is not a threat to any honest person. If there is a need for it, I will use it. If there is no need, I will not use it." His fake plea fell on deaf ears. We parted and that was the end of that case. The report favored me. Oluigbo had reported that I warned him about intervening with the students without a written request and it proved correct. Now I outsmarted him in the case of Fred. I became a target.

It was about time for Amadi my brother's son to go to Lyndon State. I was to sponsor him. I needed someone to attest that I could take care of him. I sent Amadi to Mrs. Ann Akpofure in the Federal Ministry of Education in Lagos. She again came to my aid and wrote the letter. The American Embassy refused to give him visa because he only showed them his grade two certificate without his high school certificate. He said he was going through Canada. I refused to take part in the venture. "When you get to Lyndon, write me and I will send you the money." He made it, and a few weeks later, I heard from him. I began to send his fees every semester. About his third semester, I went home, and people were telling the false story of his father. "Your brother said you don't send your nephew his tuition fees. Why?" He rationalized, "Obed was older than Amadi when he went to the U.S." But he did not add that is why he sent me money instead of me sending him money. I could not believe what I heard.

Being in the village I unburdened myself to my mother. I recalled how God saved me from a certain crash with a trailer on Oyo Road on my way to Lagos to send him money. Even now, when I remember the incident, I jerk. I thought, if I died that day leaving my young family, this would have been my reward. To make sure that the money was sent, I went to Barclays Bank in Lagos. Fortunately, Ekeledo from my village worked there. He checked the records, was shocked to hear it, and asked, "Why is Amadi doing this?"

Armed with the fact that he did actually receive every penny I sent, I wrote to him and demanded an explanation. In reply, he apologized and said he was not doing well in school, and he looked for an excuse. As stupid as he was, I could not leave him stranded in America. I continued to pay the expenses. I took the letter home, read it to my mother, and left it on her small table. I told her to tell her son to read it when he visited home. He never apologized orally or in writing for scandalizing my name. I don't even think he rebuked his son.

Teaching Practice is one of the most important activities of every department of every teachers' institution and special education was not exempted. A part of the arrangement at Oyo called for the college bus to carry all the students going to Ibadan, Bendel State, and the eastern part of the River Niger. Those for Ibadan would be dropped at the School for the Deaf at Ibadan and the rest would continue to the east. I was the only member of the faculty on the bus. I sat on the row directly behind the driver with Fred next to me on my left side. Across the aisle on my right were the Acting Principal's wife and the student President. On arrival at the University of Ibadan gate was the common scene at Nigerian universities i.e., the police in riot gear. We passed without any comment. When I returned to Oyo the student President and the Acting Principal's wife had filled Oyo with false rumors. They claimed that when Fred saw the riot police at the University of Ibadan gate, he promised to start a riot when he returned to Oyo at the end of the teaching practice. I took Mr. Mensah, a Ghanaian member of the faculty, to the bus and showed him where the four of us sat on the bus. "If Fred said anything while on that bus, I would hear it before any of those two. When they realized I was interested in the case they dropped it. Shortly after that Fred received a Federal Government scholarship. I recommended him to the University of Nebraska, Lincoln and he was accepted and left the College. Several years later the student President requested me to recommend him to a university in the States. I told him I would never recommend him for anything and cited the lies he told about Fred. He said, "But that was politics." I became the sole target for the Acting Principal, Dean, the chair of the English department, and anyone else they could recruit.

New members of the faculty arrived. By the time the government allowed them to spend in the hotel expired, the College had rented a small apartment complex building. Two of the new members taught the Christian religion. The man, Mr. Akanihu was the chair of the department, an Igbo married with his family. The one under Mr. Akanihu was a single Yoruba woman. As a rule, the senior officer gets a bigger and better apartment. The Acting Principal would not play fair. Mr. Akanihu insisted on his right. The Acting Principal invited me to his office and pleaded with me to plead with Mr. Akanihu to accept the apartment the College gave him. When I asked why he rejected it, he claimed to have given him the right apartment, but Mr. Ogedengbe, the EO, gave him the wrong one. Knowing the EO could not do that I repeated him. "Ogedengbe changed the assignments you made?" He confirmed it. I called his messenger to get Ogedengbe. When he entered the office, I greeted him with, "Who do you think you are to change the apartments the Acting Principle assigned to the faculty?" He asked, "Who me?" and went to his desk and brought a list again in the Principal's handwriting. It was not the EO's writing. I apologized to him and said to the Acting Principal, "When you are ready to tell me the truth invite me, then I will help you." I left the office. Mr. Akanihu applied for a transfer and left the College.

The Acting Principal got bolder with his embezzlement. He went to claim ₦192,000, which at that time was worth at least $284,000. The Accounts Section of the Federal Ministry of Education caught him. His Yoruba people in the Administration in Lagos tried to protect him. They knew of a Benin man, Mr. Azodo, the founding Principal, who used to order special education equipment from Britain and called him to submit a special education equipment order worth the amount. The man came to the College, and the Acting Principal was away to Lagos, and I was in charge of the College. He wondered aloud to me, "What kind of a person did they send here as the Acting Principal? He went to the Ministry and told them that he ordered special education equipment worth ₦192,000 through me and he did not even tell me." He said he was up all night trying to come up with equipment worth the amount. I interrupted him. "Don't tell me. I don't want to hear about it." I asked one Assistant Chief Education Officer who helped to protect the Acting Principal why they did not come to investigate at Oyo. He asked, "Come to Oyo because of ₦192,000?" Though the contractor made the list, not a single piece of equipment was brought to the college. But though they covered their tracks with the Internal Auditors they controlled, they did not succeed with the Federal Auditors.

I was the second most senior to the Acting Principal at the College. Whenever he was away from the College, he told me to hold down the fort. Still, I had no office. They decided I would never be allowed to use the Vice Principal's office again. God granted them their request. I completed my first study proposal and took it to the ADE. He asked me to submit it to the Secretary for Research. The ADE also told the Acting Principal to give me an office and assigned one of the typists to me. Instead of giving me the empty Vice Principal's office next to his, the Acting Principal sent me to one empty classroom with a typist away from the Administration building. Shortly after that, I received a confidential letter from Lagos. They had appointed me the Acting Vice Principal.

Such a confidential letter would be sent simultaneously to the Acting Principal and me. Whether he wanted to campaign for his brother to get it or not did not make any difference to me. I did not tell him about my letter about the Acting appointment. Thinking it was the Igbo people I knew before I went to America, I called Obani, the Igbo man who lived below me, and showed him the letter. His face revealed his heart. Besides he added, "I went to Mr. Osunkesi and reminded him that he sent me to Britain to study Special Education Administration. Since they have appointed you the Acting Vice, they will promote you." That was his congratulations. This was a man I helped to get his promotion to level ten. I met Professor Ogan at the Federal Service Commission. He was the Chairman of the Commission at the time and was delighted that I was from Amafo and taught at Akanu Item. He said, "Amafo Isingwu the home of Emelike?" "Yes Sir," I said. These were his good friends at Uzuakoli Methodist College. As we reminiscence, he pointed to a file before him with the stamp, From the War Zone." It was the file of Obani. He asked, "O gburu madu?" (Did he kill a human?) I spoke well of him. He got his promotion to level ten.

More than two weeks later the Acting Principal saw me coming from the library and told me that he received a letter from the headquarters, and I had been appointed the Acting Vice Principal. "I have had the letter for over two weeks," I said. He asked why I did not tell him. I said, "I know they sent you a copy." He called the student assembly and announced it. He still kept me out of the Vice Principal's office and decision making of the College. He assigned me Ayeni, a Yoruba Christian, as my messenger.

The Dean's power drunkenness seemed to have no boundary. One day he saw the Principal's official car carrying the gardeners. One of them, also a Yoruba, sat on the seat the Principal normally sat. The Dean slapped the man so hard that his false teeth fell off. The man fought back. They suspended him for two weeks. The administration that claimed to come to protect the Yoruba junior officers was terrorizing them. The gardener came and reported to me. I told him to go home and nurse his wound. If they fail to pay you for the two weeks, then report to me. Again, once they knew I was interested in the case, they paid him for the period.

The military even sent a few of their junior officers to the College. One of them came from Cross River State. The Acting Principal sent his messenger with a message and the man asked me to solve a problem he had. It was close to vacation. I undertook to solve the problem but did not complete it before the start of vacation. While the students were on vacation the matter came up. He denied ever sending the student or assigning the problem to me. When the College resumed, he sent the student back to me with the same problem. I sent the student back to him and demanded the assignment in writing. He was beside himself and sent his messenger to call me. He repeated the student's statement to me and demanded to know if I actually said so. I confirmed the statement and reminded him of his denial earlier. "If it is not in writing I will not touch it." I walked out. The student watched as we talked. Having learned that his writing convicted him in the previous cases and that I would not undertake any assignment he did not put in writing, he started to write on two lines or three without a date or his signature. Then He tore off what he wrote and sent the scrap to me. But each time, I made his messenger write the date and the source and sign it. I kept all the pieces of paper in a big envelope. If he thought I would throw them away, the day came when I told him and the faculty that they were safe and secured.

He sought another way to make money and found it in the purchase of drugs. But he would not do it on the day he was at the College. Unlike him, he wrote a detailed instruction about what I should do while he was away. There was nothing said about the purchase of drugs on the sheet he gave me. However, he wrote another paper and instructed a Youth Corps, the equivalent of an AmeriCorps, and sent him to Ibadan to purchase drugs and other hospital equipment he already arranged to buy. I noticed Ogedengbe, the head driver, driving the college van up and down. I sent and instructed the gateman not to allow the van to pass the gate without my written permission. The gateman denied them passage unless they had permission from me. When they came, I told them the Acting Principal did not include the trip in his instruction sheet and denied the request. I wrote a report stating why I prevented the purchase.

The Acting Principal read my report and gave it to the youth corps to reply to. He filed my report and the reply with his abuses on me. But instead of sending the youth corps to Ibadan on the day he was in, he wrote to Dr. Williams, who was in charge of Oyo General Hospital, to sell some drugs and equipment to the College. Dr. Williams refused to sell drugs to the College. His reply said the College was only a few yards from the hospital. Besides the College did not have any trained personnel who could diagnose and treat diseases. But since the Acting Principal had made up his mind to make that money, he went ahead and bought the drugs and any other thing he wanted from Ibadan in spite of Dr. Williams' objection. He put the Yoruba youth corps person, who was a special education teacher, in charge of the infirmary he created.

Promotion for level twelve came out and I was not even aware of it. The ADE for Secondary Schools came to the College. He walked into the class I taught. I stopped to greet him. He congratulated me and announced to the class that I had been promoted to Assistant Chief Education Officer. He added, "It is because of his good work." The Dean was also promoted to the same level but mine was retroactive to several months. That meant the question of seniority between us was forever settled. That did not sit well with the Acting Principal and his click. For the moment, the Acting Principal, the Dean, and I were Assistant Chiefs. That also removed Acting from my title. I was the Vice Principal. Still, I did not know what went on in the Administration but whenever he traveled, he put me in charge of the College.

As the only psychologist in the College, I still taught psychology courses. Again, the consequence of his purchase occurred in his absence. I was walking to teach my class when I saw the special education youth corps, the Acting Principal put in charge of the infirmary, walking out of the infirmary with Rakia a female student. It was like any ordinary scene. Several minutes later there were shouts and commotion in one of the classrooms. When I rushed to the scene there were about three or four male students trying to hold Rakia steady. I called a driver to bring the combi bus. We rushed her to the hospital. I also took the youth corps with me. As we arrived at the hospital the presence of a female wrestling with four male students to steady her was enough to alert the staff. Dr. Williams promptly ordered an injection to sedate her. Soon she went to sleep.

Dr. Williams turned to me and asked for a description of her behavior before we brought her. I asked the youth corps to give it. He started with, "I diagnosed her." I stopped him and reminded him that the description of her behavior did not call for his diagnosis. Dr. Williams confirmed my statement. He complied. We left the patient at the hospital and returned to the College. I wrote my report and left it for the Acting Principal. Once more he read it and gave it to the youth corps to reply. The Acting Principal did not discuss the report or event with me.

It was time to give admission tests to prospective candidates. The Acting Principal, the Dean, and the Head of the English Department (all Yorubas) decided where to send the faculty. Besides they did not construct any tests. They decided to conduct interviews. They sent me to Jos in northern Nigeria. Many Igbo people teach there. The best candidate at the interview was an Igbo woman. On my return, I submitted my report to the Acting Principal. When the freshmen came, the best candidate, who was Igbo, was not admitted. They had discriminated against her, and others based on their Igbo names.

It was time to prepare the students for the external teaching examination. I was teaching when the Acting Principal walked in. At one time during my teaching, I said that teaching is a twenty-four-hour-a-day job. It is not like an office job where one puts in the eight hours in the office and goes home to rest. The Acting Principal, who was in the class, walked back to his office and sent his messenger to call me. When I walked into the office, he said, "Dr., you were talking about me when you contrasted teaching to office work because you looked towards my office." I was angry that he stopped me from teaching to ask such a senile question. I asked if that was why he called me. When he said yes, I told him to write it down if he wanted an answer and walked away. I was still angry when I reached the classroom. I told the students, all of whom were teachers before they were admitted why the Acting Principal called me to his office. I concluded "I am not teaching this class anymore. You go and tell him to come and teach it." Before I took a step, they were all pleading for me to stay until he came. They sent a delegation to his office. When he came and confirmed my story, they blamed him and told him to apologize to me. He did and I continued with my teaching.

Chinyere, my brother's daughter, attended high school and failed the school's final certificate examination. I took her to live with us at Oyo and repeat high school. The Principal of Olivet Grammar School admitted her to the school.

Chapter 37

Acting Principal Destined for Removal

How Did I Leave Oyo Alive

Judges 7

It was evident the Yoruba people in the Ministry and the Acting Principal read the handwriting on the wall. They knew the days of the Acting Principal at the College were numbered. But they determined to resist his removal by all means. The first line of attack was to remove me from the College. If I went safe and sound, my application was already in the Federal Commission's office, and I would still be invited to the interview. How about poisoning him?

Nigerians believe they can kill by poisoning someone. The Yoruba people believe they can poison people by any means besides eating and drinking it. The Acting Principal, who would not allow me to use my Vice Principal's office, invited me to the Principal's office one day. Having painted the chair with "poison," he told me he was going to Lagos and asked me to sit down. I looked at him, doubting what I heard. "You want me to sit down on your chair?" I asked. "Go ahead, sit down," he said. I sat down. He waited for a few minutes as though he was saying to himself, "Nothing is happening to him." Then he left.

Another time he painted a chair for me. The bursar, who came from the same state as the Acting Principal, walked into the office and was about to sit on it when the Acting Principal shouted so loud that most people in the administration building rushed to see what was wrong. They carried the chair outside and left it there. I believe the day the Acting Principal told me to sit on his chair was the day he handed over the College to me, no matter what else he intended.

Our last baby was born on August 29, and a week later, it was our tenth wedding anniversary. We invited a few friends and had a celebration in Nigeria without alcohol.

Poisoning had failed. They tried to get me involved in a fight they faked with the former Vice Principal. The Acting Principal traveled to Lagos, and I was in charge of the College. I asked the Dean a question about an assignment I gave him. He barked abuses, turned round, and pushed me. Students in the library saw him. I told him that he was finished and walked away. I wrote my report and demanded a written apology. The Acting Principal invited me to his office to receive the apology. When I got there, he and the Dean were seated. I saw them and left the door open so that the typist and the messenger would hear us. The acting principal offered me a seat. I declined. The Acting Principal started to apologize for the Dean. I demanded to hear it from the Dean. The Acting Principal stood up and slowly walked towards me with his hands raised. I jumped out of the room and threatened to report to Lagos. He called an emergency meeting of a select few of the faculty. At the start of the meeting, he said there would be no minutes of the meeting. But he took minutes throughout the meeting. The meeting was inconclusive. At the end of the meeting, he gave Mr. Makinde, the chair of the English department and one of his Yoruba people with whom he misruled the College, the notes he took to work on it as the minutes. Unfortunately for them, Mr. Veerasingham saw them and told me about it. When I got home, Obani came to me and asked me not to report to Lagos. He said the students supported what I said. "When these people lie, they sound like the truth." Knowing where his loyalty lay, I declined his advice and dismissed him with, "I will do it my way."

The Acting Principal opened another front of attack on me. Unfortunately, he chose the church as his avenue. My arrangement with Ogbomoso Baptist Seminary called for them to choose the Sunday to preach. I then made the schedule to include all the preachers. Every preacher received the schedule. Except for the Principal of the Seminary and the man who scheduled the faculty from the Seminary, I never saw any other preacher from the Seminary before the day they preached. On this one Sunday, a young Yoruba doctor who returned to Nigeria from Texas U.S.A. preached at the College. Because he was late, I drove to the academic site to see if he went there. He did not, so I drove back to Durbar. On arrival, he was conversing with the Acting Principal in their Yoruba language. Introductions were made, and we went in for the service. The man preached a God-glorifying sermon. He condemned the sinful practices he was witnessing in Nigeria. He said, "If Adam was really the first man to sin, he must have been a Nigerian." Thinking that everyone enjoyed the sermon, we went home, giving no thought to the fact that the acting principal was offended. First, he thought the young doctor was the President of the Seminary. Second, he vowed to himself that the doctor would never be allowed to preach at the church again. But he would not announce his decision until the Friday of the week the President was scheduled to preach.

The week I scheduled the President of Ogbomoso Baptist Seminary to preach arrived. The Acting Principal waited till the Friday before the Sunday to talk to me. I was on my way to teach my class when he stopped me. Like the enemies of Daniel, he acted as though the only way he could get me in trouble was through the church. He said, "Dr., I want to preach on Sunday." I told him he could not preach on Sunday because he was not scheduled to preach. He insisted on preaching, and I said, "You have the schedule, and you know the

President of Ogbomoso Seminary is preaching on Sunday." He denied I gave him the schedule. I said, "When will you stop lying to people?" He walked away. Joan said, "Dr. Onwuegbu, you just called him a liar." I said in reply, "What do you call someone who does not tell the truth?" I went to teach my class.

An emergency meeting of the faculty was in session when I walked out of the class. I was invited to it. He called the meeting to condemn me in absentia. Some members insisted on my being present. When I arrived, I gave them the two conditions under which I would participate. "The Yoruba faculty secretary who takes minutes during faculty meetings would not be the recorder." A youth corps from the north took the minutes. "I shall not limit myself to his accusation." Then he repeated his charges. "He accused me of telling the young doctor from Ogbomoso all the sins of the College and asked him to preach against them ("Blessed are you when people insult you, persecute you and falsely say all kinds of evil against you because of me." Matthew 5:11). He did, and I invited him again." Thanks to God, he acknowledged that the truth undermines the sins of the college. The faculty asked me to reply. In reply I said, "Of the two of us, if one of us told the preacher what to preach, it was him. He saw him before I did."

The President of the seminary was from Benin and a much older person. I continued with his lying about his lecture to the junior staff, about Oluigbo, Fred, Akanihu, the youth corps, the soldier, the schedule, and why the students compelled him to apologize to me. For the first time, I told him that the pieces of paper he sent through his messenger were in a big envelope in my desk. Also, I told him why I jumped out of his office the day he called me to receive an apology from his dean of students. "With only three of us in the office, you might bite yourself and claim that I bit you." Obani, who was not at the service, claimed the church was used to undermine the acting principal's authority. Mr. Ayoku, a Yoruba man who was at the service, said, "I was there. I enjoyed the sermon. If anyone was convicted, he should not blame Dr. Onwuegbu; he should change."

The acting principal threatened to take the case to Lagos. "He has finished his marathon. I will put him in his cubicle," he said. (As King Saul said, "David must die.") I became his David. I challenged him to take the case to Lagos. "Those who kept you here after the report of the first inquiry and you will justify your stay at this College. The report said you lied much of the time, recommended your immediate removal, and prevented you from heading any institution for at least the next two years." He asked if I wrote the report. "No," I replied. "I did not. But I know the content." The faculty became divided. Some claimed the case was beyond them. Others said if the students could make the acting principal apologize to the Vice, why could they not decide the case? One after the other, they left. If he went to Lagos with the case, he did not receive any encouragement. Like the enemies of the four Jews in Babylon who plotted their demise and were burnt by fire and eaten by the hungry lions they intended to destroy the Jews; and also like Haman in Esther 7:10 that says, "So they hanged Haman on the gallows that he had prepared for Mordecai. Then the wrath of the king abated." As the Bible says, "...If God is for us, who can be against us?" (Romans 8:31 ESV)

The faculty emergency meeting, the Acting Principal called to remove me from the College and terminate his presence at the College. The man who wrote the minutes took it to Lagos. He gave the minutes to the Secretary for The Commission through his Northern representative in the House of Representatives. The Principal of Ogbomoso came that Sunday, and I asked the Acting Principal to read the Bible lessons, and he did.

Sweetie was pregnant at the time. Instead of registering with Oyo General Hospital she registered with Ogbomoso Baptist Hospital. All or most of the medical doctors were Americans. Joan, another American member of the faculty married to another Igbo on the faculty, was expecting and, for medical reasons, also registered with Ogbomoso. I drove them to the hospital one day. As we waited to see the doctor, I heard, "Obed, Obed," and when I turned, it was Allen. He asked if I had seen the Daily Times of the day. I had not. He told me the post of the Principal of my college was advertised, and he encouraged me to apply.

Usually the college newspaper was available for the faculty to read. But that was not the case that day. When I walked into the administration building, the Acting Principal and the Dean of Students were standing at the door of the building discussing the publication, and their gloomy faces told the story. When I asked to see the Daily Times, the Dean angrily replied, "you can't." The Acting Principal said the paper was not in the office. I left them, sought and found the vendor, and bought a copy. I applied for the job. Almost two years after the report was issued to the Federal Ministry of Education, the Yoruba people controlled, they ignored it. The Federal Service Commission, which controls all the federal ministries, heard about the report through the youth corps, which took the minutes of the emergency meeting. The acting principal called to condemn me. It reprimanded the Ministry of Education, declared the post vacant and advertised it in the Daily Times. I applied.

Months had passed since I applied for the position of the Principal of the College, and nothing happened. I went to the Commission to find out why. I discovered that a Yoruba was in charge and was sitting on the applications. When I asked why he had not invited applicants for interview, he said there were not many applicants. I asked how many he expected for such a high office. I added, "Are you interested in numbers or quality?" He had no answer. I walked away, knowing it was Yoruba planned tactics. I decided I would not spend one more academic year at Oyo.

Ibadan, once the largest city in West Africa, had a problem accommodating the Federal College for Special Education. The inhabitants of the proposed site refused to budge. They complained that they lived where the University of Ibadan was built and were forced out to build the University. Then were compelled to yield to the College of Agriculture. This third time, they vowed would be over their dead bodies. The Acting Principal said he and some people from his state in the Ministry were discussing about moving the College to his state on a land close to Ibadan. I was not prepared to move again, especially since I was comfortable in rural Oyo town. I went to Chief Ogumola, the proprietor of the Alliance Hotel, and told him the conversation. Besides, I requested that he take me to Alaafin to see if he could provide land and keep the college in Oyo. He agreed and, without delay, took me to the Oba. I was not prepared for what I witnessed.

When we got to the door, I lifted one leg to step in, and the chief held me back and gently pushed me out of the way. He folded his flowing agbada around him and prostrated flat on the floor facing down while he greeted the Alaafin until he ordered him up. Then we walked in. He was delighted to hear the news and prepared to donate the land. The Alaafin and his people donated land for the College permanently at Oyo.

The University of Ibadan started a diploma in education course at the College. Its policy was to make the Provost, i.e., the head of the institution, the Associate to the Director of the Institute at the University. It was left for the Provost or, in the case of Oyo, the Acting Principal, to choose his second in command. He chose the Dean, my junior, over me. They asked for lecturers. I refused to teach. The lecturers were paid, but I refused to participate. However, I offered to give free lectures on topics of my choice. They did not accept knowing why I refused to teach. Their game boomeranged when conditions changed.

I decided that I would not work under the Acting Principal for another year. Therefore, I applied to two state institutions for employment: one in Awka, Anambra State and Port Harcourt in Rivers State.

I bought a new car and became mobile again. Before I insured it, I carried Melody and Chinedum in the car to take Chinyere to her school. A drunk motorcyclist hit me. One of his eyes popped out. I told Chinyere to take my children home. She stayed to watch the mob gather. I felt helpless and wondered what I would do if they attacked my children. I left the car at the scene, walked my children home, and asked a Pakistani to take me to get insurance before the police arrived. As I expected, the police vainly wanted a bribe from me. The man was treated at the hospital, and his eye set back to the socket. Then, the police demanded a bribe from him. He pleaded with me to go with him to get his motorcycle from the police station. Seeing us coming surprised them. They laughed and said, "What do you know, they have become friends." I requested them to release his motorcycle. They did.

I had thought of going to see Mr. Iteke, my teacher and headmaster, in standards five and six. I did not know Aguneri, his village. However, I knew it was in the Awka area. I bought some gifts for him and his wife and drove off. I got lost in one place. But I found the village and his home. A woman who directed me to his home identified him as a Scoutmaster, not a teacher. He was delighted to see me. His wife was not home when I arrived. He sent for her. Once she saw me, she smiled and said, "Obed Isigwuzo." I stood up and greeted her. Mr. Iteke asked her, "What did you say yesterday?" Her reply was, "I said my umbrella is torn." He said to her, "Obed bought you a new umbrella." She expressed her delight. Her big smile said more than her thank you. I also bought a bottle of White Horse Whiskey for him. They were extremely and pleasantly surprised to see me. When it was time for me to leave, he gave me three yams and three shillings and said, "On your way home, ask anyone you see what my gift to you means." Unfortunately, I did not see anyone as I drove away, and I have yet to find out.

The New Year seemed to be pregnant with expectations. Our three-month-old baby was asleep, and so was everyone else on New

Year's Eve. Our normal routine was for all of us to gather in the living room and pray from about a quarter to 12 into the new year. Since everyone was sleeping, that left me to pray alone. I took my Bible and asked God to give me a passage to read. When I opened the Bible, Psalm 46 looked me in the face. Part of verse ten says, "... be still and know that I am God." I thanked God for my family and His goodness through the passing years. I prayed for the three possible positions before me in the coming year. I could continue as the vice principal of the college, become the principal of the college, or be employed by any of the two state institutions to which I applied. I asked for His will be done. Then I prayed for other things and other people.

I decided to go home and see my mother, who lived alone. I had not driven thirty minutes on a journey that took almost a whole day when I started to shake all over my body. That was the first time I experienced such a thing in my life. I stopped by the side of the road and prayed. The shaking stopped. When I reached home, my mother was very sick. I waited till the next day to take her to Amachara Methodist Hospital. When we got there, the diagnosis surprised me. Mr. Isaac Nduka, who took her blood pressure, asked what I did to prevent her from having a stroke. "I only prayed," I said. Both her high and low pressures were off the chart. The doctor admitted her. I paid some amount and drove to my aunt Ukachi, who lived nearby, and informed her. I gave her money and drove her to the hospital to see her sister. She took care of my mother, and I returned to Oyo. It was certain she would have had a stroke if I did not go home. Worse still, in the absence of anyone in the house, she could have died. Providence worked.

My two applications to the two-state positions were successful. Each offered me a better position than the Assistant Chief Education Officer position I had at Oyo. However, Awka was a better position than Port Harcourt. Besides, Awka is in Igbo land, while Rivers State people had become hostile to Igbo people since the Biafra Nigeria War. It was, therefore, easy for me to choose Awka over Port Harcourt. The

Acting Principal and the Yoruba people knew about my job offer at Port Harcourt but not Awka. I went to Awka to see what housing arrangement Awka had. I was not satisfied. We planned to meet again while they searched. A telegram from the Federal Service Commission awaited me at home on my return. The Federal Service Commission invited me to attend an interview for the post of the Principal of the College.

Only my Sweetie and I knew about the telegram and its content at the College. Two days before the day of the interview, the acting principal handed the College over to me and traveled to Lagos. One day before the interview, he was still away. Before the first scheduled interview, the ADE Schools said to Professor Obanya, Director of the University of Ibadan Institute, and one of the interviewers, "We want our man (Yoruba man) in that position." I left a note for the acting principal that I was invited to Lagos on official duty and would not be at the College. We met at the Federal Service Commission building. We were among the applicants invited for the interview. We waited for over an hour only to be told that there would be no interview. The rest of us received refunds for our traveling expenses. For the first time, the Acting Principal rejected money. He said he traveled by his official car. He and his Yoruba people in the Ministry used his two days in Lagos before the interview to concoct another lie. They claimed to have interviewed people and filled the post. The following day, his Yoruba brother, who was the Chief Education Officer at the Federal Ministry of Education, came and congratulated him. I felt that was the last straw. I was on my way again to Awka. This time, I stayed overnight. They showed me an apartment I felt comfortable with. When I returned, another telegram from the Commission was waiting for me. It was another invitation to attend the interview the Ministry canceled. The Commission had castigated the Ministry officials for thinking they could fill the post the Commission advertised. Again, we went to the interview. The Acting Principal was there, and even his former Vice was there. I was the first applicant the panel interviewed. I was there for over one hour. When they indicated the end, I said, "With all humility, this job is not a level fourteen job, and I am not a level fourteen officer. If it is not at level fifteen, give it to someone else. But please let me know your decision as soon as possible." The chair smiled and dismissed me. The acting principal was called in, and within twenty minutes, he was out and looked unhappy. His former Vice said to him, "What is the matter? You did not even spend half the time Dr. Onwuegbu spent." The acting principal asked him if he was the timekeeper. I waited until the interview was over. Soon I saw Mr. Inyang, the Ministry representative, walking away. He was almost out of the fourth floor when I caught up with him. He shook my hand firmly. That told me that I had the job. However, to make assurance doubly sure, I said to him, "I can leave the Ministry now." He replied, "No, no, no." With that, we parted. Soon, the Secretary walked out, and I followed and asked who got the job. "Who else, with all your theories and answers, you." I returned to Oyo believing I was the Principal.

After about one month and the letter of employment had not reached me, I drove to the Ministry to know why. One of those "I know it all" told me the letter was at the Honorable Minister's desk. I ignored him and drove to the Commission's office. On reaching the fourth floor, God brought the gentleman who said I was blackmailing the Commission when someone told him on the day of interview that I demanded level fifteen instead of fourteen. He is Igbo and a high official. He smiled and congratulated me. To which I asked, on what? He asked, "You have not received the letter?" No, I said. At that point, God brought the Yoruba man who was the Secretary at the interview to walk by. The Igbo man stopped him and asked him why I had not received the letter. He claimed the officer to sign it had been on leave. Okay, he will come and get it tomorrow. He pleaded for forty-eight hours and received it.

I returned to Oyo believing the problem was solved. The Yoruba man alerted the Yoruba people in the Ministry and informed them about the new development. At about 5:15 am the following morning, I had a dream that woke me up. I woke Sweetie up and said to her, "The letter is not ready, and trouble is looming over it." I left Oyo immediately after I taught my one lesson of the day. When I met the secretary, it took him ten minutes to walk ten yards. The man he said was on leave was the same Yoruba middle officer who delayed the interview in the first place. When we got to his office, he "discovered" the man was too junior to sign the letter. He started another five-minute stroll to another office. This time, it was to a Bendelite Igbo. The man was too busy and told him so. His legs became so light he almost flew. I waited till the Bendel Igbo man returned to his office and gave him the history of the case. He told me to come back the following day. Before I left his office, he called the secretary and told him to bring my letter of employment. Also before him was a petition from the chair of the English department at the College, who was a Yoruba and denied promotion. Because he was one of those against me, he did not uphold his petition.

I returned to Oyo and dreamed about the letter at about the same time the following night, and this time the letter was ready. I woke up and said to Sweetie, "The letter is ready." That day, I took Isiaka, one of the College drivers, to drive my car. When I entered the office, the officer used the exact words I heard in my dream, "Congratulations your letter is ready." He was not even qualified to sign it. The Secretary for the Commission signed it. Before I left his office, he advised me to reply with the date of the following day. He said that was important because promotion was based on the date of acceptance. I thanked him and went to the Ministry and informed Mr. Inyang. We were back to Oyo by 3.00 pm. If the faculty meeting the acting principal called is compared with Joseph getting sold to the Ishmaelites, my taking over the administration of the college is equivalent to Joseph becoming the ruler of Egypt.

In fulfilling its obligation, the Commission sent a copy of my letter of employment to the Ministry. Believing that my copy would arrive by mail the Yoruba people promptly instructed the Acting Principal to watch out for my letter and destroy it before I saw it. From that day the Acting Principal behaved like King Saul, and I became his David. Knowing how they operate even at the Commission, I developed my own strategy. I wrote a letter of acceptance immediately and registered a copy. A few days later, I took a copy and gave it to the Igbo man who gave me the letter. I requested him to keep my file in his office because these people might destroy my reply. He told me that the Secretary called for my file that morning. The Yorubas in the Ministry were already protesting that I was going from level 13 to 15. I made copies of my letter. After a week when the Acting Principal should have seen the letter and did not, he came to my classroom office and sat on my desk just as he sat on his former Vice Principal's desk the morning he rejoiced over his transfer. His intention was to find out if I had received the letter. Instead, he pretended to seek my advice and asked what should be done to improve the College in the coming year. In my heart I said, God has done it. You are out of here. But with my mouth, I told him to give me about two weeks to think about it. He left.

Having prematurely convinced themselves that I had become history at the College and was going to accept the job at Port Harcourt, they behaved as though I had, in reality, left the College. They celebrated an assumed victory by redistributing offices. The Dean became the Vice Principal designate. The Dean assumed they would still control the College the following academic year and said to Ayeni my messenger, "Dr. Onwuegbu will soon go away, and you will suffer here." Ayeni was a Yoruba. He was a Christian and loyal to me. That was his crime. He was almost in tears when he walked to my office and asked me, "Where are you going Sir? The Dean said I would suffer when you leave in a few weeks." My reply was, "Are you not a Christian? Go home and pray." He walked out dejected.

Since they had prematurely convinced themselves that I had become history at the College, a man came to the College one day and requested to see the Vice Principal, Ayeni, my messenger, brought him to my office. He took one look at me and declared, "Not him. The one who drives the red Volvo." That was the Dean of Students. Ayeni said to him, "We have only one Vice Principal here." The man left. On hearing about the man's visit, I wrote a warning letter to "whom it may concern." I am the only legitimate Vice Principal at this College. Someone from this College has made it his duty to impersonate me and my office in this town. That must stop forthwith. If it continues, I will report the matter to the police." I put a copy in my file and sent it to the Acting Principal and pasted a copy in the staff general office. Neither the Acting Principal nor the Dean reacted to my letter.

By the end of the second week, I felt it was time to shock them. I put a copy of my letter of employment in my file and took the file to the Acting Principal, showed him my letter as the Principal of the College, and asked him to read and sign that he saw it. He read it and looked at me dazed. Confused without speech for a few minutes and then said, "This letter is supposed to come through me." "O no. Look at the address. It is addressed directly to me, not even through the Ministry, and I have had it for two weeks now." He refused to sign it. I left the file with him and walked out. A few hours after I went back, he was with the Dean plotting, and Veerasingham was there with his file. He signed Mr. Veerasingham's file and still refused to endorse mine. I took my file and left. They declared full war; skirmishes were over. If I thought my letter settled the matter, they told me to think again.

Chapter 38

Lost Wars

The three Yoruba senior officers at the College, led by the Acting Principal, planned a three-front attack. One was at Oyo. The Acting Principal and his men first planned and met the Alaafin through the Chief who owned the Alliance Hotel. They claimed the Igbo man came to drive a Yoruba man away from an institution in Yoruba land. He was doomed to failure here because the Alaafin reminded them it was the Igbo man who kept the College at Oyo. They went to the legislators. The President was a Hausa, and the Vice President was Igbo.

Though a Yoruba was the deputy leader of the house, an Igbo was the Speaker of the House. The Yoruba Deputy Leader also came from Oyo and could not do anything that concerned Oyo without first consulting the Alaafin. So, he lost in both cases. His only hope lay in the Ministry and my leaving to take my position at Port Harcourt. They convinced themselves that my patience would wear out and I would leave. My people say if a doctor's child dies of poison, why is he a doctor? If these non-psychologists frustrate me, why am I a Christian psychologist?

The Acting Principal made one of those blunders for which he was known and called students back to campus two weeks earlier before the due date. The government fed the students and did not provide the funds. The Acting Principal did not know what to do with them. The students were reluctant to carry their luggage home. I called

Briggs, the Students Union President, and told him I was the Principal. But the Yoruba people were unwilling to hand over. The Acting Principal would not listen to any advice from me. Ask him to allow the students to put their luggage in the vacant and unused Vice Principal's office. He did and the Acting Principal accepted.

Having suffered two deadly blows at the legislature and at Oyo, like a dying snake the Yorubas at the Ministry and College continued fighting a losing battle. The Minister at the Federal Ministry of Education was also Igbo.

Two weeks later, the students came back. Transport was not a problem because the government paid them traveling allowance. The students were on teaching practice and Joan and I supervised the students at Ibadan. I gave her a ride. On our way to Ibadan, she said, "If it were Oke (her husband), he would have said he tried and let them have it." That offended me. "I allow them to take what belongs to me because they demand to have it?" She is white American like my wife. When I reported to my wife, she sounded like Joan. I took my pen and accused the Director in the Ministry of flouting the order of the Commission with impunity and warmed him to be prepared to answer to the Federal Commission Office. I drove to the Director's office and gave him the letter. He gave me a copy of a letter to the Acting Principal ordering him to report to Lagos for posting or face disciplinary action. But it was all a fake. He used my file to write the letter so that it could not be traced to the Acting Principal's file. The Director sent his assistant to the ADE Secondary Schools as a spy to survey Oyo and report back to him. Though the ADE recommended the removal of the Acting Principal, he rejected his recommendation. I refused to attend any meeting the Acting Principal called.

Isiaka drove me to Lagos one evening. I stopped at my friend Emedom's house where I spent the night. I called Mr. Inyang from Emedom's home. He wanted to know where I was. "In Lagos," I said. He warned me not to come to the Ministry. This sounds like Elisha warning the king of Israel to avoid the traps of the Syrian military. (2 Kings 6:9). I left early in the morning and returned to Oyo. Isiaka and I were on the outskirts of Oyo when we saw the Acting Principal and another driver driving toward Ibadan. His driver said he asked if Dr. Onwuegbu did not say he was going to Lagos? I went home, ate and went to the College.

Less than twenty minutes after I sat down in my classroom office, the Director of Education walked in. He laughed and said, "Is this classroom your office?" "Yes, Sir," I said. He asked where the Acting Principal was. I did not know. He was surprised that nobody knew where he was. He invited me to come to Lagos the following day to receive the letter of transfer for the Acting Principal. He added, "We all support you." I thought, "If I were a fool, you could fool me." Still, I went to get the letter. On my arrival, he sent me to the Secretary for Education, also a Yoruba. In my attempt to locate his office, I entered the office of the Permanent Secretary by mistake. I requested the letter before I realized it was the wrong office. Mr. Inyang was there. I walked out only to hear the Permanent Secretary repeatedly ask Mr. Inyang, "Who is that guy? Who is that guy?" Finally, I found the office of the Secretary for Education, also a Yoruba. My presence offended him. He wanted to know why I should be the bearer of the letter. I walked back to the Director. The Secretary had talked to him on the phone. When he saw me, he smiled and said "You shouted at him." I asked what reason I had to shout at him. He promised to post the letter. They lost all respect if I had any for them. I determined to fight it out with them.

President Shagari came to Oyo. The Acting Principal wrote a petition against me to read to him. He was not even allowed to come near the President. Instead, the Oyo State Presidential Liaison Officer (PLO), Dr. Balogun, also a Yoruba himself, reported to the Minister of Education the Acting Principal's refusal to hand over to me. Things got hot in Lagos. I told all the Igbo students at the College that I was the Principal. The Acting Principal was resisting to hand over. He would hand over one of these days. When he does, do not clap your hands or applaud. If you do, the Yoruba lecturers will hold it against you.

Then I learned where he was the day the Director came to the College. At least those three Yorubas at Oyo had convinced themselves that I would not pack and leave the College for them. Their next move was a plot to undo the arrangement already made for the final year students' teaching examination. The Acting Principal was on his way to the University of Ibadan to foul up everything. God intervened. His official car broke down on the way. He used the day to repair the car.

Some Federal colleges of education, including Oyo, are affiliated to the University of Ibadan (UI). As a result, the Institute of Education at the University of Ibadan supervises the final teaching examination for our senior students. The colleges pay the traveling and hotel expenses for the UI examiners. Believing he could cancel the students teaching examination arrangement, the Acting Principal was on his way to the University of Ibadan to demand a refund of the money he paid UI to conduct the teaching examination. He realized too late that his chances of continuing as Acting Principal were below zero and took the official car to demolish the teaching examination arrangement. God broke down the car on his way. Besides, Professor Obanya, an Igbo, succeeded Professor Yoloye, a Yoruba, as the Director of the Institute of Education at UI. Also, Dr. Mba, an Igbo from my district, was the Acting Chair of the Department of Special Education.

Isiaka drove me to the Institute one day. I went to see Dr. Mba the Acting Chair. I was sitting in Dr. Mba's office when the Acting Principal walked in. He told Dr. Mba to refund him the money he paid for the students' teaching examination. I could not believe the man was so selfish to sacrifice the students' future like that. It was my turn to take advantage of my language. I told Dr. Mba, in our Igbo language, which the Acting Principal did not understand, that I was the

Principal. "He is out to play havoc. Do not listen to anything he says." I left them and walked to Professor Obanya's office. A few minutes later, he came there also. I also spoke to the Professor in our Igbo language. "I am now the Principal. He is here as a spoiler. Don't listen to anything he says." I left them and walked away (2 Kings 6:19-22).

Having been defeated at every corner and turn, the Acting Principal decided to surrender. I drove to the academic site one morning and stopped at the gate for the gateman to open for me. One small bird flew to the windshield of my car, "sang and danced" on my windshield. But it did not mess up the windshield. I parked my car and walked towards my classroom office. The Dean, and the chair of the English department lined up and walked towards me. It was a big surprise when the Dean, who had not talked to me since they transferred the former vice principal, muttered good morning. Not sure he actually greeted me, I muttered back. Then, the chair of the English department confirmed the first greeting with his. I greeted him and wondered what they had up their sleeves. It unraveled after 8.00 a.m. The three had decided it was not in their best interest to continue to fight a lost war. The Acting Principal called an assembly of faculty and students. To me, anything he did at the College was illegal. Therefore, I refused to attend. I was in my classroom office when I heard him say, "I want to inform you that I am no longer your Principal. Dr. Onwuegbu is the best-qualified person to head this institution. He has been appointed the Principal and I will soon handover the College to him..." He was still speaking when I went to the hall, walked half the distance, and left. A few minutes later, he dismissed them.

On the academic side, I completed two research studies and submitted them to the Secretary in charge of research who was also a Yoruba man. One was about special education, and the second was a survey of the ten best, ten middle, and ten worst secondary schools in the country based on the school certificate results. The study intended to compare and contrast the qualifications and experiences of the teachers, the libraries, laboratories etc. of the schools. Though the Secretary had accepted and promised to fund the studies before the interview, once he heard that I had been selected to replace his Yoruba brother he held both studies hostage. On the other hand, my book, Discover Teaching, has been accepted for publication. I also had self-published Practice Teaching for Grade Two Teachers. By the end of 1979, both of them were on the market. The Acting Principal bought ten copies of Discover Teaching for the college library.

One would think that once the Acting Principal announced he was no longer the Principal he would hand over the College to me. That was not the case. He locked the Principal's office and went on his four week' vacation, which he spent there at Oyo. He also took the Principal's official car and parked it in the Principal's official residence. He did not even tell me that he was on leave.

While the Acting Principal was still on vacation, the PLO for Oyo State invited me to Ibadan to award contracts for the College. The bursar and the Acting Principal came from the same state. The PLO and I planned to award college contracts. Then I looked for the bursar to get some information. We could not find him. Aware of the games they played, I told Isiaka, the driver, to drive by the Acting Principal's house. When we reached the Acting Principal's residence, we saw the bursar's car parked there. I sent the driver to call him. I made him know I knew the double game he was playing. When I reached the PLO's office, I became aware of what the game was.

The PLO represented the President in each state. He presided over the award of federal contracts. That was one way of rewarding party loyalists. The College had ₦240,000, over $360,000 to spend. It was November and the fiscal year ended in December. Since he could not spend it, they tried to prevent me from spending it. According to the Acting Chair of the Department of Special Education at the University of Ibadan, the Acting Principal could have spent the money before the appointment of the PLOs. However, he alleged that the

Acting Principal insisted on getting twenty percent of the money as a bribe. We were able to spend all but twenty thousand naira.

A few days after we awarded the contracts at Ibadan, the bursar brought a voucher to my classroom office. He requested me to sign it. I asked what it was. He said, a voucher for a bus the College bought. Aware of his plot and looking offended, I asked if he and his brother had handed over the College to me. "No Sir. But we know who is in charge," was his answer. I warned him never, ever to try it again and ordered him out. He left.

Having exhausted all avenues of protest without any success, and knowing the money was spent and that their patience had failed to outlast mine, the Acting Principal came out of vacation. It was the last week of November. He used it to write his handing over notes. He promised to hand over the College to me on December 2. About mid-morning that day, his messenger called me to the office. He was not willing to attend a sendoff party in his honor. At the last minute, he changed his mind and accepted to attend. He gave me the handing over note. I read it and requested to see certain equipment and materials he listed but that I doubted existed. As I doubted, they did not exist, and we deleted them and initialed the lines. We returned to the office and signed the document. He left the office. He left one document on the desk. It was the petition he wanted to present to President Shagari, which he was not allowed. I believe he left it for one reason, namely, to show that Mr. Veerasingham co-signed it with him instead of the Dean or the chair of the English department, the tribesmen with whom he misruled the College all along. But that did not subtract from the good deeds Mr. Veerasingham did to me. Immediately after he left the office, I called the college carpenter and told him to change the padlock to the office. I waited while he changed it. I locked the door and took all four keys from him. The Acting Principal released the Principal's official car while his family still occupied the Principal's residence.

A committee was formed and put in charge of the sendoff. One of the outsiders invited to the sendoff was the Principal of the Federal Agriculture Institute in the town, also a Yoruba. I sat him between the Acting Principal and me. Towards the end of the party, I invited speeches. The Principal praised the Acting Principal for raising the bar with his successor. Then his brother, the bursar, spoke. He really rebuked him. He told him to read or even study what he signed, especially if it was a voucher. That bursar waited and watched until the Acting Principal was in the car to drive off before he ran to him and gave him vouchers to sign. Many of the vouchers were fraudulent. The Acting Principal was in trouble with the audit department. He was telling the Acting Principal what got him in trouble at the sendoff party. As usual, I had nothing to add except to thank everyone present and dismissed the party. In the meantime, I remained in the classroom office he gave me.

Ibadan had two good hospitals in those days. There was the University Teaching Hospital and another hospital that specialized in the treatment of tuberculosis. Dr. Whitaker at Aba Christian Hospital was not sure why our son Chinedum coughed so much. The English man put him on a TB treatment course. When we heard about the TB hospital, I took Chinedum to see the doctors. They tested him and asked us to come back on a specified date. When we returned, the Dr. was annoyed that some doctors put our son on TB treatment. Chinedum did not have TB. We thanked God.

At another time, Chinedum could not hear well. I took him to the University of Ibadan Teaching Hospital. The Dr. examined his ear, gave him a tube, and asked him to drop the liquid into his ear. Again, we were given a date to return. We did. When he came out, he asked me, "Why is everyone shouting?" "Son, no one is shouting. The wax prevented you from hearing well."

Chapter 39

In a Lion's Den with God

As I ask the Holy Spirit to teach me how to start this chapter, many verses in the Bible flood my mind. They include the stories in Daniel, 2 Corinthians 12:9, "My grace is sufficient for you, ..." However, I decided to quote Isaiah 43:2-3, "²When you pass through the waters, I *will be* with you; and through the rivers, they shall not overflow you. When you walk through the fire, you shall not be burned, nor shall the flame scorch you. For I *am* the Lord your God, The Holy One of Israel, your Savior; I gave Egypt for your ransom, Ethiopia and Seba in your place." First, let me describe the atmosphere, both physical and psychological, where I was to operate.

Federal Colleges of Education in Nigeria at this time were not autonomous. The Federal Ministry of Education practically took every decision for them and carried it out. The Ministry employed lecturers and staff for them. The Ministry promoted and disciplined those faculty and staff. The Principal must report any of the officers under him three times for wrong deeds before the Ministry discusses the matter. It decided how much money to allocate to each college and, in most cases, how to spend the money. At one time, the Principal could not award any contract above ₦5,000. The Ministry bought and distributed vehicles. It awarded all contracts above five thousand naira, and that included rents for houses. The Yoruba people were in charge of all aspects of these as a result of the Biafra-Nigeria War. If they did not like a Principal, they withheld the payment to any or all of these to cause trouble for the Principal. One can now understand why the Yoruba Director was bold enough to boast to Mr. Adigwe my fellow Igbo man in his office, "Let me see how he can succeed without my help." In the hierarchy at the time, from the highest were the Permanent Secretary, the Director, the Assistant Director, the Chief Education Officer, the Assistant Chief Education Officer, and almost all of them were Yoruba. Mr. Inyang an Anang from Cross River State were the odd man. They also controlled the financial section. Besides, the College is in Yoruba land. By human calculation, they considered me doomed for failure.

With the removal of the Acting Principal certain, the Dean tried to maneuver himself to the position of authority at the University of Ibadan. As stated earlier, UI established a diploma in education course at Oyo. The policy was for the Provost or the Principal of the college where the course was taught to become the Associate Director. The Associate then chose his Assistant. It was treated as a tribal matter at Oyo, and the Acting Principal chose the Dean, a Yoruba, as his Assistant, though I was the Vice Principal. I refused to teach any course but offered to give free lectures. Realizing the end of the Acting Principal at the College, the Dean went and campaigned to replace him as the Associate Director of the College. He almost succeeded, but Professor Obanya, who was the Director of the Institute and an Igbo, overruled them.

I went to Lagos and walked into Mr. Inyang's office. He complained that his Chief Education Officer Osunkesi told people that he was Assistant Director. He wondered where he would get the staff as though Osunkesi determined the appointment by his power. I walked over to submit my budget request to the Controller of Finance and Accounts (CFA) also a Yoruba. He looked at me with an angry face that said, "We will show you who the boss is," and said, "You don't go to Inyang anymore. You go through Mr. Osunkesi." He is now your ADE.

They tightened the nook. Osunkesi was to make sure I failed. There was still one open window left for me. The Chief Accountant was Igbo and he helped me with my first budget proposal. I went and greeted the man who had been charged to ensure my failure. We returned to Oyo.

I called the first faculty meeting since I took over and made certain changes. I removed the Yoruba man who was the Secretary and replaced him with Father Ekpo a priest from Cross River. Knowing that allowing the Dean to keep the two offices he had used to promote himself would cause disaster, I stripped him of the two. I appointed Mr. Mensah from Ghana as the Dean of Students. To avoid the perception that I was against the Yoruba people, I gave the Dean's Assistant position for the Ibadan diploma course to Mr. Ojo, another Yoruba man. I formed college committees such as library, curriculum, and agriculture, three disciplinary committees, one for students, one for the junior staff, and one for the faculty, a committee to receive contract awards, and asked departments to form equivalent committees where appropriate.

My first challenge came from the former Dean. As the furniture and other materials the College ordered started to arrive, I wrote a common letter to the former Dean, the Chair of the English department, and Mr. Veerasinghan to vacate rooms they illegally occupied. The rooms were not parts of their apartment. The last two complied. The former Dean thought he was still in charge and wrote an abusive reply to me. I knew he was not in charge. So, I ignored his abuse and invited him to come to the classroom office they gave me for discussion. When he refused my invitation, I wrote a directive to the bursar. "From the moment you receive this note start to charge Mr. Babalola the total amount or the rent for the room he is illegally occupying. You must withdraw the whole amount before you pay his salary. Should it rain and any damage is done to the furniture, that amount must also be deducted before you pay him. Make sure he receives a copy of this note promptly." It was delivered.

Less than one hour later he was in my classroom office with Obani and Mr. Mensah. These were the two who supported the Acting Principal the day he accused me of telling the preacher the sins of the College. Obani waved the letter from the bursar and said, "You wrote this letter to the second most senior officer to you?" When he stopped rattling, I asked if that was the only letter he showed to him. He muttered yes. I looked at him and told him if it were just you two, I would send you out and tell you to go and do your worst. I turned to Mr. Mensah and gave him a copy of the letter I wrote to the three officers. "This is my first letter to them and the other two complied." I gave him the reply the former Dean wrote to me. Halfway through the letter, Mensah became angry. "You wrote this letter to the Principal? Would you like someone to write you this kind of letter?" I said in spite of his insult I invited him for a discussion. He felt too big to honor my invitation. That letter is final. Without even seeing the content of the reply, Obani said he did not blame either of us and they walked out. The former dean removed his belongings from the room and started to look for a job somewhere else.

Bearing in mind the bursar's speech at the sendoff, I called him to my office and gave him my first instruction. "Whenever you prepare any voucher or document that requires my signature, it must be on my desk for at least twenty-four hours before you ask for it. Do not ask me to sign anything that stayed on my desk for less than that." That put a damper on his face. One of our students was a nun from Cross River State. She gave the college mailman her letter to register. The mailman stole the money and asked her for more money. She gave him the money. He still used the money without even sending the letter by ordinary mail. The post office said if the man had mailed the letter, it would have sent it and charged for it. With all the evidence before the Acting Principal all he said was, "That's what they do even in Lagos."

He did not make him refund the money. The man did not deny the accusation. He allowed him to continue as the mailman. I removed him and replaced him with Akinlalu. I promoted Ayeni, my messenger.

After I published my two books, I sent two copies of each to Lyndon State College (now named Northern Vermont State University at Lyndon). About a month later I received a letter from the librarian. She wrote and thanked me for sending the books. She also informed me that she put a copy of each of the books in the college archive as the first books authored by a Lyndon graduate. I became the first Lyndon graduate author. Meanwhile, one of them, Discover Teaching, was selling like hot cakes. Some lecturers called it "the Bible of Education." I also concluded a nationwide study on how Nigerian cultures perceived and treated the handicapped. Mrs Culcrick, an Assistant Chief Education Officer in the Ministry, asked for my permission to review it for the United Nations (UN). I gave her the permission. She got paid for it. I received requests from even non-English-speaking institutions for copies.

There were many educational problems to be solved in Nigeria. However, the personnel in the Ministry were concerned with positions and stealing money. The first set of our students would graduate in May or June of my first year as the Principal of the College. In every sense, they were my students. I planned two other projects. First I planned a national workshop for special education elementary teachers. Each of the nineteen states was asked to send an assigned number of students. Our students would be on vacation. Our kitchen staff would be available to serve the participants who would also use our hostels. My budget included remunerations for my faculty who would teach the courses. Two factors worked in my favor for the workshop when I reached Lagos.

The first factor was the availability of special education funds in the hands of the ADE. That meant he did not have to consult with the Director and other Yoruba people in the gang. The second factor was what he saw as his monetary gain from the project. He immediately offered to produce the big envelopes each of the participants would receive. I accepted. The deal was sealed before I left his office. I set the faculty to work.

Nigeria had a national policy on education on paper only. Secondary education was part of the policy. Every state carried on as though it was Nigeria and no one in the Federal Ministry of Education tried to coordinate the state activities. I invited all the 19 special education heads in the Federation to the College for a two-week national conference in May prior to the graduation. They all accepted the invitation with enthusiasm. I also developed a questionnaire for them that helped the College to know the needs of personnel for each state. Since Oyo was the only Special Education College in Nigeria or even Africa, the answers helped the College to determine courses to develop and who to admit based on state needs. Within the period of the conference, they learned what each state was doing, what worked and what did not. They worked out remedies. They requested the Federal Ministry of Education to establish a braille press in Lagos. It was so successful that they decided to meet at the College every May and appointed me the permanent chair. At the end of the conference, I invited them to the graduation ceremony. They declined because the states allowed and paid for only the conference period.

One of the projects the College requested funds for was to build a small safe in the bursar's office. The bursar budgeted ₦1,200 for it. The government provided the safe free. Building it to the wall should not cost more than ₦200. When the check came, he invited a Yoruba man at the Federal Ministry of Works to claim the money. He did and they shared the excess. Some of the Oyo landlords refused to rent to the College because of the high percentage bribe the bursar charged. When I cautioned him, he told me I was not his boss. He worked for the CFA in Lagos. The more I cautioned him the angrier he became. Soon he was trying to poison me. Somehow the psychology of their ability to kill by poison had also frightened me when I took over the administration (like Elijah and Jezebel). My fear became so apparent that someone wrote an anonymous encouraging letter to me. The letter encouraged me. I opened Isaiah 54 and left it on my desk. Verse 17 says, "No weapon that is fashioned against you shall succeed, and you shall refute every tongue that rises against you in judgment. This is the heritage of the servants of the Lord and their vindication from me, declares the Lord." The first thing I did when I entered my office every morning was to read my Bible and pray. I also had a cross on my desk. God had defeated the main enemy in Lagos as He defeated Baal and its prophets for Elijah (1 Kings 18:22-19:1-3). Like Elijah, who became afraid of Jezebel after God defeated the main enemy, I became afraid of their poison.

One day the bursar and the EO were in my office. As I decried the bursar's insatiable appetite for bribery, one could read death in his eyes. I looked him squarely in the eye and, pointing my finger to his face, I said, "You have been trying to poison me. If you try one more time, I will throw it back at you and you shall know who you are dealing with." I dismissed them. The following day the bursar wore a big cross on his neck. Seeing him with the cross, I said, "You now wear a cross?" He replied, "Yes Sir, this Ibadan- Oyo road I drive every day is dangerous. I need some protection." I thought about the seven sons of Sceva in Acts 19 and the evil spirit who said to them, "Jesus I know, Paul I know, but who are you?" (Acts 19: 15).

The Yoruba who controlled the Ministry suddenly decided to surprise me. For almost the four years the College had existed, there had not been a single visitor from the inspectorate except for the inquiry. Within a few months after I took over the administration of the College, a team of inspectors descended on the College without warning. I mentioned the bursar and his behavior and illustrated the fact with the case of the safe. They said it could not cost up to ₦200 to build it to the wall. By the afternoon of the third day, they had written the preliminary report. They contrasted the learning and peaceful atmosphere of the College to the chaos, which existed in the recent past and told the bursar to cooperate. They commended my style of leadership and the committees I set up. If those who sent them thought they were or wished to prove the College was still the laughingstock of the Ministry or worse, they were disappointed. We received at least A grade.

Of the three projects I listed earlier, graduation was the most important, because it exposed the nation as my audience. I formed a graduation committee. For the fact that the Ministry had not appointed a Vice Principal, I made the Dean of Students the chair of the committee. When the former Acting Principal left the office, he carried every College record, including the names of the graduating students, with him. As Providence would have it, I, the Vice Principal, was present at the signing ceremony in Ibadan, and Professor Yoloye signed a copy for me. I gave it to the committee. That is what the committee used for printing the program.

Our first graduation day was less than twenty-four hours away when Mr. Inyang, the ADE Teacher of Education, and his Assistant Chief arrived at Oyo. I booked them at Labamba Hotel, the best at Oyo at the time. Before the evening was over, I received an urgent message from his Chief Education Officer. It was not good news. Mr. Inyang's only son was at Enugu Teaching Hospital, a ten-hour drive from Oyo. I could not tell him that night, and cause him sleepless night. I waited until he went to bed and met the Assistant Chief and told him the news. We planned to wake him up by 6:00 am. I woke him up earlier and we woke Mr. Inyang up. The poor man was confused about where he was. We corrected him, and by 6:00 am, they were on their way.

The graduation was well attended by our graduates, their relatives and our students. Two factors determined the class of Yoruba people who attended the graduation. The first was the Alaafin's political affiliation. The Action Group Party exiled his father. The leader of that party led the party in government in Oyo State at this time. The Alaafin did not support this party. He aligned himself with the NPC party, which was the senior partner in the Federal Government. For this same reason, the state government was reluctant to accept the land the Alaafin offered as the permanent site for the College at Oyo. To complicate matters, he supported an Igbo as the Principal of a Federal Institution in Yoruba land instead of a Yoruba. As a result, the state government sent only a chief education officer. The Director of the Institute and the Chair of the Special Education Department of UI came because they were Igbo men. I made the Alaafin the chair of the ceremony.

The former Acting Principal was at the platform at the invitation of the committee in spite of all his efforts to prevent me from taking office dead or alive. The committee printed certificates for the founding members of the faculty. These were those who were at the College from the start till at least the end of the first term. Neither the Acting Principal nor his Vice qualified for the award and did not receive the certificate. I did not mention his name in my address. I ridiculed the posturing of the state and federal governments over the permanent site for the College. Nigeria had what it called the University of the Air at the time. It also had a home. I said, "All institutions of higher learning in Nigeria, including the University of the Air, have homes. Jesus said, "Foxes have holes, the birds of the air have nests, but the Son of Man has no place to lay His head" (Matthew 8:20). The Federal Advanced College for Special Education has no place to call home. I called on the Oyo and federal governments to accept the land His Highness the Alaafin had provided. I asked for advice on how to run a College like Oyo with one- and one-half vehicles. When we left the hall, we took the graduation group photograph with the Alaafin and the former Acting Principal.

It was prearranged that the senior officers of the Ministry and prominent people at attendance would be entertained at my residence. Obani's sister-in-law was one of those from the Federal Ministry of Education. She came outside my house and was among the Yoruba people and said to Dr. Adima, "He did not mention the former Acting Principal's name. They will kill him here. If they fail to kill him by poison, they will use matchet." Dr. Adima saw me behind her and simply laughed. He could not say to her, he is behind you. However, I did explain why the Acting Principal did not receive the certificate to him.

After the graduation address, Lagos was divided. The Yoruba Director and his men who wanted to move the College to their state were angry. The northern people laughed off the matter of the College being homeless. However, the Director wanted to know if I submitted my graduation speech for approval before I gave it. The Assistant Chief Education Officer, who was an Igbo and came to the graduation, volunteered to have read and approved it. However, the address achieved its objective. The Federal Government accepted the land the Alaafin donated and that became the permanent home of the Federal College of Education for Special Education today. When Mr. Osinkesi saw me, he asked if the Alaafin made me a Chief.

The bursar still behaved as though he was still in charge of the College. He and the former Acting Principal sent the vouchers to Lagos and refused to get the money until they received their bribe from the landlords and contractors before they released the checks. The bursar and the former Acting Principal at one time quarreled over what share each should get. But with the Acting Principal gone, the bursar thought he had the opportunity to get richer. So, he told the officers in Lagos to withhold the checks. Many months passed, the checks did not come, and the bursar did not give me any explanation. My patience was running out. I promised to go to Lagos and have the officials dismissed. Then the bursar went and reported to Mensah, the chair of the housing committee, that I was going to Lagos to have those officers dismissed. He complained that the people I was going to report to share in the bribe. If he thought that would change my mind, it made me angrier. Realizing the chairman could not change my mind, twenty-four hours before I traveled to Lagos the bursar took a sick day off and went and alerted them. His visit removed the element of surprise. They were busy with it when I arrived. Seeing that Mr. Mensah was in support of the bursar, I removed him and replaced him with Mr. I. K. Ojo as the chair of the housing committee. Soon the checks arrived. The landlords and contractors received their checks without paying bribes. If the landlords gave the bursar anything it was out of gratitude.

About two weeks after graduation the states student participants for the workshop arrived. We had about 190 participants from the nineteen states. The Special Education Department represented the Federal Ministry of Education. Having learned much and enjoyed the three weeks, the participants became good ambassadors for the College. Suddenly the College that was the laughingstock of the Ministry became a shining example. The Yoruba team took notice and reacted accordingly. My success was their failure, and they would not allow that to continue.

The Director who promised me failure was also in charge of the purchase and distribution of vehicles. Aware that he was distributing vehicles the Ministry imported to colleges and schools, I met him in his office and requested two. He refused to give me even one. When I looked him in the eye and said, "I'll return to Oyo and pray," he laughed so loud as to say, "Let me see God send vehicles from heaven to you." In addition, they cut the funds they allocated to my College. However, they left the rent paid to the landlords intact because they got a share of it. They also refused to send lecturers and staff to my College. I depended on the offices of the Youth Corpse in Lagos and

Ibadan for faculty. Because the first workshop was very successful, they refused to sponsor another one.

Chapter 40

Entrance Examinations And After Effects

At least five federal colleges of education in Nigeria were affiliated with the University of Ibadan. While the rest of them paid a set amount each to the UI Institute to construct a common entrance examination paper for them, I opted to construct the examination paper for my college. My lecturers received the test to travel to different centers to give the tests. Two of the lecturers gave the test to two women there at Oyo, one to his wife and the other to his lady friend. One scored 98% and the other 96%. We confronted the candidates. One lecturer confessed. However because he came from Oyo, he requested the Alaafin to intervene on his behalf. The Alaafin sent him to the chief who owns the Alliance Hotel, who in turn sent his associate. When I denied the request, he left the College. The other woman reported to the Ministry. The Director compelled the College to give the candidate another test. The College constructed another test, which was easier than the first, and gave it to her. This time Obani's sister-in-law and Miss. Emeruwa from the College administered the test. The candidate who scored 98% failed badly. They showed her the result and confirmed the denial of her admission.

While this was going on, the Director reported the case to Honorable Gbambose, a Yoruba Junior Minister of Education, and I was called to see the ADE in Lagos. On reaching his office, he sent me to see Director Olaniyan. When I saw the Director, he told me to see Honorable Gbambose. No one told me why the Minister wanted to see me. I walked into his office, greeted him, and introduced myself. He offered me a seat and said to me, "You are accused of practicing apartheid against Yoruba candidates at Oyo." I said I did not understand what he meant. He explained and I lay the facts before him. He apologized. Before I left his office, another Junior Minister, this time a northerner, walked in. Honorable Gbambose introduced me to him. "This is Dr. Onwuegbu they accused him falsely." The Minister replied, "Congratulations! Now that you have been accused falsely you are fully a Nigerian." I left Lagos without telling either the Director or his ADE the result of my interview with the Honorable Minister.

Like every other department in the Ministry, the Yoruba people controlled the Internal Audit Department. For as long as the Yoruba man presided over the College the internal auditors closed their eyes to all his faults. When the federal auditors disclosed the fraud at the College, the internal audit department tried to protect the man. But when the internal auditors came to audit the College during my era, they were determined to find fault or manufacture one. On the first visit, when they found nothing against me, they went into the town and investigated my character. They found nothing against me, they returned to my office and confessed. "We went round and asked about you. Everybody said you are honest." They praised me and went back to Lagos. I thought that character investigation was a part of auditing. When they sent the final report they accused me of not recovering the debts officers who borrowed money from the Ministry before they went on transfer owed. All the bursar was required to do was to state how much any officer on transfer owed and the monthly deductible on the last pay certificate. The Principal then signed it. In my case, all the officers went on transfer before I became the Principal. A Yoruba woman in the Ministry signed for the Dean when I refused to sign his. In reply I threaten to take them to court if they mess with my name.

Riots were common on Nigerian university and college campuses. To my knowledge, food was assumed to be the cause. Food was a coverup. The real culprit was politics or money. Money reared its ugly head at Oyo. Two Yoruba students were elected President and treasurer. They schemed a way to become rich. They planned to "buy a bus for the student body." They collected donations. Even the Alaafin donated five hundred naira. For some reason, they plotted with the bursar to get me to sign over students' feeding money to them. The bursar told them other Principals do it. When they came to me, I told them to go and tell him, "I am not other Provosts and Principals. I am Dr. Onwuegbu." Soon the bursar schemed with the student President and the treasurer and wrote a letter of protest against me.

Before they took the letter to Lagos, they complained to Mr. Ojo, who discouraged them. He came to my office with them. During the discussion, he said to the President, "I know you made election promises. Dr. Onwuegbu does those things before you even think about them. Before he took office, he used to write. Now he concentrates on improving things here for you." But when they reached Lagos the director did not even bother to read the letter of protest. He thought I was in trouble and came to say, "I told you so." He marched into my office on arrival. I welcomed him. He demanded to know what was going on. With disappointment written across his face that I was right, he managed to say, "That is not done. You are right." I took advantage of his presence and showed him the library and art rooms I was extending. His former Yoruba Acting Principal claimed to have extended both buildings and claimed money for doing so. For the next seven years, I was at the College, he never showed his face again. After he reached Lagos he sent his ADE to come to Oyo to investigate. Though the ADE was told that Mr. Ojo had held two meetings with the President and treasurer before they went to Lagos, in his report, he wrote, "The students are wrong. But the Administration should have open door policy …"

Before the report was out the student President was diagnosed with tuberculosis. The doctor ordered him suspended from the College. Aware of the fact that the student government had campaigned and collected money to buy a bus for students' use, I ordered the bursar and the Dean of students to audit the students' accounts according to government rules and regulations. They discovered the treasury empty. The treasurer told the Dean and the bursar what happened to the money. The student government President and treasurer had shared the money. It was close to finals. When the report reached me, I informed the student union treasurer through the Dean that he could not take the finals unless he refunded every kobo of his share of the money. He did and was allowed to take his finals. A few months passed and the doctor declared the Student President noncontagious and allowed him to return to the College. The College confronted him with how much he owed to the students and told him that he could not be readmitted until he paid the debt. He left the College and never returned again.

There was a fellow Igbo man in the financial section of the Ministry. When the Yoruba people realized that as the chief accountant he was in a position to help me, they removed him. They had completely encircled me (Judges 7:7). They cut deeper into the funds they provided for the College. As if that was not enough, when they itemized where I should spend the money, they made it impossible for me to spend the money. For example they knew the College did not own buildings to maintain because it rented. Half of the funds for the College were allocated to maintain buildings. The fund went back unspent. The bursar was enriching his pocket with the little his tribesmen sent. He claimed to have deposited money with a gas station where the drivers filled the tanks. Besides filling his tank there, he also claimed to pay interest on the money he deposited. When I called the owner of the gas station, he defiantly confirmed the lie. I blacklisted him and his business. The College deposited money in a bank. The bursar and the manager charged the College interest. As far as the bursar was concerned, the mentality that I was not his boss gave him the license to do whatever he wanted. For me, I decided talking was useless and determined to act.

I noticed in my first year of administration that only seven students in the whole College registered for the education of blind and sight impaired. The same was true of the hearing impaired and deaf. My investigation revealed that students feared sign language and Braille. I decided to make both courses core courses to be taken during the first year before students declared majors.

When I ordered the first batch of furniture for the students, faculty and my office the owner of the factory, an Italian asked what percentage of the cost he should credit me with? Mine? He said yes. "Nothing," I said. There were improvements everywhere. The students wondered aloud as to where I got the money. God opened another avenue to use the little amount they allocated to the College. The Permanent Secretary, who was a Yoruba, called a meeting of the Federal Provosts. I raised the question of funds. "I don't care how much this Ministry gives my College. If you can trust me with that College, you should trust that I should be able to identify the needs according to the priority of the College and spend the money accordingly. You should give me a one-line vote. The Provost of Abeokuta spoke in favor of my statement. The Permanent Secretary asked if that was a common opinion. They all agreed. That took care of most of my financial problems.

The landlords had become accustomed to ignoring requests to repair the houses because they shared their excessive rent money with the former administration. They unfortunately thought they could do the same thing with me even when I did not share their excess money with them. It backfired. After two requests to a landlord to repair his house and a warning, the chairman of the housing committee reported to me. We refused to renew his rent and sent our faculty somewhere else. He decided to wait until the current lease was almost over to act.

It was time for the bursar to take his vacation. He handed over the office to his assistant. That was a suitable time for me to act. I ordered the college carpenter to change the padlock to the bursar's office and give the keys to his assistant. Once the padlock was changed I issued two instructions to the assistant. 1. Make sure the bursar's hand does not touch any of the keys. 2. Prepare his last pay certificate and give it to him when he returns. Let him go and work for his boss in Lagos. Shock awaited the bursar when early the morning of his vacation ended, he tried to enter his office and could not unlock the door. It seemed like a nightmare when his assistant came, unlocked the door, and gave him his LPC and the rest of the story. At first, he thought he could bluff himself out of it. When he realized how serious I was, he pleaded with some members of the faculty to beg me on his behalf. When that failed, he pleaded to be allowed to request a transfer. I gave in. However,, before he returned my letter, he copied it and took the copy along with his letter. Having presented the two letters, the Yoruba in control ignored his letter and replied to mine. They told me I had no authority to transfer the bursar and returned him to the College. His dream that the case was settled was dashed after I replied to the letter. I acknowledged my lack of authority to transfer him but asserted my right to send him to Lagos for transfer. They sent him back to the College without further instruction or threat. He sat at the general office with the typists doing nothing for three months without pay. By this time, Lagos had employed Dr Hill, an American black, as my Deputy Provost for Academics to oppose me. Dr. Hill announced publicly that Dr. Onwuegbu would have to transfer him before he transferred the bursar. Finally, Lagos got tired of the stalemate and sent Mr. Onogoruwa, another Yoruba officer, to come and investigate. Within one hour after he started looking into the books he came into my office and said, "Dr. you are a Christian." "Thank you," I replied. That was the end of the bursar at the College. God gave the victory that earned me the respect of Oyo town and the College. However my success galvanized the Yoruba group in Lagos.

Chapter 41

Glaucoma Treatment

About the same time my sight was getting worse because of glaucoma. I knew I needed surgery. But an Indian ophthalmologist at the Oyo Hospital did not have the facility to perform surgery at Oyo. One alternative was the University of Ibadan Teaching Hospital. Dr. Mba gave me a letter of introduction. Though a Yoruba woman was the chair, the man I saw was also from India. He gave me forms for some tests. The nurses who took the tests were very complimentary about my good health. The Indian Dr. gave me a date for the surgery. Because I suspected the Yoruba, who hated my presence at the College, might poison my food or even water at the hospital, I kept my appointment a secret. Also for the fact that we boiled our drinking water, I took a gallon of water from home. When I got to the hospital the Indian Dr. told me that he could not perform the surgery because the hospital lacked anesthetic. As Isiaka drove to Oyo, I prayed. "My gracious, loving Father God in heaven, dear loving Jesus my Immanuel and dear Holy Spirit Three in One, I thank You for the delay. Trinity, You are all-knowing. If this is successful, let the Dr. perform the surgery when I come next time. But if not, let him give me another excuse, in Christ's name. Amen." On my second visit, the Indian doctor repeated himself. I said goodbye to both the Dr. and the hospital. Believing that God ruled out Ibadan, I decided to return to my doctor in New Britain in Connecticut USA.

Assuming that I would pay the costs, I wrote a letter to the Permanent Secretary and requested permission to travel to the U.S. for treatment. I had my doubts that the Yoruba man would allow me to go. However, it seemed God was saying, "When I shut the door at Ibadan, did I not have another door open?" The Bible says, "When a man's ways please the Lord, He makes even his enemies to be at peace with him." (Proverbs 16:7). After reading my application, the Yoruba man said, "You wrote this as though you want to pay for this." He advised me to get a letter from the Dr. at the University Teaching Hospital Ibadan. He also advised me to request the government to sponsor the trip and pay for the treatment. When I got there the Yoruba woman who chaired the department and who sent the Indian man to me at my last two visits showed her angry face. She accused me of patronizing foreign doctors over Nigerian doctors. I wondered where she was all the time I was greeted with cancelations; was that a part of the Yoruba protest over my presence at Oyo, or did she want me to bribe her? I walked away, and the Indian doctor at Oyo General Hospital gave me the letter.

Initially I requested four weeks, and the Ministry did not change the time. The Permanent Secretary did not change it. The Federal Ministry of Health did not change it. But when I reached the Federal Ministry of Finance the Yoruba officer reduced the period to three weeks. I returned to the Ministry of Education for the Ministry to calculate the total cost based on my level and salary. The CFA was uncooperative. I went to the Permanent Secretary who called him to his office. He spoke to him in the Yoruba language. After the CFA left, the Secretary told me what he said to him, that if I was a Yoruba, he would have done it without hesitation. The CFA must have made an occult sign while I was in his office. I did not respond. He said, "People think that when they belong to an occult, they can make signs even in a court of law and still receive a reply." I still said nothing. I realize they suspect me to belong to one of those. A short time later he included two extra days for traveling and my first-class fare.

Of the nineteen states that made up the Federation, ten were in the northern part of the country. Admissions to higher Federal institutions in the country were on a quota system. The people in the north were the least educated. Yet they would not take their quota. Touring all ten states in one week was impossible. Flying would take a much longer time. One driver alone would amount to suicide. I took two drivers. Isiaka was a Muslim and Ezekiel was a Christian. It was an interesting experience. One of the days, we reached Sokoto, after 2.00 am, was hungry and needed a bath. The hotel did not offer any food service. I had my shower, sent the drivers to the town to look for food, and went to bed. By 9 a.m. we were at the Sokoto State Ministry of Education office. Like all the other state offices I discussed the need for them to fill the quota allocated to the state and gave them the paper I prepared with the information about the College. At the time it cost the student nothing to attend the College. The Federal Government even paid the students monthly allowance besides a traveling allowance based on distance to the College. Our discussion at every station ended once they promised to send students at the beginning of the next session.

Achieving my goal at Maiduguri was almost mission impossible. First, the distance between Sokoto and Maiduguri was too long for the time we had. Second, it was a Thursday, and I had scheduled Jos and Kaduna for Friday. To make matters worse, there was no line of communication. After traveling for a long time and realizing how far we were from the city, I knew we could not reach the office before 5:00 p.m., the time offices closed. There was neither a paid telephone booth nor a post office from where I could call the state education office. I told the drivers to follow the telephone line and stop where the wire entered a house. The drama started when I entered the house. The light-skinned man, probably an Arab trader, could not speak one word of English nor my language. I mimicked my way through. I called the office in Maiduguri and told them where we were. The officer assured me I could not reach the office before five when offices closed. He promised to have someone to wait for me. But when we got to the building every door was locked. We began the search for the home of the Permanent Secretary through the city. When we found his home, he was not home. We left the paper I prepared with a message and left for Jos. We reached Jos after midnight. Once again, the hotel had stopped serving meals. For the second night, I went to bed without food. I was able to finish with Jos by 10:00 a.m. on Friday. We reached Kaduna in time that Friday afternoon and completed my discussion before offices closed. Having traveled through the vast northern nine states in five days, both my drivers and I were tired to go one more mile. I checked into a hotel, and they took care of themselves. I ate a good dinner that night. Early Saturday morning, I ate a good breakfast, and by midafternoon on Saturday, we were at Oyo.

For almost two academic years I had managed the College without a deputy provost. If the powers that were in Lagos thought the College would fall and crumble, they were completely disappointed. On the contrary they had suffered defeats on several fronts. Yet they had not given up. One evening Mr. Azado, the founding Principal, came to our house. He said he came from Lagos. Believing he actually wanted to spend the night with my family, I suggested it and he accepted. He had actually come to tell me two things. The first was that the Yoruba people in Lagos were up in arms because the Federal Commission made me the Principal at level fifteen, thereby giving me a double promotion. They told him, "He is now your senior." That was not new to me. His second reason was interesting. His Vice Principal at his school was perceived as a troublemaker and had reported him to the Ministry for embezzling money. The Director who was plotting my failure had promised to send him to the College as my deputy for administration since he has an M.A. in Special Education. He had come to warn me about the man. I thanked him. He left the following morning.

My ticket was ready for the flight to the U.S. and the Government had given me over three thousand dollars as my spending money. It was an evening flight. I was in my office signing the vouchers when my messenger walked in and told me about two people who wanted to see me. I told him to let them in. When I looked up, it was Alhaji, the associate director of Alliance Hotel, with an unknown face. I welcomed them, offered them seats and asked them to tell me why they came to see me while I continued to sign the vouchers because I was traveling. The Alhaji introduced the man as "The Honorable Deputy Leader of the House of Representatives." I looked at him again and apologized that I could not give him one hundred percent of my attention because of the pressure of time. However, I promised to listen. The Alhaji who owned the house the College rented and who refused to repair it, which forced the College to deny him renewal had gone and asked for his help. He came to ask me to renew it. He pleaded for the renewal of the rent. His reason was the man was a generous financial party contributor member. What he did not know was the wife of the Alhaji had told me he belonged to a different party.

At that juncture, I stopped signing and looked at his face. Taking the pen, I signed the vouchers with; I drew a thick line on a piece of paper. As I drew the line, I continued to thicken it and said, "You see this line, above this line is politics. You make the law. Below the line is implementation. I carry it out. Don't cross the line and I will not. You are here now pleading for me to renew the rent. Do you know what would happen if I did? No one would ever say you pleaded. They would claim that you ordered me to renew the rent or else. As a result discipline would be the first casualty at this College. My messenger will not obey me again and as for you, there will be no more rest for you. Someone who does not like how I cough will come to report to you. I will not renew the rent." He asked if I would rent from him again if he owned a house. I told him we still rented one from him. What he did not know was the house the founding Principal rented for ₦6,000, which was inflated to about ₦27,000 belonged to the man. The rent for the house we rejected was also inflated by the last administration, who shared the excess with the landlords, officers in Lagos and officers of the Federal Ministry of Works. As they walked away, I heard the Alhaji say to him, "I told you he would not change his decision." To which the Deputy surprised me with, "I like that." I completed my work at the College that day.

It was time to travel, and I bade my family goodbye. Isiaka drove me to Lagos first to my friend Emedom's house and then to the Lagos airport.

Chapter 42

In The USA

Nigerians surprised me at JFK Airport. I traveled first class and was privileged to reach the window before the lines formed. Noticing that my passport was renewed in New York the man at the window gave me a form to fill and told me to return to the window. When I returned the form, "those Nigeria mobs at the Lagos Airport" quietly formed lines at JFK and were even offended that I did not fall in line. I wondered if they were the same people I saw in Nigeria. I flew to Salt Lake City and spent a few days with my parents-in-law. After I dropped their suitcase, I bought a new set of suitcases. I flew to New Britain only to discover that my doctor was on vacation. I used the week to visit old friends at their homes by invitation and to drop in at some offices.

Soon the week was over, and the doctor was back in his office. My three weeks were almost spent. He decided to give me laser treatment. When he finished, and I read what he gave me to read, both of us were delighted. He said, "Obed you have near normal vision." He prescribed drops and glasses for me. Within twenty hours the glasses were ready. I paid and received them. Though I was a few days late, I could not come to the U.S. and went to Connecticut without a visit to Lyndon State. So I added two more days to my stay. I traveled by bus to Lyndon State.

My first surprise was the location of the bus stop. It was closer to the College. A soccer game between Lyndon and a visiting team had just ended. A former student who was a senior when I arrived at Lyndon and who informed Nwabusi at Springfield College that I was at Lyndon was the coach at Lyndon. After a brief reacquaintance, I went to a motel. Recall that on my arrival at Montpelier by plane in 1963 I missed the bus and was rescued by Mrs. Gallagher and Mr. Michaud. I decided to remind Mr. Michaud of the incident in a funny way. I called his home, and his wife answered the phone. I asked if her father was in. It was past 7 p.m. When he came to the phone I greeted and introduced myself as a Nigerian student at Montpelier. Then I made my request. "I have no way of getting to the College. Could you and Mrs. Gallagher come and get me please?" Without hesitation, he said, "No." I said, "No?" He said "No." I said, "I forgive you this time. However, this is Obed." He laughed and asked where I was, and when he heard Burke Motel, he asked if I wanted him to come and get me. With a no answer, we planned for him to pick me up the following morning on his way to the College. I called a few members of People's Methodist Church and chatted with them. I also called and talked with Fay, one of those female friends I mistreated.

The following morning I checked out of the motel and waited for Mr. Michaud. He arrived within a short time and gave me a ride to the College. In the short time I had, I went around and greeted some of the professors and staff who were there when I was a student. I walked into my favorite former English literature Professor Mary Bisson's class, and she planted a big kiss on my cheek. It was not all well. Emeka, one of the students I recommended, had also brought his brother to the College. They fought over money, and the police were called in. While I went around greeting people, Mr. Michaud gathered some staff to take me to lunch. It was delightful. We joked and reminisced. I had a brief telephone conversation with an elderly woman I knew from People's Methodist. On hearing my voice, she said, "Oh,

Obed, your voice sounds like the voice of an angel." Her husband was dead by this time. I also met Budd, my summer job supervisor, and asked how he survived without me. Mr. Michaud drove me to the bus station. I thanked him and we said goodbye. Unfortunately, I heard the sad news about Marjory Streeter, who I succeeded as the President of the Protestant Christian Club, who had cancer. I remembered the snowy day she turned twenty-one.

Jim and his wife Tracy were the best hosts I could have, and they hosted me for the two weeks plus I spent in Connecticut. Tracy celebrated one of her birthdays while I was with them. I bought her flowers and paid for the family dinner. Don Bennion another friend took me to Bradly Airport from where I flew to JFK. I could see again when I left New Britain.

Boarding the Nigerian Airline reminded me of Lagos. Even the first class was packed full. I sat next to the wife of the Hon. Minister for Education i.e., my boss. The Nigerian Airline gave first-class passengers the Daily Times of Nigeria. One interesting item concerned Federal Colleges of Education. The paper reported that the Federal Ministry of Education had decided to grant Federal Colleges of Education autonomy. After I read it, I knew a fresh war had started in the Ministry. However, how the battles would be fought depended on me. When I arrived at the airport Isiaka confirmed the arrival of the Deputy Provost for Administration. He was the man the founding Principal told me would be sent. To my surprise, even the drivers knew he was sent purposely to cause trouble for me. Mr. Mensah, who deputized for me while I was away confirmed the story. However, the man reported and went home to bring his family. I decided to behave as though I did not know why he was sent to the College. Instead, I gave him time to prove who he was.

There was another surprise waiting for me when I entered my office. My study about how Nigerian cultures perceive and treat the handicapped was making waves in the special education world. The

United Nations and the Commonwealth of Nations had called by telephone and sent telegrams and letters asking me to go to Nairobi, Kenya, to evaluate the Eighth World Conference on the Mentally Handicapped. They suggested I buy my ticket and present it when I arrive and receive a refund. While I hesitated, the Vice Chancellor of the University of Ife, whose house the College rented, came to talk about the payment of his rent money. I presented my dilemma to him. He urged me to go. I took the little gifts I bought for the Permanent Secretary and Mr. Inyang and gave them to them. As I expected the Yoruba officers were reluctant to let me loose again, but they could not prevent me from attending. I bought my return ticket and flew to Nairobi. The organizers refunded my ticket money with a check. After the conference, I flew back to Nigeria with a white nun and took her to Oyo in my car. She was going to the Roman Catholic school where our two youngest boys attended. Because it was dark, I accompanied Isiaka to drop her off after we saw my family. I wrote and submitted my report to the U.N. secretariats.

About this time Amadi, my brother's first son, visited Nigeria from the U.S. He visited us at Oyo. I introduced him to Joy a member of my faculty who later became his wife. I also signed the check the UN gave to me and gave it to him to cash and use. He did. Unfortunately, because I failed to report to the Nigerian consulate in New York, I paid my doctor's fees.

Chapter 43

Court Cases

Another college landlord was out to make money without providing the service. The chairman of the housing committee invited him to meet with the committee. He refused to see any of them. Unfortunately for him, the houses were rented for one year at a time. A clause in the contract specified a three-month period within which a party must inform the other it wished to terminate the contract. The water tank fell and there were other interior repairs to be done. The landlord avoided both the College and the Committee. My frustrated EO came and complained about his inability to reach the man. I was annoyed with him for allowing the man to outwit him. I ordered him to register the letter at the post office. The landlord went and claimed the letter and met with the committee. When he failed to get a renewal, he sued me.

When I reached the Ministry the lady in charge of the judiciary was an Igbo woman. She assigned a young Igbo woman lawyer to the case. Because of the people I dealt with in the Ministry, I developed a taste for the law and bought two law books, one criminal and one civil. When the young lawyer came, I told her the landlord could not sue me. He could call me as a witness. She disagreed and planned to go on with the trial. Then she discussed the case with her boss, the Attorney General; he agreed with me and teased her with, "Maybe we should give him the hood to defend himself." Meanwhile, I dreamed in one night,

442

the case was dismissed five times. The lawyer told the court he could not sue me. If he wanted to sue, he should sue the Federal Government, not its agent. The case was dismissed. When he and his lawyer read that Federal Colleges were about to become autonomous, they served the lawsuit to me, again.

God had given me great success during my first two years. However, the Yoruba plot and even the threat to my life were there. They would not bother me if I were single, but I had a young family. I applied for a job at the University of Jos. I had asked Professor Obanya and Dr. Mba, two of the three people I intended to ask to recommend me to the University of Jos to do so. God intervened. I dreamed. I was in the most beautiful orchard with various kinds of fruit trees. The grass was cut to carpet level. Three white clergymen dressed in the Anglican Bishop's white robes I refer to today as angels came to me, each holding a Bible in his left hand. They told me I could not leave the College. The reason is, "You have a duty to perform at this College." Note: *First, Jesus Christ gave me everything I needed at Umukabia. Here at Oyo, He assigned me a duty to perform.* End of Note. This is a reminder of Jesus Christ instructing Paul to stay in Corinth because He had followers in the city (Acts 18:10). I had met Dr. Ukpabia, a former Dean of Students at the University of Nigeria Nsukka and who was a teacher at Mission Hill when I was in standard three. He told me he was a member of the Trustee Board of the University of Jos. He encouraged me to complete the application. Like Paul in Acts 18:8-9 where the Lord promised Paul safety and instructed him to stay in Corinth, I did not complete the application.

Following the tour of the nine northern states earlier in the year, the College scheduled the entrance examination for the whole country later in the year. We sent information about the date, the center where the examination would be conducted, and the time for the test and requested a state representative to be present. A day before the examination our faculty arrived. After the examination, the member of the faculty returned with the results. The admission list is submitted to Lagos for approval. With Lagos' approval ensured, each state received the names of its candidates who were admitted. The states had at least five weeks to inform the candidates before classes started. This procedure was followed in every case. All the states including eight of the nine I toured in the north, but one carried out the instructions and sent their candidates to the College on time.

Three weeks had passed, and the freshmen class matriculated. My Registrar, Mr. Ojo, walked into my office with a concerned look on his face. His report explained the look. About ten students from Plateau State were in his office for admission and students had matriculated. What should he do? I told him to send them back to Jos with a letter that explained why they could not be admitted. He did. The officer in Jos became belligerent. He claimed to deal with an entire state, etc. Among other things, I wrote to him in reply, "I deal with nineteen states. If I can complete my task with these states, you should be able to do your duty with one state. It is only in Nigeria that people like you can keep their jobs. I should recommend you for dismissal." A short time after, I received a letter from the military governor of the state's office demanding that I admit the students. I refused, and among other things, I reminded him of the excuse they gave for the coup. "One of the reasons the military gave for taking over the government is lack of discipline. I am trying to instill discipline in the lives of Nigerians at this College." I promised to admit their candidates the following year as long as they reported on time. That was the end of the matter. My enemies rejoiced and comforted themselves with the thought that I met my Waterloo. However, they were disappointed.

The unofficial policy of the Yoruba people who control the Federal Ministry of Education was to "use the Igbo people to start Federal colleges of education, and when they became functional, the Yorubas replaced the Igbo Principal with a Yoruba." That happened in at least four instances including Oyo. Three instances of this happened in the north. One of the cases was so violent that the police became involved. As a result, the Ministry transferred most of the faculty to other colleges. Two of them were sent to my college and two of the members of my faculty were transferred to the college because of their Yoruba names. Of all Nigerians, the Yoruba people are the least to want to serve in any part of Nigeria that is not a Yoruba area. Of the two from my college, one was a Yoruba and deaf and taught in the department. I explained his condition to the Ministry and his transfer was cancelled. The other one taught English. Knowing that I did not transfer him and reporting me to the Federal Ministry would boomerang on him, he wrote a petition against me to one Oyo Yoruba state Commissioner and accused me of hating and transferring all the Yoruba members at the College. The Commissioner summoned me to his office for a hearing. I almost refused to go. At the last minute, I decided to go. I took Mr. Ojo, a Yoruba, with me instead of an Igbo.

On arrival, the English lecturer was in the office with Akindele, another Yoruba lecturer. The Commissioner read my offense to me. I was tribalistic and wished to transfer all the Yoruba lecturers out of the College. I looked at him and told him I was there out of respect for his office. Before I said one more word, he assured me that he had the power to have me arrested. I told him I was a federal not a state employee. Any question about a federal employee should be referred to the Federal Ministry not to a state commissioner. However, since I was there, I told him that I did not have the power to transfer, nor did I transfer him. He knew that and that was why he did not petition the Ministry. The Commissioner listened to him and said he was a Principal of a school prior to becoming a Commissioner. He had someone like my lecturer on his staff. He gave him six strokes on the bottom and my lecturer deserved six strokes. He said he understood what I meant when I said I came out of respect for the office and ordered the lecturer to report to his new station. We left the office.

Having failed to achieve his objective through false accusation, the lecturer returned to Oyo and the Chair of the English Department (his tribesman) assigned him courses to teach. That earned him a rebuke and he assigned the courses to other lecturers. Then the lecturer came to my office to plead for help. In the office were the bursar and the EO. I challenged him to state one thing I did to discriminate against him as a Yoruba before the two Yoruba men. He confessed I had never discriminated against him. He said he knew the former administration excluded me in decision-making even though I was the Vice Principal, and he spoke against it. I refused to intervene with the Ministry on his behalf. He attended my faculty meeting. When I ordered him to leave, and he refused, I called the police, who removed him. He went to his new station.

Chapter 44

They Were God's Angels

"If anyone stirs up strife, it is not from me; whoever stirs up strife with you shall fall because of you. Behold, I have created the smith who blows the fire of coals and produces a weapon for its purpose. I have also created the ravager to destroy; no weapon that is fashioned against you shall succeed, and you shall refute every tongue that rises against you in judgment. This is the heritage of the servants of the Lord and their vindication from me, declares the Lord." (Isaiah 54:15-17)

Looking back at events at Oyo I can now state with certainty that God planned my going and staying at the College. When I turned to Isaiah 54 and left it open on my desk, I believed it. When I saw those three angels I also believed their message. In addition, everything that happened at Oyo strengthened my faith in my God of salvation and my Rock. A full account is found in *When The Saints Pray 1977-1987 A Decade of Courage*.

Once the Yoruba people in charge of the Federal Ministry of Education removed the bursar from the College, they became extremely antagonistic. My vouchers were not processed, and I could not pay customers including rents. The landlords who wanted their rent paid went to Lagos and bribed the officials to receive the money. One day, I went to Lagos with my officer, who covered the duties of the bursar. The senior accountant in charge of issuing the checks asked me to sign the check for my college. I did and left my officer to receive the check. He snubbed my officer and gave the check to the bursar of the Federal Girls' Secondary School in Oyo to deliver to the landlord. That was the last straw. I returned to Oyo and wrote a five-page petition against the entire accounts section. When I reached the office they knew they had trouble on their hands. The ADE promised to take care of it. I refused to leave it with him. I promised to take care of it myself. He sent his Assistant Chief with me. I insisted on seeing the Permanent Secretary with my petition. They started to prepare every voucher my college submitted that laid untouched for months. I decided I had enough. "Stop preparing anything. Let us go to the Permanent Secretary and ask him to call a news conference and announce that Oyo Federal College of Education for Special Education is closed because Dr. Onwuegbu, an Igbo, is the Provost." Obani's sister in-law, who the ADE sent with me, urged them to go on. As they prepared to give me the checks, the Nigerian perineal problem called student riots reared its ugly head. Students from one of the federal institutions in Lagos surrounded the Ministry building and the order came to vacate and lock everything. My officer came the following day and collected all the checks.

In my petition, I warned them that I knew my constitutional rights and would not hesitate to use them. When those high officials, including the Secretary for Education and Director, saw me, they claimed ignorance. They transferred the Principal and Senior Accountant and replaced the senior accountant with an Igbo lady.

By the time I returned from the U.S. my Deputy for Administration had arrived. I pretended not to know either his history or why the Director sent him to the College. I assigned him certain responsibilities and watched him carry them out. I wrote a letter and asked him to take it to the CFA. He was afraid to take the letter to the

CFA. He said, "I am not going to that man's office. He disgraces Provosts and Principals, and you want me to go to him." I said to him, "Take this letter in your right hand. When you enter the office pass those women in the first room. Knock at his door, open it, and greet him. Before he says anything to you, stretch your right hand with the letter and say, "I am from Oyo FCE." When he returned, he asked what I did to the man. I replied, "God disciplined him." That impressed my Deputy. I believe if he had come to make any trouble, he said to himself, "I had better think twice." Even when I disciplined him, he did not protest.

There were three members of the faculty on study leave. Mr. Ayoku and Mr. Ozuzu were in the U.S. Mr. Obani was the last to go and he went to Britain. Each government employee's performance is evaluated annually. For those members of the faculty on study leave we had no way of judging their performance. For the fact that they were on the payroll, we simply filled in "on study leave." Both Mr. Ozuzu and Mr. Ayoku received "on study leave" as evaluation and were promoted. When it was time to evaluate Mr. Obani, the College filled out the same "on study leave" and submitted the form. Mr. Obani's sister-in-law, who was in the ADE's office, objected and insisted that we gave the same rating he received the previous year. I wondered why she did not object in the cases of the other two. Besides those two also received their promotions. In addition, my understanding of 'annual' excludes last year or next year. I refused to yield.

To make assurance doubly sure, I went to Mr. Inyang, who had become a Director, and told him what the woman demanded. He confirmed the rating and added, "His performance at the course would be his rating." Many of them considered Mr. Inyang "my partner in crime," because he is an alumnus of Uzuakoli. I went beyond the Ministry. I met Mr. Ezeife, a high officer at the Federal Service Commission, and asked for his advice. He confirmed what Mr. Inyang said. Mr. Obani was also promoted.

Before Mr. Obani left for Britain he was the Acting Chair of the Special Education Department. When Mr. Obani traveled he handed the department over to Mr. Akindele.

Meanwhile both Dr. Ozuzu and Mr. Ayoku had earned their respective advanced degrees and returned to the department, which I had organized as a school. Mr. Akindele was still the Acting Dean of the school. The Ministry had also recruited Dr. Hill, an American, as my Deputy Provost for Academics. The Yoruba people who controlled the Ministry hired him as Assistant Chief, though they denied me the level. The ADE SE kept him in Lagos for two weeks and indoctrinated him on how to oppose me. His first open attack was when I locked the bursar out of his office. Dr. Hill told everyone who could hear his voice in the open field that Dr. Onwuegbu could not lock the bursar out. He declared, "He would have to dismiss me first before he can transfer the bursar from this College." To his dismay those who told him they had the last word at the College watched the bursar disgraced and transferred. He still did not learn from that.

After Dr. Ozuzu returned from the U.S., the chair of a department at the University of Ilorin approached him for employment. The Ministry employs and promotes longevity. The university pay is based on merit. So Dr. Ozuzu was offered a more attractive position than the one he had at the College. I refused to accept his resignation. Only part-time lecturers were allowed to hold classes on weekends at the College. The Deans were to enforce the rules. If the Deans had any problem, they reported to the Deputy Provost for Academics. When I rejected Dr. Ozuzu's resignation, he went to the ADE in Lagos. As he negotiated with the ADE in Lagos, at the same time he accepted the job at Ilorin and taught his classes at Oyo on weekends against college policy. Both the Acting Dean and the Deputy Provost for Academics did nothing about it. The ADE's influence was still in control of Dr. Hill. The idea that doing his job brought honor only to me, the Provost, prevented him from performing his assigned duty. One day the

Acting Dean and the Deputy Provost walked into my office with a complaint. They reported Dr. Ozuzu. They claimed he had not given his test and asked me for advice. To have a witness listen to them, I sent my messenger to call the Registrar. When he came I asked them to repeat their request. Shamelessly they did. The Registrar was angry and said, "If you people will not do your job, will you allow others to do theirs?" If the college was autonomous I would have dismissed them on the spot. I said to them, "If you two were in a university, would you have taken this case to the Vice Chancellor?" Would you please leave?"

Sometime later I received a letter from another Yoruba state Commissioner. Mr. Akindele had accused me before him. He made outrageous charges. 1. I discriminate against the Yoruba members of my faculty. 2. I abused Honorable Minister Gbamgbose from his state. 3. I would not allow him to discipline an Igbo member of the faculty in his school. He gave a date when a meeting was called at the College, and he sought permission to discipline the person, and I denied him the permission, etc.

Read Isaiah 54:1 again. Of all days, Mr. Akindele chose one of the days I was in Nairobi, Kenya, as the day I called a meeting at Oyo. In reply, I said he could have attended a meeting. But I did not call it and was not even in Nigeria to attend the meeting. I was in Nairobi, Kenya, where I evaluated the Eighth World Conference on the Mentally Handicapped for the UN and the British Commonwealth. I enclosed photocopies of the pages of my passport to show the dates of my arrival and departure. With reference to his accusation that I refused to give him permission to discipline his lecturer, I enclosed a page of the minutes of a faculty meeting where I urged the Deans to supervise members of the faculty in their schools. He was the only Dean who opposed me. Of course, I had no reason to speak ill of the Honorable Minister, who apologized to me after he realized people accused me falsely. I concluded by asking the Commissioner to decide if his time should be wasted on a liar like Akindele. That was the end of the case. Then I sent copies of his report to the Commissioner and my reply to the Federal Ministry of Education through the ADE.

One of the reasons Mr. Akindele reported the case to a Yoruba state commission was the change of tide at the Federal Ministries. The northern soldiers were completely in control of the military. They turned their attention to the civil service. Within a short time, they swept the Yorubas aside and even created top new offices. They were Secretaries for Education and Finance and a Coordinating Director, all from the north. They took over lucrative ministries such as Petroleum, Finance, and Education. Responsibilities were realigned. For example, the Director who said I could not succeed without his help stayed in the Ministry. But he was removed from awarding contracts. The CFA was no longer the head of the Finance Department at the Ministry. The Secretary for Finance was. He was from Cross River State.

When I received the allocation to my College they had cut it again. I could not understand the rationale. The student population was growing, and we were still on a temporary site and needed special education equipment. I went to Lagos to find out the reason for the cut. The Secretary for Finance said, "They say you are a miser." That meant I did not steal and share with them. I decided to hit them back. The only money they did not cut was the rent because they still got their share from the landlords. I decided to kick them in their pockets.

There was the Secretary for Finance who would not advance the course of special education in Nigeria, pleading with me to help him get a scholarship to send his mentally challenged daughter to study in Britain. I ignored him. After I returned to Oyo I called a meeting of the landlords and the chair of the housing committee. I told them the Ministry had cut my funds to the bone. I could not pay them the inflated prices anymore. I would cut some by as much as fifty percent. They would be told the exact amount before the rent was due for renewal. I kept my promise. For instance, I slashed the house that went from ₦6,000 to ₦27,000 down to ₦13,500. There were two houses I did not cut because the landlords did not inflate the rent and the ministry men did not get bribe from them. The Alaafin's house was one of them. Even at the prices I gave the landlords they still received more than double what they could receive in the open market. The objective I achieved was the cut made it impossible or at least unjustifiable to demand a bribe or at least as much bribes from the landlords. As I expected, the news received a hostile reaction in Lagos.

A landlord went and reported to the officers in Lagos. He returned and claimed to have formed The Oyo Landlords' Association and declared himself the Secretary. Though other landlords accompanied him to my office, they disagreed with his intent. Having met with a lawyer he returned to make sure that I did not tape the discussion with the landlords. Once he was sure about that he sued me for devaluing his property. He thought he was fighting the Igbo Provost. But that cost him a lot in the future.

Dr. Ozuzu made many trips to Lagos that I did not authorize nor was I aware of them. Finally, Lagos accepted his resignation. He came to my office one day with two requests. After he informed me that he was leaving the College, he presented me with many tickets from the checkpoint near Lagos and asked for a refund and traveling bill. I denied his request. Second, he presented me with the salary the College paid him for all the months he worked at Ilorin and Oyo. I refused to touch it and told him to take it to the bursar who paid him. He did. Soon the Ministry was investigating Dr. Ozuzu for violating a military edict, which prevented any civil servant from holding two jobs at the same time. When Dr. Ozuzu became aware of the investigation he sold his belongings and returned to the United States with his family. In a subsequent communication that informed us of their whereabouts, his wife explained they did not want us to know so as to avoid people finding us guilty by association.

After my graduation speech and the attempt of the Yoruba Director to convince the northerners to punish or even censure me failed, the Ministry accepted the land the Alaafin donated for the permanent site for the College. When the ADE saw me in his office he asked me if the Alaafin had made me a chief. I had deprived them of the chance to move the College to the state of their choice. They sent an architect accompanied by Mr. Obani's sister inlaw. I described faculty and staff quarters, the classrooms and laboratories we needed including the one-way mirror testing lab. Because Braille books and special education equipment were to be used and stored there, the library was fairly large, the Director took issues with that. More than three years after the initial contract award, they ignored the College because I was the Provost. They also thought they would remain in charge forever. Suddenly the northerners swept them aside.

I took advantage of the new arrangement and applied for funds to drill a well at the permanent site. It happened that the officer in charge was an Igbo. His two Assistants graduated from Uzuakoli Secondary, and I knew them at Uzuakoli College. Also they earned their Ph.D.'s from the U.S. My request met rapid approval and was funded without delay. We built the best well in all Oyo. With its generator independent of NEPA electricity, the college was able to supply water to the faculty, staff, and student kitchen at all times. Having great success with the first national workshop proved an offense to the Yoruba officials in Lagos. As a result, the powers that were in Lagos denied my request for funds for a second national workshop for tertiary instructors and state Ministry of Education employees. I asked for permission to conduct it without asking them to fund it. They granted me the permission. I went to work. I invited the colleges and state employees and charged the institutions and state governments. Within a few weeks after we sent the invitation, everyone we invited paid for registration. We wrote a book for the workshop, and I included my first book on intelligence entitled "The Structure and Phases of Intelligence:

A Construct." Again it was conducted during the long break. It was even better than the first workshop. We were doing what no other college of education in Nigeria was doing or ever did. Since they could not stop me, they imitated me, and the Special Education Department in Lagos set up a workshop. It lasted one or two days in contrast to our three weeks. I sat in the audience and the ADE invited me to the head table. Mr. Obani's sister-in-law, who attended the two workshops at the College, opened the workshop and called it "the real national workshop." Yet they did not have as many people, nor did they cover as many subjects as we did.

Unfortunately the fate of the untrustworthy bursar did not teach his successor any lesson. I had recommended him for a double promotion, which he received. However, before the promotion was announced, the College embarked on a teaching practice. The chairman of the committee presented a budget of ₦13,000. The pay officer at Ibadan gave the money. The teaching committee spent ₦2,500. With the remaining ₦10,500 in the safe at the College, the officer in charge of finances felt it was time for him to become reckless. He decided to divorce his wife, deny her the license the College gave her to sell soft drinks and food on the campus, and marry another woman. When I asked him to account for the money he claimed to have returned it to Ibadan. I asked for a receipt from Ibadan, and he could not produce it.

The College refused to transfer the license to his girlfriend. Meanwhile, a more unfaithful bursar was sent to me. One day my new bursar and the officer who covered the duties of the bursar came to my office. When I asked about the receipt the two claimed to have it. I demanded to see it. The bursar brought a receipt. Being familiar with the paymaster's signature, I asked, "Who signed this?" The officers claimed the paymaster signed it. I refuted the claim. When he insisted the paymaster did, I called the chairman of the teaching practice committee, the EO and a driver and gave them a college car and sent them to Ibadan. Delighted to see the receipt, the pay officer declared he discovered the receipt missing and had reported to the police. The police arrested Caleb my finance officer. Caleb was in jail for about two years before the trial.

After about two years a high court at Ibadan convened to try Caleb. About five minutes into the case the Judge realized the crime was committed at Oyo and not at Ibadan. He stopped the trial and transferred the case to Oyo High Court A. But before the judge announced the transfer, the defense lawyer had played his trump card by asking the question he thought would win the case for him. "Was ₦10,500 the only money he handled?" That was the first question he asked me at Oyo, and I was ready for him.

As usual, my government lawyer was at hand. Following the entry of the Judge, the court clerk announced our case. I was called to the stand. The clerk took the Bible to swear me in. I said, "My Lord, I am a Christian and do not swear. That notwithstanding, if you want me to swear, I will." The lawyers went Huuuuuuh! He looked at me, and it might be because of the cases I brought to his court and how they had been decided, he did not make me swear. My lawyer asked me a few questions and then it was the defense lawyer's turn. He turned my statement to something else. When I started to correct him, the Judge read my statement to him. Then he took the question he thought would save his client and asked, "₦2,500 is not the only money you took from him?" I answered him with my own questions: "What are you talking about? Is ₦2,500 plus 10,500 not ₦13,000? That is the money in question, not every amount he handled while performing that duty." At this point the Judge warned him that the only thing to help him was the law because the facts were against him. He had no more questions and the Judge dismissed me. I was in Lagos when the Judge delivered the verdict of guilty.

While Dr. Ozuzu was in Nigeria he told me that he once applied for an extension of time, but the Ministry denied it. After he left I received an envelope from Mr. Obani with two letters enclosed: one official and one unofficial. The official letter said the Ministry refused his request for an extension and payment of salary so to allow him to pay his expenses. The unofficial letter reported the same thing. In addition, it requested me to pay him his salary. It ended with a double message. Don't let the Ministry know your decision. But inform Mr. Osinkesi. Mr. Osinkesi is the Yoruba man the Yoruba people in the Ministry appointed ADE SE to make sure I failed. The plot would accuse me of embezzlement. Once I wrote and denied the incriminating request and copied Mr. Osunkesi, the ADE. Then Mr. Osunkesi, the ADE, wrote a "good try" reward letter and extended his study leave with pay.

Mr. Mensah and I went to Lagos on official duty. I went to see Mr. Obani's sister-in-law. She said to me, "God hears your prayer. Will you please pray for me so that my tragedies stop?" This is the woman who did not know I was behind her when she told the Yoruba to kill me by poison or matchet. Her husband was paralyzed, and her brother had been killed by armed robbers and they took his car. I sympathized and prayed for her. After we accomplished our mission in Lagos and were on our way to Oyo, Mr. Mensah confirmed what I had believed. He said he was tired of the ADE telling him how to do his work. The ADE told him to take it easy and stop working hard, the Provost was the only one who got the praise for achievement at the College. In addition, the ADE told him he would be at the College the following day to investigate Akindele's report against me and told him to keep it a secret from me. I thanked him for letting me know.

I was in the office the following day when my messenger walked in and told me that Mr. Osunkesi was outside waiting to be allowed in. Pretending I did not know anything about his visit and thereby giving him the satisfaction he craved, I asked, "Which Mr.

Osunkesi? Did he not see me in Lagos yesterday? Did he dream about coming to this College last night?" I made sure he heard every word. He had no answer. He said that he came to investigate a report the Acting Dean of the school of special education made. He called his man who came in with a pile of papers. Mr. Osunkesi asked if he knew that Dr. Ozuzu taught at the University. Mr. Akindele said, "Yes." Asked what he did, his answer was "Nothing." He said he allowed him to teach on Saturday because Dr. Abosi a part-time lecturer taught on Saturday. "But Dr. Abosi is a part time lecturer," said the ADE. Then the ADE asked why I refused to take the money from Dr. Ozuzu? I said I did not pay him. He wanted to know the system of payment. I described how the bursar paid. Mr. Akindele came up with a "guilty by association accusation." Dr. Onwuegbu and Dr. Ozuzu are Igbos and they married Americans. So he knew everything Dr. Ozuzu did. Having failed to find fault with me in the body of his report, the ADE concluded with, "If the Provost wanted to know that Dr. Ozuzu taught at the University, he would have known."

God's Miracles at the College

The Permanent Secretary invited Provosts of Federal Colleges of Education to Lagos for a meeting. During the meeting the Permanent Secretary said the Ministry had returned four million naira to the Federal Government for two consecutive years that should have been used to award contracts at my College because of me. In other words, the Yorubas refused to award the contract because this Igbo man was the Provost.

Following the meeting, I protested in writing. The ADE invited me to Lagos. He did not tell me why. When I saw him, he told me to go and see Director Olaniyo without telling me why the Director wanted to see me. When I saw him, he demanded to know who told me about the contract. "The Perm Sec," I said. He told me to go and see him. When I walked into the Permanent Secretary's office, he said to me, "You do not have to fight them all the time. I am not going to be here forever." I thanked him and left. When the northern personnel took over the Ministry, I took two actions.

I decided it was time to remind the Ministry that my College was still on the temporary site. The Yoruba officers at the Federal Ministry of Education wished to wait till I went on transfer before they awarded the contracts at the permanent site. One way to get me transferred was to get people who work for me to refuse to do their work. So far those people suffered. Now the Lord gave mass transfer including the Permanent Secretary. I met the new Permanent Secretary, a Hausa from the North. He sent a woman in his office with me to the Yoruba Director. When I met him he was angry. "Did he forget he took the assignment from me!" I asked if that was what he wanted me to give as his answer. He immediately, even if it was grudgingly, gave me the information I wanted. The kickback the Director would have received from the contract had he awarded it also vanished with the reassignment.

In one of the annual meetings of the heads of special education held at Oyo, a number of decisions was taken. As the chair of the conference, I was delegated to lead a delegation to the Federal Ministry of Education to facilitate the implementation of the decisions. A date was secured through the office of the ADE. When we reached the office of the ADE, he told Dr. Ekeleme from Imo State and me that he sent other participants back home because the meeting was cancelled. We were still talking in his office when the phone rang. It was the Permanent Secretary's secretary asking why the ADE and the delegation kept his boss waiting. The three of us hurried over. We discovered it was the Director and the ADE who had a change of mind about the meeting as the ordinary secretary castigated the ADE. He claimed the Director told him. Only three of us met with the Permanent Secretary.

After Dr. Madubuike, the Hon. Minister of Education, left the Ministry over a dispute about the transfer of the capital of Nigeria from Lagos to Abuja, Dr. Ugo, another Igbo, became the Minister. He was from Mbaise the same town as Mr. Obani. I went to welcome him to the Ministry. He said some people wanted him to replace me with somebody simply because the person came from his town. I simply smiled. At this time the Yoruba ethnic group had four states. The Igbo ethnic group had only two but formed the minority in two other states. The Federal Government had admission policy for Federal universities, Federal colleges of Education, and Federal secondary schools. It based the admissions on ten percent by merit and the rest on quota. The ten percent merit could come from one state or all the nineteen states. The Yoruba officers who controlled the Ministry at the time formulated the policy. They had thought or even believed the ten percent would come from the four Yoruba states. To their dismay, Anambra and Imo, the two Igbo states, continually earned almost the entire ten percent. That was embarrassing and unacceptable to the Yoruba officers. Instigating trouble on the campuses did not solve the problem.

To satisfy themselves the Yoruba officers in the Federal Ministry of Education called a meeting to solve the "ten percent merit problem." They honestly stated the problem. They said only Anambra and Imo, the two Igbo states benefit from the merit system, and it created problems on the campuses. The solution was to do away with it and to admit everyone on quota. All the participants, including Mr. Obani's sister in-law, agreed. I spoke against it. To do away with the merit system would deprive Nigeria of the best brains in the country. It would mean discriminating against the two states that produce them. With that I cast the only no vote. Mr. Obani's sister-in-law attacked me and accused me of "trying to be different." I ignored her.

At the end of the meeting, I walked into the Honorable. Minister's office and reported to him. I added my main reason for my objection. "The Igbo people have only two states. They make up what they lack in states in merit. This is a plot to deny them that benefit." He was angry and said, "Let them bring it here for my signature. Do they think I am here to rubberstamp whatever they decide?" When I left his office, I went and also informed Mr. Inyang. He was equally offended. The policy remained unchanged.

Since the ADE and Mr. Akindele failed to prove a case against me in connection with Dr. Ozuzu, they planned big. I had banned all tribal organizations on campus and even instituted a Nigeria National Day. For whatever reason Mr. Akindele flouted it. He called a meeting of all the Yoruba students and some Yoruba members of the faculty. It was during a break, and I told my driver to take me to the place. I caught him red-handed. At another time I requested something from him in a file. He would not comply and instead abused me. I dismissed him as the Acting Dean. He accused me before the ADE thinking he would come to investigate. The ADE against Ministry policy received the petition without it passing through me. He asked me to reply. I did and demanded that no Yoruba or Igbo should be a member of the team of the inquiry. Less than twenty-four hours before the inquiry the ADE sent to inform me. Again, he hoped to catch me unprepared.

A little after 9 a.m. the following day, the four-person team walked into my office. The leader was an English woman married to a Yoruba man, the second woman was a Yoruba woman by birth and marriage. The last woman was born in Cross River and married to a Yoruba. The secretary was a man and from Cross River. They seemed to say, "If he does not want a person from his tribe that's fine with us. Let us fill the team with Yoruba people." After the team leader introduced members of the team, I made my first request. I wanted the Dean of Students and the Registrar to be present. She granted it. She became irritated when I said I had a second request. "What is it Dr. Onwuegbu!" "I wish to record the procedure," was the request. She also granted that. We moved to a bigger room. Mr. Akindele came with Makinde, the chair of the English department, who had been working from behind the scenes from the time of the former Acting Principal. I was glad to have him in the open.

Mr. Akindele started reading his accusation. According to him, I discriminate against the Yoruba people at the College. He listed the names of the people I had transferred, including my predecessor, the former Dean of Students who resigned to take a job in his state with better pay. The team leader stopped him and asked him two questions. 1. Did he know who transferred staff in the Ministry? 2. How could Dr. Onwuegbu transfer the person he succeeded? He had no answer. He said I was the chair at the sendoff party, and I allowed the former bursar to abuse the former Acting Principal and did not stop him from speaking. He accused me of treating the junior officers better than the faculty. Though the team leader found the accusations ridiculous she asked me to speak.

I continued from where Mrs. Sukuade, the team leader, stopped. To emphasize that Mr. Akindele gave false accusations, I said he knew I could not and did not transfer the man I succeeded. I gave the instance for which I invited the Dean and the Registrar to my office. He flouted my no-tribal organization and called a Yoruba tribal meeting. I called him to my office. The Dean and the Registrar, who are his senior came to see me. I asked them to wait outside until I finished with him. When I finished with him and opened the door he started to shout. They confirmed the story. I took out two sheets of paper and gave them to the team leader. They were my note to him and his abusive reply. That settled it for her. She was red in the face and said, "Mr. Akindele, who do you think you are, and what level of officer are you? The Provost cannot talk or write to you without getting insulted." She told him he would be on transfer. The rest of them had nothing to say. Mr. Akindele complained that I dismissed him verbally without written instruction. Besides, he said it was Mr. Obani who handed the school over to him, not me, implying that I did not have the right to remove him. Mrs. Sukuade asked me to write him. Before they left she came to my office and sympathized with me. She said I was dealing with a mental case. He will not be happy under any person who is not a Yoruba as the Principal at this College. Before the report was out Mr. Akindele wrote a report against the team leader before the day was over. He had to submit it through me. No one at the headquarters would touch it without my signature. Unlike when he reported me to the Yoruba ADE, he submitted it through me, and I read and countersigned it. When I reached Lagos people were in sympathy. "We understand you are dealing with a mental case," they said. I handed in his petition. The ADE who misled him wanted him in the Department of Special Education. The team leader refused and sent him to Abeokuta Federal College of Education under a Yoruba Provost.

The Yoruba in Lagos had learned they could not remove me with other Yoruba staff and students. They found an ally in Mr. Obani. But they had to wait till he came back from Britain.

God performed one of those miracles in my office one day that confirmed His presence in my life and stay at Oyo. I invited the college electrician to my office one afternoon. We discussed a matter I do not remember now. Suddenly fire erupted. When we looked the air conditioner was on fire. The electrician ran out and I jumped out of my seat. Running to the wall, I pulled out the air conditioner plug from the socket. The fire disappeared. While I thanked God and congratulated myself, the electrician resurfaced with a smile on his face. Annoyed at his disappearance, I asked, "Where were you?" Grinning from ear to ear he said, "I went to the fuse box to turn the electricity off." Both of us wondered what would have happened if neither of us had been in the office. There was no doubt in our minds the entire administration building could have burned down. The College would have been lucky if the damage stopped there. The thought of such a disaster caused me to buy fireproof filing cabinets for the Provost's, the Registrar's, and the bursar's offices.

Chapter 45

"Dr., You are clean."

"No man shall be able to stand before you all the days of your life. Just as I was with Moses, so I will be with you. I will not leave you or forsake you." (Joshua 1:5)

"Keep your life free from the love of money, and be content with what you have, for he has said, "I will never leave you nor forsake you." (Hebrews 13:5)

Bear in mind that Isaiah 54:10, 15, 17 quoted in the last chapter is very relevant to this chapter and even to my story as a whole.

In spite of the disgrace and transfer of the bursar Dr. Hill witnessed, he still believed that my success or failure depended on the Yoruba people in Lagos. Therefore, they dictated what and how he performed his duties at the College. His wife asked why I didn't return to my part of the country so that something could be done for the College. Confident that his three-year contract would be renewed as long as he satisfied the ADE and the Director, he carried on a nonchalant attitude at the College. At about this time, Mr. Obani returned from Britain and spent more than one week in Lagos.

Four of the five senior officers, including the bursar and the Yoruba officers in the Ministry in Lagos, hoped to use to cause my failure or at least transfer had been disgraced and removed. Though the Director and the ADE were still in the Ministry, real power was in the hands of the northerners. Still those two would not give up their attempt to remove me. They promised Mr. Obani a promotion if he would join their do-nothing group. On his return to Oyo, the EO checked him and his wife into Labamba Hotel while the chair of the housing committee prepared an apartment for them. I took a short vacation. I was in our living room when Mr. Okeke, the Deputy Provost for Administration, walked in with a letter in his hand. He read it to me. It was addressed to the manager of Labamba Hotel. Mr. Obani had refused to move into the apartment the College rented. He refused to leave the hotel until the College rented a bungalow for him. The letter instructed the manager of Labamba Hotel that from the moment he received the letter Mr. Obani was responsible for any expense he incurred at the hotel. A footnote on the copy Mr. Obani received advised him to rent any house he wanted, and the College would refund him the usual eight plus percent of the rent. He asked for my permission to deliver the letters and I gave it. Mr. Obani vacated the hotel immediately after he received the letter.

Federal and state elections were about to begin. Dr. Balogun, the first Presidential Liaison Officer (PLO) for Oyo State, resigned to run for the Oyo State Governorship. His successor came from his town also. His successor insisted on my giving him the students' feeding money to give the purchase of my students' food on contract. Having denied his demand, I asked how much his breakfast cost him. He admitted his breakfast alone cost more than twice the amount the government gave to feed an adult student for a whole day. I asked what percentage the contractor would take as gain. He had no answer. When he argued that the Perm. Sec. wanted him to award the contract, I told him, "If he wants you to award contracts, he should give you the money." A short while later, he saw me and said he saw Dr. Balogun, and he sent greetings. He added, "I should take your yes as yes and no as no." He noticed we had Utah in common. I graduated from the University of Utah, and he from Utah State University.

Dr. Hill's contract was up for renewal. He went to the ADE in Lagos, and he renewed the contract for him. On his return to Oyo, he proudly displayed it before me as if he was saying, the people who matter gave me the right to stay here. I wrote a letter to Lagos through him. "Sirs, you have the right to recruit and renew all contracts. However, I do not have any duty for Dr. Hill to perform at this College. You may send him to any other institution. He thought it a bluff until he discovered the ADE, and the Director could not override my objection. When he returned to Oyo, he came to my office and declared, "I don't hold any grudge against you." I told him he had no grounds to. He and his family left Nigeria. While Dr. Hill was getting ready to leave, Mr. Obani left for Britain to complete his dissertation. On the eve of his departure, he asked for permission to move to Dr. Hill's bungalow. I gave him conditional approval because there were two other officers senior to him. None of those asked for it. So I gave it to him.

There was a meeting of Provosts at Maiduguri. Some Provosts from the northern states attended the meeting. Some of the northern state college Provosts did not understand English. I made a statement of fact. One attacked me. Another one from the north came to my defense and said, "You didn't even understand what he said." When there was a break, I told my driver to go back to the hotel. There was nothing to achieve at the meeting. I checked out and returned to Oyo. When I reached the academic site I saw the Benin man the founding Principal used as a contractor. He greeted me with, "Dr., you are clean." I wondered what he was talking about. Soon I learned they flooded my office with water from the adjacent toilet room. In the pretense to dry the office, they searched for native medicine they thought protected me from their poison. I do not know why they did not think that if I had such a thing, it might attack them. But they found none.

Meanwhile the case of the first landlord who took me to court had been dismissed four times. Remember that I dreamed the case was dismissed five times. The landlord and my EO belonged to a club. As they drank beer one day, the landlord said to the EO that the College did not owe him anything. He sued the College to prevent the bank from seizing the buildings. The landlord warned the EO against telling anybody what he said because if he did, he would deny it. The lawyer decided to get the EO to swear an affidavit to that effect. When we got to court, the landlord denied it and the court continued with the case. At the same time, the case the so-called Secretary of Oyo Landlords Association brought against me at the court was pending. It, too, was dismissed at the first trial. The fifth dismissal of the first case was sweet. We were in court when the case was called. Neither the landlord nor his lawyer was in court. My lawyer allowed them some time to arrive. After another case was mentioned and they were still not present, the judge said to our lawyer, "In Oyo State, the law allows you to ask for the dismissal of the case." She did and the case was dismissed. We were less than one mile away from the court premises when we saw them driving to the court. We cheered them and clapped our hands as they passed. We did not know what transpired at the court when they got there. However, when I received the next court papers, they sued us at High Court B on the same premises.

I was surprised that after five dismissals at High Court A, the landlord sued me at High Court B at the same premises. I went to the lawyers in Lagos and informed them. I informed the Director of the Law Department that the suit had gone from claiming damages to permission to inspect the buildings. She decided not to send a lawyer from the department to Oyo. Instead, she advised me to hire a lawyer already at the court for two or three hundred naira to say he had permission. When I requested one of the Yoruba lawyers to grant the request, he refused and told me to pay the fine. Before I could ask another lawyer, the judge entered the court. My case was the first the court clerk called. I stood up and said, "My lord he has our permission to inspect the building." I said a short silent prayer. God, please let him write, no costs. Looking at me he said, "That's what your lawyer said to tell the court?" I replied, "Yes my lord." He wrote and announced, "No costs. Permission granted." They did not come to inspect the building during the period I was at the College. Before I went on transfer, Lagos issued an order to Provosts and Principals to cut the rents they paid by one-third of what they paid.

At one of the faculty meetings, I asked the Deans to meet and review a handout the College prepared for the students on how to write a thesis. Mr. Obani claimed there was no such guideline except the one he wrote. I wanted to see it. He went to his office and brought a paper. When I read it, I asked if he had written it. He said, "Yes." I told him the history of the paper and the three people who wrote it, namely, Dr. Ozuzu, the former Dean of Students, and I, who wrote the paper and why. He argued that the first group of graduates did not write a thesis. I took some copies of the thesis he claimed were not written and placed them on my desk. He insisted on his claim. He thought Dr. Ozuzu wrote the guideline alone, and since Dr. Ozuzu had returned to the United States, he could plagiarize it. After the meeting, I posted a copy of the guideline to Dr. Ozuzu. "Someone on the faculty claimed to have written this paper. Would you please identify it?" He did and returned it. When the faculty met again, I asked Father Ekpo, the secretary, to read Ozuzu's letter. Ozuzu's letter confirmed what I said. Mr. Obani asked why I went that far instead of going to the former Dean? Then he geared up and was ready to carry out every order from the ADE.

As a student at Lyndon, Nebraska, and Utah, and as an Assistant Professor at Central Connecticut State College (now University), I learned a few things. One of those things is the catalog and its contents. I had also written Discover Teaching, which was a best seller. I believed that though there was nothing like national accreditation in Nigeria at the time, the day would come when it would be required. Therefore, I directed each Dean to work with his school to write the general, specific objectives and the description of the courses each lecturer taught in the school. Mr. Obani refused to participate and argued that as a dean he should supervise rather than contribute, even though he taught courses. He complained that special education did not require instructional objectives. Finally the Deputy Provost for Administration directed him to collect the finished materials from the lecturers in his school. He refused and claimed to start his vacation soon. The Deputy brought his reply to me. I wrote him vide his file to complete the assignment before taking his vacation. My messenger took it to him. He ignored the instruction and went on leave. My query awaited his return and greeted him the first day he was in his office. Playing the game of do nothing the ADE instructed him to use against me, he was sarcastic and asserted vacation was his right. Pointing to the civil service regulations, I showed him that leave was a privilege, not a right. I ordered him to hand over the property of the school to the Deputy Provost for Administration within twenty-four hours and vacate the office. He obeyed and went to the staff general office. A short time later, he announced that I had dismissed him as the Dean of the staff. The Registrar came to plead for him. "Now he knows you are serious." Mr. Obani was to experience what the Yoruba antagonists before him suffered. He wrote a petition against me and took it to the ADE. He did not have me sign it nor did he obtain permission to travel to Lagos. When I walked into the ADE's office he and Mr. Obani were standing with their faces looking defeated and doomed. For the first time in his life, Mr. Obani muttered, "Good morning, Sir," to me. I muttered morning back to him. Knowing they discussed his dismissal, I did not mention it, nor did the ADE. After I left his office, I went to the Coordinating Director a northerner, and reported to him. The

Coordinating Director promised to dismiss him if the case reached his desk.

It was not long before Dr. Abosi came to my office. Mr. Obani had reported to him. He came to plead on behalf of Mr. Obani. I refused to restore him. "Listen, he had written a petition against me, and I have to reply to it." Then I learned why they wore mourning faces. The ADE had probably blamed him and rejected the petition. Dr. Abosi assured me he did not submit it. When he read what I wrote he said even if Mr. Obani's father owned the Ministry, could he get away with what he did? He pleaded with me to desist from replying to the petition. "What! He wrote a petition against me, and you do not want me to reply to it?" He pleaded more and told me Mr. Obani did not submit his petition. I said, "Get him here to tell me so himself." They came and he said so himself. I demanded an apology from Mr. Obani, and he wrote it. I reinstated him. Having learned that the ADE could not protect him from dereliction of his duty, he asked me a foolish question, "Do we owe allegiance to you or to Lagos?"

Mr. Okeke, the Deputy Provost for Administration, whom the Yoruba Director sent to the College to oppose me, saw nothing to oppose. The Director and his group started to attack Mr. Okeke. Obani was the first instrument. He came to my home one Saturday morning with Mr. Usim. He complained that a thief came to his house one night. The man tried to force the door open and ran away when he heard him draw his matchet. He could not recognize the person. However, he suspected Mr. Okeke's nephew who also worked for the College. With the devil working overtime in his head he asked me to accompany them to go and complain to Mr. Okeke to warn his nephew. I was more disgusted with Mr. Usim than the devil I knew. You were not sure who you saw? He said the person looked like him. I said to Mr. Usim, "You want me to follow you to talk to Mr. Okeke, even if you were sure?" I asked Obani why he did not report to the police, especially since the inspector was from his town, and I dismissed them (Nehemiah 6).

Special Education was a new field of study in Nigeria. The College had lost two Ph. D lecturers to two universities because universities paid better. To my knowledge, Oyo was the only college of education in Africa specifically established to train special education personnel. I believed that if I did not do something the College might become the recruiting ground for the universities. My first task was to get the faculty trained and bound for a number of years before they could leave the College. I drafted a proposal and requested help from UNESCO and submitted it to the Director of Education for approval. Six months later there was no reply. When I showed my angry face to his office he took it out and asked me to go and work with a reputable university. I met the Acting Director of the Institute at the University of Ibadan. Our schedule called for me to meet him in his office at 7.00 a.m. on a certain date. It was about 6:59 a.m. when I walked into his office. He and another man in the office started to laugh. I wondered what was funny about my greeting. He explained why they were laughing. The man had come from the University of Nigeria Nsukka the previous day and said there was no way I could be in the office from Oyo at seven. To his surprise, there I was before 7 a.m. They asked for some time, and I gave it.

When we got to the UNESCO office, a Yoruba man whose cousin was on my faculty greeted us. My presence as the Provost of Oyo College of Education got him excited and antagonized. I had requested $270,000. He told me I was asking for too much money. He had never seen anyone ask for so much money before. I told him what his duty was. Your duty is to forward the proposal to the UNESCO Office not to determine the amount. While I spoke, a woman officer from the north came by and asked what was going on. I explained. She looked at the proposal and dismissed the notion that the amount was too much. She took it and asked me to go to the Department of Special

Education and get a letter of support. The ADE was away. I asked the Chief Education Officer, an Igbo, and the former Vice Principal of the College to write the letter with a warning: "If I don't get the letter, you will see children with special needs rioting here." We left. We dropped the Acting Director at Ibadan and returned to Oyo. On my next visit, the support letter was ready. At UNESCO was an English man who was the UNESCO representative in Nigeria. He was delighted to see the proposal and encouraged me to increase the amount. However, he advised me that any amount from five hundred thousand dollars would delay the project; because the UNDP would send its officers to inspect the College first. On the other hand, if you include a research project, you could ask for more than $800,000. I went home to work on it. It was evident there was no way the Yoruba people in the Ministry could stop me. There was another coup. Another dynamic Minister in the person of Dr. Jibril Aminu replaced the able Dr. Ugo. But at the same time the Permanent Secretary and the Director for higher education came from the same region as the Minister. I had my first encounter with the Director of Higher Education soon after he arrived at the Ministry. Mr. Mensah's contract expired a month before the end of the semester. He had courses to complete and to give tests. I extended his stay for a month so that he could complete his work. The Ministry signed the contract with the lecturer, not the College. It should have known that he was teaching. If he left and the students rioted, people would blame the College, not the Ministry. The man they said was a Deputy Vice-Chancellor before he came to the Ministry could not reason. He could not see why I extended the contract for one month to allow the lecturer to complete the semester. I left him convinced that I knew why Nigerian students rioted.

    The perennial students rioting in Nigeria was on. Most of the federal universities and colleges of education were closed. The Honorable Federal Minister of Education ordered the closure of all the Federal colleges of Education and universities and summoned all the

Federal Vice Chancellors and Provosts to Lagos for a meeting. Though it seemed food was always the cause of the riots, to me the real problem was politics. The problem was tribal, faculty, and student politics and the killer was where Nigerian lecturers were educated. I said at the meeting, "Nigeria is already confused. It does not need any more confusion. This is the only country I know that sends her best students to democratic countries, communist countries, and socialist countries in the name of scholarship to study and bring all of them to teach conflicting ideologies in the same classroom to the same students. What do we expect? If our students cannot reason at this level and instead resort to violence, we should evaluate the faculty, what we teach, and how we teach instead of the students." Everyone who spoke supported the idea. That was the first time I met the Minister face to face. Soon the Honorable Minister appointed a committee to study the situation.

Before the meeting with the Honorable Minister, the Oyo Commissioner of Police called a meeting in his office of all heads of federal institutions in Oyo State. A police dispatch brought the letter of invitation to me. People speculated I had a ministerial appointment. After the meeting, the Commissioner invited me to his inner chamber. Because he was from the same eastern region as I am, the police officers present took special notice. Unfortunately, I could not admit his candidate. However, he briefed us on special agents who were ready to take advantage of the riots and what actions to take.

Almost five years after the Ministry announced its intention to grant autonomy to the federal colleges, it began to act on it. It set up a committee chaired by the Coordinating Director to evaluate the Provosts. The purpose of the evaluation was to determine which of the Provosts was qualified to remain as the Provost in an autonomous college. The committee was also required to consider the names submitted for various boards to govern each college. It was not an accident that God took me to Lagos the day the committee met. Even more miraculous was the fact that when I reached the floor where the meeting was being held, the lawyer who represented the College at the trials in Oyo opened the door and greeted me. She was going to get something and gave me two news items. 1. She was proud I was rated number one of all the Provosts in both qualification and performance. 2. I had not submitted some of the information requested. Then, in passing, she said the Yoruba Secretary submitted the name of the landlord who named himself the Secretary for the Oyo Landlord Association and took your College to court as a member of your college board. When she pointed out the name to the chair, he ordered the removal of the name, and it was deleted.

Of the three news items, two favored me. Yet I was angry. The Yoruba people were still determined to sabotage and soil my reputation. I told her I submitted everything the Committee asked for, thanked her, and opened the door without invitation. "Sorry, I understand certain documents are missing from my file. I submitted every item you demanded. The chair looked at it and confirmed what I said. I left. It was another total defeat for their plot (Elijah and the 50 soldiers, 2 Kings 1 10-12).

For some reason, the Honorable Minister decided to set up a committee to work on intelligence. I was not surprised that my college was not even informed. When I heard it I asked the Permanent. Secretary why the responsibility for organizing it was not given to the College? I presented a chapter on intelligence to the Nigerian Psychological Association at the University of Benin in 1978 and even wrote a book *The Structure and Phases of Intelligence*. He included me in the Committee. Professor Obanya was the chair of the committee, and a Yoruba in the Ministry was the secretary. After the inauguration, we invited a few more participants. The next meeting was at Kaduna in northern Nigeria. I used my official car and driver. On arrival at Kaduna, I asked my driver, Isiaka, to fill the tank, and he did. The secretary, who was also charged with the responsibility of fueling the vehicles, claimed to have filled the tank I filled and had not used it simply to claim the money. Besides he sent my driver to the airport without my knowledge or permission. I told him my car was not to be used without my permission. When he argued, I warned my driver that if he drove my car to anyplace without my authorization I would take the key from him. Unexpectantly the worst news struck.

Of my maternal aunts, the oldest had only one surviving child, a daughter. The aunt died exactly one week after the daughter's wedding. The last statement of my aunt was to me when she said, "Obida take care of your sister. You are the only person she has on earth, you, Enoch (my brother), and Godwin (my cousin)." Nnenna, the daughter and cousin we were to take care of, died suddenly. I shook at the news but had to stay till the end of the meeting without telling anybody. By the end of the conference, every participant was assigned a topic to study. Instead of going to Oyo, I told Isiaka to drive to Umuahia. When I got to her home, her children and other mourners were there. Her husband did not make sense. I broke down and wept. I gave the husband money to help with the burial and went back to my village, then left the following morning for Oyo.

Meanwhile another military bloodless coup had taken place. Babangida ousted Buhari and put him under house arrest. The Nigerian Academy for Education planned a conference to be held at the University of Lagos. A former member of my faculty at Oyo who was teaching at the University informed me. I prepared two papers to present. When we arrived at the University there were armed soldiers everywhere. Soon I learned why.

Brigadier Abacha came with his entourage which included the Honorable Minister of Education. They left immediately after Abacha declared the conference open. The chair followed with a short address. Thereafter, the Academy went into small groups. I presented one of my two papers in my small group because of a shortage of time. The Conference went for a break. The Executives met during the break. Unknown to me was that the executives had chosen my paper entitled,

Special Education: The Lonely Voice in Nigerian Education, as the Academy's number one project to discuss with the Federal Ministry of Education. When the afternoon session resumed, the Chair announced the decision. That was to my delight. The chair also allowed individuals who wished to say more about their papers five minutes.

When it was my turn I thanked them for the honor. However, I asked for permission to speak about the other paper I did not get time to present. It was granted. I suggested that the scholarships Nigeria received from foreign countries tend to do more harm than good. I illustrated the facts with the medical field. "Take the example of the medical doctors who are trained in the U.S. They diagnose with the most modern machines and operate with the best precision equipment during training. They return to Nigeria to practice without any of such equipment. They become ineffective, frustrated, and drop out. They return to the U.S. Is there no better way of using these scholarships? Would it not be better to arrange for some of those foreign professors to come and study what we have here and teach our students according to what we have and can use?" I told the participants I had to stop since I was allowed only five minutes. The chairman said, "Yes but you took ten." There was laughter. This recommendation is practiced today. Meanwhile, the Director of the Ministry perceived the honor the Academy bestowed on me as a threat to his position. He was threatened and shaken that the Academy had put another feather in my cap. I did not know what transpired between him and the Academy until the Ministry transferred me to the headquarters. That will be discussed in the next chapter.

When I included agriculture in the college curriculum, I approached and sought advice from an Austrian, Chief Siebert. The College began to raise chickens to provide eggs for the students and sell the excess. I employed the husband of my youth corps, Mr. Udosen. a Ph.D. candidate in agriculture at the University of Ibadan, as a part-time instructor at the College. I requested him to design, and we planted an orchard for the College. To mechanize the farm I took the EO to Ibadan and purchased two farm tractors. We already had a water tanker. We were able to irrigate the farm and had two harvests. Later the college drivers used the water tank to draw water from the college well for the college community when Oyo town water ran dry. We somehow commercialized the farm tractors.

As long as the federal colleges of education were not autonomous, the Federal Ministry of Education treated the college employees as civil servants, and promotion was based purely on longevity. At level fifteen I was the highest-paid Federal Ministry of Education Provost. Three months after I assumed duty, the rest of the Provosts were upgraded to level fifteen. True, I was on level thirteen for less than one year before I became the Provost at level fifteen, as proved appropriate during the Ministry evaluation of the Provosts, where I was rated number one in qualification and performance. But the Director and his Yoruba people in the Ministry would hold my "double promotion" against me forever. The Federal Service Commission called for a promotion interview. Chief Inyang was retired. The Yoruba Permanent Secretary was on transfer. The Yoruba Director, who vowed never to allow me to succeed, represented the Ministry at the interview.

Before we were called in, the Director had briefed them on every candidate. He told the panel that I spent too many years in the U.S. and had been over-promoted. My interviewers did not mention either my qualifications or performance or the Ministry rating. My attempt to mention them was ridiculed. A few days later, the result was out. I was not promoted. When I saw the Coordinating Director he expressed dismay that the Commission did not promote me. He said, "You are the best. I wonder what criteria they used. My advice is don't waste your time to petition. As the Provost, you are already at level sixteen, and there is no one in the Ministry qualified to replace you at Oyo." So I did not petition against the decision. His last statement was because of the new policy in the Ministry. The new policy determined that Provosts of Federal Colleges must come from the states or ethnic group in which the college is located. If not, they would lose their positions. That was the chance the Yoruba in the Ministry had prayed for eight years. However the Coordinating Director based his forecast on the perimeter of the Ministry. By this policy, four Yoruba Provosts in the north would lose their positions. That notwithstanding, the Yoruba officers were more than willing to sacrifice four for me. Shocked that the Ministry ruled there was no Yoruba in the Ministry qualified to replace me, they went to the universities to search for one.

On a set date I went to see the Special UNESCO Representative in Lagos. He told me about the conversation he had with the Yoruba Director. The Director was elated when he told him they got rid of the Provost. They would replace him with a Yoruba. He said that he asked him, "You are removing Dr. Onwuegbu because he is not a Yoruba? What about the project he is developing?" He told him that I could take it with me. On that basis, he advised me to change the project author and director from the Provost to Dr. Obed I. Onwuegbu and I did. He asked if I had a study proposal to go with the faculty proposal. The cost could almost double from the origin. He said if I did, we could increase the request to over eight hundred thousand dollars. I promised to consider his suggestion. I left Lagos disgusted with Nigeria. When I learned who my successor would be, I refused to include the study knowing how much he loved the Naira.

Each time they failed in their plot to implicate me in wrongdoing or through refusal to perform their duty, they seemed more determined to succeed. The next two bursars they sent to me exemplified the strategy. One would think that the fact that the second bursar heard how his predecessor left the College in disgrace and was there when the one who handed over to him was jailed should serve as a warning to him. It might have but it did not stop him from stealing. He decided to enrich himself with the sales from the chicken farm. The employee in charge of the farm handed the money from the sales to the bursar to deposit with the bank. Instead, the bursar pocketed the money. It was almost too late when I discovered it. The Ministry had served him with his transfer paper when I discovered his mischief. He prepared his last pay certificate (LPC). On the arrival of his successor, I instructed him to withhold the LPC until he withdraws the amount the predecessor owed the College. Then pass on the LPC for my signature. After three months, the LPC came to my desk. He quietly left the College.

Did his successor learn anything from what he witnessed? I would not say no. First he thought he had a better way of stealing the money. Second he believed he would not be caught. Unfortunately for him, he was wrong on the two counts. I called him to my office and confronted him. He muttered nonsense. I called the police and reported the bursar was embezzling the college money. Soon an inspector and a sergeant walked into my office. He wept as he confessed in reply to their questions. I asked what his wife did. His answer was nothing. He promised to refund a determined amount every month. I agreed and the police warned him and left. The next thing he did was make students sign for the same amount they received twice. My anger was more on the students than on him. I asked if they would sign for the same amount twice if they worked for it? They were all teachers before the College admitted them.

After about two years they transferred the bursar. Again I had to keep him for some months to recover the money he stole before I signed his LPC. One of the accounts clerks decided his time had come to steal from fellow junior employees. The Federal Government imported rice, stockfish, beef, and a variety of fish. It sold the commodities to federal institution employees and departments at the price they cost to import them. This accounts clerk was assigned to collect the money from other junior employees. He did and spent it. When it was time to collect the commodities, he did not produce the money. The junior staff could not pay and did not get their share. I had the authority to fire junior staff of his level. I instructed the bursar to withhold much of his salary every month until he had enough to refund every contributor. Once that was accomplished, I directed him to dismiss the clerk and he did.

Rotary International was established at Oyo and I was a chartered member. I was also an international officer. The official inauguration day was a Saturday. As was always the case when I spent Saturday at Oyo, a driver took me to the office. He drove me from the office to the hall where the event was held. Less than two weeks later I received a letter of inquiry from headquarters demanding to know why I used my official car for private business. I thought the person had nothing to do and wrote so to him. I said to him if, with all your spying, this is the only thing you can come up with, I must be an angel. You should be fired. I ended up with a quote from the Bible, "From now on let no man bother me for I bear the mark of Jesus Christ on my body" (Galatians 6:17). A few weeks later I was in Lagos. I walked into an Igbo senior officer's office. He looked at me, shook his head, and smiled. He had read the communication. I asked for the office of the officer who wrote the letter. He asked me to forget it. That was the end of the matter.

Lagos believed it could do anything it wanted and no one in the field had any right to question it. I tried it at the permanent site. They did not inform me when they awarded any contracts at the site. One day, as my driver drove by the site, I saw poles about four feet long, one inch thick, and one- and one-half inches wide lying on the northern side of the site. I suspected the Ministry had awarded the contract for the perimeter fence of the college. We traced the source. People we saw confirmed they worked for the contractor. I wanted to know the purpose of building fences. I told them the poles they made could not withstand a push from a chicken, a goat, or a sheep, let alone a cow. Though no one gave me any right or authority, the College was under me, so I stopped them and wrote a report to Lagos. They fumed, but with the record of my report, they could not do me any harm. To get even with me, the Director stopped contract awards at the permanent site. I undertook three more minor projects at the permanent site, namely, electrification, paving the street between the few houses nearing completion, and survey of the site. NEPA supervised the wiring and installation of electric power. We asked the Federal Ministry of Works in Ibadan to make a sketch of the street and give it to the Federal Committee at Ibadan, which I chaired, for an estimate. They left out the last two houses on the street and estimated the cost at ₦72,000. They had planned to use their own contractors. My committee opened it up for bids. I included the last two houses and a contractor charged ₦55,000. We awarded it to him. The Federal Ministry of Works officials took offense and refused to supervise, and I did it. We looked for surveyors and received bids. When one of those who submitted bids for the survey failed to get the contract, he told me that his company had surveyed the site for the Ministry. Asked why I did not have a copy in my office, he gave me no answer. I ignored him.

My Igbo people say that a sheep suffering from dysentery was messing its tail and ignorantly claimed to be messing the owner's yard. The Yoruba people in the Ministry claimed they were working against me and refused to develop the College when they were in power. Suddenly the northerners swept them out and took over the Ministry. Then it was too late for them (Jeremiah 25). When the military took over, it declared Nigeria too poor to begin any new projects that were not already awarded. That stopped a ten million naira plan the Ministry was about to award at Oyo. I decided to take the initiative. The UNESCO Representative had made my case with the United Nations Development Program [UNDP]. With that secured, I listed eight embassies in Nigeria, namely, Great Britain, Canada, China, France, Germany, Japan, the United States, and the Soviet Union, and planned to apply to each to build one house at the College.

One of the committees I created when I took over the administration of the College was the disciplinary committee. It had three branches. One for the students chaired by the Deputy Provost for Academics. One for junior staff, and on rare occasions I chaired one that involved a senior staff and a junior staff. This was the case one day in a case that involved the Deputy Provost for Administration and the junior staff in charge of the farm sales. After the bursars had tried to enrich themselves with the proceeds from the farm the auditors recommended that receipts continue their numbers in subsequent books instead of beginning afresh with number one. I made the junior officer report to the Deputy instead of to the bursar. On one occasion, the junior officer claimed to have given the Deputy more money than the Deputy acknowledged. The junior officer had his receipt book and his farm book. He did not ask the Deputy to sign the books when he gave him the money. The Deputy claimed to receive a lesser amount and failed to have the junior officer sign what he received. I invited two officers in my office, the EO to represent the junior officers and the Registrar to represent the senior officers. After the Deputy and the junior officers stated their case, I excused them. The Deputy was from my tribe. The junior officer was a Yoruba. The Registrar and the EO were Yoruba. Both the Registrar and the EO recommended the Deputy was believable. Therefore, the junior officer should pay the difference. I asked if they knew the message they were sending to the junior staff. You are telling them that because they are junior officers you cannot trust them. Both of them failed to use the receipt book and their signatures. They will pay the difference. The EO and the Registrar agreed with me. I instructed the bursar to divide the amount into two and deduct half from each salary. Neither of them liked the decision. But it was carried out.

Before the Ministry formed State councils that awarded contracts, federal colleges of education could not award any contract above five thousand naira. The Biology Department requested permission to buy materials worth ₦5,000 and received it. It was awarded to a friend of the chair of the department. I was about to travel to Lagos one morning when suddenly I decided to make a new arrangement about who should receive the materials. I called Mrs. Udosen and asked her to receive the materials. Worse than I expected had happened when I returned. Mrs. Udosen brought me the sad news. The chair, who was a Yoruba woman, had given her friend materials from the college biology laboratory to deliver to the College. Mrs. Udosen recognized them and confronted her with the fact. Both the chair and the contractor confessed. A short time after I received the report the chair was in my office. She confirmed the report and pleaded for mercy. She claimed her intention was to help the friend to receive the money and then buy the materials. She did not mean to steal them. "I don't know what I thought I was doing," she said. She was Yoruba. I had been falsely accused of ill-treating Yoruba members of my faculty and she recently had twins. If I let her go free, the Yoruba people would accuse me of being an accomplice or, at best, afraid of them. I told her she would not receive her annual raise. She asked if that would affect her promotion. When I said no, she expressed her gratitude and left. The contractor bought the materials and was blacklisted at the College.

    Another unfortunate incident happened at the College while I was on official duty in the north. When the military took over the government it decreed cheating in an examination a crime. I was on a national duty and the students were taking the midterm examination. A female student was caught cheating. By the time I returned to Oyo, the police had investigated the case and determined that the lecturer was innocent. The student was punished. When the report reached me I invited the lecturer to my office. I let him realize why I would discipline him. 1. If you had not been fooling with the woman she could not have seen the test. 2. She is punished. He said I should consider the fact that he came from the same town and forgive him. "That's why you should have behaved better; You are not getting your annual raise."

Four years had passed since the Director transferred the Deputy Provost for Administration to the College. His intention of creating an opposition against me failed to materialize. On the contrary, he became a strong supporter and defender of me and my administration. They turned against him. Though he misstepped at times, it was nothing serious. First, the College bought a cow for the kitchen instead of buying meat from the market. The kitchen staff killed it but the woman in charge of the kitchen failed to record the price. They killed, cooked, and served the students the meat. When the woman in charge of the kitchen brought the accounts book to the Deputy's office, they discovered the price of the cow was not recorded. The Deputy wrote the price in his handwriting. It was the exact price, not more or less. At another time palm oil cost a lot more in the West than it cost in the East. The Deputy requested to use the old Provost's official car to travel to the East. He bought tins of palm oil at a cheaper price and brought them to the kitchen. Up till now, I do not know whether he sold them to the College at a higher or the same price. One thing was sure. The College paid less for it than it would have cost at Oyo. Unknown to me was that some junior staff, including the woman in charge of the kitchen and the man in charge of the farm sales, had reported the Deputy to the Oyo police station. The police at Oyo told them they had no case. Unhappy with the verdict of Oyo police, they took the case to the police state headquarters at Ibadan.

As usual, when my messenger walked into my office, I never knew what was in his mouth until he opened it. This day was not different. He said a police officer from Ibadan wished to see me. The man walked in and introduced himself as an Inspector from the Criminal Investigation Department (CID) in Ibadan. By his name, I knew he was an Igbo man. He told me about his mission and went to work. By the end of the second day he had completed his work. When he searched the house of the man in charge of the farm sales he found college files illegally stored in his house. Accusing a person falsely was a crime under the military rule. Having found nothing against the College, the Inspector determined to arrest them all. He came and told me his decision. If he arrested them that Thursday afternoon, they could only be bailed on Tuesday because Friday and Monday were Muslim holidays. I pleaded with him. God would not be pleased. The woman in charge of the kitchen had a baby recently and the father would be miserable. The officer could not believe me. "That's where they wanted you and your Deputy." He allowed them to report on Tuesday morning at Ibadan. But he insisted on my telling them myself. I did. With the report out and the Deputy exonerated, I dismissed the man in charge of the farm sales for illegally storing college files in his house and misusing them. That was the sixth inquiry since I took over the administration.

Though there were a number of elementary schools at Oyo, I felt that the College should have its own elementary school for our students to practice. The College worked with the Oyo State Government, which approved and registered one in the name of the College. A committee chaired by the Deputy Provost for Academics a Yoruba supervised the school. The fees the students paid was sufficient to pay the staff and feed the students lunch. The records of registration that showed ownership and accounts were available for inspection.

Once again the Yoruba who controlled the Internal Audit department came to audit the College. At the end and before they gave me the preliminary report they went to audit the Federal Girls Secondary School in the same town. Having completed the auditing there, they returned to give me the report. The leader said to me, "Sir, we were warned about you before we left Lagos. They told us you are difficult to deal with. But you have been very cooperative. I even told Federal Girls to come and see your store. Thank you, Sir." I was pleased and warned him and his group. "If Lagos falsifies this record, I promise you a fight." True to their character, when they reached Lagos, they claimed that an Alhaji owned the College practicing school. I seriously considered taking them to court with all the records. But I had to go to Lagos first. On arrival at Lagos, I lined up to enter the elevator and in front of me was one of them. I asked him how they concluded that an Alhaji owned the school. He said a woman in the kitchen told them. "Were you not expected to ask me about it while you were at the College, you liar?" He left the line and walked the stairs. After I replied and threatened them, I did not hear from them again.

My third international project was with the European Economic Council (EEC). With my success at the UNDP registered, an Igbo man at the Nigerian National Planning gave me the address of the EEC in Nigeria and encouraged me to apply for aid from the organization. I had to pass it through the Ministry, and I did. One of the items I requested was a Braille press. The reply from the Ministry through the Acting ADE to the Director for Higher Education was a classical, typical anti-Onwuegbu. As usual, it turned out to be anti-Nigeria. It said the ADE for special education claimed that the Ministry should establish a Braille press in Lagos. I could not believe my eyes. I wrote them a letter I believed they deserved. I started asking if there was any thinking person left in the ministry. How many years ago was this decision taken? Did the decision at Oyo determine there would be only one Braille press in Nigeria? Finally, I described them as dogs in the manger. As graduation drew near and all the other Provosts who were transferred with me had been moved, I decided to spend the money I had in the bank at Oyo because of my successor's love for money.

My first priority was the multipurpose dam to raise fish and irrigate the farm during the dry season. At this time the Oyo Federal Ministry of Education Committee that I chaired was authorized to award any contract not exceeding one hundred thousand naira. We awarded it for ninety-eight thousand naira. The hall had always been too small for our events. We rented a tarpaulin for seating extra visitors. I decided to buy tarpaulin and poles and did so.

Now recall at least three of the dreams I reported in this book. One is about the letter of appointment. Another one is the instruction to stay at Oyo and perform the duty assigned to me. The third is about the case of the landlord, who was dismissed five times. If the message to stay at Oyo was not from God and delivered by His angels, I could not have left Oyo alive.

Six inquiries had failed to remove me and instead removed those who made the false accusations. Court cases were dismissed. Poison failed. They started anonymous false petitions against me. In one case a member of the faculty wrote the petition under a fictitious name but signed his real signature. All I had to do when I got the letter was to walk to the police station and prove with his file and signature that he was the author of the petition. Instead, I called him to my office and showed him the petition with his signature. He pleaded for forgiveness. In the midst of all this, I walked into the staff general office one day. Someone must have seen me and talked about me. I walked in and heard Mr. Ayoku, a blind member of the faculty, asking, "What wrong did Onwuegbu do?" He did not know I came in. I withdrew immediately on hearing him, hoping whoever was concerned would answer his question. I still do not know whether he received an answer or not. Ohiari, an Igbo member of the faculty, reported to Elijah, his friend who is from my village, that I did not steal the money and did not allow others to steal. Elijah reported to my brother. My brother said to him, "What do you want me to say? If he stole and refused to allow others to steal, you would have a case."

Isiaka and I were on our way from Ibadan to Oyo one afternoon. Heavy on my mind was why people would waste their time writing false petitions against me. The sun was shining. Isiaka slowed down to pass the bump by Fiditi High School. I heard the voice of the Holy Spirit say as clearly as though the person sat next to me, "Obed, why do you bother about false petitions? Do you know the number of saints petitioning God on your behalf?" There were only Isiaka my driver, and I in the car. I almost jumped out of my seat and asked my Muslim driver, "Isiaka do you know the saints petition God on behalf of the innocent?" His answer was, "Sir?" I told him not to worry. From Fiditi High School to my office is about fifteen minutes drive. I entered my office and was about to sit down and call my wife to tell her my experience when my messenger walked in and handed me an envelope from the Alaafin of Oyo. It was a copy of his letter to the Federal Ministry of Education in support of me. Copy below. It seemed as though God was saying that if you are in doubt of the voice of the Holy Spirit you heard in your car, on the road, here is the confirmation. Students also got into the act of writing. Below are two examples from two students and one of them is a Yoruba.

Since every other attempt to kick me out alive had failed, they tried to kill me. Isiaka and I usually left Oyo town by 6 a.m. to travel to my village in the East. Did Isiaka knowingly or inadvertently give the enemy the plan for our trip; It is unknown to me. Recall that Isaiah 54 is open on my desk in my office. Isiaka drove my official car from the academic site to my residence before six that morning. Is it a possibility he could have given the plotters a ride? Instead of going on the trip, I told him to drive me to the office. Once in the office I read my Bible and prayed. I don't know why I went to the office when my prayer stand, and a few other versions of the Bible were in the house. On arrival at the house, I decided to wait and take our two youngest boys to school. It was unnecessary because other drivers would take them to school in my absence. It was about 7.00 am before I kissed Sweetie goodbye. I thought I was making those decisions. However, fifteen minutes after we started the trip it became evident that God had been controlling my movement all along. Four armed policemen stopped us and asked for a ride to Ibadan. Surprised that they did not even have their police car, I asked why they were there and about their vehicle? They told me there had been armed robbers there for the past hour, harassing every vehicle traveling from Oyo to Ibadan. That was the hour I used to go to the office and take our sons to school. The armed robbers had been hired to kill me, just as the Spirit prevented Paul from going into Asia (Acts 16:6). My brother's wife was the first to ask if my driver was a part of the plot. I told her that did not even cross my mind.

Thinking about that incident today, if the armed robbers had succeeded, they would have dumped my body in the nearby river. Thus, God prevailed. The armed policemen became my bodyguards (2 Kings 6:15-19). We passed Obani on the road between Ibadan and Ife driving slow as though he was listening for some news.

As I celebrated the sixtieth year of my Lord's visit to me in a dream on July 31, 2023, I read a book entitled A Treasury of Christmas Miracles by Karen Kingsbury; I realized that the four policemen were God's angels sent to protect me. That is why they had no police vehicle. In addition to having no police vehicle, where they asked my driver to drop them made no sense. There were no buildings, only trees and bushes on both sides of the road.

I had one more encounter with officers of the Federal Ministry of Works at Ibadan. One of the officers who supervised the building at the permanent site came to my office one day and dumped a bunch of keys on my desk and demanded I sign his book for them to indicate the contractor had completed his work. I refused to sign without inspecting the building. The Works officer left the contractor at the permanent site. I took the EO with me. Both of them knew the house could not pass inspection. The plot was if I accept the keys the contractor would go home and enjoy his pay for unfinished work while the Ministry of Works man enjoyed his bribe. After inspecting the floor, I rejected the house. The Federal Ministry of Works man said, "The Federal Ministry of Works determines when a building is finished and acceptable. I am the inspector here." I looked him squarely in the eye and said, "The Federal Ministry of Education hired the Ministry of Works to do a good job. I am in the Ministry of Education here now. I can fire you on this spot right now." The contractor asked me what he should do. "Correct the unsatisfactory work I pointed out." We left the site and returned to the college.

Though all the Provosts in the north designated for transfer had been replaced, I was still at Oyo. I was not even officially informed of my impending transfer. A lingering doubt set in because of the words I heard in the car at Fiditi that said the saints were petitioning God on my behalf.

Obani told anyone who would listen to him that I refused to go on transfer. He said I insisted on being audited before I handed over. True, I had written two letters, one to the audit department and a second one to the Permanent Secretary, to send the auditors to audit the College before I handed it over. But that was not the condition for my leaving the College. Eventually an Assistant Chief Education Officer delivered my letter of transfer a few days before the college graduation. It confirmed that I was going to the headquarters to replace the ADE for Special Education, the office that was created to make sure I failed. That weekend was the graduation. The Acting ADE for higher education represented the Ministry and announced the changes. As rumored a Yoruba audiologist at the University of Ibadan had been picked to replace me. But it would be about two more months before he reported at the College.

While we waited the Nigerian Television crew came and did a documentary on the College. It showed the college logo I created in the shape of the globe with the rising sun, depicting the global nature of handicapping condition, the rising sun signifying the dawn of the education of the handicapped in Nigeria; surrounded by the Nigerian green and white flag that indicated ownership of the College by the Federal government of Nigeria and a handicapped child. The broadcast presented a very positive image of the College on national TV. At about the same time, some hunters from a village near the permanent site went hunting at the site and set it on fire. The fire helped them to kill the prey but also damaged the college orchard. I stopped them from entering the site. They had previously been allowed to harvest the palm tree fruits. The ban stopped that. I was in my office one day when a Yoruba Concord Newspaper correspondent walked in to interview me on the issue. I did not trust him. I told him to go to Lagos and get permission from the headquarters before I answered his questions. When he insisted on my answering his questions I called in the EO. After some minutes without achieving his objective, he reluctantly left. On a later date a lawyer came in and pleaded to know what happened. He was from the village. He was satisfied with my actions and explanation. That was the end of the matter.

The ADE Special Education was retired in December. I traveled to Lagos in February expecting to see someone else acting before my arrival. He was still in the office distributing special education materials to some Yoruba state officials. They knew me and acted uneasy. I passed them and spoke briefly to the ADE. Then I walked to the Coordinating Director's office and reported what was going on. He took his phone and called Director Alaniyon. "Was ADE SE not retired last December? What is he still doing in the office two months after he was retired?" The ADE left the office that day without handing over anything to any officer and never returned to the office again.

I inherited a Yoruba woman who was in charge of the kitchen. Shortly after I became the Principal, she left without resignation or notice. She went to one of the universities. About three years later she showed her face at the college again. A Yoruba man had rehired her and sent her to my College to be in charge of the kitchen. I refused to accept her. When I reached Lagos and the man who sent her pleaded and was ready to take her back instead of the fight I expected. I allowed her to stay. She became impossible. In one case she took the whole head of a cow the College killed to feed the students. In another case, she highjacked the water tanker for private work. At another time, she left her work and, without permission, went to mark GCE examination papers. I ordered the EO to give her a fifteen-item query. She ran away. I put her assistant in charge.

The sixth inquiry backfired on the accusers. More importantly, the Deputy Provost the Director sent to oppose me had allied himself to my course; they retired him. The Government had retired the former Yoruba Permanent Secretary. We met at the Ministry, and he wanted to know where I was. He was surprised to hear that I was still at Oyo. Months passed after the graduation, and my successor did not come.

Mr. Obani filled the air with falsehoods about why I was transferred. My phone rang one day, and it was a Yoruba veterinarian lecturer at the University of Ibadan. He talked about Mr. Obani claiming to be much better than you. He asked, "If he is as good as he claims, why has the Ministry not ordered you to hand over to him and report for duty in Lagos?" I told him to ask him that question. While I waited I wrote my handing over note. Once the Yoruba contractors heard I was going to head the special education department at the headquarters, some of them started to be friendly and even brought gifts. The hope was that I would award them contracts. However, I had made up my mind to retire and return to the States with my family. My sight was getting too bad, and I had buried my mother. God had helped my brother through me with the education of most of his ten children, giving him his first graduate, first daughter-in-law, and first grandson. My mother knew about the birth of her great-grandchild before her death. The late Dr. Ufere Torti introduced me to my brother's boss at Owerri. I asked him why my brother was still at the level he was. "Do you know what he was with the Federal Government before the Biafra-Nigeria War?" He asked, "What was he?" "He was Assistant Forman," I said. He promised to promote him. He was true to his word. I had firmly written my history not only at the College, as Professor Yoloye said in his address at the graduation, but also in the history of special education in Nigeria. I had contributed ₦400 to my brother when he bought his plot at Ebite and another ₦400 when his age group went to the square, and that did not include the bags of rice, stockfish, and corned beef we took home every Easter and Christmas besides helping to educate most of his children in secondary school. I made a suit for him and bought a special wrapper three times for his wife and once as a uniform for his wife and his son's mother-in-law.

The handover day arrived, and my successor came. He and I read through my handing-over note. I took him to the stores to see the materials I listed in the note. I showed him our latest acquisitions that included the tarpaulin. I briefed him on the UNDP and embassy projects. We returned to the Provost's office and signed the paper.

Mr. Obani was in his best suit. He assumed to be in charge and tried to dictate the order I addressed the faculty and students through a misfit Yoruba deputy provost. Suddenly, the deputy provost walked into my office, telling me to address the faculty before the whole assembly. A few minutes later, the Provost designate walked into my office. "What is the matter? Let him address the College as he wants." Mr. Obani and the misfit were trying to dictate who I addressed first. I went and addressed the students first as I planned, to Obani's shame. I mainly thanked God for what He achieved at the college through me. I told them that Oyo had gone from the laughingstock of the Ministry to the number one College. I have written my history. It is your college, so make it what you want it to be. I introduced my successor. His impression of what he saw can be summarized in one of his statements. "Dr. Onwuegbu is a miracle worker." Then we went to the general staff room, where I addressed the faculty. I spoke to Mr. Obani in my address to the faculty.

One or two of you here have specialized in lies. I looked at him while I spoke. "He has gone everywhere and lied about everything, including a small building at the site. He said the Provost thought his office was more important than other buildings and built himself an office. That small office is called the site office. The Federal Ministry of Works built it. That's where their officers hold meetings with the contractors, the architect and the Provost. They build such an office wherever they supervise federal contracts. Besides the Provost does not award building contracts. The Federal Ministries of Works and Education award building contracts at the site. The Provost will be lucky if they inform him after they award the contracts. A lecturer at UI called me and asked why the Ministry has not told me to hand over to him if he is as good as he claims?" Even an Army Captain from his town called me and complained about his boasting. I advised the Provost to read the files in the office and discover the facts for himself. I added that he had qualified people to serve him and wished him good luck. I promised to write about the history of the college for the last ten years. I have written it and is entitled When *the Saints Pray ... 1977-1987 A Decade of Courage*. I asked Isiaka to drive me home. When I reached home I told him to come the following morning to take me to Lagos to assume duty.

Chapter 46

Last Days in the Ministry of Education

Isaiah 55:8 states that we do not think the way God thinks, nor is His way our way. The voice I heard in the car was specific, and I thought I was limited to the false petitions. But like my Lord's visit, God extended the meaning to cover other areas, including my impending transfer. Isiaka drove the Provost's official car to my gate the following morning to take me to Lagos. I bade goodbye to my family, and we left. When I reached Lagos on June 3, no senior officer was available to report to. We returned to Oyo. The same thing happened on the fourth. By this time, the Provost took possession of his official car and made an older car available to me.

Before the handover and because of the lies of the internal audit department about the College, I invited the Chief Auditor to come and audit the College. The Chief did not respond. I wrote a second letter of invitation through the Permanent Secretary. He did not reply either. I made both letters a part of the handing over document. If the Provost thought the handing over document was only for him and me, he was mistaken.

Isiaka came again on the third day to take me to Lagos. As was my manner at the time, I took up my Bible as he drove and opened it to read any passage God gave me. When I looked, it was Mark 11, The Triumphant Entry. I read it but did not know what to make of it. However, I knew I was not Jesus. We drove to Emedom's and took him with me to pray in the office with me. The senior officers were in their seats that day. Not even knowing what God had already accomplished, he read God's promise to Moses and Joshua that He would drive the enemy out one after the other, and we prayed. The Acting Principal, the Dean, the bursars, the chair of the English department, the Acting Dean of the school of special education, the lecturer, and now the office of the ADE created and filled to ensure my failure have all fallen by the wayside. The College was then under me. I went to report. I distributed copies of my handing over notes to the Honorable Minister's office, the Permanent Secretary, the Coordinating Director, the Director for Higher Education, and the Controller of Finance and Accounts. After I had distributed the handover note, I walked to the secretary for finance and requested money to check into a hotel. He authorized an officer to give me a check for four weeks. The officer was also a Yoruba man. He was all smiles when he saw the amount. He promised to send me to a "nice hotel." When I asked the name of the hotel and its location, he told me a story. I rejected his offer and simply asked to receive the check. His smiling face turned sad. He gave me a cross-check. I had a bank account in Lagos, but for over two years since I paid the last fee for my nephew in the U.S., I had not used it. I went to the bank to cash the check. They told me my account had been dormant for too long, and I had to reactivate it. To do so, I had to see the manager. I went to the third floor and saw the manager. I told him I was on transfer to Lagos and desired to cash the check. He looked at me and said, "Whoever gave you this check does not wish you well. He wants you to work and sleep in your office." He promised to do the first thing first. After he reactivated my account, he gave me ₦2,000 and told me to come back in two weeks for the rest of the money. Isiaka took me to the American Inn Hotel. I stayed there for almost six weeks. While I was with the CFA, the Igbo woman Director of the Inspectorate walked in and I gave her a copy of the handing over note. I did not give any copy to the auditor, the Director of Schools and Services, who was my boss.

Then I went and informed him that I had arrived. He pretended to be nice and asked me to go and inform the Permanent Secretary of my arrival. I walked into the Permanent Secretary's office, greeted him and said, "I am directed to report my arrival to you." He laughed and asked, "How did you escape?" I smiled. When I returned to my office and called the Chief Education Officer to hand over the department to me, he said no one had told him to hand it over to me.

I walked to the Coordinating Director's office to greet him. He asked how I was settling down. "I am not doing anything. The Chief Education Officer told me that no one has told him to hand over to me." He was angry and called the Director for Schools. He told him what the Chief Education Officer said and told him to order him to hand over to me immediately. He then told me what the Chief Education Officer reported to him when he heard I was going to be his boss. The Chief Education Officer was an Assistant Chief at Oyo and my senior. As an Assistant Chief Education Officer, he also applied for the position of Provost but did not get it. Therefore, when he heard that I was going to be his boss, he went to the Coordinating Director and complained that he was my senior at Oyo. The Coordinating Director asked him, "So what?" When I returned to the office, the Chief Education Officer was waiting for me. He told me he had nothing to hand over. He said that the ADE came to work one day and left and never came back to work. He did not hand over anything to him. That was how I took over.

Soon, I called a meeting of the department or section, as some called it. At this time, the sister-in-law of Obani had been retired. I needed to know the responsibilities each officer, from the Chief to the junior officer at level seven, who was my graduate, performed. There were accusations about who awarded contracts and who did not. I told them to go and read the National Education Blueprint and study the special education section. We are going to plan how to implement it at the federal, state, and local government levels. It will be a three-part operation. 1. We start it and send our product to states and institutions to critique and submit their products to us. 2. We read and assess. 3. Invite individuals from states and institutions to produce the final product. Finally, we would present it to the Nigerian Council on Education through the Honorable Minister. We met once a week during the period I was in the Ministry. It was still at the planning stage when I left.

A few weeks later, I distributed copies of my handing-over note. Dr. Anugwelem saw me and told me the Honorable Minister asked him to summarize and send a precis of it to him. He did and a week later he told me the Minister had ordered the Ministry to write me a letter of commendation. Within a week, a secretary in the office of the Director for higher education walked into my office beaming with smiles; she was an Igbo. She greeted me, gave me her mail delivery book to sign, and the letter with, "Congratulations, Sir." Of all the five Provosts the Ministry repatriated (transferred), I was the only one who received a letter of commendation. I thanked God and wrote a psalm and pasted it on the door of my office. Things seem to be falling in their right places. I became convinced that the passage I read in the Bible about the triumphant entry, namely, Mark 11, was real.

Aware that my Director would not appreciate my letter, I took a copy and two other files to his office. He opened the files and read the contents of the other two files. When he read the title of my letter, he said he did not have time to read it. Knowing that he vowed that as the Provost, I would not succeed without his help, I walked out of his office but more determined to force him to read it. About 9.00 a.m. the following day I took the file myself again to his office instead of sending my messenger. He was doing nothing, and I opened the file and placed it in front of him. He had no other choice but to read it.

After he had read it, he did not say one word. He closed the file and handed it back to me. Smiling broadly I said goodbye and left. I gave a copy to the Imo State newspaper, which published it in its entirety. I believe he perceived my letter of commendation as a threat to his position and wished I was not in Lagos.

Mr. Adigwe, a fellow Igbo, was in the Director's office the day he said, "Let me see how he can succeed without my help." When Mr. Adigwe read my letter of commendation in the newspaper, he came to my office. He congratulated me and expressed his surprise that I survived eight years in Yorubaland. He added, "I thought we would see you in a coffin within six months. And here you are after eight years with a letter of commendation. How did you do it?" I said in reply, "I didn't do it. God did it." Again, this is a reminder of Judges chapter seven.

About a month after I arrived at the headquarters the Director for Higher Education sent a file to me. It was a request from a special needs organization for a scholarship to the Ministry to send four of its members to study in Britain each year. I was told the problem had been on the table for at least four years. I did not blame people who wished to be educated. I blamed the ministry personnel for a lack of foresight and planning. Then, I suggested a solution. I rejected the request of sending four special needs students overseas each year. Instead, I recommended upgrading Oyo to a degree-awarding institution in arts subjects. I also suggested the Ministry choose three Federal universities to specialize each on how to teach science in different science subjects to students with different handicapping. Then, award the scholarships to Nigerian institutions. I returned the file to the Director. It took a few weeks before someone returned the file to my office again. When I opened it, the Director of Higher Education had filled a page with objections to my proposal. His reasoning was as though it came from a colonial clerk waiting for Westminster to issue orders. He claimed the Ministry did not have the authority to do what I suggested without orders from higher authority, etc. But he did not name the higher authority. This is the same Director who could not understand why I extended Mr. Mensah's contract for a month in order for him to complete the semester. He sent the file to the Perm. Sec. and the Coordinating Director. Both agreed with him, and they sent the file to the Honorable Minister. He overruled their objection and upheld my recommendation. The only obstacle he saw at that time was a lack of funds. From then on, I became their oracle. The common expression became, "You know it all."

The Permanent Secretary convened a meeting of the ADEs, the Directors, the Secretary, and the Coordinating Director. This is the highest authority in the Ministry. One of the items on the agenda was the budget for the Colleges of Education. When the Permanent Secretary announced the budget for Oyo, what I suspected was confirmed. Oyo received exactly one-half of the amount each of the other colleges received. The evidence was before all of them. "Are you going to continue to punish that College? I am no longer there?" I said. The Director, who was the architect of the small budget for my college, muttered a statement in defense. But no one paid any attention to him. I believe he realized his days were numbered as long as I was there. The Permanent Secretary asked me if adding 10 million was all right. Since I said at least ten million earlier, I said that would not even bring the College to par with other colleges. But because my successor was a Yoruba who loved money, I thought, I said that was better than nothing. Both the meeting and my handing over note revealed much of what and how the Yoruba people in the Ministry, especially the Director, dealt with the college and me as the Provost.

A northerner who was a student in the UK came to ask for more money. The Director sent him with his file to me. I requested information on him from the assistant chief education officer in charge of scholarships, and he gave it to me. Both at Oyo and then in Lagos I told those who work under me to forget the colonial language of ending every assignment with please advise. So based on that, I recommended three solutions, and the Director sent the file back to me. Afraid that none of the three solutions might be acceptable to his northern bosses, he returned the file to me, accusing my officer of giving me the wrong information. After reading it, I sent it back with the following: "My officer gave me the correct information. Based on that, I made three recommendations. You may choose one of the solutions or develop a new solution." The file did not come back to me. He learned I was not there to make policies to suit individual wants but national policy.

A short while after, his tribesman came up with a fake science workshop for teachers of the handicapped. He walked into my office and asked for permission and funds to conduct it. I liked the idea. Though I went through teacher education without a real science education background in Nigeria, my first degree in the U.S. was in teaching science and mathematics in junior high. Besides, I took a special course on teaching science in junior high at the University of Utah with Dr. James. So I said to the man, "Give me an outline of what you want to teach, the objective, and how you intend to achieve the objective." He left my office and did not return. Unknown to me was that he had gone to the Director, his tribesman, and they agreed that he should go ahead with the Director's approval. Sometime later, the Director called me and told me to go and represent the Honorable Minister at the University of Ibadan and declare the workshop open. He also asked me to draft a speech to be read at the opening and show it to him for his approval. When I showed it to him, he deleted the "negative points the press would find fault with." The day arrived, and my driver took my friend Emedom and me to the University. There was no trace of the man or any workshop. I went to the Dean, who gave the man a letter of recommendation, and asked about the man and his workshop. He looked dazed and defensive. He was the Acting Director of the Institute I worked with when I was at Oyo. He confirmed giving the man a letter of recommendation and that was all he knew about the workshop. I gave him a copy of my letter of commendation to read, and he was pleased. "You were the best of the Provosts I worked with," he said. I also showed it to Dr. Abosi. He could not believe what he read because of the lies Obani told him about the reason I went on transfer, and he made a copy for himself. It seemed God was against the Director. When he heard the report the following day, he was beside himself. He asked, "What would happened if the Honorable Minister had gone there himself?" He directed me to write a serious warning letter to him. I gave him the look that said I told you so and left.

Apart from the first week I was in Lagos, I did not spend any other weekend there. I checked out every Friday morning and did not return to the hotel till Monday afternoon after work. My driver drove me to Oyo every Friday after work. I traveled by taxi every Monday morning from Oyo to Lagos. It was during such trips to Oyo that I learned what was going on there. Though I had left millions of naira for my successor to spend, something unheard of in the history of handing over in Nigeria. He wanted the money the Federal Contract Committee awarded for the multipurpose dam. He wrote Alhaji Ajisafe, the contractor, to stop building the dam. The contractor ignored him and continued with his work. Recognizing that he had made a fool of himself, he wrote a second letter requesting the contractor to return his first letter and continue his work. The Alhaji made a photocopy of the first letter before he returned it and showed it to me when he reported to me.

I took a copy of the letter of commendation to Oyo and sent it to the Rotary Club of Oyo. The President could not believe the content because of the false story Obani told as to why I left. As we traveled from Oyo to Lagos one Monday morning, we reached Jobele almost opposite the spot where my car had a flat tire about ten years earlier. The taxi car stalled. The driver went back to Oyo to get another vehicle. Then, the Concord newspaper correspondence man who visited me in the office and I recognized each other. He asked if I had false rumors about me. When I said no, he told me the story. He said the college said I did not purchase the tarpaulin and poles but billed for them. He said someone even offered him one thousand naira to print it, but he refused. He continued, "The Provost of Oyo State College of Education, a sister college in the town, appealed to me to take it easy on you. Then they claimed to find it. "I asked him why he hadn't published it. You are one of those who keep me poor. I would have sued you and your paper for fifty million naira. "But the court would not have awarded you that amount," he said. I showed him a copy of my letter of commendation and told him this letter and others like it would have made it costly for you. He congratulated me. Soon, the driver arrived with another vehicle, and we were on our way to Lagos.

I had planned to leave Nigeria with my family in August. A month and one half after I submitted my letter of retirement without any response from the Perm. Sec., I went and requested for the approval. He claimed to have misplaced it. I submitted a second one. Somehow, he thought that if he did not approve it, I could not leave the Ministry. I informed the Coordinating Director of my intention to leave the Ministry. He said the Ministry was planning to make me the Director of Special Education. To me, that was already too little and too late. Another northerner, the Secretary for Education, said, "Nigeria needs you." I thought Nigeria needs me to work as a slave without promotion. This is the time to leave, now that they realize they need me. That was confirmed when the Hon. Minister started to pass files directly to me instead of through the Permanent Secretary and Directors. In order to give the impression that the plan to seek help from foreign governments was his, my successor came to the Ministry to seek approval for my plan to get the embassies and their countries to build houses such as the library, classrooms, and hostels at the College. He bypassed me and went to the Director. The Director did not know what to do with it. Finally, they told him to wait until the College Board was established. In their attempt to deny me the honor as the initiator of the project, they denied Nigeria the benefit. At about the same time, a messenger brought a file to me. When I opened it, it contained the final approval of my project for the development of the faculty at Oyo. The UNDP promised to fund my project for $400,000. It was sent to Dr. Onwuegbu through the ADE Special Education. At this time I was both the ADE and the Director of the project. I took it to the Director i.e., my boss. I showed him the letter and asked him how to proceed. As I expected, that was a dagger to his heart. He lost it and shouted, "Go away with it!" Slowly, I walked away.

Though I had doubts about how my successor would spend the money, that would not keep me in Nigeria. With this UNDP Award, God established the three most important features of the College through me. First, by my appeal to the Alaafin and his provision of a permanent home, the College is now permanently located at Oyo. Second, I created the curriculum for the College, and the multi-purpose dam, and planted the orchard. Third, with the $400,000 UNDP Award for the training and development of the faculty, the College was now firmly able to function. The college that started with about thirty students serves sub Saharan Africa with more than ten thousand population today.

By the middle of August I had bought six plane tickets for the family to fly to the U.S. I returned to Oyo one weekend and sold our family car that I bought for less than ₦6,000 and received ₦13,000 because the naira was falling in value. My family still lived at Oyo in the house the College rented and furnished. Unfortunately the military government had decreed that Nigerians traveling out of the country to the U. S could only be allowed to fly to the east coast of New York JFK or to Los Angeles and without any spending money. Since my destination was Salt Lake City Utah, I bought tickets to L.A. A friend of the family from Europe gave my wife fifty Swiss francs besides the $100 we bought from a Nigerian who was visiting from the States.

It was imperative that I handed the house and furniture over to the College when my family vacated. So, I asked for permission to travel to Oyo on the day. My messenger came back with a negative answer from the Director. I took the file to him myself and told him I had to go in order to hand over the property to the College. He changed his negative answer to yes and pretended to become my adviser. "Even when your Chief Education Officer asks for permission you make him give you a reason." I walked out.

My driver came on the morning I went to Oyo and drove me to the house. By the time we arrived, the EO, who had been promoted to senior executive officer while I was at Oyo, was in the house with two junior officers from the store checking the furniture. I wondered if they checked the Acting Principal when he moved out and replaced the college furniture with his old chairs and carpet. While they checked, my driver took me to the College, where I made forty copies of my letter of commendation. No one said anything about the tarpaulin to me. When I returned to the house, there were many people helping Sweetie pack, more people than I expected to know about the move. One of the surprises was a sendoff for the graduating class on one of the Sundays I was at Oyo. Because I declined two previous invitations for sendoff parties, the church I founded on the campus planned one for the graduating seniors that included my family but kept the part about my family a secret. Sweetie received a big copy of the 1916 version of the King James Bible at the party. I contributed fifty naira to the seniors' party. Before we were ready to leave the house, Mr. Gupta, our Indian neighbor, offered his car and his driver to drive our children to the airport. Once they finished the checking, I signed the papers. My Yoruba driver took Sweetie and me with the suitcases to the airport. My family traveled to the States without me. Friends were also at the airport to say goodbye. It was almost midnight before we sent everyone home.

Realizing that nothing happened after the Nigerian Academy For Education chose my paper as its number one project and planned to discuss it with the Federal Ministry of Education for implementation; I submitted an abridged copy to the Director in writing. He lied on paper and sent the lie to me. He claimed it was an old idea. I assumed that to be how he dismissed the Academy and challenged him in writing. "Tell me where you saw or heard this before I presented it at the Academy. Quote the book, magazine page, and author or minutes of a meeting. The only place you will read this is Issues In Nigerian Education Vol. 1 where this paper is chapter 19. The editor called it the catalyst of the book. The book is not even on the market. The only people who have copies are the contributors who wish to use it to support requests for promotion." As usual, I took the file to him myself. After he read it he took his pen and wrote TKU and signed his name. Then he said, "You were not supposed to reply to this." I said to him, "If you do not expect a reply don't write." I learned later that TKU means thank you. My Assistant Chief Education Officer II, also a Yoruba, inadvertently told me why the Director lied to the Academy. Doing what I proposed would take a job he did not even know existed and reduce his prestige. When I asked if Nigeria needed my proposal or not, he said yes.

Then there was a test of will between the Director and me. His Yoruba real spy in the department had planned to travel to Syracuse, New York, U.S.A. He brought his file to me for approval bypassing the Chief Education Officer. I sent it to the Chief. After going through the file, he determined neither the country nor the department would benefit from the trip. I refused to approve the trip. Soon my telephone rang, and I picked it up. At the other end was the Director. His tribesman was in his office. The only reason he gave me to allow the officer to travel was that my predecessor approved it before he retired. I told him that I was there at the time, not the former ADE. "The officer should try to solve his problem here instead of running to you." That was the end of the discussion, and the officer did not travel. As the ADE in charge of special education in Nigeria the College I left was also under me. Yet the Provost had been to the headquarters several times and avoided me each time. He discovered the Director could not solve his problems. One day, he, his Deputy for Academics, and the Dean of Students surprised me with a visit to my office.

The Provost called me Oga-katakana (master of all), and we greeted him. He said he had been reading the files and wondered why people lied about what I did. I told him to read on, "You will discover the truth." Then he told me the real reason they came to see me. First, with the northerners in power, the Yoruba Director was not the authority he made them believe he was. Second, the colleges gave the entrance examination, marked the papers, and ranked the candidates. Then they recommended and submitted the candidates they selected to the Ministry for approval. My office should facilitate the process for him. By bypassing my office he was almost late getting his results. Then he realized he could not avoid my office and still succeed. I sent the officer in charge with them, and the result was released. After they left the Dean of students came back to my office. He reported that Obani was still writing petitions against me. I told him not to bother because it would come to my desk. He told me what I believe was his reason for coming back alone. He told me Mr. Obani was still claiming seniority over him. Dismissing him, I said, "If you have any complaint, send it in writing to me through the Provost. Otherwise, it is a rumor, and I will not entertain it." Alright, Sir, he said and left.

There was still one more hurdle left to jump and that was the straw that broke the camel's back. A file came to my desk one morning and it was through the Secretary for Finance. It contained another petition that reached him through my Director. It was purposed to have been written against me to the Honorable Minister by a former Yoruba student who stole a library book. It made all kinds of accusations against me. But the most annoying was the fact that the Director had given it to the Secretary to file it in my confidential file without asking me to respond to it. However contrary to the wishes of the Director, the Secretary sent the petition to me for my response. I shocked the Director.

My reply consisted of two parts. The first part accused the Director of soliciting the false petition, the seventh in the series. I supported my accusation with facts beginning from when the Commission appointed me the Principal of the College. He refused to transfer the man from his tribe because I am Igbo. It took my letter of threat to report him to the Federal Service Commission that employed me and whose order he was flouting with impunity before he transferred him after three months. I discussed his treatment of the College during my tenure as the Provost, his refusal to send lecturers, the drastic cut in college funds, the six previous inquiries against me and the results, and the immediate cause for the seventh petition. He was threatened by my successes since his arrival at the headquarters. First was my letter of commendation, which he did not want to read. When finally I got him to read it, he did not say one word but frowned. He even falsely claimed that a paper I presented to the Nigerian Academy, which the Academy chose as number one and discussed with him was an old idea. When I confronted and challenged him to show his support for his claim, he could not and chose to thank me with TKU, and more. Then, I addressed the petition in the second part.

I began with the address and the date of the letter. It was addressed to the Honorable Minister. This letter is addressed to the Honorable Minister. The petition should have gone from the office of the Hon. Minister to the Perm. Sec. to the Coordinating Director before it reached the Director. I accused him of promoting himself and usurping the office of the Hon. Minister. I took up the date. The petition that was supposed to be written at Ilorin in June took seven weeks to reach Lagos, incredible. My qualification is not in question. Someone had accused me of being an English major at one time and the former ADE demanded my transcript. So the Ministry had the transcripts in my file, including my Ph.D., where I have only one B grade; the rest are A's. Besides, I went through all stages of teacher education in Nigeria, namely, PTC, ETC, HE, and B.S.Ed. Even the chair at Central confessed he had not seen anyone with as many psychology courses as I. I had been sent to Kenya by the UN and the British Commonwealth in recognition of who I am. I was the founding Vice President of Educational Psychology of Nigeria (NEPA). I defended my Acting Registrar, who made a recommendation for admissions. When I answered all the questions, I called for an inquiry to investigate the Director once, since he enjoyed setting up inquiries to investigate others. I limited the scope to his activities at Oyo and the special education I administered. Though of all the Provosts the Ministry ranked me number one in qualification and performance, he told the Commission not to promote me. I also accused him of sneaking the petition into my file to prevent my promotion again. As usual, I sent copies to the Honorable Minister, the Permanent Secretary, the Coordinating Director, the Secretaries for Finance and Education, and the Director.

    The Director saw the handing-over note I attached to the copies of my reply for the first time. He was alarmed and confused when he saw my reply and called my office. My typist reported the call when I returned to the office. When I returned his call, he told me not to bother. Later on, I discovered that he had pleaded with the Secretary for Finance to intervene on his behalf and get me to change the tone of my reply. Instead of requesting an inquiry to investigate him, he wanted me to ask an inquiry to investigate the allegations. Later in the week, the Secretary for finance asked me to see him. When I reached his office, he pleaded for a change in the tone of what I wrote. When it seemed I was about to do what he wanted he spoke the forbidden sentence. He said I could ask for the investigation of the points of accusation, not the Director. That did it. I refused. He said to me, "Well he is a difficult man to deal with anyway." I left him with the reply and returned to my office.

Realizing that I did not have one penny in my pocket to travel with and my plane ticket could only take me to L.A. when my destination was Salt Lake City Utah, there was only one way to solve my problem. The same decree, which prevented me from having any spending money also allowed me five hundred dollars as pocket money if I bought a return ticket. So I purchased a return ticket and got five hundred dollars to help me travel from LA. to Salt Lake.

Meanwhile, I evaluated the annual performance of my Chief Education Officer and gave him A's and B's, which he could not have received from the former ADE or the Director. He came and pleaded for more A's. I told him I rated him better than he deserved and reminded him how he rated me at Oyo based on the Dean's advice. He took it to the Director to sign. He would not countersign it because it was too good. He took it to the Coordinating Director who sent him to another Director who signed it for him.

Someone stole my leather suitcase, and its contents included my permanent residence card. My wife and I went to the American Embassy to renew it. The woman at the desk wanted a guarantee that if I had to be deported my father-in-law could afford to pay for it. I waited for the document to arrive. Sweetie's arrival in the U.S. hastened everything. The big envelope arrived within a short time after she arrived in the States with the Children. I took it to the Embassy and the woman at the desk almost did not open it and gave me the paper. I rescheduled my flight. I applied for vacation and went to the Permanent Secretary and asked for the approval of my retirement. He gave me the sheepish smile again and said he misplaced it. About this time, Mr. Ojo, who I made my Acting Registrar but who left to work for his state, came with his evaluation sheet. I asked him to leave it on my desk. Unfortunately, I did not rate him before I traveled. I hope he will forgive me. When I told Mr. Ojo about the false story that I claimed to buy the tarpaulin, he was dismayed and said, "Even if you were in the grave you would rise to defend your integrity." The phone rang and invited me to the main Ministry building.

There was an officer from the Civil Service Commission in the Ministry, and I did not even know that. He was an Igbo and might even have been an old boy of Uzuakoli or had relatives who attended Uzuakoli. My reply to the petition had reached his desk. His duty in the Ministry was to take care of such cases. As I walked into his office, he expressed mixed emotions. He was offended that the Ministry even entertained such a petition and well pleased at my reply. He congratulated me and showed me his decision. Among other things he wrote, he asked the Ministry who is believable, the thief who stole a college library book and was mad he was caught and punished for it; or the distinguished Provost who is rated number one and given a letter of commendation? That the Secretary who passed the file did not make any recommendations or call for the inquiry I asked for further demonstrated its ineptitude. That strengthened my resolve to leave the Ministry. I thanked him and left.

It was time for me to take my annual leave. I wrote my letter and indicated that the Chief Education Officer would be in charge in my absence. Also, I indicated that I was waiting for the Permanent Secretary's decision on my retirement application. I took the file to the Director to sign before I took it to the Perm. Sec. He offered to pass it on to him. I left it with him. He knew I was leaving for good and thought his position was secure without me in the Ministry. But his last action against me in my absence hastened his demise in the main Ministry than if I were present. See the next chapter. After I left his office I walked to the Honorable Minister's office. He had two other Ministers with him. As he opened the door for his visitors to walk out, he saw me and, with delight, said, Dr. Onwuegbu! His visitors looked at me as though I was some special person. He invited me in. I told him I came to thank him for the letter of commendation and to say goodbye. He wanted to know why I was retiring. "Are you fifty-five years old?" When I said no, he asked if I had worked for thirty-five years. Again, the answer was no. Then he said, "Please let us know what you will be willing to do for us." I told him I was leaving the country. He gave me his visitor's book to sign. I thanked him for recognizing my little contribution and signed it. He said and wrote, "You contributed a lot. We shook hands and I left.

It was a weekend, and I planned to leave the office by midafternoon. I had left the hotel and was spending the last few weeks with Emedom and his family. I instructed my official driver to come and pick me up at Emedom's apartment the following Monday. My brother and his wife were surprised to see me, and more so when he heard that my family was already in the U.S. He was delighted to see my letter of commendation. He incorrectly told Nwoko, his next-door neighbor, that I was on level seventeen. Soon, there were him, his wife, and me. I told them I was returning to the U.S. I had been on level fifteen for more than eight years and I am tired of fighting the Biafra war all over again. I was rated the best of all the Provosts and the only one to receive a letter of commendation. Yet my juniors are my seniors today.

As I expected once people heard that I was in the village, they started to come. One of them was Mr. Umunnakwe Amaefule. As they drank and talked, I took out a twenty-naira note and gave it to him. He looked at it and asked, "What is this for?" I reminded him of what he did for me when I was in standard three. I had an ulcer that prevented me from attending school for the whole of the third term. He gave my mother the medicine they called German potash that healed me. My mother carried me on her back to go to take my final year examination. Still, I took the first position. He said, "See these boys, Ezeka also reminded me that I did the same thing for him. I continued to send small amounts to him till his death. I spent only one full day at home and returned to Lagos that following Sunday.

Part Six
Back To The U.S.A.

Chapter 47

Back to the USA

This was the second time I had returned to the U.S. since I had returned to Nigeria almost twelve years earlier. However, unlike the time five years earlier, this time, I came to stay. The British Caledonian office in Lagos called my office and changed the date of my departure. The second time the office called I ignored them and went to the airport. Believing they wanted me to bribe them, which I refused to do, I went to the airport and got a seat on the plane. This time, after an exchange of a few words at the Lagos airport with two English men, they allowed me to board the plane. We were to change planes at London Heathrow Airport. For a short time, it seemed like I would spend the night in London. Then, a gentle English lady asked if I had my green card. When I said no, she put me on the plane. I expressed my gratitude.

A pleasant surprise awaited me at the Los Angeles airport. On arrival, I went to the immigration office at the airport to get my permanent residence status. I presented my passport and other papers to the official in the office. He looked at them and consulted his computer. Within two minutes, he stamped my passport and gave it back to me, and congratulated me. "Is that it?" I asked. "That is it, and you can fly back to Nigeria now and come back whenever you want," he said. I thanked him and left. My permanent residence card contains a part of my history in the U.S. It contains the year I received my social security number in the early sixties and my current green card without an expiration date.

It was time to make use of my $500. I had to travel from one gate to another to buy my ticket to Salt Lake City though the pilot told us that we were flying over Salt Lake City on our way to L.A. I bought my ticket and soon I was at Salt Lake International Airport. I called the home of my parents-in-law. My daughter answered the phone. She was excited when she learned I called from Salt Lake City Airport. Sweetie was equally or even more excited to hear the news of my arrival. I heard her ask, "Is my husband at the airport?" I asked them to come and get me. It was late in the evening when the two came and got me. That cool September evening gave way to warm hugs and kisses. In less than one hour we were in the house. The reunion was complete. I showered and ate my dinner.

Sweetie brought me up to date about the condition of things in relation to my family. She was still looking for a permanent job. Working part-time also meant she did not have health insurance of any kind. She and our children had been in the country for about one month when I arrived. Our children were all in school. Melody, seventeen, had completed one year of higher school in Nigeria, was a student at the University of Utah, and was working part-time. Chinedum, fifteen, who would have graduated from high school if he stayed in Nigeria, was sent back to repeat his junior year because he had no American history courses. Munachimso, ten, who would have been a freshman in secondary school in Nigeria, was sent back to grade five because of his age and some courses he did not take in Nigeria. He later graduated as a President's scholar from Junior High. Uchechi, who turned eight at the end of August that year, did not escape downgrading.

We still attended Christ United Methodist church. Munachimso and Uchechi were of age for confirmation in the church. Thomas, the associate Minister, read the "creed" to me. Part of it read, "I owe allegiance to the United Methodist …" I strongly objected to it. "My sons will not owe allegiance to any denomination. They owe allegiance only to Jesus Christ. If not, forget it and confirm others without them." The church changed it and announced during the service that the change was because of Obed's objection. Our sons became members of the church.

One of the reasons I left Nigeria was the sacrifice of my sight to serve an ungrateful people. My glaucoma was getting worse every day, and there was no effective treatment anywhere in the country. However, my arrival in the U.S. did not provide immediate remedy because we did not have jobs and consequently did not have health insurance. I started my daily journey to the University of Utah library to read the newspapers and professional journals in search of jobs. Many facts are stacked against my goal. October was a bad month to search for jobs at colleges and universities. Because of the bad economy at the time, many colleges and universities had retired senior members of their faculty and hired new graduates. When I wrote my former institution, where I taught prior to leaving the U.S., the chair told me they recently hired someone at the Assistant Professor level. There was only one thing to do about my sight. My father-in-law took me to his eye doctor. He confirmed what I already knew i.e., I was almost completely blind in the right eye. That was the eye the soccer ball hit, and the left eye was bad, too. The doctor said I needed surgery badly and as soon as possible, but I did not have a job, which meant I had no health insurance. I did not have the money to pay for the surgery either. He prescribed drops and pills.

As we walked out, I saw Bud Krider's ex-wife. Bud is the son of Mary Krider, a Professor at the University of Nebraska, who adopted me as her son and was instrumental in my coming to Utah.

She and her husband represented my parents at our wedding. I saw their former daughter-in-law who had divorced their son at this time. I said to her, "Hi sister." She looked at me with a frown that said, How can I, a white woman, be a sister to this black man and then said, "Who are you? I am not your sister, and I don't know you." I smiled big and asked, "Are you going to deny me in public? She stood there confused. All the white faces present stood and watched the drama. "I am your adopted brother-in-law from Biafra." She smiled, and we got reacquainted and talked about Mother Krider and how she passed away.

Knowing that the Permanent Secretary was expecting me in the office, I called him and asked for an extension of my stay for a month because my wife did not have insurance to pay for my surgery. He granted it and asked me to put the request in writing. I did. It was not too long before Sweetie got a job with a bank through our son Chimso's teacher. However, the insurance would not become effective until after six months. Since the Ministry refused to give me a one-year sabbatical, I asked for a three-month extension. The Permanent Secretary sensed I was not coming back and took two actions.

First, he stopped my salary. Second, he instructed the Director to write to me. Instead of writing to me, the Director believed this was an opportunity to threaten my brother. My brother's letter to me sounded as though I had committed a crime, and he was going to be arrested for it. For me, that was the straw that broke the camel's back; the Director had crossed the line of no return. I typed a four-page letter and told the Honorable Minister how the Director treated the College and me and drove me away from serving Nigeria because I was not a Yoruba and did not steal and share with him. He was not satisfied with that. Beyond that, he was threatening my brother. He and his supporters wanted me to work without promotion even though of all the Provosts, the Ministry rated me number one in qualification and performance and gave me a letter of commendation. My juniors became my seniors. Even if you promote me to level seventeen now, I would have to pray hard before I accept it. To prevent even his secretary from opening it, I registered it in the Honorable Minister's name. Again, I called for an inquiry into the conduct of the Director. A few weeks later, I received a letter from the Ministry. The Honorable Minister had approved my retirement. When I called the Ministry later, Alhaji Hamsa, the Coordinating Director, had replaced the Permanent Secretary, and the Director had been sent to the Inspectorate. An Igbo woman replaced him. With the removal of the Director, who, though I did not replace him, God had routed eight Yoruba officers who wanted me out dead or alive. I know at the time of this writing, Nigeria still owes me millions of naira as retirement benefits from October 1987.

Sweetie has two siblings: a sister, Kay, and a brother, Rick. Kay lived in Seattle, Washington. She met and married a "fellow Christian student." When I arrived, my family of six lived with my parents-in-law. We did not pay rent and contributed little to our feeding. Kay's abusive husband was making great monetary demands on her parents, which was nothing short of extortion. Kay and her husband claimed her husband was sick and needed an operation. But they would not allow the parents to talk to or see his doctor. I advised against it, but with my family depending on them, being forceful could be misconstrued as selfishness on my part. The parents sent $25,000 from their savings. They demanded more. The parents flew to Seattle to see Kay and her husband. Both husband and wife DISAPPEARED, and her parents flew back to Salt Lake without seeing them. Realizing his source of free income had run dry, he smashed Kay's hand with his hammer and left her unconscious in their apartment. After a day or two and by the advice of his lawyer, he carried her to the hospital and pretended to be the good Samaritan. He claimed to see the unknown body on the street and brought her in. The nurse at the hospital became suspicious, pretended to get more information, and detained him. The hospital called the police and had him arrested. They put my sister-in-law in a drug induced coma. By this time, she was unable to breathe on her own. The hospital got in touch with Ted, Kay's cousin, in Seattle, and he called my parents' in-law.

My brother-in-law Rick, his wife, and I drove from Salt Lake to Seattle. It was an all-night drive. We arrived at the hospital early the following morning. I had my Bible and Kay's Bible that I planned to leave at her sick bedside. Rick married Annette, a Roman Catholic nurse, and joined the denomination. Annette acted offended by my decision to pray for Kay. She said to me, "Whatever you want to do, wait until we come out, and then go and do your thing." I was taken aback but complied. When they walked out, she declared, "You can go and do your thing. But she is going to be a vegetable." When I saw her, she was breathing with the help of a tube and snoring loudly. She was still in a coma. I placed her Bible on the bedside, raised my right hand, and prayed. A few yards from where I stood sat two nurses. When I finished praying, a voice on my right side said, "Amen" with me. Thinking that one of the nurses had joined me, I opened my eyes and looked. There was no human by me. I thanked God and walked out. She was in the hospital for a few weeks. She recovered and went to a junior college and earned two degrees. The husband served his term in prison.

Back in Salt Lake, Sweetie began to work for a bank. For the fact that we did not pay rent and other household expenses such as electricity and water bills, we took over feeding expenses. It was evident my father-in-law was in heavy distress. That influenced his treatment of my family. My heart almost broke one day when my daughter confided in tears to me confidentially, "Dad, we must leave here and find our own apartment." My mother-in-law also commented on what she thought was the misplacement of her husband's anger on our children. Soon, we found a three-bedroom apartment and moved before Kay left the hospital and returned to live with them. I found a part-time teaching job at Salt Lake Community College. To my disappointment, I discovered that 14 years after I demanded and received $1,000 to teach a three-hour course in Connecticut, I would teach two courses of six hours for about the same amount I charged for one course. My sight was getting worse by the day. I could not read sixty term papers and did not assign topics. The head of the department did not like that and did not invite me back. Also, I had a funny experience.

There was a lady who taught a class immediately following my teaching. She walked into the class one morning as I got ready to leave and ordered me to stop. She said there was a standing rule for every lecturer to clean the board at the end of the class. I apologized for my ignorance and cleaned up what I wrote. But that was a very small portion of the board because someone had filled the whole board before I walked in. There was fire in her eyes as I tried to put on my coat. She barked another order at me. "You are to leave the board clean! Clean the whole board! Who are you?" I thought this is one of the black haters. I am Dr. Onwuegbu. If you saw what I cleaned and compared it with the writing on the board, you know I did not write what you insist I clean." She persisted in my cleaning the board. I thought she was acting as though slavery still ruled and said to her, "Go and find whoever wrote it and make him or her clean it." When I turned to leave the class, some of her male students winked at me. I smiled and walked out.

By the time I arrived from Nigeria, Melody was employed part-time at a Burger King near where we lived. She worked there for about three months before the end of the year. She so impressed the management that she was awarded the Employee of the Year over those who worked all year. On the other hand, Chinedum came home one evening with tears in his eyes. He had a serious disagreement with another employee, and they fired him. He was in the bathroom weeping and washing his face when I saw him. He felt they fired him because he was black. I tried to comfort him. This is Utah I said. All these happened before they rolled in the "forbidden fruit human sexuality course." Chinedum had a 3.8 grade point average in his senior year in high school. Mathematics was his best subject. His Math teacher claimed he disturbed his class and stopped him from attending class without telling his counselor, the Principal, or us parents. At the end of the term, he gave him a C grade. When I learned why he got the grade, I was angry and demanded a meeting with the school. At the meeting were the Principal, Chinedum's counselor, the teacher, and me. The teacher made an unprofessional statement at the meeting: "Chinedum is so smart he did not need the class." That made me angrier. I had one of my books, Discover Teaching, with me. Waving it in his face, I said, "See this book, I am the author. Get a copy and learn how to be a teacher. I demand you teach my son all the lessons he missed because of your arrogance and at his convenience. If not I will act against you. You are so bold to refuse to report to the Principal, his counselor and even his parents. Who gave you that absolute authority?" They were amazed that the father of this black boy was a doctor and an author. The Principal pleaded for forgiveness. The teacher pleaded for forgiveness.

Meanwhile, Chinedum had turned seventeen. Because I had not found a permanent job, I chose to sell Rainbow (a brand of vacuum cleaner). This was a product people used to clean homes, but the manufacturers did not want to call it a vacuum cleaner. At the same time, Chinedum decided to join the National Guard in order to help to finance his college education. Since he was not eighteen years old, his mother and I signed for him. He was still underage when he graduated from high school. He went to boot camp and returned. Shortly after, Saddam invaded Kuwait. His unit was called to active duty. My eighteen-year-old son was going to war. The news devastated me, and I felt I betrayed his trust and signed away his life for money with my signature instead of educating him.

On the morning his unit flew to Washington State from where the unit would fly to Kuwait, his friends and siblings gathered in our living room. Before they left, I asked them to hold hands for prayer. I sobbed as I prayed. I thanked the good, gracious, loving Father God in heaven that He knows and controls everything. I thanked Him for the gift of His Son to my son. I thanked Jesus, the Son of God, and my Immanuel for dying on the cross to forgive my sin and give me eternal life. I thanked him for giving me the Holy Spirit to indwell me, pray for, teach, help, and remind me of all things. I told the Trinity that I had no one else in the air, on land or sea, but the Three. I handed my son over to God and asked Him to please bring him home safely in the name of Jesus Christ and for His sake. Amen. By the time I stopped praying, everyone in the living room was sobbing. His sister and all his friends drove to the barrack with him.

At this time, Sweetie had a car. She also worked two jobs. Besides she drove me to wherever I had an appointment to demonstrate how to use the Rainbow. At the end of my demonstration, I called her to come and get me and my equipment. It was about early in the second week of December when Chinedum's unit flew to Washington State. Friday of the same week Sweetie drove me to a home where I demonstrated how the rainbow worked. I called her at the end of my demonstration to drive me home. As we parked the car and walked to our apartment, this peace I could not and still cannot describe suddenly overwhelmed me. I walked closer to my wife, put my hand around her shoulder, and said, "Sweetie, I have this peace I cannot even describe to you. There is no iota of worry in me, not about our son, job or anything else. It must be the peace of God." She said, "Praise God." I replied, "Hallelujah, Amen!'Come to me, all who labor and are heavily laden, and I will give you rest.' (Matthew 28:30)" We went to church service on Sunday, and I told Brenda, who taught the fifth grade Sunday school with me my experience. She surprised me with the comment, "Obed, you always have these experiences," when that was the only one I ever told her. I also told Thomas, the Associate Minister.

Our Monday came and went like every ordinary Monday. We were relaxing in our living room peacefully on Tuesday evening when the phone rang. Sweetie answered it and our son was at the other end. It was a collect call and Sweetie agreed to pay for it. The military had authorized his unit to go home and celebrate Christmas with their families. He requested a round trip ticket. We obliged. He came and went back after Christmas.

Sweetie and I attended Christ United Methodist where we were married more than eighteen years earlier. It was natural for us to attend there when we returned to Salt Lake City. However, either the sermons had changed, or we changed or both, and were not what we expected. Besides teaching the fifth grade, I introduced Bible study. But when the senior Minister started to preach a series on "The Things Jesus Shouldn't Have Said," and challenged anyone who disagreed with him to call him. I called him. This particular Sunday, his topic was Jesus' rebuke of the apostles after He calmed the storm: "You of little faith, why do you..." He claimed that was not the appropriate reaction from Jesus.

There were two secretaries and an associate Minister in the office. I hoped one of the secretaries would answer the phone. I would ask her to connect me with Thomas, the Associate Minister. Then, I would tell him what I wanted to discuss with the senior Minister and get his reaction. Then, decide what to do based on his advice. So I called. Guess who answered the phone. Tom, the senior Minister, answered the phone. I laughed so hard and said, "Tom this is Obed." He wanted to know what was so funny. I said God has a sense of humor and told him my plan before I talked with him. But God wanted him to answer it himself. Two of the points I raised in our discussion were 1. The disciples did not know who Jesus was. If they did, they would not be afraid and this is borne out by the question they asked, "... What sort of man is this, that even winds and sea obey him?" (Matthew 8:27). If they knew who Jesus Christ is, that He told them to cross to the other side would have been the assurance of success and safety. 2. "Perfect love casts out fear." (1 John 4:18). His answer, "Our love is not perfect." We had different understandings of whose love this love refers to. I believe it is God's perfect love not mine. We started to look for a new church.

In about the last month we attended Christ United two persons came to the church to ask for volunteers in their different ministries. One was Bruce B. He led a prison ministry involving a group of protestant churches in the Salt Lake area. I volunteered and was there for over two decades, even after Bruce retired. Even after the churches disbanded and all the original volunteers retired. I continued alone with the help of Joe Incardine and Paul Hewitt who shared the responsibility of taking me to the prison because of my blindness. The second visitor came from the University of Utah campus. He was also looking for volunteers. He was in charge of the protestant campus ministry. I made myself available. He looked at me and decided I, as a black man, could not teach the Bible to university students and determined what this black man was capable of doing. Looking askance he said, "I don't have any plumbing job for you." I smiled and said, "I have no experience in plumbing either." He asked, "Then what can you do?" When, at last, he knew me and what I had done, he covered his face with his palms and apologized. I helped him until he went back to the university for his advanced degree. Through the activities of this group, I became involved in an international students' Bible study.

Our son did go to war and fought in the first Desert Storm. My peace from God proved to be His true peace. For example, within 24 hours after my son's unit left the building they occupied, an Iraqi scud missile slammed that same building and killed 28 American soldiers from Pennsylvania who replaced his unit. Within a few months after the war started, President George H. W. Bush declared it won and over. I was typing one lonely midmorning when the phone rang. I picked it up, and our son was calling. He said he was sorry he missed his flight and would be flying to the U.S. by the next plane. Unawares he was playing his prank, I calmly replied, "Take care. God will bring you home safely." He said he was calling from New York City. They would be in California for about two weeks for debriefing. Then I got excited, thanked God, and called Sweetie. On the eve of his departure, he was promoted to specialist. His grandfather, who was a World War II veteran, entertained us with pizza on his return. When I wrote the story, a member of my Christian Writers group asked how I understood and explained the peace. My answer was, "God promised to take care of my son." However, the more I think about it today I believe God simply told me to have His peace and leave the worry to Him.

My wife's insurance matured about the same time the first Desert Storm started. The doctor at the clinic knew I needed surgery he could not perform. He referred me to the University of Utah Ophthalmology Department. After a few visits, I was scheduled for my first operation at the University. Sweetie drove me there and stayed with me until they wheeled me to the operating room. When the operation was over, and the doctor brought me out to Sweetie, he apologized for the long time the operation lasted. He said the operation took a little too long because I stopped breathing, which delayed them for twenty minutes. After a while, he used laser surgery on my right eye. He also performed another surgery on my left eye, but he applied local anesthetics to my face. As he talked to me while he operated, I asked him if he talked to the animal he operated on in the zoo. He said no. Of course, all I hoped for at this time was my sight would not get worse. However, that would not be the case.

Sweetie and I went to the state employment office. They gave us a psychological test. A few of the items looked silly to me, and I refused to answer them. When the result was out, it placed me at the 95 percentile. The white woman who gave the test was impressed and willing to help me find a job if she could. However, with my first eye operation, my Rainbow sales ended abruptly.

I was in a position to do what I had actually not done in my life i.e., look for a job. I attended Preliminary Teachers College immediately after grade six, Elementary Teachers College after one year of teaching, and High Elementary Teachers College. I never looked for a teaching job because before I completed teacher training, the Methodist Synod had assigned me to a school and provided transport for me. Even when I completed my Ph. D. program, all I did was submit my resume to the University and went to one interview, and I had a job. This time, as an applicant, I was on my own. I applied for one position in Pennsylvania as the vice president of a junior college. I knew I was late and said so in my application. My resume impressed them, and they encouraged me. When they rejected my application, the reason they gave was they chose someone who would be the vice president and teach. Another university called and asked if I was coming to a psychological conference. I was a member, but I could not afford to attend the conference. I forfeited the interview. I qualified for two or three others. One was in Kansas, and two were in Utah.

Kansas's advertisement was on the administration of special education. With my experience in founding the only special education college in Africa, developing the curriculum, the review of my study for the United Nations, and evaluating the Eighth World Conference on Special Education in Nairobi, Kenya, at the request of the UN and the Commonwealth, etc., they would at least invite me to the interview. I am not sure they asked for letters of recommendation, and I did not send any. The office later sent me a sketch of what the responsibility of the person who got the job would be; it was almost identical to the one I developed for Nigeria, except that I had better organization and interdepartmental participation in teaching practice. The plan was already published as chapter 19 in *Emergent Issues In Nigeria Education Vol. 1*. I planned to take the book with me to the interview. It was a great disappointment when I was not invited. If I was knowledgeable about telephone interviews at the time, I would have requested a telephone interview. But I did not.

Another job was at the University of Utah. The African American Studies department wanted a chairman. I applied for the job. My white American wife was working at the University at the time. A black woman at the personnel office recognized her as my wife. At the same time, the man at the President's office who received the applications and was probably the outgoing chair was also black. What I did not know was that my marriage to a white woman was offensive to them. I was in the office of another black man at the University discussing my application when he looked at my resume. He saw that one of my publications on intelligence was by the University of Ibadan Press. He called the black woman at the Personnel office. Her husband had attended the University of Ibadan. He raised the question of my candidacy for the job. That was when she spoke about the problem of my marriage to a white woman. My complaint to a popular black pastor in the City did not change anything.

Then, there was another job with the state board of education. One of the requirements was teacher certification. I wrote to Lyndon State College to confirm that I am a certified teacher. The reply was negative. I considered but did not have the moral courage to sue my beloved Lyndon for fraud. I called Professor Bisson. She was angry and contacted Esther who was the chair of the education department when I graduated. The next thing I saw was the best letter anyone could receive. By then, it was late. I wondered if God was saying something to me.

Having decided not to return to the Federal Ministry of Education in Nigeria, I sent my return ticket to my brother in Nigeria. He wrote to me and said he received ₦2,162. Later on, I sent him a check for ₦2,500 against my account at Oyo. He also acknowledged the receipt of the money. He later wrote to me and claimed Nwoko told him that someone had told him that I had walked out from an office, an indication I had a job. He followed that up with a list of expenditures totaling more than nine hundred thousand naira and asked me to send him the money. I ignored him. Thinking about it today, he believed that if I could send gifts to those thirteen families in Umuahia, Nigeria through him, I could give him whatever he demanded. Then he concocted another lie. He wrote to me and said the government ordered him to survey my plot at Ebute. Sweetie took the only amount of one hundred dollars in our account and sent it to him. I dreamed that he lied to get the money and wrote to him about it. He confirmed my dream. I wrote an angry letter reminding him of what I had done for him and his selfishness. All he did was accuse me of claiming to sustain his life. Surprised that I remembered the gifts I sent to him, he asked me if I wrote down every gift I gave him and reminded me that Jesus said we should not expect reward when we do a good deed. I refused to reply. I know he forgot that Jesus asked where the nine other lepers were when only one of them came to thank Him for healing him and God's warning to Israel for ingratitude.

There was a non-denominational protestant Christian conference in Salt Lake City. Sweetie and I attended the first two of the three-day conference. Each of the two days, the leader walked up to me and talked at length how God showed him how He planned to use me as an evangelist in a big country. He also called me to the platform to say something. Uchechi played organized soccer at this time. Still not satisfied with the church we attended; Sweetie met Ann the mother of Eric, who played soccer with Uchechi. However, the conversation started, and she invited Sweetie to her church. She was surprised when Sweetie asked if they preached from the Bible. That is how we started to attend Evangelical Free Church in Salt Lake City.

Chapter 48

Living with Blindness

My sight was not improving. However, the rate of deterioration was slow in the left eye. I went to see Dr. Crandall the eye doctor. He looked into my right eye and said to the nurse with him, "There is nothing we can do for this eye. We will send him to Dr..." He told me to go to the doctor from India. As I walked towards the room, I wondered what the doctor would tell or do to me. He was on the phone, I assumed, with Dr. Crandall. He completely ignored me as I walked in. When he was through, he ordered me to sit down. With an air of arrogance, and without even touching my face, said to me, "I am going to remove your eyeball and replace it with an artificial eyeball. I looked at him indignantly and, with dismay, said, "You can't, and I will not allow you to do it." I walked out thinking whether they had placed themselves in the place of God to decide my fate without even asking my opinion. I was more offended when the office called me a few days later "to remind me of my appointment with the doctor." I told whoever was on the phone that I made no appointment with the doctor and had no intention to see him. I called Crandall and asked him if that was the only option available. He said no and made an appointment for me. I did not know that he became angry because I refused to accept the artificial eye.

Sweetie drove me to the clinic on the day of the appointment. The doctor took me to a small room, gave me a sheet of paper marked

X on a dotted line, and asked me to sign on the dotted line. I did. The nurse in the room showed me a small bed in the room and asked me to lie on it. The doctor came back and injected two substances into me: one into my arm and the other into my eye without any explanation. The first one put me to sleep. The last one was in my right eye. Within a short time, a white substance covered my right eye. It felt hard, and it was frozen. I was angry, but I have a Ph.D. and have signed his paper. I did not have the means and could not sue him. Even if I sued him, a black man might not win in Utah. My only choice was to look for another doctor. Also, I had already been mistreated by the woman at the desk. Twice I was to see the doctor at 1:30 p.m. Each time, they bypassed my file and called white people. When I asked why I had not seen the doctor, they said he was busy. Once, I made a fuss about it. Paula a woman who was at Christ United when we were there, saw me and called me Dr. Onwuegbu. Their attitude and behavior towards me changed.

Some members of Evangelical Free met on Wednesday evenings to pray. I was one of them. Don, another member, saw my eye and inquired about it. After I told my experience, he recommended Dr. Wooldridge and gave me his telephone number and address. My Sweetie drove me to the office. When we reached the office, Dr. Crandall's name was also on the door. Dr. Wooldridge called Crandall's office at the University and requested my file. When he looked through it, he suggested surgery by Crandall. The file was scanty. I asked if Crandall was the same one who felt he could do anything he wanted with my eye with or without my approval. He said yes. I said to him, "I would rather go completely blind forever than have him look into my eye again. He had two interns in his office. Before he told them what Crandall (now late) did to my eye, he asked me to block my ears to prevent me from hearing him. Then he suggested Dr. Zabriskie. I accepted. I have been with Dr. Zabriskie for more than twenty years as I write this sentence. He refers to me as his best patient. I still enjoy him. Dr. Wooldridge also referred me to the Utah State Eye Services. From there, I learned about the library for the blind and other services for the blind. I have read more books from the library than I ever read.

Though Braille was taught at my college, I did not think I would be blind and did not take it. So here I am, blind and unable to read Braille. I have authored at least thirteen books and wish to continue writing. I could not touch type when we left the U.S. on January 3, 1976, to return to Nigeria, and offices were not equipped with computers. After twelve years, when we returned, typewriters had become obsolete. Even Sweetie had to learn to use a computer at the bank. She then convinced me to use her dad's computer. The big problem with her dad's computer was he bought parts and put them together. As a result, whatever computers emit that affects the eye adversely seriously damaged my right dying eye. The left eye got worse. The doctor declared me legally blind. I was still able to read a little with my left eye.

Our financial state became problematic. While our son was in Saudi, he called collect as often as he could. Before long, our phone bill was over $480. The phone company cut off our long-distance connection. He could not call, and we could not call any long distance either. Unknown to us was the fact that before he left for the war, he signed his military pay over to his civilian roommate. To his dismay, on his return, the money was gone. Did they think he would not return from the war? He did not ask us, his parents nor inform his siblings before he assigned his salary over to them.

About this time, a man who attended Christ Methodist Church visited me with a project. Three officials of the Nigerian National Petroleum Corporation (NNPC) sent him a proposal. They selected his name from a catalog. They claimed the previous military government officials said they bought materials worth $32M. They asked the man to send them a bill for $32M. They would pay the money into his account. He would get twenty percent of the total. He offered to pay me ten percent of his share. I refused to participate.

I applied to the Granite District for the job of a substitute teacher. I also took two of my books with me. The official who hired me promised to pay me fifty dollars each day. However, when I received my first paycheck, it was calculated at thirty-five dollars. When I protested, the person who paid me did not know I was a doctor and readjusted the pay. Still, we did not make enough to pay for our two youngest sons' lunches at school. The district supplemented their feeding at school. When Chinedum joined the military he tested so high that they told him he could choose any field of study. He chose to drive the truck. When I expressed my displeasure, he told me he chose what he would enjoy. So he drove the tankers right behind the tanks in Kuwait. On his return from the war, he was overjoyed to discover that his mother had bought a car. Unfortunately, my wife does not know how to say no to her children's requests. Chinedum took advantage of that. What we did not know was that he had collected unpaid speeding tickets along the way. He had an Iranian friend, Page, who we later learned was an illegal immigrant. It seemed their mission was chasing girls. His world was falling apart, and he did not know it. I knew he was in trouble when I warned him and he said, "I am only nineteen." At another time, he asserted, "It is my life."

I knew from my psychology of human development that a strict father or mother with a permissive father or mother does not produce the best children, which is our situation. Chinedum took undue advantage of the situation. For example, when he asked to take the car and I said no, his response was, "It's my mother's car, and I am asking her." She allowed him to use it.

We started to attend Evangelical Free Church and liked the sermons. Also, I attended a Bible study session at Jim's house with some other members of the church. Members of the group were the first to know a little more about my background than the rest of the members of the church. From Jim's knowledge of me, he requested me to accompany him to the Rescue Mission. Some of the time, I preached, but most of the time, I prayed. A couple from the Church followed us one Sunday. She was really short, almost half as tall as her husband. I prayed and she could not get over the prayer. So many times, she repeatedly said, "Your prayer was anointed." She told me the Church met on Wednesday evenings for prayer and invited me to be a part of the group. That's how I became a member of the Wednesday prayer group. A short time after that, she and her husband left the state.

We could not meet our financial obligations at the first apartment we lived in and had to move. At this time, I was contributing financially. We moved to a duplex. Sweetie worked one and a half jobs. Our daughter lived on her own while the three boys lived with us. It was December, and Christmas was near. As poor as we were, I thought about poorer people at home and how many of them would go without unless someone helped. My mental calculation brought the number to about thirteen families. One elderly woman had no child of her own. Two lost their adult sons before we left, and one lost her son, who was my classmate throughout elementary school. My aunt and brother were there, along with his family and others. Thanks to God, a small amount could go far. We bought the check and were about to post it when we had a major car problem.

Both Sweetie and I would not receive any other check until after Christmas. Both of us could wait till after Christmas. But what should we say to our two youngest boys who live with us? Even if we cashed the check, it would not take care of the car. We decided to mail the check and promise the boys gifts worth fifty dollars each when we received our checks after Christmas. That was what we did. The boys accepted our offer.

It was a few days before Christmas, and as we sat in our living room, the doorbell rang. It was already dark. I decided to answer the door myself. I turned on the porch light. When I opened the door, there was nobody anywhere. On a second look, I saw a basket. I carried it in, and we opened it. There was a dress for Sweetie, a shirt and pants for me, a big turkey, and $120 inside the basket. That was twenty dollars more than we planned to spend for our two sons. God had given us more than we planned for Christmas, and it was not even over. A few days later, the owner of the car dealership my wife worked for held a Christmas party for his employees and gave each of them a turkey. Sweetie came home with her turkey. We gave it to the lady who occupied the other side of our duplex. She and her son had a good Christmas, and that started an exchange of Christmas gifts for the time we lived there.

All of a sudden, our two oldest, who were students at the University of Utah, registered for what qualified as a pervert cause they called human sexuality. That became a license for promiscuity. The first time I heard about it was when I was typing, and Chinedum was in the kitchen using vulgar language. I could not believe what came out of his mouth. I called from my room, "Chinedum if I hear one more dirty word out of your mouth, I will kick you out of this apartment." It was still winter when he brought his friend Paige home. He introduced him as his best friend. He asked us to allow Paige to stay in the duplex for two weeks. He promised that Paige would feed himself for the two weeks and then leave. He knew he was lying because Paige had no prospect of getting any job soon. We were not even feeding five mouths, let alone a sixth. After almost four weeks and Paige was not contributing, I called Chinedum and reminded him of his promise. He became angry. I gave him a twenty-four hour ultimatum for his friend to leave. He promised to go with him. I accepted his challenge. He called Paige, who was in the basement bedroom, and told him they had to leave. They departed.

About three days later, Chinedum returned without his illegal alien friend. We learned what happened later. They were homeless for two nights, and Chinedum got the worst of it. The first day, he called his sister, who allowed him to stay part of the day but not at night. His friend advised him to return home. He still did not learn anything from the experience. My wife's car was still available to Chinedum, and he continued to drive as though there was no speed limit. It was about 2:00 am one Saturday when the telephone rang. It was Paige at the other end. Chinedum had been arrested for speeding. This time, a ticket was out of the question, and he would be tried on Monday morning unless he was bailed before then. I had saved some amount in the bank, but I could not go to the bank on Saturday. By the time we found out how much he owed, he had been tried and sentenced. We went to the bank and withdrew the money. Sweetie went and paid the money, and they released him. His thanks was to blame Paige, his friend, because he told him not to tell us as he planned to find someone else to bail him. I thought he lost it all. I warned him that he would pay me back every penny of it.

Chinedum came home one day and announced he was one of many applicants for a scholarship Nordstrom was interviewing for. He expressed an air of optimism. A few days later, he said he had received it. It paid his tuition and bought all his books. Besides, he was employed and clothed with a smart uniform, jacket, pants, shoes, and tie. He was making as much as if not more than his mother who was employed by the University of Utah College of Nursing. We were still struggling to make ends meet. I waited for him to initiate financial help. When he failed, I suggested he contribute one hundred dollars every month to feeding. He did not see why he would live with his parents and, as an adult, contribute to his feeding and free accommodation and decided to move out. He rented an apartment for over three hundred dollars a month and fed himself. Besides his regular employment, he also traveled with his National Guard unit some weekends. One of those weekends, his unit was in California. The phone rang. Uche was closest to the phone, and the operator said, "Will you accept a collect call?" Uche asked if he should accept it. When I asked who was at the other end, it was Chinedum. No was the answer. His unit returned to Salt Lake. Knowing that the family attended church service on Sunday, he lay low until we were at church. He came to the duplex and entered through the window. When we entered our bedroom he had spread three twenty-dollar bills on our bed to complete the payment of the money I paid to bail him out. That was his way of saying goodbye. From then on whenever he called and I answered the phone, he hung up.

Meanwhile, I was trying my hands at a number of things, including writing. My Christian activities also increased. Bruce took me to the prison ministry, where we joined two other ladies and held service for the inmates on the first and third Sundays of the month. When I started with them, we met for two hours each Sunday. The choir came for the first hour, after which the rest of them came for the service. After a while, I suggested having all of them come for the two hours. I would lead a Bible study during the first hour while the choir practiced. Bruce, who led the group, agreed. That was how we started the Bible study. About the same time another older lady who attended EV Free told me about another prayer group that met once a week and invited me to it. The gentleman who led the group came from Texas with his family. He was a pastor without a church. The group was what one would call a Christian community for as long as he led it. Again, there were predictions about me. One of them said she had a vision of me as a preacher, and the Pastor's wife said she saw me as Aaron the high priest. He moved from state to state. I left the group after he left Salt Lake City. I also joined the Christian Writers Association of Salt Lake. I taught Sunday school and Vacation Bible study at EV Free. Evangelical Free also sponsored a Christian school. There was a couple at the church at this time who had two daughters. One of the daughters died in a car accident. I did not know them at the time.

As one little girl asked her mother, "Mother, do you know Mr. Obed? He is the only chocolate man at our church." I became known as the only black man at the church. While many of the people knew me, I scarcely knew but a few. However, Joy Holder's name came up every Wednesday evening at the prayer meeting. It was not only that they lost their daughter but also she was sick, so sick that the doctors did not know what to do for her. Her sickness was so serious, she took sick leave from teaching. Each time someone brought up the problem, I suggested the prayer group should go to her house and pray for her. Each time I received the same discouraging answer. "It is the duty of the elder board to go and pray for her." I decided Satan was having a good time at the cost of the family and it must be stopped.

Jesus said to His disciples, "This can only be cured through fasting and prayer." (Mark 9:29) So I decided to fast and pray. One day, I fasted from morning till 2:55 p.m. and prayed to Jesus Christ, "Dear Lord Jesus Christ, I am doing this in obedience to You. I am going to call Joy and pray for her. If You are in this, she should answer the phone after it rings twice. If she answers it at the first or third ring, I will not pray. I will only pray if she answers at the second ring, in Jesus name Amen." I dialed the number and she answered at the second ring. I thanked God and told her my prayer to Jesus and prayed as she wept. I did not know what happened till Sunday.

I was waiting for Sweetie at the church corridor after service the following Sunday when Donna walked to me. She was one of about four families that migrated from Christ United Methodist Church to EV Free. She said to me, "Obed, now I know one thing you can do." "Really," I said, wondering what this one thing was. Joy told the women's Sunday school class what happened after I prayed for her. Her temperature that had ranged between 103-104 F subsided and she felt as though cold water was poured on her. She went to her doctor who said, "I do not know what you did. Whatever happened to you, you are healed." More than four years later two women friends from another state visited the church. She brought them to me and said to them, "This is Obed, the man who prayed for me and I was healed."

One of those incidents about my color I did not expect in church greeted me one day. Mr. Harldson the financial officer of the church was distributing cards for a dinner evening at the church. The cards cost $12 per couple. Some paid as they received the cards and others promised to pay when they were served. I was one of those who did not come to church with money. As he stretched his hand to me with the card I said, "I'll pay when the meal is served." He withdrew the card and gave it to someone else. That white person did not pay him immediately either. On the evening of the event, I took Sweetie out to make sure she did not cook though it cost me more.

On the following Bible study evening at Jim's house, many members said they missed Sweetie and me at the event. I assured them we missed them also and told them why we were not there and where we ate. Jim asked Harldson if he knew who I was. When he saw me in church the following Sunday, he came over to me and addressed me as Dr. But he fell short of offering an apology. He also told the senior pastor. The wife saw me and asked if they should address me as Dr. I ignored her. Then there was pressure from certain members of the church for me to join the church. "Obed join the church so as to become a member of the leadership team. But it would be more than two years before we joined the church. By this time, almost everyone with a prayer need had come to me.

While we lived in the duplex, SueAnn, our friend from Connecticut, paid us a second visit in Salt Lake City. This time, she came with her son Matthew, who is three months younger than Uche, our youngest. At the same time, Uche had a friend who was about three years older than him. The boy came over to stay for some days with us. Unfortunately, he was a dubious character, but we did not know it. We did not know where Uche met him. The boys slept in the basement. Matthew noticed the boy took Uche out through the window after midnight to smoke cigarettes and told his mother. SueAnn told us. When we confronted Uche, he confirmed it. We sat Uche down and made him call the boy at his home. I warned the boy to never come to our duplex again. We thought we had stopped Uche from smoking, but we did not know he was already hooked. He continued to smoke secretly. I unintentionally encouraged it by giving him and his brother money for any A they earned in school.

It turned out the owner of the duplex was a Shylock. I was not aware that Sweetie was not able to pay the rent on time. He charged us such exorbitant past-due fees; it might have been more than two or three hundred percent, and she paid it without telling me. When I learned about it and reported to him, it was too late. However, we went to arbitration.

Soon our daughter was living what she learned in her human sexuality class. It seemed I was about to lose the two oldest children. When I heard where she was living, I took the phone and called her. I gave her a twenty-four-hour ultimatum to return to our apartment or change her name to something else and never to be associated with my name again. She moved back to our apartment within the time I specified. A few days before she returned to the apartment, a man who went to Desert Storm with her brother rang our doorbell. When I opened the door, he was carrying a basket full of dirty clothes. He told me Melody sent him to come and do the laundry at our apartment. I warned him to turn back and never to show his face at the apartment again. He never came again. Soon, my daughter, who had a double major and was doing well at the University, decided men had become more important than education. She decided to get married.

One day, as I typed one of my books, my wife called me to the living room of our apartment. Melody was there wearing the diamond of a man she brought to show me as her future husband. Sweetie and her siblings were seated. He was not a student. I knew this black American man could not have lived this long without being married before. After voicing my objection, I went straight to the point. "Is this your first marriage?" He said, "No, Sir." "And you are divorced?" His reply was, "Yes, Sir." "How many children are involved?" He said, "No children." He was in the Air Force. I left them with my "No" hanging in the air and went and resumed my typing. She wrote her uncle in Nigeria and complained about me. Eventually, they got married. One of the main reasons I brought them back to the U.S., namely education, was slipping away. I could not stop it. Within a short time after the wedding, she flew to Japan to meet him in Okinawa. I shed my secret tears at the Salt Lake Airport.

    Once we became members of EV Free Church, it did not take long before someone nominated me to the elder board of the church. The church voted me in. Chinedum talked about a girlfriend named Pam. He drove a vehicle to our duplex apartment one evening and showed it to us as a car he was buying for himself. It turned out he was buying it for Pam his girlfriend. Yet he had no car of his own.

    The woman who occupied the other half of the duplex with her son moved out, and two families moved in. They had two daughters about the same ages as our two youngest boys. The girls waited outside and watched for our boys. However, we seemed suspicious of the activities that went on in their home. Suddenly, they moved out. One late night after midnight, there was sawing and knocking in the apartment. We could not sleep. We called the police. The police came and arrested the man, and he was one of the last occupants stealing from the house. We found a new apartment and moved.

    Our experience the first hour in the new apartment was unpleasantly unexpected. As we carried our furniture into the living room, we noticed water dripping from the first floor through the ceiling into our basement apartment. Within a short time, water filled the apartment. Worse still, the man who took care of the apartments locked the unoccupied apartment where the water leaked from and went away. We had only one option, Sweetie called Rick her brother. He came with his big water vac. It took him hours to dry the carpet. By then, the tank upstairs was almost empty. By late afternoon, the man we thought was the owner of the apartment but who was only the caretaker came. He unlocked the door and turned off the water. The good news was we were to witness everything, and our furniture was not damaged.

Shortly after we settled, I was alone typing when the doorbell rang. When I opened the door, I saw a tall woman looking at me. She introduced herself as Jill. She and her husband had come to see the apartment above us but could not get inside. She asked if she could come in to see what ours looked like. I allowed her to go around and went back to my typing. Then she came to our bedroom and saw the special computer inbuilt space where I typed. It impressed her, and she called her husband to come and look. They rented the place. She looked into our apartment one day and saw Sweetie and proclaimed in surprise, "Sue what are you doing here?" She did not know Sweetie was married to a black man. Jill turned out to be a student nurse at the college of nursing where Sweetie was employed.

As is the case with children, Uche told his classmates that his dad wrote books. When his Vice Principal heard that his father was a doctor and an author, she became angry. This white woman with a Ph. D. concluded there was no way this black boy could have a father with a Ph. D., be an author, and a president of a college. She is determined to prove him a liar. The phone rang one day, and I picked it up. The voice at the other end introduced herself and asked if I was Uche's dad. When I confirmed that I am, she requested to see some of my books. Without thinking or asking why, we arranged for a day. The day came, and I took Discover Teaching, The Structure and Phases of Intelligence: A Construct, and Special Education: *A Lonely Voice*, which is a chapter in a book of readings. I met the Principal, introduced myself, and told her why I was there. She called her vice principal. I walked to her office, and she was confused. She glanced at the books. After some time, she went and made a copy of *Special Education's A Lonely Voice* and said, "We even need a program like this here in Utah." It was almost graduation time before I learned why she called me. She did not even expect me to come to the school, let alone bring books.

Chapter 49

In the Will of God

> When you pass through the waters, I will be with you;
> and through the rivers, they shall not overwhelm you;
> when you walk through fire you shall not be burned,
> and the flame shall not consume you. Isaiah 43:2 (ESV)

This chapter is a classical demonstration of spiritual and demonic war being waged simultaneously. The war was waged at home, at church and at the prison. There were successes and there were failures.

Melody and her husband were in Japan and left their car with Chimso who was a senior in high school. He had graduated as a President's scholar in junior high. He had made up his mind to study architecture at the university and was taking advanced placement (AP) courses. On the other hand, Uche appeared uninterested in education. Even when Chimso tried to help him with his math homework, he looked angry and uninterested. Though he was good in sports, especially soccer and basketball and acting, and even music, he would not get along with the instructors. I was called in, and I laid it down for him. That term, he made 3.8. He was even invited and participated in a national television show, Touched By An Angel, that was filmed here in Salt Lake City. Unfortunately, the friends he made in school had a bad influence on him. Ironically, he was interested in law enforcement and the only A.P. course he took was a police course. He rode and still goes on rides with police officers as I write this chapter.

It appeared that Chinedum was doing well at Nordstrom and at school. He even got his younger brother Chimso a job there. Sweetie was still working full-time at the College of Nursing and part-time at a car dealership. Chinedum bought a new car there, and Sweetie co-signed for him without my knowledge. It was not long before Sweetie had major surgery. No one heard from Chinedum. I called him and asked if he knew where his mother was. He did not. We were still at the hospital when he came with a girlfriend he introduced as Pam his wife. They were not engaged, and I thought he was joking. However, Pam was pregnant, but it was not showing. That was just the beginning of the problems. Sweetie recovered from the surgery. But Chinedum was out with as many girls as he could find creating problems. With Pam pregnant, one would think that Chinedum would settle and take care of her. She urged him to inform his parents but without success. Bang! Chinedum was arrested. Pauline, another so-called girl friend, told him that another man Chinedum knew kissed her. Chinedum went to his house to beat him up. He locked his door and Chinedum forced it open. The man called the police, and he was arrested. The judge considered his service at Desert Storm, our presence in the court, and God's mercy in her heart and gave him a suspended sentence and good behavior for a period of time.

I completed my first Christian book and submitted it for publication. The publisher read it, and before I received his reply, I had dreamed that he would reject the book. His reason was I had not published before. When I talked about the manuscript and my dream at our Wednesday prayer meeting, the pastor in his unbelief insisted I tell them the dream. I refused to please him. When finally I received the letter, I had actually read the letter in my dream with a few additions.

For example, the publisher wanted me to pay him over two thousand dollars for him to publish the work. I requested he return my manuscript, and I received it.

There must have been a misunderstanding at the church of which we were unaware. Shortly before the pastor preached an emotional sermon on his last Sunday, he told me that Chinedum had come to his church office for counseling. He said that he had disobeyed his father and he was in trouble. He got two women pregnant and did not know what to do. When I called him that evening, he was at Pauline's. Where are you? He told me. When I asked who she was? He said she was a girlfriend. Finally, he told me she was pregnant. "Does she not know about Pam?" She did. I decided not to have anything to do with her. Even after he chose her over Pam, I refused to attend the wedding. By the difference in the ages of the children, she was not pregnant when she claimed to be. His problems with her were just beginning.

Chimso had graduated from high school and earned 24 advanced placement hours. Harvard University wrote and asked him to apply for admission. He refused to go that far. He chose the University of Utah over Arizona and California Polytechnic State University. He was also working for Nordstrom and had bought his own car. I completed my second book and did not even have money to mail the manuscript. At this time, Pam had given birth to Chidi, our second grandchild. I was alone in our basement apartment one day when the phone rang. When I answered, it was our son-in-law in Japan. He announced the birth of our first grandchild. "Congratulations, Grandpa." I shouted, "Praise the Lord. Halleluiah! Boy or girl." He said a boy.

Since I did not have a penny to post my manuscript, I arranged with Chimso to come during his lunchtime to take me to the bank so I could borrow a hundred dollars. 12 noon is one of the hours I pray during the day. As long as I could read, I read the Bible before I prayed. As was the case at times when I read the Bible, I simply asked God to choose a passage for me. I took my Bible and said, "Dear Lord, please give me a passage to read in Jesus' name. Amen." When I opened the Bible, Proverbs 22 was looking at me. I started to read it. Soon, I was at verse seven, and it read, "The borrower is a slave to the lender." I stopped reading. I prayed, "Okay Lord, if You don't want me to be a slave to the bank You have to solve this problem Your way so that I will be a slave only to You, in Jesus' name. Amen." I called Chimso and told him not to come. When he returned home, he asked why I stopped him from coming to get me? I told him. His reaction was, "I wondered what happened."

Bett, a member of EV Free church also attended the Wednesday evening prayer meetings. She was a teacher in the Midwest. She moved to Salt Lake City after her divorce. Her ex-husband sent her about eighty-six thousand dollars as a part of her share of their business. She offered to give me one or two thousand dollars. I told her one thousand was enough. She gave me a check for one thousand dollars at the next Wednesday's prayer meeting. God gave me tenfold the amount I would have indebted myself to the bank. I thanked God and gave about thirteen percent of it to God's work.

I woke up one morning and saw Sweetie and the children off for the day. After typing a few pages I walked to the kitchen to eat my brunch. The sun was shining when I walked to the kitchen. It was spring. I looked at the Rocky Mountains. They looked majestic and gorgeous with all the flowers sprouting everywhere. I was overcome by God's creation and the beauty of it all. I decided to fast and praise God for His creation. That was one of the most meaningful fasts I ever had. Sunday came and the preacher based his sermon on Psalm 90.

As my spiritual life grew the enemy was busy attacking my flesh through my oldest son. It was not only that he had two women pregnant at the same time, he had decided to marry the Mormon woman. He also asked me to attend his wedding. I refused though his mother and the younger siblings attended. Sweetie and I went to bed one night. Suddenly she was sobbing. For the first time, I learned we were so much in debt that the only way out was a declaration of bankruptcy. Chinedum had failed to keep up with his car payment. Sweetie cosigned with him. She also borrowed from "instant loan" to pay part of the debt. Worse still, though she had paid the amount she borrowed with some interest, the bank was demanding much much more as interest. The car dealership repossessed the car. We declared bankruptcy.

As if that was not enough problem, the apartment became problematic. Our shower began to flood. I called the caretaker. He would not answer his phone. I wrote to him and there was no reply. Finally, I sent him a certified letter. He showed up angry that I sent him a certified letter. When I confronted him about his avoidance behavior, his excuse was he had many other apartments he took care of. However, he employed someone who repaired it.

Meanwhile, it was a midterm break, and Chinedum and Pauline planned a trip to California. By this time Chinedum had a second daughter. I thought he had enough earnings from his employment. Unfortunately, the money he was going to waste was his tuition scholarship money. On his return, he went back to the University and completed his courses but did not receive his grades. With the discovery that he did not pay the tuition also came the end of the scholarship. He continued to work but living with Pauline was daily becoming like living in hell. He came over to our apartment with TaMia, his daughter, one day. He lay on Uche's bed and talked to Pauline. He wept and told her he regretted meeting her. The daughter ran to me weeping and said, "Daddy is crying. Daddy is crying." The worst was still to come.

One evening, the phone rang, and Sweetie answered it. It was bad news. Chinedum overdosed himself. He was on his way to an emergency room. Sweetie was almost in tears. It was Chinedum and he said he loves you and me. When I asked why Sweetie's eyes were teary she replied, "That's what people say when they want to commit suicide." I asked Chimso to get ready and drive me to the clinic they took Chinedum to. On arrival, the first person I met was the doctor in charge. I introduced myself as Dr. Onwuegbu and the father of his patient. His statement was "He is hurting." I said, "I know." He told me that Chinedum overdosed. But he had taken care of that problem and took me to his bed.

When I reached his bedside Pauline was with him weeping. He was awake and said he was sorry. Chimso was there while Pauline described what happened. One of his friends walked into the room and took me aside. She said Chinedum had cried all week and recounted all the bad things his marriage had done to him and his future. Once we were sure he would be okay, we drove home. He was released after a short time. Of course, the marriage ended in divorce. He called me one day and requested to return to our apartment. I told him he must fulfill two conditions if he wished to come back. He asked what they were. "1. You must join the four of us every morning in our morning devotion. 2. You must go to church every Sunday with us." He accepted the two conditions and came to live with us.

Meanwhile, the prison ministry was progressing well, but my experience in the elder board was anything but satisfactory. After about two years without a pastor, the new pastor was well-received. The church gave him a ten thousand dollar gift to help him purchase a house. The church grew from over three hundred to over five hundred. The church also owned Intermountain Christian School (ICS). A man donated land to the church in Draper. Salt Lake City was growing in population. The church was located at the center of that growth. As the population of the church grew so did the financial state. Pride and materialism reared their ugly heads.

First the senior pastor proposed to hire more staff and build more offices to accommodate them in anticipation of more growth. Four more members of staff were added. The elder board was in session one day when he introduced another item. He introduced the topic by saying, "The spirit has been speaking to me." What the spirit was saying to him was the church should sell its property at the present site and develop the land at Draper. Even some businesspeople had approached him and made an offer. However, the man had said he would not pay anything for the property except for the piece of land. Only about two elders spoke in favor of the proposal.

I could no longer hold on without saying what I believed. I started by saying "The Spirit did not tell me what I am about to say. I am opposed to moving the church to Draper. If we want to move anything to Draper, let us move the high school and leave the church and the grade school at its current site. If, in the future, we discover the need to expand, then we can build a satellite church by the high school for people in Draper. At the end of my speech, the pastor for evangelism said he had thought about the same thing. That put cold water, but not ice on the topic. No decision was taken that day. On our way, the chairman who gave me a ride said he thought the pastor's idea was good. I said I did not see anything good about it. At the next meeting, more people agreed with me. The pastor said, "Maybe I have been listening too much to my staff." I said to myself, "Your staff is the spirit that spoke to you."

Later there was a problem between him and the choir director. I called him and pleaded for peace. He had told her to leave the church. I told him the church was bigger than either of them. It is the church of Jesus Christ. I promised to go to see the lady with him. He promised to go but did not. I think his attitude was, "My presence increased the membership and raised the money; therefore, I can spend the money my way and keep or send away any member." That created a problem.

Salaries took almost all the money. His salary was more than seventy-nine thousand dollars not including health insurance. He hired a music pastor for sixty-five thousand dollars. We had an associate pastor, a youth pastor, and an evangelism pastor. The Principal of the school got sick at one time. The elder board wanted to help him financially. The board did not know how much to give him. It took the matter to the general meeting. The church asked the board to come up with a specific amount for it to consider. At the next meeting of the board, the pastor said he gave the Principal so and so according to what the church decided. No one challenged his claim. I did. I said the church told this board to present it with a specific amount at its next meeting to consider. The man who took the minutes at the church general meeting was not present at the Board meeting. The rest of them would neither dispute nor support my statement. The chair said, "Obed listens very well. If he said so, that is what happened. I believe him." I thought the rest of them were lying in their silence. Soon the pastor became sick. He was in the hospital for a few days. The Sunday he came to church the elders went to his office to pray for him. He stood up and hugged everybody. When I stepped forward to hug him he sat down. His friend walked in, and he stood up and hugged him. Then he thanked everybody who called and left a message. He concluded: I returned all the calls except Obed's. By their own designation, I am the hugger and prayer warrior." But I did not pray. I waited till the end of the prayer time and walked out of the office. I felt that the devil was on the four corners of the ceiling controlling the hearts of men, and I determined to resign from the board. But I had to pray and give them time.

At the next meeting of the Board, the secretary was there and read the minutes, which confirmed what I said. I suggested a letter of gratitude to the choir director. The chair and the pastor were to get together and write it. But they did not. The pastor blamed the chair when I called. At this meeting, the pastor was still inviting those who disagreed with him to leave the church. He supported his action with Paul's rejection of Mark. I called the chair one evening and resigned my membership of the board. He asked me to reconsider my decision and promised to keep it a secret until the next board meeting in case I changed my mind.

Someone made a statement in church the following Sunday that prompted me to mount the pulpit and speak about prayer. A week or two later, the phone rang, and by the time I got to it, it had stopped ringing. When I removed the receiver there was a message. I listened to it. Whoever called heard me speak about prayer in church and called the church office for my number. She requested me to call her, and I did. She came over. In less than two hours we read as much of the Bible as we could. Tears ran from her eyes as she called me the blind who led her through the Bible. She gave her life to Jesus.

There was a church general meeting that weekend. A few people gave their witness including the Vice chair of the board. The chair made no remarks. I stood up and spoke about a lady who got my number from the church office and called me. She came over to our house and, in about two hours, gave her life to Jesus. Before I completed my last sentence the chair was up and talking. The one thing that remained for him to say was to call me a liar. He demanded to know if the person existed and the name of the person. I did not even know that Kari the lady was sitting behind me. She stood up immediately, raised her hand, and said, "I am here, and my name is Kari." The man shut up and sat down as the people roared, cheered, and clapped their hands.

As time went on things got worse. The staff was not getting along. The pastor said he stopped the youth pastor from attending the elder board because he was too outspoken. Soon, the music pastor, who the senior pastor called executive pastor, resigned. The church had a general meeting before he resigned. I asked Sweetie to take me to the meeting. I went to the meeting to voice my concerns. By this time the church had gone from over the five hundred peak to about three hundred. I asked the leadership to consider what it is doing to the church. "I had been reminded several times that Paul sent away John Mark. We should read the entire Bible. It was that same Paul, not Barnabas, who told Timothy to bring John Mark because he was profitable to him (2 Timothy 4:11). Mark is even more profitable to us than he was to Paul. Without him we might not have the Gospel of Mark today. I don't know how many Marks we are driving out from this church." Before I stood up to leave, Randy, a former elder, spoke and supported what I said. Sweetie and I left. It was very quiet when we left.

The following day, the pastor went to Randy's wife, who was a secretary at the school, and asked her if he should resign. She did not have a yes or no answer for him. My prayer ministry was prospering. Gloria, a lady at the church, was diagnosed with breast cancer. Because I had left the board she requested prayer. She asked the elder board and Obed to come and pray for her after service. We did and God healed her. The board that had nothing to say about the pastor while I was a member rated him C's and D's. He saw the handwriting on the wall and started looking for a job elsewhere. He invited me to come and pray for him before his sermons on Sundays. He said to me, "Do you know you draw people to yourself?" I felt sorry for him one Sunday when he came to hug me, and I shook his hand instead, and he said, "You would not hug the unhuggable?" By the time he was ready to leave Utah, he had completed a house in Draper that he put on the market for more than three hundred ninety thousand dollars. One wondered if the house influenced his choice of moving the church to Draper. Gloria was completely healed of the cancer.

God was also performing miracles at the prison. Some Muslims and Mormons came to my Bible study. A Muslim claimed Jesus predicted the coming of Mohammed. He promised the baptism of the Holy Spirit. I asked if Jesus predicted that in the Koran. He said no, in the Bible. I turned to Acts 1:8 and he read it. He confirmed the reading. I asked how a few days turned out to be almost six hundred years. Then we turned to Acts 2:2-4 where the baptism of the Holy Spirit occurred in ten days after the promise. That was the end of that.

The Mormons wanted to know the difference between them and Christians. I started him with the cross. 1 Corinthians 1:18, "For the word of the cross is folly to those who are perishing, but to us who are being saved it is the power of God." You believe that you will do ninety percent and Jesus will complete the remaining ten percent. I asked him to show me where that is in the Bible. He could not. I asked him to turn to Isaiah 64:6, Haggai 2:28, and Habakkuk 1:13. Then I told him to turn to Ephesians 2:8-9 and Colossians 2:13-14. Then I asked him to turn to John 3:5, and verse 16. After the discussion I told them I had to use the remaining hour for the rest of the class and my lesson for the week. However, the best miracle at the prison was with Pat. Unfortunately, it started well but ended in failure.

Pat was serving two five-to-life sentences when I met him at the prison. He came to me and wept as he told me how much he missed his two young sons and wife. He requested me to pray for them to visit him. I prayed for him and advised him not to cry before them when they came. What we did not know was that on Sunday, he was weeping, and I was praying for him; the family was coming to visit him. But the car broke down on the road. Then God brought them the next time, he saw them without crying. That encouraged him to be more open and ask for more prayer. He told me he was taking college courses. He was afraid of failure. It was a struggle for him to make C's in high school because of illegal drugs. Again he wanted me to pray for him. "Pat, it takes more than prayer. You have to put in the effort it requires." I prayed for him. He promised to try. At the end of the course, he had A's and B's. Then he wanted me to pray for his release. Before the end of the fifth year, Pat was released from prison. He had his own enterprise, and the government gave him money to hire labor. He pruned and cut trees in people's yards.

About this time, my sister in-law informed Sweetie that Todd, who worked with her at Snowbird, had a house to rent. He was moving to Minnesota but did not want to sell the house. He was afraid of renting it to someone who might abuse it. She wanted to know if we were interested. The price was reasonable, and it was the best house in the area. We rented it. The caretaker of our basement apartment was offended to hear of our move. He confided to his wife that he would not refund the money we deposited with him. However, when he saw the house we rented and remembered that I am a doctor he changed his mind. When I called to give him the address, his wife said, "I thought he would not return it to you." I told her to give him the address. He refunded much of the money and claimed to have used what he kept to clean the apartment. We were in this house when Pat called me.

Pat reported how well his business was thriving. Then he requested to start Bible study with me. I must have forgotten or did not know I was not supposed to be in contact with a parolee as long as I was a prison volunteer. I granted his request. For a time the study went very well. Even when his mother visited him from another state, he brought her to the Bible study. Sometimes he brought some ex-convicts with him. Also, He brought two other women with him. His mother was very proud of her blue-eyed grandsons. We even found him some customers, including my parents-in-law and their neighbor.

The first sign of trouble surfaced when I asked about his wife. They had become estranged. He claimed the wife followed him wherever he went to work and shouted to anyone in hearing distance that he used drugs and that they should not hire him. He put a restraining order on her. Then he came with another woman twice. She was on drugs. He bought her a diamond for two thousand dollars. Like him, the woman had been in prison. She had also lost her child to the state because of drugs. They had fights and the neighbors called the police. They even shared drugs at least once. He claimed he had Jesus. He would not listen to my advice to leave her. One day I called him and told him to choose between the woman and coming to the Bible study. He was angry and told me he was over forty years old and could keep any company he liked. This was in spite of the fact the woman had sold the $2,000 diamond for two hundred dollars to buy drugs. The next time I heard from him, he was back to prison. By then I knew I should not write him, and I did not reply to his letter. The last I knew about him was his letter to my church with five dollars enclosed as his tithe.

By the time the Pastor left, the church had dwindled to about three hundred. We started to rebuild. The church needed someone to lead prayer. They asked me to be the leader. I gave one condition. I wanted an all-church prayer on the first Sunday of every month without Sunday school. The elder board met and offered me the first Sunday of every quarter. I accepted. So, in addition to Wednesday evening prayer for the few who attended, there were no Sunday school classes on the first Sunday of the beginning month of every quarter. Everyone was at the prayer room that Sunday. I also offered my telephone number as a substitute for the office for anyone who called the office for prayer after office hours. One lady called after midnight one morning. Her rich boss wanted her as his mistress though he was married. She said after she refused, the rich man found another woman who worked with her in the same company and gave her all the things he promised her including a furnished house. The worst part was they made her life miserable. Among other things, I reminded her Jesus said, "What will it benefit a man to own the whole world and lose his soul?" ref. We talked for almost one hour. We prayed. She asked how she could identify me if she came to the church. "I am the only black man there," I said. I also became active in the Sudanese ministry and led their Bible study when they came to the church. The Wednesday small prayer group organized a women's group and provided meals for sick people who needed meals.

With the dwindling number at the church also went the pastors. The Superintendent recommended one. During the period it took to hire a pastor, we had two interim pastors. One of them, Dr. Hanson, came to me a few weeks before he left and said to me, "Someone came to me and said: 'Before you leave this church you should hear

Obed say the pastoral prayer.' Would you please lead the pastoral prayer next Sunday?" I accepted. That was the beginning of our friendship.

I soon discovered another way to use the staff room we used for meetings and the Wednesday prayer meeting. I stood at the door after Sunday service. Anyone who had any prayer need came in and we prayed. It was about this time that we employed a new pastor.

Chapter 50

New Pastor And Results

He was young and had recently completed a master's degree in theology. Some of his answers during the interview drove some members out, including my friend Dr. Matlack and his wife. He shed tears when he asked me to pray for them. They walked out of the building that day and never came back to EV Free. At this time, I was reelected to the elder board. I was still in charge of prayer. The first elder board meeting was a little surprise to me.

The pastor said he had the last say on matters. The board talked about electing officers but postponed it until the next meeting. The pastor bypassed the board and appointed the chair, the vice, and the secretary by the next meeting and announced it through the man he chose to be the chair. My first open disagreement was when he announced that the elders would give the pastoral prayer. He followed it up with, "It should not last more than two minutes." I waited for a few minutes, and nobody said anything. I spoke up. "When I get up there to pray, I use the first thirty seconds for silent prayer to ask the Holy Spirit to pray for me, with me, and through me. That leaves me with one- and one-half minutes. You want me to pray for one- and one-half minutes?" He said yes. I told him to count me out. He said fine. His chairman said, "This church will not allow Obed to be in this church and not pray. He said, okay, let him pray, but not too long. Then we had two theological problems.

The pastor distributed a handout and asked members of the board to read it and be ready for discussion at the following meeting. I asked Sweetie to read it to me. I was puzzled by what she read. I requested her to highlight certain declarations with yellow marker. At the meeting most members claimed they did not read the handout. I said I did. I gave my copy to Don who sat on my left and asked him to read the portions marked yellow. He read two examples. I asked the pastor if that was what he wanted to teach at the church. When he said yes, I told him he could not say anything like that outside that room. "This is worse than the LDS doctrine. LDS claim they do ninety percent through good work and Jesus completes the remaining ten percent for them. You want members of this church to do all one hundred percent. That is unbiblical. What happened to Ephesians 2:8-9?" When I finished Joe quoted John 6:29. I asked him to start with John 6:28. The pastor who said his word was the final withdrew the article and claimed to be testing what the board would say. I said, "Thank God we did not allow it to go without a challenge."

Shortly after that, he took up salvation. This time, it was not saving; it was the retention of salvation. It became a war between him and me. When at first the members' silence became unbearable, I wrote a paper entitled: "I Never Knew You" (see Matthew 7:21-23) and emailed it to every board member.

I absented myself from the meeting. When I returned to the next meeting, he complained that Millie, a woman in the church who was going through a divorce with her husband, had refuted him. He had told the woman she would lose her salvation. She replied, "Go and talk to Obed about salvation." From then on, I became the devil to the secretary. He made fun of me whenever I walked into the room. One evening, I determined to tell them off and resign. Dennis who gave me a ride walked into the room and sat down. I stood up, waiting for the secretary to make his off remark and receive the payback. He did not. After a while, I thought, okay, God, if You still want me here, I will serve you. I walked to the chair and sat down. Sunday came and I discovered why the secretary was silent. The pastor preached on salvation. He confirmed that once a person is saved, the person remains saved for eternity. But that was not until he had told Shirley Wilson that people lost their salvation. She was the choir director who left the church before the last pastor left the church. Dennis and I interviewed her for readmission. She said, "What I don't understand is how someone can lose his or her salvation." Dennis said, "When you read the passages he (the pastor) gave, it makes sense." Without hesitation, I replied, "It is not true, and it does not make sense." Before the end of the year, the secretary returned to Missouri, his state. He thanked me for being on the board. For a long time after, he sent us a Christmas card.

There was another threat of divorce in the church. The man was a drug addict. His wife had checked him into a drug rehab facility. He did not take it seriously. He made and broke many promises to his wife and children. He made birthday promises to his children and failed to keep any. The woman was on the point of divorcing the man. Bill, who was the contact person, reported his frustration with the man to the board. Again, the pastor wanted to punish the woman. When I suggested more counseling to the man, the pastor suggested me. I accompanied Bill to the rehab residence. It happened the owner was a drug addict and served a prison term and attended the prison Bible study before he was freed from drugs and established the rehabilitation center. Bill and I met with the husband. He was not serious about leaving drugs. The pastor told the woman the punishment. She said she had enough problems to think about. She would not include the guilty feeling to her problems and left the church. Unfortunately, the pastor's parents' divorce had an influence on him, complicated when his white mother divorced his white father and married a black man.

Finally, there was the Sudanese problem. There were really two problems. The Sudanese were refugees who had lived their entire lives as refugees, first in Ethiopia before coming to Utah. They lived in camps before coming to Salt Lake. They got married at the age of fourteen. Worse still, they started having children immediately. So, children of the camp have children in the camp and bring them to "civilized" U.S.A. Some members of the church saw the children as running wild when they should be in Sunday School. The pastor asked why they did not go to a Sudanese church he heard was somewhere in the City. At the time, the one thing the church provided for them on Sunday morning was transport to and from church. Many acted as though they were the worst children in the church. I reminded them I had three white boys in my Sunday school class who were worse than the children they complained about. This is the meaning that "it takes a village to raise a child." I believe this is the reason the Pastor asked you to stand up when a child is dedicated at this church and make you promise to help the parents bring up the child. Asking members of the church to help raise children should include these immigrants."

Then two ladies, Donna and Sissy, wanted to start a pantry for the Sudanese. They asked the elder board permission to start it. The pastor refused to allow it. His reason was lack of space, "There is no room to store the items." It seemed I was on the board to plead the cause of the Sudanese. So I did not say they would share them every Sunday. That was the end of the matter. Miraculously, the Sudanese disappeared from the church.

Before the end of my three years on the elder board, each elder was assigned a topic to teach the church. Each topic was to be completed on one Sunday. At first, Joe wanted me to teach salvation. When he announced it at the meeting, the pastor said he wanted to teach that and asked me to teach prayer. I accepted. When my time came to teach, I started with What is prayer? Who prays (Romans 8:26), to whom, and when do we pray? I planned to finish with answers to prayers. But time ran out. By unanimous agreement, the class decided for me to use a second Sunday to complete the lesson. On the second

Sunday, the pastor was busy with some people in his office and came late to my class. I teased him as he teased me when I pronounced certain words e.g., Noel. I told the class the lesson my mother taught me when I was a little boy. "Listen, you latecomers. My mother told me that if I wished to be counted as being present at church, I had to be in church before 9.00 am because God's angels come to church at 9.00 am. They count the people in the church. Anyone who is not in church at that time is known as absent from church that day." The class laughed. Sweetie gave me a kiss after the teaching and declared, "I forgot you are a teacher." At the end of three years, I refused to renew my membership on the board.

Many members of the church had some serious health problems. I retained my prayer and visitation leadership. See James 5:14. There was great satisfaction when three of us visited June in the hospital, and she said, "I told my doctor the prayer team from my church will visit me, and here you are." Then one Sunday, Steve, a family friend of Lee and Shirley, came to me weeping as he reported to me. Lee and his family are our friends also. I had prayed for their pregnant daughter, who was epileptic, and their youngest son, and God answered the prayer. Steve could not even control his weeping. Finally, he said Lee had cancer and the doctor gave him only a few months to live. The small prayer group went to the hospital and prayed for him. The doctors were pleased with his progress and extended the time to a few years and sent him home. The three of us, Dennis, Curt, and I, visited him at his home and continued with prayer. When I put my hand on his head and said, "I mess your hair with my hand." He said, "Obed, you can mess it as much as you want." I said, "God now takes complete control." After so many years, he is still alive. Those few months turned into more than eleven years. The last we heard is that he is free from cancer. Then there were Bruce and Virginia, his wife. They also had cancer. Through prayer and medication, Virginia is completely healed. Bruce's went into remission but came back. He suffered from cancer for about ten years. According to him, of all the people who got the cancer at the same time, he was the only one alive. He even acted as a pastor to the team that took care of him at the hospital. In the midst of all this, their son committed suicide. They called the pastor and asked him to bring me along. We spent the night with them.

At about the same time, God's real miraculous healing took place in the lives of three little children. Curt, one of the three elders of the prayer and visitation team, and his wife Gloria were visiting Heather, their daughter, who was also a nurse. Their grandchild was seriously ill. They were flying the child in a helicopter from one state to another to a children's hospital when they called me while they were in flight. I prayed with them. The child was healed. The mother, being a nurse, knew what the doctor did wrong and told the hospital to pay her expenses in place of suing the doctor and the hospital for millions of dollars. The hospital agreed and refunded her the expenses. The other two children were cancer patients and took more time.

Reilley was about eight years old and had leukemia. He and his parents live in Montana. However, his maternal grandparents live in Utah. Primary Children's Hospital in Salt Lake City has a cancer treatment department. The Shaw's, i.e., the child's grandparents, attended EV Free. The boy was treated at Primary Children's Hospital throughout his period of sickness. He was asleep one evening when our prayer team visited him. Our prayer woke him up. When he realized what was going on, he said, "I was thinking of another treatment again." Just before we left, Curt said, "We shall come to pray with you again." I said to Curt, "I prayed for him to get healed and leave this place. I don't want to make a habit of coming here." We visited him at home and prayed with the family at home and church.

Sweetie was praying at one of our morning devotions. She said Reilley was to have another surgery. Recalling what the young boy had gone through and and still suffering, she started to sob. I took over and completed the prayer. When we got to the general prayer meeting the following Sunday, we learned the boy was undergoing surgery at the time. Sweetie and I were praying. It was successful. His mother shed tears one Christmas because there was no money to celebrate Christmas for him and his sister. He said to her, "But I am here and alive." His mom cleaned her eyes and hugged him. The church was yet to experience the most radical of miracles.

Elizabeth Loop was about four when she was diagnosed with the rarest form of cancer. We met the family first when we interviewed the parents for membership in the church. The Huntsman's Cancer Treatment Center in Utah could not treat it. The cost for the treatment was far beyond what the parents could afford. Her parents planned to sell their house to pay the expenses. Led by the prayer team, the church took two actions. The first action the church took was to organize prayer. The second was to start raising money. One Sunday of every month was set aside for people to donate money toward Elizabeth's Fund. At emergency times when she could not even eat, the three of us, Curt, Dennis, and I, rushed to her home and prayed for her and the family. I adopted her as my granddaughter spiritually. No matter where I was at the end of the service, her father brought her to me. Either I carried her or stooped down, hugged, and prayed for her before they left. By the end of the first six months, many thousands of dollars had been raised. Getting close to the time of the surgery, with still more thousands raised and more needed, the miracle happened. Like the angel that released Peter from jail, the cancer was gone. The only treatment she needed was what she had received earlier. The only money the church paid was the amount it deposited at the time. The family moved out of state. As of this writing, the parents have written to inform us that Elizabeth has graduated from high school.

I started to receive my Social Security money in November 2001. It was only a few hundred dollars. By then, our daughter and her husband had planned for us to visit Japan at their expense. I declined to go for two reasons. The first was my partial blindness. I did not see the reason to go when I could not see much. The next was I had not been to Nigeria since I returned to the U.S. and my brother would not believe that my daughter and her husband paid for the trip. So, I tried to save as much as I could in order to visit Nigeria. Sweetie went alone and enjoyed the visit. If she learned any Japanese she forgot it by the time she walked off the plane.

I had another crisis on my hands. This time, it was Munachimso. The phone rang, and it was the hospital. He and his date were in a car accident. He drove her car, which tumbled a few times. When we saw the date, and I asked where they went to, she said she did not know. I was disappointed in her lie and thought if my son died, that's the answer she would give me. I did not believe she did not know where they went. We sought for the room Chimso lay. When he saw us, he started to weep and apologize. We comforted him. "There is no need for apology." As one of the nurses said, "Many die from this kind of accident." The car rolled several times. As the car rolled, the car window broke, and the tendons on the back of his left hand were severed when the broken glass cut his hand. It was necessary to do a skin graft. He was in the hospital for several days. Chimso and Tiffany met at one of their classes at the University. When it appeared they were getting serious, knowing Utah and its religion, I asked if she was a Christian. His answer was no. "Are you going to marry a Mormon?" He said she was not a Mormon. "She is nothing. She does not believe in God." I objected to the friendship and suggested his classmates in junior high and senior high. The girl's father had also independently suggested Chimso to her when she tried to date someone else. She even came to see him at the apartment when he was recovering from the accident. But he was not home when she came, and because of my blindness, I could not recognize her until she told me who she was.

One Wednesday evening Chimso drove me to the Evangelical Free church building where the prayer group met. We were on the church grounds, and one or two minutes before he dropped me, with tears in his eyes, he told me he was serious about marrying Tiff. He was going to propose to her. I told him I would not be a part of it. By this time, I was not able to read the Bible. The following Saturday, I called him to our bedroom, gave him a Bible, and asked him to turn to 1 Corinthians 6 and asked him to read verses 18-20 to me. He read the verses and became angry. "If someone asked you to give up your theory of intelligence that you had spent so much time developing, would you?" I wondered if he was raising the woman he wanted to marry and who was at least three months older than he. How could you compare marriage with the development of a theory? Our pastor would not marry a believer and an unbeliever. Later, I learned that the pastor who agreed to marry them, a divorcee himself, told them they were not going to live with me after their wedding. They should go ahead and get married.

    Nordstrom decided to open a store in New York City. It also decided to send our sons as the foundation staff. It was summer, and even Chimso, who was still in school, traveled to New York City and participated. For a time, that became Chinedum's station. Even Pam and Chidi went to work in New York City, where Pam worked for M.A.C. Cosmetics in Nordstrom. Chinedum and Pam fell in love again. They returned to Salt Lake City and after a while got engaged. Pam took out everyone, including her parents, to throw a party on Chinedum's birthday. Sweetie and I did not go. However, Chinedum surprised Pam with an engagement ring at the birthday party she held for him. I did not know that Pam had become a Christian. She and her family were Mormons. I invited her over one day to discuss her religion. She confessed she had become a Christian. When I asked why? She said Christianity is practiced in our family, and she had seen the difference. Though she and Chinedum did not get married, when she married her husband it was our youngest son Uchechi who married them. She still lives as our daughter. Her parents are still our friends and have left the Mormon religion and are Christians today.

Don is an architect who attended EV Free. Chimso was doing well at the College of Architecture and enjoying his work at Nordstrom. But he needed some experience in his field of study. I asked Don if he could employ my son at his firm. He was gracious, and Chimso worked for the firm throughout his undergraduate and master's programs at the University.

Chapter 51

Living With Enlarged Prostate

I started frequenting the bathroom to urinate. It was not easy either. The first doctor I visited thought I had kidney stones. Joking with him I said to him, "My wife does not feed me stones. How can I have a kidney stone.?" After he looked through me with a narrow tube, he said it was a muscle. He did not do anything, nor did he prescribe any treatment. Then, someone recommended Doctor Barman in internal medicine. After he examined me, he said I had one of the largest prostrates he had ever seen. He added, "But it is healthy." He prescribed medication and sent me to the lab. The PSA was 24. The next time I went to see him, the PSA had gone up to 36, but the prostate was still healthy, according to him. Taking precautions he sent me to a urologist. He still kept me on the pill he prescribed.

It was the month of December when I went to see the urologist. He took me to his office and requested help for his son who was gathering counting numbers in different languages. Once he finished writing the numbers in my Igbo language, we walked to his examination room. When he saw the PSA, I became statistics. He declared me a cancer patient. I looked at him with distaste and told him I did not have cancer. The only uncertainty in his mind was whether or not it had spread to my bones. He decided to send me to the lab to find out. While he was making the appointment with the lab and filling out the papers, Uche, my youngest son, walked in. The doctor said to him,

"Your dad has cancer." I was angry. I scolded him. "You have no right to tell my eighteen-year-old I have cancer. Even if I had cancer, my wife should know first. You are not the one to tell him." He did not have a thing to say. When he completed the arrangement he made a separate appointment for me to see him in his office for a test of cancer of the prostate. Uche drove me home.

I got to the lab for the test and met a man and a woman. The man asked me if I knew what I was there for. Before I answered, he added, "Your doctor said you have cancer and wants to know if it has spread to your bones." I responded, "No, I am here for you to find out if I have cancer." I lay down. They ran the machine through me twice and asked me to get up. I asked what they found. The man said, "I am not your doctor, but I did not see any cancer." I thanked them and left. Later in the day, the doctor called and told me the cancer had not spread to the bones and confirmed his own appointment for his own test.

It was more than a week when Sweetie took me to his office. He took me to the test room. He applied his hand machine six times. Then he said, because of the size of the prostate he would do it eight times. I did not object. He applied it two more times. When we returned to his office with the result, he declared, "There is no cancer. However, I would like you to come for another test. Make an appointment with the nurse at the front desk to see me in two weeks." When we reached the front desk, I wished them Merry Christmas, and that was the last time I was there.

My people say whatever feeds grow. So it was as I fed my prostate, it grew, and the PSA increased. My problem aggravated. Sweetie worked at the College of Nursing at the University, and through her, a urologist at the University was recommended. The PSA had increased to 46 at the time. The diagnosis corroborated the finding of Dr. Barman, my primary doctor. It was large but without cancer. Joking with me, one of the doctors said, "Don't come back unless the PSA is 100."

Later on in the year, I bled. After examining me Dr. Barman's assistant suggested they send me back to the urologist. Dr. Barman refused and treated it. The bleeding stopped.

The EV Free Church team went to the Salt Lake Rescue Mission (a temporary home for the homeless) to conduct church services, counsel, and pray for individuals at request. One member of the team said, "If parents were to be blamed for all their children's bad behaviors, then we would blame God for all human bad behaviors since He is the Father of us all." That was a little comforting to me. Meanwhile, Chimso had planned his wedding, and I was almost certain I would not attend.

As the date of the wedding drew nearer, I struggled with my perception of my situation. I considered many options. I could tell my wife she would not attend the wedding, and if she did, I would return to Nigeria before the end of the week. However, I prayed and prayed. It seemed I had lost my family and my sight, and I was without a job. Twenty-four hours before the wedding, I still had not made up my mind about whether to attend the wedding or not. Our daughter Melody and her family had arrived from Maryland. She reported my situation to her former pastor. He told her he would not marry them. That told her I was not being unreasonable. At the last minute I went to the wedding and saw the pastor who married them. He proudly announced that he had married hundreds. The bride's mother thanked me for coming to the wedding.

Chapter 52

Visit To Nigeria

More than thirteen years after our family returned from Nigeria, I decided to visit home. I had saved enough to make the trip and still make some progress in the house I had almost completed before I left home. It was 2002, and the Twin Tower destruction had changed traveling rules. I had to obtain a visa to pass through London. Though on the eve of my travel,, my enlarged prostate was still large, there was no sign of trouble, and I still had my pills to control my urination.

I had everything I needed for the journey on the day I traveled except the visa to enter Britain. However, we were assured that I would get the visa in L.A. the same day before I traveled. Sweetie and I flew to L.A. on the morning I traveled. By noon I had my visa. Sweetie and I ate our lunch and waited to fly to our different destinations, she to Salt Lake and I to Nigeria vide Britain. I was still well when we parted.

More than halfway to London, I felt the first discomfort. I looked at my watch. It was not time for me to take my pill. But I took it anyway. I went to the toilet several times before we landed at Heathrow. It got worse. I had not experienced such pain before. I could not pass urine. I walked to a pay telephone and asked the operator if it was possible to call collect in the U.S. from there? She said yes. I called Sweetie collect. "Please call Onyema to come to the airport and take me to the hospital. I am sick." She called Onyema. He did not come, nor did he call to ask how I was doing. That was the first sign he showed he owed me a grudge. But I missed it. I was hungry but without any appetite. I ordered food and tried to force myself to eat. I managed to put a spoonful in my mouth. Both the smell and the taste were unbearable. I walked away from the table. I walked to a policeman who checked my passport and green card before directing me towards the gate. Not too long after, the plane loaded. When the plane arrived at the Lagos airport, Emedom, my best friend, and Akachi, one of his sons, were waiting for me. He had bought his ticket to fly to Port Harcourt with me. Ihuoma one of my nieces and the last one to live with us at Oyo was at Port Harcourt with her husband to drive us to Umuahia.

Still very uncomfortable on arrival, the news of my arrival brought many people from the village to the house. Politics was in the air. Unawares of my condition as they drank and chatted, Ago one of the chiefs, suggested I run for the Presidency. Ihuoma and her husband gave Emedom a ride when they left. It was after the visitors left that my brother and his wife realized how serious my condition was.

Mr. Ibegbulem had a heart problem. So I went to see him and his wife. On arrival at their home, I was surprised to notice how seriously ill he was. Another better and pleasant surprise was that their youngest son, Chukwu, was visiting from Britain. He had a car at home and a driver. We were delighted to see each other. He was about to return to London and made the car and the driver available to me. He said to the driver, "This is my uncle. He should use the car while he is at home. Take him wherever he wants to go."

After spending some time with the Ibegbulem family, I was referred to a medical doctor at Amachara village. We discovered his clinic was at the township. After I described my condition, he asked me to lie on his examination table. He proceeded to push a rod-like thing into my penis. I asked where he was trained. He said U.S.A. I wanted to know if he was a urologist. He said no. I told him to stop, and he did, and I asked if he knew any urologist in town. Because my mother is from his village, we become blood relatives. When he said yes, I asked him to take me to the doctor. On arrival, he introduced me as Dr. Onwuegbu, his uncle visiting from the U.S.A. If that required good care of me, it was also understood to mean that I had money. Unfortunately, the catheter the doctor fixed on me to help me to urinate had been used on a former patient. I became infected. My condition grew worse. By this time I had paid my "nephew" ₦5,000 and ₦40,000 naira to the urologist.

When I left the U.S. I took enough money to continue to build my house. I changed some of the dollars in Lagos and arrived home with ₦185,000 naira. Because of my sickness, almost everyone who visited me came to the bedroom I stayed, and there were many of them. Even some other people from other villages who went to Mission Hill with me decades ago visited me. Besides, my brother's wife was spending the money. So I gave her the money to keep. She suggested giving ₦2,000 to each of their four of the five children in Nigeria and ₦2,500 to Ihuoma and her family. I agreed. Amadi, the first son, was also visiting Nigeria at the time. His children needed money to buy school materials and he did not have it. I asked if seven would buy what they wanted. He said, ₦700? I replied, ₦7,000. He said yes and I authorized his mother to give him the amount. She suggested giving every woman in the compound about 15 of them ₦500. I said no. I gave them ₦300 each. Sweetie bought my brother and his wife gifts that I took home with me. I also bought some gifts for the church besides the cash I gave, though my sickness did not allow me to attend service. I also gave a few people cash as a gift. My sickness got worse by the day. Instead of spending the six weeks I planned for, I decided to return to the U.S. by the end of the third week.

Because of how serious my illness was, my brother proclaimed, "They brought him here to kill him." Amadi, his oldest son, said to me, "He is melting away. Call him and talk to him." About that time, the

Reverend Minister and a person from Umuda, i.e., the next village, who was going to succeed my brother as one of the church circuit leaders, came to visit. I invited all three to my room. Emedom was already in the room with me. I became an evangelist. "Why are you miserable?" I asked my brother. "Your worrying does not help you or me."

He justified his worry with, "Even Jesus wept over Lazarus" (John 11:35). I said to him and his two visitors, "Jesus did not worry about and did not weep for Lazarus. I shall return to that. I think I am sick because God wants to teach you a lesson on faith. I asked Emedom to turn to Roman 8:28." He turned to it and read it. "And we know that in all things God works for the good of those who love him, who have been called according to his purpose." I acknowledged the bad side as my being sick and the good side as building his faith. Then I asked Emedom to turn to Isaiah 43:2-3. He did and read it. "When you pass through the waters, I will be with you, and when you pass through the rivers, they will not sweep over you. When you walk through the fire, you will not be burned; the flames will not set you ablaze. For I am the Lord your God, the Holy One of Israel, your Savior; I give Egypt for your ransom, Cush and Seba in your stead." I explained it with the examples of the children of Israel crossing the Red Sea, the three Jews in the burning furnace in Babylon, and the four policemen and me on the Oyo road. First, I explained the two passages. *All things* in Romans 8:28 comprise good and bad. Isaiah 43:2 starts with *when*, not *if*. Besides, I cited my personal example. Some Yoruba people tried to ambush and kill me on the Oyo road. Do you remember God sent four policemen who chased them away before my car arrived at the spot? We gave the policemen a ride, and they became my bodyguard. At the end of the discussion, I turned to Lazarus.

I started with the statement Jesus made when He heard that Lazarus was sick. "This sickness will not lead to death. It will bring glory to God and His Son." Why should Jesus weep for such a glorious event? Jesus wept for the unbelieving dead mourners who were mourning for sleeping Lazarus. When I finished, I asked him if he wanted to be born again. He agreed and Emedom led him through the sinner's prayer and prayed with him. As sick as Mr. Ibegbulem was, he and his wife came to see me before I traveled to Lagos.

By the time I decided to cut short my stay in Nigeria, I had about ₦100,000 left with my H and Amadi had returned to the U.S. I had his youngest brother travel with me to Lagos. We stayed with Emedom and his family. Once again, he called Sweetie, who then contacted Onyema in London. The plane stopped overnight in London; the Airline charged me ₦40,000 extra because of the change in my original date of travel. I exchanged my travelers check to naira. By the time I completed my transactions in Lagos and paid the fare for my nephew's return ticket to travel back to the east, I had over seven thousand naira left. I gave it to my nephew as pocket money.

As the Provost of the Federal College of Education, I developed an interest in politics. Dr. Azikiwe's leader of the NPNP party, which was a junior partner in the Federal Government, withdrew from the government because the Military Government decided to move the capital of Nigeria from Lagos to Abuja in the north. Lagos is in the west, a Yoruba land. The Yoruba people, who should have protested and revolted, did not. Their party replaced the NPNP in the federal government. I wrote an anonymous article against the NPNP decision and took it to Dr. M. I. Okpara and distributed it in the east. Dr. Okpara agreed with me. I determined to run for the Presidency if I was still the Provost in the next election. However, I was not nor was I in the country during the election. So before I traveled in 2002, I drafted my paper declaring my intention to run for the Presidency. The first person I told about it in Nigeria was Mrs. Ibegbulem. Like Sweetie, she opposed it. However, when Emedom read it, he was all for it. He wanted me to return after I got well. I left him with some copies. Several years later Sweetie saw it in the computer published by Daughters of Biafra. After I got sick, I decided God has other assignments for me, not the President of Nigeria.

Having informed Sweetie of the date of my departure from Lagos, she knew when our plane arrived in LA. She planned to meet me at the airport. She also informed Onyema and Chikara, my cousin, both of whom lived in London. They met me at the airport. They took me to a hospital that reminded me of my days in elementary school in Nigeria. The patients filled up the small hall waiting to see the doctor. I did not see any doctor that night. The nurse I saw mishandled the catheter I arrived with and asked me to report the following day when there would be a doctor. The catheter became useless and could not hold my urine anymore. On our way to Onyema's, we dropped Chikara, and his family came out and greeted me. That warm greeting was missing when we reached Onyema's. He showed me the bedroom to sleep in and his wife brought me a plate of rice with fried plantain. They showed me the bathtub. I did not see them again. I used one of my undershirts to collect the urine throughout the night. I thought Onyema would take me to the hospital early in the morning. He left me and went to work. It was after midmorning when he showed up. I said to him, "Could you not take me to the hospital, leave me there and go to work?" He looked at me like, who are you, and for what?" He took me to the hospital. God provided a doctor. He attached a catheter. The instant he finished, there was an ambulance. He left the nurse and me and ran to the ambulance. I asked the nurse to discharge me. She would not. I told her my flight was leaving for the U.S. in a few minutes. She insisted on my waiting for the doctor. I signed myself out and left.

On arrival at the airport, passengers were already boarding. The man at the desk took one glance at me and rejected me as a passenger. "You are too sick to travel alone. Unless someone travels with you, I shall not allow you to travel by this plane alone." I asked him if he knew that I had traveled from Nigeria. By the time I finished talking, Onyema engaged him in a serious argument. He stood his ground. I lifted up my right hand and said a silent prayer. "Lord, this is Your problem, not mine. Please solve it, in Jesus' name. Amen." When I lowered my hand, he asked me to go on the plane. I was surprised to see that someone was assigned to take care of me between London and LA. I paid Onyema $130 before we reached the airport. The difference between the catheter I received in London and the one the doctor at Umuahia gave me was like day and night. I realized that if I had been to the London hospital on my way to Nigeria, I could have avoided the infection and spent my six weeks in Nigeria.

The man who took care of me on the plane wheeled me out to the waiting area. I saw Sweetie and said to him, "That's my wife." He handed me over to her. Getting on to the plane from L.A. to Salt Lake was another story. I carried my carry-on bag. Because of the 911 air attack in New York City the airport staff checked everyone who was different. They allowed Sweetie to pass with a minimum check. They went through my bag and made me take off my shoes, and ran the little thing they held in their hand over me. Sweetie was irritated. Finally, we were in Salt Lake City. Sweetie drove me straight to the University of Utah Emergency Room (ER).

Even a few days before I left the hospital, I could only see the shadows of the nurses, members of my family, and members of the church who visited me. I remember someone giving me a bath and telling a nurse to lower her voice. I was sedated most of the time. After about three weeks Sweetie brought me home and became my nurse. It took me a good 24-hour period before I recognized our home. I also lost my taste. One of our friends, Mary Alice, volunteered to come and help while Sweetie worked. I gratefully declined. The first church service I attended after my return was either the Christmas or New Year service.

Sweetie became my nurse and treated me at home. A home health nurse also visited once a week. I called my brother, Emedom and

Onyema, and Chikara and informed them of my release from the hospital. Onyema was amazed that my prayer worked a miracle. "It was wonderful. Immediately you lowered your hand, the man told you to go on the plane." He forgot that I gave him his citizenship through prayer. At the time, his wife said, "Immediately you stopped praying I know he will get it." He woke me up after 2:00 am to give me the news. That was the same case with his job.

It was about three months since I went to the prison before I traveled to Nigeria. I missed the inmates. I did not know they missed me more than I missed them. However, they knew I would be back this particular Sunday. When we arrived at the prison chapel, my fellow volunteers expressed doubt as to how many inmates would attend the service that day. They said only one inmate attended service the previous Sunday. I thought they were joking. But they were serious. Then the inmates came, about twenty-seven of them. Micky, one of the volunteers, said, "Now we know who they come to see." One of the inmates said to me, "We know who loves us." I taught the class and was grateful God spared me to continue the prison ministry.

Having understood that I was not born to be a President, I decided to publish one of the books I was writing. I completed Affixing Fragmented Nigeria the Scramble for Africa Must Stop in early 2003. Only one publisher agreed to publish it. His terms of the agreement, which included making me responsible for the sales, were unacceptable. About the same time a woman who heard about my book from a common friend wrote me and expressed interest in the book. After she read the manuscript, she made me a generous offer. We signed the contract without dates. When I called the publishing house she claimed to own, someone told me she had been fired. Soon she called me to tell me about a delay in the publication. I was surprised and confronted her with the information. "I understand you are fired." She claimed the people got jealous. When she refused to return my manuscript I asked a lawyer friend to write the Attorney General of her state. He could not prosecute her since she had not published the book. I self-published the book.

The book traced the history of the creation of Nigeria to the Amalgamation of Nigeria under Captain Lugard. Though Britain seized parts of Nigeria during the Scramble for Africa, it chartered the United African Company to administer the territory for her till the end of World War I. The book also traced the problems Nigeria suffers today to the creation of an ungovernable federation in the country. It listed the ten most dangerous enemies of Nigeria. Then, it suggested solutions. It concluded with the fact that the Scramble for Africa is ongoing. The Organization of African Unity was the number one tool Europe used to continue to enslave Africa. It called Africans everywhere to make Africa south of the Sahara a country. I regret to say that many Africans have not read the book. The continent is still suffering. The OAU is a tool of the EU.

By the end of the same year, I completed another book entitled Humanizing Education for The Twenty-First Century. For some reason, members of my Christian Writers group could not read the entire book for the time I had. One of them recommended a woman editor to me. By the time I called, she had been contacted. Sweetie and I were in the house one evening when she came. The book contained eighteen chapters. She glanced through the double-spaced pages with sub-headings within the manuscript. Her only question was, "Every chapter has sub-headings within it?" I said yes. She said I would pay her $320. As a Nigerian I tried to bargain. But that was her last price and I yielded. She surprised me when I called to find out what progress she was making. She said, "I have spent more than eight hours, and I am not even halfway." I wondered what hours had to do with completing my manuscript. When I called next, she claimed to have worked too many hours for $320 when she completed the first eleven chapters. She said I had to pay her more money if I wanted her to do more. I thought of taking her to court. But I was in Utah. She is white and a woman, and I am a black man. It would be a jury of ten whites and, at most, two blacks. I sent her $320 by certified mail. She returned my manuscript.

One day as I waited to hear from my publisher, our telephone rang. When I picked up the receiver, someone at the Lyndon State College Alumni Office was at the other end. She said something and quickly turned to: "Let's talk about something more important. Congratulations you are the 2004 distinguished alumnus." "Really. Thank you." She gave me the information I needed to attend the ceremony. One problem I solved was the hiring of a gown for me because I have mine. At the end of the conversation, I called Sweetie and informed her. Part of her responsibility at the College of Nursing is to deal with distinguished alumni awards. So she knew more about it than I. I was in a celebratory mood when she came home. The restaurant we went to almost spoiled the evening with bad food. I decided never to go there again.

Graduation at Lyndon in 2004 was in May. That was the day of the award. Our daughter, our son-in-law, and two grandsons from Maryland, Chimso, our son from Salt Lake City, and SueAnn and her husband from Connecticut were among the people from out of state who witnessed the ceremony. Before the day of the ceremony, my next book, Humanizing Education for The Twenty-First Century, was published. I took a copy, which I gave to the Alumni Office. There were a few surprises before the ceremony. The last interim President came and introduced himself. He had been to Nigeria and heard about the famous hospital at Umuahia, my hometown, and I named it, The Queen Elizabeth II Hospital. He confirmed. After he read the piece on which the award was based, he said, "Only people in education will fully appreciate your achievement." "Thank you," I said. Then the Vice President of the Alumni Association came and demonstrated how I dribbled and danced with the ball in the field when I played soccer.

The ceremony itself was only a small part of the graduation. The chair lady of the Alumni Association read the citation and gave me the beautiful, engraved crystal bowl. I introduced Sweetie, our children, and friends who traveled with us. I gave my short speech. I thanked the college community that was so friendly and made my stay at Lyndon the best years of my school years in the U.S. I thanked the family of the former President, Dr. Long, with whom I spent my three Christmas days in Vermont, and others, especially fellow students. When I narrated my experience with the bus and how Mrs. Gallagher and Mr. Michaud came to rescue me from Montpelier, the students cheered. Then I told the trick I played on Mr. Michaud in 1982. The hall rocked. After more than three decades since graduation, most of the professors who were there when I was a student had retired or left or even dead. However, guess who came out to talk with me?

When I walked out of the hall the Art lecturer who gave me D- because of my opposition to his atheistic views followed me. Beaming with a smile he said with a stretched hand, "Congratulations." I shook his hand and thanked him wondering if he had been converted. Later on, I discovered he mistook me for my nephew. Behind him was Janet McKnight, the lady who gave me a grade four Sunday School class to teach the first Sunday I was in the U.S. She had good and bad news. Her daughter-in-law graduated with an M.Ed from Lyndon, but her husband was suffering from cancer. Our visit was cut short by a former student. She said I asked her to iron a few shirts for me, and when she came, I gave her thirty. That is what men know as women's exaggeration. I did not even have half of that. But she was one of those female students who helped me with ironing and typing. Then Mr. Michaud, who came to Montpelier with Mrs. Gallagher to rescue me the day I arrived in Vermont and the bus for Lyndonville left without me., complained he did not hear his name. When I claimed that I said his name, he said I did not pronounce it well. Probably, I did not. But at eighty could his ears have played a trick on him?

We visited a few places of interest. The little Lyndonville and even Lyndon Center had grown. People's Methodist was at a different location. Our friends from Connecticut went with Sweetie and me to see Mary Bisson, my favorite retired English Professor. She was recuperating from a serious illness. The lady taking care of her said they almost lost her. She was the same Mrs. Chatting Chaucer I nicknamed her. After we left them, we went to the maple factories. My father-in-law used to weed every dandelion he saw in our yard in Salt Lake City. Unknown to me, even after I lived in Vermont for three years, there is a festival of dandelion wine. They said the wine was the best. The festival would start a day or two after we left. We wished we were there to buy my father in-law a bottle. Of course, we could not go to Lyndon without shopping at the college bookshop.

We enjoyed the hotel the college arranged for its visitors. Even a better news item awaited us at the checkout desk. Because our son-in-law who booked the stay is a retired Air Force man, we received a discount of a certain percentage from the normal charge. Chimso drove to Lyndon from Burlington in a rented car, and we were all flying out of Vermont from Burlington. We decided to ride with him to the airport. The three of us went to Burlington but flew to Salt Lake City by different airlines and planes.

Checking in our suitcases at Burlington Airport proved a difficult matter. Sweetie and I had two suitcases. Mine was the bigger one and contained most of our possessions and, therefore, weighed more than the airline allowed. However, the combined weight of our two suitcases was within the weight the airline allowed. When I refused to transfer some of the items from my suitcase to Sweetie's suitcase they surcharged me. I paid for the "excess weight." That I refused to open my suitcase before them became an excuse for them to suspect that I had contraband in the hard suitcase. They had three other reasons to suspect me. First, my color was not pink like their color, and these are people who spend half of their summer in the sun trying to look like me. Having failed to look like me, they call it tan. Their second problem was the inability to pronounce my simple last name. They could not tell from what part of the globe I came. Finally, I had my beard. They took out their frustration on my suitcase and stopped it from flying with us. I am sure when they forced the suitcase open and saw the distinguished alumni award, a mounted crystal bowl, the graduation gown, and read the writing in the graduation handbook about me they knew what a gentleman scholar they were dealing with. They blamed themselves and called Salt Lake City air port and informed them that my suitcase would be coming by the next plane the following day.

We boarded believing that our suitcases were on the plane with us. I was dismayed to discover that after I paid the surcharge, they still withheld my suitcase. On reaching the window to complain, a form was waiting for us to fill. Sweetie filled it. They brought the suitcase to our home the following day with a confession that they opened the suitcase. I tolerated their excuse since nothing was missing. About one year later Sweetie and I visited our daughter and her family in Maryland. I made my third attempt to reach Mrs. Gallagher by phone and succeeded. She was the Admissions Officer when I was admitted to the college and came to Montpelier with Mr. Michaud to rescue me the day I arrived in Vermont. She was over ninety and retired. As we reminisced, she said, "And we (the college) loved you." I said, "Thank you. I know." I even spent one Thanksgiving with her and her husband. But by the time of the conversation, he was dead.

Chapter 53

Experiences

This chapter is the most difficult to write. The events described here shook me and revealed things I never expected and changed the course of events and relationships.

One day in early 2005 as I listened to one of my books on tape for the blind, I heard a statement that shook me. The author made a reference to "the late John Ogbu of Berkeley ..." I reversed the tape and listened again. I heard correctly. I stopped reading and asked Sweetie to google John. She did and the statement was confirmed. It was sad news.

John was a brilliant scholar and my classmate at Uzuakoli Methodist College. He had been dead for more than one year at this time. Thinking he was still alive I gave his name to Lyndon State College as one of those to be informed of my distinguished alumni award the previous year. But I did not hear from him. Unfortunately, I do not know any member of his current family. Linda the wife we knew, and John were divorced a long time ago. So I could not get in touch with any member of the current family.

Nordstrom transferred Chinedum and Uche to Denver. Chinedum was a manager. Soon Pam and Chidi were also in Denver, but Pam's and Chinedum's engagement was faulting. Both boys visited Salt Lake City with their girlfriends. Aware of the family rule, they did not ask to stay with us. Shortly after the visit, Chinedum, in a reversed order, told us that his girlfriend was expecting, and they were getting married. By this time, Sweetie, our daughter, and two grandsons had visited the boys in Denver and reported a very bright future for Chinedum in Nordstrom. The store manager liked him so well that he planned to take him when he became a regional manager. Boom! It happened again.

As usual, whenever there is any bad news from our children, it reaches me through their mother. They are sure of her sympathy. Chinedum called her and told her he had been fired from his job. He had an affair with his subordinate. She pleaded with me to call him and be gentle with him. It took many hours before I called. Still annoyed and uncertain what to tell him, he answered the phone. Before I said one word, he sobbed and apologized. "Dad I am sorry. You taught me the right way to live, but I disobeyed, and each time, I put myself in trouble. Please forgive me." I asked if he learned anything from this. He said yes. He added that he was thinking of returning to Salt Lake City. I told him that running would not solve his problem.

Between these events our nephew Amadi in Oklahoma City found a wife in Texas. When he introduced her as Joy, I thought he made a mistake because the name of his late wife was Joy. But that was the name. Amadi and his bride invited us to their wedding and sent us return tickets. When we asked them to find us a nearby hotel, Amadi told us his bride had enough rooms in her house. Onyema and his family came from London. My brother and his wife were surprised to hear that I helped to carry and arrange the chairs at the church where the wedding took place because of my poor health when I left home to fly back to the USA. That was the first time I met Onyema's family, though I had spent a night in his apartment. Sweetie and I flew back to Salt Lake City a day after the wedding.

No, Uche, the last born, was not missing. He was the least interested in education. As far as education is concerned Uche was the horse you can lead to the stream but cannot force it to drink. He might have been good in soccer and basketball, but his smoking ruined his chances there. He dabbled into acting and, even as mentioned earlier, acted in Touched by an Angel, a national television show. But that also involved reading and cramming. He was also employed by a hotel while he was acting. His part in the show required him to grow facial hair. That was in violation of the hotel rules, and they fired him. He enjoyed his ride along with the police, even as I write this today. He went to a junior college but even when one majors in law enforcement, one still has to take other courses. He did not complete the two years.

Before he joined Nordstrom as a full-time employee, he sold cell phones. After a while, he reported a crisis at the workplace. The store manager planned to take the case to court but decided to take the case to arbitration first. I accompanied him. It turned out someone in the store had tried to take advantage of what he saw and misconstrued to be stealing. He said the contract Uche signed allowed him to take out a phone to any potential buyer without signing it out first. When Uche did exactly that, he accused him and said, "I can prove that you took out a phone without signing it out." The whole thing looked silly and a waste of my time. Looking at the lady who chaired the meeting, I asked if I could say something. "Please do Dr.," she said. I repeated the terms of the clause in the contract. The contract allowed him to take the phone out without signing it out. The accuser said, "Yes." I asked again, "He took out the phone without signing it out.?" He said, "Yes". Then I asked him, "Then what do you mean when you said, you can prove? You want to prove that he obeyed the terms of the contract?" That was the end of the case. Then against my advice, Uche bought a car with a beautiful body but a dead engine. Before making Denver his home, he gave it away and received a tax rebate. Uche and Chinedum lived together in the same house when Chinedum lost his job. He was also engaged.

Chinedum was without a job, income, or savings. I considered sending him a small amount of money anonymously. But Sweetie suggested I send it in my name. I sent him $150. He found a job in a shoe store. Uche and his fiancé had set their wedding date. Sweetie held a shower for them in Salt Lake City. Uche's future parents-in-law also came from Denver.

Many of our relatives from different parts of the U.S.A.: East, Midwest, South, and West came to the wedding. Sweetie gave the catering service the menu for the Nigerian stew, and they did a good job of preparing it. Late at night on the eve of the wedding, when almost all the relatives who had come for the wedding were about to leave, the phone rang. It was Amadi announcing the arrival of him and his wife. Everyone delayed their departure to see them. On arrival, his wife left the women who waited to see her and sat with Amadi and the men. I said to her, "Do you know that these women waited to see you and you are sitting here with us?" She hurried to meet them with her bare feet. I kidded her, "They don't want to know how short you are. Put on your shoes." We all laughed as she put them on and went to see them. She and Amadi gave us Nigerian clothes. I thanked them and added because of the tension between them, "The best gift you will give to us is to love each other and live in peace."

It was a beautiful wedding with a Nigerian flavor. We played Nigerian *high* life music and the Americans tried to keep up with the rhythm. If Sweetie were Igbo by birth or even knew the custom she would have performed the Igbo marriage customary ceremony. However, Ngozi, my cousin's wife who came from Maryland, performed it. Uche's wife was given her Igbo name. Also, Chimso's wife, who did not receive her Igbo name at her wedding, received it in Denver. Sweetie, her mother, sister and I were the last visitors to leave our boy's home on the day of departure. Chinedum stood near the steps that led to the house and Sweetie stood outside near the vehicle we drove, about five yards away from him. Suddenly she was crying uncontrollably. There was Chinedum standing and looking dejected and helpless. I knew he was hurt to see his mother in such pain that could have been avoided. I felt sorry for him. However, I walked to Sweetie and consoled her. Soon, the four of us, Sweetie, her mother, sister, and I, were on our way to Utah. It seems the experiences of the period changed him. He got a job and wrote letters of apology to the two other women he got pregnant with earlier and asked for forgiveness. Worse still, as if to punish himself he took a job with a gas and oil mining company in Utah in one of the coldest parts of Utah. He spent the week there and went home for the weekend. His pregnant girlfriend gave him her good car and drove his bad car. We continued to pray for all our children. God trained Chinedum in the school of difficulty in the mine. Then he learned there was a need for an assistant manager at a Verizon retail store and applied. He got the job. Later he became an assistant pastor.

Thank God because of my blindness. I learned to touch-type, something I could not do when I had my sight. The Bible says, "My grace is sufficient for you…" (2 Corinthians 12:9). Having published Humanizing Education for The Twenty-First Century, a teacher at the church asked to read it. I had criticized the method of teaching and practice of a teacher having a class just for one year and suggested three grades instead. I compared schools with mothers who have worked with their children for 18 years. I stated the advantages such a system should have over the current practice. After she read the book, and before she discussed her concern with me, she became the crusader of "What happens if the students get a bad teacher?" When I heard it, I wrote another book entitled, Teaching that Guarantees Learning for School and Home Teachers. I reemphasize teaching as an environmental arrangement, etc. A teacher does not have the right to be bad. Bad coaches lose their jobs. Bad parents lose their children to the state. Why should a bad teacher be paid to be bad? Fire any bad teacher. One of the readers told me that she went to the University of Stanford summer school just to learn about the method of teaching I described in the book.

Though Joy was a Nigerian she had become an American citizen before she married Amadi. She wanted a baby badly. Her inability to become pregnant frustrated her very much. She became unreasonable. She was a nurse herself and about 47 years old. She accused Amadi, her husband, of being impotent and, at the same time, accused him of getting a Yoruba woman pregnant. As she complained on the phone to me I told her to stop talking. I reminded her that Amadi had four children before his first wife died. You accused him of getting a Yoruba woman pregnant. But he cannot get you pregnant.?" I did not even know that Amadi was her third husband. She never got pregnant during her previous marriages. She went to Nigeria and adopted a daughter. Amadi joined in the adoption but the American embassy in Nigeria denied the little girl entry at the first request. Later Joy called and told me me what Onyema told her. She said that Onyema told her they all had decided not to have anything to do with her. I did not and still do not know who "they all" are. Whomever they all are, Onyema became the spokesperson. Onyema did not tell me who made the decision, and I did not ask him. Finally, Amadi and Joy were divorced. Not too long after the divorce, the daughter they adopted from Nigeria saw Amadi in a store and ran to him calling "Dad, Dad." She had finally made it to Oklahoma City.

Many of my Oyo students wrote me after I returned to the U.S. One of them informed me they named the church I planted The Church of Reconciliation. One day my phone rang. It was a Yoruba woman and a former student. When I answered the phone she called me daddy the formal way a Nigerian would address an older person loved and respected. It was Nike. She was still a student at Oyo in June 1987 when I left the College. She said that she had her master's degree and was in the U.S. She asked for a recommendation. I gave her a general recommendation but when she asked for evaluation of her as an employee and rating her against others, I told her I had no basis to do it. Dr. Paul Ajuwon, who was a youth corps at Oyo when I was there, had found my address and even visited us in Salt Lake City and had the same experience with her. Quite a few of the former students from Oyo called from time to time. Amazingly, they still think that after about three decades, even when I did not teach them, I can still remember them enough to write a letter of recommendation for them. This was the case with a woman who had been to Britain, who told me she earned a master's degree in the U.S. and applied to do her Ph.D. Even someone in the institution told her time was no problem. The individual forgot that I had not kept abreast with her activities all that period and could neither be fair to her nor to the institution. I responded to many of the questions with, "can't answer this."

I started writing a few books. Each time I started a new one I said, "When I finish this one, I call it a quit." Sweetie responded with, "I heard that before." She was always right. At one time I had eight of them. I wrote all the chapters but needed someone to critique them. Sweetie had a full-time job that, at times, required as many as twelve hours some days. I had more than five Christian books. I hired Kay, my sister-in-law, as a part-time secretary, though she had a full-time job also. She did not have some of the skills required to move sentences and paragraphs from one page to another. So I stopped using her after a period of time. There were also other books on intelligence, teaching, children's books, the history of Oyo Federal College of Education, and my autobiography. While I worked on some of these books, Sweetie was interviewed for another position in the College. She got it with an excellent raise. At the same time, our children were doing well. I asked them to send money to their uncle and aunt in Nigeria. They did. Melody's husband put humor to it. When Melody asked him if they should send one or two hundred dollars, he replied, "Since we owe him a goat, let's send him two hundred dollars." That is what they sent to him. Others sent less.

Before I left Oyo, I carried my belongings to Amafo Isingwu, i.e., my village, and stored them in the room my mother occupied in my brother's house. One day, our phone rang. When I picked it up, Onyema was at the other end. He said his niece went home on vacation from the university. As she walked out from one of the bedrooms to the living room she saw a snake that coiled around the leg of the chair her grandmother used to sit on. Then people came and killed it. I asked if anybody was bitten. His answer was no. He then went on to tell me the real reason he called. He told me his sister Uzoma, who lives in Britain, told him the belongings I left in the room my mother used were breeding the snake. I should move them out. I said, "Really!" He said, "Yes." I told him to tell his parents to carry my furniture out to the street, maybe some people might use them. He must have been surprised at my willingness to part with the furniture and other things in the room so willingly. He said nothing. As I think about everything in the room, almost all of them, the bed mattress, couch, chairs and cushions, the lamps, small desk, Yoruba agbada for Sweetie and I, wall pictures including the last supper, were all gifts. Onyema and his siblings were already using the hideaway bed, which he retrieved from Uncle Onwumere's house. That was the bed he slept in at Aba while he lived with my family. His odor still smells on the bed. According to Onyema, that is the bed his first daughter was conceived in, in my house in the village. Another announcement he made was "People are talking about the huge amount you gave for Mr. Ibegbulem's burial." When I asked him who the people were, he did not say.

It was about seven years since I visited Nigeria last. The naira was falling in value. I decided it was time to revisit the country. Prices of oil were falling worldwide. I called my brother and asked him the price of a bag of cement. He said it cost ₦2,550. He thought I was about to send him money. I asked Emedom in Lagos. He said he did not know but was sure it was below two thousand. I asked my nephew at Port Harcourt. He said it cost ₦1,560. Even when I was in the village and told my brother the price his son quoted to me, he made his famous statement, "What does he know?" His son also told me the naira was ₦168 to the dollar. I sent eight thousand dollars to my brother's account about two weeks before I traveled. A few days before I traveled I called his son at Port Harcourt and told him how much I sent and my itinerary. Also, I told Emedom in Lagos my time of arrival. My two calls to Nigeria led to two persons welcoming me to the country.

Unknown to me was that my sister-in-law was at Port Harcourt when I called her son but in the home of her daughter, who was not far from the son. The result was she went home earlier than she had planned to prepare for my arrival. Emedom was well aware of the attitude of the employees at the Lagos airport. He also had a relationship with the Chief Immigration Officer at the airport. Chimdi, Emedom's son, arranged for the Chief to take care of me on arrival at the airport. Emedom was there to identify me to the Chief. Chimdi was in South Africa.

Our arrival to Lagos was without a hitch. Emedom and the Chief were waiting at the luggage claim when I arrived, and he introduced him. The Chief must have been off duty and took off his tie and jacket. He took my ticket and started looking for my suitcase. Soon he located it with the bold letters and the junior employee who carried it. Suddenly the man dropped the suitcase and walked out. Not knowing who the Chief was and that he was waiting for that particular suitcase, he left it and tried to walk past him. The Chief stopped him and demanded to know why he left the suitcase where the passenger could not retrieve it. He became abusive and dropped my card into the pocket of the shirt of the Chief and told him to go and get it. Two intermediate officers grabbed him. He realized he was in trouble and started pleading for mercy. He left the suitcase because he had stolen the cover my wife placed on the suitcase. Things were already complicated, and I did not want to add more. He pleaded while someone else went and brought out the suitcase. I gave Emedom $300 to change to naira. He gave me more than ₦47,500. I bought my ticket to Port Harcourt and tipped the second man who brought the suitcase. Because of the presence of the Chief, he had to be persuaded to accept the tip. But he accepted it when the Chief urged him. However, when we drove to the local airport the last flight for Port Harcourt had left. We drove to Emedom's home. We called Sweetie from his home to tell her where I was.

I left Lagos the following morning by the first plane to Port Harcourt. My nephew was at the airport when I arrived with a taxi driver from the village. The taxi driver also lived at Port Harcourt. The three of us drove to the village. The road was exceptionally bad. It took more than twice the normal time to reach home. So when I asked my nephew how much to pay the man, he suggested ten or twelve thousand naira. I gave him twelve to pay the man. Soon they were on their way back to Port Harcourt. People started to gather. The first sign of trouble showed when I asked my brother how much naira the bank gave him for the eight thousand dollars I sent to him. He claimed the bank gave him ₦900,000. "What!" I asked. I want to go to the bank tomorrow with you. He declined my offer and volunteered to ask the bank himself. When I insisted on knowing the exact amount later, he said he had about a million naira in his account. He added, "I had ₦300,800 before you sent the money. I told him that he had three thousand and eight naira, and I sent over ₦1.2 million to him. He said he would ask his bank when he went back. He went to the bank but never told me the exact amount he received. Even a few weeks later, when I gave his son $200 to buy me naira, he still gave me more than ₦32,000 since they said the value of the naira rises against foreign currencies as Christmas draws near. I went with the gifts we gave them. I asked them to take ₦40,000 for feeding and the same amount for other expenses. He wanted to be the contractor. Worse still he insidiously determined the percentage he would take without negotiation. He became angry when I refused to go along. His anger and frustration spilled to other areas. I grew up in that village and experienced suffering, which I refer to today as growing pains in life's education (Romans 5:3). I also know what it means to be denied help.

Nigeria owes me millions of naira as arrears for my retirement from October 1987 as I write this statement in March 2013. I live on social security, depend on Sweetie, and at times a meager sum from my books. Yet I send the money I give. Let me say from the onset the money I sent is God's. Here is another example.

Once, I called Udobi, my cousin who lived in Maryland, U.S.A. I inquired about another distant and younger cousin Ikwuagwu at home. Ikwuagwu is the only son of his father just as his father was the only son of his grandfather. I understood he needed some help. I sent $200 (₦25,600 at the time) to Udobi and asked him and his two brothers to add whatever they could and send the money to him. A short time after, a Christian lady who attended the same church with me went home to be with the Lord. She designated me to conduct her funeral service. Though she was in Arizona, a different state, they brought the body to Salt Lake City. I know her relatives were surprised that I was black in a congregation where I was the only black, but they carried out her wish. A few days later, I received a check from the daughter. It was exactly $200, the exact amount I sent to Ikwuagwu. I believe it was God's doing.

The news that I sent the money to Ikwuagwu did not sit well with my brother for two reasons. First, it was too much, and second, I did not send it to him. That God gave me back the money did not make any difference to him.

He was still struggling with that when his granddaughter came home from the university. Still angry and wishing to get even with me, he gave her ₦36,000 of my money. Then turned to me and said, "One pastor said if you educate your children without educating your grandchildren, you have not educated anybody." I asked him, "Do you know that I have grandchildren?" He said, "No!" "You don't know I had grandchildren," I repeated. He said, "No!" I did not say one more word.

My brother believes his wish is law in my father's family because he is the oldest. He feels the same about his family. Any resistance to that boils his anger. My people say an elderly person does not watch a goat give birth while on a leash. That is exactly what my brother did one day. Two cousins, the grandsons of Eziaku, one much younger than the other were fighting. The older and bigger boy was beating up the younger boy who was helpless and cried for help. That cry should wrench the heart of anyone who heard it. My sister-in-law and I got up to go and separate them. My brother was outraged and ordered me to sit down. "Where do you think you are going? Sit down!" By the time he stopped yelling, I was out of the room. One would think he was a Roman watching the gladiators. That fight reminded me of the way he used to beat me.

I spent about five weeks in the village. One day my sister-in-law said that the women of the compound decided not to give her and her husband my wife's and my share of baby birth ceremonial gifts. She wanted me to do it. My brother chimed in because we had not performed our own. He claimed that our daughter Melody used to call and talk with them, but since he talked about performing the ceremony she stopped calling. I asked how much it would cost. He said ₦50,000 for each. This amount is for each of my grandchildren he did not know I had. I made a mental calculation of all the people who live in the compound. There was not a single one of them who made half of that amount a year. If each of our three children with children would send that amount, they would have fifty thousand naira times nine. My compound is the smallest of the four that makeup Amafo Isingwu village. There again is the contractor work. I ruled that out. Were they demanding ₦50,000 from each of our children based on their estimate of how "rich" they thought the children to be especially since he said others in America were building factories at home? They could not have based the demand on normal practice of childbirth celebration. I denied his request. Neither did he demand that amount from his children at the birth of any of his grandchildren. He neither told any member of his family about the gifts from our children nor me, nor did he express any gratitude.

These two incidents that happened while I was home illustrate the wealth of the whole people in this compound who were supposed to spend ₦50,000 each time a new baby was born. One of them lived at Calabar the capital of Cross River State. For some reason, he spent more money than he should. He needed ₦500 to pay his fare. No one could afford to lend him ₦500. His mother Eziaku came and told me about it. I gave him ₦1,000. Chukwuma, another man in the compound, hired a truck that carried some materials he had bought and, in the process, damaged the street gutter. I asked my brother to contribute ten thousand naira of my money to help repair the road. He refused. In spite of that, I heard his wife saying to her husband, "Cursing him is not going to repair it. You said more than you should have said." For her to say that meant he must have cursed heaven and earth. This was a much younger person. I offered to contribute ₦10,000 towards the repair. My brother would not allow it. Yet his car drives through it every time it ventures out.

Nwoko was my cousin, my age mate, and lived next door. He was not employed, nor did he receive any retirement. He was sick. He visited me the first day I came home. My brother expressed his anger when I told him that I wished to give Nwoko ₦1,000. To avoid a fight, I said nothing. But I determined to give Nwoko the money and told his wife that. Two days later, when I asked him to justify his objection, he said if I had decided to give Nwoko the money, I should go ahead. I did.

The pattern did not stop with me. Uzoma, his daughter in Britain, sent money through her sister at Port Harcourt. My brother and his wife were to give the money and a bag of rice to another woman married in the same compound as my niece. The money became a bone of contention between the couple. My brother arbitrarily determined he would keep the money and give the woman only the rice. To avoid getting involved, I left the living room and retired to the room where I stayed. Realizing I was not happy with his love of money (1 Timothy 6:10) he came to the room to justify his decision to keep the money. My response was, "Hum." He walked out.

The one maternal aunt who died many years ago was the oldest of the siblings and outlived the brothers. Her daughter, who was older than my brother, also died. Her son, who is our second cousin, lived in our village and was fixing the iron doors and windows and railings in my house. He had offered to bring some Yoruba men living in the compound to perform a little job in my new house. My brother rejected his offer and decided to find people himself. I was sitting in the room the day the cousin came to find out the cost of doing the work. My brother told him it was over eight thousand naira. Reading the disappointment on my cousin's face, as he asked, "On what basis?" My brother reduced it to six thousand. Trying to convince me about how costly things were my brother overbid the plumber and ordered his wife to pay the plumber ten thousand naira in advance. She paid it with protest.

It was not too long after my arrival that a bad odor filled the living room. It was a dead rat. That reminded me of Onyema's statement that my belongings in his parent's house bred snakes. I asked his mother about the claim. She was embarrassed and said it was not true. She remembered a snake I killed in the yard years before the birth of Onyema and described how I killed it. She also recalled two recent incidents when our neighbors Nwoke and Emeuwa chased snakes out of their houses. The fact is that snakes chase lizards and rats into the houses. I asked them about other stories Onyema told me about Chikezie and Jacob. They were all lies. I asked where he got the stories, and she said, "It may be from Ik, the son at Port Harcourt."

I was lying down in the room I stayed in while at the village one day when my brother walked in. He said to me, "You said that you sent more than ₦1.2M. I have spent more than one million. You have to bring more money." He was not ready for what followed. I disputed his claim. When he insisted he was right, I asked him two questions. 1. "How many times have you gone to the bank since you received the money?" He said, "Three times." 2. "How much did you withdraw each time?" His answer was ₦200,000. For all intents and purposes, he might have gone to the bank three times. But he did not withdraw up to ₦200,000 at any given time. Suddenly he realized that three times two is six. Mr. Uku, one of our teachers at Mission Hill, said, "When you tell one lie, you tell ninety-nine more lies to cover the first one. But they all turn out to be lies." That was the game my brother indulged in. He said, "No, four times." Four times two did not give him over one million. He said five times. Five times two did not exceed one million. He added, "At one time I withdrew ₦200,700. One would think that as smart as he claimed to be, he would leave. But he stayed to convince me that he had spent more than a million naira. He got tired of my silence and left.

Chiko, the cousin who was fixing the railing, came over one day to report on the progress he was making. He had one more railing to do and the work would be done. My brother seized it as another opportunity to talk about more money. First, he said I should put four air conditioners in the house. He said Nnamdi, the brother-in-law, said he used my money to help at Uzuakoli secondary school and was spending millions to build his house. By implication, I was not spending millions. My brother did not and, at this writing, does not have an air conditioner in his house. I said, "That is my house. I want only one air conditioner in the master bedroom. If you intend to build a hotel where people who would come to bury you would stay, my house is not a hotel. I have given you between ten and eleven million naira to build this house. Would you explain why I can't go there and sleep?" He said, "You can go there and sleep." About a week later Chiko came back and said, "You can move in now. But that could not happen because the plumbing, electricity, water system, plastering, and painting were still to be done. Another cousin wiring the house was making a mess. Chiko discovered it.

Meanwhile, I had given Ik another $2,000 to change to naira because, as I said to him, "I don't know what your father and his bank are doing with the money I sent to him." Between the two of them, they had ten thousand dollars. When I discovered the game they were playing I decided to return to the U.S. with $1,110. If they wanted, they had enough money and more to complete every single thing that was required in my house. I resigned myself to go to Nigeria at any appropriate time with Chimso, one of our sons who is an architect, and do whatever I need to do.

Then came a shocker. A relative had visited us one time and said her brother-in-law, who was a millionaire, neglected them. Instead of sending their children to the university, he had suggested sending them to become vehicle mechanics. The rich relative was dead and could not defend himself. So the matter died there. My brother and his wife could not charge me with similar offense since everyone in the village and even the Isingwu clan knew I educated their first son in the United States and married for him; not to mention his two daughters who lived with my family and attended secondary school at my expense and the thousands of naira I sent to him.

Immanuel: a second cousin was about to get married. To fulfill the custom, he brought a bottle of wine to my brother to formally inform him. My brother took the opportunity to accuse me of not buying wine for him. Before this time, I did not see him drink except when he entertained visitors, and even then, he only offered them beer.

When he received the drink he asked, did I not know he drank? I said nothing. His wife and son said that most of the bottles of wine the Yoruba people gave me, which I gave him were still there. I told the son, who still was in possession of the two thousand dollars, to buy him two bottles of wine. In his usual manner, he said nothing when he received them. His wife told him the sermon that Sunday was saying thanks to show gratitude. He mumbled thanks. Then he said, Chikara takes care of me." This is the same Chikara he accused along with me to Kema of not helping him. I looked at him but said nothing.

I turned the page to talk about the Mercedes Benz he owned. "I wonder what my mother would say today if she knew you go to the farm to harvest cassava with this car," He praised Ngozi and her husband, who gave him the car as the only two who took care of them. "People claim that Uzoma bought me the first car. But it was my money. All she did was to help me." One of those times the wife could no longer keep quiet. She said, "Ihuoma and her husband also helped." This is the same claim Onyema made when he bought clothes for them. Onyema said he bought the clothes because only his dad and mom struggled to educate them. I turned and looked at my brother. He knew I had enough and was ready to talk. He blamed the dead relative again. He said *one of the times* I sent him some dollars, he took it to Enyeremadu to change for him, and he cheated him. That was an admission it was more than one time. I kept quiet.

I live in Salt Lake City. The people who know me call me a prayer warrior. I get calls for prayers from people who live as far as California in the west to as far as Connecticut in the east. Even my niece in Nigeria called me to pray for her safe delivery. This is my brother's daughter. I dreamed after the first prayer and called her and informed her she would have a safe delivery and a baby boy. As told earlier it happened. Before I left to travel to Nigeria, I learned that my brother's oldest daughter, who was sick, had stopped talking. For many years she did not speak. When I left, I took my anointing oil with me.

A few days after I arrived I fasted and called her. I anointed her and prayed for her. She still did not talk. On the following Sunday, my brother, my sister-in-law, and I were invited to speak about my condition the last time I visited home. In the process, I mentioned my three spiritual gifts, namely, prayer, teaching, and healing. See *Experiencing God's Gracious Shepherding* by this author. My brother like the Jews who ridiculed Jesus Christ, poked fun of my healing gift. I mentioned prayers of healing God did not answer the way people asked for in the Bible including that of Paul himself (2 Corinthians 12:9), Timothy and the sick man Paul left in his house (2 Timothy 4:20). When I prayed on the morning I left home, I was emotional and almost in tears because of her.

About a week after I returned to the United States the phone rang. When I picked up the receiver it was my niece at Port Harcourt. She told me that Chinyere, her sister, was speaking again. We rejoiced and thanked God. I wondered what pandemonium would have taken place at the house if God had healed her immediately after I prayed. Every sick person in that village and even a ten-mile radius would have come to his house, and all or most of them would not be healed. Who knew what chaos would have resulted? Later, Anuri, my youngest niece in Britain, called and told me that her dad asked me to call him at 9:00 a.m. on Monday their time. I calculated and remembered the wife would be at Aba at that time for treatment. Whatever amount of money he planned to demand from me was a lie and he did not want his wife to hear it.

I called on Sunday when I expected everyone to be home. He was angry. "Is today Monday and is now 9 a.m.?" Pretending not to know why he wanted me to call at the time, I said to him, "Do you know that your 9.00 a.m. is 1 am here in Salt Lake City, and you want me to keep awake till then?" He had no answer. Finally, he said, "Chinyere is talking." I told him I knew. He wondered why I did not shout Hallelujah! I believed he wanted to ask for more money. But the presence of his wife prevented it. When he gave the phone to her, I asked, and she confirmed that she would be at Aba for treatment at 9 a.m. the following day. I talked with Anyadindu one of the two daughters who lived with them. She lamented, "While you were here we joked and laughed. That is all gone now." I tried to console her.

Though Chiko knew the house was not ready for occupation, with the doors and the windows firmly installed, our property could be safely stored there. Sometime after I returned to the U.S. I dialed Onyema and asked if he had the phone number of Chiko. He did not. Without telling him that his mother and the facts disputed his claim that my property bred a snake in the house, I said to him, "You said my belongings bred a snake in your parent's house. Could you call Chiko and tell him to move them to my house? I will refund whatever the move costs." He said there was no need to ask Chiko. He would tell Ik, his brother at Port Harcourt, to do it. They never moved the belongings, nor did they ask for any payment.

Before the school year began in Nigeria in 2011, I called Ezihe, my niece who is a teacher, and asked her to find out if anyone in our compound needed financial help in school. She frankly told me she did not know. We agreed that she should consult her mother; when we talked again she told me that Okechukwu may need ₦1500 per term. Knowing what to expect if I got my brother involved I totally avoided him in the transaction. Since the amount was not small, I sent more than ₦4,500, the total sum for the year, in my sister-in-law's name, plus money for her use. I doubted that Okechukwu was the only person who could use some help. I accepted and acted on the recommendation.

In the early part of December 2011, Onyema called me. He told me that he and his siblings in Europe and Nigeria and their father had decided to hold a memorial service for my father. They planned to kill a cow. The grandchildren in America should contribute $50 each.

I asked why he wanted to do this now? Did Chikara i.e., my cousin in London with him do this for my uncle who in comparison with my dad died recently? He said yes and added, "If he did not kill a cow for his father they would not have made him a chief." He said his father promised to contribute what he could. I promised to contribute $200 to the $200 our daughter and her brothers would give. However, I made it plain that I had celebrated my father's memorial service twice in the village, once in 1972 when I visited Nigeria and again in 1976 when my family and I returned to Nigeria. The $400 I would send could not be used as any part of the payment for the cow. It must be for what I call a memorial scholarship in my parent's honor. I instructed him to write down the names Jeremiah Isigwuzo and Rachel Iheomadinihu Memorial Scholarship Fund. I gave two qualifications for winning an award. The first is the child is in need. The second is the child is a Christian and respectful. He said he would increase his contribution to add to the fund. When he informed me of the date, it was not on December 25 when many people from the village come home from all parts of the country and overseas to celebrate Christmas. When I asked why, he said there would be Izaha (A most famous and important celebration when members of an age group demonstrate that they are fulfilled and become recognized in the village). It takes precedence over every other event. So on Friday of the Sunday, they scheduled the ceremony, Sweetie went to the bank after work, which was between 5:00 and 6:00 p.m. Salt Lake City time and was between 1:00 and 2:00 a.m. Saturday Nigerian time. The exchange rate was ₦161.75 to the dollar. To my knowledge banks are closed in Nigeria on Saturdays and Sundays. For that reason, there was no justification to wake them up at about 2:00 a.m. in Nigeria when Sweetie came home. When I called the following day Saturday after 10:00 p.m. Salt Lake City time, it was after 6:00 a.m. on Sunday Nigeria time. They were already up and cooking in preparation for the festivity.

In the conversation that followed, I said to my brother, "I sent $400 (₦64,700) to your bank account yesterday. Not a penny of it should be spent on the killing of a cow, a goat, a sheep, a dog, or a chicken. I told him what the money was for. To emphasize the point, I asked him to put the phone on speaker. With the speaker on, I asked his wife to listen as I repeated my instruction. She said, "Anunam" (I heard). I repeated my instructions to his son. I asked my brother to announce at the church that morning at the same time as he invited the church to the feast. His reply unveiled his hidden agenda. He said, "Let us finish this first."

Two weeks later it was Christmas. We called them to wish them a Merry Christmas. I asked my brother if he made the announcement. He said, "I told the committee." I told him I would call Mba a member of the committee. My answer was intended to warn him knowing he did not tell me the truth. Easter came and we called them to wish them Happy Easter. Again, I asked him about the money. He said he gave it to Mba. Dismayed that he would hand over the money to Mba, I repeated what he said. He confirmed it. I asked if he had Mba's number. He called Chinyere and asked if they had the number and she said yes. On second thought I told him not to worry about the number. I would get it from Mba's son here in the States. I got the number and called Mba. I left a message and when he called, I did not recognize the number my phone announced and did not answer it. He also left a message.

As I waited for Sweetie to come home and dial Mba's number for me, two thoughts occupied my mind. Is my brother lying to me? Did he get angry with me and decided not to have anything to do with the project? Sweetie came home and dialed the number for me. This time Mba answered. He said the only conversation he had with my brother was whether he heard from me or not. That confirmed my suspicion from the onset that he did not intend to use the money for the purpose I sent it. I told Mba the amount (₦64,700) and the purpose for which I sent it. Also, I told him the name of the fund and asked him to meet my brother. We agreed that the financial help should be limited to elementary school students.

A few days after our son Chimso posted one of my books *ABCD of Intelligence and Behavior*, I was typing when the phone rang. I answered the phone. It was Onyema. Thinking it was a friendly call I told him about the book. He wanted to know where he could get a copy. I told him how to get it. Then he started: "That is how it started, from Anuri to Uzoma and to me. Professor Uzoukwu was abusing my father, and you were supporting him. As a Christian, you should defend your brother against outsiders. Only he and Mama struggled to educate us. I don't want you or anyone else to kill him before his time. I asked Onyema what Mba said to his father. He said, "I don't know. I was not there; I was not in Nigeria." I said to him, "If you don't know what he said, what do you want me to defend?" He had no answer. If you want your money back, we will send it to you." I said whatever you heard, the fact is he told me that he gave Mba the money. If you were told that, would you not call Mba and ask him what he is doing with the money? He said he would. But added, he did not know if his father said that or not. In reply to refunding my money, I told him to send it to Amafo if he wished to refund the money. He ridiculed the meager amount of ₦50 I give to individuals in the compound and said they laugh at the gift and the giver. He claimed to have told his father to use the money and spend all on the feast. I asked if his instruction should override mine. He said, "No." To his ridicule of my gifts, I said, "If you don't like my widow's might give them ₦5000." He said that's nothing. "That's nothing" was his answer to giving ₦1,000,000. Then I said give them ₦100,000,000. He laughed. Then I said to him if you think that you are rich, don't compare yourself with me. Compare yourself with my children. When I talked to Sweetie she asked, "What did Mba say?" I had no answer.

I asked her to give me Onyema's number. She asked if I could cram all eleven numbers. I did and called. His wife said she could not wake him up because he was on night duty. She left a note for him to call me when he woke up. When he called, he warned me he had only five minutes for me. I asked if he meant what he said when he claimed only his father and mother struggled to educate them? He said, "Yes," and repeated it with emphasis. I said I helped and came home and helped more. He said, "You are lying. I had packed my suitcase to go to Turkey when you came back." I said what? He repeated himself, "You are lying. I am over fifty years old." I said, "Now I know why you treated me worse than a beggar when I was sick and spent a night at your house in London. Thank God, I paid you $130 for the night." I dropped the phone and later called his brother in the U.S. He is older than Onyema.

I had a short conversation with him. My first question was, "Before I came back in 1976 did my brother at any time tell any of you that I was sending money to help him?" For the next minute, he was silent. I asked, "Are you there?" He said he was thinking. Finally, he said, "No," and added, "At one time he said you told him that you would send him a car." I asked him about the first two gifts I sent in December 1964 ($10) and August 1966 ($300). No, he did not tell anyone. I called home and my brother answered the phone. I asked him what Mba said to him? He said Mba told him to give him the money. "Did you not tell me you gave him the money?" I asked. He said, "No that he said he handed over the matter to Mba." I told him to hand over the phone to his wife. He did. I asked my brother's wife, "Before we came home in 1976 did my brother ever tell you that I sent money to him?" She did not say one word. I explained that I asked because Onyema called me a liar when I said I helped. She repeated to me. Referring to me, my brother said, "Didn't somebody help him?" Then, I became specific. "Did he tell you in December 1964 that I sent him money because he said he had no money to celebrate Christmas for his family, as the result of defending his family against his Yoruba enemies?" She said, "It would be all right." That was her way of saying no. Again I asked, "Did he tell you that I sent $300 in August 1966 when Amadi passed to attend Government Secondary school at Umuahia?" She said, "Odinma" i.e., her way of saying he did not. My brother wrote to me and said the bank gave him 107 pounds, six shillings, and five pennies for the $300. These two are a drop in the bucket when compared with the total amount I gave him before 1976. In 1975 alone I sent him $2,000 to buy me a plot of land. He said the bank gave him 714 pounds, five shillings, and eight pence. Note: The pounds mentioned in this chapter are not the same value as the current British pounds. Each pound is more than double the value of the current pound: twenty shillings as opposed to the ten shillings, the current value of the British pound, and twelve pence instead of ten of the current shilling. End of Note. Also, I sent him $200 to take care of his family at the same time. I said to his wife with tears in my eyes, "Put the phone on speaker." Referring to me, my brother asked his wife, "Did someone not help him?" I said to his wife, "Does someone not help him," a justification for calling me a liar? Even if he paid for my education in the U.S.A., which he did not. Would that justify seizing the money meant to help the poor children in the village and lying about it?" She said her husband had been sick for about a month. Now his wife felt telling the truth to his hearing while he is sick would kill him. I bade her goodbye. With tears running down my cheeks, Sweetie came and comforted me. I could not believe I was being persecuted for punishing myself and my family for helping my brother, his family, and the poor children in my village. At church that Sunday I asked Sweetie to fill the prayer portion of the bulletin. Ask them to pray that my brother will tell his family the truth. As for me, if not the Bible, I would have run crazy. For example, 2 Timothy 3:12 (NKJV) says, "Yes, and all who desire to live godly in Christ Jesus will suffer persecution." 1 Peter says, "For what credit *is it* if, when you are beaten for your faults, you take it patiently? But when you do good and suffer, if you take it patiently, this *is* commendable before God" (1 Peter 2:20 NKJV)

I told Sweetie not to tell our children Onyema called me a liar. I called Amadi my brother's first born and gave him certain passages of the Bible to give his father to read. The first was Proverbs 6:16-19. These are the seven things God hates. I wanted him to see what his pride was leading him to do, including getting some of his children against my father's family. I asked him to read 1 Timothy 6:10. I gave him 1 Samuel 3; my money was a sacrifice to God.

Again when I called him early 2010 and he demanded more money, I told him I would not send a penny until he gave me an account of how he spent the more than ten thousand dollars I already gave him during my last visit. He told me the old story that Chinyere wrote everything down. "Send more money. Ik is coming home this Saturday. He will send you the record." Ten years later that report has not reached me.

Besides ridiculing my gifts Onyema made two other statements that defined his motive. He said his grandfather contributed to his prosperity. Right there is ancestor worship. He added, "I started the ball rolling." The same pride that prevented his father from telling his family the gifts I gave him. Well, Onyema might have started his ball rolling, but I started my balls rolling and completed them. What about my brother, what motivated him to kill a cow? These two stories explain his motive.

Dr. M. I. Okpara, a former Premier of the Eastern Region of Nigeria, suddenly fell down and died as he celebrated the memorial celebration of his dead father. He was overweight and suffered from other health problems. Suddenly he fell in the middle of the celebration and died, probably of a heart attack. In a society such as ours, where people always find something to blame when someone dies, the people speculated that his grandfather, who died earlier and whose death was not celebrated, killed him because he did not celebrate his death first. His village and mine are in the same clan and practice the same custom. My mother's passing with funeral were at the door. I paid the expenses for the burial. I bought five northern goats at Oyo and Alhaji Ajisafe gave me a cow. Amadi and Ogini transported the cow and five goats in a college pickup truck. On arrival at home, the older men in the compound vehemently objected to the killing of the cow. They contended that since I did not kill a cow at my father's memorial service, I could not kill a cow at my mother's funeral and still live. They were not ready to bury another person. We sold the cow. My brother who wants not only one or two cows but as many cows as possible to be killed at his funeral, wanted the cow to be killed in honor of the father he hated for blessing me instead of him. May I ask the reader to please read 2 Corinthians 11 and 1 Corinthians 9 before reading what follows. These are the balls I started and finished. I did not ask Onyema, his father, or any other person to contribute. I bought Onyema's mother three sets of clothes and a wrapper. I bought the first suit he and his older brother wore. I sent the money for the family's 1964 Christmas celebration. I sent $300 (more than 107 pounds) in August 1966 to his father for Amadi's secondary school education. I sent more money, $150 in November 1967, and in 1968, I sent him $50, part of which he said he used 240 Biafran pounds ($10) to bail his wife from jail. I sent him $50 in 1969 to inform him of my marriage. I sent $50 in January 1970 after the war. If the only thing I did for Onyema and his father during that period was to provide money to give back his mother from jail, any other human being should be grateful. Still, as a private student in debt, in January 1970, when I saw the picture of Biafran children on the TV naked and running everywhere to pick up some candies newsmen scattered, I was crushed. Though wondering whether the Nigerian victors would seize the money, I still sent $50 to him. He acknowledged the receipt. I graduated in June with Ph. D. I put $50 and my picture in a big envelope. This is the money he told his wife Enyeremade cheated him of. I sent him $150 in December 1970. In May 1971 an American went to Port Harcourt. I was an Assistant Professor. I gave the man $150 and enclosed a sweater my brother requested. I also gave the man five dollars to register the parcel to my brother when he reached Port Harcourt. My brother acknowledged receipt of both the money and the sweater. In 1972, I traveled to Nigeria with the Educators To Africa Association. I bought three hundred Nigerian pounds at JFK. Having completed the first memorial service for my father, I gave my brother 150 pounds to take care of his family. Among other things, I killed a goat. Grateful to God that they were all well and even my mother, who was sick when I reached home, was well again. I sent more money with copies of the pictures I took. In 1973 and 1974, I sent him a total of $300 and $200 in 1975. I also sent him $2,000 to buy me a plot of land. He acknowledged the receipt and said the bank gave him 714 pounds, 5 shillings, and eight pennies for the $2,000. On my return to Nigeria in 1976, I asked him about the land. He said he did not buy the land and added, "I used the money to educate the children and to help Nnamdi (his brother-in-law) at Uzuakoli with the hope that he will help me to educate these children." We were with my mother at the time. I wondered aloud as to how he could use such an amount within such a short period. I decided on the basis of what I had done so far, besides a poor salary, that it was time to take care of my family. Should I be persecuted? My salary was not enough to feed my family and pay rent. I protested and requested the government to upgrade my position based on my education, experience, my position in the U.S., and, in comparison, with officers who graduated with bachelor's degrees after me and the level they were at. When they refused, I resigned. My brother's sympathy was to tell everyone he met that Chikara and Obed he helped had refused to help him. Even at this time when I was without a job and without income, Onyema, his second son, lived with my family at Aba, and Sweetie cooked for him, and he was not charged one penny. I did not stop helping him and his family.

Following my resignation, the government upgraded me and sent me to Oyo. Though living on borrowed money, Onyema still lived at Aba with my family at my expense. I educated my brother's first son at Lyndon State College, Vermont U.S.A. Chinyere, my brother's oldest daughter who failed her school certificate examination, came and lived at Oyo with my family and attended Olivet High School at my expense. She obtained her GCE certificate, but her behavior was unbearable. I sent her home. I initiated and again paid all the expenses for the second memorial service for my father. Instead of asking my brother to contribute I bought a suit for him for the occasion. I married my nephew, my brother's first son (paid bride price wedding gown, and bought a set of clothes and wrapper for both mothers of the bride and groom, and bought and paid money for the customary things for the marriage). Ihuoma, another one of my brother's daughters, also failed her final year school certificate exam. She also came and lived with us at Oyo. She also attended Olivet and passed the school certificate exam at my expense. I employed her at the college, housed her free and finally admitted her as a student at the college. I paid for the training of Aunt Ukachi's two grandsons. I gave my brother ₦400 to help him pay for a plot he bought for ₦1,000 and another ₦400 to help him defray the cost of his age group celebration. I took care of my mother and paid the expenses for her burial. As the first son, that was my brother's responsibility. The money he found in my mother's room and promised to give to me, he never told me the amount, nor did he give it to me. I did not stop here. I carried one-half bag of rice, stockfish, and corned beef to my brother's family each time I went home at Easter and Christmas, even after the burial of my mother's body.

Before my family left Oyo, the police bought our big dog for ₦1,200. We sent the money to my brother through his son at Oyo towards the building of my house. I helped his son who was in search of a job after his youth corps service. When we returned to the United States, I sent my return ticket to my brother. He said the airline refunded him ₦2,162. I sent him a check for ₦2,500 to draw money from my bank at Oyo. He acknowledged the receipt of the cash. The last amount before my visit in 2002 was the $100 he received by lying that the government ordered him to survey my plot at Ebite. I dreamed it was a lie and wrote him. He confirmed the dream. Amadi, his first son, took over my Pontiac Grandville I left at Oyo. I regret writing this part of my story, but I am compelled to write it. God provided the means, and I enjoyed doing them. Instead of acknowledging them, Onyema accused me of not helping his parents to bring them up. When I said, "I did help," he called me a liar. Let anyone with conscience deny any of these gifts before God. So far nothing has happened that encourages me to believe that the truth will be told.

Note: What is Onyema's problem? He visited Nigeria from London when I was at Oyo. I had all the responsibilities listed above. I still gave him ₦40 transport money to Umuahia. He wanted me to add his education to the list. I could not do it. He even said, "I see you have all these responsibilities." I was in the U.S.A. as a private student and sent money to care for them. I never asked his father for one penny. Instead of working to earn money, he wasted money and flew to Nigeria and exchanged visits with a girlfriend and owes me a grudge for not stealing to satisfy his aggrandizement. End of note.

Chapter 54

What's Your Name

In more than two decades of prison ministry there had been only two incidents when our safety was of concern. The first was a Sunday when we actually conducted the service. On our way out the red and yellow lights were flashing. Having left the chapel, we saw the light, and a guard ushered us into a room and told us what was going on. He warned us it was not safe to go to the parking lot. Even if we got to our cars, the guard at the gate would not allow us out. Some prisoner or prisoners had tried to escape. He gave us the cell phone to call home and tell our families why we were delayed. We obeyed. The delay did not last too long before we were released. Our second experience was such that we were not even allowed to enter the prison premises.

As said earlier in this book we held our Bible study at Ann and Jim's house. One day, we had two visitors, Rich and his wife Georgianna. He was a cancer patient. It was advanced and he did not feel the doctor was having any success. Someone had asked him to come to our group for prayer. I put my hand on him and prayed. One or two others also prayed. After a while, I saw him in church and asked how he was doing. He said the doctor said the cancer was in remission. However, he was still giving him radiation treatment. I expressed my concern he may kill all the white cells. If the cancer returns, it will have a free ride. Because of how serious the cancer was, the doctor had given him the date of his death. He told his relatives in the eastern part of the U.S. When his people arrived in Salt Lake City, he had gone fishing with his doctor. He apologized for "not dying."

Later on, the cancer returned with vengeance. He called me a prophet. He invited me to be present the Sunday the church was to pray for him. I told him I could not because of my prison ministry that was at the same hour. As we drove close to the prison gate, we saw the yellow lights flashing everywhere. Bruce said, "They may not allow us in." He was right. On our arrival at the gate, the guards turned us back. Bruce turned around and drove me to the Evangelical Free Church building. When I walked into the room, Rich said, "Obed I thought you could not make it." I explained why I was able to attend. The short nurse who invited me to the Wednesday prayer group called him "our Lazarus." Unfortunately, he did not recover.

Sweetie and I have friends scattered throughout the U.S. We correspond with most of them during Christmas. However, SueAnn is an all-season friend. Though she and her family live in Connecticut, we still exchange visits. We participate in some important decisions in her life through advice but more by prayer. Sweetie and I were on our way to see our daughter and her family in Maryland and stopped in Connecticut to see her and her family. She and her husband drove us to see her daughter who was having a problem with her husband. She took offense at her mother for revealing her secret to us. My advice against divorce offended her more because she was ready to marry another man. Shortly after the divorce, she remarried. The new man was worse than the first and she divorced him. We could claim her as our adopted daughter, and she knew the relationship was there. She called and emailed us. We responded favorably.

In 2011, I determined to complete a few of the books I started. There were three Christian books: The Christian and Christian Life, Jesus: Humankind's Only Hope, Why God Became a Man and my book on intelligence. I hired Kay, my sister in-law, as a part-time secretary. However, her knowledge of the computer was limited. She and I worked only on The Christian and Christian Life. When I submitted some of the Christian books for assessment, they suggested I tell stories to enhance the effect. We continued to attend Evangelical Free Church, but it had become a struggle. I was still actively leading the prayer group, visitation and greeting. Preaching from Deuteronomy the pastor said, "You see after you go through the New Testament you come back to the law." I wondered what happened to: "For the law was given by Moses, but grace and truth came by Jesus Christ" (John 1:17). The last blow came after the death of his father in-law. He preached from Ecclesiastic 9 and told everyone in church they would die. I walked out because death means separation from God. John 3:5-18, 5:24, 4:25-26, John 6:47, Romans 8:1, 38-39, Jesus has abolished death (2 Timothy 1:10), Romans 6:23, 1 John 5:11-13, which all say I have eternal life. But I had been scheduled to greet one more time at the church. Sweetie and I were flying from Baltimore to Denver when the decision was made for me. Get out from that EV Free. I fulfilled my greeting obligation and told Sweetie I was out. She said she felt the same. We left.

I was not sure about what to do about worship. If we were not in Utah, I would start a nondenominational church. So, being in Utah, we attended a church close to us. Sweetie told me the name is Southeast Christian Church. We met a couple who used to attend EV Free. The sermons seemed to agree with our beliefs. Then we were invited to a newcomers meeting to hear what they believed. The senior pastor made two statements about water baptism that contradicted what I know and believe. I reacted to water baptism. "Did you say water baptism completes salvation?" I asked. He said yes and added, "Jesus said preaching and baptizing." When I asked who baptized the thief on Christ's right, he said who knows what Jesus did. Because of the other people, I did not want to drag on the discussion.

With the topic still lingering in my mind, we still attended service the next Sunday. In the absence of the senior pastor, the worship pastor baptized a boy. When the boy emerged from the water the worship pastor said, "This completes your salvation." The following day I called the senior pastor, and he was evasive. This time, probably because a number of people in his church who knew me at EV Free, including one elder, had told him about me. Also, because we gave a sizeable sum of money that Sunday, he said, "Obed, you know, sometimes we have one thing in mind, and we say something else. I will find out and talk with you on Sunday." Sweetie and I attended service that Sunday and he avoided us. That was our last visit to the building. A few people from there asked why we were not coming again. We told them that we disagreed with the teaching. At this time, a friend invited us and we attended Risen Life Church and enjoyed it.

In 2012 I determined to publish a few of the books I have been working on. I know that sometimes I write against the grain. I believe the system will catch up with me someday. For example, in the summer of 1967, when I called intelligence tests cultural tests and incurred the wrath of Dr. Orton, I did not know anyone else who questioned the validity of I.Q. Today, many do, and I now label I. Q. a misnomer. I name it Quotient of Items on the Test (Q.I.T.). Also, I disputed the statement that people forget because the cells that carry the information die off. Research now confirms my reasons for forgetfulness, namely, the impact of first impression at the onset, how often the knowledge is used or not used, and the importance or unimportance of the knowledge in the frame of things. So the first book I registered and submitted to Amazon as an E-book was my book ABCD of Intelligence ... As the reader knows by now, education has been my trade since I graduated from grade six. To me, teaching and learning have come to mean quite a different thing from what is practiced in most classrooms. I have published in the area both in Nigeria and in the U.S. I published one more for the benefit of home teachers entitled

Teaching That Guarantees Learning for School and Home Teachers. A few months before Christmas, I submitted Why God Became A Man. At this time, I still had more than five to submit, including The Christian, Christian Life, and When the Saints Pray 1977-1987 A Decade of Courage (the history of Oyo Federal College of Education for Special Education.)

 Several months after I called home and asked my sister-in-law if my brother had told her about the money I had sent, I only mentioned the first two gifts of December 1964 and August 1966; she answered evasively with, "It will be all right." I asked her to turn on the speaker. She said, "Your papa has been sick for about a month now. It is ok." I understood that saying the truth would upset and kill her husband. I decided not to call them again. Then Ngozi, one of my nieces, called from Ireland. In the course of our conversation, she said her father complained that I did not call again. I told her why. She promised to talk to her father and brother and call me. After the birth of Chimaraobim our grandson, I called Ngozi in Ireland to inform her. When she informed me that her father refused to discuss the matter, for the first time I told any of the children that I sent him $2,000 to buy me a plot. When I asked him about the plot in early 1976, he said he used the money to educate his children and his brother-in-law at Uzuakoli Secondary School.

 Note: After I realized that my brother did not tell any member of his family about any of the money I gave him, not even his wife, or the more than fourteen-hundred-pound sterling I sent to him between December 1964 and October 1975, I made a painful decision. He used the money to play pool. That confirmed my suspicion that he purposely lied to people when he said, "Obed and Chikara I helped, have refused to help me to educate my children." Considering the condition I was in as a private student when God enabled me to earn and send the money, I further resolved he was a dangerous man especially since he said he did not know I have grandchildren. Yet he demanded ₦50,000 for the celebration of the birth of each of the nine grandchildren. I refused to call him. I wrote on my computer, "If I go home to be with my Maker while he is still on this earth, my body should be cremated and taken home for burial only after his death. I fear he might poison my family or plan their kidnapping. He could do these to own my three plots and my house, which he occupies at this writing, while his children add a second floor to his house. Unfortunately, he gave me cause to feel this way. End of note.

Chapter 55

July 31

Usually, I did not answer any phone call that said, "name unknown." But for one reason, I determined to answer every call on July 31 the night I saw Jesus Christ in my dream in 1963. I usually fast and pray each year on this day. So on July 31, 2013, when the phone rang and said, "name unknown," I picked up the receiver and answered it my way. "Praise the Lord, I am blessed and grateful." I added, "Do you need a prayer?" The voice at the other end replied, "Yes, I need a prayer. Yes, I need a prayer." I recognized the voice. It was Chikara my cousin in London. It had been about six years since we talked. He had cancer and called home and my brother complained that I did not call home anymore. However, he did not tell him why. If Chikara was not aware of the thousands of pounds and dollars I gave him, he knew that I educated my brother's first son in the U.S. and married for him. So he was offended to hear that Onyema, my brother's second son, called me a liar when I said that I helped his father. He was surprised to hear that my brother and his wife alone brought up their children without help from anyone else. Notwithstanding, he pleaded with me to call him. I refused to promise anything. Of Enoch's denials and misdeeds, I regard his denial of the knowledge of the existence of my grandchildren as the expression of his hatred for me and everyone in my family. I will not call him.

On August 24, 2013, Chimarobim (My God knows my heart's desire), our ninth grandchild, came into the world almost five weeks premature. I called Amadi, my nephew in the U.S., and informed him of the birth. Also, I called Joy in England and left a message. Ngozi in Ireland was absent when I called, but I talked first with the oldest son, Chima, and then with her husband. She returned the call when she came home, and Sweetie answered it. I did not call Nigeria. When I helped their father, I thought it a favor to help them to live a good life and get educated. Now I realize God did it all through me to have a record for me in His book. My suffering is sweeter. Thanks to my God.

About the last week of August 2013, a publisher called me and also sent an email. This was the third contact about my books. The first contact was because their researcher saw my books registered as e-books. I rejected their offer and dismissed them. About two months later they wrote me again. This time they charged me about $2,000, about one-third the original charge. I still refused to reply. About the last week of August, they called again. This time, they offered to publish all three books without any charge. They also sent me a contract. Considering where they started and the fact that it is a subsidy publisher, it sounded too good to be true. However, Sweetie and I decided to take them seriously. We submitted the contract to a law firm.

While we waited for the feedback from the lawyer, Mindi, our daughter-in-law in Denver, Colorado, read my book and texted Sweetie to watch a CBS documentary entitled, *Teach* on September 6, 2013. I joined Sweetie to watch it. It was about four teachers in three different states in the U.S. The students had certain things in common. One of them was they were two or three grades below their current grades in the subjects the teachers taught. These teachers grouped the students according to their abilities and taught them from where they were. Each of them avoided the current classroom arrangement of lining the chairs and students up with the teacher standing in front of the class and lecturing. More importantly, the teachers knew the subjects they taught. The students succeeded. Some became medical doctors and some lawyers. By the end of the two-hour program, every topic they discussed was addressed in my two books, namely Humanizing Education for The Twenty-First Century and Teaching That Guarantees Learning for School and Home Teachers, in the manner I described. Yet they covered only a percentage of the contents of my books. More importantly, the students succeeded.

Looking at Sweetie I said to her, "Isn't God gracious and wonderful? Though they did not mention my name or the title of my books, they have advertised my books. Where would I get money to pay for a two-hour advertisement for my books? Yet they did it and it did not cost me a penny. I called Nicole, the publisher's representative, the following Monday. On answering the phone I asked, "Do you believe in miracles?" "Yes," she said. I asked if she watched the documentary Teach on CBS last Friday. She said, "No." I said to her, "Though they did not mention my name or the title of the book, they advertised the content of the books free of charge for two hours. She asked for the title of the documentary. 'Teach," I said.

On the fourth Sunday of September, we had our son Chimso and his family over to celebrate his wife's birthday. I asked what kind of grades the two girls in school brought home. He gave me another pleasant surprise. "They are moving away from A,B, C,D and F grades." I interrupted him. This is what I advocate in *Humanizing Education for the Twenty-first Century*. God wrote these books through me. Grandchildren, you can tell people your grandfather was a pioneer in modern education." Unfortunately, not long after the publication the publisher went out of circulation because of lawsuits. Then I mentioned my book on intelligence. I am going to win the Nobel Prize with my intelligence book. I am done with education. I have one more assignment from my God to complete. That is to complete the Christian book I have already started.

What would make a man malign and debase his dead mother just to falsely uplift himself to greatness? As a psychologist, I should know the answer. Yet, after my telephone conversation with Enoch, my oldest brother, on September 24, 2013, I find myself asking this question.

As I listened to a sermon one evening the phone rang. Waiting for it to identify the caller, I heard Enoch. I hesitated and it repeated Enoch. I picked up the receiver and answered it my usual way: "Praise the Lord. I am blessed and grateful." He responded with, Hello, Hello." I dropped the receiver. He called again and I repeated my answer. He repeated his hello. I asked, "Who is this? Who is this?" He said, "Me, how are you?" I thought he would say Enoch or your brother or Papa, the name I call him. "We are fine and what about you?" "I just came out from the hospital, but I'm well now." When I asked why he was in the hospital, he said it was for stomach trouble and high blood pressure. Then he stated why he called. Chimso, our son, and his wife had a baby boy, and I did not call to tell them. Chibuikem, his grandson, and his wife had their baby, and I did not call. He demanded to know why?

"Would you listen if I tell you?" He asked me to tell him. "You took ₦36,000 from my money without my knowledge and gave to your granddaughter. To inform me, you turned to me and said, 'The pastor said anyone who educated his children but failed to educate his grandchildren has not educated anybody." I asked if you know that I have grandchildren? Your reply was "No!" Dismayed at your answer I asked, "You do not know that I have grandchildren?" You replied more emphatically, "No!" If you don't know about the other eight, how can you know the ninth?" He said nothing. Then I continued. My father-in-law died. We called you and informed you. My wife was on the phone. Your sympathy was, "Take two corns, boil them, eat one, and give one to your husband, and you two return to Nigeria. When I asked what you said, you repeated yourself. He said those were not the current issue.

Okay, Onyema called me a liar. As I discussed it with your wife, you interjected, "Didn't someone help him?" He claimed that only you and his mother suffered to educate them, the same claim your wife made when I visited home in 2009. He made the same argument that Onyema defended his abuse of me. "Onyema had graduated from secondary school and had gone to Calabar and returned before you came back in 1976. I was offended. I calculated the money I sent to him from December 1964 to Summer 1975 and put them at a total of more than fourteen hundred pounds sterling. First, you did not tell anybody about them. I was a private student and neither dated nor bought a car. I waited in Lincoln's wet snow for the bus. He asked if I wrote down every gift I gave him and if he should announce to the world that I sent him gifts. I could not believe him. "You are telling me that informing your family, your wife, and children is telling the world? If for nothing else, when you received the money you used to bail your wife out of jail. Also, that January, the war ended, and we watched Biafran children on TV. I had little more than $50 and I debated what to do. First I thought Nigerians would open the envelope and take the money. I decided it was better that Nigerians stole it than have it here and you starve. I prayed and sent it. Sweetie and I were overjoyed when you wrote and said you got it. You mean, you did not tell anyone about any of the money I gave you including the $2,000 to buy land for me? When I asked for the land your reply was, "I used the money to educate these children and to help Nnamdi at Uzuakoli College so that he would help you to educate these children. You called me a liar before Onyema. You are telling me that you received all the money but never used any of it to buy Onyema books and clothes, to pay his school fees, i.e., tuition or feed him. You told your children and others that I did not help you. He jumped in at this point.

I never told anybody that you did not help. Yes, you did. You told Nkemaakolam. He asked, Nkemakolam Ugenyi? When I said yes, he replied, "I don't remember saying that to him." Whether he knew it or not, his answer indicated he said it to more than one person. Nkemakolam was angry when I told him that Enoch had told me that he used all the money I sent for his use, including the $2,000 I sent to him, to buy land for me to educate his children and brother-in-law. He told me to demand a refund of the $2,000. That was Uncle Onumere Ikeji's reaction. He acknowledged the receipt of all the sums, including the one he used to bail his wife, but said he could not remember the money I gave him when I came in 1972. I told him where we were sitting when I gave it to him. Then he came with the killer.

He claimed to have bought a plot of land for me at Ovoghovo. That was too much to swallow. I shouted at him. That is a lie! My mother bought the land for me! He claimed that she bought the land with the money he gave to my mother. I told him she might have saved it from the money I gave her. He said, "Well your mother is dead." I wondered what kind of a man would lie against his dead mother to uplift himself. I reminded him that I gave him four hundred naira to help him pay for his own plot.

Note: I visited my mother from Oyo my station in western Nigeria. My mother presented me with the land. She explained the gift to me. She had paid for the membership of my brother to Okonko. As a Christian, she did not want me to be a member of that organization. So, the plot is what she could do for me in place of Okonko. Since she refused to accept the refund, I increased the amount of money I normally give her. When she went to be with the Lord, this man found the money she saved in her room. Since I paid the burial expenses, he promised to give me the money. He never gave me the money nor told me the amount. End of note.

In an attempt to defend himself, he revealed the real reason they decided to kill the cow. He said I brought a cow from Oyo to be killed at my mother's burial. But because the elderly people in the compound prevented me from killing it for the fact that I did not kill a cow at my father's memorial service, I could not kill the cow and still live. So the cow was not killed. They gave the example of Dr. Okpara who they claimed died suddenly for celebrating the father's death when he did not do so for his grandfather. He said they agreed to "do this in case anything happened to him (he dies). Yet when his first son, who is a Christian, asked him why they killed the cow, he denied the fact. If their suspicion were true, would he be willing to sacrifice his son to have cows killed at his burial let alone me? Soon he said he had one minute left on the card he bought. I refused to call him to continue. Sincerely I don't think my brother in the flesh believes he owes any human being any gratitude. I would not be totally surprised if he changed "The Lord is my Shepherd" to Enoch is my shepherd. I have said that there is no self-made Christian. But my brother does not know that God hates pride and ingratitude.

The false claim my brother made when he said he gave me the land my mother bought for me reminded me of another false claim Onyema, his son, made. When he called to tell me about the plan to kill the cow he added, "We have paid to name a street after our grandfather." Though I did not know who "we" were, I was flabbergasted and offended at the same time and asked, "What?" He repeated himself. "Onyema, I am a member of the village committee that decided the plotting of the area, the streets, and the names. The committee decided that my father, Jeremiah Isigwuzo, Iroegbu, Uwaezuoke, and Onwuegbu, our grandfather, should each have a street named after them in their honor for their service and sacrifice. You or anyone else could not have paid one penny for the street. To claim that you or anyone else paid for the street amounts to saying my father is unworthy of the honor the village bestowed on him." Realizing I knew everything about naming the streets, he did not say one more word about the payment for the street. Since he claimed *we*, I called his siblings to find out if they contributed to the payment. They did not, and I do not know what he meant.

Chapter 56

Celebrations

Sweetie and I got married on September 5, 1969. Our fiftieth wedding anniversary was in 2019. We are enjoying our retirement. We also enjoy our church activities. With my blindness from glaucoma, communicating the arrangement for the celebration fell onto her shoulders. She had sent invitations out to relatives including nephews and nieces in the U.S., Britain, Ireland, and Nigeria. We received the terribly shocking sad news. In the middle of the preparation, a tragedy struck.

Our telephone rang. It announced the name of the caller, Amadi. Sweetie picked up the receiver and gave it to me. Amadi is my brother's oldest son who lives in the U.S. When I answered the call he said, "Your H left." "My H," is the name I call his mother. There was no previous discussion about her visiting the U.S. His statement made no sense to me. Therefore, I asked, "What?" He said, "Your H is gone. Isn't that what you call her, she is gone." He described what happened. When he finished, I concluded that she suffered a heart attack.

It appears the Igbo people in Nigeria devised a stupid way of wasting money even when they cannot afford it. Before the era of mortuaries, people buried their dead the very day they died. In the last days of the twentieth century, dead bodies did not stay in the mortuary for more than one week. Today, dead bodies stay in the mortuary for months before they are buried. Amadi's four siblings in Europe planned a three-month delay before the burial. Meanwhile, Amadi and his family in the U.S. planned a celebration of life for her. This took place about a week before we celebrated our fiftieth wedding anniversary.

Instead of one celebration, my brother's family and mine prepared for three, two in the U.S. and one in Nigeria. Amadi planned a celebration of life for her in the state of Georgia. Sweetie, Melody, and Chinedum, two of our children who knew her, went to the celebration. A week later Amadi and members of his family in the U.S. came to our anniversary celebration.

As much as I would have loved to be in Nigeria for the burial of my Happiness, I could not and did not. I am blind and travelling through four airports before I reached home required some assistance. To me, it was meaningless to go to the burial where I could not see any person nor any of the events. Overriding all other reasons is the custom. My father left this earth before I could recognize him. That notwithstanding, I celebrated his memorial service twice, first in 1972 and second in 1976. Recall from earlier chapters of this book that my mother brought me up as a single mother. She went to be with the Lord in 1985. Elderly men in our compound vehemently refused to allow me to kill a cow at her burial because I did not kill one at my father's memorial service. The reason is that I would die if I did. Therefore, I did not fly to Nigeria for the burial of my Happiness. Her children and brothers killed four cows. The children also paid the three bishops who conducted the funeral service ₦150,000. I called and talked with my brother and members of the family several times before, during, and after the funeral.

My brother called me about a month later. He relayed what he called the needs of our two late aunts' families. He said he needed ₦250,000 to accomplish those needs. The one need he mentioned was the burial of a nephew. When I questioned why he wanted such a huge amount of money, he got angry. "My wife died, and you did not send me any money," he said. I warned him never to ask me for money again.

I had a dream before his call. In that dream were my brother, Amadi his first son, and I. We were at Umuahia market. My brother listed a number of things he needed for the ceremony. We bought all and some excesses. We could not carry them home. We were trying to hire a taxi to carry them home when I woke up. The dream, like the one I dreamed when he lied to get my money for his use, revealed he did not need the money. When I confronted him with my dream, he confirmed he did not need any money for my services. Therefore, I was ready when he demanded the ₦250,000.

Amadi his first son who lives in the U.S. and Uzoma, one of the daughters in Britain, each killed a cow at the funeral of their mother. My brother said that Onyema who did not kill a cow during the funeral had contributed one hundred thousand towards the two hundred and fifty thousand. Instead of asking him how much he wanted from me, I told him never to ask for money from me again.

Almost one year later our telephone rang. It was an unknown number. Our telephone said, "Name unknown." I refused to answer it. It left no message. Because Nigerian telephone numbers start with 234, we investigated the call.

We discovered that my cousin Godwin's wife died. Her children had buried her. They wanted money. I had no address to send the money; I sent it through Amadi, my nephew here in the U.S., to his father with specified amounts to my brother, my nephew's two sisters, and my nephews who lost their mother. My brother called me and reported the receipt of more than ₦21,000 for him. He said, "The money came at the right time for the memorial service of my wife's first-year death celebration."

Sometime in the third week of August 2021, I received a call from Amadi. He reported that my house in the village leaked, and "they" want ₦675,000 to replace the zinc roof. He further asked me not to do anything until after his investigation. I had been suspicious of my brother and his son at my village in Nigeria. I called Emedom, my friend in Lagos, Nigeria, and told him about the demand. He laughed and said, "You have trees that yield money." That was also the reaction of Uzoma, my niece, in Manchester, England. In my attempt to find out the source of the quotation, I discovered that my brother's houseboy, his family, two or three distant nephews, and their wives live in my six-bedroom house without my knowledge and permission. I called my brother and ordered them to vacate the house.

My attempt to find the source of the quotation was frustrated. All I heard was *they* said. I insisted on knowing whether *they* had names or not. My brother's son at Abuja said Chiko and his sister at Port Harcourt said, "The carpenter." None of these two live in my village and must be invited to give the bid. Somebody in my family must invite either of them before they come. None of the informants was willing to name who invited either the carpenter or Chiko.

Believing that something was fishy, I took two decisions. First, no one should do any repairs to my house without my authorization, and I do not authorize this. Second, vacate everyone in my house today. All my brother said was "okay." I believe the prank to get ₦675,000 from me is because my family had given more than ₦284,000 to help people in my village (Amafo Isingwu and Umuegbe compound) because of COVID. "They" calculated that if my family could donate that amount to help the people in our village, I could afford to send them the amount. I would not be surprised if this is a cynical way to get me to contribute to the number of cows he planned for his funeral. When that failed, my brother tried to get money from me in another way. He claimed that someone was trying to claim and farm my land at Ebite. Knowing the game he plays, I called several people including two of his children. He was forced to tell the truth and complained that I was calling everybody. It turned out no one was claiming my plot. Less than six months later when I called him, he demanded ₦1.4 million to repair the roof of my house. I warned him to leave my house alone. I would not be surprised if that is his way of claiming to spend the money the tenants in my house paid him.

Chinyere, my brother's oldest living daughter, called me on June 30, 2022. When I answered the call, she said her sister Anyadindu had something to say to me and handed the phone to her. She became the spokesperson for a "committee." It was about my house. While she spoke, a voice said, 'Or we repair it and the cost will be in two installments, and Amafo is laughing at us." She relayed the same to me. I told her that Amafo laughs at my brother, his hate for me, and his hatred and misuse of the funds I gave him and his son, who were more interested in stealing the money I gave them to build my house than building it. The condition of the house is a witness against them. I have Jesus Christ. I came into the world with nothing and will leave with nothing. I thank the Trinity for everything I experienced in this life. I wished I knew that God was using each one of them to make me reach who He planned for me to be. I am very grateful to God for every experience including the defeat of my Goliaths that you read in this book. I would not change any.

Today, I thank the Trinity for every experience in this book and more. I wish I had known earlier in my life that God was using the experiences to mold my life. I would have praised the Trinity more and lived a more enjoyable life. Better late than never. Glory and honor to our God. Amen.

Note: On May 9, 2024, about eleven months after the death and burial of my brother, I called Amadi my brother's first son. One of the two questions I asked him was, "What is the condition of my house?" He answered, "Fine." He added, "I painted the wall before the burial." This is the house my brother demanded ₦1.4 million to repair.

Indices

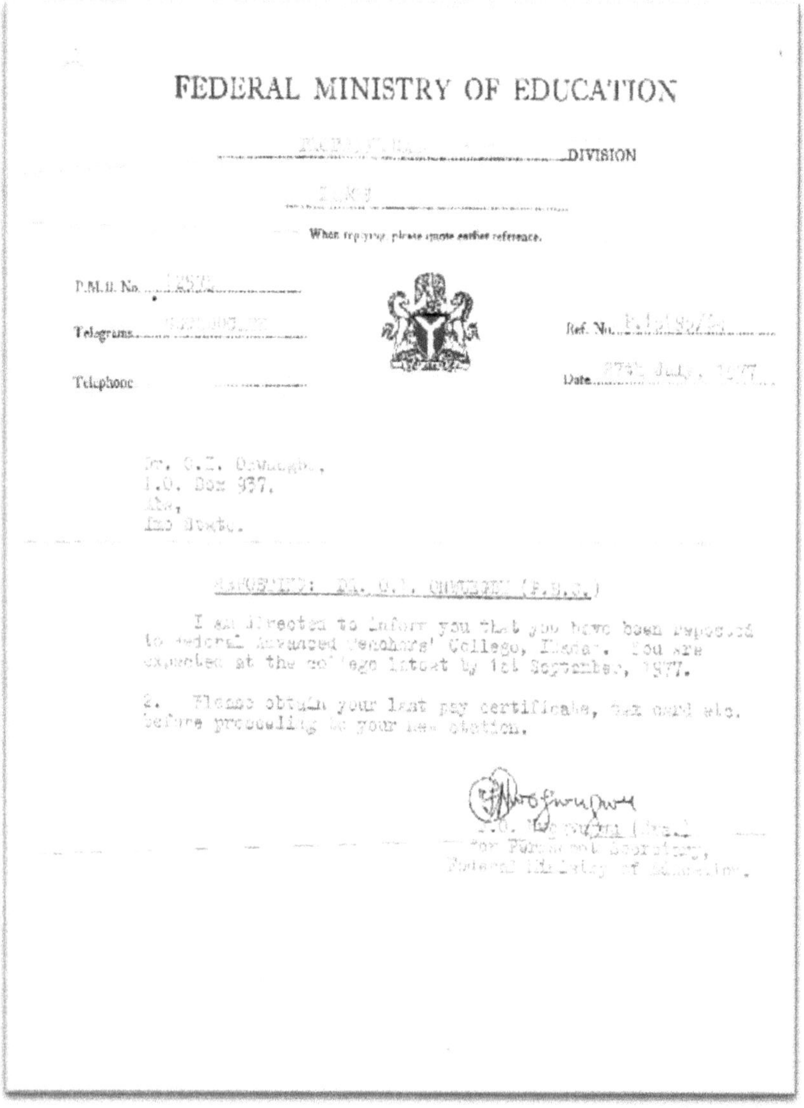

Tel. LAGOS
Telegrams :
*All communications should be
addressed to*
The Secretary,
Federal Civil Service Commission,
Private Bag No. 12586, Lagos

*In replying please quote the number
and date of this letter.*

No. FC.1300/C.5802/T/25

Federal Civil Service Commission,
Private Bag No. 12586,
Lagos, Nigeria

15th October, 19 80

Dr. O. I. Onwuegbu,
Federal Advanced Teachers' College
for Special Education,
P. M. B. 1039,
Oyo.

Dear Sir,

Appointment As the Principal (FATC, Special Education)

With reference to your application dated 3rd August, 1979 and your subsequent interview, I am pleased to inform you that the Commission has approved your appointment as Principal, Federal Advanced Teachers' College for Special Education, with effect from the date you assume duty. The post is on salary GL. 15. Congratulations.

2. Notice of your appointment will be published in the Official Gazette shortly.

3. This approval will be regarded as having elapsed in the event of your failing to indicate within two months of the date of this letter whether or not the offer is acceptable to you.

(GAMBO GUBIO)
Secretary
Federal Civil Service Commission.

Telephone: Oyo 038-230105.
Our Reference: APO.13/Vol.XV/5.
Your Reference: ....

Aafin, Oyo Nigeria

19th January, 1987.

The Permanent Secretary,
Federal Ministry of Education,
Lagos.

Dear Permanent Secretary,

Re - Allegation against Dr. I. O. Nwuegbu,
the Provost, Federal College of Education,
(Special) Oyo

I am writing on behalf of myself, Chiefs and the generality of Oyo people. We have just received information to the effect that certain elements, who described themselves as representatives of the people of Oyo, have written letters of protest containing some grave allegations against Dr. I. O. Nwuegbu, the Provost, Federal College of Education (Special), Oyo. Such letters were said to have been addressed to Federal Authorities amongst which you happen to be one.

We were also informed that among the demands of the said disgruntled elements was the removal, and or transfer, of the Provost from his present Post in Oyo.

We hope this is not true. However, if any such letters had reached you, we categorically hereby say that we in Oyo have no hands in it. We strongly detest the practise whereby any one single cultural Organisation, or group, where there are over one hundred of them, will be arrogating to itself the prerogative to speak for a whole Community where there is established Traditional Authority and functional statutory bodies in the town duly recognised by both the State and the Federal Governments.

What is more, no allegation of misconduct and impropriety against the Provost, Dr. I. O. Nwuegbu, had been brought to the knowledge of myself, my Chiefs, my Traditional Council and the Oyo Local Government of which I am the President by any person or group of persons in and outside of my domain.

In the circumstance, therefore, we honestly believe that the Provost is trying his very best for the College and should be allowed to continue most especially in order to allow continuity in the present phase of the development of the College.

Lastly, we believe it is our duty, and a sacred one indeed, to protect officials of Government, either Local, State or Federal, from intimidation, harrassment and blackmail in the honest discharge of their duties. We shall not shirk our responsibilities in this regard.

Thank you.

Iku Baba Yeye,

OBA LAMIDI OLAYIWOLA ADEYEMI III, J.P.; C.F.R.; LL.D.,
(THE ALAAFIN OF OYO).

cc. Mr. J. A. Adeosun, (Permanent Secretary),
Federal Council Office, Lagos.

cc. Chief S. A. Olopoenia,
18, Ekololu Street, Surulere, Lagos.

cc. Dr. I. O. Nwuegbu, (Provost) Fed. College of Education, Oyo.

FEDERAL COLLEGE OF EDUCATION (SPECIAL)
OYO

P. M. B. 1089, OYO

Telegrams: FECSPED

Telephone: 038- 200917

Your Ref..................

PROVOST:

O. I. ONWUEGBU
B.SC. (SC.) M.A. (NIGR.), Ph.D. (UTAH.)

Our Ref........FCES/OY/6/8.47/65

Date.........6th January, 1987

The Permanent Secretary,
Federal Ministry of Education,
Victoria Island,
Lagos.

Attention: T. M. Bala.

I am writing to reply to the letter Ref. No. SAP: 36/S.311/27 dated 16th December, 1986, received today January 6th, 1987, copy attached for easy reference. There are three paragraphs, paragraph one demands confirmation, second paragraph demands awareness of "the" braille press being under the special education section of the Ministry and the third paragraph states the persons present at the time the so called decisions were taken.

Please with all humility and with all respect, I wish to state my thoughts. I hope we will all put away emotions and be objective. The Romans cut off the head of Hannibal's brother and threw it into his camp. He exclaimed, "The Doom of Carthage!" The doom of Nigeria is spelt in chasing shadow and leaving substance.

Paragraph One:

I cannot honestly confirm or deny such a meeting or decision. I have looked through the file to locate the minutes of such a meeting but cannot locate it. Please send me a copy of the minutes.

Comments on Paragraph One:

I will try very hard to make my comment very brief. Let me assume that such a decision was taken. I am now quoting the writers "........ that the braille press should not be attached to any institution,...." Does the word, "the" not refer to a specific braille press? Can any living and rational person and or group of persons decree that no institution in Nigeria can acquire a braille press, let alone special education institution? If "the braille press" refers to a specific braille press, does that not refer to a braille press bought and owned by the Federal Ministry of Education? Does such braille press prevent any person or organisation from owning one? Am I requesting Mr. Onwukwesi to transfer his braille press to my College? The Federal Government has its own press. Does that prevent the universities from establishing university press? I enclose here the minutes of the conference of Heads of Special Education Units/Sections/Divisions held at Oyo College in May 1985, page 4, where the AIM expressed his inability to acquire a braille press. May I ask one more question can the Federal Ministry of Education, ie, alone ADE (SE) and a few people legislate against the constitution of Nigeria, i.e. freedom of expression?

Paragraph Two:

The question is whether, "...., you are aware that decision was taken that the said braille Press should be a separate establishment under the Ministry ...."

Again, I cannot say whether this decision was taken or not.

..../2.

All official correspondence should be Addressed to the Provost.

FEDERAL MINISTRY OF EDUCATION

HIGHER EDUCATION DIVISION

TEACHER EDUCATION SECTION, LAGOS

P.M.B. No. 12573
Telegrams: SECEDUCATE
Telephone: 612567

Ref. No. SAP.36/S.261/1/297
Date: 22nd July, 1987

Dr. Obed I. Onwuegbu,
Assistant Director of Education,
Special Education Section,
Federal Ministry of Education,
Victoria Island,
Lagos.

Dear Dr. Obed I Onwueghu,

Letter of Commendation

This letter is in recognition of the personal efforts which you demonstrated in executing your duties as Provost, Federal College of Education, (Special), Oyo from 1980 until May, 1987.

2. After going through the handing over note to your successor, the Honourable Federal Minister of Education appreciated your sense of dedication and a most judicious use and management of available financial and other resources to sustain a viable College of Education.

3. Your personal initiative in the provision of facilities, equipment, and other necessary tools which were effectively utilized is commendable. The development and administration of a meaningful academic programme is appreciated. The quality of performance reflects the amount of collective cooperation among all cadre of college personnel in serving the students. This is encouraging.

4. You are therefore greatly commended on your achievement and we all wish you success in your new assignment.

A. A. GWANDU (DR.)
DIRECTOR (HIGHER EDUCATION)

UNITED NATIONS   OFFICE OF THE RESIDENT
DEVELOPMENT PROGRAMME   REPRESENTATIVE IN NIGERIA

P. O. BOX 2075
LAGOS

REFERENCE:
NIR/87/008
PRO/300/CP

14 July 1987

Attention: Mr. J.A.O. Olawiyi

Dear Sir,

Project Formulation Mission:
NIR/87/008 – Training of Teachers of Handicapped, Federal College Of Education (Special Education), Oyo State

As you are aware, the Third UNDP Country Programme (1987 – 1991) provides a total of $400,000 for an estimated duration of two years for the above-mentioned project.

In this context, the Executing Agency (UNESCO) for the project, in consultation with the Federal Ministry of Education, proposes to field a consultant/technical adviser on a mission to Lagos to assess the needs of the Federal College of Education (Special) and assist in the formulation of a project document. Already, a draft project document has been prepared by the Provost of the College, Dr. O. I. Onwuegbu but needs to be reviewed and reformulated.

We would appreciate it if you would sign and return to us the attached Project Development Facility request form for further processing, in order to finance the above mission.

By copy of this letter, we are informing the relevant Government departments of the above action.

Assuring you of our full cooperation and with kind regards.

Yours sincerely,

Chandra Malik
Resident Representative a.i.

Permanent Secretary
Fed. Ministry of National Planning
Federal Secretariat
Ikoyi/Lagos

cc: Permanent Secretary (Attn: AIE Special Education Section)
    Fed. Min. of Education, V/Island, Lagos
cc: Dr. O.I. Onwuegbu, Provost, Fed. College of Educ. (Special Educ.), Oyo
cc: Mr. A. Callaway, UNESCO Representative, Lagos

AN OPEN LETTER TO THE PROVOST

Some of my readers might be wondering why I'm not even afraid to write to the highest authority so openly. Well, don't be carried away, for a clear conscience they say, fears no accusation, just read on, you will see what I mean.

My dear Provost, though there are many people and I have met a few, who could administer, govern, even rule. But to lead, really to lead a whole people, takes something more, and it is not learnt in schools or from books. It is not to be judged by fine clothes, big cars, money in the bank or the shouting of slogans. It is not just the capacity to start a crowd cheering; a demagogue on a street corner can do that. Leadership takes more. It involves the possession of a series of qualities that are possessed and seen to be possessed and which make others prepared to follow the one who owned them.

But the natural qualities are in the man, strength without brutality, courage without recklessness, honesty without priggishness, intelligence without sentimentality, the ability to dominate other men by sheer personality or the capacity simply to inspire. I know Winston Churchill had it, Charles de Gaulle had it, John Kennedy had it, David Ben Gurion the father of Israel had it, Emeka Ojukwu had it, but I have never known other Nigeria till OKWUECHU, C.I. of the Federal College of Education (Special), Oyo.

My dear Provost, I'm only writing this piece to show my sincere appreciation for all your various activities since the beginning of this session, to see to the well being of Students of this noble College. Though you have been doing these things for the past years but this year outnumbered the past years'.

Even without the Student Unionism, the relationship with the Students is so cordial which is a very great achievement compared to the past years, or the new hostels for better comfort of the Students, more chairs for lectures and what is more the reduction in the academic work load, which has been generating bitter cries from every nook and corner of the College and from every mouth of every Dick and Harry. These things are really worthy of praise and that is why I have picked up my pen to say a BIG THANK you and more grease to your elbow. My words of thanks also go to the Deputy Provost, the Deans and all others for being so imaginative.

My dear Provost, remember the battle is HALF won if the greatest is not achieved, which is our movement to the promised land, - The PERMANENT SITE. I know you have been struggling for this, but this is to remind you to keep the flag flying HIGHER than ever before.

May God help you to carry and bear the cross of SPECIAL till the GREATEST is achieved Amen. LONG LIVE MY DEAR PROVOST, LONG LIVE SPECIAL OYO, LONG LIVE NIGERIA.

OLOGBENLA, M.T. AND O.
ENGLISH/THE.

Federal College of Education
(Special)
Oyo
29th May, 1986

The Provost
Federal College of Education
(Special)
Oyo

The Registrar
Federal College of Education
(Special)
Oyo

Sirs,

THANK YOU AND GOODBYE
AS IT TOUCHES MY PERSON

I enclose here with copies of acknowledgements in my project book. When I think of people who have helped me in life, your names come first in my mind.

The admission you granted to me will go a long way to solve my life's problems. But a lot more remains to be solved by my environment. These problems are (a) my position as a family head with about eleven brothers and sisters as well as my six children; (b) my deafness and ageing which I see as a double challenge and a double jeopardy. Now I wish that members of my family would under go training here so that they can easily understand and communicate with me.

APPEAL:

People from the North are granted remedial course because of the so called imbalance in Education. As their ageing member I appeal that the deaf from the South should be included in this Educational imbalance and granted remedial course or made to undergo four year course.

MY IMPRESSIONS:

When I came here in 1983, Students informed me that the Provost was one of Nigerians recalled from foreign countries to help integrate the various tribes after the civil war hence he banned tribal meetings in the College. The whole thing has turn to be the integration of the handicapped people with the normal people, and the extension of Christ mission on Earth. "Are you the one to come or are we to expect for another Messiah" was John's message to Christ.

FEDERAL MINISTRY OF EDUCATION

................ADMINISTRATIVE................DIVISION

................LAGOS................

P.M.B. No. 12573

Telegrams: Seceducate

Telephone: 630630/121

Ref. No. F.15198/90

Date 1st May, 1980

Dr. O.I. Onwuegbu,
u.f.s. The Principal,
Federal Advanced Teachers College,
(Special Education)
Oyo.

Dear Sir,

PROMOTION TO GRADE LEVEL 13

I am pleased to inform you that the Federal Civil Service Commission has in its letter No.FC.2010/S.5/156 of 2nd January, 1980, approved your promotion to the grade of Education Officer Grade IV (Assistant Chief Education Officer) Grade Level 13, with effect from 1st April, 1979.

2. Congratulations. Notice of your promotion will soon be published in the official gazette.

A. SOTTKARE
for: Permanent Secretary,
FEDERAL MINISTRY OF EDUCATION

Uzuakoli Higher Education School – 1958

Obed as Acting Headmaster at Akanu Item – 1959

First and Second Teams at Methodist Central School - Umuahia
1963

First Summer in the U.S., 1964 - Camp Counselor in Massachusetts
- Campers with Parents

Graduation with Bachelor's Degree in June 1966

Wedding Reception 1969

National Psychological Conference Attendees, Benin City, Nigeria - Late 1970's

Group Photo of Amafor Isingwu People living in Enugu, Nigeria. Taken at a reception for our family when we returned from U.S. in 1976

Mr. Azado - First Principal of Federal College of Special Education, Oyo, Nigeria 1977-1978

Obed's Brother Enoch, Enoch's Wife and Sue's Parents when they visited Nigeria in 1981

Obed I. Onwuegbu – 1996

Uzuakoli Days - Obed 2nd Row, 2nd Person from the Right

Brother Enoch - Wild Enoch the Boxer

Godwin Anozie - Friend, Colleague and Neighbor

Mr. Mensah, Ghanian Faculty Member at Federal College for Special Education, Oyo, Nigeria

Obed and Sue

Obed I. Onwuegbu, Provost, Federal College of Special Education, Graduation Day

Obed using a picnic table as a bed on a camping trip with College and Career Group from Church

Obed's Best Friend, Emedom Ogbonna

Obed's Mother and Cousin Nnenna

Obed's Teacher, Grade 4 at Mission Hill

Obed and Sue in Traditional Dress – 2003

Distinguished Alumni Award from Lyndon State College, Vermont – 2004

40th Wedding Anniversary 2009

Obed and Sue Aug09

Family Photo 2014

Our Children 2014

Christmas 2016

2018 - All the Grandchildren

2018 - Family Photo

2018 Us and Four Children

Our four children 2018

Grandchildren 2018

Our Children 2018

2018

All 9 grandchildren with first great-granddaughter. 2022

50th_Wedding_Anniversary

Grandchildren minus one granddaughter and one great-granddaughter. November 2024

Family Photo 2024 minus Obed

Distinguished Alumni Award

www.ingramcontent.com/pod-product-compliance
Ingram Content Group UK Ltd.
Pitfield, Milton Keynes, MK11 3LW, UK
UKHW021451240225
455493UK00007B/605